HARVARD STUDIES IN BUSINESS HISTORY

1. JOHN JACOB ASTOR, BUSINESS MAN by Kenneth Wiggins Porter
2. JAY COOKE, PRIVATE BANKER by Henrietta M. Larson
3. THE JACKSONS AND THE LEES: TWO GENERATIONS OF MASSACHUSETTS MERCHANTS, 1765–1844 by Kenneth Wiggins Porter
4. THE MASSACHUSETTS–FIRST NATIONAL BANK OF BOSTON, 1784–1934 by N. S. B. Gras
5. THE HISTORY OF AN ADVERTISING AGENCY: N. W. AYER & SON AT WORK, 1869–1939, and revised edition, 1869–1949, by Ralph M. Hower
6. MARKETING LIFE INSURANCE: ITS HISTORY IN AMERICA by J. Owen Stalson
7. HISTORY OF MACY'S OF NEW YORK, 1858–1919: CHAPTERS IN THE EVOLUTION OF THE DEPARTMENT STORE by Ralph M. Hower
8. THE WHITESMITHS OF TAUNTON: A HISTORY OF REED & BARTON, 1824–1943 by George Sweet Gibb
9. DEVELOPMENT OF TWO BANK GROUPS IN THE CENTRAL NORTHWEST: A STUDY IN BANK POLICY AND ORGANIZATION by Charles Sterling Popple
10. THE HOUSE OF HANCOCK: BUSINESS IN BOSTON, 1724–1775 by W. T. Baxter
11. TIMING A CENTURY: HISTORY OF THE WALTHAM WATCH COMPANY by C. W. Moore
12. GUIDE TO BUSINESS HISTORY: MATERIALS FOR THE STUDY OF AMERICAN BUSINESS HISTORY AND SUGGESTIONS FOR THEIR USE by Henrietta M. Larson
13. PEPPERELL'S PROGRESS: HISTORY OF A COTTON TEXTILE COMPANY, 1844–1945 by Evelyn H. Knowlton
14. THE HOUSE OF BARING IN AMERICAN TRADE AND FINANCE: ENGLISH MERCHANT BANKERS AT WORK, 1763–1861 by Ralph W. Hidy
15. THE WHITIN MACHINE WORKS SINCE 1831: A TEXTILE MACHINERY COMPANY IN AN INDUSTRIAL VILLAGE by Thomas R. Navin
16. THE SACO-LOWELL SHOPS: TEXTILE MACHINERY BUILDING IN NEW ENGLAND, 1813–1949 by George Sweet Gibb
17. BROADLOOMS AND BUSINESSMEN: A HISTORY OF THE BIGELOW–SANFORD CARPET COMPANY by John S. Ewing and Nancy P. Norton
18. NATHAN TROTTER: PHILADELPHIA MERCHANT, 1787–1853 by Elva Tooker
19. A HISTORY OF THE MASSACHUSETTS HOSPITAL LIFE INSURANCE COMPANY by Gerald T. White
20. THE CHARLES ILFELD COMPANY: A STUDY OF THE RISE AND DECLINE OF MERCANTILE CAPITALISM IN NEW MEXICO by William J. Parish

HARVARD STUDIES IN BUSINESS HISTORY

XX

Edited by

HENRIETTA M. LARSON

Professor of Business History
Graduate School of Business Administration
George F. Baker Foundation
Harvard University

The CHARLES ILFELD COMPANY

A STUDY OF THE RISE AND DECLINE OF MERCANTILE CAPITALISM IN NEW MEXICO

By William J. Parish

HARVARD UNIVERSITY PRESS
CAMBRIDGE, MASSACHUSETTS · 1961

Distributed in Great Britain by Oxford University Press, London

Library of Congress Catalog Card Number 61-9687
Printed in the United States of America

To
Porter and Eveline Gifford
and their daughter
Edna May

Foreword

This history of a mercantile firm that operated for nearly a century in the American Southwest is presented by the *Harvard Studies in Business History* as an unusual contribution to the history of business and to general American history. This study, though concerned with a well-known type of organization, deals with a segment of American business which has had little attention from business historians: business on the frontier and in the developing hinterland of metropolitan centers of the American economy. And it presents a revealing example of the contribution of businessmen to the development of the great American Southwest, a region which in American literature and history traditionally has been pictured as the land of the Indian, the cattleman, and the *Padre* with his missions. The story of successive generations of the Ilfeld firm epitomizes the contribution of the merchant, in establishing and developing a system of trade, toward building and maintaining the economic life of a region.

The Charles Ilfeld Company, a Study of the Rise and Decline of Mercantile Capitalism in New Mexico, is an especially welcome and appropriate addition to the *Studies.* It is fitting that this volume, which grew out of a thesis started under the direction of the late N. S. B. Gras, Straus Professor of Business History, and which so realistically presents examples of certain historical types of businessmen associated with his work, should be published in the series he established and for nearly twenty years edited. The present editor considers it a happy circumstance that this volume broadens the historical reach of the *Studies* by dealing with a region and a kind of business new to the series. The author and the members of Charles Ilfeld Company, who so fully cooperated by making their records available without restriction, deserve our gratitude for this venture in regional business history. May it serve as an example for others to follow!

William J. Parish is dean of the College of Business Administration of the University of New Mexico. He is a graduate of Brown University and received the MBA and the DCS degree from the Harvard Graduate School of Business Administration. He has an intimate acquaintance with the region in which the Ilfeld firm operated and with the past and present business of the Southwest.

HENRIETTA M. LARSON, *Editor*

Author's Preface

It has been the purpose of this study to present a meaningful picture of the changing structure of business enterprise in New Mexico from the days of the Santa Fe Trail to the present time; to describe in some detail the transitions from petty to beginning, and then mature, mercantile capitalism, and finally to industrial capitalism; to draw significant parallels with the history of economic development in western civilization; to accomplish these objectives by building upon an intimate analysis of the activities and policies of one pervasive company and its dominant personalities. These objectives have seemed the more important because so few stories of enterprise in New Mexico, since the days of the American occupation, have been told from firsthand access to business correspondence and records. Fewer still have attempted to place economic development in a meaningful context.

Some of the satisfaction that comes from the completion of this self-appointed task is dulled as I look back over the 14 years of its doing. Since 1946, when I discovered the Charles Ilfeld correspondence in a dark corner of a loft in one of Ilfeld's old Las Vegas warehouses, death has taken several of those friends whose contributions to this study have been immeasurable. What mistakes of fact and interpretation they might have helped me avoid is a matter for conjecture. They probably would have been many.

Professor N. S. B. Gras, whose hard-bitten criticisms of my now appreciated weaknesses, died without having seen the finish of the work he encouraged. He had been unmerciful and gentle at the right times. At the point of his severest goads and my lowest ebb, he initiated a research grant from the Business History Foundation to help me forward. I am grateful that he lived to see the discovery of a unique collection of records of a sedentary merchant and an analysis of those records to a point that seems to support through modern history the theories he had spun from a lifetime of brilliant research. Though this work borrows heavily from the pioneering studies of N. S. B. Gras, it is suggested throughout that environment may play a greater role in the shaping of business policies than traditional concepts of the entrepreneur would embrace. Such evidence concerning the "why's" of change in the business structure, though involving new emphases, should add strength to and appreciation for the basic contributions of this inspiring teacher and scholar.

Louis C. Ilfeld, son of Charles, spent many patient hours answering my letters and submitting to interviews—the latter bringing opportunities for pleasant week ends in his Las Vegas home. It was he who made the gift of the invaluable Charles Ilfeld business records to the University of New Mexico. Some recompense was granted me for the loss of this friend when I learned he had received the manuscript of my first eight chapters in time to read them and to express his enjoyment during the last few hours of his life.

Earl L. Moulton, who followed the progress of the manuscript throughout, apparently never saw those concluding chapters that concerned him in his capacities as general manager, president, and chairman of the board of the Charles Ilfeld Company, though we had discussed at length the problems that these sections covered. As president he gave me access (as later did Frank A. Mapel and Robert J. Nordhaus) to all the company records I wished to explore. He set the pattern for executives and employees to discuss freely with me historical and current matters pertaining to the company. Part of his letter of February 25, 1950, to Louis C. Ilfeld expressed a viewpoint he followed without exception in his experiences with me.

> I have talked with him [author] at various times about the completion of his work, that is, bringing it down to a later date. He explained that the farther you get along in a thing of that kind the more difficult it is because of personal angles that develop. Of course it finally will have to be whatever he decides on. He naturally must maintain the objectivity with which he started; namely that of writing about the development of business and business practices as exemplified by the growth and progress of the Ilfeld Company. The basic significance of business as performed in the Southwest is his theme. I assume that he would have to go along in that way and "let the chips fall where they may."
>
> It will be interesting to watch, and if he does go ahead and do it and have it published, I hope that it will be in our time so that you and I may enjoy it, or at least observe it.

To the three who have passed on I must add a fourth—Rodney B. Schoonmaker—who even in his nineties was still clear of mind. He drew heavily upon his intimate experiences with Charles Ilfeld's enterprise to unlock many an intriguing problem presented only in outline in the records.

Others to whom I owe great debt, happily, and who will be able to render opinions on the accuracy of fact and interpretation, are Charles S. Brown, William A. Keleher, Louis A. McRae, Frank A. Mapel, Robert J. Nordhaus, A. C. Ortega, Julius H. Rosenthal, and William H. Stapp.

Of my colleagues on the University of New Mexico faculty, I wish to pay special tribute to Frank D. Reeve, France V. Scholes, and Cecil V. Wicker. A former colleague, George P. Hammond, now director of the Bancroft Library, kindly gave his permission to use an extensive quotation from the Quivira Society's publication by Carroll and Haggard, *Three New Mexico Chronicles.*

Research assistants—Jane Blumenfeld, J. R. Hagy, Thomas J. McLaughlin, Charles W. Morton, and Martyn R. P. Naylor—who performed some of the more tedious tasks, have my deepest gratitude. Katharine Nutt—now doctor of philosophy and professor of history—gave special services in performing the basic research for the 1870 map of New Mexico. Appendix 7 is her description of the methods used and the problems encountered in her splendid achievement. The map was drawn by Professor Richard G. Huzarski who also drew the street map of Las Vegas. Shirley Huzarski drew some of the other exhibits.

The long chore of typing the final manuscript was the dedicated task of Lynette Wilson, who, with Mary Saner, put earlier portions of drafts in usable form.

The sacrifices my family has made over years of evenings, week ends, and summers, that I might finish the task we all hoped could be accomplished, are more easily understood than explained.

I have left for the last the expression of my appreciation for the continuing interest and encouragement of Professor Henrietta M. Larson and Hilma Holton. A grateful accolade is due Hilma Holton who edited the entire manuscript. As only a skillful artist can do, she removed blemishes, smoothed unpleasing expressions, but left the complex of her subject true to its strengths and weaknesses. My gratitude also is extended to Mrs. Barbara Shapiro who, in that last pressured period of time, prepared the index.

A final statement, in all conscience, should be made. The freedom accorded me by all the officers and employees of the Charles Ilfeld Company to ask, speak, see, and write as I pleased throughout this long stint, not only deserves unrestricted credit but it adds clearly to the responsibility that is mine for the facts and interpretations I have recorded.

WILLIAM J. PARISH

June 1960

CONTENTS

PART TWO

FOUNDATONS OF MERCANTILE CAPITALISM: CHARLES ILFELD, 1867–1887 (EARLY PHASE)

PART THREE

TOWARD MATURE MERCANTILE CAPITALISM: THE ESTABLISHMENT OF MONOPOLISTIC AND PROTECTIVE DEVICES: CHARLES ILFELD AND MAX NORDHAUS, 1887–1929 (LATER PHASE)

PART FOUR

DECLINE OF MERCANTILE CAPITALISM AND THE RISE OF A NEW ERA

APPENDICES

Tables

Illustrations and Maps

PART ONE

Transition from Petty to Mercantile Capitalism to 1874

I

SANTA FE: DEVELOPMENT OF AN ECONOMIC TOWN TO 1865

Restless Capital

The tale of traders on the Santa Fe Trail is an old story retold. One is struck by the almost perfect parallels with the traveling merchants of ancient, medieval, and later days. The Arabs of the first century A.D., trading with the east coast of Africa, who "brought to the restless West the surplus from the ordered and industrious East," certainly had the same desire for profit and adventure as those early traders like Josiah Gregg, who made the perilous trip from the border of Arkansas to Santa Fe in 1839 and thence on to Chihuahua and return.[1]

The large seventh-century caravan of Mecca, operated by a syndicate of merchants, is seen on a small scale in the caravan of 81 men who left Franklin, Missouri, in May, 1824, and returned from Santa Fe in September with $180,000 in precious metals and furs.[2]

Can that typical caravan leader described by Gras who "with an effective backing of armed clansmen was hired to beat back the Bedouins or other pirates of the inland" be a much different individual than Charles Bent who in the 1830's captained many a caravan and who saw to it that "every able-bodied man . . . had to stand guard regularly" against possible Indian depredations?[3]

The souls of the traders of Carthage, Alexandria, or Rome, as well as Mecca, Genoa, and Lübeck, lived again in the like of the McKnight brothers, John and Robert, the Magoffins, Samuel, James, and William (not to forget Susan), and of Henry Connelly and Alexander Majors. These and others like them were the traveling merchants of the Santa Fe trail whose capital, as restless as they, was as likely to be tied up in the merchandise of New York and Baltimore as it was in the furs, blankets, and silver of Chihuahua, Santa Fe, and Taos.

Capital was "footloose and fancy free" on the Santa Fe Trail. The Missouri River could overflow its banks (it did in those days, too) but cause little concern. Mules, oxen, "Murphy" wagons, and merchandise comprised the bulk of the investment and neither "hell nor high water" harmed this mobile capital: it merely moved it on.

Author's Note: An economic town is defined by Professor Gras as follows: "When there came into being a class of traders who resided in a market village, and who had stores which not only supplemented the market place but became its rivals, then the economic town was born." N. S. B. Gras, *An Introduction to Economic History* (New York, 1922), pp. 91, 105.

In 1828 the capricious Missouri extended the terminus of the old Cumberland and Boone's Lick Roads when it inundated the town of Franklin some 200 miles above St. Louis. The Cumberland Road wound its way from Baltimore and Washington to Vandalia, Illinois; the Boone's Lick extension pointed on to St. Louis and the new town of Booneville, two miles beyond, flooded Franklin. Booneville was bypassed as the traders used the steamboat to ply their wares beyond to Independence, the storied "jumping off" place for Santa Fe and Chihuahua.

A swollen Missouri served to speed the inevitable westward movement of termini again when it removed the Independence landings in 1833 to give the focus of trade to Westport. So the ceaseless pressure to be "on" found Westport overshadowed and then absorbed by Kansas City, which in turn was threatened for a short period before and during the Civil War by the trade flowing through protected Fort Leavenworth.[4]

Kansas City and St. Louis remained the home of the larger sedentary merchants—those wholesalers who "sat down" to use their energies more in administration than traveling. Meanwhile, the railroad in the 1860's and 1870's moved the termini of the mule-team and ox-team ever westward to Hays City, Sheridan, Kit Carson, Granada, La Junta, El Moro, Otero, and Las Vegas. Indeed, the shrinking Santa Fe trail became only a folk tale about Indians and Indian fighters. The rooting of capital, however, and its flowering into permanent towns and businesses is another story.

The American Trader and the Development of Wholesaling

It was inevitable that the American trader would sooner or later dominate the Santa Fe market. He had the advantage of superiority in variety and quality of domestic and imported goods brought at competitively low costs to St. Louis by barge and on to Independence by steamboat. To be sure, it was farther to Santa Fe from Independence than from Chihuahua in Old Mexico, but the merchants in the latter place were handicapped in acquiring the bulk of their stock by long overland treks either from Durango, a manufacturing center some 400 miles to the south, or from several times that distance through the ocean ports of entry, namely, Vera Cruz on the Atlantic or Acapulco on the Pacific. Although the American traders found the dangers of Indian depredations great, and the burdens of tariffs and taxes, and the costs of bribery-on-the-side, high, the competitively low cost and enticing quality of their goods permitted high enough mark-ups—100 per cent it has been estimated—to permit frequent occurrence of substantial profits.[5]

It may not have been inevitable—or perhaps it was—that American arms would follow the growing dominance of the American trader, but they did—an occurrence that was not at all surprising to the Mexicans.

Nor could the Mexicans do anything about it. Whatever rationalization is needed to uphold the Americans, Charles and Mary Beard have produced: [6]

> Without capital and without stability, harrassed by revolutions and debts, Mexico could not develop the resources and trade of the northern empire to which she possessed the title of parchment and seals. More than that . . . she did not have the emigrants for that enterprise.

General Kearny, with James Magoffin and his dollars softening the way, took over New Mexico for the United States in August, 1846.

It was inevitable, also, that the American trader in Santa Fe speeded the change from a village economy to that of an economic town. As late as 1800, Santa Fe, a community of 4000 inhabitants, had been predominantly agricultural, with most of its people wringing a living from small plots of irrigated soil. The market place of the itinerant merchant was still at this date the principal place of trade, and the settled petty capitalist with his store was still two or three decades in the future.

Chittenden says wholesaling in Santa Fe sprang up about 1830 principally because the small traders, mortgaging their property at home to finance their trip from Missouri to the Southwest, could not tarry long enough to sell all their goods at retail.[7] Céran St. Vrain, later to have a forwarding house with the Bent brothers, wrote from Taos a revealing letter to Messrs. B. Pratte and Company, September 14, 1830: [8]

> Gentlemen:
>
> . . . I was the first that put goods in the Customhouse and I opened immediately, but goods sold very slow, so slow that it was discouraging. I found that it was impossible to meet my payments if I continued retailing. I therefore thought it was best to hole saile & I have done so. . . .
>
> Your obdt., servant,
> CÉRAN ST. VRAIN

The small traders found themselves squeezed if they failed to turn over their stocks rapidly. Though many of them persisted in selling their goods at retail in the market places of Taos and Santa Fe, proceeding on to Chihuahua with whatever balance remained, these markets were easily glutted and made this practice uncertain of profits.[9] It is not surprising, therefore, to find the most successful merchants to be those who set up shop, carrying on their traveling habits as before, but using partners and agents for selling their wares in an orderly manner at established stands. Under such arrangements there was less distressed merchandise and the temper of the market could be judged at first hand.

The Magoffin brothers and Henry Connelly early established stores in Chihuahua and Santa Fe.[10] The *Santa Fe Republican* of September 10, 1847, carried an advertisement of William S. McKnight, wholesale and retail merchant. In subsequent issues of that year, advertisements appear of many such retailers including the famous firm of St. Vrain and Bent, which carried dry goods, clothing, groceries, and liquors. Unlike the sedentary merchant, however, whose heart and soul was in the building of a permanent business based on a well-calculated balancing of risks, these early Santa Fe retailers were both transient and narrowly exposed to the hazards of acquiring and marketing eastern merchandise. Either through lack of foresight or, more probably, desire, they failed to establish reliable local sources of produce and consequently sent their wagons eastward empty or only partially filled.[11]

Though many of these early wholesalers were manifestly successful for a varying number of years, not a single one established prior to 1848 was in existence in the 1860's, so far as can be learned. Many of them fell by the wayside for lack of adequate capital, or because of heavy losses of merchandise at the hands of the Indians along the Santa Fe Trail, or as the result of poor administration.

There is, however, a more fundamental reason for their leaving the scene. Almost universally these merchants entered the Santa Fe trade for speculative reasons, and, like Sombart's eighteenth-century businessman, had no thought of remaining permanently.[12] James J. Webb, for instance, typical of this group, retired to his comfortable Connecticut environment when he had accumulated sufficient capital.[13] These merchants were generally of Anglo-Saxon stock, eastern American born, who still retained their fondness for the more settled sites of former years.

The German Immigrant and the German Jew

A sweeping change took place in New Mexico from the 1850's on—the same change that 100 years before in Europe had ushered in a new state of business capitalism. Sombart has described the businessman who dominated this earlier scene as one who had acquired a changed profit objective.[14] He no longer worked toward an early day of retirement. Rather he sought to build a thriving and more permanent business enterprise. When this phenomenon occurred in Territorial New Mexico, it became manifest through the German immigrant and, especially, the German Jew.

This Jewish influx, new to the West, had been forceful in the eastern states for a decade and a half.[15] These people had fanned out as peddlers and merchants until their influence had been felt in almost every town and village.[16] Their appearance in the West, however, was not noticeable until the close of the Mexican War. They came first in the late 1840's to the Gulf communities of Texas and to the gold rush areas of California. A number of them converged on Salt Lake City from the East and West in the 1850's to fill the nonmercantile bias of the Mormon settlers.[17] At approximately the same time, and in significantly larger numbers, they traveled the Santa Fe Trail or moved through the southern states and Texas to establish themselves in New Mexico. Those German Jews who settled in this new Territory, many to become eminently successful merchants, soon approximated 0.5 per cent of this oldest of populated areas within the continental United States. They constituted, perhaps, more than three-fourths of the German immigrants of the Territory in contrast to an estimated 7 per cent for the nation as a whole.[18]

Among the first of the German Jewish immigrants who subsequently became prominent merchants was Solomon Jacob Spiegelberg. He came to Santa Fe in the middle 1840's, joined Colonel Doniphan's regiment, and participated in the capture of Chihuahua, March 1, 1847. Upon his return to Santa Fc he was appointed sutler to his regiment, a position fraught with opportunities for profitable specialization as it had been to the army purveyors before him: in Spain before 1492, in England during the sixteenth and seventeenth centuries, and on the Continent somewhat later.[19] Spiegelberg's new position aided him greatly in the establishment of a mercantile firm in October, 1848.[20] Four brothers, Emmanuel, Levi, Lehman, and Willi, and possibly a fifth, Elias, followed Solomon and became members of the firm. Two of the brothers remained in New York City permanently to carry on the eastern activities of this growing enterprise: the buying of eastern merchandise and the selling of western produce.

The Seligman brothers, the first of whom, Sigmund, reached Santa Fe in 1849, produced a similar history by establishing Seligman and Clever, which in 1856, a few years after the arrival of Bernard, became Seligman Brothers.[21] Zoldac and Abraham Staab of Westphalia started a general merchandise firm in Santa Fe in 1858 which Twitchell has described as the largest wholesaling house in the Southwest in the 1860's.[22]

Elsberg and Amberg

The most important of these early German immigrants, who provide a thread and setting for our story, were two cousins: Gustave Elsberg and Jacob Amberg.[23] When they came to this country is not known, but they founded a partnership for the purpose of conducting a dry goods and general merchandise business in the town of Westport, Missouri, March 7, 1855. Elsberg at that time was a resident of Philadelphia and Amberg of Santa Fe. We can assume with little fear of error that the two had been carrying on business dealings prior to their new venture, Elsberg probably acting as Amberg's eastern purchasing agent. Such was the agreement anyway in the articles of partnership. The fact that Amberg contributed $1250 capital in cash and Elsberg "his name and reputation" indicates the latter's previous acquaintance with the purchasing function. Nothing could convey more the spirit of empire that pervaded these Santa Fe merchants than the clause in the partnership agreement suggesting an expansion of the business to other places in or out of the United States.[24] This plan subsequently became more than a dream, for the store in Westport was abandoned and transferred to Santa Fe sometime during 1856, and in October, 1866, a branch was established in Chihuahua.[25]

Santa Fe had not grown greatly in the first 60 years of the nineteenth century but its economic complexion following the Mexican War had taken on a new hue. Elsberg and Amberg were typical of the new merchants who had made this alteration permanent. In 1800, when the town had little more than 4000 inhabitants, few people earned their livelihood from the income of the community. Santa Fe was a town, socially and politically, but from an economic point of view it was still a village. People lived as an organization but their income came directly from the ground. The wealth and influence was in the hands of the "ricos," the owners of the large cattle and sheep ranges, who controlled a feudal society.[26]

After 1830 a rapid change took place.[27] The settled petty capitalist, a general storekeeper or shopkeeper, appeared and attracted to him the farmers and ranchers of the surrounding area now willing and anxious to trade where stores and shops would offer a year-round selection of goods and services. Then in the 1850's came the sedentary merchant, not content merely to sell but desirous to enlist and control the petty capitalist farmer and his supply of produce for eastern shipment. Like Zoldac and Abraham Staab they took the "hay, grain, chili, beans, flour, and buffalo meat giving employment to many of the native citizens of New Mexico who gained their livelihood as sub-contractors." [28] From 1830 to as late as 1890 Santa Fe remained supreme as the most influential economic town in New Mexico, losing its commercial prestige only as the railroads bypassed it to spur the growth of the towns of Las Vegas and Albuquerque.[29]

Among those firms that contributed heavily to this commercial change was the partnership of Elsberg and Amberg. As far as can be gleaned from Santa Fe newspapers of 1864–65, this mercantile house prospered and grew large principally through the efforts of its local partner, Jacob Amberg. Amberg was not one to overlook the possibilities of public relations as a method of building business, and the newspapers, conscious of the growing importance of the merchant, found in this particular individual much worth publicizing. Jacob Amberg sensed this mercantile influence in the building of a town and the wisdom of letting others know of his activities, as is evident from the following quotation:[30]

Elsberg and Amberg . . . are pushing on their work upon their large and splendid building so imposing in its position and appearance. . . . These men might have sent the profits of their trade to Europe or elsewhere but they have chosen to add an enduring species of wealth to the city of Santa Fe.

The firm opened its doors for business in September, 1864, though the building was not fully completed until December.[31] The *Gazette,* in somewhat immoderate language, described the edifice:[32]

THE NEW BUILDING

Of Messrs. Elsberg and Amberg referred to in our article on the Masonic Dedication, requires more than passing notice. It is by far the most commodious and elegant building in New Mexico and we doubt if it has its equal west of the Missouri River. It is situated on the Northwest corner of the Plaza, is two stories high, 90 feet front, 130 feet in depth, with a portal around the entire front and side. In its construction was consumed the enormous amount of 300,000 feet of lumber, 150,000 adobes, and 90 kegs of nails. All the articles used in its construction were of the best material and quality; lumber being brought from their own mill where it had been prepared especially for the purpose. The house contains 26 rooms. The lower story is divided into store rooms and occupied by the Messrs. Zeckendorf, James Hunter, and Elsberg and Amberg. The corner store occupied by the latter firm is 24 feet by 31, with a wareroom attached 33 feet wide and 80 feet deep, and has a commodious and spacious cellar. The upper story, leading to which are five winding staircases, elegant specimens of workmanship, is laid out for private apartments and warerooms, and contains two magnificent halls, occupied respectively by the Masonic and Odd Fellows' lodges. The entire building is well lighted with large windows, which with the judicious arrangement of the rooms, gives it a peculiar light and tasteful appearance for a building of its strength and solidity. Altogether it is a fine specimen of architecture, a credit to Santa Fe, and an enduring testimony of the sterling business men and gentlemen, Messrs. Elsberg and Amberg.

It is perhaps noteworthy that such news items as these and others were obtained, as far as can be determined, from extant newspapers, without a single advertisement being placed in either *The New Mexican* or its competitor, *The Gazette.* Elsberg and Amberg's competitors, however, advertised frequently with no such reward.[33]

Even the advent of a mule train, a most common occurrence those days in Santa Fe, brought Elsberg and Amberg more than ordinary recognition: [34]

The train of Elsberg and Amberg of ten wagons, loaded with their own goods, came in last Monday. The mules belonging to this train looked extremely well considering their trip, and were said by good judges to be the largest and best mules that have come to Santa Fe this year. But it is a failing that this firm is affected with, that they always will have the best in the Territory without any exception.

Jacob Amberg did not miss an opportunity for publicity even in grief. Some time after the founding of the firm he had brought his young cousin, Herman Elsberg, a native of Prussia, to manage the firm's mercantile and mining properties at Pinos Altos, an operation some nine miles north of Silver City. In 1861 a band of Apaches stole the mules and other animals belonging to the establishment situated near the mines. Young Elsberg gathered a party of 12 men and gave chase, but the Apaches ambushed and slaughtered the group.[35] Four years later Amberg made the trip to the mine, disinterred his cousin's body, and reburied it in Santa Fe. *The Santa Fe New Mexican* carried the story with color and detail.[36]

The operations of Elsberg and Amberg were extensive. In 1865 the Pinos Altos Mining Company was incorporated with Jacob Amberg as president.[37] In addition to the lumber mill and company store mentioned above, Gustave Elsberg listed in July of 1869 stock in Pinos Altos Mining Company, part interest in the Hanover Copper Mine and other mines, a small interest in coal mining shares, interest in the San Eulalia mine in Mexico, and over $100,000 of merchandise stock in Santa Fe and Chihuahua.[38] The partnership liabilities were given as approximately $210,000 to New York creditors.[39]

When the petty capitalists, settled and traveling, were retreating before the stronger and more permanent mercantile capitalists, and when the restless capital of the trader was taking root with these sedentary merchants, it was this company of Elsberg and Amberg (representing the transitory decade for Santa Fe from 1855 to 1865) who invited Herman Ilfeld, another German immigrant, to become a partner in 1865.[40] It was Elsberg and Amberg, too, who in the same year gave Charles Ilfeld, younger brother of Herman, his first employment on the frontier. It was this same company that, through the next three years, financed the new firm of A. Letcher Company, antecedent to the Charles Ilfeld Company and subsequently to become the largest mercantile house in New Mexico.[41]

II

CHARLES ILFELD COMES TO TAOS, 1865

Migration

Charles Ilfeld was the seventh child of ten born to Lester and Bettie Ilfeld of Homburg vor der Hohe. William, the oldest living son, having inherited his father's butcher shop, was little inclined to tear up his roots to plant them in the new environment.[1] The younger brothers had no such restraining influence. With Prussian conscription to escape and the new world beckoning, Herman, the second son, already had made his choice, and Charles, of like mind, was soon to follow him.[2]

Charles had just turned eighteen when he sailed from Hamburg on or shortly after April 29, 1865. His passport describes him as five and one-half feet tall, with brown eyes, dark hair, long nose, broad chin.[3] Already he had acquired an excellent knowledge of English and a fair competency in bookkeeping.[4] Surely with these qualities it would not be long before he could find his way in the new land. With such tools for confidence it was easy to sever his ties with the Fatherland.

We can envision Herman arranging for Charles to meet Gustave Elsberg in New York City. Elsberg, as purchasing partner for Herman and Jacob Amberg, had been buying heavily during the Civil War and, with prices still on the rise, Charles may well have received an earful of optimism concerning the prospects of trade in the Southwest.[5] He left New York almost immediately, determined to take advantage of the opportunity that awaited him.

We do not know for certain his exact route to Santa Fe. Those who had money and did not wish to endure the hardships and dangers of a caravan "chaperoning the patient ox," went with comparative speed and comfort via the Burlington and the Hannibal and St. Joseph railroads, ferrying the Missouri River to Fort Leavenworth.[6] Here a steamboat could be boarded for Kansas City. A Barlow-Sanderson stage, protected by United States Cavalry, would deliver its passengers in Santa Fe in 15 days.[7]

Charles Ilfeld, however, left Westport, Missouri, by ox-wagon, probably accompanying an Elsberg and Amberg caravan, making the arduous trip in 90 days.[8] He very likely reached his destination in early August of 1865.

Selection of Taos

The young immigrant arrived in Santa Fe at a propitious time. The Civil War had ended only a few months before. Civilian trade, which had been completely destroyed between Santa Fe and Arizona, Chihuahua, and Durango, and which to Missouri had been profitable only in the summers, was now growing with the large influx of people from the East and from Europe.[9] Government contracts to supply the forts, a lucrative business during the war, continued to be a boon to larger merchants. As bidders on this type of business, Elsberg and Amberg must have wished more than once for a direct contact with the plentiful crops of corn and wheat growing some 95 trail miles northeast in the fertile valley of Taos.[10]

The temptation to tap this grain source was enhanced by the depressed prices prevailing in Taos—a condition brought on by the difficulty of transporting crop surpluses by wagon over the mountainous terrain. Céran St. Vrain, along with 138 others, in an open letter to President Lincoln in 1863, pleading for a public road between Santa Fe and Taos, complained: [11]

> The valley of Taos, almost unbounded in extent, unvaryingly fertile, and rich in agricultural products, has long been considered, as it promises ever to remain, the principal granary of this Territory; yet inhospitably shut in by natural barriers, wanting available artificial outlets, and thus, in great measure, isolated from interior marts of trade, in vain has plenty reached abundance, and an over-supply cheapened prices far below demand elsewhere. On this point it will be sufficient to refer your Excellency to the statistics of our last census report, to show our annual grain product, while we beg leave to remark, that corn and wheat which bring at this time $1. and $1.50 a *fanega* (about two and a half bushels) in Taos, is from six to eight dollars in Santa Fe.

These spreads in prices were in large measure absorbed by the 3¼ cents per pound transportation charges between the two towns, a cost that the mercantile capitalist, with his own equipment, could reduce.[12] This was a situation ripe for the sedentary merchant, who thrived on the inertia and timidness of others.

Those merchants who could buy grain "on the ground" were in a most favorable position. The mercantile houses of Santistevan, St. Vrain and Company, and the Beuthner Brothers, as well as Lucien Maxwell, who had "a very prosperous business as merchant and contractor for troops" in Taos, were such people.[13] This competition, no doubt, encouraged Jacob Amberg and Herman Ilfeld to seek an agent in Taos. Such an agent could be both a buyer of grain and an outlet for merchandise. Why not make possible the establishment of such a firm closely tied to Elsberg and Amberg?

We do not know actually who was responsible for this idea. Perhaps it came about substantially as we have indicated above. Perhaps, however, Jacob Amberg and Herman Ilfeld were greatly influenced by a thirty-six-year-old trader from Baltimore, Adolph Letcher, of whom we know very little.[14] Letcher may well have been employed by or connected with one of the Taos firms. Probably he was impressed, because of the success of men like Solomon Beuthner and Céran St. Vrain, with the profit possibilities existing in that area. It would be interesting to know his background and the circumstances under which he obtained support from Elsberg and Amberg and thus became associated with Charles Ilfeld.

A. Letcher Company

Letcher started a new firm in Taos in September, 1865.[15] It was well stocked with merchandise on credit from Elsberg and Amberg. Charles went with Letcher, but did he also go with the merchandise? Letcher had known the young man but a few weeks, and Charles was only eighteen. Ilfeld was a willing applicant for any first-rate opportunity, a loyal protégé of Elsberg and Amberg, and a promising apprentice for Letcher.

The confidence of the Santa Fe firm in Adolph Letcher is significant. The volume of merchandise supplied can only suggest that Letcher was well known in those parts, highly trustworthy, and considered to be a man of real ability. The opening inventory of A. Letcher Company, bought entirely from Elsberg and Amberg on credit, amounted to $13,864. Eleven days later, before any remittances had been made, this stock had been increased by $2225. By the first of the year purchases of goods through this source grew to $34,800.

Almost $13,000 of the opening inventory had been purchased for Letcher by Elsberg in New York. The account ledger reveals its route and cost of transport:

Account Ledger

Expenses on $12,769.83 from New York @ 15%	$1916.48
10,895 lbs. from St. Louis to Leavenworth @ 75¢ per 100	81.71
Storage commission and drayage in Leavenworth @ 17¢	18.52
Insurance from St. Louis to Leavenworth of $1065.00 @ 1%	10.65
Freight from Leavenworth to Santa Fe, 10,895 lbs. @ 14¢	1525.30
	$3552.66
Cash paid on above from Santa Fe	351.00
Total Cost	$3903.66

Freight, drayage, insurance, and storage commissions from New York, therefore, added slightly more than 30 per cent to the cost of merchandise delivered in Taos.

The merchandise was varied. A selected sample sold before the end of the year is interesting both as to kind of goods and price:

Clothing: Silk dress $100.00; silk cloak $35.00; shawls: silk $8.00, wool $15.50, muslin $3.00; pair of silk hose $2.50; boy's suit $12.00; straw hat $1.25; balmoral shirt $9.00; shirt $3.25; pair of boots $12.00.

Dry Goods: Manta 27¢ per yard; calico 33¢; linen 27¢; cambric 75¢; poil de chevre (mohair) $1.00.

Groceries and Dairy: Coffee 60¢ per pound; sugar 45¢; butter 75¢; lard 50¢–60¢; pepper $1.50; eggs 38¢ per dozen.

Miscellaneous: Razor $3.00; bar of soap 35¢; saddle $35.00; gallon of whiskey $6.00; bottle of castor oil 25¢.

Customers and Trade Area

One of the firm's good customers was Solomon Beuthner, who, together with his two brothers, had built a very successful mercantile business in Taos.[16] It was still operating in May of 1864, and probably a year later.[17] The firm of Scheurich and Ritz, freighters on the Santa Fe Trail, patronized A. Letcher Company and paid for its purchases in freighting services.[18] Scheurich was related to Kit Carson by marriage.[19] Céran St. Vrain, famous frontiersman, merchant, and owner of a flour mill, made occasional purchases.[20]

The account of Major Pfeiffer, aide to Kit Carson and perhaps the most ruthless Indian fighter of his day, clearly bears out a weakness ascribed to the man in a letter cited by Sabin: [21]

Santa Fe, May 8, 1863

Dear Pfeiffer:

. . . I have been making inquiries of every person who has seen you and they all tell me that your face is not yet well, and that you are again drinking. When will you have sense? Can't you try and quit whiskey for a little while, at least until you get your face cured? If your face ain't well when I next see you, you had better look out.

. . . Remember me kindly to Mrs. Pfeiffer, and remember also what I say about your drinking.

Yours Truly,
C. Carson
Col. N. M. Vols.

Pfeiffer purchased 39 bottles of whiskey from Letcher in 34 days. If it were not for this letter of Carson's, we could be pardoned for assuming his consumption to have been above normal at this time, a consequence of the brutal killing of his wife by the Mescalero Apache Indians.[22] To his credit, or good luck, it should be recorded that in February of 1866 he apparently met a reforming influence, for his whiskey purchases dropped to one bottle in the next three months. Substituted therefor were such items as 12 yards of calico, 12 yards of linen, one skirt, chocolate, and an accordion. As suddenly as the whiskey had stopped, however, it started again, and he was off to Fort Garland, Colorado, to help his friend and superior, Kit Carson.[23]

The great majority of Letcher's customers were local, of course. Many, however, were ranchers and farmers who came in from an area 25 to 40 miles north and south of Taos, principally along the trail which the military used in transferring supplies and men from Fort Marcy, Santa Fe, through Taos to Fort Garland, Colorado, 80 miles north in the San Luis Valley. The weakness of Taos in continuing to exist as a prosperous economic town, serving a surrounding trade area of dependent villages, is clear from these book accounts. The outlying customers were few and scattered, stretching in linear fashion along a route on which commerce was insecurely supported by the military, and riskily dependent upon the continued flow of trade along the Taos branch of the Santa Fe Trail.

Money Barter

Through one of his customers, Letcher kept in close contact with Elsberg and Amberg in Santa Fe. He was Felipe Lidu, the mail carrier. He was employed by Elsberg and Amberg, but his wages of $70 per month were paid by A. Letcher Company and deducted from the firm's liability to the Santa Fe firm. Felipe, like many others who sold services or merchandise to Letcher, was seldom paid in cash. What good was cash but to risk losing? Credit, against which needed merchandise could be drawn, was available at both Taos and Sante Fe. Many customers made frequent withdrawals of from $1.00 to $10.00; seldom would anyone have need for more.

These barter accounts were in many cases both a necessity and an advantage to Letcher. This method of trade was permitted and encouraged when a drain on cash would otherwise result. The purchase by Letcher of wheat, corn, oats, fruit, beef cattle, and lumber, all of which usually would have had a ready market in Santa Fe, were paid for in merchandise. A double profit resulted, and a maximum reduction in liability to Elsberg and Amberg was effected.

In his youthful exuberance, Charles Ilfeld, serving as clerk and bookkeeper for Letcher, made a detailed credit to the Elsberg and Amberg account which shows the possibility of money barter.[24] Letcher sold wheat in Santa Fe for $1050. It was entered as $550 cost and $500 profit. The merchandise bartered for the $550 worth of wheat probably yielded another $275 gross profit.

Letcher and Ilfeld carried cash conservation to great lengths. With the exception of rent, which was $30 per month, there was no other regular-expense outlay which was not bartered. During the first month in Taos, Letcher and Ilfeld boarded at the house of Albino Chavez at a cost of $60 for the two of them.[25] Chavez' purchases from the store, however, were meager, not quite reaching the $60 mark by the end of the month. The young men, therefore, transferred their patronage to the more affluent John LeRoux, rancher, agreeing to pay $100 per month.[26] Though the charge was higher, they did somewhat better, for John LeRoux was purchasing well-marked-up merchandise at the rate of $150 per month. In the meantime Chavez had to wait until his debt to Letcher surpassed $60 to receive his offsetting claim.

The personal needs of these two bachelors were small, and their demands upon the business were slight. All of Ilfeld's withdrawals were charged to wages, indicating he was not a partner during the Taos period.[27] Apparently Ilfeld withdrew $250 in cash in 20 months, which sum, when coupled with the gross cost of his board properly chargeable to wages, amounted to $1210 or a wage of about $60 per month. Letcher in the same period withdrew cash in the amount of $673 and merchandise valued at almost $300.

The clear objective of every transaction was to garner and conserve all the cash possible in order that it might be sent to Elsberg and Amberg. If neither Letcher nor Ilfeld found it convenient to make the five-day trip to Santa Fe, there was always a trusted friend passing on his way south who would gladly carry the greenbacks for them. At various times Aloys Scheurich, the freighter; Goldbaum or Kirchner, butchers; or Joseph Hirsch, Colonel St. Vrain, J. Clothier, merchants; or Colonel Carson, rancher, and others delivered as much as $2000 per trip in greenbacks as a convenience for their friend Letcher.

Analysis of Total Business

A falling price level and declining sales, however, were a cause of great concern to the new firm. Total sales fell from an average of $3912 per month in 1865, to $1526 in 1866, to $816 in 1867. Cash receipts during the Taos experience declined from $2726 per month to $904. Despite an almost complete abstention from credit sales in November, 1866, and the following months, the accounts receivable the next April were down only one third from their peak and were higher than the total had been 15 months before (see Table 1).

Letcher's financial condition might have been precarious had it not been for his unusual frontier experience of being able to make two thirds of his sales in cash. Atherton estimated this cash ratio at less than one half and typically one third or less for the early merchant in mid-America, a fraction considerably higher than that experienced by the merchant of Colonial days.[28] Two factors could account for this marked difference in Letcher's experience. Soldiers traded a good deal in Taos, and for the most part paid cash and, as will be shown presently, the prospects for good credit risks in this area were not great.

TABLE 1. A. LETCHER COMPANY CASH RECEIPTS, SALES AND RECEIVABLES, TAOS, NEW MEXICO, SEPTEMBER, 1865–APRIL, 1867 (DOLLARS)

Date	Cash receipts	Cash sales	Charge sales	Total sales	Receivables
1865					
Sept.	2,718	2,718	693	4,461 [a]	693
Oct.	2,859	2,427	1,385	3,812	1,443
Nov.	3,271	2,620	1,841	4,601 [a]	2,035
Dec.	2,056	1,585	1,187	2,772	2,530
Total	10,904	9,350	5,106	15,646 [a]	
Monthly average	2,726	2,338	1,277	3,912	
1866					
Jan.	1,916	1,629	316	1,945	1,997
Feb.	1,348	1,030	410	1,440	1,977
Mar.	583	447	375	822	2,055
Apr.	932	815	419	1,234	2,242
May	1,465	1,266	497	1,763	2,498
June	734	653	143	796	2,485
July	895	839	381	1,602 [a]	2,748
Aug.	571	504	142	873 [a]	2,778
Sept.	1,562	1,359	488	1,847	3,013
Oct.	1,702	1,579	98	1,677	2,848
Nov.	1,672	1,377	1,758	3,135	3,273
Dec.	1,336	895	281	1,176	
Total	14,716	12,393	5,308	18,310 [a]	
Monthly average	1,226	1,033	442	1,526	
1867					
Jan.	756	746	62	808	2,861
Feb.	841	715	14	729	2,660
Mar.	505	414	—	414	2,355
Apr.	1,515	1,291	12	1,314 [a]	2,084
Total	3,617	3,166	88	3,265 [a]	
Monthly average	904	792	22	816	
Grand total	29,237	24,909	10,502	37,221 [a]	

Source: Derived from Cash Receipts Book I and analysis of Account Ledger A of A. Letcher Company (University of New Mexico Library).

[a] Total sales increased by sales to Elsberg and Amberg of grain totaling $1810 which were offsets to accounts payable.

More than half of Letcher's receipts on accounts had been in merchandise and services, and the former had not been convertible, readily, into cash since the rapid decline in prices which had begun in the early part of 1866. Losses on accounts were running high: 8.5 per cent of charge sales; 2.5 per cent of total sales.[29] Elsberg and Amberg, suffering from the same ailment but on a larger scale, would not be patient long. Letcher's liability to them had been reduced more than $31,000 by April, 1867, of which approximately $27,000 had been through the medium of cash—a figure only $2000 less than the total cash receipts since the start of the business. And still a balance of $11,375 remained.

Commercial Decline of Taos

These figures were most discouraging and yet they told but half the story. Underneath it all Letcher and Ilfeld now saw clearly much that could have been seen in 1865 had their vision not been directed by older heads in Santa Fe, and perhaps in Taos. Eighteenth-century Taos had gone forever. The great fairs, which had been held in July of each year, complementing the January fairs in Chihuahua, had marked the commercial terminals of the old North-South trail.[30] The Taos fairs, held as late perhaps as the 1820's, passed away coincidentally with the decline in the fur trade.[31] Taos had been trapped out in the middle 1820's as far as practical support of any large trade was concerned.[32]

The Santa Fe Trail and Bent's Fort on the Arkansas River had temporarily revived the commercial glories of another day. The Cimarron Desert to the East constituted as great a hazard as the Indians, and it was safer to follow the northern, well-watered route, turning south from Bent's Fort to the Cimarron River, and thence westward directly to Taos.

The ox-wagon caravan had changed all that. Since William Becknell had introduced this mode of transportation on the Trail in the spring of 1822, the Santa Fe trade had ignored Taos to an ever-increasing degree.[33] This change must have been quite obvious by 1865. Only two years before, St. Vrain and his fellow townsmen had publicly described the isolated position of Taos.[34] In the fall of 1864 the *Rio Abajo Weekly Press* of Albuquerque had editorialized: "Taos is also a centre for a considerable local trade, and would rival Santa Fe as a commercial centre were it not for its inaccessibility by wagons." [35] These heavy laden vehicles were difficult for drivers to control and for animal power to pull over the double ridge of the Sangre de Cristo Mountains.

Letcher determined to move to greener pastures in the spring of 1867. Packing his inventory on the backs of nearly a hundred burros, a caravan was prepared to wind its way eastward over the mountains and south to Mora and Las Vegas.[36] The mode of transport was significant.

As for the old men of Taos—they were about to leave, too. Kit Carson died in 1868, William Bent in 1869, and St. Vrain (who had already moved to Mora on the other side of the mountains) in 1870, the same year that Lucien Maxwell departed upon the sale of his famous Maxwell Land Grant.[37]

Commercially, Taos had been dying for years.[38] Adolph Letcher and Charles Ilfeld witnessed the death. They slipped away just before the burial.

III

LETCHER AND ILFELD, LAS VEGAS (1867–1874)

Las Vegas in Retrospect

On their journey away from Taos across the mountains to the Mora Valley, Letcher and Ilfeld had plenty of time to contemplate as they rode beside their plodding caravan. Taos County lay behind them—ancient, decadent, isolated, one seventh of its prewar population gone, its once dynamic leaders sapped of their strength, or dead.[1] Ahead were the wheat fields, the flocks of sheep, the energetic and prosperous farmers of the Mora Valley. Even the donkeys would "perk up" when they refreshed themselves in the tall grasses and watering places along the Mora River.

The town of Mora, with its 800 inhabitants, would give a preview of the commercial prospects of this whole area to the east of the Sangre de Cristo Mountains. The German merchants, who dominated the town, had brought the beginnings of mercantile capitalism to this grain-growing region.[2] They had prospered, largely because of the location of Fort Union just 20 miles to the east. A traveling reporter, writing for the *Santa Fe New Mexican,* described the Mora merchant as one who exchanged goods for grain to the extent of need: "The merchant then makes a heavy advance upon his goods, and he profits upon selling the grain to the government, or those who have contracts with the government."[3]

Beyond to the south was the County of San Miguel, with the largest and fastest growing population of any area in the Territory. Its administrative heart was the bustling town of Las Vegas, standing in the path of the stagecoach and wagon train bound for Santa Fe some 70 miles beyond. More and more, however, the caravans had been stopping in Las Vegas to unload their wares for the distributors who, in that location, were taking advantage of the shorter route. These same distributors had lower freight costs and found that the extensive plains and mesas, fanning out from east to south, provided vantage routes to a productive and populous region. Many of the cattlemen and sheepmen in eastern New Mexico, from Fort Bascom in the north to Roswell and the Pecos Valley in the south, had been driving their stock to Las Vegas and in turn purchasing their supplies in that center. Las Vegas was becoming a gathering point for wool, hides, and metals from the Pecos and Mesilla Valleys and from the

Grant County region near the Mexican border, as well as for the grains and lumber of San Miguel and Mora counties. Now a town of well over 2000 people, serving a trade territory of more than 30,000, Las Vegas encouraged comparison with Taos.[4] The new town, expanding and open to the flow of commerce, promised a permanency of a different character.

Such thoughts as these were a bit incongruous in the light of Las Vegas' brief history. Gregg could not have forecast this development in 1831 when, upon reaching the Gallinas River, he reported seeing "a large flock of sheep grazing" and "a little hovel at the foot of a cliff." [5] The settlers on the second Vegas Grandes Grant could not have foreseen the change to come when they selected their townsite in 1835.[6] This "dirty mud town of some seven hundred inhabitants," described by Davis in the early 1850's, did not foreshadow the metamorphosis which commerce was to bring at the beginning of the next decade.[7]

In all probability, however, these historical considerations were not among the thoughts of Letcher and Ilfeld as they watched the burros grow weary under their 200 to 300 pound burdens. Their hopes were pinned to the future—a future that boded well, but was to require of them more than average ability. Las Vegas already had a full complement of able, established merchants, many of whom had acquired a loyal following. It would not be easy to become accepted commercially in the same company with Emanuel Rosenwald, who had built a large mercantile business since his coming in 1862, or Michael Des Marais, who had been merchandising and contracting since 1852.[8] Trinidad Romero and brothers had done well, as had John and Andres Dold—the last named being one of the more prominent and well-liked merchants in the Territory.[9]

Then there was the genial Marcus Brunswick, merchant, freighter, and contractor, of Brunswick and Hecht, whom everyone loved and respected and whose advice in all matters was widely sought.[10] Already established there, too, were Charles Emil Wesche and many others, all with going mercantile businesses; the newcomers would have to prove their worth.[11]

The New Business Site

The burro train filed into the Plaza of West or Lower Las Vegas early in May of 1867, and the slow process of unloading began. One by one the sturdy little animals were led in front of Frank Kihlberg's old store, midway on the north side, and relieved of their burdens.[12] It was a small, one-story adobe building that Kihlberg had occupied for several years while carrying on a mercantile and freighting business with his partner. Kihlberg was an "old-timer" in Las Vegas, having lived there since 1852.[13] Letcher was fortunate to find this vacancy with the expectation of keeping some of Kihlberg's customers and good will.

The Plaza itself was an excellent location. Ranchers and traders made this their stopping place, usually with headquarters at the Exchange Hotel.[14] Wagon and mule trains from the hinterland could drape themselves conveniently around the oval while the grain or hides were being "weighed in."

Letcher had agreed to pay $100 per month rent for this location, though he reduced this amount somewhat by subletting Kihlberg's old office to Henry Schwarz, a jeweler.[15] Perhaps he was a little optimistic in view of the experience he had just been through, coupled with the continuing decline in prices. But he had several factors on his side now. His trade area was an expanding one; his location was such as to attract a large number of customers to him; Elsberg and Amberg had agreed again to tide him over with merchandise; and, perhaps more important than anything else, Charles Ilfeld was no longer the apprentice to be tested.[16] This young man of twenty had demonstrated ably his willingness and capacity to share responsibility.

Partnership

Shortly after the opening of the Las Vegas store on May 13, 1867, Adolph Letcher "agreed with said Carl Ilfeld to receive him as a partner in his business." [17] Charles Ilfeld placed this date at about one month after the establishment of the store.[18] He became a partner in the concern on or before July 1, 1867.

There was no public evidence of such an agreement, so far as can be determined, until July 1, 1868, when a letter in Charles Ilfeld's handwriting was signed "A. Letcher and Company." [19] All letters of this company from this date forward were so subscribed. The reason for delaying the announcement, of course, was that the younger member of the firm could not carry his responsibility legally until his twenty-first birthday, which had occurred on April 19, 1868.

There is no clue to be found concerning the partnership agreement for the division of profits or net assets. No accounting was made in the records of profits or their distribution. Letcher, apparently, received 7 per cent on his investment, and Ilfeld an undeterminable rate.[20] The recording of capital (Letcher $7672.64 and Ilfeld $517.70, including interest) was not made until March 22, 1869, though each had posted his respective amount with Elsberg and Amberg in Santa Fe as partial guarantee for the payment of merchandise.[21]

Sales and Profits

The new firm met with immediate success. Its sales soared to more than $40,000 in the balance of that first year, upon which it was claimed and the partners admitted profits of $18,000.[22] Inasmuch as the expenses of the firm during that first 7½ months were only $3600, exclusive of partners' salaries, it would appear, if the profits figure was soundly conceived, that the mark-up was more than 100 per cent in spite of a falling price level (see Table 2).

TABLE 2. A. LETCHER AND COMPANY GROSS MARGIN, MAY 13–DECEMBER 31, 1867

	Dollars	Dollars	Per cent
Total sales		40,299.76	100
Expenses	3,626.64		
Profits	18,000.00	21,626.64	
Cost of merchandise		18,673.12	46
Gross margin		21,626.64	54
Mark-up on cost			116

Source: Cash Book, 1863–1868, and Ledger A.

ELSBERG AND AMBERG RELATIONSHIP

As A. Letcher and Company prospered, its chief supplier of goods and capital, Elsberg and Amberg, was finding the road a bit rocky. It will be recalled that their branch in Chihuahua had been established in October, 1866, and hence the inventory for that store must have been purchased at near peak prices.[23] Large amounts of merchandise had been furnished to Letcher in Taos upon which substantial credit balances were carried. Losses in their copper mines from 1861 to 1864 may have been heavy because of the Indian depredations.[24]

Gustave Elsberg brought the condition of his firm into the open in July, 1869, following a hurried trip to Santa Fe when he filed suit against his partners, Jacob Amberg and Herman Ilfeld.[25] When the debts of the partnership had grown to unbearable proportions, Amberg absconded from Santa Fe in late March or early April, apparently destined for Chihuahua; and Herman Ilfeld returned in April from a visit to Germany to find himself heir to a bankruptcy.[26] Elsberg's Bill in Chancery makes the progressive embarrassment clear: [27]

. . . during the years of One thousand eight hundred and sixty six, One thousand eight hundred and sixty seven, and One thousand eight hundred and sixty eight the remittances sent your orator [Elsberg], fell far too short to meet the liabilities when falling due and for necessary expenses, thereby necessitating on the part of your Orator, in order to maintain and uphold the credit of said firm, to resort to various expediences for the temporary raising of money, thereby in the end entailing losses on the firm, and that ever since the month of October One thousand eight hundred and sixty eight, the said defendant Amberg failed to send remittances in sufficient amounts to meet the liabilities of the said firm. . . .

While these developments were occurring, Gustave Elsberg was appointed eastern purchasing agent for the firm of A. Letcher and Company. In July, 1867, Ilfeld and Letcher began sending all funds they could spare to this agent in New York City, both to reduce their obligations and to make possible the purchase of merchandise. More than $25,000 was sent between July and December.[28]

In January, 1868, a letter written by Adolph Letcher suggests that some knowledge of the financial situation of Elsberg and Amberg was seeping through: [29]

January 29, 1868

Gustave Elsberg
314 Broadway
New York
Dear Sir:

I've received by last mail a letter from Jaraslowski Bros. written by Mr. Amberg of said firm, requesting me to send money for my Note, which has been due for the last 3 weeks. This letter is by no means a polite one, it is written in a most severe language. Now I would ask you how it stands with this note, *is it paid or not.* I wish you to informe [*sic*] me of this matter by return mail, as I would not answer this most insulting letter till I hear from you. I have inquired at your house in Santa Fe about the Note and Herman said in his letter that you had paid the amount there. It appears that Jaraslowskis have but very little confidence in your firm as they express themselves *not* to send the money to Elsberg as it will reach us sooner [direct?]. Inclosed you will find a copy of the letter.

With kind regards,

I am Respectfully,
and truly yours,
A. Letcher

By January, 1869, the financial condition of Elsberg and Amberg should have been obvious because A. Letcher and Company had posted bond with the United States government guaranteeing the fulfillment of a corn contract which Elsberg and Amberg had not been able to complete.[30] Yet the full import of this did not come to Letcher and Ilfeld until Gustave Elsberg passed through Las Vegas, on the morning of March 11, on the Santa Fe stage.[31] Herman Ilfeld, who might have kept his brother and Letcher better informed, had left Santa Fe the previous September for a visit to Germany and had not yet returned.[32] Elsberg, not in a happy frame of mind because of Amberg's dilatory remittances, apparently broke the news. He must have acquainted his listeners sufficiently with the true situation, because a draft for $1000 dispatched to New York by coach the night before, was the last transaction A.

Letcher and Company ever had with Elsberg and Amberg.[33] Relations were not to be severed completely, however, until the young firm had weathered a legal scare which threatened to drag it down with the older house.

Herman Ilfeld returned from Germany in April, "and being informed that said Elsberg and Amberg was greatly embarrassed [Elsberg] . . . being in the City of New York, and . . . Amberg in the Republic of Mexico, and finding his information correct . . . he at once devoted himself to settling the business of the same." [34] What he did, and how his actions were interpreted by Elsberg, make interesting reading (see Appendix 1). The effect on Charles Ilfeld and Letcher, however, came close to being disastrous, for Elsberg filed suit in Santa Fe, claiming these two men not only to be copartners but partners in Elsberg and Amberg as well.

No documentary evidence was presented to uphold this contention; there was only Elsberg's word that such had been the agreement. Amberg's voice was not present to verify or refute the charge, but Herman Ilfeld denied that "Adolph Letcher and Carl Ilfeld . . . ever were partners in the business of Elsberg and Amberg." [35] The point of debate turned on whether A. Letcher and Company had agreed to share its total profits permanently with Elsberg and Amberg, or only those profits arising from the sale of merchandise furnished by Elsberg and Amberg. Letcher denied categorically the former agreement, and he probably was supported in his claim by a document drawn in Santa Fe, March 22, 1869, purportedly releasing Letcher and Charles Ilfeld from "all claims and demands against them, and especially all claims as profits arising from their business in the future." (See Appendix 3.) The release was signed "Elsberg and Amberg," without a partner's separate signature, and in view of the absence of Herman and Elsberg, it could have been signed only by Jacob Amberg, whose disappearance tainted the entire development with fraud.

Whatever the whole truth may have been, several damaging letters written by Charles Ilfeld could have caused irreparable harm had they been available to the court. Two examples are given: [36]

November 8, 1867

Mess. Saml McCartney and Co.
St. Louis, Mo.
Gentlemen:

Enclosed please find drafts . . . total $148.50, which amount was paid to us for your firm of Mess. Dittenhoefer, Hamburger & Co. by order of our house in Santa Fe. Please acknowledge receipt and send Balance in two cents revenue stamps
and oblige yours

Elsberg and Amberg
by Charles Ilfeld

March 5, 1868

Mess. W. H. Chick & Co.
Ellsworth City, Ks.
Gentlemen:

We have ordered today some groceries of Mess. Sam'l McCartney in Saint Louis to which will be shipped to your care. Please forward same by first train at rate of eight cents per pound.

Respectfully yours
Elsberg and Amberg
by Charles Ilfeld

These letters and others like them indicate that some suppliers of A. Letcher and Company considered the firm to have been part and parcel with Elsberg and Amberg. One wonders whether Ilfeld and Letcher did not think likewise. Regardless of the facts in the case, whatever they may have been, the business historian can only look upon the quarrel as a logical, and not surprising, outgrowth of an economic system typified by interlocking partnerships. It was a confusing aspect of the structure of mercantile capitalism that the many relationships of the sedentary merchant with others, as either partners or agents, were not easily understood by outsiders.

Letcher and Ilfeld: Mercantile Capitalists

The passing of Elsberg and Amberg completed the transition of Adolph Letcher from a petty to a mercantile capitalist. It is perhaps unfair to place him, at any time, in the petty capitalist category, for at heart he had never been a part of it. His willingness and ability to assume large debt; his alacrity in moving from a small, country, general merchandise store in a decadent area, to a location amid mercantile capitalists in an expanding market; his alertness in seizing opportunities, as exemplified in the assumption of the Elsberg and Amberg corn contract, are evidence that he was consciously pointing toward economic freedom and varied risks.

This is not to ignore Charles Ilfeld as a force in this change, though his contribution was less direct. When he became a partner at the age of twenty, it was more a manifestation of Letcher's desire—and opportunity—to devote his energies to other profitable pursuits, than an indication that the young man had attained business maturity. Charles emulated Letcher's propensities and adapted himself quickly.

The failure of Elsberg and Amberg could not have come at a more convenient time as far as Letcher and Ilfeld were concerned. A much earlier collapse might have been most embarrassing to them, for it would have meant pressing the young firm to meet a rather heavy obligation before the business had become established in its new environment. A later failure might have postponed "the cutting of the apron strings" until the depression of the 1870's set in. Not having established independent credit lines and sources of supply, particularly in the East, Letcher and Ilfeld could have been placed in a difficult situation. As it happened, the partners were forced to take the initiative while business conditions were not too depressed, and, fortunately, at a time when the young firm had freed itself of debt.

As a stopgap, Letcher and Ilfeld purchased their needed eastern goods through David Letcher, a Baltimore merchant and brother of Adolph.[37] Their groceries were obtained through McCartney and Company, St. Louis, a firm that maintained an agent in the Territory with whom both men were well acquainted.[38]

It was necessary to cultivate personal association with suppliers if Letcher and Company were to receive merchandise of the quality desired at competitive prices. As far as practical it was wise to select goods personally, since eastern wholesalers had little "feel" of the southwestern markets, and the time element in replacing poorly selected merchandise was long, and involved heavy cost. Clearly, then, one of the partners would have to make at least one eastern trip a year.

Letcher spent much of his time traveling to various Army forts, soliciting what business he could.[39] Then with Ilfeld striving to collect accounts, Letcher left for the States in December, 1869.[40] He was gone until May, by which time he had established several connections with eastern firms, particularly S. Rosenthal of Baltimore.[41]

In the meantime Ilfeld was augmenting sales by filling Army contracts. He delivered oats to Fort Craig, beans to Fort Defiance, corn to Fort Wingate, and lumber to Fort Union, getting in return the needed money exchange to finance Letcher's purchases.[42]

The senior partner was off again in January, 1871, for six months and again in October.[43] The latter trip was short and for personal reasons. He returned with "his Lady" in December.[44] In June, 1872, Mr. and Mrs. Letcher left by stage for Kit Carson, Colorado, where they boarded the Kansas-Pacific Railroad for the East.[45] Ilfeld was left alone this time for nearly a year.

It was during this period that the younger partner's initiative and foresight become apparent to the historian. By January, 1873, he had rented (most certainly with Letcher's knowledge and approval) a property located at Tecolote, some nine miles south of Las Vegas and at the branch of the Santa Fe Trail, the south fork of which led to Anton Chico, Puerto de Luna, and Roswell.[46] Here he established a store and corral to service the Army and commercial travel.

Beginning in September, 1870, A. Letcher and Company had been operating a store and corral at El Monton de Los Alamos, about nine miles north of Las Vegas, a property rented from F. O. Kihlberg, landlord also of the store property in Las Vegas.[47] In April, 1872, Ilfeld completed arrangements to buy this property.[48] The "Alamos" branch served a similar objective to the one held by Elsberg and Amberg, when that firm sought a collection point for the grains of Taos. Letcher and Company could store grains of the Mora County region for profitable use in the servicing of the Army trains on their way to and from Fort Union, and for the horse teams of the Barlow-Sanderson stages operating between Santa Fe and the end of the Kansas-Pacific Railroad.

As this long period of sole responsibility wore on, Ilfeld must have given much thought to his position. He was facing and solving all the local problems, while his partner was making and strengthening the commercial connections upon which Ilfeld might be solely dependent sometime in the future. It is indicative, therefore, of the young man's initiative to learn that he departed shortly after Letcher and his wife returned in April, 1873, to see the East for himself and to make a long-delayed voyage to Germany.[49]

Upon reaching his home town of Homburg, Ilfeld was treated to a warming surprise at the sight of pretty Adele Nordhaus, daughter of Rabbi Nordhaus of Paderborn.[50] Now nineteen, she presented a delightful contrast to the little girl he had known eight years before.[51] Charles lost no time in proposing marriage, and before he embarked for New York with his fifteen-year-old brother, Louis, as company, Adele promised she would follow him as soon as a proper waiting period had transpired.[52]

Ilfeld returned to Las Vegas in November, 1873, but not until he had made the acquaintance of merchants in Baltimore and New York.[53] On his way west he cultivated ties in St. Louis, particularly Joel Wood of McCartney and Company, and then took the train to Kit Carson, Colorado, where he could spend some time studying the powerful forwarding houses of Otero and Sellar and Company, and Chick, Browne.

In the spring of 1874 Charles dropped all business and left for that anticipated reunion with Adele Nordhaus, who was to meet him at the end of her voyage to the States. The two were married, probably in New York City, on May 24, 1874.[54] (See Genealogy, Appendix 16.)

Charles Ilfeld: Proprietor

It is more than probable that Ilfeld knew when he left on his wedding trip that upon his return some agreement would be reached concerning his buying of Letcher's interest in the business. This seems certain in view of the following letter in Ilfeld's handwriting: [55]

March 20, 1874

Mess. S. Rosenthal
No. 76 Hanover St.
Baltimore, Md.
Dear Sir:

Enclosed hand you sight draft . . . Four Thousand eighty-five 87/100 Dollars which amount please place to Private Account of our Mr. A. Letcher. As he has no use for this amount at present, he wishes to state that you might loan the same out, on as good rate of interest as possible. . . .

Truly yours
A. Letcher & Co.

This was the first sizable withdrawal of capital by Letcher, and it reduced his original investment to less than $1000.

There were several likely reasons for Letcher's desire to leave. He was forty-five, and like many of the merchants of the Southwest before him who had accumulated some capital, he had a desire to settle down in a less strenuous atmosphere and to invest his capital for a more regular return. Marrying at his age, he was less willing to forego the personal use of his savings that the business might expand, and it can be presumed that Mrs. Letcher might have pressed the point that living on the frontier was "no life for a lady." [56]

The Ilfelds reached Las Vegas in early July, and the sale of Letcher's interest in the firm to Charles Ilfeld was consummated September 14, 1874 (Appendix 4). In the meantime Letcher had withdrawn the remainder of his original capital, as did Ilfeld. The purchase price of Letcher's interest was $36,000—$12,000 in cash and six notes of $4000 each, payable in consecutive four-month periods. Ilfeld assumed all known debts and acquired the entire property of the firm.

Where Ilfeld obtained the funds for the down payment is not clear. There is no evidence in the Charles Ilfeld Company records that any part of the $12,000 was borrowed, for no future payments on such a loan were ever made. Ilfeld had never withdrawn more than a pittance from the business. The cash balance of A. Letcher and Company just prior to Ilfeld's purchase of Letcher's interest was roughly $5000, no part of which was used to pay Letcher.[57]

A probable source of Charles Ilfeld's capital, however, can be detected in certain large receipts of the partnership that do not appear in either the cash or personal accounts. Cash in the amount of $7000, for instance, was received from Samuel B. Wheelock of Santa Fe in 1871 in payment for merchandise, without thereby increasing the book cash on hand.[58] The copy books reveal several Army contracts fulfilled with no record of compensation, though it is a certainty that monetary exchange must have been received. Undoubtedly Charles Ilfeld and Adolph Letcher made it a practice to divide "other income" occasionally when a "windfall" came their way. Ilfeld's share from such sources could well have equaled the $12,000 down payment on the Letcher purchase.[59]

The basis of valuation of the business can only be surmised. A reasonable assumption could be made that the price represented one half the value of the assets—cash, real property, and inventories at the three stores in Las Vegas, Tecolote, and Alamos less the known debts of the

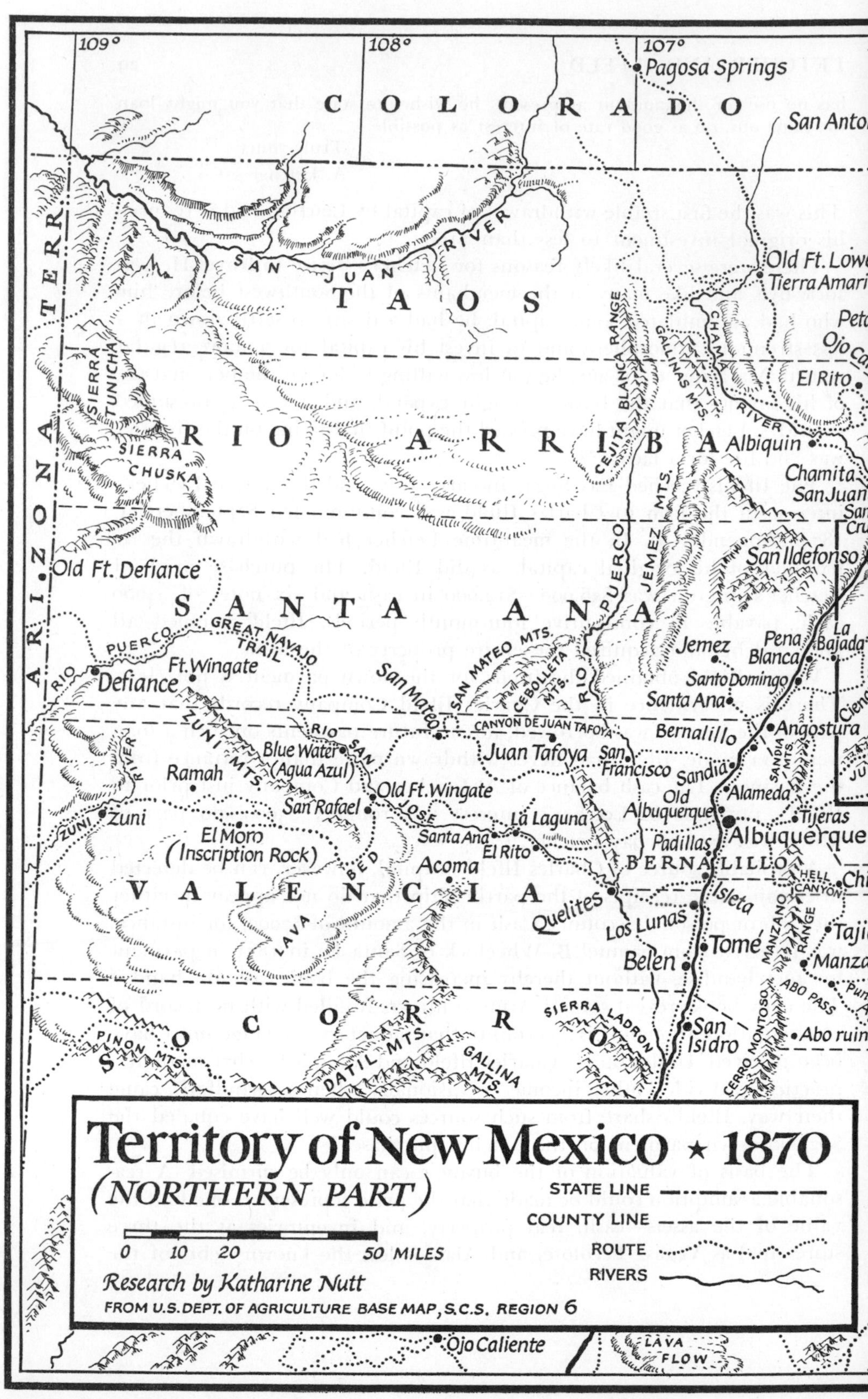

Territory of New Mexico ★ 1870

(NORTHERN PART)

Research by Katharine Nutt

FROM U.S. DEPT. OF AGRICULTURE BASE MAP, S.C.S. REGION 6

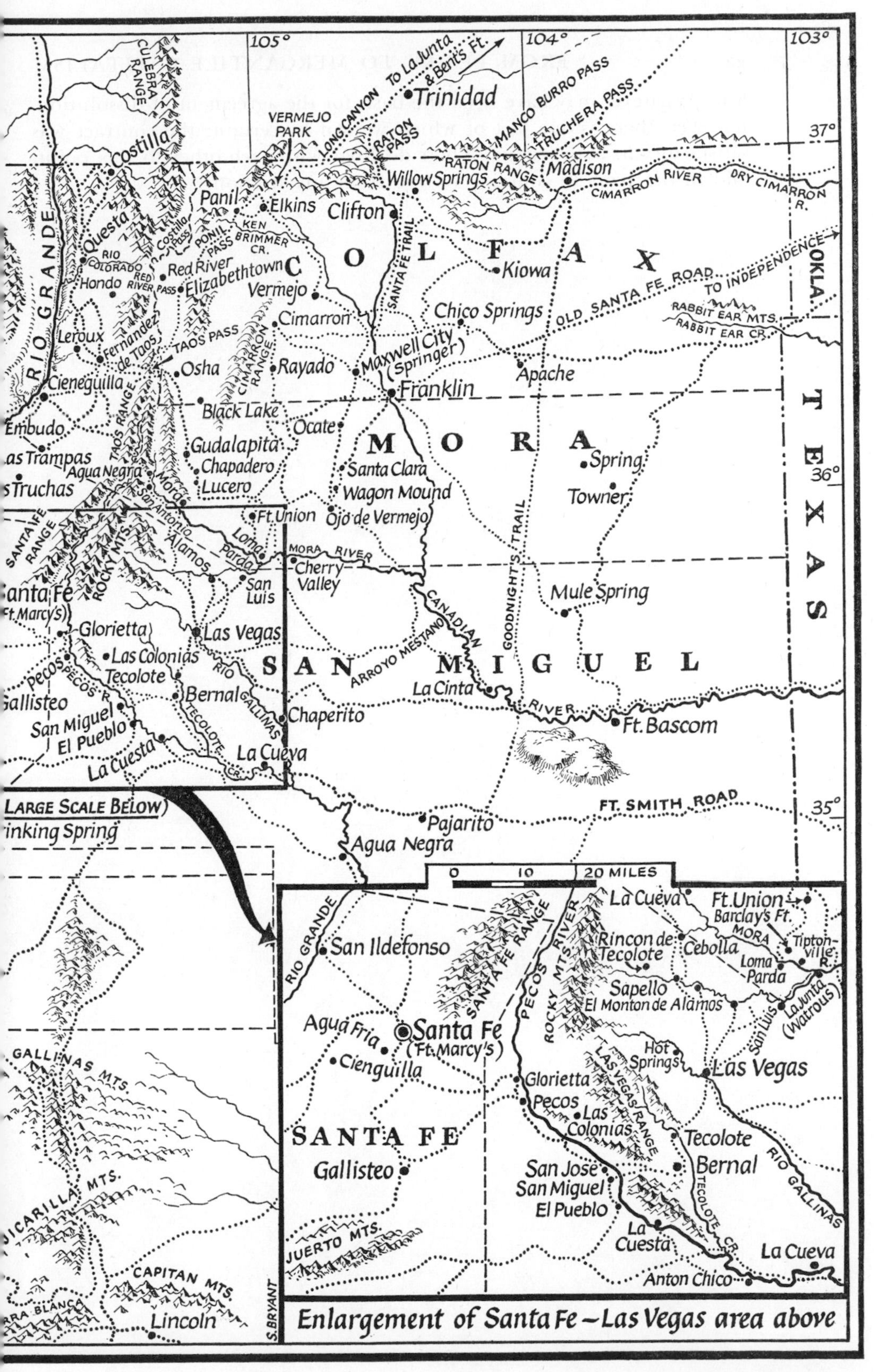

Enlargement of Santa Fe – Las Vegas area above
COLFAX
MORA
SAN MIGUEL
SANTA FE
TEXAS
OKLA.
Trinidad
Santa Fe
Las Vegas
Ft. Union
Ft. Bascom
Cimarron
Maxwell City (Springer)
Franklin
Taos
Lincoln
S. BRYANT

firm. Whatever may have been the basis for the agreement of dissolution, however, there is one fact of which we can be certain: the contract was satisfactory to both parties. Their dealings with each other to this point. and in the years to come, were free from any friction.[60]

PART TWO

Foundations of Mercantile Capitalism: Charles Ilfeld, 1867-1887 (Early Phase)

Introduction

In many outlying, less-developed regions of the world during the nineteenth century, mercantile capitalists were flourishing contemporaneously with industrial capitalists—those large specialists of the metropolitan centers. The success of the former rested solidly upon three foundations: the ability to acquire scarce monetary exchange acceptable for the purchase of foreign goods, the absence of an efficient system of indirect lending of capital, and the necessity for hauling purchases over vast stretches of water or sparsely settled land.

The significance of monetary exchange as a foundation of mercantile capitalism is in the method by which it had to be acquired. Either raw materials were sent to the industrial areas for credit against which drafts could be drawn, or capital, already invested in the hinterland by industrial specialists (such as the Army or transportation companies), served as a market from which monetary exchange could be obtained. In either case the petty capitalist farmers, loggers, trappers, or other small specialists became tools through which the sedentary merchant assured his sources of supply.

In the absence of an efficient system of indirect lending of capital, the sedentary merchant became the dominant source of credit for the petty capitalist. The merchant credit system of money barter, therefore, gave the sedentary merchant the controlling position in the hinterland hierarchy of business capitalism.

These two factors explain the reasons for the dominance of the mercantile over the petty capitalist. But what of the encroachment of the larger specialist of industrial capitalism? How could the mercantile capitalist, having been overshadowed in the metropolitan centers, survive and flourish in the distant, less developed areas? The answer is to be found in the third foundation of mercantile capitalism. The large specialist was dependent upon a substantial market for his goods sufficiently near the point of production to permit ready sales at low prices. The advantages of capital concentration and division of labor, tools of the larger, single-risk enterpriser, were lost if slow, inefficient transportation over long distances was to be used.

In the period 1867 to 1883, and for many years thereafter, Charles Ilfeld prospered as a general merchant, while his contemporaries in the East were concentrating on a single risk: such merchants as specialized wholesalers of either dry goods, hardware or groceries; manufacturers of congruous goods; or vendors of banking, transportation, or insurance services. Ilfeld's success as a multi-risk merchant can be traced directly to his intuitive use of the three foundations of mercantile capitalism. He dominated the petty capitalist through his drive for monetary exchange and his granting of merchant credit. He was protected against the low-cost specialists of the East by distance; and, when they came west as banks and railroads, they became for a period of time as subservient to him through their inherent weaknesses, as he, in other respects, grew dependent upon them.

Each of these foundations deserves a separate analysis, and the first to be chosen, because it was uppermost in the mind of the mercantile capitalist, is the acquisition of scarce monetary exchange.

IV

MONETARY EXCHANGE, LAS VEGAS AND THE EAST

Role of the Forts

The Red man and the White man played their respective parts in obstructing the progress of New Mexico's trade: the Red man by prolonged though intermittent carnage, and the White man by fringe skirmishes in his Civil War. With the notable exception of the Apache tribes to the south both had found peace by the close of 1866, but the public works arising from their fracases, the forts, remained to give the sedentary merchant his most needed tool for business—exchange.[1]

It cannot be said that the forts supplied this need fully or adequately. One can only be apprehensive of the consequences had these monuments to posterity begun their decay before their more constructive contribution had been recorded. A dozen or more military establishments not only helped to bolster Territorial income, thus permitting greater capital formation, but they remained for some years a principal source of eastern exchange, the only domestic exchange acceptable to eastern suppliers of merchandise.[2] Any dependable and ready source of New York drafts would obviate the expense and risk of shipping currency and would place less dependence upon the long, slow consignments of raw materials for eastern credit.

The sutler attached to each fort became the liaison man between the merchants of the immediate area and the fort with respect to the exchange of greenbacks for drafts. The fort could use currency for payroll purposes and would gladly remit drafts in exchange.[3] Merchants, needing drafts to pay eastern bills, would forward their currency to the sutler with a request for an eastern draft, which was usually obtainable by return mail. As long as drafts were transferred between merchants, there is no evidence that any service charges were made.[4] This service was merely an accommodation typical of the camaraderie of the frontier. We will see it again in matters of collection, servicing of freight, and communications.

Charles Ilfeld dealt with W. H. Moore, the sutler at Fort Union, some 25 miles north of Las Vegas.[5] Moore, who had a number of mercantile establishments at one time or another, using different partnership arrangements, built his store at Fort Union with the problems of monetary exchange in mind.[6] Two stories high with brick walls, this sutler's store enclosed a plaza large enough for wagons to be driven within and unloaded. A safe room had been constructed for the payroll money Moore would hold and dispense for the soldiers and mechanics in the vicinity of Fort Union.[7]

During Ilfeld's first two years in Las Vegas, he purchased most of his exchange through this source. After accumulating $1000 in greenbacks, Ilfeld would send them to Moore who would remit within two to four days with a New York draft for like amount signed by the assistant quartermaster at Fort Union.

Ilfeld and his partner Letcher, it will be recalled, were reducing their Elsberg and Amberg debt as rapidly as possible at this time. In his anxiety to obtain New York drafts, Ilfeld began imposing upon Moore. In December, 1867, we find Ilfeld enclosing $800 in currency while requesting a $1000 draft, promising to forward the balance upon receipt of exchange.[8] This practice was repeated three times during January, but on the last occasion Moore failed to respond.[9] Waiting nine days without answer, Ilfeld wrote again forwarding the remainder due.[10] Moore's compliance was immediate. Henceforth, without exception, the full amount was forwarded with the request.

The payrolls of the forts were a minor source of exchange, however. The need for supplies gave many individuals a greater opportunity for acquiring large amounts of eastern credit through direct sale of goods.[11] Some of these people, like Colonel St. Vrain, who had a ranch and flour mill in Mora, in addition to his contracting business, were frequently in need of currency to pay wages. Consequently, it was possible for Ilfeld to buy drafts from the Colonel.[12] In other cases some of these contractors were able to build up eastern funds beyond their immediate needs. John Dold, merchant, traded such exchange for currency on several occasions by issuing Ilfeld a sight draft on the mercantile house of Leon Arnold and Company, New York City.[13]

Whenever possible, however, exchange was obtained by contracting directly with the forts. Ilfeld was never a large contractor in this respect. Others, like Maxwell, Brunswick, Kihlberg, Otero and Sellar, and Chick, Browne and Company, were much more involved.[14] From 1871 through 1875 Ilfeld's cash books show receipts from this source as follows: lumber, $5678; oats, $5371; grain, $1468; corn, $8549: total, $21,066.[15] Inasmuch as these supplies were purchased for the most part from customers indebted to Charles Ilfeld, these contracts amounted to a conversion of otherwise nonliquid accounts into eastern exchange. The profit in the process was twofold, one from the original sale of merchandise and the second from sale of raw materials to the forts.

Occasionally Ilfeld subcontracted with his debtors to carry through an Army commitment. For instance, Louis W. LeRoux, of Gallinas, delivered lumber from his sawmill, at Ilfeld's direction, to Fort Bascom and Fort Union.[16] In fact, we begin to see in these examples a growing dominance by the mercantile capitalist. In his efforts to obtain eastern exchange, he was creating markets for the petty capitalist—in this case the farmer, rancher, miller, or lumberman. These small tradesmen submitted to the domination willingly until financial control, which inevitably followed, deprived them to a great extent of their economic freedom.

Servicing Transport

The forts of the West were a stimulus to this inevitable change, but their importance declined measurably, not only because they were progressively abandoned, but because new sources of exchange became available, and transportation of raw materials to the East was speeded with the building of the railroads.

As movements of goods and men increased, Ilfeld saw an opportunity for profit and for acquisition of eastern drafts. Like the modern tourist court of the western highway, forage corrals were needed to rest and feed the power animals used in early transportation, together with their drivers and passengers. The stagecoach horse, the army mule, and the freight oxen were bedfellows with their masters in the frontier corral.

For the purpose of servicing the traffic of the trail, Ilfeld rented a house and property at Tecolote south of Las Vegas on the road to Santa Fe, a convenient location to catch many of the freighters who used the southerly route through Anton Chico, Puerto de Luna, and Roswell. The property belonged to Willi Spiegelberg of Santa Fe, and the rent was $12.50 per month.[17] In conjunction with the corral Ilfeld operated a store for general merchandise. The Tecolote venture, which began no later than January, 1873, must have been reasonably successful. Its receipts during that first year were just shy of $6000, with wage expense probably not exceeding $50 per month.[18] The net to Ilfeld and Letcher during that year must have been no less than $2500.

A large portion of this revenue came from the Barlow-Sanderson Stage Lines, which company, because of its express and mail contracts and eastern passengers, was able to remit from Atlantic seaboard depositories.[19] Less important to Ilfeld was the Army transport through Tecolote, for which Ilfeld had the agency, but which accounted in 1873 for a mere $75 in forage though it contributed more than its share of troubles.[20] A theft of some collars and bridles belonging to the Army occurred one night from the Tecolote corral, and a question arose about liability which Ilfeld attempted to disclaim. He wrote Colonel A. I. McGonigle, assistant quartermaster at Fort Union, that "the man in charge of the agency could not in any manner control [those in charge of the transportation], and the property was entirely under their charge, and not the agent. If we are to be held responsible for any loss occasioned to property while in our corral, and when we are not absolutely in control of it, we would prefer not having the agency." [21]

Although Ilfeld seemed to have proof that the men in charge of the Army transportation "stole and disposed of said missing property," the Colonel complained that his superiors would have to be satisfied.[22] Ilfeld reluctantly made good the loss but "respectfully declined to be held responsible in future for any property missing." [23]

Mail Contracts

Another source of exchange as well as revenue was available through participation in mail contracts. To Ilfeld this was a minor source but it was helpful. For Barlow-Sanderson Stage Lines he conducted the Las Vegas Postal Office prior to the coming of the railroad and, after the trains came, he subcontracted this firm's route between Fort Union, Tiptonville, and Watrous (La Junta) where, at the last-named spot, the Las Vegas mail was received and delivered by the railroad.[24] H. C. Griffin of Pueblo, Colorado, later paid Ilfeld for continuing to manage this contract.[25] John T. Elkins of Kansas City, Missouri, used Ilfeld as his agent for getting the mails delivered over the route from Las Vegas to Mora through Alamos, Sapello, and Rincon.[26] The next year this franchise became the property of the Texas and California Stage Company of Little Rock, Arkansas, but Ilfeld continued to watch over the operation.[27] In all of these cases Ilfeld's fees were $75 a month payable quarterly.

It was not until the 1890's that Ilfeld seemed to lose interest in this source of revenue although he had evidently expanded his activities in this field considerably in 1889.[28] Much later he was subleasing the contract from Las Vegas to Santa Rosa to his indebted customer, A. A. Sena.[29]

New Private Investment

Other sources of exchange came gradually as opportunity for capital investment became known to outside interests. Promoters like Wilson Waddingham, who with others persuaded Lucien Maxwell in 1869 to give them an option to purchase the Maxwell Land Grant, were instrumental in encouraging British and Dutch capital to come to New Mexico. Waddingham and associates obtained the option to buy the Grant for $650,000 and exercised their privilege in 1870 by selling the ranch to an English and Dutch syndicate for $1,350,000.[30]

The new corporation was styled the Maxwell Land Grant and Railway Company, the purpose of which was to sell land piecemeal to prospective settlers. The company kept its ranching and agricultural interests, stocking the Grant with fine imported breeds of horses and cattle. This necessitated a sizable payroll for which greenbacks were welcomed. Ilfeld frequently shipped his excess currency to Cimarron, headquarters of the Ranch, and received in return New York drafts.[31]

The railroads, as they came into the Territory, offered a profitable source of eastern exchange. The Atchison, Topeka & Santa Fe Railroad, operating through its subsidiary, the New Mexico and Southern Pacific Railroad, crossed the Colorado–New Mexico line early in 1879 and reached Las Vegas on July 4, 1879.[32] The Denver and Rio Grande, Western Railroad, seeking to compete with the Santa Fe, extended its tracks south in New Mexico at the same time, reaching Espanola in 1880 and Santa Fe in 1885.[33] The Atlantic and Pacific Railroad Company, owned jointly by the Santa Fe and the St. Louis and San Francisco Railway Company, began extending the lines of the Santa Fe westward from Albuquerque in the summer of 1880. The Southern Pacific Company was building its lines eastward from southern Arizona through Lordsburg and Deming to El Paso in the period 1879 to 1881.[34]

Otero writes that as a result of railroad construction in 1879 and 1880 "money was plentiful in Las Vegas. . . . All the contractors from Raton tunnel to Lamy, did their business in Las Vegas with either Otero, Sellar & Co., or Browne and Manzanares . . . so there was a considerable amount of money in very free circulation." [35]

Charles Ilfeld, through Jacob Manthes, owner of a sawmill, supplied some of the railroad ties to the Santa Fe during its construction through New Mexico. Manthes was heavily in debt to Ilfeld and others. It became necessary on one occasion for Ilfeld, in order to protect his source of supply for the railroad contract, to pay Manthes' debt and to take his sawmill as security.[36] The Santa Fe was extremely slow in paying because of one of Ilfeld's notes which it held and which he refused to pay, having charged the Santa Fe with breach of faith.[37] Ilfeld's relations with the railroad had not been cordial for several years, and when the Santa Fe refused to accept lumber for delivery on his contract with the Atlantic and Pacific Railroad in the fall of 1880, he would gladly have severed relations with the monopoly had such a move been prudent.[38]

In 1881 Ilfeld obtained a contract to supply lumber to the Mexican Central Railroad, which extended south from El Paso, at $20 per 1000 board feet f.o.b. Las Vegas.[39] He bought the lumber from William Kroenig of Watrous for $15 per 1000 board feet.[40] Such opportunities as these arose from time to time, some serving as liquidators of slow accounts, but all functioning as creators of monetary exchange.

Banks and Exchange

When banking institutions made their appearance, the problem of acquiring eastern exchange for immediate delivery was solved, except in those cases when banks simply sold all the eastern credit they had possessed. The First National Bank of Santa Fe was founded in 1870; the

Second National in 1872.[41] Ilfeld made little use of either bank, however. The only exchange he purchased in this manner prior to 1876 was from his Tecolote landlord, Willi Spiegelberg, cashier of the Second National Bank of Santa Fe. The exchange rate was 0.5 per cent, and this, to Ilfeld, was an unavoidable expense.[42] He did not use his account in the Raynolds bank in Las Vegas for checking purposes until more than a year after the bank's founding, and when he did on occasion use the account, it caused his manager Dunn to complain of the exchange charges that some Colorado banks were making.[43] For instance, it cost him 40 cents for a $40 check to clear Denver.[44] The Stockgrowers' National Bank of Pueblo, Colorado, extracted 74 cents on his check amounting to $232.74, although the First National Bank of Pueblo made no charge on $298.06.[45]

Shipment of Raw Materials

The most consistent, reliable, and profitable method of acquiring eastern credit, against which drafts could be drawn, was through the shipment of raw materials, livestock, and other items. Wool, hides, and metals comprised the bulk of these commodities.

Ilfeld was too far from the copper mines of Grant County to deal conveniently in metal ores, although others, like his friend Don Mariano Barela of Mesilla, did.[46] Poor transportation facilities made the shipment of livestock hazardous, and until the railroad came in 1879 the only big market for cattle and sheep from New Mexico was Colorado.[47] Ilfeld kept a flock of from 3000 to 5000 sheep from which he made occasional sales to Colorado points, but in the early days he was not enthusiastic about the business. By 1875 he had sold most, if not all, of his sheep.[48]

Likewise he did not have much personal or financial interest in the cattle industry in these early years.[49] He was first of all a merchant who sought quick turnover of his inventories. It was better to buy the wool and the hides after others had tied up their capital. He would make his profits in short jumps to avoid the risks of violent price fluctuations typical of longer periods.

To help finance his grocery and liquor purchases in St. Louis, Ilfeld shipped wool and hides to that center. Gradually, however, his interest turned almost exclusively to the wool market, the center for which was Philadelphia.[50] His principal outlet in that city was through Gregg Brothers.

Many of these eastern houses employed buyers of wool who worked on a commission basis, and Ilfeld tried on several occasions to make such a connection but did not succeed, partly because his terms were too high. He did reach an agreement with Gregg permitting him to draw some money in advance for the purpose of financing purchases, but this was short lived because Ilfeld objected to paying interest on his drawings.[51] His manager, Richard Dunn, in charge of the Las Vegas office while

Ilfeld was in the East, wrote Gregg Brothers: "have no intention of buying [wool] regularly. Any of my customers who decide to ship I will recommend you." [52]

Before the buying season of 1877 had come he tried through his friend Joel Wood of Tyra-Hill, successors to McCartney and Company in St. Louis, to find a company willing to finance him in the purchase of wool. A. Krieckhaus and Company of that city would have been willing to advance money, but when they offered to pay Ilfeld one cent per pound on all purchases of hides and wool, Ilfeld objected, stating that he should receive in addition one half the profits from all sales of hides and pelts he sent.[53] Deliberations were dropped.

A letter to Allen Hoffman and Company of St. Louis, also referred to Ilfeld by Joel Wood, reveals the procedure followed in the buying and shipping of wool: [54]

March 22, 1877

Allen Hoffman and Co.
St. Louis
Gents:

In reply to yours of the 17th inst. would say that the money I proposed to borrow was for the purpose of buying wool this season, and in order to secure large lots it is generally necessary to make cash advances before sheering time (June and July). Of course where advances are so made we close a contract for the entire clip. Philadelphia is the best market for our wools so we could not draw on you with Bill of Lading, nor would this be necessary, as any Commission House is willing to advance 75% on B/L. My wants are for money at the present time *to advance* for when wool is delivered and payment required I can draw for its payment here, on my Commission Merchant. Now if you can devise any other means by which you can satisfactorily secure yourself and furnish the money I would be glad to have it. Your early reply will oblige as I desire to make some arrangements before the season is to fare [*sic*] advanced.

Respectfully yours,
CHARLES ILFELD

During the years from 1873 to 1875 Ilfeld shipped $15,000 in wool to Gregg Brothers, Philadelphia, plus several thousand more to Lewis and Tuttle, Chicago.[55] Minor shipments were made to other houses.[56]

This need for eastern exchange cannot be overemphasized. Letter after letter written by Ilfeld makes this point. In one case he could not send his balance due on "cegars" because eastern drafts were not available.[57] In another he would have been willing to cash drafts of Otero and Sellar's traveling representative, M. Friedman, if Otero and Sellar would have furnished an equivalent amount of eastern exchange.[58] Never an opportunity was missed to acquire exchange.

When the Bland-Allison Act was passed in 1878, enabling the Secretary of the Treasury to buy no less than $2,000,000 worth of silver in the markets per month, a new opportunity arose for profit and eastern credit.[59] The price of silver fell from $1.28 per ounce in 1874 to $1.11

in 1884, enabling merchants in the southwest to buy Mexican silver dollars, heavier than the United States coin and fullbodied, at a discount.[60] These could be melted down, taken to the mint, and coined as domestic dollars.[61]

Ilfeld sent $400 in Mexican dollars to Lewis and Tuttle, Chicago, and $600, "valued at $450," to L. Levenson and Company, New York City, in 1879.[62] A letter to C. H. Moore of Puerto de Luna states that Ilfeld would pay 80 cents for all Mexican dollars "but would have you keep this private as it might raise the price of them should any of your competition hear it." [63] Many more of these dollars were sent east during 1880.

Significance of the Drive for Monetary Exchange

Because of the possible volume and variety of raw material shipments, the southwestern mercantile capitalist continued to lean heaviest upon this method of acquiring eastern credit. By so doing, however, he inevitably attained a firmer grip on the small petty capitalist who was gradually committing himself to production by contract to the large merchant. The mercantile capitalist sold him supplies on credit, advanced him money, found him his markets, and in turn demanded a commitment on his production.

The social repercussions from such an alteration in commercial methods, involving a question of economic freedom, were great and lasting. Immediately, however, the surface eruptions showed themselves in the smaller towns of southeastern New Mexico, where the sedentary merchant, through his control of large areas of cattle land along the Pecos River, and his contracts with Fort Stanton, obtained a degree of monopoly which made possible a serious exploitation of the small farmer and rancher. Particularly was this the case in the town of Lincoln, 10 miles east of Fort Stanton. Here the firm of L. G. Murphy and Company, later becoming J. J. Dolan and Company, held a tight grip on the economy of the area.[64] Murphy and his partner Emil Fritz, through friendship with the Indian agent at Fort Stanton, had become, as one researcher has put it, "business dictators." [65] Because of their monopoly position, Murphy and his partners were able to grind down the prices of produce of the small growers, and like the "company stores" of near modern times, forced many an individual into perpetual debt. So general was this that Murphy was able to build his new store in Lincoln, "a magnificent two-story structure," through the forced labor of those who had become indebted to him.[66]

Like all artificial monopolies, protection became a major expense of operation, and when others like Chisum, and the Englishman, Tunstall, began to offer competition, a period of lawlessness set in the like of which

New Mexico has not seen before this time nor since.[67] The Lincoln County "War" of 1877–1878 consisted of little more than a bunch of subsidized outlaws (from Billy the Kid down), who were paid to rustle the cattle of rival factions.[68]

Some of the aspects of industrial capitalism can be seen in this eruption. Murphy and his arch opponent, Tunstall, had begun to specialize in the raising of cattle, the big market for which were the Army forts—the local opportunity being Fort Stanton. It was soon discovered that once specialization occurred on a large scale, a vulnerability developed which, through possible loss of markets and great risk of lower prices for a single product, coupled with heavy cost commitments, provoked competition of the most damaging type. These merchants of southeastern New Mexico were peculiarly susceptible to this weakness and some, like Tunstall and McSween, paid with their lives in the "War" that resulted; and, as usually happens, so did several innocent bystanders.[69]

Charles Ilfeld, in these early days, never made the mistake of permitting himself to be placed at the mercy of a single dominating risk, nor did many of his competitors in the larger centers of Santa Fe, Las Vegas, and later, Albuquerque. Fortunately for this sound development, the monopoly position of the sedentary merchant attained in Lincoln, New Mexico, was not typical of the Territory. And yet one would be blind not to see the quiet resentment, which has persisted to a great extent to this day, of the petty capitalist who felt the impact of this new and dominating form of business capitalism.[70] Unlike the bloodshed which such a change caused in London in the riots of 1327, and in later years in various commercial centers across the Continent, no explosions occurred in New Mexico.[71] The smoldering resentment of docile people, however, can in the long run be most dangerous. The idea is not without foundation, though perhaps it embodies some exaggeration, that the more difficult social problems of present-day New Mexico can be traced to this economic change which began in the 1850's and accelerated through the balance of the nineteenth century.

Mercantile capitalism in its maturer phase, the subject of later chapters, led to the full-fledged development of merchant banking, and to the partido contract, an agreement for the raising of sheep and the production of wool akin to the share-cropping system of the South. It was these later developments that brought the petty capitalist to a full realization, if the beginnings of mercantile capitalism had not, that they who produced with their hands were under the control of those who sold by their wits.

And to those of us who have the privilege of hindsight, it was the need for the acquisition of monetary exchange, or its equivalent eastern credit, that was at the root of it all.

V

THE MERCHANT CREDIT SYSTEM: INDEPENDENT OF SPECIALIZED BANKING

The Late Appearance of the Banking Specialist

The drive for monetary exchange, as described in the previous chapter, embodied so many difficulties and inconveniences to the sedentary merchant, that he is typically thought to have borne the banking function as a burden.[1] A ready assumption follows, therefore, that the specialized banker missed an opportunity in not offering his much-needed services sooner than he did.

Why was it that the commercial bank was slow to make its appearance in towns on or near the frontier? The Italian cities, serving the frontier of Europe as early as the eleventh century, had reached an advanced state of enterprise before the Bank of St. George was established, perhaps as late as 1407.[2] The Revolutionary War had been fought before Philadelphia, New York, or Boston boasted a commercial bank.[3] The merchants of Missouri were for all practical purposes without a bank until 1837.[4] It was 1871 before a bank was operating in Santa Fe, and 1876 in Las Vegas.[5]

The fact was that the mercantile capitalist solved his problem of exchange so efficiently through his own organization that he delayed the arrival of the banking specialist for many years, and then prevented him from dominating the scene for a long time thereafter. This sedentary merchant, who in England had so successfully borne the "White man's burden," apparently was able, also, to bear the burden of the banking function efficiently enough not to wish to release it to others.

The merchant credit system, that overlapping bridge between the direct and indirect methods of lending capital, was the positive force that delayed the rise of the banker. Fortunately we are able to give a rather detailed picture of the methods the sedentary merchant used in accomplishing this feat, but, before we do so, it would be wise to describe the negative influences at work that discouraged the banking specialist from making an earlier appearance and that handicapped him when he did come. These drawbacks were the simple society that existed on the frontier with its unfavorable balance of trade, the liberality of credit terms granted by metropolitan wholesalers, and the high profit margins which the mercantile capitalist was capable of obtaining.

Handicaps to the Banking Specialist

(*1*) *A simple society with an unfavorable balance of trade.* Bankers serve as intermediaries for people whose relations are distant and impersonal. When merchants function as the principal dispensers of credit, they serve as intermediaries for people of common interests who, at least in their own community, are well known to each other. It is quite probable that banking, in the real sense, has little or no place in a community of simple relationships, whereas the merchant credit system will tend to disappear in a more complex group.

In a simple economy of face-to-face relationships, a loan and deposit banker is likely to find himself a crippled and unappreciated economic element. He will be more abused than used. The unfavorable balance of trade, which runs heavily against such a community (only a very primitive group could be self-contained), drains the cash resources and creates an insistent demand for monetary exchange. Under such conditions, if a banking institution does arise, it becomes scarcely more than an exchange brokerage house operating almost entirely on its own capital.

Raynolds Brothers Bank in Las Vegas, founded in October, 1876, following an abortive attempt to start a commercial bank with local capital, approximated this exchange status during its first two years of operation.[6] Ilfeld and others bought exchange when it pleased their purposes, and some of the merchants undoubtedly made deposits, but little evidence exists that these accounts were used for any purpose other than the conversion of temporary funds into eastern exchange. A careful analysis of collection items received by Ilfeld during this period, as revealed in his records, shows only one private check drawn on Raynolds, this by Otero and Sellar and handled by Ilfeld on April 6, 1878.[7]

Charles Ilfeld made large deposits almost immediately after the bank opened for business, but withdrew his funds through eastern exchange drafts almost as fast as he deposited them.[8] However, he did begin to increase his balance in May, 1877, in preparation for meeting the cost of a hotel he was planning to build on the Plaza.[9] Ilfeld probably was exceptional in this respect, in that at this early date he had obtained surplus funds which he might choose to invest in specialized activities. Not until December, 1877, though, did he start the practice of paying some of his local and territorial accounts by check, and this did not become a settled practice until March, 1879.[10] He, like most merchants who dealt with the hinterland, was expected to loan small amounts of cash to customers as they came to town to shop or "cut loose," and this custom encouraged the merchant to maintain in his store a goodly cash balance from which he paid the few local credit balances he might have with other businesses.

Because of this close relationship of customer and merchant, any permanent funds from the outlying areas were likely to be deposited with the merchants instead of the bank, and the merchant in turn usually converted this money into eastern exchange at his first opportunity. In rare cases these funds might be deposited with the bank to cover specific payments, as in the case of Coleman and Williams of Roswell, who ordered merchandise from Ilfeld prior to obtaining credit standing with him.[11] But to the extent that this happened it only emphasizes the temporary nature of the funds placed with the Raynolds bank. It appears, therefore, from the spotty information that is available, that this bank had little more success in attracting permanent deposits in its beginning years than the First National Bank of Santa Fe had had a few years before. It took the Santa Fe bank more than three years to acquire deposits equal to its paid-in capital despite the fact that Santa Fe was the largest distributing center in the Territory, the seat of the Territorial Government, and the administrative center for Army operations.[12]

The surprising fact is that the Raynolds bank was used only sparingly for exchange purposes. During the first 40 months of operation it sold, on the average, only 3 drafts per day. Most of Ilfeld's monetary exchange was purchased from other sources than the bank, and it was not until January, 1878, 15 months after the establishment of this local institution, that Ilfeld used its facilities for this purpose often enough (12 times) to indicate that this service was at all necessary to him.[13] During those first 15 months he purchased an average of 3 drafts per month through the bank, and the average size of these purchases was $469.[14] His customary purchase of eastern exchange was no less than $1000.

An interesting fact concerning Ilfeld's neglect of commercial banking services appears in his cash book on August 1 and 3, 1877. Approximately $4000 in cash is recorded as having been "taken to the East." This may be evidence that at this particular time monetary exchange was not purchasable at the bank or elsewhere. Indeed, no paper had been bought since July 24, though a draft for $1000 was sent to St. Louis on August 9.[15] Perhaps, however, this was simply the exercise of a preference—a reversion to older methods. Certainly it was not the fear of banking institutions that influenced Ilfeld in this neglect, for we have recorded that he did deposit with Raynolds the savings he expected to invest locally. The fact, though, that Raynolds was a private bank, the first in Las Vegas, and that it operated outside the regulatory restrictions of the National Banking Act without a single Territorial banking law to guide its conduct, may have accounted in part for the minimal use of this institution by the merchants in general.[16]

The Raynolds bank did develop a little business from eastern merchants as they learned of its existence. Where credit risks were great, or when the custom of certain industries was to sell for cash, sight drafts were sent with the shipment of merchandise. A. Anheuser Company of St. Louis used the bank for this purpose upon shipment of a full car of beer to Ilfeld. Ilfeld objected to this pressure and succeeded in making arrangements to pay one half in 90 days through his St. Louis agent, Wood and Lee (successors to McCartney and Company), and the other half in 6 months.[17]

Even the founding of National Banks in Las Vegas, following the coming of the railroad, failed to elicit any real interest from Ilfeld for commercial banking. In the late months of 1879, he avoided an opportunity to become a director and a stockholder in the San Miguel National Bank.[18] Miguel A. Otero, Jacob Gross, L. P. Browne, and others were the founders, and Charles Ilfeld had agreed to associate himself with them. However, a week after the organization of the bank, we find Ilfeld asking to be relieved of his commitments: [19]

December 22, 1879

M. A. Otero
Pres. of San Miguel Nat. Bank
Las Vegas, New Mexico
Dear Sir:

For private reasons I do hereby request you as Prest. of S. M. Nat. Bank to remove my name as stockholder in the above named Bank and desire you to accept my resignation as director of said bank.

Respectfully yours,
CHARLES ILFELD

The "private reasons" referred to were his deteriorating relations with the Atchison, Topeka & Santa Fe Railroad, and his preference not to have to deal at close quarters with the representatives of either Otero and Sellar, or Browne and Manzanares (successor to Chick, Browne and Company).[20] He was sure both had received favors from the Santa Fe railway not granted the merchants of Old Town Plaza, and he had a feeling that Miguel A. Otero had used his position as vice president of the New Mexico and Southern Pacific Railroad (construction company of the Santa Fe), to further the interests of the large commission houses.[21]

It would be a grave error of emphasis, however, if the slighting or ignoring of financial institutions by the early sedentary merchants were to be traced to personal fears, idiosyncrasies, or prejudices. There were forces stronger than individual bias that directed these men. The controlling factors were the close relationship of merchant and customer, typical of a simple society, and the heavy unfavorable balance of trade that permitted few permanent cash surpluses to be available to the banks.

(2) *Liberality of credit terms granted by metropolitan wholesalers.* If the banker in a simple frontier community could expect little merchant support in the form of permanent deposits, he was equally handicapped

in finding a market for loans of sound variety. His logical customers were the merchants who were expanding their inventories to meet the needs of the growing town. Unfortunately for the banker he was confronted with the competition of liberal credit offerings of metropolitan wholesalers. Long periods of grace in which to pay obligations gave the sedentary merchant much opportunity to obtain the necessary monetary exchange without charge through his usual sources of supply.[22] The terms he received varied from one to six months in the 1870's, somewhat shorter than they had been 20 to 30 years before, but the merchant succeeded in extending his period of credit and obtaining his cash discounts, too, by employing purchasing agents who carried the merchants beyond these time limits if necessary.[23] Ilfeld wrote his New York agent, Solomon Beuthner, in November, 1873, at which time Ilfeld still owed this agent $2556, "discount our Bills, we shall remit more in a few days." [24]

H. B. Claflin, New York dry goods house, gave Ilfeld varying terms, depending on the merchandise. On some goods payment was not due for four months, on others 60 days, and on still others 30 days. The last-named carried discounts varying from 1 to 5 per cent.[25] When Hammerslough Brothers of New York asked Ilfeld to give them a note on his account of short standing, he paid the account, less 5 per cent, and enclosed a letter explaining his understanding with "Julius Hammerslough that my terms were four months less 2% or six months net, and I also told him that I never give any notes." [26] One Louisville firm, Davis and Haden, gave six months' terms, and C. O. McLain, a shoe firm of Haverhill, Massachusetts, offered the same with a 2 per cent discount for early payment, which Ilfeld stated were "the terms of all our purchases made in your city [Haverhill] and Boston." [27]

Thus the mercantile capitalist was, creditwise, too independent to present the specialized banker with a ready demand for borrowings. In other directions the banker was not offered much encouragement, either. The petty capitalist farmers were not good risks, as a class, to the money middleman because, by and large, they were lacking in the necessary intelligence and initiative to reach a stage of liquidity. Furthermore, the same factors that deprived the banker of the bulk of the merchant market discouraged his entrance here. The farmer was permitted long periods of credit by the sedentary merchant and he was enabled to pay off his debts with his crops as they matured.

The shopkeeper and storekeeper, also petty capitalists, were an unlikely market for the banker because they were small, and, for the most part, stagnant. Only the large cattle and sheep ranchers, large specialists, offered a possible source for sound borrowings. In the 1870's in the arid Southwest this industry had grown to a sizable scale, and although the

1880's saw it expand tremendously and become a speculative craze, it was of sufficient size in 1876 to present Raynolds with a substantial market for secured loans. This development probably accounted for the ability of the Raynolds bank to succeed in an otherwise discouraging environment.

(3) *Profit margins to the sedentary merchant.* The extended credit terms offered by the merchants to their customers had much to do with restricting the market for loans by the specialized banker, but it was the high profit margins of the sedentary merchant (see Table 2) together with the expansiveness of his business that made the long credit terms possible. These same profits adversely affected the banker in his ability to acquire deposits. When the successful sedentary merchants in the towns began to accumulate cash surpluses, it was the merchant bankers, existing principally in the metropolitan centers and as an integral part of mature mercantile capitalism, who, in seeking these funds, outbid the banks, both as to interest and services.[28] McCartney and Company of St. Louis, for instance, paid Ilfeld 6 per cent on the funds he deposited with them, gave him free checking service, and absorbed all charges on collecting or sending drafts.[29] When this opportunity was coupled with that of using purchasing agents who would carry the local merchant, while paying his discount bills, a clear example existed of the phenomenon of "having one's cake and eating it, too," and all without leaving the halls of the merchants. This was precisely what Ilfeld did, for he was able to maintain substantial balances with McCartney at interest while he was withholding funds from his New York and Baltimore agents (see Table 3). A year or two later, however, his New York agent, Solomon Beuthner, began to charge interest of 10 to 12 per cent on unpaid balances.[30] Although in almost all the months during the period from 1870 to 1874 Ilfeld could have met all his bills on a cash basis, he was able to get his eastern agents to discount his bills while he collected interest on funds which he owed them. No wonder Charles Ilfeld preferred to keep his depositing and borrowing within the merchant system.

In March, 1875, the German Bank of St. Louis sought to tempt Ilfeld away from this attachment to merchant bankers, and Ilfeld replied to its letter: [31]

March 16, 1875

P. Weiss, Esquire
Cashier of German Bank
Saint Louis, Mo.
Dear Sir:

Your favor of the 9th inst. has come to hand and contents noted. Please advise me what rate of interest you are willing to allow me on running account, giving me permission to draw on you at any time when I am in need to make remittance East, but will have a Balance due me all year around. I shall remit you

TABLE 3. A. LETCHER AND COMPANY END-OF-MONTH CASH POSITION AND BALANCES OWED AGENTS, 1870–1874
(FIGURES ROUNDED TO NEAREST DOLLAR)

	Cash		Accounts Payable				
Date	Las Vegas, N.M. office	Samuel McCartney St. Louis	Samuel Rosenthal Baltimore	Solomon Beuthner New York	Otero, Sellar Kans. Pac. R.R. points	Kihlberg, Bartels W. Animas Colorado	Net cash position
1870							
July	5478	222 [a]	767	—	327	—	4163
August	3635	535	233 [b]	—	466	—	3937
September	2456	659 [a]	1175	—	91	—	531
October	850	352	1087	—	405	—	290 [a]
November	1578	444	574	—	41	—	1406
December	4214	932	845	—	160	—	4140
1871							
January	63	825	1314	—	172	—	598 [a]
February	486	5292	1312	—	410 [b]	—	4876
March	212	4802	1945	—	1019	—	2050
April	1168	54 [a]	794	—	1019	—	699 [a]
May	2254	584	325 [b]	—	9 [b]	—	3172
June	564	2000	820 [b]	—	129	—	3255
July	1864	3602	90	—	271	—	5105
August	3301	2075	700	—	362	—	4314
September	1149	4274	1836	—	1001	—	2587
October	1305	5276	836	—	1097	—	4649
November	2253	5889	468	—	0	—	7672
December	1441	592	467	6398	0	—	4831 [a]
1872							
January	1679	936 [a]	648	5398	346	—	5650 [a]
February	306	404	562	4994	380	—	5227 [a]
March	463	410	562	3832	503	—	4024 [a]
April	3729	1102	562	3848	790	—	368 [a]
May	1593	254	562	1095	1134	—	944 [a]

June	353	3083	0	1173	835	—	1429
July	2582	2155	0	823	340	—	3574
August	355	4438	235	323	751	—	3483
September	591	1437	235	2492	451	—	1151
October	1283	2208	235	2492	129 [b]	—	893
November	959	3291	90 [b]	2492	1394	—	453
December	1259	1943	90 [b]	2492	779	—	20
1873							
January	1462	3662	2057 [b]	2492	104	—	4585
February	128	3531	426 [b]	2116	475	—	1495
March	641	2840	662	621	1568	—	630
April	2633	4053	662	621	1323	—	4080
May	1117	5764	791	621	583	—	4886
June	1035	4204	859 [b]	621	553	—	4924
July	1282	3565	868 [b]	3557	1399	—	760
August	657	3321	390 [b]	2557	575	—	1236
September	371	4459	890 [b]	2557	1321	—	1842
October	2616	4459	890 [b]	2557	1329	—	4079
November	4048	3422	10 [b]	831	318	—	6332
December	3395	3415	434	20	1706	—	4649
1874							
January	2477	4082	845	20	1506	—	4187
February	7628	5983	843	0	2133	—	10635
March	3757	8077	194 [b]	—	916	51	11061
April	1150	8600	914	—	1202	0	7634
May	1749	7713	1910	—	623	357	6572
June	267	8375	1099	—	39	43	7462
July	1987	8772	599	—	367	671	9122
August	1949	8030	0	—	415	759	8805
September	732	4036	20	—	145	759	3844

Source: Ledger B and Journal A.

[a] Credit.

[b] Debit.

in N. Y., Philada., and St. Louis Exchange and shall pay off East by sending a Draft on your Bank. Up to date I have made by Deposit with one of your Businesshouses, who allowed me six per cent on running account, but I prefer doing my dealings with some good Bank. Awaiting your reply I remain yours,

CHARLES ILFELD

Ilfeld's desire to deal with some good bank was a passing one, not too strong at best, and probably stated for bargaining purposes only. The German Bank evidently did not desire to meet the competition, for there is no further correspondence in the records.

Although Ilfeld's purchases of eastern merchandise were continuous, his abstention from eastern banking connections continued, with one minor exception, until 1882, when he began settling his seaboard balances, and later all his extra-frontier accounts, through the National Shoe and Leather Bank of 271 Broadway, New York City.[32] Prior to this date Ilfeld satisfied his eastern banking needs through merchant bankers or commission agents.

Thus the environment of beginning mercantile capitalism proved itself a severe handicap to the banking specialist. And yet it was more than just a handicap. This environment gave rise to a positive opposing force —a thoroughly dependable system of financing, adequately and profitably serving the sedentary merchant and his customers. We have chosen to describe this as the merchant credit system because the financing of supplies from a distance or locally was accomplished entirely, in its purest form, by the sedentary merchant and his agents and partners.

USE OF AGENTS

Slow communication over long distances presented a handicap to the mercantile capitalist that would have been insuperable, from the standpoint of control of operations, had not extensive delegations of responsibility to far-flung agents and partners taken place. So generally, in fact, was this delegation of authority practiced that agencies and partnerships became the dominant form of organization within mercantile capitalism. Distance and slow communication, therefore, were characteristics of mercantile capitalism that placed emphasis upon individual responsibility and responsible individuals.

As long as the partnership of Ilfeld and Letcher existed, merchandise could be selected by one or the other of them on their frequent trips east. In spite of this arrangement, though, it seemed wise to employ a commission agent to handle eastern purchases, to make payments on accounts when due, and to serve as a depository against which sight drafts could be drawn.

The experience that the young partners had had with Elsberg and Amberg as their eastern purchasing agent had been a relationship of compulsion, and it was not strange, when this association ended, to find Letcher selecting an agent in Baltimore, a city in which he was well acquainted. Baltimore and Philadelphia had long been the chief supply centers of the West, though by this time, 1870, both had lost much business prestige to New York City.[33]

The first connection with the Middle West had been over the old Cumberland Road, and when the Santa Fe trade became a factor, the Boone's Lick Highway extended this supply route to St. Louis. These roads gave Philadelphia and Baltimore the advantage in transportation, though much of it was lost upon the opening of the Erie Canal in 1825. Nevertheless, the wholesalers of Philadelphia and Baltimore were still vigorous and plentiful in the 1870's.[34]

During Letcher's first eastern buying trip, he made arrangements with Samuel Rosenthal, dry goods merchant of Baltimore, to handle Letcher and Company's account, and in June, 1870, upon Letcher's return to Las Vegas, he wrote Rosenthal: "I shall send you in future all my orders, buy as cheaply as possible." [35] Apparently no commissions were paid by Letcher and Company for this service, Rosenthal being satisfied with the mark-up on his own goods he was able to sell, plus whatever discount he could receive from other merchants on the goods he had to purchase to complete Letcher's orders.

In December, 1871, an additional agent, Solomon Beuthner of New York City, formerly of Taos, was engaged.[36] Beuthner was a close friend of both Letcher and Ilfeld and had married a cousin of the latter.[37] His commissions, paid by Letcher and Company, appear to have been 2.5 per cent of the cost of goods handled.[38]

A third agent, Samuel McCartney and Company of St. Louis, with which an agreement was reached to pay interest on Ilfeld's deposits, was used in the Elsberg and Amberg days, but the agreement to pay interest was made, apparently, as of July, 1870.[39] Thus Samuel McCartney became Ilfeld's midwestern supplier, purchasing goods for him from other merchants if McCartney did not have the needed merchandise in stock.[40] Quite logically Ilfeld purchased heavily of McCartney those goods carrying large freight charges or narrow profit margins. These items comprised, for the most part, hardware, groceries, and liquor. The last named, although of higher profit potentiality, was used in part as a "loss leader" in the sense that the tin cup always hung free to the thirsty customer as he dropped in from his hot and dusty trip to town.

It was important to keep the freight costs on all merchandise as low as possible, and St. Louis, situated on the Mississippi River, was in a position to obtain many goods at comparatively low transportation cost from a variety of sources. Later, some staples were purchased by Ilfeld through McCord, Nave and Company of Kansas City, but in the 1870's St. Louis was by far the dominant midwestern distribution center for the

Southwest.[41] Ilfeld reserved for the East the lighter and higher valued items, such as shoes, clothing, dry goods, musical instruments, and specialty goods which were shipped overland from New York and Baltimore.[42]

Once the goods reached the end of the railroad on their trip west, it became necessary to employ another commission agent to take care of the drayage, assembling, and shipping to destination. Ilfeld used Otero and Sellar for this purpose, although Chick, Browne, and Company and Kihlberg, Bartels were also employed, but infrequently.[43] These firms were paid a commission for their services, although Ilfeld's records do not reveal the relationship of commission to value of merchandise handled.[44] In addition to performing a forwarding business, these houses became wholesalers of staples. Ilfeld frequently requested Otero and Sellar to fill any unused space in the wagons with sugar, flour, coffee, liquor, or lead shot so that, in a sense, this company became a fourth supply agent.[45]

In Table 4 an analysis of A. Letcher and Company's sources of supply for the years 1870–1874 is given. These figures represent over 90 per cent of Ilfeld's purchases of finished goods during this period and show clearly the importance of Baltimore and St. Louis as his supply centers. In addition, the figures shed some light on the effect of the crisis of 1873.

Upon the purchase of Letcher's interest in the firm, Ilfeld dropped Baltimore as a supply center, although he continued to place an occasional order there with various wholesalers. The last order given to Rosenthal was entered on September 14, 1874—the very day Ilfeld be-

TABLE 4. A. Letcher and Company purchases from eastern sources of supply, 1870–1874

Location	Number of firms	1870	1871	1872	1873	1874
Baltimore	(42)	$7,855	$13,320	$14,188	$9,314	$7,328
Philadelphia	(5)	1,261	—	—	—	—
New York	(20)	—	1,736	3,721	231	2,774
East total	(67)	9,116	15,056	17,909	9,545	10,102
Louisville	(1)	—	—	—	—	335
Pittsburgh	(1)	—	—	84	—	—
St. Louis	(41)	6,257	26,459	16,155	5,360	6,198
Kansas City	(7)	—	783	1,779	2,163	85
West total	(50)	6,257	27,242	18,018	7,523	6,618
Total	(117)	15,373	42,298	35,927	17,068	16,720

Source: Charles Ilfeld records of remittances carried in his Copy Books.

came sole proprietor.[46] From that day on, New York became the principal supply center from the eastern seaboard, and Solomon Beuthner his only agent there.[47]

Ilfeld did most of his own buying on his annual and semiannual trips through the East, but Beuthner made all the account payments, gave credit for all discounts taken, arranged shipping, and took care of any freight rebates Ilfeld could arrange. These services were performed as late as September, 1874, on a straight commission of 2.5 per cent, but sometime later Beuthner also began to charge 10 to 12 per cent per year on unpaid balances.[48]

Beuthner went to the Riviera in the winter of 1877–78, and Charles Ilfeld, rather than employ a new mercantile buying and banking agent, experimented with the private banking house of Donnell-Lawson and Company of New York City as his depository, preferring to buy his goods himself, either while on his eastern trips, or by means of letters.[49] The experiment was not satisfactory, for we find him returning to the merchant, as combination buyer and banker, after using the private bank for approximately six months. He established relations with L. Levenson and Company, New York wholesale clothiers, in July, 1878, maintaining this association until 1882, when he opened a checking account with the National Shoe and Leather Bank.[50]

These agents served as intermediaries of far-flung merchants who, in most cases, had little acquaintance with one another. They served, however, to make the mercantilist philosophy of balancing imports and exports workable. The agent, who was most frequently a merchant himself, extended long-term credit to a distant client, and, in turn, because the agent was well known in his locality (usually a metropolitan center) he was able to buy from others on similar terms. By permitting credit terms of at least six months to the sedentary merchant in procurement areas like that surrounding Las Vegas, sufficient time was given for the distant merchant to acquire the necessary produce and monetary exchange to balance his purchases.

Use of Partners

While Ilfeld used agents to perform his bidding in the East, he preferred the partnership arrangement at home. He operated stores at El Monton de Los Alamos (Los Alamos), La Junta (Watrous), and Tecolote, as outlets for merchandise, and as assembling points of raw materials.[51] El Monton de Los Alamos, being only nine miles north of Las Vegas, could be supervised from the home office, and so a clerk-manager, William Frank, brother-in-law of Adolph Letcher, was placed in charge. La Junta and Tecolote, however, were managed by junior partners.

Geronimo de Vega, partner, whom Ilfeld later described as a man of "honesty and capacity" and as one who "speaks the Spanish perfect and knows every dog in the country," opened the La Junta store in the early part of 1875.[52] De Vega was not content, however, with the restricted possibilities for income in this country store, where he felt he could not "make his salt," so he resigned to specialize in the wool buying field.[53] A partnership was again established in January, 1876, with William Gellermann whom Ilfeld had known first as a salesman for A. Letcher and Company and who remained with Ilfeld in this location until the partnership's dissolution in 1880.[54]

The Tecolote store, which was opened no later than January, 1873, was placed in the charge of a manager until November, 1874, when the following contract was made with David Winternitz: [55]

PARTNERSHIP AGREEMENT

Articles of agreement, made and entered into this the 23rd November, A.D., 1874 between Charles Ilfeld, of the first part, and D. Winternitz, of the second part witnesseth: That the said party of the first part have a starte [*sic*] and commenced a business of selling goods and Merchandise at Tecolote, New Mexico under the name and Style of Charles Ilfeld, and the said party of the second part to wit the name D. Winternitz is to superintend and manage said business with Industry, Economy, and Correctness and to give for said purpose his personal labor, for the good and beneficial Management of the same, and it is hereby agreed, that the said party of the first part, furnish all the goods and Merchandises, for said Business and at cost prices, adding freight and such expenses on them as are actually necessary to deliver them to this place and it is furthermore agreed that after paying at Las Vegas, New Mexico for all Goods and Merchandise so purchased and delivered by them the nett [*sic*] profits of said Business at Tecolote, if any, shall be equelly [*sic*] divided, as follows, one half of said nett [*sic*] profits to be given to said Charles Ilfeld, party of the first part, and the other half to be given to the said D. Winternitz party of the second part, of all what is on hand or remaines [*sic*].

It is hereby agreed, that the said party of the first part, the said Charles Ilfeld, can and have a right at any time hereafter to dissolve said Business, and settle up the same, if any reason, or good ground should present itself, for him to do so.

In witness whereof I have hereunto set mi [*sic*] hand and seal and his, this the day and date above mentioned at Las Vegas, New Mexico.

In presence of
W. Frank

CHARLES ILFELD
D. WINTERNITZ

In addition to his junior partners who made distribution and procurement easier, Ilfeld frequently entered into partnerships for the purpose of liquidating enterprises, fulfilling supply contracts, acquiring produce, or carrying on specialized activities.[56] Ilfeld always employed partners or agents where responsible supervision was necessary.

Local Procurement Area

Through his branches and home office Ilfeld carried on the merchant credit system with customers who were as adept at postponing payment to him as Ilfeld was in delaying remittance to his eastern agents. Most of his larger customers paid only when he pressed them, something Charles Ilfeld could do graciously but firmly, and made a point of doing before each eastern trip. One of his large customers was Captain J. C. Lea, who had a general merchandise store in Roswell and a sheep ranch in that vicinity.[57] Lea offset his purchases from Ilfeld by shipping him wool and Mexican beans. The beans, it appears, Ilfeld stored free of charge if the market was not favorable, pending orders to sell, and the wool was shipped on to Gregg or Coats in Philadelphia.[58] Ilfeld found it necessary to seek payment of Captain Lea on numerous occasions, payment that always was made in sufficient quantities of produce to keep his account within safe limits.

On the trail to Las Vegas from Roswell, Ilfeld had many other customers who paid their debts in lumber, cattle, sheep, wool, bran, corn, wheat, hay, and oats. Pat Garrett of Lincoln, the famous sheriff who killed Billy the Kid, was hard to catch himself when bills were due, yet he was respected and trusted, and Ilfeld was willing to stretch Garrett's credit to a year without too much complaining. Garrett reciprocated the favor by collecting for Ilfeld one all-but-hopeless account, that of Judge Lenard, and then reduced his own balance by shipping Ilfeld 7000 pounds of beans.[59]

A. Grzelachowski (see Appendix 5), a former Polish priest turned merchant, freighter, and rancher, sent his wool from Puerto de Luna. With his partner, Richard Dunn (Ilfeld's erstwhile office manager), Grzelachowski used Ilfeld as his purchasing agent for eastern goods.[60]

From the southwesterly trail, down Albuquerque way, Ilfeld received wool and wine, the latter from the vineyards in the Rio Grande Valley near Bernalillo. He sold Ben F. Perea's wine on a commission basis of $5.00 per barrel.[61]

To the north his barter customers were strung out along the Mora, Sapello, and Gallinas Rivers, and on the Santa Fe Trail to Cimarron, New Mexico. Ilfeld received lumber, corn, flour, and oats from these areas, and a few of the well-known people who supplied him were William Kronig, S. B. Watrous, Henry Göke, Andres Sena, and H. M. Porter.[62]

From nine miles northwest of Las Vegas, at Rincon del Tecolote, came lumber, hay, corn, and wool from Juan Pendaries, Telesfor Jaramillo, M. Rudolph, and S. A. Clements. Ilfeld's supply area, therefore, extended from Roswell and Albuquerque to the south, to Mora and Cimarron on the north. Occasionally hides from El Paso were received, but usually Ilfeld's customers living as far distant as that point found more advantageous places to dispose of their surpluses.

In order to encourage the supply of raw materials, wool in particular, Ilfeld advanced either cash or needed supplies. In writing a prospective supplier he said: "I advance them [suppliers] goods and all the money they need during the quarter." [63] A few customers, like Juan Perea of Puerto de Luna, received cash advances frequently, but most of Ilfeld's customers preferred goods, paying back their debts with their produce.[64]

The sedentary merchant, thus cognizant of the advantages of the merchant credit system, faced his problem squarely. He bartered his finished goods for raw materials, and seized his opportunity for a profit in both directions. The general cash shortage, plus his intimate knowledge of customers and raw material markets, led him to prefer the direct method of putting out capital.[65] He advanced the necessary materials, including food and clothing, and then awaited the repayments in kind. This was hardly an atmosphere for a money middleman, for in such a community money barter predominated, not for lack of a bank, but in spite of a bank.

Declining Emphasis on the Merchant Credit System

When the railroad came to Las Vegas in 1879, industrial capitalism made its first deep impression upon the sedentary merchant in that area. The superiority of the steam engine over animal power was so marked that the mercantile capitalist gave up the function of transportation wherever the railroad could be used. We shall see in the next chapter that he was far from dominated by this new influence and he certainly profited from its use.

The rapid growth in population that followed the speedier mode of transport opened an opportunity for the commercial banker he had not possessed before. Less capital needed to be tied to inventories for there was now assurance that replacements could be obtained within a short period of time. The railroad, itself, brought new capital and dispersed it through local contractors, their employees and suppliers. There was, consequently, a greater liquidity within the community that manifested itself in bank deposits. For the first time the banker could count on the savings of others, in liquid form, in large enough amounts to permit a substantial expansion of loans and discounts.

Equally important in the rise of the commerical banker, however, was the new character of social relationships. Las Vegas was no longer so small a community as to permit commerce to be carried on almost entirely by intimate contact of merchant and customer. A complicated society was arising in which impersonal relationships assumed a growing importance and the banker found himself in the happy position of being needed. It was under just such conditions as this that the indirect putting-out system of capital was able to display its efficiency.

The impact of the railroad had been felt for only a few months when the Raynolds' private bank obtained its charter to become the First National Bank of Las Vegas.[66] Four months later the San Miguel National Bank was qualified to do business.[67] In contrast to the indifferent success the Raynolds brothers had experienced before 1879, both banks flourished from the beginning. Tables 5 and 6 show the tremendous growth that took place in the period from 1880 to 1883, but particular note should be made of the percentage increase in loans and discounts, and total deposits. In both banks the growth of these items varied from 100 per cent to more than 200 per cent. The effect of the railroad is quite clear when we compare this experience with that of the First National Bank of Santa Fe, which opened for business in 1871 in the largest town in New Mexico, and which during a similar period of time, three years, succeeded only in acquiring deposits equal to its paid-in capital.[68] The San Miguel National Bank accomplished this in a matter of five months.[69] Otero, however, makes the picture more vivid.[70]

> The banking establishments in the West had little to worry about during those early days, for money was plentiful and there was never such a thing as a bank failure. The profits in buying and selling cattle, sheep and horses were enormous, so those who engaged in that line of business were quite willing to allow the banks to take a good share of their profits. Frequently a customer would see an opportunity to buy a bunch of cattle at a low price and then hold them for several months. On such occasions he would go to the bank and borrow $10,000 for six months, paying eighteen per cent interest, the note reading "from maturity" so the interest, amounting to $900, was deducted and an additional ten per cent commission was charged; for the banks would stress the fact that they were short of money and would have to rediscount the note in the east. So the borrower would get $8100 for his $10,000 note. The note was re-discounted in New York at four per cent interest. Banks readily earned twenty per cent to fifty per cent on their capital stock each year. Losses were few and far between. Dividends were usually twelve per cent and the remainder of profits was passed to the surplus account, which gradually increased the value of the stock to many times its par value.

That Otero was not exaggerating the earning power of these banks is shown in Table 7 in which the growth of net worth for each Las Vegas financial institution is given for several short periods of time during which dividend payments do not appear to have been made. As we might expect, the San Miguel National Bank in its beginning years did not measure up to the record of its older and well-established competitor, though the sample time periods we were able to use for both institutions show very substantial returns on not only the capital stock but the total net worth as well.

TABLE 5. Comparative balance sheets, First National Bank of Las Vegas, 1880–1883

Dates	2/29/80	12/31/80	6/30/81	12/30/82	10/2/83
			Assets		
Loans and discounts	$120,012	$173,999	$203,843	$333,979	$364,909
Per cent of 2/29/80	(100)	(145)	(170)	(278)	(304)
Overdrafts	2,087	4,914	687	4,220	11,930
U. S. bonds to secure circulation	50,000	50,000	50,000	50,000	50,000
Stocks, bonds and mortgages	1,471	822	1,534	9,822	13,063
Due from banks and reserve agents	98,498	105,494	174,599	253,175	215,610
Case items	284	2,629	11,057	22,402	5,818
Bills of other banks	11,381	8,105	1,500	1,230	1,275
Fractional currency and specie	2,310	2,611	1,778	13,117	8,650
Legal tender notes	25,000	35,283	28,471	34,788	32,554
Redemption fund and due from U. S. Treasury	2,250	2,271	2,250	2,950	2,270
Real estate, furniture and fixtures	4,434	13,566	17,083	17,721	17,872
Other assets	3,518	844	844	844	5,148
Total assets	$321,245	$400,538	$493,646	$744,248	$729,099
			Liabilities		
Individual deposits subject to check	$177,660	$141,769	$231,185	$313,709	$318,945
Demand certificates of deposit	18,058	10,310	15,487	25,163	27,305
Time certificates of deposit	16,430	33,450	27,334	67,899	45,520
Due to other national banks		9,539	6,257	34,100	30,655
Due to state banks and bankers	8,636	100,091	103,312	148,140	141,135
Total deposits	$220,784	$295,159	$383,575	$589,011	$563,560
Per cent of 2/29/80	(100)	(134)	(174)	(267)	(255)
National bank notes outstanding	45,000	45,000	45,000	45,000	45,000
Capital stock paid-in	50,000	50,000	50,000	100,000	100,000
Undivided profits	5,461	379	71	237	8,539
Surplus		10,000	15,000	10,000	12,000
Total liabilities	$321,245	$400,538	$493,646	$744,248	$729,099

Source: Las Vegas Gazette.

TABLE 6. COMPARATIVE BALANCE SHEETS, SAN MIGUEL NATIONAL BANK OF LAS VEGAS, 1880–1883

Date	4/23/80	7/1/82	12/30/82	10/2/83
Assets				
Loans and discounts	$ 49,551	$111,838	$ 86,816	$109,652
Per cent of 4/23/80	(100)	(226)	(175)	(221)
Overdrafts	214	4,294	2,183	1,511
U. S. bonds to secure circulation	50,000	50,000	50,000	50,000
Stocks, bonds and mortgages		2,057	1,247	4,182
Due from banks and reserve agents	14,485	82,429	49,552	32,434
Cash items	2,535	2,002	8,299	5,895
Bills of other banks	3,610	735	4,340	5,975
Fractional currency and specie	237	7,693	14,078	22,940
Legal tender notes	9,032	9,252	8,526	9,789
Redemption fund and due from U. S. Treasury	2,250	2,250	2,250	2,250
Real estate, furniture and fixtures	2,062	3,079	3,093	3,741
Other assets	3,795	6,456	1,452	10,330
Total assets	$137,771	$282,085	$231,836	$258,699
Liabilities				
Individual deposits subject to check	$ 33,520	$108,050	$ 96,829	$106,949
Demand certificates of deposit	—	6,842	1,240	951
Time certificates of deposit	6,026	3,595	5,040	8,920
Due to other national banks	665	48,211	12,441	11,966
Due to state banks and bankers	—	684	872	167
Total deposits	$ 40,211	$167,382	$116,422	$128,953
Per cent of 4/23/80	(100)	(416)	(290)	(321)
National bank notes outstanding	45,000	44,000	45,000	44,500
Capital stock paid-in	50,000	50,000	50,000	50,000
Undivided profits	2,560	10,703	10,414	15,246
Surplus	—	10,000	10,000	20,000
Total liabilities	$137,771	$282,085	$231,836	$258,699

Source: Las Vegas Gazette.

TABLE 7. Return on invested capital of Las Vegas banks during selected periods, 1880–1883 [a]

Dates	Net worth (dollars)		Rate of return (per cent)		
	Beginning of period	End of period	Per period on net worth	Per annum on net worth	Per annum on paid-in capital
First National Bank					
2/29/80–10/ 1/80	55,461	66,975	20.8	35.4	39.2 [b]
12/31/80– 5/ 6/81	60,379	72,705	20.4	59.2	71.5
6/30/81–10/ 1/81	65,071	75,277	15.7	61.2	89.6
3/11/82– 5/19/82	77,406	85,668	10.7	56.7	87.6
7/ 1/82– 8/ 3/82	76,571	91,928	20.1	223.1	340.9
12/30/82– 6/22/83	110,237	131,993	19.7	41.4	45.7 [c]
San Miguel National Bank					
4/23/80– 6/11/80	52,560	53,724	2.2	16.3	17.2 [b]
7/ 1/82–10/ 3/82	70,703	76,862	8.7	33.9	48.0
5/ 1/83–10/ 2/83	78,002	85,246	9.3	22.3	34.8

Source: Bank statements published in *Las Vegas Gazette*.
[a] The longest period during which no decrease in net worth occurred.
[b] $50,000 paid-in capital.
[c] $100,000 paid-in capital.

The merchant credit system, therefore, faced a formidable competitor in these commercial banks as soon as the railroad opened the town to a sudden increase in population and capital. But, whereas the mercantile capitalist relinquished his function of transportation gladly, he met the banking specialist with stubborn resistance. Being able to capitalize on the confidence his customers had acquired in him, he offered to pay interest on any credit balances they could keep with him. He maintained the merchant credit system of money barter but at the same time competed directly with the banks for the liquid savings of the community. Browne and Manzanares, wholesalers, had a separate building for its banking operations.[71] Rosenwald Brothers, retailers of dry goods on the Plaza, competed with Ilfeld for these funds and was purported, on occasion, to have paid 0.5 per cent more to get them.[72]

The merchant credit system died hard, for though the indirect lending of capital, the essence of commercial banking, was a necessary development as towns grew and relationships became more complicated, it could do no more than serve in addendum as long as the environment for mercantile capitalism persisted. The railroad was still but a thread in a woof, and poor communications remained to plague the specialist. His opportunities for tapping business beyond the immediate concentration of population were meager and costly. Only the sedentary merchant had the facilities to supply the hinterland with necessities, to offer the necessary credit, and to bear the risks of collection.

The commercial banker in seeking to attract this outlying market recognized the great risks attached thereto. In many instances, therefore, he required these rural customers to obtain the guarantee signature of the merchant before permitting a loan. In such cases the merchant, in effect, was serving as middleman, and it was only natural that he would prefer, except in the cases of large loans, to carry this paper himself.

He did, and interest became a new wrinkle in the merchant credit system—to such an extent, in fact, as to give rise to the merchant banker, a facet of mature mercantile capitalism. The key to the question, however, of why the banking specialist was so long delayed, why he failed to dominate the scene when he did come, and why the merchant credit system persisted even when the mechanisms for the indirect lending of capital were available, is found in an understanding of the significance of a slow and painful process of transportation—the third and the most stalwart foundation of mercantile capitalism. It is only by a study of this problem that we can appreciate the tough and stubborn qualities of the merchant credit system.

VI

SIGNIFICANCE OF SLOW AND COSTLY TRANSPORTATION

Protection against the Specialist

The "burden" of banking which the mercantile capitalist bore was not the only handicap adroitly turned to bring him profit. With the rise of the specialist in the nineteenth century, the mercantile capitalist's very existence was dependent upon another "burden"—that of slow and costly transportation. The industrial capitalist of New England and New York, specializing and operating at low unit costs, had obtained the upper hand by 1830 in his contest with the mercantile capitalist of that area.[1] By 1870 he had spread his domain westward, locating principally in three centers: Cleveland, Cincinnati, and Chicago. A decade later he had become well established in St. Louis.[2] When conditions warranted it, he would not hesitate to push his advantage into the arid Southwest as well.

But the industrial capitalist depended upon large populations, metropolitan centers, and speedy disposal of his production. Otherwise his volume output at low cost would not be justified, and the marketing delays encountered would make his single risk unbearable. The mercantile capitalist depended upon a balancing of risks, gaining on most of them sufficiently, he hoped, to more than offset his inevitable losses. Slow and costly transportation over long distances made multifarious functions under one manager possible without fear of any important displacements by the specialist.

In New Mexico this specialist came in the form of the banker and railroad during the early and late 1870's, but the mercantile capitalist lost little to either of them for many years. The banker, as we have seen, was slow to demonstrate his superiority, and the railroad, as far as industrial capitalism was concerned, was only a ribbon of adumbration. The main structure of mercantile capitalism was to be intact as long as speedy and efficient local distribution of large volumes remained an impossibility.

Temporary or Sporadic Impediments to Commerce

Most tales of the frontier have emphasized the difficulties of transport convincingly enough to obviate the need of further proof here. And yet such information may not be unwelcome if it has the advantage of truth and freshness.

Commerce along the trails of New Mexico in the 1870's was more vulnerable to weather than to any other single factor of a sporadic nature. Heavy rains could mire the wagons and delay their arrival for days. In July, 1880, Ilfeld wrote his friend and recent junior partner, Gellerman, that because of the rains there had been no mail from the East for three days.[3] When snow came to the northern part of the Territory, disruption could be great. Sometimes it even caused embarrassment as it did late in the winter of 1875. Ilfeld had been foraging livestock shipments for Z. Staab and Brothers, a sizable mercantile house in Santa Fe, and there had been a delay in delivering one of the consignments. Apparently a member of the Staab firm had written an accusing letter which Ilfeld answered as follows: [4]

> Gents: Your favor of yesterday has come to hand, and contents noted. The teams left Tecolote this morning, it was impossible to move any sooner on account of the snow, and if anybody told you that the delay was caused to fatten up the stock, would state that it is a false information. The teams traveled during the storm, and were several miles from Tecolote when I sent out orders to them to return, as it was impossible to get through. I am sorry about this unusual delay, but the fault was not on my side, the teams made the trip from Animas to here in 16 days.

The Indians, of course, were always a possible source of trouble. We have noted before that the Indians in the northern part of the Territory had been quieted for all practical purposes by 1866.[5] The Apaches to the south, however, continued their depredations for some time. It is an exaggeration, though, to say that their activities greatly impeded trade in New Mexico after 1867. The possibility for disruption of trade was there, but Ilfeld, though he made many shipments to the southwestern, southern, and western parts of the Territory, took note of Indian troubles only on one occasion, and that affected him but indirectly. He complained in a letter to J. C. Lea that a firm in Roswell had expected "to get freight for 2¢ when people were paying 3 and 3½¢ before the Indians broke out." [6]

A third type of interruption hit the Southwest in 1873. The Post Office Department had done its share in the early 1870's to improve and extend communication facilities so that the people and merchants of New Mexico need not feel isolated. A daily mail route to Santa Fe from Missouri was operating as early as 1869, and in the next five years, mail routes within the Territory had increased in length from 1506 to 2052 miles, and were being covered with "celerity, certainty, and security"—a proud boast of the government service arising from the subjugation of the Indians.[7] Because the operation of the routes was dependent on man and beast, however, the service was peculiarly vulnerable to disease.

In January, 1873, the "epizootic," or horse influenza, hit Las Vegas and the Southwest with paralyzing fury. It had come from the Middle West, carried by the horses of the stage coach and Army.[8] For three or four weeks Charles Ilfeld was unable to communicate with the East except by telegraph and personal messenger, as the stage line could not operate. Those horses that escaped the malady were kept out of areas where the disease prevailed.

Ilfeld sent a letter to McCartney in St. Louis on January 21 by a private party: "We sent you the other day a Telegram in regard Perea Dft. on Matthews as for the last two weeks we had no way of sending letters east, on account of the epizootic the coaches stopped running and we do not know when they will commence running again." [9] He wrote McCartney again on January 30: "Epizootic still here but we have a weekly mail from the East again." [10] In the first week of February, Ilfeld managed to bring Letcher and Company's train through with their assortment of spring goods in spite of the lingering disease.[11]

In 1877 it was man that succumbed, this time to smallpox. This malady was frightening and was kept as quiet as possible lest people and trade boycott the area. Most of the damage to trade, however, was caused by the delay the disease brought in the harvesting of crops. Ilfeld had written to Otero and Sellar in October that "small pox is very bad among the natives," and in November to a firm in Santa Fe he wrote that "on a/c of small pox everybody is behind with harvesting their corn." [12]

More Serious Impediments to Trade

Weather and disease were only temporary handicaps to business. It was the everyday multiplication of errors, lapses, delays, and losses, however, that would have proved too costly and risky for the large-scale specialist. An example of what can happen when two or three of these possibilities gather together is seen in the incidents growing out of an order for a buggy.

A buggy had been ordered by Letcher and Company sometime prior to September, 1874, from Messrs. Coan & Ten Brocke of Chicago, to be delivered to Solomon Brothers of Denver. R. Baca, a customer of Ilfeld, had agreed to accept delivery there, but when the vehicle was unduly delayed in transit, Baca found it necessary to buy another one.[13] Rather than have the buggy on hand as dead inventory, or incur the added expense of shipping it to Las Vegas, Ilfeld asked Solomon to sell it at a loss, if necessary, of no more than $15 to $18.[14] As a last resort, however, Solomon was to send it on to Kihlberg, Bartels of Las Animas, Colorado. Shortly thereafter, though, another Baca, Benito, having reason to journey to Denver, agreed to take charge of the buggy when he got there and to bring it back to Las Vegas.[15] Immediately, Ilfeld sent a second set of instructions to Solomon and enclosed a draft for $63 to pay the freight charges incurred on the vehicle from Chicago to Denver.[16] Unfortunately the second letter was lost in transit, a rather common occurrence, and Solomon, not having found a buyer, sent the buggy on to Kihlberg.[17]

In the meantime, Benito Baca, arriving in Denver the early part of October, and finding the buggy had gone on, went about his personal business without informing Ilfeld of what had transpired.[18] And Solomon, who had washed his hands of the entire transaction by passing the freight charges on to Kihlberg in Las Animas, did not bother to write a letter concerning his actions.

The buggy should have reached Kihlberg by the middle of the month, but it was not delivered to him and he refused to pay more than the freight charges from Denver. On November 28, a month later, Ilfeld received a frantic wire from Solomon wanting to know what was going on.[19] It was obvious from the bewilderment in its wording that Ilfeld's second set of instructions had not reached its destination, and with it, of course, the draft in payment of the Chicago-Denver freight charges. Another 10 days passed before Solomon confirmed he had not received the draft and before Ilfeld was able to stop payment through Appleton, Noyes of St. Louis, the drawee.[20] Ilfeld then instructed Kihlberg to pay the full amount of the freight charges.[21]

At this point Ilfeld must have relaxed, expecting to see his buggy roll in any day, but he was jolted on January 6 by a wire from Kihlberg stating that the buggy had not been received in Las Animas.[22] A hurt letter from Ilfeld to Solomon offered to pay the freight charges direct if that would release the buggy, but before any answer was received, Ilfeld heard from Kihlberg that the vehicle was on its way, having been shipped from Las Animas with a Mexican train.[23] As no further correspondence on the matter appears in the records, we can assume the buggy finally reached its destination.

The point of the story is not alone that the industrial capitalist would break under such delays and uncertainties; it is also that the mercantile capitalist was organized to take them in his stride. He did this in part through delegation of responsibility to partners and agents; he did it principally by building a system of cooperation among merchants which the large specialist, in his youthful independence, overlooked.

Interdependence of Merchants in the Arid Southwest

Not only were distance and inefficient transportation indigenous to mercantile capitalism; they also combined to make every sedentary merchant, subjected to these conditions, dependent on, and thus responsible to, every other sedentary merchant. The significance of this fact should not be overlooked, for it breathed into mercantile capitalism the fresh air of constructive effort, of responsibility, and of simple honesty. A highly individualistic system of private enterprise became noted for its cooperative and accommodating members. It has been noted that this quality of responsibility was fostered through the almost universal use of partners and agents strategically located. But these arms of the sedentary merchant were not long enough, and it is not stretching a good story to say that every merchant became, in a sense, the agent of every other.

When Charles Ilfeld sent his wagons, laden with oats, to Fort Craig, a distance of 225 miles, he did not hesitate to write for assistance from William V. B. Wardwell, merchant and, very probably, sutler at the Fort, though he had not had prior dealings with him: [24]

> Will you be so kind enough to receive from Francisco Lucero and Aarsiso Otero, Freighters, and deliver to the Quartermaster at Ft. Craig, N. M. 42,478 pounds of Oats. In case the freighters should want anything from your store, please let them have it and charge the same to us. Any expense that you are put to, and the amount that the freighter may receive from you, we will gladly remit on the presentation of your order. We also wish you could be so kind and send us a separate memorandum of the amount cash Freighter has delivered. Any time we can do you a favor at our place please command.

Two years later, 1871, on a similar shipment, requiring a month to deliver, Wardwell was called on again.[25] He informed Ilfeld that some of the oats had been rejected, and Ilfeld answered Wardwell's letter of December 24 on the 28th: "If you can sell the oats or keep the same for your own use, we will charge you contract price." [26] Later Ilfeld made up his deficiency with Fort Craig by shipping 3707 pounds of oats—"one hundred and seventy pounds over." [27]

Ilfeld was not always on the receiving end of these favors. Often he was given the opportunity to help others as in the case of his good friend and customer Mariano Barela, a large rancher, freighter, and merchant of the Mesilla Valley, near the southern border of the Territory. Barela, on one occasion, suffered substantial losses in cargo near Anton Chico, probably because of irresponsible drivers. Ilfeld immediately took charge, employed new freighters, appointed R. J. Hamilton of Anton Chico, his agent, to salvage what he could of the damaged merchandise and sent the wagons on their way to Mesilla.[28]

One never knew on the frontier what the next call to duty might be. When the wagon train of Morrill and Kellner of Silver City stopped at Ilfeld's corral for servicing, Ilfeld took it upon himself to warn the firm never again to employ Elijio Domingues, their freighter, as he "is the meanest and most worthless Native I ever met in charge of the train and if I had received your instruction to act in this matter according to my notion I would have unloaded your freight and shipped by other teams." [29] Ilfeld's premonition was well founded, for a few days later he wrote H. M. Porter of Cimarron, who must have had an interest in the Silver City firm, that "the freighter for Morrill and Kellner is six miles from town . . . staying secretly at a house of ill-fame . . . will do all I can to protect M & K interest if you say so." [30]

If business history should occasionally squint an eye at brothels, so must it reckon with drinking and murder. Six months after Don Mariano's wagon train had been waylaid at Anton Chico, Ilfeld had the unpleasant task of burying Manuel Barela, brother of Mariano. Manuel, while acting as major-domo of his brother's train, left a saloon in Las Vegas, shot two men without provocation, and was hanged by the vigilantes that midnight.[31] Ilfeld took care of the burial and sent the following bill to Mariano:[32]

Cash for washing body	1.50	
1 suit clothes, shirt and socks, slippers, necktie & 1 pr. drawers	21.00	
Digging grave	4.00	
Taking provision to train	1.00	
Enclosed bill of Frank Ogden (undertaker)	37.00	64.50.

An earlier letter to Mariano explained the arrangements Ilfeld made to forward the leaderless wagon train to Mesilla: [33]

Damacio Baca, major-domo, personal services 25.00 per month.
Allowance for use of horse 6.00 per month.
Return trip both 12.40 equal to 12 days wages for himself and horse.
Monseis Baca, teamster 20.00 per month.
Return trip to Las Vegas 10.40.

Perhaps this last service was a bit unusual for even the sedentary merchant to perform, but the dispatch and thoroughness with which it was handled was not in the least surprising. It was the common, everyday requests, however, that show the camaraderie of the merchants of the frontier, whether friends, acquaintances, or strangers. Ilfeld's first dealing with Franz Huning, successful pioneer merchant of Albuquerque and Belen, was to request him to collect a debt from a freighter on his way to Huning's store.[34] Another such favor was asked by Ilfeld of his landlord Kihlberg, a forwarder at Las Animas, to be "on lookout for Preciliano Maris and load him as he is indebted to me and this is the only way to collect." [35] The weather, which might delay a train, was thoughtfully described, as when Ilfeld reported 17 inches of snow to George Maxwell of Las Cruces, son of Lucien Maxwell of Maxwell Land Grant fame: "Your freighters went by the 8th Inst . . . heavy snows since they left." [36]

Charles Ilfeld, typical of the sedentary merchant, was a purveyor of news and a doer of helpful deeds. His letters, and those of his assistants, have frequent notations of weddings, births, sickness, and death; of business failures and law suits. He was called upon to write letters for the illiterate, to collect pensions for those not familiar with government red tape, or to send cash for customers to relatives in Germany. He responded graciously to those who asked, and thoughtfully served those who perhaps unknowingly became dependent upon him. Distance and slow communication instilled in the sedentary merchant a sense of responsibility and thoughtfulness that in degree was not approached before this stage in business history, and which will be difficult to attain again under the impersonal and limited liability corporation.

Problem of the Backhaul

Once the sedentary merchant of the Southwest acquired his own wagons and teams he had committed himself more deeply than ever to the practices of mercantile capitalism. Not only did he make markets for local produce for the purpose of acquiring eastern credit and liquidating local accounts; it became necessary for him to find raw materials to fill the empty or partially filled wagons on the light side of the haul. It was costly to pay drivers to accompany trains over long and circuitous routes with only space to pay the freight.

Before the railroad came to New Mexico in 1879, the backhaul to the merchant of Las Vegas and Santa Fe was usually the initial haul. His problem was to fill his wagons with raw materials to meet the eastern goods he had purchased. Actually, however, he was never sure of the exact poundage awaiting him at the end of the railroad, nor if he knew could he very often send the correct amount of capacity just to meet the need. Each wagon was capable of carrying 4000 to 5000 pounds which meant extra space was usually present after the eastern goods had been loaded. Many are the letters in Ilfeld's copy books asking the forwarding houses to reserve freight for his wagons upon arrival.

The prize fill in freight, if it could be arranged, was government supplies destined for the forts because such a cargo meant payment in eastern exchange, or credit with a large forwarding house. The forwarders had leeway to play favorites with this tonnage, for they were, by and large, government contractors themselves and could, if they wished, ship by customers' wagons. When Otero and Sellar in Kit Carson, Colorado, filled Letcher and Company wagons with private freight destined for Santa Fe and other places, it brought an immediate protest from Ilfeld: "Would prefer government freight." [37] Private cargo could mean re-shipment from Las Vegas and perhaps an added collection problem, though Ilfeld did not object to carrying it if he had the opportunity to make the necessary arrangements in advance. He was happy, for instance, to make such contracts with Spiegelberg of Santa Fe, for he often, in the early 1870's, was in debt to that merchant.[38]

The sedentary merchant solved this backhaul problem in part through the use of independent freighters, who were as reliable a group of "boomers" as can be found in history.[39] It is a significant fact that Charles Ilfeld did not suffer, so far as can be seen in his records, a single loss by theft at the hands of these men during the period from 1867 to 1883, although occasional examples of losses occurring to other merchants show this experience to have been exceptional. When one considers, however, that these men were in full charge of the freight, and fully responsible for it from the time it was checked out until it was checked in, this record is not so surprising. This was just another example of delegating responsibility to encourage responsibility, so typical of the mercantile capitalist stage of business history.

In contrast, freight handlers working for the railroad were of a different sort. Their responsibility was no less than that of the wagoner, but they were employees of industrial capitalism and were treated as common laborers without an effort having been made to give meaning and character to their work. Theft of freight from the railroads by employees was common in the 1870's and 1880's, but sometimes it reached such a state as to be ludicrous. Ilfeld wrote the Kansas Pacific Railroad one day as follows: [40]

> I have repeatedly received packages from which there were articles stolen ere they reached Las Animas and so boldly of late that upon one package of Champagne there were short 4 bottles and marked upon the box!! "Here we drank this to your good luck."

The wagoners were able men in their line and quite capable of driving a good bargain. If Ilfeld were to obtain the lowest rates, he was still faced with the problem of guaranteeing a backhaul to the freighter. Ilfeld, for instance, upon filling a merchandise order from J. C. Lea of Roswell, was obliged to plead with this customer to "prepare yourself to have some freight for them [freighters], otherwise am obliged to pay them anyhow." [41] He asked Lea to buy hides and pelts from his neighbors if necessary.

The sedentary merchant in the Southwest was not in the business of finding markets for local produce solely for the purpose of obtaining profits from their sale. Domination of the petty capitalist would never have reached significant proportions had this part of his business been an independent function. The protection of his profits from eastern merchandise was also a cause in forcing him to seek control of the output of his smaller, specializing brother. The problem of the backhaul must stand with the necessity to acquire eastern credit, and to liquidate the accounts of his local customers through money barter, as one of the fundamental propellants of mercantile capitalism in the arid Southwest.

Wagon Rates

Freight rates were, of course, a serious problem to the sedentary merchant in the Southwest, for, unlike many of his ilk in other times and places who had the advantage of water transportation, he had to haul long distances overland with his freight costs thus becoming a major item of expense. In 1865 it had cost Ilfeld and Letcher 14 cents per pound to bring merchandise by wagon from Leavenworth, Kansas, to Santa Fe.[42] When, in 1868, the Kansas Pacific Railroad moved westward to Ellsworth, Kansas, the wagon rate was 8 cents per pound.[43] The next year some freight came from Sheridan at 2 to 3 cents, and by 1871 Kit Carson, Colorado, had brought the wagon haul costs down to 1.5 cents per pound, and lower.[44] This last-named rate, over a distance of 275 miles, the equivalent of 11 cents per ton-mile, was unusually low. The rule of thumb has often been given as 1 cent per pound per 100 miles or 20 cents per ton-mile.[45] It is not surprising, therefore, to find that Ilfeld was rate conscious in the extreme and was constantly seeking ways and means to cut this item of expense.

Freight rates varied widely from the rule of thumb, depending on several factors, which though not always given conscious weight, were, generally speaking, a part of the quotation given. As in present-day transportation, distance, speed, volume, bulk, value, perishability, and backhaul were important considerations. But unlike the present time, the season of the year, condition of the road, supply of and demand for equipment were far more important. There was even the question, long since ruled out, whether payment was to be in goods or cash, spot or time. Charles Ilfeld, for instance, wrote his forwarder in La Junta, Colorado, F. O. Kihlberg, to "explain to Felipe Chavez that the Freight is payable in goods or make Time contract with him for cash."[46]

Clear examples of wagon rate determination can be gleaned from Marcus Brunswick's Wagon Bill of Lading books, two volumes kept while he was agent for Wilson and Fenlon, government contractors in Leavenworth, Kansas.[47] Wilson and Fenlon were awarded the bids to supply Fort Stanton from Las Vegas during the two years ending June 30, 1883, although Marcus Brunswick appears as the official contractor in the second year. The contract rate for 1881–82 per 100 pounds was $3.25, and for 1882–83, $2.50 for the official distance of 182 miles, though the actual mileage was nearer 230.[48] The actual rates paid by Brunswick to freighters, however, varied from 1.25 to 3 cents per pound, with the vast majority of the hauls being at the rate of 1.5 cents per pound. On the basis of 100 miles these rates would range from about 6 to 13 mills per pound.

For some inexplicable reason Wilson and Fenlon paid Brunswick the full contract rate each year with the exception that a cash discount of 1 per cent was deducted the second year. The gross spread between the contract rate and actual amount paid the freighters gave Brunswick a profit of more than 1 cent a pound before some rather moderate shrinkages of perishables and occasional losses.[49] The total poundage carried in the two years exceeded a million, and the Board of Survey at Fort Stanton, charged with the responsibility of inspection, refused to pay for only a few hundred pounds of this amount. All delays beyond the contract time were forgiven.

The low rates of 1.25 cents were paid in periods of good weather, May and October, when the cargo was of good bulk, including such items as flour and steel products. The peak rates of 3 cents a pound were paid only once on a special haul of perishables in which a shorter time period for delivery was required. The standard time allowance was 12 days per 100 miles, but on special hauls the maximum was cut to 8 days per 100 miles. Actually, barring unexpected difficulties, the 230 miles were covered in 15 days, a rate of 15 miles per day, more than equal to the speed required on special contracts at the official distance of 180 miles.

There was a tendency for rates to be higher on furniture and perishables and on light loads; on cargoes when horses were used in place of mules and oxen; in winter than in summer.[50] The last observation was not always likely to hold true, however, because frequently wagoners and their teams were in demand during the good weather, forcing up rates, whereas in the winter, frequent periods existed when freighters were plentiful.

Ilfeld's experience with independent freighters was similar to Brunswick's. If the cargo was heavy and compact, of low value and with little care needed in its preservation, the rates were low. When Ilfeld sent some freighters to La Junta, some 200 or more miles distant, to bring back a load of mixed eastern purchases, he sent more than 4000 pounds of sheepskins as ballast at a freight cost of 0.75 a cent per 100 pounds.[51] On the return trip, though the cargo of merchandise weighed 10,000 pounds, the rate rose to 1 cent per 100 pounds.[52] A shipment of flour only from Las Animas, about 20 miles east of La Junta, was contracted at 1.25 cents per 100 pounds but delivery had to be guaranteed in 15 days or the rate dropped to 1 cent. [53] Ilfeld's rates to Roswell, 180 miles, usually on assorted groceries and merchandise, varied from 1.5 to 3 cents per pound depending on his ability to get a backhaul and, on one occasion, upon the disposition of the Mescalero Indians.[54]

On short hauls the rates were close to the rule of thumb—1 cent per pound per 100 miles—but substantial differences could occur between light and heavy loads. The rates between Las Vegas and Tiptonville, 25 miles, varied from 20 to 25 cents per 100 pounds; to Santa Fe, 70 miles, 40 cents to more than $1.00 per 100 pounds; to Puerto de Luna, 80 miles, 50 to 70 cents per 100 pounds.[55] With such variations, bargaining was the accepted method of reaching a figure, and sometimes the freighter had to accept a lower than fair rate. On one such occasion, Ilfeld admitted to a customer that the reason for delay in the delivery of his goods was the low rate he had contracted to pay the freighter.[56]

Railroads and Rebates

Ilfeld's chief concern, however, was not with the animal-powered train but with the "iron horse." He could hold his own with the best of his competitors where he had a fair degree of control over transportation. With the approach of the railroads westward from the Mississippi River, he faced a different problem. The railroads of the West, as in the East, during the 1870's and 1880's, were willing to grant rebates to favored customers and to those whose bargaining position was strong—a situation that left each merchant worried and suspicious lest his competitive position be undermined behind his back. As long as animal power was the only substitute for steam, all merchants had some control over their freight costs albeit the tariffs represented relatively high charges. But when railroad competed against railroad, a different set of conditions arose. Then it became possible for a merchant who could be responsible for a good volume of freight to play one road off against the others, and neither Ilfeld nor his competitors hesitated to play this game for all it was worth in obtaining substantial refunds on their freight bills.

There was nothing illegal about granting or receiving rail rebates at this time. Viewed in an economic sense it was not even unethical. The railroad happened to be among the first of the high fixed cost industries, each of which, because of its absolute dependence upon volume, has experienced at one time or another suicidal price competition. The unrealistic attitude of the public toward condemnation of rebates on the one hand and toward price agreements or basing point systems on the other, is to miss the economic nature of industrial capitalism. Rebates have been tied opprobriously to railroads, but no other aspect of high fixed cost industries, in a competitive situation, could be more typical or inevitable.

The Kansas Pacific Railroad, part of the eastern division of the Union Pacific Railroad, had built as far as La Junta, Colorado, in 1876, and though this branch was subsequently torn up for lack of business, it became important to the trade of New Mexico for a few years.[57] The Atchison, Topeka & Santa Fe paralleled this road, constructing from

Topeka to Burlingame, Kansas, in 1869, to Emporia in 1870, to Newton in 1871, to Hutchinson and Dodge City in 1872, to Granada, Colorado, in 1873, and to Las Animas and La Junta in 1875, the same year that a terminal eastward was established at Kansas City.[58] It was not, therefore, until 1873 that competition between these two railroads for New Mexico trade became severe. Otero and Sellar and Chick, Browne, forwarding houses, recognized this change and located on the Santa Fe in Granada in the fall of 1873, keeping for the time being their houses at Kit Carson on the Kansas Pacific.[59] Ilfeld probably began to obtain rebates on his eastern freight shortly after this time, but no evidence of such appears until February, 1876 when S. W. Eccles, western freight agent at La Junta for the Kansas Pacific Railroad, informed Ilfeld all rebates had stopped as of February 1.[60] Ilfeld's only concern at this turn of events was to make sure he would collect his rebate on goods which had been shipped before this order came through. In a letter to Kihlberg, in West Las Animas, he added a postscript: [61]

> The R. R. Company [Kansas-Pacific] must allow me the rebate on all goods which had been in transit during last month. I had letter of Eccles stating that from the 1st Feby he could not allow any rebate anymore.

R. F. Oakes, general freight agent in Kansas City, wrote both Kihlberg and Ilfeld assuring them these rebates would be paid.[62]

Ilfeld was not greatly concerned over this development, probably because he knew the weakness of the railroads and realized that a few shipments over the Santa Fe would change the Kansas Pacific's mind. As a matter of fact, a new agreement was soon made and the railroad again began secretly to pay rebates to Ilfeld. The confidential aspect of these transactions was well illustrated when Ilfeld requested the railroad to forward copies of his freight bills to Otero and Sellar in order that that house could check eastern rates—presumably an auditing service performed by commission houses for their customers. The railroad immediately objected, not wishing others to know of its separate agreements. Ilfeld replied: [63]

> *November 29, 1876*
>
> D. B. Keller, Esq.
> La Junta
>
> . . . In regard to your remark about sending your statement to Otero, Sellar would say that I always kept my Rebate as a strictly Private matter but in order to check off my eastern rates O&S requested me to forward them monthly my RR statement. In sending me in future my statement you could put an extra slip of Paper in your letter on which you can write down the net sum so the Commission House don't know anything about our arrangements.
>
> Truly yours
> CHARLES ILFELD

Time and again, because of this agreement, Ilfeld reprimanded his eastern suppliers for not honoring his order to route via the Kansas Pacific. He wanted Solomon Beuthner in New York to obtain refunds of $20.35 because goods had been routed Santa Fe where the freight charge was $81.37.[64] When Tyra-Hill, successors to McCartney in St. Louis, shipped him 25 barrels of whiskey via the Santa Fe, he wanted to know where the mistake occurred that he might collect $36.65 on a freight bill of $146.60, as the Kansas Pacific would have charged $109.95.[65] A letter from Ilfeld to Beuthner confirms these figures as typical when he stated his contract with the Kansas Pacific Railroad permitted him "a 25% rebate." [66]

The St. Louis, Kansas City, and Northern worked in close association with the Kansas Pacific, and Ilfeld generally requested routing over these two roads from St. Louis. His rebates from this company were paid separately and credited to his Tyra-Hill account in St. Louis. His letter to A. C. Bird, general freight agent of the St. Louis, Kansas City, and Northern makes this arrangement clear: [67]

> Enclosed hand you B/L for my shipment up to the 1st inst over your route, on which please calculate the Rebate as per our contract. By your books you will notice that I shipped more freight than I send B/L for, as several houses send only to my commission house a Duplicate. Be kind enough to pay amount due me on Rebate to Mess Tyra Hill & Co. of your city and advise me of sum paid.
>
> Truly yours
> CHARLES ILFELD

Charles Ilfeld was not content to obtain rebates from western railroads only. Through the use of eastern forwarders, or "eveners," he was able to keep freight charges on the first part of his haul at a minimum. Though the Santa Fe had not given him preferential treatment before 1879, Ilfeld, without this company's direct knowledge, obtained rebates anyway. He worked through William Bond, 319 Broadway, New York City, of H. K. and F. B. Thurber Company, contracting agent for the Blue Line, which company gave favorable rates through its contracts with the Chicago, Rock Island, and Pacific, and Santa Fe railways.[68] Another eastern forwarder used was the Star Union, which generally routed via the Kansas Pacific.[69]

The firm of H. K. and F. B. Thurber quoted rates from New York to El Moro, Colorado, as of May 15, 1878, as follows: first class $2.00, second $1.80, third $1.70, and fourth $1.40 per 100 pounds.[70] (These compare with present rates, July, 1958, of $7.40, $6.29, $5.18, and $4.07.) In addition Thurber gave rebates, though evidence of such does not appear until 1880, and they may not have been associated with the rates quoted above. Charles Ilfeld's younger brother, Noa, who was in New York at the time, took waybills to Thurber for collection of rebates.[71] At an earlier date, 1876, Solomon Beuthner, Ilfeld's New York agent, collected rebates from the railroads for Ilfeld's credit.[72]

The only clear example of a rebate obtained from the Santa Fe directly was in November, 1879, when Ilfeld, then engaged with others in the building of a hotel at Hot Springs, New Mexico, sought and received "30% off first class rates from the Missouri River." [73] A letter to J. F. Goddard, general freight agent, Atchison, Topeka & Santa Fe Railroad, later confirms the fact that this was a rebate and not a special quotation to be paid upon delivery of the goods.[74]

Enclosed please find way bills for goods shipped over your line for the Hot Springs Hotel amounting to $1409.72 on which is due us a rebate of 30% as per arengment [*sic*] made with Dr. J. M. Cunningham amounting to $422.92 for which please send us your voucher and oblige.

Yours Resp't
J. M. Cunningham & Co.
c/o Chas. Ilfeld, Las Vegas

Of course, rebates on freight were not the only form of refunds. These emoluments also were given to the shippers in the guise of free personal transportation. The railroads gave these privileges reluctantly as necessary bribes to retain tonnage. The competition for freight among railroads was so intense that such a small item as an occasional free ticket to a customer who could influence the routing of goods was given in New Mexico without question during the 1880's.

In the early 1870's, even though the railroad had not yet reached New Mexico, Ilfeld got his passes in a roundabout way by working through his agent, McCartney, in St. Louis and, later, through Kihlberg in La Junta, Colorado.[75] By the time the tracks had reached Las Vegas, if not before, Ilfeld began receiving an annual pass.[76] This privilege had become so natural by 1885 that he was forward enough to ask that his family be accorded free travel, too, though on his broaching he did ask for the favor only "if consistent." [77] He and his brother-in-law, his general manager, Max Nordhaus, had each received "commercial permits" before 1885 and by 1886 Ilfeld was requesting the same privilege for his wool buyer, Sol Floersheim.[78]

Evidently the Santa Fe railroad, by 1890, had chosen to use the second section of the Interstate Commerce Act of 1887 as a bolster for its nerve to abolish or curtail the granting of free travel privileges to customers.[79] In a letter to Ilfeld which apparently gave the impression the railroad was not exactly leading from strength of conscience, Ilfeld's request for passes had been refused. Certain that his competitors were still receiving this privilege, Ilfeld encouraged his well-read and imaginative bookkeeper,

Rodney B. Schoonmaker, to frame a retort. Ilfeld signed it and F. C. Gay, Esquire, general freight agent of the Atchison, Topeka & Santa Fe Railroad, Topeka, Kansas, received it.[80]

My dear Sir:

Pardon my apparent neglect in so long delaying a reply to your most esteemed favor of the 23rd ult. which I find to-day in cleaning up some correspondence that has been necessarily put off during our wool-season push. But to use the old adage "Better late than never," I trust you may kindly accept this later acknowledgement of your solicitude in my behalf, shown by refusing to furnish the passes I requested and thus averting in all probability the social and financial ruin of yourself—"The great Santa Fe Route" and even my own insignificant self.

I shudder to think of the frightful chasm of destruction into which my iniquity (had you in a thoughtless moment issued these passes) would have plunged us—and I await with deepest dread and heartfelt sympathy the discovery, that some of my friends and neighbors have accepted and used these direful passes, since the passage of the Interstate Commerce Act—May it be well with them in the Great Beyond, for their names will evidently be Dennis with a collosal D, should it ever be known ere they take their departure "To that bourne from whence no traveler" (D.H. or not) "returns."

Since the receipt of your benevolent letter, I have spent so much time in pondering on your consideration of my welfare that twenty cars of my wool, which should have been shipped from Springer [Atchison, Topeka & Santa Fe] were by some hook or crook loaded at Clayton [Denver, Texas & Fort Worth R. R.]—and should you learn of other blunders of this kind, please be fully impressed that it is all for the best, and is only a mysterious way of doing you and the "Santa Fe Route" a very small favor in meek acknowledgement of the magnanimous one you have conferred on

Yours very truly,
CHAS. ILFELD

It was not long before the passes were being issued again not only to Charles Ilfeld, but, as in the past, to his associates and family as well. From two to three requests were made each year from 1892 to 1897, for free trips to and from Kansas City, Chicago, and New York, while many other shorter gratuitous trips in New Mexico were asked for quite regularly.[81]

By 1897, the Santa Fe, like a good many other railroads in the West, had adopted a plan for free passes that had as its intent the avoiding of interstate law. By issuing state passes, as opposed to interstate, and by appointing individuals to positions holding a temporary or merely technical relationship with the railroad (the Interstate Commerce Commission described them as "nominal employees"), the unlawful aspects of such discriminatory actions could be evaded.[82]

Ilfeld became a nominal director of the Santa Fe along with a number of other individuals for purposes of obtaining free transportation. A revealing letter from Schoonmaker to Ilfeld in March of 1897 shows again, as in the letter of 1890 quoted above, the pressures which the merchants of New Mexico brought on the Santa Fe.[83]

C. F. Jones (R.R. agent) called this morning to have me sign these routings . . . but I declined to do so as I understood you were favored by the Frisco with a pass while the Santa Fe would not give you any. He says the New Mexico directors have received their passes within the last ten or fifteen days. None has come here for you.

In May, Ilfeld was still seeking his pass while claiming that several of the local directors had received their annual transportation.[84] By August he had been so favored, though he noted that his pass was good only for the Territory of New Mexico, so he sought another for his eastern trip.[85]

Earlier in the year W. B. Biddle of the Santa Fe had informed Ilfeld that a new policy was in effect and that no more passes would be issued.[86] Although this new policy was not immediately enforced, it is interesting to note that in the 1913 investigation of the free pass practices in Colorado, the Sante Fe received favorable recognition as one railroad that had successfully competed for traffic over a period of 10 years without giving free passes to its shippers. Subsequently, however, this railroad had been forced to resort to such practices again as a "means for stimulating the good will of shippers." [87]

It is significant that the indictments levelled against Colorado shippers by the Interstate Commerce Commission were directed at industrial capitalists: the Colorado Fuel and Iron Corporation, the Victor American Fuel Company, the Colorado and United States Portland Cement Companies, and the Great Western Sugar Company.[88] These relatively high fixed cost industries, so dependent upon volume in a severely competitive market, took full advantage of the oversupply of railroads that also were grasping for great volume.

In New Mexico this rebating episode in transportation was more easily brought under control. There it was the sedentary merchant who was dominant, a businessman whose cost structure was flexible enough to permit reasonable adjustment to market prices and whose control over market prices was aided by the isolated areas he served and the merchant credit system he employed. These factors took some of the verve out of his continuous efforts to seek rebates on his transportation costs. The near-monopoly position of the Atchison, Topeka & Santa Fe Railroad, of course, further limited his bargaining position.

Looking Ahead

The decline in the strategic position of the mercantile capitalist, vis-à-vis the new specialist in transportation, was more than a story of abuse eventually brought under control. It was only one aspect of the losing struggle this merchant was to fight for another half century with the forces unleashed by the railroad—forces that shook the foundations of mercantile capitalism. The growing liquidity that the railroad helped to bring to the economy lessened the dependence of the small petty capitalist ranchers and storekeepers upon the general merchant for scarce monetary exchange. The spur this new form of transportation brought to population growth in old and new economic centers made indirect lending by banking specialists more practical. The direct access it brought to and from eastern markets for larger volumes of goods permitted the establishment of specialists in various trades who were able to bypass the general merchant.

The shaking of the foundations of mercantile capitalism, however, is more a twentieth-century story. Meanwhile the quality of success achieved by Charles Ilfeld in the face of this changing environment is more the story of his business policies, strong and weak, with which he impregnated his organization during the closing decades of the nineteenth century.

VII

SOME EARLY POLICY DECISIONS OF CHARLES ILFELD

Given the environment conducive to a particular stage of business capitalism, the enterprisers who are willing and able to meet its challenge find themselves drawn inevitably along certain well-defined paths of policy.[1] Many important and basic decisions, involving little or no choice, are made naturally in the process of conforming to that system. These decisions, however, lack that positive flavor so often, and rightly, associated with the term *business policy*. Rather they represent an acquiescence to a compelling environment.

The foundations of mercantile capitalism gave rise to the sedentary merchant and willy-nilly forced his kind into common policies: use of partners and agents, control of sources of supply through money barter, and the assumption of varied risks. In short this was the entire institution we have chosen to term the merchant credit system. To the sedentary merchant these were not matters of choice.

The term *business policy* as it will be used in this chapter, however, involves management actions which are neither so automatic nor so generic. It embraces those individual decisions made for the purpose of seeking or maintaining a competitive advantage. Thus, in an appraisal of such policies there can be no gospel for comparison. Men of different aptitudes are able to attain similarly successful objectives through divergent policy programs. For purposes of analysis, therefore, it has seemed wise to separate these individualistic, character-reflecting decisions of Charles Ilfeld from the foundation policies indigenous to the sedentary merchant.

Credits and Collections

It should be clear, in view of our detailed analysis of the merchant credit system, that the sedentary merchant faced a great and ever-present problem in his efforts to remain liquid. His cash sales were likely to be less than half his total sales, and his charge accounts were, to a large degree, paid in produce.[2] His most important individual policy decision, therefore, involved the whole question of credits and collections. No merchant could long succeed who did not extend credit readily beyond present-day concepts of prudence, and yet that very fact schooled him to acquire a firmness and tact in dealing with men that may have been measurably lost in our modern emphasis upon balance sheets and financial ratios. In the case of Charles Ilfeld, his credit and collection policy came as close to being an explanation of his long-term success as any single factor, in isolation, could have been.

Before we attempt an appraisal of Charles Ilfeld's credit policy, however, we should first appreciate the opportunities that he possessed for the abuse of credit. His small, agricultural customers, practically all of whom were uneducated and ill-informed, were easy prey for the man of resources who, through overextension of money and merchandise loans, could bring many of these people to do his bidding or force them to relinquish their property. The "East Lynn" stories of frontier New Mexico are likely to be overdone and too generally applied, but when they have a basis in fact they stem from the unequal relationship that existed between the petty and mercantile capitalists.

Intuitively or deliberately, it matters not which, Charles Ilfeld steered a clear course away from such practices. Old employees and customers alike will vouch for the truth of this statement, though they are likely to do so with stories more apocryphal than factual.[3] Impressions gained from reading 3000 to 4000 business letters written prior to 1884 by Charles Ilfeld and his associates, however, leave no doubt of the accuracy of this conclusion. Ilfeld was inclined to be gentle and understanding in his dealings with others. His wrath, seldom displayed, was reserved for those who took advantage of him. Even in anger, however, his letters display a tone of hurt that others should fail to act in accordance with their promises. Only on the rarest occasion does a vengeful epithet appear to salve his feelings, though many were the provocations to justify one. Here was a young immigrant American, only thirty-six years of age in 1883, who believed deeply in dispensing fairness, and who had an abiding faith that justice would be reciprocated—yes, even in the form of profits.

None of these observations are meant to minimize in the slightest degree Ilfeld's practical approach to the mercantile business. He "never lost sight of making money" his old bookkeeper, Rodney Schoonmaker, has said, and that was true, but he also had the wisdom to guarantee a continuity of profits through calculated moves to create a loyal and growing list of customers.[4] Men learned through experience that Ilfeld would meet their legitimate needs for credit, but they knew also that, patient as he was, he would not tolerate careless or deliberate procrastination of payments. If in spite of honest efforts to repay their debts these men fell behind, they learned, too, he would seek a method to unburden them without loss of face or property. He lent his signature to their bank notes that they might renew their credit.[5] He even bought their notes from private parties who were pressing for payment, and then gave those debtors time and a fair opportunity to repay.[6] Many of these transactions proved immediately profitable to Ilfeld, of course, but many turned to losses, too. In the process, though, he guaranteed his sources of supply and kept his customers.

A Definite Policy of Collection

Ilfeld's collection policy evolved slowly as he put on years and judgment. His Taos experience, for which, presumably, Adolph Letcher should be held responsible, had ended with substantial uncollected balances.[7] Though the bulk of the blame for this can be traced to environmental forces, a good share must have been the result of an emphasis upon sales without a considered credit policy.

In the early days of the Las Vegas partnership, however, there appears to have been more discernment in the granting of credit. There are few names in the account book which are not recognizable as having been those of substantial citizens of Las Vegas or the surrounding trade territory. Though balances in some cases were carried for years without complete settlement, sizable payments in cash or produce were commonly made quarterly or annually, and few accounts prior to 1873 became a problem. Two factors were responsible for this. Wool, the chief export of the Territory, had had its price break of 1866 checked by the imposition of a national tariff in 1867, and the Franco-Prussian War, which strengthened the price of wool in 1870, sent it on its inflationary spiral throughout 1871 and into 1872.[8] Secondly, the population of Las Vegas and environs, growing rapidly, was sustaining a brisk retail and wholesale trade.

The beginning of a collection policy for Charles Ilfeld came in 1873 with the break in wool prices and their subsequent decline through 1878.[9] In contrast to his early collection techniques, which consisted mainly of offering a profitable market for a debtor's produce, or humorously shaming a customer into making payment, Ilfeld now began to take more positive measures.

As a first step he stuck to his old methods. When an account was slow Ilfeld generally appealed for funds that he might meet his own debts. If the balance remained unpaid he would write in a jocular vein of that "old and weary account" or "to date have no sign that you reside among the living." [10]

When these measures failed, the third step was to solicit the aid of other merchants who were in a better position to bring pressure. In such a case, however, Ilfeld was careful not to make his demand on his customer final nor to place his merchant friend in an awkward or untenable position. In asking M. Rudolph of Sunnyside, New Mexico, to collect Alejandro Segura's account, he gave explicit instructions: ". . . should there be any delay please charge interest. . . . Should he sell his sheep and refuse to settle . . . take the necessary legal steps . . . should he not have the means to make settlement you may let the matter rest at present." [11]

Though in the above case the collection was made, there were others in which a fourth move was taken without recourse to the courts. If the customer's patronage and produce were likely to be desirable in the future, Ilfeld would sacrifice possible immediate gains by seeking to reach some friendly settlement. For instance, his firm wrote William Kronig, a large rancher of La Junta, New Mexico: ". . . will take 30¢ on a dollar as your offer to our Mr. Ilfeld with the expectation that you will pay on the Balance in full whenever you think you are able to do so." [12]

A last step, which was taken only rarely, was to resort to the courts. When such action was taken, however, it was usually an effort to garnishee the wages of some soul who had "skipped the country" with no intention of paying his debts.[13] Ilfeld's collection policy, repeated over and over again in these early years, was to reach an agreement through patience and persistence and without the use of legal force. He had a firm faith that all problems could be solved if at least one party were consistently fair.

Interest

In the early 1880's, however, this collection routine was strengthened, partly perhaps because faith and persistence are not always enough, but principally because much opportunity for profit was being bypassed. In 1882 he began, as a matter of policy, to require an interest-bearing note of any customer whose balance had been due more than 30 days. If Ilfeld were not successful in obtaining the signature of his customer, he accrued the interest on his books anyway. The rate charged was usually 12 per cent per annum but occasionally it reached 18. This technique of collection is well illustrated by a letter to Domingo N. Baca of Las Conchas, New Mexico: [14]

> As I am settling up all my outstanding accounts for last year by taking notes in order to balance my books, I herewith hand you one note for your private account for $23.25, other account of D. N. Baca & Bro. for $201.00 requesting you to be kind enough to sign both of them at your earliest convenience if you should desire to let the account run.

Only the day before he had written to another customer that "goods are sold on a thirty day basis and I am enclosing a twelve per cent note upon which I have already accrued four month's interest." He added, however, "you can pay small amounts on note as fast as you can and it will be alright." [15] Actually these rates were less than the going bank charges of the period, which ranged from 1.5 per cent per month up.[16] Ilfeld had no intention of discouraging credit nor was he losing sight of the greater profits to be made from the exchange of produce and finished goods.

This change in January, 1882, to charging interest as a method of collection, and more than incidentally incurring a profit, had a double significance. First it marked a recognition of the fact that the Las Vegas area was passing from the early phase of mercantile capitalism, in which the merchant credit system of bookkeeping barter holds full sway and in which commercial banks play a minor role. It was becoming possible, and therefore practical, for a mercantile business to see a greater liquidity in its accounts.

Secondly, this change represented a major, deliberate step by Ilfeld toward merchant banking, which often played so great a part in the mature phase of mercantile capitalism.[17]

Labor Policy

Ilfeld's genius for creating and keeping profitable trade was handicapped somewhat by the little attention he gave to a constructive labor policy. He looked upon his employees much as he did commodities, paying no more than market prices. His general clerks received from $15 to $20 a month—some of whom may have received board in addition—though an offer of $25 and board was once made.[18] Those employees who were expected to assume some managerial responsibilities received only slightly more. A promising young Canadian, A. W. Cleland, Jr., who occasionally was placed in full charge of the store when Ilfeld was out of town and who helped to keep the accounts, was paid a salary of $25 a month including, probably, his board.[19] In 1880, and until he left the company in November, 1881, Cleland was placed on a salary of $1000 per year—a break in wage policy that was extended to others within a few years.[20] William Frank, who managed the Monton de Alamos branch for a while, received $35 a month but apparently no board.[21] These were not very good wages, even with board, when one considers that a man could obtain his meals at the local hotels for $5.00 a week or only $8.00 with lodging thrown in, that common laborers earned from $1.00 to $1.50 per day, sheep shearers close to $2.00 per day, and carpenters as high as $3.25.[22] Some of Charles Ilfeld's clerks received the equivalent of from $40 to $45 a month in the late 1870's and early 1880's, about the equivalent of public school teachers at that time, a somewhat invidious comparison.[23]

Ilfeld coupled his low wage policy with a demand for extremely long hours, as did his competitors. Schoonmaker, his bookkeeper, recalls that the average work week in the 1880's included 12 or more hours per day with some work on Sunday for the office force.[24] This was some improvement in hours over those that prevailed prior to October, 1874, when the merchants of the Plaza agreed to Sunday closing hours. The following notice, signed by A. Letcher and Company and 14 other merchants, appeared in the *Las Vegas Gazette:* [25]

> In order to give the young men employed in the respective business houses of this place an opportunity to have some leisure time at their command, we, the undersigned business men of Las Vegas do hereby voluntarily agree to close our respective stores on Sundays at 1 o'clock P.M. to commence the first Sunday in October next.

That this concerted move may have been more a measure of protection against what would have been considered undue reduction in working hours, is evidenced by the complete abolition of Sunday hours in May, 1876.[26]

This practice of paying bottom wages was typical of the sedentary merchant. Gras lists it as one of the weaknesses of mercantile capitalism, in the sense that it kept purchasing power low and that it restricted markets to the middle class, but it was a weakness as unavoidable and as necessary in that stage of business capitalism as labor unions and higher real wages are today.[27] In our analysis of the foundations of mercantile capitalism we have pictured an economy in which there was little technological development and a heavy reliance upon hand labor. Capital was scarce. Labor was plentiful. Under such conditions wages were certain to be low, for men simply lacked the tools to produce the goods and services which could make them valuable beings in the eyes of others. Inevitably and concomitantly, under such conditions, a lack of interest in the common man prevails, and management's concern for the average employee is likely to be minimal.[28]

Those who abhor the growth of fascism and totalitarian governments should recall the destruction of capital in two major wars in a part of the world where capital, freedom, and standards of living grew side-by-side for 400 years. It is not a coincidence that the wages and the dignity of the individual declined with the capital destruction that took place. Fortunately, under mercantile capitalism in the nineteenth century, labor's plight was temporary because the sedentary merchants were building markets for the petty capitalists, and were paving the way for industrial capitalism with its capital concentrations and high wages.

Indeed, the parallel of this change manifests itself in the Charles Ilfeld Company to a surprising degree in 1883 when Ilfeld completed the building of his Great Emporium, a department store with at least five distinct specialized divisions.[29] As soon as specialization appeared wages rose appreciably. As an employee in the millinery section in May, 1882, prior to the building of the department store, Mrs. Mary P. Ellis received $25 per month and $33.33 per month for the rest of the year.[30] However, in 1883, her replacement, Mrs. Hollenwager, though hired for $40 per month, was raised before the year ended to $60, and in 1886 was put on an annual salary of $800.[31] In February, 1883, Sol Floersheim was employed at a salary of $1000 per year and in 1886 was raised $350.[32] Schoonmaker, the bookkeeper, received $1000 per year, and later $1200.[33] By 1887, in addition to Max Nordhaus (his brother-in-law who drew what he needed), Ilfeld had at least five employees who were paid a minimum of $1000 per year.[34] Even the porter, Manuel Delgado, who perhaps had commissary responsibilities as well, was raised in salary from $35 per month in 1882 to $62 in 1883.[35]

The change from mercantile to industrial capitalism, reflected in only one aspect of Ilfeld's early business policy (a problem to be discussed subsequently in this chapter), sharply focuses two factors of great economic importance. First, capital concentration, in this case a large building, demanded volume business to support its fixed overhead. Secondly, volume demanded greater division of labor to bring out the capabilities of employees in the most efficient manner. With increased production came higher wages. It matters not that labor had this latent capacity under mercantile capitalism. It is important to note that it did not have the tools to use its capabilities efficiently.

Of course to the enterprising employee of the sedentary merchant low wages was no handicap. A little experience, a sense of responsibility, and a desire to work would open many opportunities for junior partnerships and chances for higher incomes. Perhaps this assumption convinced Charles Ilfeld he could not hold a good man anyway without some profit-sharing arrangement, and that as long as the town was full of labor he might as well bargain for the best he could get at a competitive cost. Of course, under this policy, he got what the town was full of as is evidenced by the failure of any of the employees of his general merchandise store to rise to the rank of manager of a department in his new store.

All this is not to excuse, though it may condone, Charles Ilfeld for his policy of low wages. As a business policy it would have been wiser, probably, to improve the caliber of his clerks by offering more than the going rate. By paying higher wages, he might have been better off in the 1880's when he needed specialists in his department store, or later still when, with Max Nordhaus directing policy, managers were needed for a branch mercantile business on a large scale. But Ilfeld had not begun to think in terms of the future usefulness of these young men. As far as can be determined, Charles Ilfeld in the 1870's and early 1880's hired solely to meet present needs.

A business policy of buying labor at the market was unwise in another respect. Had Ilfeld adopted a conscious program of improving the caliber of his clerks he might have reaped the same reward in internal control that he had so successfully obtained through growing numbers of customers.

Internal Control

During this early period Charles Ilfeld was appallingly weak in his policy of internal control. Like most of his competitors, he operated a business small enough to make a cash journal and an account ledger seem sufficient. This ledger contained his bookkeeping barter transactions in the same manner which Baxter so well describes in his story of Thomas Hancock, colonial merchant of the eighteenth century.[36] Ilfeld added a general journal to his record-keeping in June, 1870, from which he posted faithfully to the ledger, but many entries, some explained and some not, were original with the ledger. The cash receipts and expenditures noted in the ledger were not tied in with the cash book; consequently it was impossible to balance the records.

The result of this single entry system was, as one would expect, a plethora of errors, many recognized at a later date, but many never discovered. Two substantial errors appear not to have been brought to Ilfeld's attention by his agents, and it is certain he did not find them himself. His balance with Samuel McCartney and Company of St. Louis on December 31, 1872, was $1942.50, and yet it was erroneously calculated as $942.50 and carried forward with no correction as late as September, 1874, when the account disappears into a lost ledger.[37] Again, a draft, number 753, issued by the Second National Bank of Santa Fe on the National Park Bank of New York for $1000 was sent to Samuel Beuthner, Ilfeld's agent, on November 1, 1873, but was never recorded.[38] Adolph Letcher wrote, "place amount to our credit," but he failed to ask for confirmation.[39] The account of Beuthner was closed in February, 1874, after Ilfeld asked for his balance, with a payment of $20.47, which apparently should have been a receipt of $979.26.[40] There is scarcely an active account that cannot be shown to have been in error in some respect, a not surprising discovery considering the volume and variety of transactions made without check against human frailty.

Another source of error was the practice of handling transactions for others without recording them in permanent records. Such was the case of William Tipton, who left funds with Ilfeld with which to pay Tipton's St. Louis accounts.[41] Occasionally a service was performed for another merchant, such as provisioning freighters, but because no account had previously been placed upon the books, or because the existing one was inactive, no entry was made.[42] Sole reliance for the record of such occurrences was the correspondence in the copy book.

Ilfeld further complicated his problem of control by purchasing merchandise from a particular firm both directly and through an agent. McCartney, for instance, representing Charles Ilfeld, bought merchandise from J. J. Beakey Company of St. Louis. This transaction was recorded by Ilfeld as an account payable through the Samuel McCartney account with a notation, "J. J. Beakey," but McCartney was held responsible for paying the bill.[43] In other cases Ilfeld bought directly from Beakey, posted the credit to Beakey's account, and paid the invoice by drawing a draft on McCartney.[44] Inasmuch as there were many such accounts, it must have taken constant vigilance on the part of Ilfeld and his employees to make certain that invoices from each firm were correctly separated according to method of purchase in order to avoid duplication of payment. Under such conditions a man with less capacity for detail would have found himself floundering in a welter of confusion and unexplained losses. Ilfeld's talents for minute supervision, however, were apparently too accomplished for him to worry greatly about an inadequate system of internal control.

In 1884, the young bookkeeper, Rodney B. Schoonmaker, fresh from his training at Marshall Field and Company in Chicago, appraised the shocking state of this system of accounts and recommended a double entry procedure. Schoonmaker claimed many years later that the price of his effort was an admonishment from Ilfeld that the method then in use had served the enterprise well. As a result, Schoonmaker kept two sets of books for a short period of time until the superiority of his suggestion could be demonstrated.[45]

Emphasis on Retailing

What appear to have been weaknesses in Ilfeld's business policy, low wages and minimum internal control, may actually lend credence to observations made by people who knew him, and particularly when these people contrasted his policies with those of Max Nordhaus of a later date. Nordhaus was the wholesaler and expansionist. Ilfeld was at heart a retailer.[46] Certainly Charles Ilfeld would have seen the wisdom of paying a higher wage for the purpose of training and keeping employees for key positions had he envisaged the need for such positions in the first place. Even his stubbornness in not seeing the value of a double entry bookkeeping system implies a narrow retailing concept.

In the eyes of those who finally turned the firm to wholesaling, and of the economy which later benefited by this change in policy, Ilfeld's decision to remain a retailer, in Old Town, was an error in judgment. Ilfeld, however, as long as he held actively to the reins of management, would never have agreed to this interpretation. Nor should the historian do so either unless he believes business to be an institution apart from the people who comprise it.

Charles Ilfeld was not an accurately milled piston which can be placed neatly in the round hole of mercantile capitalism, though mathematically he fits fairly well the mold of a sedentary merchant formed by Gras.[47] Ilfeld's policies and his functions were not astray of those practiced by the mercantile capitalists of the thirteenth-century Italian States; of fourteenth-, fifteenth-, and sixteenth-century England; or of seventeenth- and eighteenth-century America. He spent comparatively little time on the road, unlike the traveling merchants before him. Ilfeld made use of partners and agents to reduce his risks of procurement and supervision in outlying and distant areas. He exercised some control of the petty capitalist to insure himself supplies of raw materials for distribution. The special privilege he sought and got from the railroads, stage coach, and the military were typical of his earlier prototype.

Ilfeld functioned as an exporter and importer between the undeveloped West and the industrial East. He owned his teams and wagons for transport though he used the petty capitalist freighter and the industrial capitalist railroad extensively. Occasionally he stored goods for others. Ilfeld was a prolific letter writer both in his own interests and as an aid to other merchants and friends. His tendency toward banking and his investments in other enterprise were typical of the mercantile capitalist.

But Ilfeld differed from the model sedentary merchant in one important respect, and that was the emphasis he placed upon retailing. It is true that in time he became a wholesaler, but it was not from preference, and unlike Gras's sedentary merchant who "was forced by circumstances to perform the *task* of retailing," Ilfeld clearly was at home in this field —so much so that he took the task and made it his first love.[48]

This is not meant to imply that the wholesaling function was ignored, but it most certainly was consciously avoided. Ilfeld served the satellite towns with their wide rural areas, but he did so, for the most part, in a retailing manner. He sold to J. C. Lea's store in Roswell, but the prices were f.o.b. Las Vegas. Ilfeld acted as purchasing agent for Grzelachowski and Dunn at Puerto de Luna, but he sold them their fill-in orders at retail.

The accounts that were strictly wholesale, in the sense that they were in bulk at preferred prices, were very few. William Gellerman of Springer received his goods from Ilfeld at cost plus 10 per cent.[49] Some individuals, like Brunswick, who was a contractor and freighter, retailer, prospector and what not as it pleased his will, occasionally bought goods on the same terms.[50]

Others who received lower prices were the large ranchers. Ilfeld catered to this group and advertised himself as an "outfitter." It was this class of business that gave Ilfeld the right to think of himself as a wholesaler. It is important to note, however, that only two advertisements in the *Las Vegas Gazette,* one A. Letcher and Company, in 1874 and the other

Charles Ilfeld, in 1881, bear the captions "Wholesalers and Retailers." [51] The rest of the advertising, of which there was considerable, directs itself to retailing and outfitting.

The point to be emphasized, however, is that a very small percentage of the merchandise, certainly not over 10 per cent, was sold in bulk lots, and even less of it at discounted prices. Ilfeld relied heavily upon his drawing power as a buyer of varied produce over a wide area to bring customers to his doorstep. His branches at Tecolote, El Monton de Alamos, and La Junta had aided in reaching his market in the earlier days, but now they were gone and only one, El Monton de Alamos, remained as a customer.[52] Ilfeld was placing himself in a vulnerable position should any force step in to direct elsewhere the attention of his hinterland customers, who were, after all, his suppliers.

The Influence of Industrial Capitalism

During the fall of 1882 Ilfeld's three-story building on the Plaza was nearing completion, a structure which would house the department store he had been moving toward for more than a decade. In January, 1883, he was ready to advertise the opening of the Great Emporium with three floors and a basement fully packed with merchandise (see Appendix 6).

In the basement Ilfeld located the grocery department, which included both the liquor and hardware divisions. Dry goods and allied merchandise occupied the first floor. On the second level, in addition to dry goods (referred to in the newspaper as wholesale) was a millinery and dressmaking department. The third floor was set aside for carpeting, and later a furniture department was added.[53]

Ilfeld employed a manager for each department though in the case of the dressmaking division, where manufacturing would have to be emphasized, he hewed closely to the mercantile capitalist's policy of using an independent contractor. In seeking a competent woman for this position he wrote: [54]

> In order there will not be any misunderstanding on her arrival would repeat once more, that I want her to take hold of my Dress making room. She can have all the work she can do and shall have all what is in it. The dress making Department is attached to our store for which she has to pay a small rent [55] on which we can agree afterwards. All goods and trimming she buys out of store for the work room will be charged up to her less 10% commission. . . .

With the opening of his Great Emporium, Ilfeld had brought to fruition a long-held objective. In any eastern metropolitan center he probably would not have abandoned large-scale retailing. In New Mexico he had to compromise with mercantile capitalism and eventually bow to it completely, though it was the younger generation who bent him over in reluctant obeisance to the growing wholesale function.[56]

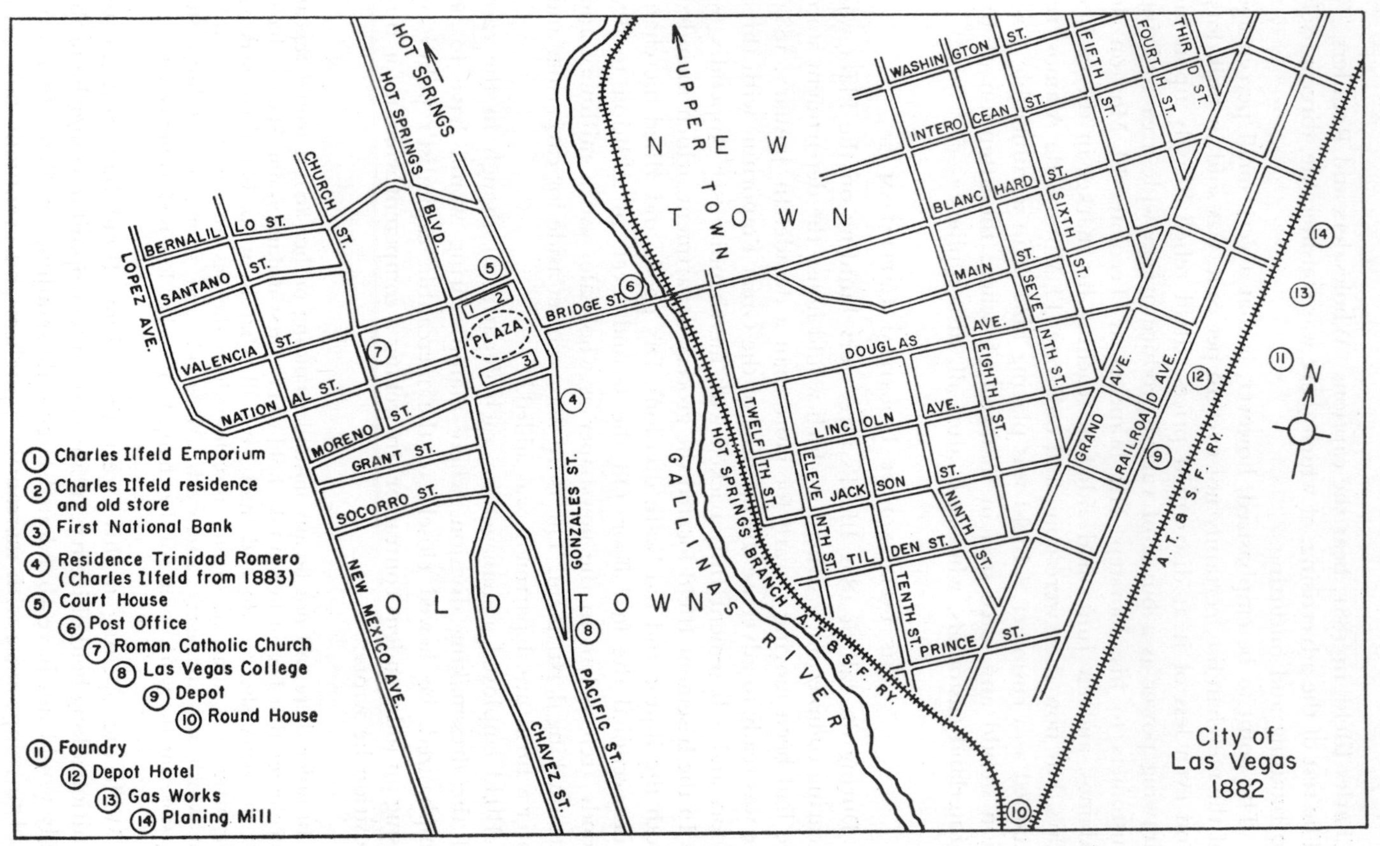
City of Las Vegas 1882
N
NEW TOWN
OLD TOWN
UPPER TOWN
HOT SPRINGS
HOT SPRINGS BLVD.
GALLINAS RIVER
A.T.B.S.F. RY.
HOT SPRINGS BRANCH A.T.B.S.F. RY.
PLAZA
BRIDGE ST.
CHURCH ST.
BERNALILLO ST.
SANTANO ST.
VALENCIA ST.
NATIONAL ST.
MORENO ST.
GRANT ST.
SOCORRO ST.
LOPEZ AVE.
NEW MEXICO AVE.
GONZALES ST.
CHAVEZ ST.
PACIFIC ST.
WASHINGTON ST.
INTEROCEAN ST.
BLANCHARD ST.
MAIN ST.
DOUGLAS AVE.
LINCOLN AVE.
JACKSON ST.
TILDEN ST.
PRINCE ST.
THIRD ST.
FOURTH ST.
FIFTH ST.
SIXTH ST.
SEVENTH ST.
EIGHTH ST.
NINTH ST.
TENTH ST.
ELEVENTH ST.
TWELFTH ST.
GRAND AVE.
RAILROAD AVE.
1 Charles Ilfeld Emporium
2 Charles Ilfeld residence and old store
3 First National Bank
4 Residence Trinidad Romero (Charles Ilfeld from 1883)
5 Court House
6 Post Office
7 Roman Catholic Church
8 Las Vegas College
9 Depot
10 Round House
11 Foundry
12 Depot Hotel
13 Gas Works
14 Planing Mill

Ilfeld detested wholesaling instinctively. It was too slow and secluded for one who loved daily contact with many people. His Jewish heritage of centuries of retailing pulsed in his veins. It is not surprising, therefore, that when petty capitalism failed to hold his ambitions and his abilities, he sought to turn at the first opportunity toward specialization in retailing on a large scale.

Rooted to the Plaza

That Charles Ilfeld was at heart a retailer, with little thought of building the large wholesaling business that later bore his name, is re-emphasized in his firm desire not to move his warehouse from the Plaza in Old Town to a railroad site in the new and rapidly growing East Las Vegas.

The merchants of the Plaza had expected, to be sure, that the New Mexico and Southern Pacific Railroad, subsidiary of the Atchison, Topeka & Santa Fe, would be built to pass by or near the Plaza. On the strength of such a promise many of the merchants gave their personal notes to the railroad agreeing to make their contributions "upon arrival of the first freight train at the depot of Las Vegas." [57] Las Vegas, in their minds, meant the old and original part of the town.[58] Charles Ilfeld pledged one of these notes for an amount of $375.[59]

As early as November 20, 1878, Ilfeld had knowledge that the railroad would not be built through Old Town. He wrote Kihlberg, his landlord, on that day.[60]

> I have been informed that Robinson will arrive here in a week from now to pick out a place for a Depot and from what I learn it will be on the other side of the river [Gallinas] close to town.

Though this letter makes it appear that the depot was going to be close enough to Old Town to satisfy the merchants of the Plaza, developments soon made it clear that this was not to be the case. Instead of greeting this fact as one would a brother, Ilfeld and the Plaza merchants reverted to a defense complex quite characteristic of most men with vested interests. They could have purchased property along the railroad right-of-way, as some merchants did in order to move with the tide, but most of them preferred to sit on the Plaza and buy their protection. A year after the railroad had been built into East Las Vegas, more than a mile from the Plaza, Ilfeld wrote a letter to Ed Wilder, Treasurer of the Atchison, Topeka & Santa Fe: [61]

> My understanding was, that this money [pledged on notes] was to be paid in order that your company would buy up all the lands at the depot here, so as to prevent the building of a new town in opposition to Las Vegas. Besides your company agreed that no one should be permitted to occupy the Depot grounds for any purpose except for a Commission house, while you are now permitting

two wholesale and retail houses there [Browne and Manzanares; Otero and Sellar] with large rebates of freight and are thereby greatly injuring and damaging this town, and all of which your company agreed not to do.

Fortunately for the merchants of the Plaza, the railroad had a commercial undertaking of its own which partially removed the sting which the main line location had caused. On the first of April, 1879, the Santa Fe Railroad bought the Montezuma Hotel at Hot Springs, six miles north of Old Town.[62] In order to protect this investment the company completed a branch line in April, 1882, through the Gallinas Cañon to the resort hotel.[63] This gave Ilfeld and neighbor merchants a spur track only a quarter of a mile distant.

Why did Charles Ilfeld choose to keep all his Las Vegas mercantile investment on the Plaza? Was it because of the cost a new warehouse and perhaps a store would entail? Possibly, yet, in 1882, three years after the coming of the railroad, he built his new store on the Plaza, hailed as the largest in New Mexico. What of the cost of handling goods from the railroad? Would not this added expense soon exceed any investment in new facilities? [64] Old-timers like to remember the difficulties of bringing the goods across town. In the winter the roads were frequently impassable. When the horse-drawn streetcar made its appearance, Ilfeld experimented with this vehicle as a freight conveyance, but all the car's horses pulling, and all Ilfeld's men pushing could do no more than encourage the car to leave its tracks.[65]

If East Las Vegas had not yet grown sufficiently to encourage a profitable retail trade, why did not Ilfeld decide to move his warehouse to the railroad? That at least would have prevented the cross haul on merchandise shipped out by rail as well as the added haul of local produce destined for eastern markets.

Was it simply animus let loose against a monopoly that had not cooperated with him in the earlier days and now threatened the welfare of Old Town? It is possible Ilfeld permitted a feeling of spite to influence him, but surely so superficial a reason could not have had so permanent an effect.

No, it is not likely that this merchant, who had displayed a capacity for seizing opportunities whenever they arose, would misjudge so obvious a chance to improve his service and lower his distribution costs. He had watched the coming of the steam engine with anticipation, as had all people of the Territory, and now with its arrival he would not disregard its potentialities without, what appeared to him, a good reason.[66]

Ilfeld's mistake was that he appraised his business in the same light in which he had seen it grow. It was a gathering place for mule and oxen trains from near and distant points. It was a general merchandise store servicing to a great extent the Spanish-speaking people, who would not wish to change their habits by trading a mile east in an "Anglo" district. Ilfeld's one objective was to build his retail business with customers who had something to give him for eastern markets. Wholesaling had no part in his plans.

From a personal standpoint, as a retailer and merchandiser of rare ability, Ilfeld proved his judgment sound for several more years. In the long run, however, his policy of emphasizing retailing was doomed to failure. The telling effect of the railroad was to limit the volume of raw material supplies delivered to the Plaza. He could somehow drag the merchandise he had purchased in the East across town at a cost, but he could not compel his sheep-ranching friends, up and down the tracks, to bring their wool clippings to the Plaza in Old Town if some gathering point on the railroad could save a long wagon haul. Eventually they would leave him one by one, and group by group.

When the Texas and Pacific Railroad completed its line westward from San Antonio to El Paso in January, 1883, connecting with the Southern Pacific, the combination of these roads with the Santa Fe put Las Vegas on the defensive as a gathering center from the southern part of the Territory.[67] In the 1890's the Pecos Valley Railroad from Pecos City, Texas, to Eddy [Carlsbad], New Mexico, which upon its extension met the road from Amarillo, Texas, and was opened to traffic in March, 1899, completely removed the Roswell area from dependence on Las Vegas.[68] In 1901, the El Paso and Northeastern Railway cut northward from El Paso to Carrizozo, New Mexico, and its extensions took the tracks through Santa Rosa and the northeastern part of the Territory.[69]

It was shortly after this time that Charles Ilfeld's decision to remain a retailer on an old and shrinking path was rescinded and a new course of branch warehousing and wholesaling was instigated. This move, however, awaited some solution to his management problem, a problem that would hardly solve itself in view of Ilfeld's weak labor policy; a problem that had become critical, by 1884, because Ilfeld had seemed unconcerned about solving it with any dispatch.

VIII

CHARLES ILFELD AND HIS MANAGEMENT PROBLEM

If Charles Ilfeld was prone to put business first it was not because he lacked for diversions. He loved excitement and entertainment. He enjoyed the dance and with the ladies played the man gallant. He preferred the acquisition of wealth to all other activities but he wanted at least a reasonable amount of leisure to enjoy it. His purchasing trips to New York were looked forward to with as much anticipation of the opera and the theater as they were toward the finding of bargain-priced goods. He wanted to extend these eastern trips, too, whenever the opportunity afforded, beyond the ocean to Europe and his native Germany.[1]

Charles Ilfeld, proprietor, did not fit this scheme of things as fully as he would have liked. From the time he bought the interest of his partner, Letcher, in the fall of 1874 until July of 1876, he was tied closely to his store with no employee capable enough to manage the enterprise should Ilfeld wish to leave.[2] His only travel in this period was confined to a few side trips of one to three days' duration to Fort Union, Santa Fe, or other nearby centers. He was forced to rely heavily upon his good friend Solomon Beuthner in New York to make his eastern purchases and to serve as his business agent.[3]

Beuthner, who knew the New Mexico market well and who possessed years of mercantile experience, apparently performed his task well. Neither Beuthner nor Ilfeld, however, would have been likely to accept such an arrangement as permanent. Beuthner was near retirement and would soon return to New Mexico.[4] Ilfeld was too restless and cosmopolitan to enjoy being cooped up the year-round in Las Vegas, much as he loved it as an abiding place.

Temporary Managers

In 1876 Ilfeld was able to make the first of several arrangements with the capable but erratic Richard Dunn to manage his business while he was away on his purchasing trips.[5] Dunn took charge in 1876 for a period of nine or ten weeks and again in 1878 for almost five months while Ilfeld traveled to New York and Europe.[6] In 1877, cigar-smoking Aaron Schutz, husband of Fanny Nordhaus, Ilfeld's sister-in-law, was mustered in at the last minute to assume control in Ilfeld's absence.[7]

It is possible that Ilfeld made a trip east in the early part of 1879 while his clerk, A. W. Cleland, Jr., a young man of twenty-three years, took care of routine business.[8] If so, Ilfeld was not gone as long as usual, and he did not make another trip until March, 1881.[9] Richard Dunn, who might have released Ilfeld for travel, had become a partner in 1879 with Grzelachowski, the ex-priest, in the general merchandising business in Puerto de Luna, and Ilfeld, by his own admission, was too short of help to permit any employee leave "except it must be." [10]

In 1881, though, he left for New York—Cleland and Dunn each assuming managerial duties, Dunn having been borrowed from a new partnership, Pendaries and Dunn, of Rincon, New Mexico.[11] In 1882, a two-month purchasing trip was made while an Albert Bloch served as store manager.[12]

Why did Charles Ilfeld continue his "catch-as-catch-can" method of obtaining managers? The answers, speculative as they may be, fall into three categories: first, Ilfeld's failure to appraise accurately the true character of his business; second, his unwillingness at this time to share either his assets or authority with anyone; and third, the possibility of finding the answer to his problem at a later date in the person of his brother-in-law, Max Nordhaus.

The first reason, involving the character of Ilfeld's business in the 1870's with its heavy emphasis on retailing and the failure of Charles Ilfeld to grasp the potentialities of the wholesale trade—so necessary for the continued growth, if not the survival, of the mercantile capitalist—was a retarding factor in reaching a solution to Ilfeld's management problem. The business, at this time, was small enough to permit reasonably effective control by one man—even with a single entry bookkeeping system—and to allow it to be carried forward by momentum for short periods of time under the direction of an honest and fairly capable manager who had had some experience in the mercantile business. Charles Ilfeld's narrow retailing complex, observed through some of his early policy decisions, caused him to overlook the advantages of division of labor and of function, and to believe, intuitively, that his business could not support more than one manager's income.[13] With this he had to compromise, as we have seen, in the hiring of Richard Dunn, who in the absence of any salary payments must have been employed on a commission or profit-sharing agreement. Some division of management had to be followed to permit Ilfeld to fulfill the specialized function of purchasing, so important to a firm which buys in a metropolitan area for a frontier demand, and, we should add, to permit him to enjoy the leisure and pleasure of extended traveling.

The second reason that caused Ilfeld to continue this policy of hiring fill-in managers is strictly a negative one. He could have solved his problem simply by acquiring a partner but he did not want to. Why, we may wonder, did he not want to grasp the solution he had seen work at first hand with his former partner, Letcher, and which was being used so successfully by his competitors, Browne and Manzanares, and Otero and Sellar? Again Ilfeld's conception of the character of his business and his failure to recognize fully the advantages of division of function enter into the picture. This, however, was not the whole story.

Ilfeld, in 1880, was thirty-three years of age and only fifteen years removed from the day he had arrived in the United States with little if any capital to further a business venture. In fifteen years he had built a business possessing a net worth as large, perhaps, as $100,000 (more than a quarter of a million dollars at today's prices). He had done so through stint and perseverance, and through a self-confidence that knew few limits. Under such circumstances, is it likely that Ilfeld, still young, healthy, and vigorous, would wish to share his future enterprise with business partners even though we grant these conjectural associates to have been thoroughly competent and compatible? Ilfeld had this solution to his management problem in these early years literally staring him in the face in the person of Marcus Brunswick, also a German Jew, who was his counselor and dearest friend.

Brunswick, eighteen years the senior of Ilfeld, was, perhaps, as shrewd and able and as well-liked a man as lived in the Territory. The two men had been partners in minor joint ventures, and Brunswick, a bachelor, in addition to boarding at the Ilfeld residence, kept an office at the Charles Ilfeld store as headquarters for his varied activities which, of course, no longer included the general merchandising business. Yet, the seemingly logical step of full business association never occurred, and even the possibility disappeared when Brunswick dropped dead on the Plaza following a hearty meal at the Ilfeld residence.[14]

Even more logical, perhaps, would have been a partnership arrangement with one or more of his three brothers: Herman, Louis, or Noa. Herman had built a successful general merchandising business in Santa Fe, and Louis and Noa had done the same in Albuquerque. Sometime before 1880 the three had formed a partnership doing business as the Ilfeld Brothers. Charles was very close to all three, familywise. Yet there was, apparently, no inclination to merge his business with theirs, though he cooperated with them frequently in purchases and sales, and even though many commercial advantages could have resulted, including a well-established branch wholesaling business with a territory-wide trade area.[15] Ilfeld probably wanted some solution to his managerial problem, and after a fashion he attained it, with temporary managers and agents—but a partnership was not in his plans. He stopped at the brink of sharing future income and wealth with men who, because of ability, age, and prestige, would force him also to share his authority. Ilfeld's failure to appraise accurately the true character of his business, as well as his unwillingness to share either his assets or authority with business partners, were dominant reasons in 1880 for his procrastination in solving his management problem.

A third reason for postponing this solution, and one that should not by hindsight discount the other two, was the prospect of bringing Max Nordhaus, Mrs. Ilfeld's younger brother, to America and, as an employee, to train him in the general merchandising business. Though this approach would take some time, and might not succeed anyway, it was a logical move. Max would live at the Ilfeld home. He could be trained on a twenty-four hour schedule. He would have no strong diversionary interests. For some time his money wants would be small. He presented a better-than-fair risk to Ilfeld that he would soon develop into a competent manager who, in addition, would be loyal, sympathetic, and, happily, a member of the immediate family.

Max Nordhaus, in 1883, was approaching that magic age of eighteen when all young German males became men, and when thousands of them avoided the Prussian draft to test the promised freedom and opportunity of the United States.[16] Max, an only son to grow to manhood, having chosen not to follow his father's profession of Rabbi, had studied instead in the *lehre,* the institution of the business apprenticeship.[17] Not having a business inheritance in Germany to look forward to, but possessing a favored opportunity in America, he was conditioned to his prospective move.

In April, 1883, with Bloch again managing the store, Ilfeld left for Germany to join members of his family who had preceded him on a lengthy visit and to bring them home.[18] He returned in June, having previously requested railroad passes for his family, "consisting of my wife, 2 Children, 2 Servant Girls, and 2 clerks for my store." [19] One of the clerks was Max Nordhaus—less than two weeks shy of his eighteenth birthday.[20]

Pending the Apprenticeship of Max Nordhaus, 1883–1886

Ilfeld's procrastination in facing his management problem found him unprepared to meet adequately the demand for executive talent created by the completion of his greatly enlarged department store in January, 1883.[21] A. W. Cleland, Jr., an assistant office manager, who had been hired in 1878 at the rather low salary of $25 per month, had had his stipend raised in 1880 to $1000 per year and was given more responsibility. He left the employ in November, 1881.[22] Albert Bloch took his place in January, 1882, at the same salary but left the company in July, 1884, though his salary in the meantime had been raised to $1200 per year.[23]

A key employee, who was to have a quiet but important influence on business policy over a span of 20 years, was one Rodney B. Schoonmaker. He was employed in July, 1884, as a replacement for Albert Bloch, the bookkeeper.[24] A few years later he became office manager and cashier.[25] Schoonmaker, a frail young man of twenty-eight years, had come to Las Vegas as a health seeker just a few days before his employment by Ilfeld. He had had previous experience with the firm of Marshall Field and Company of Chicago where he had been an office employee in the wholesale division.[26] The first task Schoonmaker set for himself (perhaps with some encouragement from Max Nordhaus but against the judgment of Charles Ilfeld) was to establish a set of double entry bookkeeping records as the only method by which he could keep accounts accurately.[27] Although this system left much to be desired it was a great improvement over Bloch's hybrid single and double entry effort, and it offered an opportunity for the first time to make monthly estimates of business results.

In this same year, 1884, it had become evident that some further division of function in management would be necessary. The wool market had been declining since 1880 and collections on the hinterland accounts were demanding closer attention. A few months before the employment of Schoonmaker, therefore, Ilfeld faced this problem and brought back to the organization a young German immigrant, Solomon Floersheim, whom he had employed first in 1880 and who had resigned in 1882.[28]

Floersheim, as later evidence indicates, was a shrewd trader, but was generally liked in spite of this because of a pleasant tongue and an uncanny ability as a medical diagnostician and practitioner.[29] Although Floersheim was quite capable of "drumming" the merchandise trade, his chief job was to make sure that customers reduced their accounts by selling their produce, principally sheep and wool, to Ilfeld.[30]

Floersheim, however, was restless and probably was somewhat concerned about his future in view of the Nordhaus-Ilfeld relationship, and a salary of $1350 per year did not hold him too long. He left, in March, 1888, for a successful business career.[31]

With Floersheim and Schoonmaker handling their respective areas of management capably, Max Nordhaus was kept relatively free to learn all aspects of the business which, considering his age and limited experience, he accomplished in a very few years with a degree of competency that is rather remarkable.

The Rise of Max Nordhaus

Schoonmaker, in describing conditions in the Ilfeld organization of 1884, wrote: "Mr. Nordhaus was acting as office man and I received from him what instruction I got on duties." He remembered him as being "a very acute business man even then." [32]

Nordhaus' rise, as detected from the records, shows him to have been writing and signing routine business letters in the early part of 1884.[33] After Bloch left in July of that year, he began to write many more, displaying a maturity noteworthy for a lad of nineteen. In March, 1885, Charles Ilfeld authorized him "to sign and endorse checks and notes in my name" at both eastern and New Mexico banks, and to act for Ilfeld in his capacity as secretary of the board of directors of the Las Vegas Street Railway Corporation.[34] In July, a notorial seal for Max Nordhaus, Notary Public, was ordered.[35]

It was not until the close of the year 1886, however, that Charles Ilfeld conferred upon Max Nordhaus full authority of management. He did so by appointing his young brother-in-law, twenty-one years of age, his agent with the broadest possible powers. A power of attorney recorded with the County Clerk of San Miguel County reads as follows: [36]

> Know all men by these presents: That I, Charles Ilfeld of Las Vegas in San Miguel County and Territory of New Mexico, do by these presents appoint, constitute and make Max Nordhaus my true and lawful attorney, for me and in my place and stead, to take charge of my business of general merchandising; at Las Vegas, County of San Miguel, Territory of New Mexico; to purchase and sell, for cash or on credit, all such articles, goods, merchandise, wares, real estate and live stock as he shall deem proper, necessary and useful to said business; to sign, accept and endorse all notes, drafts and bills; to execute and cancel mortgages, to state accounts, to sue and prosecute, compromise, collect and settle all claims or demands due or to become due, now existing or hereafter to exist in my favor; to adjust and pay all claims or demands which now exist or may hereafter arise against me, either connected with said business or otherwise; giving and granting unto my said attorney full authority and power to do and perform every act and thing whatsoever necessary and requisite to be done in said business as I might or could do if personally present.
>
> In testimony whereof I have hereunto set my hand and seal this fifteenth of December A. D. 1886.
>
> Signed and sealed CHAS. ILFELD
> in presence of
> R. B. Schoonmaker

It is interesting that Ilfeld did not choose to make a partnership arrangement. He preferred the agency relationship which, though it conferred upon Nordhaus the same powers for action a full partner would have had, and placed Ilfeld under the same risk of unlimited liability that would have been present with a partnership agreement, it stopped short of granting Nordhaus property rights to earnings and net assets. In return for his services Nordhaus continued to enjoy the privileges of drawing without obligation of repayment whatever he needed from the business without regard to set limits or to any fixed ratio with Ilfeld's drawings, and of receiving his board and room at the Ilfeld home without charge.

Although this power of attorney was never changed or revoked, a supplemental agreement of partnership was agreed upon 24 years later in February, 1911, granting Max Nordhaus a one-fourth interest in all the property, real or personal, belonging to the two men.[37] It was not until Ilfeld reached the age of sixty-four that he accepted a partnership arrangement.[38] The earlier Nordhaus agency had been created to free Ilfeld for the fuller life but also, apparently, it served to circumvent any serious misunderstandings, particularly by third parties, that Max Nordhaus, having performed the acts of a partner, could have been declared, in fact, a copartner with Charles Ilfeld in the absence of expressed evidence to the contrary.

Those employees and friends who knew both men intimately have considered this long-term relationship a most rare, if not unique, phenomenon in the business world. Beyond the rather obvious factors of trust and respect that each man held in and for the other, the key to the success of this most broadly framed agency was Max's capacity for taking responsibility and of ably executing it while being content to maintain a humble and undivided loyalty to Charles Ilfeld.

Ilfeld's implicit trust in the business ability and judgment of his young brother-in-law left the older associate conscience-free to pursue the life he wanted. By 1887, the first year of the Nordhaus agency, Ilfeld was turning forty with an increasing desire to be shed of the compulsion of business detail. He came to the store daily, whenever he was in Las Vegas, but more and more his time there was spent in consultation, in leisurely opening his mail, in rising to meet old customers or to wait on a lady as she entered the store. He continued to make his two-month to three-month annual trips to the East, combining varied pleasures with that of purchasing, but from 1889 on these trips were extended in length of time and, later, their greater frequency, twice a year, warranted the renting of a New York City apartment for himself and his family.[39]

Only when Max made his periodic trips to Europe—which he did in 1888, 1893, 1896, and 1903—was Ilfeld's freedom restricted.[40] At such times an occasional sentence in Ilfeld's letters pointed out the extent to which Max Nordhaus had assumed control of operations. In 1893 Ilfeld wrote to a customer: "I have to stay here this Spring and will be the Boss until Max returns." [41] That this was probably something more than a light statement is indicated in a harried letter to his former partner, Letcher, in 1896, written about two weeks after Max's departure in which he expressed a wish that "He [Max] was back already." [42]

Although Charles Ilfeld continued to direct major policies to 1889 or later, Max Nordhaus, by virtue of his day-to-day decisions, was the policymaker. Ilfeld, through desire and wisdom, was retreating more and more toward leisure and less positive direction and was leaning on an executive leader whom he evidently sensed was more adept at handling control problems that confronted the continually expanding business. The story of the proprietorship of Charles Ilfeld growing into mature mercantile capitalism is, in large measure, the story of Max Nordhaus, general agent.

PART THREE

Toward Mature Mercantile Capitalism

The Establishment of Monopolistic and Protective Devices

Charles Ilfeld and Max Nordhaus, 1887-1929 (Later Phase)

Introduction

The beginning mercantile capitalist was cloaked in an armor of distance and time. This natural form of protective tariff effectively insulated him from direct competition from without his territory, and prevented an excessive number of competitors from arising within. Those without his area were stymied by the practical impossibility of direct contact with the sparse and far-flung market; and those within were discouraged or prevented from substantial propagation by the sheer problems of acquisition and distribution of goods.

So protective, however, was this natural barrier of distance and time that the early mercantile capitalists spent much of their effort in seeking ways to ease the barriers to their trade. In New Mexico, and elsewhere, they clamored for the building and improvement of roads. They pressed for extension of mail routes with faster and more frequent service. They demanded and received military protection for their cargoes en route. They pleaded for public works expenditures which would not only serve to increase trade but would make the acquisition of monetary exchange easier. They resented the imposition of tariff duties on those goods which they imported. When new and more efficient forms of transportation made their appearance, these merchants were quick to adopt them if they could. And when the railroad promised to tie them closer to industrial centers, they cheered its progress and, oftentimes, subsidized its dramatic onrush.

When the railroad came to New Mexico, and later its extensions and new routes, the competitive complexion of mercantile capitalism in that area changed. New centers of population arose bringing new opportunities to more individuals. Old distribution areas were disrupted and new ones created. In many cases the new trade areas, carved out of the old, were smaller and overlapping. Often vested interests were shaken rudely. Although the sedentary merchants found themselves still striving for those aids and innovations that would cut their costs directly, they also were driven to seek protective devices that would prevent the changing environment from dissipating the control they had gained over many dependent petty capitalists. The gradual, and sometimes sudden, releasing of trade from the natural barriers of distance and time caused many beginning mercantile capitalists, who possessed substantial resources, to expand certain functions to a highly specialized state of development. This was an instinctive reaction to a threatened loss of their control over sales of goods to the hinterland and, more important (in view of large credit extensions), their control over incoming payments on account through delivery of produce from the countryside. By expanding, a more strenuous competition arose between the few more successful merchants in a fashion faintly suggestive of the often brutal competition of the specialized industrialists of the eastern metropolitan centers. This change toward a greater specialization in certain business functions also brought with it the ever-present danger of imbalance of risks as one function and then another became top-heavy in relation to others. Though this development was a compromise between the basic philosophy and the practice of mercantile capitalism, it gave the successful sedentary merchant, for a period of time, as much or even more control over the petty capitalist than he had enjoyed before.

Charles Ilfeld and Max Nordhaus moved toward mature mercantile capitalism in three principal ways. First, they took progressive steps toward specialization in sheep and wool and, to a far lesser extent, in cattle and livestock. They loaned sheep, receiving a share of the wool product and increase as interest (cattle also was used in share contracts), and sometimes leased pasturage to sheep growers. When collections of sheep, cattle, wools, pelts, and hides flooded them with inventories, they enlarged their facilities for pasturing the livestock and storing the produce.

Second, they sought and obtained a more certain control over supply and demand. This they did by specializing in the function of purchasing, not only for themselves but as agents for others, and by consciously seeking exclusive distribution contracts of branded goods. They obtained closer control of their markets through the practice of financing the inventories and credit of country stores, thus giving more attention to the field of wholesaling—a practice which for lack of control and marketing efficiency encouraged a deliberate move toward direct control through company-owned wholesale and warehouse branches.

The third step, which paralleled and grew upon the other two, was an extension of the merchant credit system. Ilfeld and Nordhaus financed their retailers and ranch suppliers by taking on many of the aspects of a commercial banker. They developed a check-writing system through which cash or merchandise could be drawn and in which system their own and other retailers served as convenient branch "banks." They accepted deposits and paid interest upon them. Inasmuch as these practices were carried on by other mercantile capitalists in New Mexico, it is not surprising to find several of them choosing to take the final step in the process—the establishment of a commercial bank separately operated. Ilfeld and Nordhaus had no inclination to do this. Those who did take the step, however, divorced their banks from the merchant credit system and, in many cases, retained this older procedure as an integrated function of the general wholesaling and shrinking retailing business. The merchant credit system remained in more liquid form, but the convenient and liberal access which the petty capitalist storekeeper and rancher had to this banking function kept him close, and often it tied him tightly to the control of the mature mercantile capitalist.

Each of these functions and combinations of functions—the move toward specialization in sheep and livestock, the creation of means of better control of supply and demand, and the development of many of the aspects of commercial banking—were protective in nature. They arose as protection against a worsening credit position in the depression of the 1890's and a threat of shrinking trade areas and greater competition. Sometimes these protective devices, such as the use of sheep and wool and often banking, became specializations to the exclusion of mercantile trade. Though this was not true in the case of Charles Ilfeld and Max Nordhaus, the imbalance of investment in and the attention given to the sheep and wool industry became very great. The story, however, can best be told by discussing each of the expanded functions separately.

IX

TOWARD SHEEP AND WOOL SPECIALIZATION

Underlying Forces

The ubiquitous sheep. Hernando Cortés left Cuba for the Vera Cruz coast in 1519 with "some five hundred men, thirty muskets, a few toy cannon, and sixteen horses." [1] If only he had included a ram and a ewe in the outfit one would be tempted to speculate that the American ancestry of the New Mexico sheep industry dated from the very beginning of the Spanish Conquest of the mainland. Ewes and rams, however, did follow and to such an extent that by 1531, nine years before Coronado started north with "a large number of cattle and sheep," the progeny were beginning to be numerous.[2] Chevalier terms the proliferation of pigs, sheep, and horned animals around some villages as "fantastic" by 1538 or 1540.[3] He further states that in the first decade of the seventeenth century Franciscans in the Province of Avalos were raising sheep for profit and were renting winter pasturage to other stock raisers farther east.[4] By the middle of the century, large numbers of sheep were roaming the high, dry plateaus of central Mexico where the Jesuits, in particular, possessed "many hundreds of thousands" of head.[5] Bancroft, evidently with some conservatism, remarks that "sheep raising was of some importance in the northern and central provinces" during the eighteenth century.[6] By 1800, with peones tending the fertile flocks on great expanses of free land, the Spanish ricos had become patrons of an industry that covered the whole of feudal New Mexico.[7]

In or about this year the Spanish governor, Baca, is purported (logic suggests with gross exaggeration) to have owned 2,000,000 head of sheep which were tended by 2700 peones.[8] A half century later, following the American occupation, the Pereas, Martinezes, Armijos, and others were driving large numbers of their sheep to California to help feed the gold miners and their families.[9] By 1880 the Far West was producing more sheep, by a considerable margin, than any other section of the country, and New Mexico, outranked only by California, Texas, and Ohio, was producing a large and increasing share of the total.[10] During the next 10 years a major part of the flocks of Colorado, Kansas, Utah, Wyoming, and Nebraska had been supplied from New Mexico—"the mother of the sheep industry of the Rocky Mountain region and the great plains." [11]

The demand for sheep in the late 1870's and early 1880's from neighboring states and territories was of such size as to foster temptations among men of all economic levels to participate in this growing New Mexico industry which still had at its beck and call vast stretches of open range where only a bare beginning had been made toward fenced and controlled pasturage. Yet, in spite of the ubiquitous sheep, free land, and trained labor cheaply hired, the established mercantile capitalist in the larger centers had resisted the temptation, as late as 1885, to invest, substantially, either in the ownership of livestock or in the business of wool and sheep contracting. Only in small measure did the established mercantile capitalist at this early date choose to pasture or range his own livestock. Rather he accepted such chattel, along with wool, pelts, and hides in payment on account, and disposed of his inventory as promptly as the market allowed.

The railroad. By the time the Atchison, Topeka & Santa Fe Railroad had crossed New Mexico from north to south and reached its terminus at El Paso, Texas, in July, 1881, the mercantile capitalists in the three centers of Las Vegas, Santa Fe, and Albuquerque found themselves in a new competitive situation in which they were encouraged, if not compelled, to reassess their policies of credit extension to customers who raised cattle and sheep.[12] Not only did the railroad give many of the livestock growers a choice of several shipping points, thus putting them in a better competitive position, but the railroad also gave rise to the specialists in wool and sheep, both as brokers and contractors. These enterprisers, who for the most part tended to settle in or operate out of Albuquerque, because of its command over the great sheep-raising territory to the west as well as much of the area to the east, offered an alternative source of financing to the livestock grower.[13] With easy access to eastern markets, and with the opportunity of financial backing from eastern commission houses or large western feeders, these specialists could afford to contract a rancher's crop of wool or sheep. They advanced the rancher funds and paid cash for the balance due upon delivery. Although this development threatened to divert from the mercantile capitalist only the trade of those ranchers who had attained a certain amount of liquidity and who were not tied to merchant credit, it promised to become an important diversion because it comprised the most desirable business.

The advantages of intimate contact with his market which the merchant possessed—that is, of tight hold over customers through financial bonds, convenient service, and personal relationships—prevented this direct competition of the independent wool and sheep buyer from becoming serious. The presence of this specialist, though, did cause the mercantile capitalist to enlarge his interest in the sheep industry, and particularly so when the demand for mutton in western slaughter markets jumped almost geometrically as a result of a rapid growth of metropolitan centers from the middle 1880's on.[14] Furthermore, the wool and sheep buyers of the North and East preferred, in most instances, to use the general merchant in New Mexico as a middleman. They found him ideally adapted to the gathering of thousands of sheep from the small and medium-sized ranches of the vast hinterland. The merchant, too, facing ever more serious collection problems as prices of agricultural products continued their long-term post-Civil War fall, gladly collaborated with these buyers for the liquidity they could bring him. Only the resident independent buyers competed directly with the general merchant, but the growth of the market for mutton was of such proportions as to dilute the impact of these newcomers.

The railroad, in opening the growing mutton market to New Mexico ranchers, offered the mercantile capitalist a further opportunity to play the role of middleman that he loved so much. The typical sheep buyer, in traveling to New Mexico from the States, was willing to offer the merchant contracts, sometimes with substantial advances, to purchase large numbers of lambs, ewes, and wethers months before the date of delivery. The merchant, in turn, could rely no longer on the deliveries of sheep his customers chose to bring to town. Rather he contracted them in advance of the season at safe prices—paying more if the customer sensed the merchant's anxiety to collect an account, or if some competitor, merchant or independent buyer, had been there first.

Those merchants who had acquired substantial resources became more liberal in the extension of credit to ranchers in an effort to assure supply, though they protected themselves with the widespread use of chattel mortgages. As we shall see in a later chapter, the larger mercantile capitalists gave selected sheep growers lines of credit and checkbooks which could be used to write drafts, payable in cash when, as subcontractors, these ranchers bought sheep; or they could be payable in merchandise when supplies were needed. The merchant thus became involved heavily in the financing of the sheep industry in New Mexico as the specialist buyer placed an enlarged source of monetary exchange at the merchant's disposal.

The railroad had been responsible, in large measure, for this happy development but it also brought with it a depressing effect as far as the mercantile capitalists of Las Vegas and Santa Fe were concerned, an effect which, indirectly, forced the merchants of these areas into even greater participation in the New Mexico sheep industry. Each of these towns was irreparably hurt as a wool center by the coming of the railroad because the southeastern part of the Territory—Lincoln and Dona Ana counties, long a part of their trade areas—became closer, economically, to El Paso, Las Cruces, and Socorro. The railroad severed this great area from the two major centers, as far as merchandise distribution was concerned, and it hampered continuance of their sheep and wool trade. In order not to be forced out of the southeastern part of the Territory entirely, these merchants, by dint of financing ability and the chattel mortgage, continued for at least a decade to receive sheep and wool from many of their old customers in that area. They kept their feet in these distant doors by direct loans and the use of the checkbook draft, and, too, by making investments in sheep and placing them among old customers on a rental-and-share-basis.

By 1885 the mercantile capitalist in New Mexico was moving toward a purposeful investment in the sheep industry. The ubiquitous sheep and the railroad made it possible. The independent buyer of sheep and the growing mutton market had made it certain. None of these forces, however, had done more than cause him to expand his role as middleman and banker. It was a third factor that pushed him, and roughly so, into the fold of sheep husbandry.

Falling wool and sheep prices and the collection problem. As we analyze from hindsight the extent of the merchant's participation in the sheep industry, it seems almost certain that the established mercantile capitalist in New Mexico would have kept the risk of sheep husbandry on the shoulders of the rancher, small and large, bearing none of it himself, had he been able to follow his business inclinations. He would have preferred to remain a broker, as far as the livestock industry was concerned, because of the minimum risk that it entailed. He would have moved toward contracting on a large scale as the independent contractor and the public's demand for mutton drove and enticed him, but he would have protected himself, as far as possible, by passing on in advance the burden of his contracts to others—usually the large feeders of the corn states. The old story, however, of the precipitous decline of agricultural prices versus the more controlled fall of industrial prices, which, as applied to wool, occurred with increasing emphasis from 1880 to 1889, to sheep from 1893 to 1896, and to cattle from 1884 to 1895, forced the mercantile capitalist to assume the additional role of sheep husbandman.[15] This was contrary to his policy of earlier years and it is questionable if he was anxious to accept the added burden.[16]

In general we can reason how this movement into sheep husbandry occurred. To the mercantile capitalist, who after all was an importer and exporter in the strictest sense of the words, this growing spread in price trends meant a worsening of his terms of trade, to borrow a modern phrase. As the prices of what he imported, indicated by a general wholesale price index, fell from 100 per cent in 1880 to 70 per cent in 1896, those of wool, which he exported, declined to less than 40 per cent.[17] In two critical periods, 1880 to 1888, and 1893 to 1896, the price of medium and coarse wools fell 3, and then 2.5, times as much as general wholesale prices.[18]

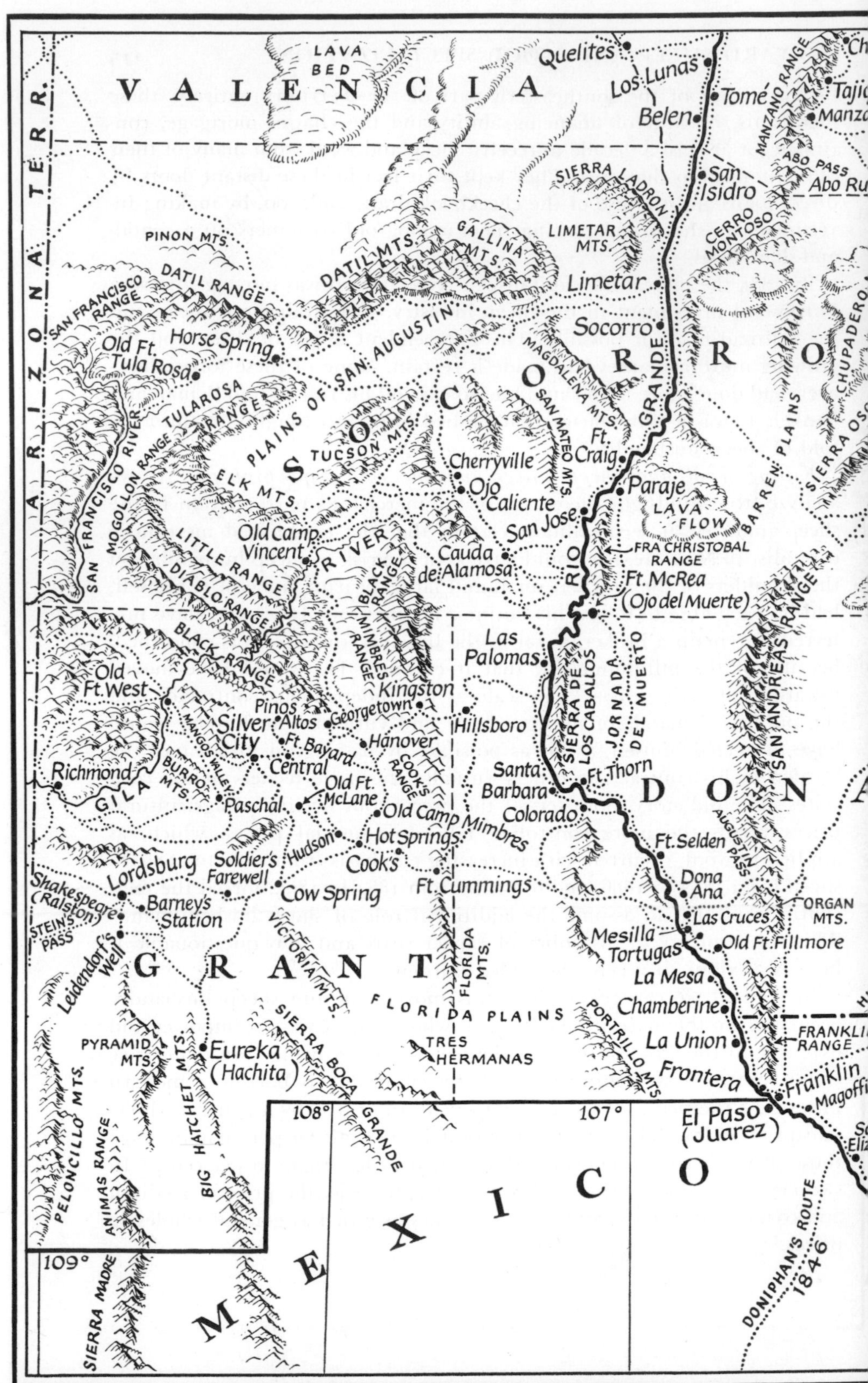

VALENCIA
SOCORRO
GRANT
DONA
MEXICO
ARIZONA TERR.
LAVA BED
Quelites
Los Lunas
Tomé
Belen
San Isidro
Abo Pass
MANZANO RANGE
ABO PASS
SIERRA LADRON
CERRO MONTOSO
LIMETAR MTS.
Limetar
Socorro
PINON MTS.
DATIL MTS.
GALLINA MTS.
DATIL RANGE
SAN FRANCISCO RANGE
Old Ft. Tula Rosa
Horse Spring
PLAINS OF SAN AUGUSTIN
TULAROSA RANGE
MAGDALENA MTS.
SAN MATEO MTS.
RIO GRANDE
Ft. Craig
CHUPADERO
BARREN PLAINS
TUCSON MTS.
Cherryville
Ojo Caliente
Paraje
LAVA FLOW
SAN FRANCISCO RIVER
MOGOLLON RANGE
ELK MTS.
LITTLE RANGE
DIABLO RANGE
Old Camp Vincent
RIVER
BLACK RANGE
San Jose
Cauda de Alamosa
FRA CHRISTOBAL RANGE
Ft. McRea (Ojo del Muerte)
BLACK RANGE
MIMBRES RANGE
Las Palomas
SIERRA DE LOS CABALLOS
JORNADA DEL MUERTO
SAN ANDREAS RANGE
Old Ft. West
Kingston
Pinos Altos
Georgetown
Hillsboro
Silver City
Ft. Bayard
Hanover
MANGOS VALLEY
Central
COOK'S RANGE
Richmond
GILA
BURRO MTS.
Paschal
Old Ft. McLane
Santa Barbara
Ft. Thorn
Colorado
Old Camp Mimbres
Hudson
Hot Springs
Cook's
Ft. Selden
AUGUSTIN PASS
Lordsburg
Soldier's Farewell
Cow Spring
Ft. Cummings
Dona Ana
Shakespeare (Ralston)
Barney's Station
STEIN'S PASS
Las Cruces
ORGAN MTS.
Mesilla
Tortugas
Old Ft. Fillmore
Leidendorf's Well
VICTORIA MTS.
FLORIDA MTS.
La Mesa
FLORIDA PLAINS
PORTRILLO MTS.
Chamberine
La Union
PYRAMID MTS.
Eureka (Hachita)
SIERRA BOCA GRANDE
TRES HERMANAS
BIG HATCHET MTS.
Frontera
FRANKLIN RANGE
Franklin
Magoffi
El Paso (Juarez)
PELONCILLO MTS.
ANIMAS RANGE
108°
107°
109°
SIERRA MADRE
DONIPHAN'S ROUTE 1846

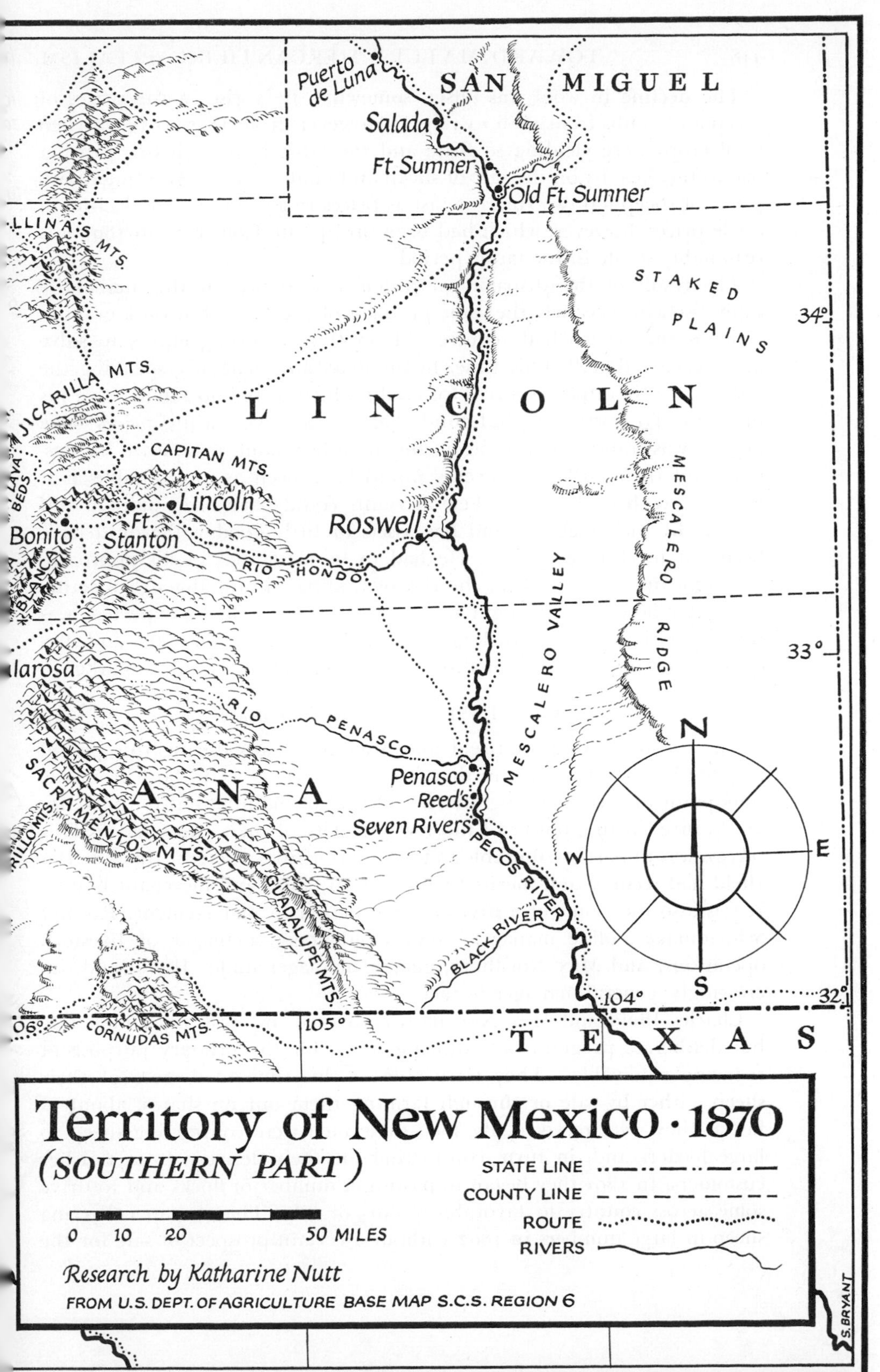
Puerto de Luna
SAN MIGUEL
Salada
Ft. Sumner
Old Ft. Sumner
STAKED PLAINS
34°
JICARILLA MTS.
LINCOLN
CAPITAN MTS.
MESCALERO
Lincoln
Bonito
Ft. Stanton
Roswell
RIO HONDO
MESCALERO VALLEY
RIDGE
33°
RIO PENASCO
Penasco
Reed's
Seven Rivers
SACRAMENTO MTS.
PECOS RIVER
GUADALUPE MTS.
BLACK RIVER
N
W
E
S
104°
32°
105°
CORNUDAS MTS.
TEXAS
Territory of New Mexico · 1870
(SOUTHERN PART)
STATE LINE
COUNTY LINE
ROUTE
RIVERS
0 10 20 50 MILES
Research by Katharine Nutt
FROM U.S. DEPT. OF AGRICULTURE BASE MAP S.C.S. REGION 6
S. BRYANT

The decline in wool was offset, somewhat, by a rise in the prices of sheep and lambs from 1886 to 1893.[19] However, from 1893 to 1897, when wool crops were yielding so little and the typical New Mexico rancher had to rely heavily on the sale of sheep and lambs to meet his obligations, prices of sheep fell two times as fast as prices in general.[20] The decline in cattle prices, however, which had been precipitate from 1884 to 1891 was reasonably stable in the latter period.

The result of this disparity of trends was to present the mercantile capitalist with precisely the same problem of exchange, but on a grander scale, as that which had required his most enterprising efforts to solve at an earlier date.[21] This time, fortunately, and generally speaking, he possessed substantial resources for credit which would go far to solve his problem. To borrow capital funds heavily, however, while prices were falling, was fraught with danger. On the other hand, to squeeze his customers of their flocks and fleeces would have been as unprofitable as it would have been heartless. Few accounts could have been paid in full anyway by such methods and few assets or little good will would have been left for future trading. He had to be farsighted in his approach, which meant he had to bear the risk of trading and intelligent collecting no matter how great it might be. The result, as might be expected, was the acquisition of sheep in large numbers and dollar amounts, and, frequently, at times when their disposal was difficult in a glutted market.

Charles Ilfeld and Max Nordhaus

The record of Charles Ilfeld and Max Nordhaus during this period may not have been typical in that they succeeded so well—both from the standpoint of successful operations and that of maintaining the solvency and future earning power of the vast majority of their customers.[22] This success was in part attributable to the superior lines of credit that Charles Ilfeld had secured and merited with eastern banks and merchant houses. It was also the result of a division of function in management: Rodney Schoonmaker, office manager; Max Goldenberg, manager of livestock operations; and Max Nordhaus, general manager under Ilfeld, and, increasingly, general manager in fact.

Charles Ilfeld and Max Nordhaus embarked, in 1888, on a moderate but deliberate program of acquiring sheep for the primary purpose of reducing receivables. They were able at this time to dispose of their sheep, either by sale or through farming them out on shares, about as fast as they were received. By 1890 these men were contracting sheep to large feeders and, in turn, contracting for their delivery from rancher customers. In 1891 they began to pasture a number of flocks and to drive some across country to favorable points of sale. They began collecting sheep in large numbers in 1892 without a certain prospect of sale for the large proportion of them. From this date on they became involved, to an increasing degree, in the business of sheep husbandry.

Max Goldenberg, Collector and Sheep Specialist

Charles Ilfeld had complained of "dull times" in May of 1884.[23] In October of that year he wrote to Elias Brevoort, a Santa Fe pioneer, that "times are very dull." [24] In May of 1886 he wrote his old friend Pat Garrett: "Vegas looks to me duller than any time for the last 15 years I can recollect." [25] By 1888 he was writing disconsolately: "times are excessively dull" and "our old Las Vegas now more despondent than ever." [26] Though his sales had shown only a slight dip in 1887, and had been rising well in 1888, his cash position had fallen to a dangerous point indicating a lag in collections.[27] Ilfeld was concerned about the situation and, apparently, had little confidence that Solomon Floersheim, the man he hired in 1884 to help in this collection problem, was the proper man for the job. Floersheim resigned in March, 1888, with some encouragement from Ilfeld, and within a few months, if not immediately, a more suitable individual, from Ilfeld's point of view, was employed.[28]

In the late summer and fall of 1888, Max B. Goldenberg, a cousin of Max Nordhaus, who had come to Santa Fe in 1876 from Germany, was working for Charles Ilfeld, traveling the east side of the Territory from White Oaks to Liberty trying to collect on customer accounts.[29] Several reasons for the employment of this particular individual are apparent.

In the first place Goldenberg needed a job and secondly he owed Ilfeld more than $3000. There seemed little hope of collecting this sum very soon if Goldenberg were left to his own devices, for he was dependent for his income upon a cattle ranch in Las Cruces, New Mexico, operated by his brother Alex, and cattle prices were falling.[30] Previously he had not been successful as a merchant in Las Cruces—with a wicker chair factory on the side—and he was having some trouble as a merchant and livestock man in Tularosa, New Mexico.[31] However, if "Big Max," as he was known to distinguish him from little Max Nordhaus, was not a merchant by qualification, perhaps his very handicaps in that direction might fit him for the sheep trade. Earl L. Moulton, when he was chairman of the board of The Charles Ilfeld Company, spoke of Goldenberg as "the dirtiest man ever seen—unke[m]pt and messy." Moulton also added, "He was a good sheep man," although one suspects Goldenberg may not have qualified as an expert in these early years.[32] Both of these qualities (his appearance, unscoured as the sheep he was to tend, and his aptitude for the trade) promised him access to the typical sheep ranch and a good chance for success after he got there.[33]

Three years of patient, and then impatient, efforts to collect Goldenberg's account had led, no doubt, to some consideration of ways to put

Big Max's abilities to work in directions where they would offer at least a fair chance for profit to the firm and, perhaps, eliminate the problem of a bothersome relative.[34] "Tired of monkeying any longer" but willing to give Goldenberg six months more in which to pay, Ilfeld employed the burly German sometime after March of 1888.[35]

We first find him in the White Oaks–Lincoln area, near Fort Stanton, attempting to hold some of Ilfeld's customers who were going elsewhere with their business. "Try to get an order for goods from Aniceto Lueras," wrote Schoonmaker. "If Narciso Otero is there and is ready to turn over sheep you may give them to Aniceto Lueras on *partido* if that should be necessary to win him back as a customer." [36] This reference to "partido," or renting out sheep, rent to be paid in wool or increase, was a common practice and Goldenberg supervised this activity. In another instance, Schoonmaker wrote him: "Take 500 sheep from Juan Hinojos at the best price you can get them for and contract them with J. Pablo Martinez." [37]

That Goldenberg's main function was to make collections becomes particularly clear in a revealing letter written by Max Nordhaus.[38]

> You ought to know that I have not the least objection to your taking or contracting Wethers from people who are deep in with us and are in any way doubtful such as the Giddings and I think you better go back to their resp. places and get or contract all the Wethers they have. Do the same with all other parties who you think can't pay up with wool. I consider this the main feature of your Trip to try to secure such accounts in any way that you think best.

The records do not reveal the financial arrangements made with Big Max, but apparently he was an employee on commission, though two credits to his account in 1888 and 1889 indicate a small salary may have been paid at the beginning.[39] A later unexplained credit in November, 1890, of approximately $4300, which reduced his account to a few hundred dollars, seems to have been either a commission or, possibly, a sharing of profits on the sale of sheep acquired through his efforts. That he may have been hired on a profit-sharing basis in the beginning is indicated by a letter written to Goldenberg by Schoonmaker as a result of some misunderstanding. It ended with the terse comment: "Trusting our business connection may continue mutually pleasant and profitable." [40] By 1893 Goldenberg was being employed on a straight salary of $125 per month.[41]

Contracting Sheep

The years 1890 and 1891 were welcome relief to Charles Ilfeld. The price of sheep had risen moderately since 1888 but had gained a momentum in 1890 that was to carry through 1892. In May, 1890, he spoke of the "sheepman's prosperity" that had begun, and in the following February Max Nordhaus wrote his friend, Francisco Vigil in Picacho, a ranching settlement near Lincoln: "Glad all is well in Lincoln. Business is also very good here and the reports from all my customers are very favorable." [42] Both Max and Charles complained of the tightness and shortage of money in general, but Charles was able to borrow almost for the asking, at interest rates of 6 to 8 per cent, from his good friends of long standing: Telesfor Jaramillo of Los Lunas, Louis Sulzbacher and H. L. Waldo of Las Vegas and Kansas City, and his cousin, Emil Wolff, of the international merchant firm of Einstein, Wolff and Company in New York City.[43] When he did not borrow from individuals, his cousin, assuming personal liability, would discount Ilfeld's notes for him at the National Shoe and Leather Bank of New York City.[44]

His general business, too, had an optimistic tone. Sales of the Charles Ilfeld Company rose from $160,000 in 1889 to $188,000 in 1890. The next two years brought further increases of $34,000 and $45,000, respectively.[45] His cash balances in New Mexico and New York banks remained lower than had been the custom, even though the business had grown, but Nordhaus managed the borrowings and cash collections in such a way as to always take his discounts. Ilfeld, with less concern than he had held for several years, chose 1890 to inaugurate his semiannual trips to New York which took him away from Las Vegas six to eight months of each year. There was an air of less caution as Max and Charles deliberately borrowed funds to expand their interests in sheep contracting.

Max Goldenberg was in his glory during these days. He traveled a great deal with full power to contract sheep and to make agreements with subcontractors. Max Nordhaus (Maquecito his Spanish-speaking friends called him) gave Big Max a relatively free hand but did a good deal of the contracting himself by letter with distant ex-merchandise customers of Lincoln County.[46] Either Ilfeld or Nordhaus, probably Ilfeld, had made firm contracts with W. W. Gleason of Cheyenne, Wyoming, and S. M. Newton of Ogden, Kansas, for one-, two-, and three-year-old wethers and ewes.[47] Newton's contracts called for 5000 to 7000 sheep and Gleason's, apparently, were as large or larger. Max Goldenberg was pressed to meet his requirements.

"Excessive drought" in the spring of 1890 had increased the already widespread sheep disease, scabies, and when Goldenberg did succeed in finding the requisite number of sheep for Gleason, Ilfeld had to write: "I shall be obliged to put up the forfeit stipulated in [the contract]" unless the "free from scab" requirement is waived.[48] Gleason waived it but it showed that the Ilfeld organization had not prepared itself fully for the business it was encouraging. It was not until July, 1891, that plans were laid for the construction of a dipping vat to bathe the sheep as they would be gathered for shipment and not until May, 1892, that all the sheep received were being treated in this manner.[49]

This was not a surprising delinquency, however. Few sheepmen in New Mexico or the West at that time were taking proper precautions to prevent the spread of this mange disease. One of the reasons, certainly, is not difficult to isolate. Dipping sheep was, and until recent years continued to be, a mean and exasperating job.[50] Sheepmen had to arise at two or three in the morning to mix a solution of lime and sulphur and then heat it to a tepid temperature of 100° or higher.[51]

When daylight came the slow process of dipping began. It must have been extremely slow for those in charge of Ilfeld's operations on the Vegoso because his dipping vat was only 10 feet long and 2.5 feet deep which must have necessitated hand-dunking.[52] Most dipping vats, however, were constructed as a long and narrow trough and deep enough so the sheep, having been led to the chute by their Judas Iscariot or forced by the cussing sheepherders, would have no choice but to swim the distance.[53] Somewhere along the vat a hired hand would completely submerge the heads of the struggling animals. Unfortunately, if the caustic bath was to be at all successful in killing the mites that had burrowed into the sheep's skins, the sheep usually had to be dipped twice. One can imagine the difficulty of persuading these stubborn bleaters, Judas or no Judas, to submit themselves to a second dunking.

Other reasons for the sheepman's reluctance to treat flocks for scabies were the sheer cost of the process, the probable loss of sheep, and the damage the solution caused to the wool. The expense of materials and labor ranged in the early 1900's from 2.5 to 3.5 cents per head.[54] Ilfeld, in 1893, had been charging 1.5 cents at his Vegoso dipping station, about 5 miles east of Las Vegas, but Goldenberg balked not only because "medicine, wood and men cost more than we get" but because the "grass is tramped out & range ruined." [55]

In the ordeal of swimming the vat some of the sheep drowned and others, their lungs and stomachs, as well as their skins, burning with a lime and sulphur solution, often re-enforced with lye, died from the effects.[56] This was particularly true if the sheep were not strong as the result of disease or inadequate food. Goldenberg had experienced such a difficult situation in 1895 when, with grass short and sheep dying, he had postponed bathing his scabied sheep and had treated them solely with blue ointment. When finally he had to proceed with the dipping he wrote: "The sheep are pretty poor and have to be extremely careful to dip. Have to carry lots of them." [57]

Care had to be taken, too, that the overheated sheep were not exposed to cool weather, a danger that in the spring and fall, especially, was ever-present in sudden drops in temperature.[58] In addition, the sheep owner suffered a loss in the quality of his wool as the lime, or lye in some cases, constricted the fibre.[59]

Goldenberg did meet his contract requirements, however, in spite of the delay in providing even inadequate facilities for the proper care of the sheep upon delivery, and in spite of his and Nordhaus' failure to organize customers for the delivery of sheep on a larger than normal scale. In the face of northern buyers forcing prices up by making offers at the ranches, all 1890 contracts were filled by July 8 of that year.[60] In November, however, Nordhaus began laying plans for the following year in anticipation of larger contracts and greater competition brought on by the feeders' growing demand for yearling wethers to be fattened into mutton sheep. He wrote to a large number of his rancher customers as far south as the town of Lincoln, as well as northwesterly along the road to Taos and beyond, setting forth the conditions under which he would contract for the following year. A typical letter was written in Spanish to a Senor Valdez of Arroyo Seco:[61]

> I send you blanks according to contract. I will pay you 10 to 15 cents per head, advanced, to which end I enclose check book. Deliver the sheep between the 1st and 10th of July, 1891, after sheering in Las Vegas. The sheep ought to be one year old in the contract as you are able to get them. If it is for 1 dollar or 1.15, always we will pay you 1.275. Without more I remain your friend.

At first these contract blanks were sent out in large numbers to subcontractors without too much check on whom these people, in turn, contracted with. The result was that many advances for commissions were made for sheep that were never delivered. Most of the individuals to whom Nordhaus wrote were native men of small means whose desires to make some easy money often outstripped their foresight. The contracts they made with their neighbors were prone to exaggerate the capacity of these people to deliver at the time stipulated.

In 1892 Nordhaus attempted to close this loophole by approving all contracts before advancing any money. To Benigno Jaramillo of Las Vegas, he wrote: "We send the contract [direct to the contractee] and we transmit one copy with our signature and check for the sum which you agree to advance if we agree with your trade."[62] Under such approved contracts Nordhaus agreed to advance up to 25 cents per head on a final price of 90 cents for lambs, \$1.25 for yearlings, and \$1.60 for two-year-olds.[63] Even this step of approval of contracts, however, was too loosely administered. Advances sometimes were made before contracts were returned with the contractor's signature. Perhaps this reflects simply the anxiety of Nordhaus and Goldenberg to obtain a large quantity of sheep because, a year later, when sheep were becoming a drug on the market, Nordhaus instituted an iron-clad policy of advancing no funds until the contracts had been signed and returned.[64]

Turning Toward the Trail

In February, 1891, the Charles Ilfeld Company had about 15,000 wethers on hand, and a temporary dip in the price of sheep scared Ilfeld.[65] He wrote his contractors not to buy any more.[66] By March, however, with no buyers in sight, Nordhaus was seeking more sheep, offering $1.25 per head, seldom in cash, for yearling wethers and ewes.[67] In June the firm was seeking the cooperation of commission houses in Denver and St. Paul to sell excess sheep that had been gathered near Las Vegas.[68]

In August the picture had changed again and Nordhaus was offering 75 cents for lambs, though he must have purchased few at this price, and contracted for 2000 wethers to be delivered to his agents, Lujan and Pinard, at Bueyeros in Clayton County.[69] By the middle of September he had filled his contract.[70]

Shortly after Ilfeld returned from New York in October, he solicited his old friend, Alexander Gusdorf, a long-term resident of Taos, to buy sheep for him on a commission of 5 cents per head, and he also engaged the services of Louis Baer, associate in Eisemann Brothers, sheep and wool specialists of Albuquerque, to "tackle all good sheep men" and "pay as high as 1.25 for yearlings & 1.50–1.65 for 2 year old wethers." [71] To reenforce the request, Ilfeld forwarded Baer a checkbook "to draw against me." [72]

Ilfeld's contracted sheep were gathered in large numbers near Las Vegas but an occasional sale kept inventories down. His agents, Lujan and Pinard, sold between 8,000 and 14,000 head of yearlings and two-year-olds at $2.00 per head. Ilfeld was more than disgusted, however, because he had priced the two-year-olds at $2.50. "For our business relations sake," he wrote, "I shall not hold nor have held you responsible for the loss I sustain by the sale as made by you but to allow commissions on a loss is unfair to ask.[73] I don't accuse you of anything but a mistake and am willing to pay for everything but mistakes." [74]

Increasingly, however, inventories became a problem as small bunches of sheep, collected from each of a large number of ranches scattered throughout the area east of the Rio Grande River and south of Taos, ambled into Las Vegas. In 1891 from 10,000 to 15,000 head remained unsold most of the year.[75] In 1892 this figure had risen until in May the unsold flocks amounted to close to 30,000 head.[76] As long as sheep prices continued to rise, and they did through 1892, this was not a matter of concern but it did require the development of a different approach to selling. Perhaps we can call it the "drive-and-probe" technique, that is, the driving of flocks toward the large markets in the northeast, along well-grassed and watered routes, while the sedentary merchant probed possibilities of sale by means of letters and agents.

The revival of the sheep drive in the 1890's by Charles Ilfeld, and probably others, was the natural result of a number of causes.[77] Ilfeld and Nordhaus had not prepared themselves for surpluses and did not own, in the early 1890's, pasturage in advantageous places to care for their sheep.[78] Nor had they the slightest desire to hold their flocks any longer than absolutely necessary for purposes of orderly marketing. The railroad was always handy and the Kansas City market would absorb all the sheep these men cared to ship, but once the unsold sheep were in transit all control of price was lost. Furthermore, the sheep from New Mexico were scrawny by Kansas City standards, and the better markets were the corn fields of Nebraska where the feeding interests made a business of overcoming this deficiency. It was this market that was not absorbing in an orderly fashion the surplus sheep of New Mexico, and which required time and probing to find enough willing purchasers who possessed the necessary financial resources.

Not only did "the drive" give management time to find a better market, but fortunately this method of marketing was relatively cheap. Ilfeld estimated his costs "of driving in bunches of 10,000 & upwards for 350 to 400 miles at ten cents per head" [79] which is not a surprising figure considering the free grass along the way and sheepherders' wages of $15 to $25 a month including board.[80] The freight on doubledeck cars, holding no more than 300 sheep, from Las Vegas to Kansas City, a distance of 755 miles, was $87.50 or, roughly, 13.5 cents per head for 350 miles.[81] Not only did Ilfeld estimate that his costs of driving sheep were somewhat less than the railroad freight; he also was aware that he had a natural advantage of rising prices, relative to Las Vegas, as he neared the major markets.

New Mexico sheep were well adapted to the drive, too. Their ancestors had been driven over the open range for two centuries or more, and the Spanish Merino, which came to the United States in large numbers in 1809 and 1810, and New Mexico in 1858—improving by 1870 the common Churro breed—were great walkers themselves.[82] Ilfeld's sheep, as described by Goldenberg in a letter to H. L. Dickinson of the Dickinson Stock Company in North Dakota, were dominantly of this cross.[83]

> The sheep I am handling are improved Mexican sheep, crossed by Spanish Merino Bucks. They are very hardy Sheep and are especially adapted to rough it. *They are the sheep for the Range,* more so than the very highly improved Spanish Merinos.

With such advantageous factors as hardiness of breed, cheapness of operation, a rising price factor en route, and time to arrange favorable sales, it was probably worth the risks of loss from weather, disease, and further deterioration of prices to take the surplus sheep to the trail rather than send them to market immediately by way of the railroad. The other obvious choice, to keep the sheep and pasture them for a more favorable day, would have been a reluctant answer for the mercantile capitalist—and especially Charles Ilfeld—who believed in and practiced the turning over of real capital into money capital as fast as it could prudently be accomplished.

In 1890 Max Goldenberg drove 14,000 ewes and rams to Springer in the northeastern part of the Territory but these had been sold, apparently, in advance.[84] In August, 1891, with 14,000 head unsold, plans were readied to drive them to Kansas if need be.[85] They were driven toward the ranches of Lujan and Pinard near Clayton, where they were scheduled to arrive in October.[86] These were the wethers, probably, part of which were sold by Lujan and Pinard at a lower price than Ilfeld had intended.

The drive of 1892, which began in July, was a larger undertaking as Goldenberg directed his sheepherders and "a few thousand yearling ewes —and about 32,000 mutton sheep" along the trail from Liberty, New Mexico, to Kit Carson, Colorado.[87] By August 1 Ilfeld was worried. He wrote: "[I] find much trouble in selling them." [88] Goldenberg, too, was concerned and was laying plans to leave the sheep and make a personal sales tour of Nebraska. Ilfeld answered: "I don't favor the idea at all, as in the first place it would be impossible for you to travel all over the state to see the feeders, as most of them live away from any R.R. Secondly it looks to Buyers, if we run after them, that the sheep are a Burden to us & must by all means dispose of them. We have them well advertised . . . you better stay with the herds." [89]

Goldenberg corralled his herds at Folsom, New Mexico, while Ilfeld wrote buyers and feeders in Colorado trying to entice them to "run down" and take a look.[90] When no luck was encountered, Goldenberg moved on with his flocks toward Kit Carson, but soon changed his objective eastward to Cheyenne Wells—a stop on the Union Pacific Railroad in Colorado.[91]

Arrangements had been made with the Union Pacific Railroad to refund "all Rail Road Fares paid on their Road by purchasers" of sheep shipped over the Union Pacific.[92] On November 6, Goldenberg sold 11 cars of sheep out of Cheyenne Wells to a feeder from Cozad, Nebraska, this evidently being the balance of the flocks he previously had not sold.[93]

The prices of sheep had remained firm during this trial and, apparently, the special efforts put forth had avoided a net loss in sheep operations and, perhaps, had yielded a small profit. It had been an out-and-out speculation, as Ilfeld admitted.[94] But even if some losses had been sustained, it still would have been a remarkable case of collecting accounts and one which may well have given Ilfeld and Nordhaus the financial strength to carry on through four trying years ahead. In 1892, cash collections on accounts and notes receivable, which included the receipts from sheep previously received on account, totaled $482,102. In the same year increasing credit sales amounted to $216,033. The net reduction in receivables, therefore, through cash receipts was $266,069. The year previous the reduction, by way of cash, had been less than $5000—the first time, incidentally, since 1886 that cash collections had exceeded credit sales.[95]

In August, 1892, after starting this first large sheep drive, Ilfeld had rationalized to an impatient rancher whose sheep were included in Ilfeld's flocks: "I am driving 30,000 sheep to Colorado in order to see what can be done with them there and then having sold them I will know well the value of sheep in the States. I think I will gather many others next year and give my customers all the advantages and experience I am going to have. I beg you to have a little patience." [96] Before the drives of 1893 and 1895 had ended, Ilfeld, Nordhaus, and Goldenberg had acquired a good amount of experience with "patience."

The Drive of 1893

The year of 1893 opened with the price of sheep still strong (slightly higher than the previous January), and optimism within the Ilfeld organization must have been high.[97] Receivables had decreased substantially and total merchandise sales, in spite of weakening prices, were still strongly on the rise, having increased $34,000 in 1891 and $45,000 more in 1892, to a total of $267,000.[98] Goldenberg was contracting sheep at the same prices as a year before, and by March, Ilfeld had signed commitments with feeders to deliver 60,000 head.[99] Max Nordhaus, no doubt feeling with Ilfeld that this was the time to take his first real vacation since 1888, readied himself for a six months' trip to his home in Germany.[100]

Demand for wethers at the ranches had been exceptionally high in February, and Ilfeld backed away from offering the prices being paid by some of his competitors.[101] Typical, though, of his reactions were his immediate efforts to contract sheep from distant markets where he had reason to believe demand was not so high and prices a good deal lower. To Pat Garrett, who had moved to Uvalde, Texas, he wrote: "There is very little of interest to report from this section of the Country & it is very hard to make an honest dollar in the Dry Goods business. I am now & have been for the last two years engaged in buying yearlings & two year old Whethers [*sic*] & also Ewes & I am told money can be made to buy them in Texas . . . maybe we both can make some money on the deal . . . I either pay you a commission or give you an interest on the profits." [102] A few days later Ilfeld thought he might get 2000 sheep from Arizona.[103]

Sometimes the strength and breadth of the demand became a little ludicrous. In March, Ilfeld bought some sheep of his customer, W. L.

Hargrave, in Puerto de Luna, only to learn that Hargrave had bought the sheep of Frank Page, who in turn had bought them from Santiago Giddings. All were Ilfeld's customers living in the same area and, presumably, Ilfeld paid three profits in the purchase. In letters of disgust he wrote: "I wish all your business direct." [104]

Though the price of mutton in early March was 50 to 75 cents a pound less than the previous March in eastern markets, Goldenberg was trying to make arrangements to sell his inventories in either Las Vegas or Kit Carson, Colorado, at the same prices he had been getting.[105] He was finding it difficult, and with the prospect of 40,000 head on hand and unsold by July, thoughts turned more and more to the organization of a large drive into Colorado.[106]

Max Nordhaus returned from Germany in June at a time when market conditions were worsening. In July, Ilfeld received a letter from a Wm. Frachen of Colorado Springs backing out of his contract and forfeiting the amount he had advanced.[107] Within a few days plans were being made for one of his major-domos, Concepcion Atencio, to gather sheep on the east side of the Territory in the vicinity of Endee and Liberty, and to drive them to Las Vegas to join other herds—all to arrive about the first of August.[108] Goldenberg was inquiring about the range and water supply conditions in Colorado around Cheyenne Wells and wondered if it would be advisable to take as many as 50,000 head to that area.[109]

On August 19, Goldenberg wrote he was starting for Folsom, New Mexico, near the Colorado border, about 160 miles away by good grass and water, with 45,000 head of sheep. He expected to arrive between September 10 and 15.[110] Hoping to sell the sheep in Folsom, if not at points along the way, for shipment east, Nordhaus began to bargain with the railroads.

"I am holding in this vicinity about 45,000 Mutton Sheep which I intend to ship from here if I can get low rates to Omaha, Kansas City and Chicago with stop over privilege," Nordhaus wrote the railway livestock agent at Albuquerque.[111] By this time the sheep were probably on their way by hoof and the letter was for effect only. Three days later he wrote again to say: "I intend to hold my herds between Springer on the A. T. & S. Fe R.R. and Folsom on Denver & Ft Worth . . . I hope not to be compelled again to drive sheep to other roads as I have been for the last years on account of better rates." [112] But drive Nordhaus knew he would have to until the sheep were sold, for to place his sheep on the railroad in the face of the stark reality that "there [was] no market for them anywhere" would have been to invite the worst kind of distressed sale.[113] To hold them and bargain at too far a distance in the face of falling prices with no bottom in sight was not an aggressive approach and would have left Ilfeld and Nordhaus in no better competitive position than many others who sat and waited.

The first show stop was Wagonmound, New Mexico, on the Santa Fe Railway on September 6. Here, in fulfillment of contracts, the flocks were to be augmented.[114] The outlook was dark. Nordhaus wrote Pat Garrett not to buy any more sheep in Texas: "Have speculated the wrong way on them and fear to loose [*sic*] a lot of money on them." [115] To others he wrote: "Am not buying any more sheep at present, they are way down in price and there is no market for them anywhere." [116] "As I am bound to sell they will go at what they will bring." [117] Nordhaus, however, saw a possibility for saving the situation should the sheep be driven as far as Nebraska where the corn crop was reported as good.[118] With apparently no success in Wagonmound the outfit pushed on toward Springer where a showing was to be had on September 10, followed by one at Folsom to the northeast on the Denver and Ft. Worth Railroad.[119]

By the time the flocks reached Folsom about September 20, their offering prices had been cut several times. The yearlings which the firm had contracted for July delivery in Las Vegas at $1.50, and which originally had been offered at $2.00 to $2.25, f.o.b. Kit Carson, Colorado, or 3.25 cents per pound, were being offered at Folsom in September at $1.50, or 2.5 cents per pound less 3 per cent for shrinkage.[120] In other words they were now being quoted for sale at less than cost.

Since almost two weeks of feeding in the vicinity of Folsom brought few if any bids, Max Nordhaus, who was now in charge of financial affairs (Ilfeld was in Boston and the East), offered to sell the sheep with half payment in commercial paper.[121] An offer for 10,000 head, about a fourth or less of the flock, was received from a buyer in Trinidad and presumably was filled about a week later.[122]

The season was growing late, and fear crept in that to push farther north, as originally planned, would be to risk an early winter storm.[123] Besides, the grass was excellent at Folsom and the sheep, having lost some weight on the trail, could rest and eat to advantage.[124] Goldenberg, losing patience, left the sheep and took to the road, traveling through Colorado and Kansas, along the Union Pacific Railroad, making stops at Trinidad and Kit Carson, Colorado, Junction City and Ellis, Kansas, and Kansas City. Sometime in November he sold the balance of the sheep, shipped them over the Union Pacific, and filed a claim for refunds on his passenger fares.[125]

The loss for 1893 dealings in wethers was recorded as $3828.19, but the probability is that many costs, properly chargeable to this account, were omitted.[126] Certainly, if the revenues and costs of the drive could now be isolated from the total figures, the loss on this operation, alone, would have been quite large. Whatever the loss may have been, however, it should be measured against the reduction in receivables it brought about. Credit sales in 1893 were $161,805 but reduction in receivables through cash receipts, including sales of sheep and wool, amounted to $336,284; $73,000 of this came in July when the large contracts were filled; $63,000 came in October and November when the driven herds were sold.[127]

The net loss of the drive would appear to have been less than the ultimate losses in receivables would have been had there been no concerted program of collections of sheep. Had the purchase of sheep from sources that constituted a cash drain on the company not been a part of the speculation, the operation would have been a resounding success in spite of net losses. As a protective device the drive was a brilliant maneuver.

Trying Again in 1895

As one might expect, following this experience, in 1894 Ilfeld and Nordhaus were timid. There was no necessity for taking great risks because receivables had been reduced and strengthened measurably. With a cash position still uncomfortably low—$5277.43 on January 1—and borrowings still relatively high, the persistent fall of all prices, and particularly of sheep and wool, dictated caution.[128]

Ilfeld spent at least seven months of the year 1894 in the East, and Max Nordhaus, with slightly more than ten years of executive training behind him, managed the business with a certain forwardness. The change, as reflected in the quantity and type of letters he wrote after mid-1893 upon his return from Europe, dates his rise to full authority and self-assurance. He sent Goldenberg around the countryside to contract wethers but only to fill the firm contracts he held with northern interests. He made very few forward contracts—generally accepting only commitments that stipulated immediate delivery.[129] By the end of the year he was actually short of the number of wethers he could have used to fill an elastic contract with Adams and Buck and Company, Union Stock Yards, Chicago.[130]

Though Nordhaus evidently had determined to avoid speculation in 1894, a policy he continued to follow during the first seven months of 1895, he was forced by circumstances to change his tactics. As the year wore on he learned he would be unable, in all probability, to dispose of his sheep fast enough at market prices to avoid large losses. The continued fall in prices that had dictated a policy of caution so weakened many suppliers financially that large numbers of livestock of all kinds were being sent to market. In addition, a short but serious drought that was not broken until late July left the grass short and forced further shipments.[131] With the July rains and the hope of better grass conditions,

Nordhaus withdrew his wethers from the market and determined to make another drive—this time with Liberal, Kansas, as the destination—a spot chosen on the advice of Michael Slattery, capable manager of the Bell Ranch who was in that area at this time.[132] Camp was expected to be made either at a point a few miles north of Liberal—at Arkalon—or east at Englewood—both sites being on the Cimarron River. Arkalon was located on the Chicago, Rock Island, and Pacific Railroad and Englewood on the Atchison, Topeka & Santa Fe.

Three outfits—two for sheep and one for cattle—left Las Vegas on August 31. Goldenberg was in charge of 25,000 sheep, 300 dry cows, 300 yearling steers, and 300 yearling heifers. His foreman was P. D. McElroy of Springer, under whom were two major-domos and 14 pastores for the flocks, and additional personnel for the cattle.[133] The route this time was through Clayton and the panhandle of Oklahoma where, in deference to the plodding cattle and aged sheep, the flat land would make the going easier.[134] Little effort was made to sell livestock en route, although a few letters were written to let prospective buyers know the path the herds were to follow. All efforts to attract buyers seemed to be concentrated on the Arkalon and Englewood destinations. The herds passed Clayton about September 17 and reached Arkalon, Kansas, choosing against Englewood, near the middle of October, where they settled down to what was to become a long winter's night.[135]

Goldenberg blew hot and cold. One day he wanted to dip the sheep and plan for a long stay, and the next he threatened to bring them back to New Mexico.[136] Pat McElroy, his foreman, wrote on October 16 that the herds were in excellent condition but Goldenberg, a day or two later, opined that they were thin.[137] Nordhaus penned a series of directives: [138]

> We can't see any other remedy for the thin stock but to ship and feed and would advise *prompt* sales of everything else at present Market prices. To judge from all indications the flooding of sheep to the market from range and feeders will continue for a long time and as long as the Medicine is to be taken we better take it without unnecessary delay.

On October 28 he sent a wire and a letter. "Sheep market reviving would sell in preference to returning can replace here plenty for sale." [139] In his letter that followed, Nordhaus, then thirty years of age, displayed some of the tact and executive ability for which he is now remembered.[140]

> I consider after meditating over the matter a return drive a very risky undertaking. I understand that you cannot avoid a long strip of unsheltered country and if so a heavy storm can destroy all the flocks. We fully appreciate your efforts in doing the best you can and the fact that it is no easy task to wind yourself out of this difficult situation. Your action in sending culls to Feed Yard is in the proper direction in as much as you procured Yards and feeding

Material at such reasonable rates, and between feeding and driving back the balance in case of inability to sell at market prices I would give the former [feeding] the preference.

In early November Goldenberg sold an unrecorded number of wethers for cash, and 7200 on time.[141] The latter bunch were contracted to two Kansas feeders at $1.85 per head for the old wethers, and $1.50 for the yearlings.[142] The purchase prices of these sheep had varied from $1.00 to $1.40 for the yearlings to as high as $2.00 for the older sheep.[143] The cattle also were disposed of through a similar sale.[144] The remainder of the wethers, which the year-end inventory placed at 8100, were driven to Lindsborg, Kansas, to the northeast on the Union Pacific Railroad, and a fewer number to a town named Ogden, at which places, as of December 31, Goldenberg calculated his sheep had accumulated feeding and caring costs of more than $2.15 per head.[145] Two months later Nordhaus wrote: "It seems you are putting a fortune into these wethers & they ought to be worth their weight in gold by the time they come out of yards." [146]

No further revenue was produced until the middle of February, and the drain on the firm's limited cash reserves was becoming serious. Nordhaus had to suffer the embarrassment in December of explaining to Adolph Letcher, who had sought to collect his demand note, that the company could not meet the payment. "Max took all our sheep and cattle to Kansas to sell," he wrote, and "so far he has hardly realized expense of driving and freight." [147]

Goldenberg's carelessness in controlling feed expenditures and in safeguarding the firm's interest in drawing sales contracts caused Nordhaus additional worry. He cautioned Goldenberg to "stay at feed yards and control stuff we are feeding as well as all that is out on Mortgage until Marketed and paid for," and admonished him to get "a lawyer to look into Papers and Contracts with Newton and to fix Matters so that all sheep are shipped in our name." [148]

Other troubles occurred, too. Scabies broke out among the sheep in January, and Goldenberg threatened to send a shipment of dressed mutton to Kansas City, but Nordhaus vetoed the idea and sent him, as an antidote, 2500 pounds of sulphur out of St. Louis.[149] Two herders, coming home for Christmas on rail tickets provided by the company, became separated in Pueblo and the younger of the two disappeared. Nordhaus had some frantic parents on his hands and his efforts through the Pueblo police had not produced any results as late as January 7.[150] A complete outfit, under the direction of an old man and boy, and consisting of 25 horses, 4 mules, 6 burros, 1 wagon, 2 sheets, 4 sets of harness, 1 camping outfit, and 155 pounds of coffee and flour, had to be abandoned at various points along the trail toward Las Vegas as illness among the horses developed.[151]

In late January and February, 1896, Antonio Joseph, former delegate to Congress from New Mexico Territory; Henry L. Waldo, solicitor for the Santa Fe Railway in New Mexico; and Marcus Brunswick were in Kansas using what influence they could to help their friend Charles Ilfeld extricate himself from potential heavy losses.[152] Nordhaus wrote Goldenberg to take full advantage of Joseph's offer to assist.[153] What influence these gentlemen may have brought to bear is not known, but coincidentally with their efforts, one fairly sizable sale of sheep was made and collections on outstanding sales contracts, which heretofore had not yielded a penny, began through the Midland National Bank of Kansas City.[154]

Fortunately for Charles Ilfeld the market for wethers, which had been showing some signs of strength since the first of the year, was favoring the seller by the end of March.[155] Goldenberg pieced out sales of sheep all during April while the balance of collections on the older sales contracts was made. By the middle of May, almost nine months after the 1895 drive had started, the last of the herds had been sold, and Goldenberg had returned to Las Vegas.[156]

As far as the entries in the wether account (which included all sheep purchases and sales and out-of-pocket expenses chargeable thereto) can be analyzed, a loss of $26,800 had been sustained by the drive on an original investment of, perhaps, no more than $50,000.[157] The sales prices obtained for the sheep, however, were considerably higher, no doubt, than would have been the case had the sheep been sold f.o.b. Las Vegas in August, 1895. This is probably true because prices must have been relatively higher as distances to markets were shortened, and because sheep prices, in general, rose in the early part of 1896. Feeding and care, however, more than made up for these differences, so that a substantial part of the loss must be chargeable to the decision to make the drive.

Again, however, as in the case of the 1893 drive, we should measure this loss against the losses it prevented. Credit sales in 1895 amounted to $164,870 as opposed to total collections on receivables, turned into cash, of $266,053 or a net reduction of $101,183. Sheep and wool collections accounted for $126,120.[158] A sizable part of this wool must have been attributable to the collection of sheep. Perhaps a reduction of as much as $100,000 can be credited to the effects of the organized program of sheep collections. It probably follows that without the protection of this specialized effort, in such an economically depressed year as 1895, extra losses from customers' accounts might have exceeded the actual losses that were sustained from the drive's operations. It should be granted, however, that had Max Nordhaus insisted on taking "the medicine" when he proposed that it should be taken—October, 1895—the outcome might have been somewhat less painful.

Perspective

The expanded program of acquiring sheep, which Ilfeld and Nordhaus started in 1888, was motivated primarily by their worsening collection problem. Because the price of sheep had held reasonably steady throughout the 1880's, except for a mild rise in 1883 and a less-than-severe break from that year until 1886, and because the supply of this commodity was plentiful in New Mexico, such a program was clearly logical and was of maximum benefit to both the firm and its ranching customers. By 1890 the coincidence of a rapidly growing mutton market in Nebraska and eastern centers, coupled with rising prices for sheep, turned some of the emphasis in incentive from collections alone to one of a primary business in which many sheep were purchased with cash.

In 1893, when the final plunge of general prices began, the collection problem again assumed acute proportions, but this time the sheep markets were glutted and the price per head was falling too fast to permit orderly disposal of inventories. This development caused Ilfeld and Nordhaus to seek spectacular answers. The sheep drive, which paralleled the railroad but did not make use of it until firm sales had been made, was the chosen marketing tool.

From 1888 through 1895, therefore, the sheep industry in New Mexico was being used by Ilfeld to meet the exigencies of the moment. This had not been the case prior to 1888 and it became a declining influence in policy in the years that followed. In turning to a more balanced picture of the relationship between this merchant and the sheep industry, a description of his trade in wool is necessary.

X

THE WOOL TRADE

Early Interest in Wool

Wool was a steady source of monetary exchange to Ilfeld in his early business days. An intermittent stream of wagons laden with this commodity—often with hides and pelts as supplement—left his Las Vegas store for northern railroad points thence to be shipped to Philadelphia. Until 1877, however, there is almost no evidence that Ilfeld used any special methods to encourage this wool to come to his Plaza store, although on one occasion, three years before, he had expressed a desire to begin buying on a large scale.[1] In that year, 1874, Ilfeld had been shipping mixed wools in lots of 6000 to 7000 pounds, and had accumulated, in July, an inventory of 30,000 pounds.[2]

We need only to recall the deflation in wool prices following the Franco-Prussian War of 1870 and 1871 to understand Ilfeld's apathy toward this commodity in the ensuing decade.[3] The break in prices of medium wool from roughly 70 cents to 48 cents in 1872 and 1873 was too fast to enable Ilfeld, who was many hundred slow miles from eastern markets, to purchase the commodity with any assurance of a profitable return.[4] Few buyers of commission houses made New Mexico a regular stopping place in these days, and firms like Gregg of Philadelphia encouraged shipments on consignment.[5] Ilfeld's desire to enlarge his buying of wool in 1874 had come on the heels of an increase in wool prices, but with the continued deflation through 1876 no apparent commitments to such a program had been made. Through most of these years he remained content to accept the wool of his customers as it came to market. He credited their accounts with the revenue he actually received, less storage costs, and made no effort to encourage a greater than natural flow.

In 1877, a sharp rise in wool prices occurred and Ilfeld's buying became aggressive.[6] It was a good opportunity to reduce some accounts that had been lagging in the depression years preceding. Too, the railroad had reached Las Animas, Colorado, in 1875, and a terminal for eastward shipments had been established at Kansas City.[7] Transportation difficulties, thus, had been lessened and wool houses evidently were showing a willingness to employ New Mexico buyers on a commission basis.[8] In 1877 Ilfeld was attempting to borrow sizable sums for the purpose of advancing funds on wool contracts.[9]

Wool prices reached a peak in 1880 and then, having fallen slightly over the next two years, broke in 1883 and 1884.[10] Ilfeld still had been consigning most of his wool to Gregg in Philadelphia with not too happy a series of experiences. In March, 1882, he wrote: "wools are & have been for the last 4 months a drug in the market. . . . Have at present about 60,000# wool in Phil. since last July, for which I can't realize cost." [11] His interest in wool collections remained a passive affair under such conditions and changed very little toward a positive program even after the year 1884, when the collection problem and other factors might have been expected to force and encourage his hand.[12] Except for the catering to opportunities presented occasionally by commission houses and independent buyers, and some efforts to extend credit at interest to his customers during the period they needed to market their wools while on consignment to Ilfeld, no special program of attracting wool to his warehouse was implemented.

Wool Contracting Discouraged

With the hiring of Goldenberg in the spring or summer of 1888, some efforts were made to contract wools but the sagging market discouraged this practice. Evidently, however, Goldenberg had been instructed to contract the wool of certain customers whose financial independence placed them under little or no obligation to the Charles Ilfeld Company or others. One of these, at this time, was the Casaus family, comprising a sizable number of able sheep growers in the vicinity of Bado de Juan Pais, a crossing of the Pecos River just eastward of the present town of Dilia.[13] The flocks belonging to members of this family were of high quality.[14] In the face of a less than satisfactory market, however, Schoonmaker cautioned Goldenberg to treat Leandro Casaus diplomatically but warned: "There is no established value for Fall wool and you will hardly be able to contract." [15]

To the extent that Ilfeld was financed by independent buyers in this practice of contracting wool he tried to foster the program. With prices worsening, however, most suppliers were reluctant to commit themselves to prices that were lower than the current market, and few buyers would fail to anticipate a further fall before advancing money. A letter to Eisemann, the wool buyer, in August of 1889, explained: "At Galisteo I arranged with Demetrio, Leiba & Bro. to look after any wools for sale. The people in that locality are not favorable to contracting as they expect same prices as received last spring." [16]

Actually commission houses showed a great lack of enthusiasm for contracting at any price. Ilfeld often found it difficult to dispose of his wool except upon consignment to eastern buyers.[17] He did this frequently but always with the greatest reluctance and usually the results caused him to regret his action. "It is another sad lesson in the consignment business which I regret very much," he wrote A. G. Mills, a prominent sheep grower in Puerto de Luna.[18] And to Letcher, four years later, he cautioned: "Let this be a warning against consigning wool in future."[19]

The Charles Ilfeld Company's action in contracting sheep for July delivery, one to two months following the spring shearing, without contracting wool separately, appears to be evidence that the firm had no need to do so. Actually the typical, small wool grower of this period was in a somewhat helpless situation. Once he sheared his sheep the wool had to come to market because he had no satisfactory means of storage. In the slow market that existed in most of the years from 1884 to 1897 his opportunity for bargaining was lessened and his logical place of delivery was to the merchant to whom he was indebted. His problem, too, went beyond the local and national level; it was international as well.

Though the peak supply of sheep in the United States—as well as New Mexico—was reached in 1884 and 1885, the greater yield per fleece in the years following was such as to cause very little reduction in domestic clip prior to 1890, and to bring about a rather marked growth after 1891.[20] Along with the growing poundage from domestic sources, imports from the rest of the world—principally Australia—rose very rapidly.[21] The fact, too, that these phenomena took place at a time when the demand for mutton seemingly could not be satiated only added to the wool problem. By 1900, 30 per cent of the wool clip from western United States, for instance, came from mutton sheep.[22]

During these early years and until 1898, at least, this combination of factors brought wool to Ilfeld and Nordhaus in such quantities as to cause them to have little interest in any fleeces that would not serve as a payment on account. Their warehouses were frequently full after the season had passed its peak, and although more wool could have been handled, the market was seldom in an absorbent enough condition to have taken it without causing further distress to the seller.

Wool Storage and Handling

The Charles Ilfeld Company had two warehouses on Valencia Street to the rear and east of the store.[23] One of these was rented from Ilfeld's old landlord, F. O. Kihlberg, until 1898 when the company constructed an "almost fireproof" warehouse directly to the rear of the store.[24]

Although these buildings were known as wool warehouses they were used, in fact, for all types of produce and, probably, merchandise as well. The Kihlberg warehouse was described as being capable of holding about 100 tons of alfalfa and half of this space once was offered on a temporary basis to Wm. Frank at $5.00 per month for the storage of 50 tons of this forage.[25] Schoonmaker was forced at one time to complain of the overloading of the warehouse with oats as he earlier had objected to too much hay.[26]

Yet when the wool season opened—usually in May—other produce was moved out as fast as possible to make room for the increasing lots of wool that came from as far away as the Lincoln area. Nearly all the wool was placed on consignment at a standard charge, covering all handling costs and commissions of 10 cents per 100 pounds.[27] This charge had not altered as late as 1903 although in that year insurance of 2.5 per cent was levied in addition.[28] When competition was severe and distant customers were tempted to turn to other rail centers, as occurred in the Lincoln area, Nordhaus offered free storage, on one occasion, until a satisfactory price could be obtained.[29] Such a practice would encourage early delivery with a good chance of making a sale before any storage costs had been charged, or before warehouse space had become scarce.

Customers were encouraged to consign wool to the company to be disposed of at its discretion. One letter to the Tularosa area stated: "It is the custom of my customers to send their wool after shearing and I put it in my warehouse until I see the proper time for sale." [30] Typical of this practice was a sale of A. G. Mill's wool after which Nordhaus wrote: "I did not think you could get this price after all other wools of this grade are in, and I therefore sold it now." [31] Often, of course, the wool was held pending the customer's advice but as a practical matter the owner of the wool seldom took the initiative.

Only rarely were lots consigned to Ilfeld at a specified price, and these usually were subject to change pending the frequent comments on the market made informally in letters from the Charles Ilfeld Company. Like many forecasting services, this company's advice was accurate only about 50 per cent of the time, but the instructions were forthright and but one meaning could have been read into them. In June of 1890, Nordhaus was advising a large customer, Hargrave, to sell because "the Wool market has a 'blue eye' & the demand is now growing less every day." [32] Prices held firm, however, and grew quite strong by October.[33] In 1894 he was advising that prices are "truthfully sad and going lower." [34] The expected did happen and when in 1895 Nordhaus wrote: "I believe break in prices coming," he was proved correct.[35] Much of this opinion was passed on from a telegraphic service received directly from an eastern commission house, but a great deal was the result of information contained in dispatches from Ilfeld who, while in New York, kept in close touch with developments.[36] Adolph Letcher, in Baltimore because of his New Mexico sheep holdings, remained an interested student of wool markets and frequently expressed opinions to Nordhaus on future wool and sheep prices.

The spring clip began arriving in May, and if the market was at all active the early lots sold rapidly. There appears, however, to have been a heavy growth of inventories in these depressed years as autumn approached. A fair quantity of fall shearing brought peak holdings in November and December inasmuch as the earlier clip frequently failed to move. In December, 1892, the warehouses still held more than 72,000 pounds, and in the same month of 1894 the inventory stood at 100,000 pounds which, apparently, was close to total warehouse capacity.[37] In March, 1897, there was more than 90,000 pounds on hand which must have been a carry-over from the previous year.[38]

The wool was brought to the warehouse in sacks of varying sizes, but the most common seems to have been 7 foot to 7½ foot lengths made of 9½ ounce bagging.[39] A sack of wool of this size weighed between 200 and 250 pounds, though in a shipment to Eisemann the weights spread from 170 pounds to 326 pounds, which indicates the variety of sack sizes used.[40] Ilfeld charged the seller 25 cents per sack at this time, though at a later date, when all his wools were sold gross weight (that is, including the weight of approximately 3 pounds for the sack itself), he deducted the sack weight at the average price per pound of wool before crediting the customer's account.[41]

Wool was usually delivered to the warehouse unsorted as to various grades. Nor were individual fleeces tied separately as is the present custom.[42] Some exception to this practice might have occurred when a particular rancher received the dominant weight of his clip from highly improved sheep, and he was careful, therefore, to sack his light and more valuable wools separately from his coarse or heavy. It was also customary, of course, to separate the black wool, which carried a much lower price, from the white. Generally, however, quality of sheep throughout a given rancher's flocks was fairly uniform, and the custom was to sell the clip as a unit with the undercuttings, dirty and coarse as they were, mixed in.

Because it was custom for eastern buyers to bid on clips instead of individual fleeces, Ilfeld did not employ any sorters.[43] Inspection was done by sampling. As a result of this practice temptation was great on the part of some suppliers to "weight" a sack of wool with sand or dirt as the bag was being filled. A stovepipe, placed in the middle of the empty sack and raised as the wool was stuffed in around it, served as a convenient method of funneling the sand toward the less detectable spots. Black or inferior wool could sometimes be hidden in larger lots of higher quality fleece.[44] But these practices, though wryly talked about, were not too common and only constituted a one-time risk at best.[45] Those who tried such "shennanigans" were discovered when their wool reached the eastern seaboard, if not before, and thereafter these people were subjected to closer inspections.[46]

Yet wool buying is a risky business. The intricacies of wool qualities are likely to escape all but the most keen and practiced eye.[47] One of the more serious risks, that only an expert can minimize, is the estimating of weight shrinkage of wool upon scouring, variations of which, among clips, can be very great. The average weight shrinkage of New Mexico wools in the years 1886 to 1891, as estimated by Joseph Truitt of Philadelphia, was 40 per cent.[48] S. N. D. North raised this estimate to 46 per cent in 1892 and 50 per cent in 1893.[49] These figures, representing a fair judgment only, appear to be minimal according to the experience of the Charles Ilfeld Company. In 1888 a shrinkage of 55 per cent on one lot was considered reasonable.[50] In 1890 eastern buyers were informed that wool in the Ilfeld warehouse would average 64 per cent shrinkage.[51] Light wools in 1892 were expected to have no more than a 35 to 40 per cent shrinkage, however.[52] One lot of 289 sacks of unidentified quality, shipped east in 1897, shrank more than 67 per cent upon scouring.[53] A loose notation in the *Gross, Kelly Company Wool Book* listed a dozen or more lots of wool, "weighing in the grease" 340,831 pounds, that were stated to have shrunk 70.89 per cent upon scouring.[54]

In 1903, by which time contracting of wool had become a general practice throughout the Territory and the Charles Ilfeld Company a substantial participant, Nordhaus expressed the problem he faced in buying this commodity in a letter to A. Vanderwart of Albuquerque, an independent wool buyer, with whom Nordhaus had a contract to buy on a commission of 0.25 cent per pound.[55]

> The result on the Lambs wool shows exactly what you say "that we don't know it all." I am willing to go further and say *I don't know anything* and feel like giving up making any estimates on shrinkages. It surely teaches me one lesson and that is in order to be safe to rather put on 2 or 3% more than 2 or 3% too little.

Wool Scouring

One method of minimizing this risk of misjudging the shrinkage of wool was to have it scoured before presenting it for sale. In the early 1890's some of the wool coming to Las Vegas was handled in this manner —being washed by hand in wooden flumes built out into the Gallinas River.[56] This was the Ludeman Wool Company which, by 1895, had two competitors operated by brothers—the John Robbins Wool Scouring Mill and the James Robbins Wool Washing Mill.[57] These mills, as well as two in Trinidad, Colorado, were used by Ilfeld in 1895.[58] The Gross, Kelly Company used Ludeman extensively in the late 1890's usually for its own account, that is, consigning it temporarily to Ludeman, but sometimes for "his account," thus indicating a sale to the scouring mill.[59] Various lots were charged differing rates for this service, ranging from

0.75 cents to 1.25 cents per 100 pounds.[60] The reasons for the different charges are not apparent.

Minimizing the risk of buying wool in the grease—that is the raw product still in its oily and dirty state—was not, however, the governing reason for the rise of scouring mills in New Mexico. The wool grower, faced with the necessity of paying freight rates on dirt and extraneous materials comprising three fifths to four fifths of the poundage, was tempted to take advantage of the favorable freight tariff on scoured wools.[61] Any wools that contained more than 49 per cent filth could be scoured to advantage as far as the cost of shipment was concerned.

The favorable spread between dirty and scoured wool freight rates gave rise to a number of wool scouring mills, particularly in the first decade of the 1900's. Las Vegas had at least four such mills in 1902, and one, the Arnot Wool Company (see Appendix 8), was wholly owned by the Gross, Kelly Company which, in 1901, is reputed to have scoured 3,000,000 pounds.[62]

In Albuquerque, James Wilkinson founded his mill in 1897 (see Appendix 9).[63] By the turn of the century, however, this mill had grown considerably, having added two individuals to the management of the firm.[64] The Ilfeld Brothers, Louis and Noa, who recently had become sheep and wool specialists, sold extensively to the Wilkinson mill.[65]

Elsewhere in the Territory, scouring mills were observed in Carlsbad in 1900, Tucumcari in 1904, and Roswell in 1905.[66]

In spite of the obvious opportunity that the wool growers and the handlers had in scouring out the 60 to 70 per cent dead weight before shipping, these enterprises, for the most part, had but a morning glory rise. With the exception of the Wilkinson mill in Albuquerque, which remained in operation until 1922, there appears to have been little or no activity of this nature in New Mexico following conversion of the Arnot Wool Company of Las Vegas into the Gross, Kelly Company Planing Mill in 1908.[67]

The reasons for this sudden attrition in local wool scouring are attributable to various causes. The all-too-apparent savings to be obtained in removing the dirt from the wool caused more individuals to go into the business than, economically, the demand could support. Few of these businesses could attain enough volume to overcome the disadvantage of the highly seasonal operation of but four to six months of the year, though in the 1890's, particularly, a fair supplementary income was obtained from pulled wool and the sale of the hides from which the wool had been removed.[68]

The primary reason, however, for the disappearance of this industry from New Mexico, and undoubtedly the reason why the Charles Ilfeld Company, unlike its competitor, the Gross, Kelly Company, which was committed to its own mill, used these scouring mills sparingly, was the desire of eastern top makers and worsted mills to select grades and staples of wool fitted for their particular blends.[69] As has been stated before, New Mexico wool growers and handlers were indifferent to the advantages of careful sorting of their clips, and, even had they not been, it was unlikely that the growing worsted manufacturers would have abandoned their desire to sort, comb, and blend their own wools and to subject these blends to their own scouring plants.[70] Therefore, though a local scouring industry seemed to offer a partial solution to the ever-present problem of high freight costs as well as an opportunity to determine exact shrinkages before the region lost control of the wool, it became apparent in a relatively short period of time that this was not the answer.[71]

Actually, the risks encountered in the buying of wools were minor when stacked against the economic and political forces that seemed determined to discourage even the most enterprising of wool growers and which, in turn, created serious credit and financial problems for the sedentary merchant who supplied their needs. The persistent cyclical decline in general prices bore heavily upon the prices of raw materials and agricultural commodities. In the case of wool, however, the added threat of national politics forced New Mexico and western sheep interests to face the contingency of downward revisions in the protective tariff on this commodity. Ilfeld and Nordhaus, not at all complacent about the situation, took up the cry of "Tariff"—the panacea for the economic ill that afflicted them.

The Protective Tariff

Raw wool had received the benefit of a substantially higher tariff in 1867 several months prior to the major collapse in American wool prices and a year or so before the fall of these prices in the London market.[72] The unprecedented rate of increase in the world supply of wool during the first half of the decade, the cessation of Civil War demands, and the increasing competition from cotton were greater forces than the tariff could stay.[73] However, a favorable result, as far as the wool growers were concerned, was the reduction of imports to less than half the average annual importation of the Civil War years.[74] In spite of this protection, prices of wool continued downward during the next few years, reviving as a result of the drain placed upon world supplies by the demands of the Franco-Prussian War, coming as it did on the heels of a diminishing rate of increase in world stocks.[75] But the downward trend returned, and, in the ensuing deflation, wool prices fell with all other commodities with little support being mustered until 1879.

Those who studied the wool market, though, knew that the tariff had stemmed a far worse collapse in wool prices, however much it may have protracted the agony. Domestic wool prices remained, on the average, 8 to 11 cents per pound above the English market during the post-Civil War period and held that advantage until wool was placed on the free list in 1893.[76] The fact that the tariff, by its own size, should have accounted for a differential greater than this only served to convince the typical wool grower that he needed higher protection. Grover Cleveland's election, however, and his messages to Congress in 1885 and 1887, which had come on top of a slight reduction in wool excises in 1883, threw the dampest kind of a blanket on any hopes the wool growers would otherwise have had. Nordhaus wrote in May, 1888, that "the Wool Market is very unsettled yet; it is impossible to predict any values for the future as the market seems to depend altogether on the passage or the defeat of the Tariff bill." [77] Within a month he pessimistically believed that protection for wool stood a good chance of being removed entirely.[78]

President Cleveland could not muster the strength necessary to reduce the tariff of 1883 during his first administration and, with the election of Benjamin Harrison, the protectionists gained a strong hand. The further fall in wool prices and the decrease in the numbers of sheep in the nation in the years following 1885 were tied closely enough in point of time to the lower tariff of 1883 as to give leverage to the arguments of the wool protectionists. The McKinley bill, passed after extended debate, became law in October, 1890, and virtually restored the wool rates of 1867.[79] The fact that the sheep industry had started its natural long-term decline, even before the slight tariff reduction of 1883, had escaped general notice because of the overshadowing growth of western flocks on lands that had had little or no competition from crop agriculture.[80] It was difficult for anyone to raise an effective answer to combat the wool growers' argument based, as it was, on the strength of coincidence.

With the passage of the McKinley bill, New Mexico wools of all classes firmed slightly in the Philadelphia market although Nordhaus wrote of a slight break which, he said, brought wools to a price level less than the tariff rates.[81] This weakness continued through 1891 and 1892, and, with the election of Cleveland to his second term in the autumn of the latter year, Nordhaus was caught with a warehouse full of wool. He sold all of it "in order to prevent any heavier losses" to his customers which he thought would arise with "the expected reduction of the tariff." [82] By the close of 1893 his worst fears had been realized as Philadelphia prices for New Mexico wools had declined another 5 or 6 cents per pound.[83] From June on, in that year, the Charles Ilfeld Company was quoting no more than 12 cents for any wools—the top protective tariff excise—and toward the end of the year the range of quotations and sales prices was between 6 and 9 cents.

Cleveland's forthright determination to remove all tariff protection from raw materials brought forth stiff opposition from the western states and territories. Charles Ilfeld was among those wool growers from Arizona, Colorado, California, Montana, Nebraska, New Mexico, and Wyoming who signed a resolution sent from Denver to the United States Senate opposing lower tariff rates.[84] In April, 1894, Charles Ilfeld was certain the Wilson-Gorman tariff bill would not pass, but in May, Nordhaus wrote Juan Maria Blea of Santa Rosa, signing, with a touch of realism—"Macquecito:" [85]

> The wool business is becoming gloomier than I have ever seen it. It appears the Democrats are finally going to free wool of the tariff and it will cause much damage to our products. But we must suffer with what comes to us and be content with our misfortune.

The United States Senate passed its version of the House tariff bill in early July, and neither branch of Congress had included a duty on wool. When the joint committee of the houses simply approved the Senate version, wool had been placed on the free list, although the tariff bill did not become effective until August 28.[86] In spite of the inevitability of duty-free wool, Nordhaus was writing in the first week of August that "demand [for wool] is very brisk" and "wool now arriving has no chance of getting warm in the warehouse." [87] A few days later he bemoaned his pre-August foresight in admitting that wools were "at least" 0.5 to 1 cent higher than when he had disposed of Letcher's wool earlier.[88] Anticipatory selling had driven the price of wool unnaturally low, and none of the prices received by the Charles Ilfeld Company from this date on were any lower than the prices that had obtained in the period of selling that took place shortly before the removal of the tariff. Until 1896, wool prices appear to have remained on a plateau slightly higher than the bottom of 1894.

The decline in importance of the wool and sheep industry east of the Mississippi River showed itself clearly in the tariff bill of 1894. The western interests received little support in their efforts to hold the tariff on wool. Though the bill was, in effect, so protective as to cause President Cleveland to allow it to become law without his signature, it singled out wool as the only commodity of importance to be dealt with so "incisively" as to remove all protection.[89]

The Democrats were to blame, and Ilfeld and Nordhaus, who were Republicans—nearly all sheep and wool men in New Mexico were, with the exception of a few Democratic ranchers, also of high tariff persuasion—began to treat their politics more seriously. In October, 1894, Nordhaus requested Chas. J. Webb & Company of Philadelphia, wool buyers, to send him some pamphlets advocating protection. Earlier he had handed a few to the Republican Central Committee, who "promised to order some and to make good use of them in the coming campaign." [90] In 1895, though the good Lord had given the ranges better than average moisture, Nordhaus wanted a little more assurance. "We have had 3 very bad years here, but the present one is a marked improvement; our ranges look fine and prospects for the future have never been better. All we are waiting for is a good republican government." [91]

In November, Ilfeld was a delegate to the Wool Growers Association Convention in Washington, but he gave his proxy to T. B. Catron, Territorial delegate to Congress and Republican boss of Santa Fe County.[92] He advised Catron: a "6¢ Duty on all Classes of wool is enough; would not ask any more for fear that it won't be considered at all." [93]

Hope for protection was strong at this time and sheep growers were anxious for the last bit of news. Nordhaus wrote to Teodoro Casaus: [94]

Caro Amigo:

Yesterday I had advice from Washington that there is a very good chance that again a tariff will be placed on wool. The House already passed a law putting a tariff of 6¢ per pound, but it is deficient until the Senate also pass the law and President Cleveland sign it. I will be very happy if the law passes soon and I think that we will know within the week if it will pass or not. To each one I am giving advice not to trade this week or next until we hear from Washington. As soon as I know with some certainty I will write again and in the meantime I remain

Your attentive servant and friend,
CHARLES ILFELD, mn

Even though the above-mentioned tariff bill failed to make further progress in the Congress, prices of wool remained strong throughout 1896. This did not dampen the ardor of Ilfeld and Nordhaus, however, for a Republican victory and its concomitant—the protective tariff. Max Nordhaus and others put forth every effort in 1896 to found a New Mexico Wool Growers Association which, beyond doubt, was sparked by the tariff issue. In May, Nordhaus had been appointed secretary, pro tem, of the prospective organization and he was busy gathering information for the constitution and bylaws.[95] On July 7, he wrote: "Wool Convention is a success; delegates appeared from all over." [96]

McKinley's nomination in June caused many a seller to withhold his wool pending the political campaign.[97] Eisemann Brothers in Albuquerque were informed by the Charles Ilfeld Company in October that the movement of wool had stopped.[98] "Everybody is holding off for McKinley's 25% better than present bids," [99] he wrote. In November, the news went out to the byways: "McKinley is elected." [100]

As the months passed optimistic sentences crept into the company letters: [101] "Now . . . there should be no trouble in disposing of wool to good advantage." [102] "Waiting for Congress to act in the tariff question." [103] Wool was expected to go to 15 cents in July if the tariff bill passed.[104] "I believe the tariff bill should be passed about the 1st of July but it may be delayed until August." [105] "The tariff bill is passed putting 7 to 11¢ on wool." [106]

And so the tariff remained until *thoseDemocrats* in 1913, with sure control of both houses of Congress, relegated wool to the free list again.[107]

The Uptrend

The strengthening of wool prices upon McKinley's election, with the strong expectation of tariff protection that was in the air, caused Nordhaus to become more aggressive in the acquisition of wool. He contracted with Thomas Ross, an independent buyer, to attain certain clips and paid him a commission of 1/4 cent a pound.[108] Some of these clips were brokered as in the past, but others, and these apparently for the first time, were bought outright as speculations.[109] The company's gross profit on one batch was a full cent and on another, 3 cents.[110] Competing against Gross, Blackwell and Company, Nordhaus bought 20,000 pounds of wool at 17 cents, a half cent higher than had been offered by Harry Kelly, partner of that firm. A profit of at least 1/2 cent was expected.[111] He invested $3500 in Rosenwald wool which he sold to a wool buyer on 60-day paper carrying 10 per cent interest upon which he made a gross profit of 5/8 cents per pound.[112]

As the speculative fever rose so did plans for a new wool warehouse.[113] Some delay in implementing the idea was encountered when land behind the Plaza Hotel was purchased from John Pendaries, who thought he owned it but did not.[114] The warehouse was started at last in the spring of 1898 and with some anxiety was pushed to completion by the middle of July—a little late to meet the opening of the wool season.[115]

By the time the warehouse was completed most of the speculative urge had been taken from Nordhaus. Although business conditions in general continued to improve, and his merchandise sales to rise, he was describing the wool market in April as being in a "deplorable condition" and "bluer than it has been for a very long time." [116] The tune had not changed much by June. "There is absolutely no inquiry for wool from the East at present," he wrote. "I never knew of a time when it was harder to answer the question . . . regarding the situation on wool. . . . We are also at sea as to value." [117]

The reason for this sudden lull is difficult to isolate. Prices in the East, supported in part, at least, by the sudden but short Spanish-American War, were scarcely down from the year before and were holding firm. Imports of raw wool were being cut almost two thirds although domestic wool production was up approximately 3 per cent.[118] General business conditions, as reflected in a variety of indices, were upward.[119]

The one explanation that seems plausible was the long-term trends of increased competition of cotton with wool and decreased consumption per capita of wool.[120] These factors must have been accentuated in 1898 as a result of the previous year's tariff on raw wool and wool manufactures, coupled with the failure of the law to place rates of relative protection on cotton goods. Raw cotton remained on the free list.[121] The pressure on wool prices until the spring of 1902 (except for the temporary speculative spree fathered in the European markets in the fall of 1899) lends further credence to the theory that the competition of cotton and other wool substitutes may have played more than a normal role in these years.[122] Whatever the reason, however, the quantity of raw wool purchased by the Charles Ilfeld Company in 1898 was substantially less than it had been during the previous two years.[123]

A major change in business policy came in 1902, when by dint of circumstances Nordhaus had to take strong steps to retain a large part of his business in both wool and merchandise. The Chicago, Rock Island & Pacific Railroad and its subsidiary the El Paso and Northeastern, had cut across New Mexico from El Paso to Santa Rosa and Tucumcari and had forced Nordhaus to "contemplate making an important change in my business." [124] By August this change had taken place in the form of a branch establishment at Santa Rosa.[125]

With this expansion in facilities and the strong upturn in wool prices in the last quarter of 1902, Goldenberg began to contract wools with vigor in fulfillment of other contracts the company had with A. Vanderwart of Albuquerque, and Brown and Adams of Boston.[126] From the former, commissions of 1/4 cent per pound were to be received, and from the latter, 1/2 cent.[127] That contracting of wool had become general is evidenced by a report sent to a commercial bulletin in Washington, D.C., in which Nordhaus wrote that "considerable of the new wool has been contracted in advance to eastern buyers at prices much in advance of last year's figures and above the present market prices." [128]

As this great surge in wool activities took place throughout the Territory, the Charles Ilfeld Company obtained more than its share of the increase. In the period 1903 through 1905, this company's annual volume was more than 60 per cent over that which had been handled as an average in the years 1898 to 1902 (see Table 8).[129] The average annual purchases during the earlier period had been more than 1,000,000 pounds. In the later years the figure had risen to almost 1,700,000 pounds.[130] Pressure for additional warehouse space was crucial. Nordhaus wrote Arthur Ilfeld, son of Charles, who was temporarily in charge of the business at Santa Rosa, to tell the Rock Island Railroad "it would be necessary . . . to put up a woolhouse at Santa Rosa to store at least 750,000# wool in order to keep the wool trade there, otherwise a great many people will

TABLE 8. WOOL RECORD, 1894–1905 [a]

Year	No. of sacks		Quantity (1000 lb)		Average weight Sack (lb)		Total value (1000 $)		Price (cents/lb)	
	Bought	Sold	Bought	Sold	Bought	Sold	Bought	Sold	Bought	Sold
1894	5,979	5,970	1,180	1,178	197	197	93.1	96.2	7.9	8.2
1895	4,354	4,306	865	856	197	199	87.5	89.4	10.2	10.4
1896 [b]	4,828	4,221	987	867	206	205	77	67.3	7.8	7.8
1897	4,922	5,944	1,003	1,263	205	212	137.4 [c]	148.9 [d]	13.7	11.8
(1898 [b])	(3,023)	(2,727)	(614)	(552)	(205)	(202)	(78.5)	(74.9)	(12.8)	(13.6)
1898/9 [e]	9,784	9,796	2,039	2,039	208	208	258.8	273.1	12.7	13.4
1900	3,899	3,143	772	627	198	199	95.7	81.1	12.4	12.9
1901	5,366	7,316	1,109	1,509	205	206	122.1	174.0	11.0	11.5
1902 [f]	(2,933)	(2,941)	(574)	(579)	(195)	(197)	(75.5)	(78.5)	(13.2)	(13.6)
1902 [g]	(4,453)	(4,452)	(1,014)	(1,015)	(227)	(208)	(121.2)	(127.9)	(12.0)	(12.6)
1902 [h]	7,386	7,393	1,588	1,594	215	216	196.8	206.4	12.4	13.0
Average (1898–1902)			(1,014)							
1903	7,728	7,491	1,827	1,760	237	235	249.3	247.3	13.7	41.1
1904	6,375	6,699	1,552	1,623	243	242	224.6	244.3	14.5	15.1
1905	6,939	6,938	1,699	1,696	246	244	325.7	344.3	19.2	20.3
Average (1903–1905)			(1,693)							
Totals	67,560 [i]	69,217	14,621	15,012	216	217	2064.7	2178.7	12.7	13.1

Source: Sundry Exhibits, Record Book, 1897–1909.

[a] Figures in parentheses embrace partial or full amounts included in other aggregates.

[b] Year incomplete.

[c] Includes $3,950 scoured wool from 1896.

[d] $3,757 in scoured wool not included.

[e] Covers two full years.

[f] Las Vegas.

[g] Santa Rosa.

[h] Total 1902.

[i] Lower than sales probably because of discrepancies in 1897 and 1901.

take their wool to Pastura, where the El Paso NE RR Co. is putting up a woolhouse now . . . we have not enough room at our warehouse to handle goods and wool at the same time." [131] The warehouse at Pastura had been put up at the request of Nordhaus, who had also asked for another one at Corona where he planned to open a branch store.[132] In Las Vegas it became necessary to rent additional space in the old Hilario Romero building on the west end of the Plaza.[133]

Wool had become big business to the Charles Ilfeld Company. Yet only part of the story of how it became so important has been told. That part was the use of the sheep drive that was forced on Ilfeld and Nordhaus as a corollary to their collection problems and the falling price level.[134] The rest of the story concerns another institution that grew for the same reason, but which led the way to sedentary sheep husbandry, a specialized business risk. This was the partido system—the lending of sheep on a rental basis—a phase of the problem to which we now turn our attention.

XI

THE PARTIDO SYSTEM

Development and Early Growth

It would appear logical that the livestock industry in New Spain would have been a necessary and desirable part of the colonization that proceeded from the conquest of Montezuma and his Aztecs by Cortés in 1519. That the industry had gained an important role within a rather few years is evidenced by the "interminable law suits . . . particularly between cattlemen and the sheep owners" that had arisen by 1536.[1] Such legal tangles encouraged Antonio de Mendoza, first viceroy in New Spain, to adopt as law the form of the Ordinances of the Spanish Mesta —those laws which grew out of that national association of shepherds officially recognized and chartered by Alphonso the Learned in 1273.[2] The Constitution of the Mesta in New Spain, comprising 17 articles, was adopted in 1537.[3] Little clue is given in this document, however, concerning methods practiced by the owners in the conduct of the livestock industry. A revision of these Ordinances in 1574, by their very length and detail, reveals how important this industry had become. For our particular purposes it is interesting to note that, in spite of the feudal slave economy of New Spain, the herder or pastor had opportunities to acquire livestock of his own, though the law (if it was enforced) prevented him from keeping his acquisition as capital. The pastor was entitled, upon his choice, to a share or partido of his master's herd in lieu of money wages providing that at the end of one year or sooner this share would have been sold.[4] Because of the colonial nature of New Spain this restriction of ownership pertaining to the herder is not a surprising reversion from a freer development that had evolved in the Old World. In Spain proper, as early as the fourteenth century, the herder was allowed to keep as part of his wages, and without charge, a certain number of sheep of his own, usually about 10 per cent of the total flocks he tended.[5]

Such an artificial restriction of ownership as the Mesta of New Spain attempted to enforce could only exist as long as enterprise within the laboring classes failed to exert itself. It is probable that more than a few pastores and estancieros (ranch foremen), as they proved themselves superior hands, were granted the privilege by their masters of keeping an agreed-upon share of the flock increase as wages. How soon this became a general practice is not known, but 200 years later in the vicinity of Santa Fe the lending of sheep as capital to individual herders, and in return the payment of so many head of increase as interest, thus permitting the herder an opportunity to profit, seems to have been an advanced stage of the earlier form of wage payments.

Several examples of what, in New Mexico, has been known as the partido system were described by Fray Francisco Atanasio Domingues in recording his journey to the missions of New Mexico in 1776. In reporting on the various confraternities, or lay orders of the Church, he noted that the capital of these religious bodies had been invested in ewes farmed out at interest, which in all but one case required an annual return of 16 head per 100 advanced.[6] The Confraternity of Our Lady of Light was able to invest its 1070 ewes at an annual return of 20 per cent in sheep plus 12 fleeces of wool.[7]

An earlier example of a partido contract, this one between two individuals, had been agreed to in 1760.[8] Don Nicolas Ortiz, "Lieutenant-General of the Kingdom," delivered 400 breeding ewes to one Juan Gutierrez for a contract period of six years with the understanding that Gutierrez was to deliver each year 30 lambs less than a year old and 70 wethers—each 100 head to be added to principal. At the end of six years the original principal was to have been augmented by 200 ewes in addition to the annual increase required. To all this was added the stipulation that 100 fleeces should be delivered annually. The rate of interest per annum, therefore, was 25 per cent in sheep, 25 per cent in fleeces, and a bonus of one third in ewes at the end of the contract.

Josiah Gregg, reporting on what he learned from his visit to Santa Fe in 1831, described the same practice: [9]

> In former times there were extensive proprietors . . . who had [on] their *ranchos* . . . from three to five hundred thousand head of sheep. The custom has usually been to farm out the ewes to the rancheros, who make a return of twenty per cent upon the stock in merchantable *carneros*—a term applied to sheep generally, and particularly to wethers fit for market.

A more precise description of the partido system, as practiced in New Mexico in the first half of the nineteenth century, has been left to us by José Augustin Escudero, lawyer and one-time district judge of Chihuahua, who visited Santa Fe in 1827 and who published his notes in 1849. He was deeply impressed by the opportunities this system offered the enterprising shepherd, though he was swayed beyond the point of reason in ascribing to it such economic benefactions as the elimination of the pauper and its granting to the poorest New Mexican the comfort and luxuries of the wealthiest. Nevertheless his description is worth repeating.[10]

> It can be asserted that there were no paupers in New Mexico at that time, nor could there be any. At the same time, there were no large-scale stockmen

who could pay wages or make any expenditure whatever in order to preserve and increase their wealth in this branch of agriculture. A poor man, upon reaching the age when one generally desires freedom and sufficient means to subsist and start a family, would go to a rich stockman and offer to help him take care of one or more herds of sheep. These flocks were composed of a thousand ewes and *ten* breeding rams, which were never separated from the herd as is the practice of stock raisers in other countries. Consequently, in each flock, not a single day would go by without the birth of two or three lambs, which the shepherd would put with the ewe and force the female to suckle without the difficulties which he would have had with a larger number of offspring. The shepherd would give the owner ten or twenty per cent of these sheep and an equal amount of wool, as a sort of interest, thus preserving the capital intact.

From the moment he received the flock, the shepherd entered into a contract in regard to the future increase, even with his overseer. As a matter of fact, he usually contracted it at the current market price, two *reales* per head, the future increase to be delivered in small numbers over a period of time. With this sum, which the shepherd had in advance, he could construct a house, and take in other persons to help him care for and shear the sheep, which was done with a knife instead of shears. The milk, and sometimes the meat, from the said sheep provided him sustenance; the wool was spun by his family into blankets, stockings, etc., which could also be marketed, providing an income. Thus the wealth of the shepherd would increase until the day he became, like his overseer, the owner of a herd. He, in turn, would let out his herds to others after the manner in which he obtained his first sheep and make his fortune. Consequently, even in the homes of the poorest New Mexicans, there is never a dearth of sufficient means to satisfy the necessities of life and even to afford the comfort and luxuries of the wealthiest class in the country.

By the time the American Occupation had taken place in 1846, the partido system had become a common pattern of sheep ownership in New Mexico. In an area possessing little specie or coin (it was drained off by the highly unfavorable balance of trade), sheep served not only as money but the procreative ewes brought interest to their capitalist owners. It was the sheep specialist, still to this day spoken of as a patron, who found the partido system useful. In 1846, José Leandro Perea of Bernalillo is reputed, no doubt with much exaggeration, to have placed 200,000 head in flocks of 2500 each with risk-bearing sheepherders known as partidarios.[11] The vast public range that permitted and encouraged the herds to roam great distances made supervision of wage labor from one central point costly and subject to high risk. Logically, the owner of large and far-flung flocks—not unlike the maritime mercantile capitalist whose cargoes rode the seven seas—gave those responsible for the wise care of the investment an opportunity to profit from work well done. The cracking of the peonage system in New Mexico during the latter part of the eighteenth century and its near disappearance in the early decades of the nineteenth were symptomatic of this demand for free labor.

The mercantile capitalist, whose dominance in the economic towns of Taos and Santa Fe was apparent by 1850, evidently did not make use of the partido system until a much later date. It may have been that some of the Santa Fe merchants with capital to invest were responsible in part for the use of partido agreements reported to have existed in the Galisteo area, some 30 miles south of Santa Fe, as early as 1854.[12] Yet it is significant that the Bill of Complaint, filed by Gustave Elsberg against his partners Jacob Amberg and Herman Ilfeld in 1869, does not list sheep as part of the property holdings of that large Santa Fe firm.[13]

It has been stated that there was no partido system in Rio Arriba County in the 1860's where, in the eastern part at least, both Santa Fe and Taos merchants would have had easy access. Later the system is purported to have appeared there under the sponsorship of merchants as it did in Mora County, to the north of Las Vegas, as an incidental part of the mercantile business.[14] The fact that the Territorial legislature, in 1882, recognized for the first time that contracts, for pay or for shares, between owners of livestock and those who herded or cared for the animals might be recorded with the county in which the contract was made probably indicates that the partido form of agreement may not have become an important commercial instrument, as far as merchants were concerned, until a few years preceding this date—probably not until the coming of the railroad in 1879 and 1880.[15]

This rather late use of the partido contract by the mercantile capitalist should not be surprising. Certainly he had little motive for using the instrument prior to the 1880's. He had not assumed the risk of sheep husbandry for reasons discussed in previous chapters and, therefore, unlike the large livestock specialists, had few sheep available for lending. The likelihood that he might have wished to use the partido system as an outlet for investment, as had been common among individuals and institutions a century earlier, does not seem probable. His need for capital to carry adequate merchandise inventories, construct the necessary store and equipment facilities, and finance the six to twelve months' credit granted his customers held important priority, and his ability to meet this demand was strained. Nor did the sedentary merchant of New Mexico want for sufficient supplies of sheep to meet the maximum demand of the mutton market. The ubiquitous sheep, raised under the lowest cost conditions, were at his threshold with little and sometimes no encouragement on his part.

Charles Ilfeld Adopts the Partido System

Charles Ilfeld did not participate in the partido system until his collection problems worsened perceptibly. The first evidence of the practice appears in the records in 1884, the same year he hired Solomon Floersheim to aid in sheep and wool collections, although it is not improbable that at least one contract existed prior to this date.[16] Some increase in this activity occurred in the next two or three years. With the hiring of Goldenberg in 1888—a year in which Ilfeld's cash position had declined to a dangerously low level as a result of lagging collections—a number of new contracts were created.[17] By 1890, apparently spurred on by the newly inaugurated program of sheep contracting, Nordhaus and Goldenberg had placed more than 17,000 ewes on shares with selected customers.[18] As the economic collapse of 1893 deepened, the number of partido sheep rose rapidly until a temporary peak of more than 33,000 head were being loaned in 1897. Though the number of sheep farmed out in this manner declined markedly over the next four-year period, this figure rose again in 1902 and by 1905 had reached a high of 38,000 head as both sheep and wool prices climbed markedly (see Table 9).

The partido system, if used on a highly selective basis and carefully supervised to prevent abuses on the part of partidarios, was a sound method of refinancing or funding debt of customers whose account balances with Ilfeld were growing unduly or were not being reduced. Not only could a rancher sell his sheep to Ilfeld to reduce his current debt, but by being permitted to retain these sheep on a rental contract he preserved his earning assets. Thus, if he were an able sheepman, he had the opportunity to improve greatly his financial position over an extended period. The funding of current debt and the preserving of earning assets of selected customers were important objectives of the partido system as adopted by Charles Ilfeld.

There were other advantages of this system, too. The sheer demand for these contracts from both indebted and nonindebted customers, as well as from large and highly specialized livestock interests, particularly during the 1890's, must have encouraged Max Nordhaus, upon whom the burden of administration fell, to enlarge the scope of this activity beyond immediate intentions. By and large, however, he resisted this temptation.

Another, and most important, reason for Ilfeld's adoption of the partido contract as an integral part of his business was the need for protection against the keener local and intersectional competition brought on by the coming of the railroad. As the trade area of Las Vegas shrank in the face of the rise of economic towns and new centers of distribution, loss of distant customers became a matter of concern, and local competition grew more severe as merchants tried the harder to recoup with nearby trade. Ilfeld accepted the opportunity that the furnishing of partido sheep gave him to hold present customers and acquire new ones.

As the market for sheep became disorganized in the acute depression years of 1893 to 1897, the partido system turned its emphasis somewhat and served, partially, as an outlet for surplus sheep, thus alleviating the

TABLE 9. PARTIDO SHEEP

Year	Year-end sheep inventory No.	Book value (dollars)	Average book value per head (dollars)	No. of partidarios	No. of sheep per partidario
1884	—	—	—	1	—
1885	—	—	—	5	—
1886	—	—	—	5	—
1887	—	—	—	7	—
1888	—	—	—	19	—
1889	—	—	—	20	—
1890	17,000 [a]	—	—	30	567 [a]
1891	—	—	—	29	—
1892	—	—	—	31	—
1893	—	—	—	31	—
1894	—	—	—	39	—
1895	—	—	—	32	—
1896	32,476	40,910	1.26	32	1,015
1897	33,183	63,954	1.93	33	1,006
1898	30,901	72,612	2.35	32	966
1899	27,215	61,234	2.25	30	907
1900	24,413	56,929	2.33	29	842
1901	31,174	62,348	2.00	39	799
1902	29,196	62,771	2.15	43	679
1903	32,193	67,605	2.10	42	767
1904	37,651	82,832	2.20	44	856
1905	38,230	86,018	2.25	44	869
1906	37,258	83,831	2.25	43	866
1907	30,405	68,411	2.25	35	869
1908	31,434	70,727	2.25	39	806
1909	25,308	56,943	2.25	31	816
1910	24,310	54,698	2.25	29	838
1911	23,399	52,648	2.25	23	1,017
1912	24,499	55,123	2.25	24	1,021
1913	23,948	53,883	2.25	28	855
1914	23,783	53,512	2.25	27	881
1915	23,991	71,973	3.00	30	800
1916	22,303	66,909	3.00	27	826
1917	15,466	46,398	3.00	25	619
1918	15,320	45,960	3.00	24	638
1919 [b]	13,548	40,644	3.00	24	565

Sources: 1884–1895, various ledgers; 1896–1898, Record Book, 1895–1909; 1899–1919, Annual Summary Book, 1899–1929.

[a] Estimated.

[b] Sold to Ilfeld, Moulton Livestock Co., as of January 1, 1920.

merchant's problem of pasturage for unsold flocks. With the turn of the century and the entering of the Charles Ilfeld Company into sheep husbandry on a large scale, the higher average prices paid for partido wool than for the average of all wools purchased by Ilfeld (see Table 10)

TABLE 10. COMPARISON OF AVERAGE SELLING PRICES OF TOTAL WOOL HANDLED AND PARTIDO WOOL, 1894–1904 (CENTS/LB)

Year	Total wool	Partido wool
1894	7.9	—
1895	10.1	—
1896	7.8	8.2
1897	13.7	13.9
1898 [a]	12.8	15.6
1899	12.7	14.4
1900	12.4	12.8
1901	11.0	11.2
1902	12.4	12.8
1903	13.6	13.9
1904	14.5	15.2

Source: Sundry exhibits, Record Book, 1895–1909.
[a] Incomplete. 1898–1899: Total wool, 12.7¢; Partido wool, 14.7¢.

suggests that the partido system may have been used as a tool to improve the quality of the sheep his customers grew. This, however, is not at all certain. The most that can be said is that, as breeders succeeded in improving the quality and size of the fleece in all parts of the West, it should have become important to Ilfeld that his customers not lose their competitive position in the world-wide wool market. To the extent that surplus sheep of high quality existed on the Ilfeld ranges and were farmed out on partido contract to certain customers, one can ascribe to Ilfeld's use of the system the motive of improving the flocks of his customers. Probably, however, it is nearer the truth to recognize that the partido system could not have borne successfully the burden of this need and that Ilfeld, pushed by Nordhaus, preferred for this and other reasons to bring the control and production of sheep and wool, as far as practicable, within the province of his own sheep husbandry operations.

A final motive for the adoption of the partido system by Ilfeld was, perhaps, no motive at all. This was the opportunity for direct profit to be attained from the rentals on sheep capital. Generally speaking, it has been assumed that this motive was dominant. To the extent that it was present, however, it must be judged minor in the total picture. It seems reasonable to assume, in the light of the evidence, that the profits obtained were accepted as less than a just reward for the problems endured and represented earnings upon a capital fund that would have been happy to expend its efforts in more profitable and less burdensome pursuits.

The Profitableness of Partido Agreements to Charles Ilfeld

Fortunately, a sufficient breakdown of figures in the Ilfeld records is available to give us evidence of the rate of return received by Ilfeld on partido contracts in the years 1894 to 1904. Table 11 shows the admitted

TABLE 11. Rate of return on partido sheep investment

Year	Year-end sheep inventory (dollars)	Net profit (dollars)	Rate of return (per cent)
1894	39,118	3,926	10.0
1895	41,415	6,305	15.2
1896	40,910	3,159	7.7
1897	63,954	10,463	16.4
1898	72,612	5,314	7.3
1899	61,234	8,298	13.6
1900	56,929	7,839	13.8
1901	62,348 [a]	—	—
1902	62,771	3,307	5.3
1903	67,605	5,047	7.5
1904	82,832	13,048	15.8
Total	589,380	66,706	11.3

Source: Sundry exhibits, Record Book, 1895–1909.
[a] Excluded from Total below.

annual return to have fluctuated between roughly 5 and 16 per cent—averaging better than 11 per cent after taxes but before capital losses and interest on borrowed money.[19] Capital losses, though not a great factor, would have reduced this figure somewhat. When interest on money borrowed for the purpose of carrying partido sheep is included, however, the rate of return can be shown to have been reduced by as much as 3 per cent.[20]

Ilfeld's average net return from partido sheep of approximately 8 to 10 per cent compares with the 12 per cent simple interest that was charged to delinquent accounts. In fact, the gross return of partido wool of two pounds of wool per rented sheep, calculated as a percentage of year-end values of sheep, would have amounted to approximately 12 per cent over the period 1896 to 1904.[21] One such contract was written to permit an annual charge to the account of a partidario of 12 per cent of the value of the sheep rented.[22]

Other things being equal, it would have been more profitable and less burdensome if the partido venture had not been tried. Of course other things were not equal. As in the case of the sheep drives, the partido system served as a protective device to forestall serious losses, though by this latter method reasonable profits were realized in the process. In contrast to the sheep drive, however, the partido contract was a more selective device—being used with favored customers only—and was limited to the credit resources of Ilfeld. Financing the partido program was costly, but it was a cost that appeared far less than prospective losses would have entailed through distressed selling of sheep on the one hand and foreclosures of customers on the other. We can be certain that the adoption of the partido system by Ilfeld was not influenced greatly by the prospect of direct profit and that, until the end of the 1890's at least, it was a long-range program to aid selected ranching customers through funding their debts and preserving their earning assets.

Debt Funding

As the economic pressures upon the rancher grew more serious, the Charles Ilfeld Company was faced not only with a collection problem of some magnitude but also with a need to protect customers whose future livelihood was most important to the mercantile business. It is not surprising, therefore, to find Ilfeld's collection philosophy of the 1870's reaffirmed in the 1880's and 1890's.[23] At the risk of extending himself too far financially, Ilfeld, through Max Nordhaus' skillful management, chose not to press collections harshly, and, in selected situations, through the use of the partido contract, funded current obligations owed him with real capital—that is, sheep. The earnings which the partidario customer could make on these sheep were expected to aid the company in future collections.

In 1884, when Ilfeld first began to loan sheep to his customers, he asked Grzelachowski, the Polish ex-priest, to collect 100 picked ewes from one José Griego, in payment of account "which I desire him to keep on shares." [24] In order to reduce the account of Pedro Sena, the company bought 400 of his ewes and left them with him on shares.[25] In 1893, when José Montano of Lincoln County balked at losing his herd of ewes in payment of his account, Nordhaus offered to purchase 1500 ewes at $1.00 per head and to credit them to Montano's account while leaving them with him on a rental basis.[26] In so doing Nordhaus offered to require only one pound of wool per head as rental—an unusually low figure.[27] Montano accepted with some enthusiasm, paying Nordhaus 2500 ewes instead of the 1500 asked for, and he was permitted to keep them all on partido contract.[28] In the case of another partidario in the Lincoln area, Esperidion Lueras, Goldenberg was instructed to "buy his ewes and contract say 500 to be credited." [29]

Many times debt funding was accomplished in an indirect manner through first receiving ewes on account from one group of customers, then placing them promptly with other debtors. Several times Nordhaus used C. H. Moore of Puerto de Luna to collect ewes from a number of specified persons to be distributed to a list of others.[30] On one occasion this practice involved not only the collection and transfer of sheep from one customer to another, but the transfer of a partido contract as well.[31]

The Partido Contract as an Aid to Customers

It would be rather naive to assume, without evidence, that this act of funding debt was, prima facie, an act dominantly in the interest of the debtor. The mere fact that the partido system has been known to flourish in company with economic recession is evidence, frequently seized upon, that this form of contract was largely for the purpose of gaining undue profits at the expense of the small rancher whose debts had placed him in a defenseless position. That the system produced no such profit to the Charles Ilfeld Company is, at least, negative evidence that his company had other objectives in view. An analysis of the terms of the standard partido contract as drawn for Ilfeld, and the implementation of the same as revealed in his records, strongly imply that the contract was drawn, primarily, for the profit and economic advancement of those partidarios who possessed the capability and willingness to take advantage of the opportunity.

The standard contract offered by Ilfeld and Nordhaus from 1884 until 1902 required a rental of two pounds of wool per ewe and permitted the partidario the right to keep the balance of the wool and all of the progeny. None of these sheep or their progeny, however, could be sold or encumbered in any manner without the consent of the Charles Ilfeld Company and until the terms of the contract had been fulfilled. This remained a typical contract after 1902 as well, although in that year quite a few examples of annual rental payments of one fifth of the partido flock in wethers appear. Also from this date on, with the general improvement in the quality of sheep, a tendency is evident to raise the standard wool rental contract to 2½ or 3 pounds per sheep (see Table 12). For the privilege of retaining all the progeny and the balance of the shearing (or all the wool and the balance of the progeny as the case might be), the partidario paid all the expense of herding and caring, which included one half the ad valorem taxes on the flocks.[32]

In most cases Ilfeld made a freight allowance of one half the wagon cost to Las Vegas, although on long hauls he fixed a maximum of 45

TABLE 12. NUMBER OF PARTIDO CONTRACTS UNDER VARIOUS RENTAL TERMS

Rental terms	1896	1897	1898	1899	1900	1901 [a]	1902	1903	1904	1905
1 lb wool per head	1	1	1	—	—	—	3 [b]	2 [b]	—	3
1½ lb wool per head	1	—	—	—	—	—	1 [c]	—	—	1
1¾ lb wool per head	1	—	—	—	—	—	—	—	—	2
2 lb wool per head	27	31	30	30	30	23	28	26	20	23
2¼ lb wool per head	—	—	—	—	—	—	—	—	1	1
2½ lb wool per head	—	—	—	1	—	—	—	1	6	10
2¾ lb wool per head	—	—	—	—	—	—	—	—	1	—
3 lb wool per head	—	—	—	—	—	1	1	2	2	1
7½ per cent wethers with wool	1	—	—	—	—	—	—	1	—	—
10 per cent wethers plus ½ lb wool per head	—	—	—	—	—	—	—	1	—	—
15 per cent wethers plus ½ lb wool per head	—	—	—	—	—	—	—	1	—	—
20 per cent wethers with wool	—	—	—	—	—	—	3	10 [d]	12	3
20 per cent wethers shorn	—	1	2	2	4	4	3	—	1	1
Cash (charged to account)	1 [e]	1 [e]	—	—	—	2 [f]	—	—	—	—
Totals [g]	32	34	33	33	34	30	39	44	43	45

Source: Wool and sheep records.

[a] Compilation for this year is not complete.

[b] Probably for fall shearing only caused by late delivery of ewes.

[c] Actually 1.4 lb per head.

[d] Two marked "shorn upon delivery." No penalty charged in one case. 7/10 lb wool per head delivered in other cases and 1/10 lb equivalent was charged to account.

[e] 12¢ per head.

[f] One at 20¢ per head; one at 22¢ per head.

[g] Totals do not agree with Table 9 for at least two reasons. In some cases partidarios had two contracts with different terms. In other cases the terms of the contracts are not known and had to be omitted.

cents per 100 pounds.[33] Ilfeld evidently did not assume the cost of shearing, though on at least one occasion he did furnish housing free of any charges.[34] Although the contract exempted the mortgagee from the natural risks of "lightning, Indians, or pest," the partidario was expected to bear the more serious risks present in wolves and weather.[35] The contract was drawn for a period of "ambos voluntarios," a succinct Spanish phrase meaning "for such time as either of the parties may desire," though either party was required to give 30 days' notice of intention to terminate (see Appendix 12).

That this was a fair contract can be shown by approximations of a partidario's income and expenses. Estimates by Nordhaus of the weights of fleeces, made at intervals over the years 1891 to 1903, stated that sheep handled by the company sheered from 3 pounds to as high as 10 pounds per head.[36] The 3-pound estimate was made on but one occasion and then it was given as "three to four pounds" on a band of Mexican improved sheep. The median estimate of the 13 cited was 5½ pounds, with no apparent trend over the period.[37] It is safe to assume, therefore, that after the partidario paid Ilfeld the 2 pounds of wool per head he had available to sell for his own account another 2 pounds or more.

For this wool, unless it was in very poor condition, he received a higher average price than Ilfeld paid for the average of all his wool purchases—indicating a better than average quality of sheep placed on shares. This average price evidently did not fall below 8 cents per pound in each of the years 1897 through 1904 (see Table 10). The partidario's income from wool in excess of his rental contract, therefore, should not have been less than $16 per 100 head (2 pounds at 8 cents) and, typically, should have ranged from $24 to $30. The median fleece of 5½ pounds, netting the partidario 3½ pounds, would have brought income from wool, alone, of $28 to as high as $50 or more per 100 head.

In addition to wool income, the partidario was entitled to the full increase of sheep progeny—either selling them to Ilfeld or holding them as security for the partido contract. The size of the lamb crop varied, of course, from year to year. When rains in the early spring brought forth plenty of grass, sheepmen had expectations of 95 to 100 per cent lambing—that is, one live lamb for each ewe that was bred.[38] One authoritative estimate for the early 1890's placed the average yield at 75 per cent within a normal spread of from 65 to 85 per cent, an average figure that seems reasonable for later years.[39]

The lowest price discovered in the records that Ilfeld paid for lambs in this general period of the 1890's and early 1900's was 75 cents per head. The more common price was 90 cents to $1.00, with much higher amounts in 1897 and later years.[40] It was probable, therefore, that a partidario would not have received less than $48 from the offspring of 100 ewes (75 cents times 65 per cent times 100), but considerably more than $100 under more favorable conditions. His total annual income, therefore, from wool and lambs, barring serious lambing losses, should have been no less than $60 per 100 ewes and, under more typical conditions, he could have received an income within a range of $100 to $125.[41]

Offsetting these estimates of revenues, the costs of caring for sheep were not high, and except under the most unfavorable conditions, permitted a net profit that at times could have been quite large. An analysis of cost estimates, submitted by a number of ranchers from all parts of New Mexico and made in the early 1890's prior to the depression of 1893 to 1897, indicates the partidario should have been able to keep his annual expenses within 60 cents per head, exclusive of ad valorem taxes but inclusive of a reserve of 10 per cent of the value of the sheep on hand. "American" owners' estimates ranged between 40 cents and 60 cents per head. "Mexican" owners' estimates ranged from 30 cents to 50 cents.[42] Ad valorem taxes in San Miguel County, where Ilfeld kept most of his partido sheep, amounted to 5¼ cents per head; hence an Ilfeld partidario would have been obliged to pay 2⅝ cents for this purpose.[43]

The only example of complete caring costs cited in the Ilfeld records occurred when Charles Ilfeld shared a one-half interest in 500 sheep with one F. J. Jones, and contracted them for care from March until shearing time to C. P. Hawley, near Puerto de Luna, at $16 per month plus $10 to $15 for lambing and shearing.[44] This cost on an annual basis would have been less than 42 cents per head which, when augmented by a reserve of 10 per cent on the value of the sheep and a partidario's share of taxes, would have brought the total cost to no more than 59 cents per head.

It would appear, therefore, that under any semblance of efficient management the partidario should have been able to "break even" under conditions of highest cost and lowest income—each extreme approximating $60 per 100 sheep per year—and he should have profited well under favorable circumstances.[45] Inasmuch as the average band of sheep or partida granted by Ilfeld was between 700 and 1000 sheep (see Table 9), it seems entirely possible that a number of his partidarios had the reasonable opportunity in most of these years of earning, net, $300 to $400 from the sheep capital invested by Ilfeld.[46] In addition, of course, the partidario generally had sheep of his own and often possessed other regular sources of income.

Whether many of these partidarios actually attained this estimate of income is difficult to ascertain. An analysis of their ledger accounts, however, would seem to suggest that, generally speaking, these people were able to do better financially than popularly has been supposed.

Analysis of Partidario Ledger Account Balances

There were, prior to 1896, 51 partidario accounts recorded in the general ledgers of the Charles Ilfeld Company with which partido contracts were in effect one year or more. Fourteen of these contracts began or were in existence in 1888 and remained active for at least six years. Ten contracts originated in 1890, all of which were still in existence in 1895. Four contracts became effective in both 1892 and 1894, and each of these groups was intact at the end of a six-year period. A study has been made of the year-end balances of each of these groups to determine what trends, if any, took place in the amounts of debt that were owed on trade balances to Charles Ilfeld.

At first glance the popular conception of the partidario slipping deeper and hopelessly into debt appears to be borne out.[47] In the case of the 1888 group, the partidario accounts receivable in the years following averaged more than 3½ times greater at the end of four years, and 2½ at the end of five. The 1890 group increased to twice the original debit balances by the end of the second year following, but these had been reduced by one half when their five-year period had been concluded. Both the 1892 and 1894 groups had increased their debit balances approximately 50 per cent in five years.

When all 51 of the partidario accounts were analyzed, covering a period from 1888 through 1900, only 1889 showed a slightly lower average account receivable balance than 1888. In no other year was an average debit balance less than 60 per cent higher than 1888. In the peak year, 1892, the figure had risen to 350 per cent of the base year. At the end of the period the average debit balance was still 70 per cent above the first year (see Table 13).[48]

A significant coincidence, however, is that the peak of balances of both the 1888 and 1890 groups was 1892, and henceforth through the acute depression years of 1893 to 1897, and then into the following period of prosperity, the average balances show a marked downtrend. Could the increase through 1892 merely reflect the loosening of credit granted because of rising sheep prices through that year? Could this have been the natural increase expected because of the newly expanded credit base of this group of customers? Does the decline in balances throughout the depression years, in spite of worsening terms of trade for these partidarios, vis-à-vis exports and imports, simply indicate that these individuals had gained a significant source of income they would not otherwise have had?

Perhaps more light can be shed on the answers to these questions through an analysis of the ultimate disposition of these accounts and contracts so far as it is possible to do so. Fourteen of the 51 partidarios were unable to pay their debts in full and their balances were written off to the Profit and Loss account. All but three of these people, however, had reduced their balances to one half or less of their debt existing at the end of the year in which their contract had started—the other three accounts having increased their balances from 1½ to 4½ times.

Thirty-three, or 65 per cent, of the partidarios terminated their contracts successfully—20 continuing their trade with Ilfeld on a normal basis and 13 closing their accounts without further purchases as late as 1907.

Three of the 51 contracts were still operating in 1907—one having

TABLE 13. PARTIDARIO END-OF-YEAR BALANCES (DOLLARS)

Partidarios	1888	1889	1890	1891	1892	1893	1894	1895	1896	1897	1898	1899	1900
Started 1885–1888													
Total balances	3,281	2,879	5,231	8,698	11,915	8,329	5,737 [a]	8,451	3,604	2,926	—	—	—
Number [b]	*14*	*14*	*14*	*14*	*14*	*14*	*12*	*11*	*7*	*6*	—	—	—
Average balance	234	277	374	621	851	595	478	768	515	488	—	—	—
Started in 1890													
Total balances	—	—	5,635	8,503	11,038	10,141	6,089	2,596 [a]	1,563 [c]	2,019	915	771 [d]	—
Number	—	—	*10*	*10*	*10*	*10*	*10*	*10*	*7*	*5*	*3*	*3*	—
Average balance	—	—	564	850	1,104	1,014	609	260	223	404	305	257	—
Started in 1892													
Total balances	—	—	—	—	1,707	2,501	2,308	2,384	2,529	2,826	—	—	—
Number	—	—	—	—	*4*	*4*	*4*	*4*	*4*	*4*	—	—	—
Average balance	—	—	—	—	427	625	577	596	632	707	—	—	—
Started in 1894													
Total balances	—	—	—	—	—	—	2,181	2,956	2,755	3,285	4,996	3,487	—
Number	—	—	—	—	—	—	*4*	*4*	*4*	*4*	*4*	*4*	—
Average balance	—	—	—	—	—	—	545	739	689	821	1,249	872	—
Total, originated 1895 and earlier													
Total balances [e]	4,887	4,795	12,200	17,639	27,468	21,900	19,244	15,503	15,384	16,512	18,031 [f]	5,297	8,110 [g]
Number	*19*	*19*	*30*	*28*	*30*	*30*	*39*	*38*	*28*	*24*	*13*	*11*	*7*
Average balances	257	252	407	623	916	730	493	407	549	688	1,387 [f]	482	1,159 [g]

Source: Various ledgers.

[a] Includes 2 credit balances.

[b] Ten started in 1888; 1 in 1887; and 3 in 1885.

[c] Includes 3 credit balances.

[d] Includes 1 credit balance.

[e] Includes all 51 partidarios originating 1895 and before.

[f] Includes A. P. Grzelachowski's account of $10,280 which soared in 1898, the year of his death, because of enlarged store and sheep operations at Puerto de Luna. Without Grzelachowski the average was $646.

[g] Includes one partidario with $5,512, paid down to $129 in 1901 and 1902 which balance was written off to P. & L. Without this account the average was $433.

existed for 17 years and two for 18.[49] At the end of that year one of these partidarios owed approximately $400 or 60 per cent more than his 1888 balance, but only one half his peak debt. Another owed $10 though his peak debt had been $1700. The third had acquired a credit or deposit balance of $2500, it having been almost twice that figure the year before. In prior years he normally had owed a balance of $500 to $900.

One can only conclude, considering the depression times and the fact that few of these partidarios had shown any ability to free themselves of debt without aid of outside discipline, that the partido system as used by the Charles Ilfeld Company in the period prior to 1888 and through 1907 attained reasonable success as a producer of income to partidarios and as a supplementary tool in the whole collection program.[50] This limited success, however, needs to be appraised in the light of the undisciplined appetites which these people held for pleasure and leisure—or as the partidarios might have expressed it—fiesta and siesta.

Troubles with Partidarios

For the amount of direct or indirect return that Ilfeld received on his partido investments, his resulting problems with partidarios were somewhat burdensome—certainly to Max Nordhaus who was always on the front line. Nordhaus, in his supervision of these contracts, found it necessary to maintain a constant watchfulness against the known weaknesses of these sheep tenders.[51] He was dealing with a situation that evidently was similar to the problems faced by the sheep owners of fourteenth-century Spain who, as members of the Mesta, relied on national ordinances to impose strict regulations of duties and behavior upon shepherds, who as a group possessed a reputation for lawlessness.[52]

The propensity to drink excessively was as indigenous to this class of labor in 1890 as it had been in 1390. Nordhaus, unfortunately, had no legal weapon to prevent tippling on the job, and when he brought threats through letters he even had to coin a Spanish word to call attention to the source of trouble. "Lay off the Juisque," he wrote.[53] To the brother of another partidario he admonished: "you must not sell him not one drop of Juisque." [54]

Whereas the ordinances of the Mesta forebade the leaving of sheep untended, Nordhaus could only threaten. "I have been informed by various persons that you have not been taking proper care of the herd. . . . All my *partidarios* assure me that they will go with the herds when they pasture afar. . . . I have commissioned the carrier of this, Bruno Martinez, to inform me about the result of my letter . . . if not perfectly satisfactory I will be obliged to take away the herd." [55]

There was the problem, too, paralleling the experiences of Old Spain, of preventing the unauthorized sale of sheep. This was a constant danger, and it was reflected in the passage of Territorial legislation in 1882 permitting the filing of partido contracts with the county clerk in order to prevent innocent or conspiring buyers from gaining ownership of contracted sheep.[56] Goldenberg wrote from Roswell in 1897 that "mexicans . . . are selling right & left regardless of Partido Contracts or mortgages." [57] To one partidario Nordhaus sent a letter to forestall the sale of ewes. "You ought to know you have no authority to sell a single head." [58]

In seeking to prevent such unauthorized sales of sheep the partido contract generally contained a clause requiring "a lien on all sheep owned by said ________ for the full and faithful compliance with all the conditions of this contract." [59] In explanation of this security, Nordhaus wrote the following to F. N. Page of Puerto de Luna: [60]

> I am informed that Ramon Campos & T. B. Giddings have sold to you some Wethers. If so, I hereby notify you that neither of them can do so without my consent, R. Campos having given me a chattel mortgage on *all* his sheep and T. B. Giddings having a Partido Contract with me which expressly stipulates that I shall have a lien on *all* his sheep and that he agrees not to sell *any* until my contract is fulfilled and satisfied. I therefore caution you against the purchase of any sheep from either of them. Santiago Giddings also gave me a mortgage on all his sheep, but I gave him my consent to contract wethers with you provided proceeds are paid to me.

A very serious loss of partido sheep occurred in 1898 when as many as 900 head, under contract and the care of two brother partidarios, Filomeno and Severo Maes, disappeared. Evidence soon developed that the sheep had been sold to certain suspected parties. The loss was particularly nettling to Nordhaus because the Maes brothers had been discovered once before selling sheep in small numbers which had been mortgaged to the company. Nordhaus had forgiven them because, as he wrote: "we did not care to take the sheep from them." [61] No doubt one of the reasons for this leniency had been the large accounts they owed the company which could not have been satisfied without taking all or most of the sheep entrusted to the brothers.

In addition to his having given these men reprieve for their earlier misdemeanors, Nordhaus had permitted them to live on Ilfeld's ranches near Puerto de Luna without charging them rent.[62] In writing to Goldenberg, who had left the employ of the company a few months before to join in a merchandise firm with his brother, Alex, at Liberty and Tucumcari, he described the Maes boys as "the most ungrateful scoundrels I have heard of yet; after being kept up the way we did . . . they ought to be sent to the Pen." [63]

A month later Nordhaus had further reason for dismay. The man he had hired in August, 1897, to take Goldenberg's place, William Hunter, and who had been described by Nordhaus as "a daisy for collecting," appeared to Nordhaus, from growing evidence, to have been in collusion with the Maes brothers.[64] Although Hunter vigorously denied he had had any connection with the illegal sale, Nordhaus fired him and brought suit in the District Court at Puerto de Luna.[65] There does not appear, however, to have been any recovery of losses. In the meantime Filomeno Maes was unable to reduce his ledger account of more than $1300 and it was charged off to Profit and Loss along with the 900 head of sheep.

The illegal sale of mortgaged sheep was also tied into the gypsy problem that had been so severe in the sheep industry of Old Spain, although in New Mexico the phenomenon, perhaps, holds more interest than significance. Nordhaus was troubled occasionally by the threat of *Los Arabes,* an itinerant group of middle-easterners, who in the 1890's offered partidarios an enticing sales outlet that, on appearance, would be difficult to check.[66] Nordhaus kept on friendly terms with several of these people, even renting store quarters to one of them (who has fathered a large and prominent family in New Mexico).[67] On one occasion Nordhaus was informed by "one of the Arabs" that two partidarios of the company, located in Salado, New Mexico, had sold the Arab some sheep which carried an Ilfeld mortgage. The sale of these sheep evoked the following letter from Nordhaus to a friend or relative of the partidarios. It sets forth strongly the protective nature of the partido agreement.[68]

> I have heard that Don Bacilio has sold either ewes or wethers to an Arab and I wish you would go to him with this in order to advise him that he must not sell any wethers or ewes until I am paid my partido and balances. I have nothing against him trading with others after he pays me but I wish that you as a friend see that he does not sell any more until I have been paid. I await your answer.

By this practice of requiring a partidario to reserve the increase in sheep for balances owed the company, many accounts were kept within bounds and made more secure. The typical partidario, perhaps unhappy at times with this regimen of forced saving, was helped by the discipline forced upon him. It was another example of the program of credits and collections which Ilfeld so skillfully developed and Nordhaus so conscientiously followed. It was the assumed obligation of Charles Ilfeld and Max Nordhaus to devise and create opportunities for their customers that would enable these people, in trying times, to remain solvent and in better times to enlarge their trade. At no time, however, were Ilfeld or Nordhaus lax in bringing persistent and firm pressure upon those who lagged in reducing their accounts.

Demand for Partido Contracts

The point emphasized, that a main purpose of the use of the partido contract was to aid selected customers, seems even more conclusive in view of the demand Nordhaus faced for partido ewes. Except in rare instances, as in the Montano case, when Nordhaus did some bargaining to persuade an individual that his debt should be paid with sheep to be left on partido, no effort was needed to place sheep on shares.[69] More times than not Nordhaus could not fill the demand without resorting to further heavy borrowings, though by waiting for inventories of ewes to accumulate, as deliveries on account were made, he was able to satisfy the need partially. This was true in the summers of 1891, 1892, and 1894, as well as in the fall of 1895 and the spring of 1898.[70] No doubt this was a normal situation, because many requests from regular customers in other years, too, were refused or postponed.[71] In the fall of 1893, when the financing of a sheep drive was bringing Ilfeld to the brink of his credit capacity, Nordhaus reiterated that he had no intention of placing sheep on shares; rather he wanted to sell them.[72] A frequent observation by Nordhaus was that no sheep could be made available to partidarios unless other partidarios would give up some of their flocks voluntarily.[73] Apparently this was not a normal expectancy.

The great majority of requests for sheep on shares came from the Spanish-speaking segment of the economy. Because these people, economically as a group, represented the marginal element and have been identified with the partidario class, the temptation often has been to assume, as has been noted before, that the partido system thrived on the unequal bargaining power of the small rancher as opposed to the large merchant or sheep patron. In Ilfeld's case, though he reserved this form of contract almost exclusively for native ranchers, it was not for lack of opportunity to place them elsewhere. Many "Anglos," some of whom were large ranchers who knew well the economic merits of the Ilfeld agreement, also made numerous requests for partido sheep.

James J. Dolan, an established and successful rancher in Lincoln County, asked Ilfeld for a partido contract in 1891.[74] Emil Fritz, also a prominent livestock man, in 1894, wanted to rent 3000 ewes.[75] In both cases the requests were not fulfilled because, as Ilfeld stated, he did not wish to invest more in sheep.[76] He refused to place sheep in El Paso, Texas, as, indeed, he refused in such distant places as Nebraska, Kansas, and Arizona, though in the last-named case Nordhaus gave the matter some consideration.[77] The Trigg Brothers of Amarillo, Texas, were refused sheep even though this firm appeared to be interested in contract terms calling for a rental of 25 weaned wethers per 100 ewes—a higher figure than the records reveal Ilfeld ever charged.[78]

A number of other requests for partido contracts of the Charles Ilfeld Company also were received from ranchers with English and North-European surnames.[79] A typical reply to these letters is an answer to Cornelio Hendron of Endee, New Mexico, stating: "We have so many applications that we have to give preference to . . . customers." [80]

The fact that there existed a rather widespread demand for Ilfeld's standard partido contract, not alone from regular customers of the company but also from a number of sheep growers who might have been considered shrewder in economic matters than the typical native rancher to whom Ilfeld contracted ewes, may be accepted as reasonable proof that the terms of Ilfeld's partido agreements were considered favorable. The fact, too, that in the face of this demand Ilfeld preferred to keep his substantial and often burdensome investment in partido sheep confined to his own customers—though in many cases his direct profit suffered for the troubles they gave him—adds weight to the conclusion offered: that direct profit was the least of the motives for the adoption of the partido system by Charles Ilfeld. The cohesiveness of these and other bits of evidence discussed in the above sections add credence to the belief that, along with the protection the partido contract gave to selected accounts receivable, it offered fair income opportunities to a group of Spanish-speaking customers whose economic plight was at least ameliorated thereby.

Protection against Loss of Customers

One cannot separate this policy of protecting receivables and aiding customers, however, from the policy of holding customers whose earning power and trade would otherwise be lost. Several examples appear in the records of partido contracts that were used as competitive weapons to hold the trade of customers who were being weaned away from Las Vegas as the center of economic nourishment, or who were being tempted to place their affection with Ilfeld's competitors.

When Francisco Garcia, who lived in Chaperito some 25 miles southeast of Las Vegas, showed signs of taking his trade elsewhere, Charles Ilfeld held him with the promise of such a partido contract. He wrote thus to Goldenberg: [81]

> The Bearer of this Francisco Garcia of Chaparito [*sic*] is a Customer of ours & has a few sheep of his own & I have given him on shares the 55 sheep of Jesus Gallegos of Chaparito, in order to keep him as a customer. If you have in the meantime rec'd any more sheep of anybody turn him [*sic*] over to him on shares at 2# Wool each year. I think about 250 to 350. . . .

Another rather evident example of the use of a partido contract to hold the wool and merchandise business of a nearby ranching family was the placing of 350 sheep on shares with Leandro Casaus in 1888, a partido agreement that remained with the Casaus family until 1901.[82] Goldenberg had been instructed to deal diplomatically with these individuals because their wool shipments were large and generally of good quality, and their financial independence was real. Leandro negotiated a contract that permitted him the privilege of having 12 per cent of the value of the partido sheep charged to his account each year in lieu of delivering two pounds of wool per head. Actually the value of the sheep loaned was set at $1.00 per head, which very likely was no more than one half the market value of the sheep. The cash entry of $42 compares with $98 to $105 that Ilfeld would have received from the Casaus wool had he demanded and received the normal rental of two pounds of wool per head.[83] In the following years the same advantage to Leandro Casaus prevailed. In view of the disparity in favor of this partidario, coupled with a later statement by Nordhaus that he did not want anyone else to purchase the Casaus wool even if it had to be handled without profit, there is indication that the partido contract was used on occasion as a competitive weapon.[84]

In Lincoln County, in the southeast part of the Territory, the threat of heavy account losses attracted the partido contract there. As the depression deepened these sheepmen, even more distant by rail from eastern markets than ranchers to the north, felt the unfavorable divergence of export and import prices to a much greater degree. The price they could obtain for their wool and sheep at the ranch was less because of distance to market, and the prices of finished goods they bought were higher. Until the railroad from Pecos City, Texas, was built northward through the Pecos Valley in the 1890's and extended to Amarillo, Texas, in 1898, these sheepmen still could be persuaded to ship their wool to Las Vegas, although increasingly they traded with such firms as Browne and Manzanares in Socorro to the east by way of the Hondo Valley. Unless Nordhaus could hold the sheep assets of these customers through contract, he ran a grave risk that other merchants, nearer at hand, would obtain payments on their receivables first. The partido contract not only offered some protection on this score but, as sound collection policy would dictate, it aided in friendly relations by offering the partidario the possibility of increased earnings.

In the years 1888 to 1893, roughly one third of the 30 or so partido contracts were given to ranchers in Lincoln County (see Table 14). Twenty-four of the 30 partidario accounts existing in 1890 possess ledger notations showing the quantity of wool these men delivered that year. Those from Lincoln County were responsible for half again more wool per contract than those few from the Las Vegas area, and more than twice that of the average contract in the vicinity of Puerto de Luna. It seems unlikely that such a disparity could in any significant measure be the result of higher fleece weights in Lincoln County. Rather we must assume that the number of partido sheep per contract in that area bore a comparable distribution to the inflow of partido wool.

Little by little these Lincoln accounts disappeared from the books,

TABLE 14. Location of partido contracts

Area	1888	1889	1890	1891	1892	1893	1894	1895
Las Vegas	6	6	4	4	3	3	8	7
Puerto de Luna	5	5	13	12	15	15	21	21
Endee	2	3	3	3	3	3	3	3
Lincoln	6	6	10 [a]	10 [a]	10 [a]	10 [a]	8	7
Total	19	20	30	29	31	31	40	38

Source: Various ledgers.

[a] Includes three contracts belonging to members of the Lueras family located in the Manzano-Pinos Wells-Red Cloud area. The last named, in Lincoln County prior to 1893, became a Valencia County post office in 1893 when the southern border of the latter county was shifted southward slightly. Another member of the family, Aniceto, lived in White Oaks.

however, but Nordhaus would have lost them sooner had he not, with the aid of the partido contract, held them reasonably well through most of the 1890's. In 1903, he bemoaned the fact that "the Lincoln wool—even our own Partido—was delivered by our Partidarios to Lincoln Trading Co. [Jaffa]." [85] This had occurred even though by this time the Charles Ilfeld Company had established a warehouse at Santa Rosa, New Mexico, on the Rock Island Railroad some 80 to 100 miles closer to the Lincoln-White Oaks area.[86] A few loyal partidarios, however, stayed with him, as, for example, Esperidion Lueras, whose partido contract was enlarged in 1899 in order to secure his sheep business.[87] But the economics of the problem, gaining an ever-increasing hand, turned this business to Roswell—the growing economic town of southeastern New Mexico.

Surplus Sheep and Land Policy

The partido system was useful to Ilfeld and Nordhaus only as long as, in one way or another, it served as an aid in the collection process. It did this, as we have seen, by increasing the earning power of certain debtor customers after having funded current obligations for easier future payments. Although prominent as a competitive weapon, the system was, even in this form, more often a protective device to hold old business in distant places until such time as debts could be liquidated.

A third method by which this system was used in the collection process was the facility it afforded as a reservoir for unsold sheep which judgment often dictated should be held for a more propitious marketing opportunity. The need often occurred in the middle or late fall, when collections of sheep could not be sold to northern feeders so late in the season, or, in the years of the sheep drives, when sheep could not join the long trek that had already started. Some herds, therefore, had to be held for many months after delivery, and the system of renting them out again was fitted to meet this development.

This obvious use of the partido contract was made the more opportunistic by Ilfeld's long-standing policy of keeping his capital at work in situations that permitted its rapid turnover—a policy that precluded any extensive investment in land.[88] Prior to 1899 the Charles Ilfeld Company did not hold much land for pasturage purposes but chose, rather, to keep surplus sheep with customers whose private ranches, though small, could be supplemented by the expanse of public range.[89]

The only need this company had for range land was at those times of the year when preparations were being made for a sheep drive or for the filling of a large contract. This necessitated the gathering of flocks from various ranches and the caring for them in some central place. In 1895 and 1896, and other years as well, when the flocks of sheep were being gathered, the favorite spot was the Conchas country on range that extended from Cabra, some 35 miles southeast of Vegas, eastward for another 30 miles or so.[90] Here there was plenty of free pasture and good places to lease.[91] By 1903, Henry Huneke's ranch, near Cabra, was overgrazed and "eaten out." [92] Nordhaus sent Manuel Delgado, who had been a general hand about the store, to this area to care for the growing herds in the spring and summer of 1896, and when this employee left the company Nordhaus replaced him with Luis Sena until the flocks could be marketed.[93]

There was a limit to which this flexible land policy could be pushed, however, and Nordhaus decided, in 1893, to acquire a ranch at the head of the Vegoso, within a few yards of the old Santa Fe Trail, some four or five miles east of Las Vegas.[94] Here he constructed corrals where, if sheepmen would deliver their flocks, thus saving the cost of gathering by the company, a bonus of 5 cents per head was paid.[95] The location, close enough to Las Vegas to enable Nordhaus to take prospective buyers to the site, was equipped as a dipping station where sheep could be freed of scabies before they were marketed.[96] Those sheepmen who wished to bring their flocks there for shearing were permitted to pasture them without charge, though shearing costs were 3 cents per head.[97] For an additional 5 cents per hundredweight—the customer furnishing the sacks—the wool was packed and delivered to Las Vegas.[98] This became the gathering point for all the partidas.[99]

The Vegoso ranch, however, had several drawbacks. Water frequently was scarce, and grass could not stand up under the grazing and the stinted moisture.[100] In either the spring or fall it was likely to be too cold on the mesa for dipping sheep, and Nordhaus found that this necessary operation had to be curtailed on occasion.[101] Because the need for the ranch was sporadic, it was only manned upon notice of a day or two that flocks were on their way.[102]

In November of the years 1897 and 1898 camp was broken—in the former year because all the sheep present were sold, and in the latter because of cold weather.[103] In cold weather the herds were taken "below the mesa" toward the Cabra—a region to the southeast.[104] In October, 1899, Vegoso was abandoned, and the herds were moved to a spot one mile west of Bado de Juan Pais near the confluence of the Tecolote and Pecos rivers just below Dilia, where corrals were set up on land which does not appear to have been owned by Ilfeld.[105]

This was the last temporary arrangement. Forces were at work that within a few years would change markedly the direction of sheep policy of the Charles Ilfeld Company. From a program of flexible operations, based primarily on the partido system and the public range, the company adopted large-scale specialization in sheep husbandry necessitating substantial investments in real estate and livestock.

XII

SEDENTARY SHEEP HUSBANDRY

Forces at Work

Homesteading. A persistent force in the ultimate passing of the partido system as a significant institution in New Mexico was the movement to settle and control the public range. The Homestead Act of 1862 had encouraged citizens, actual and potential, to file claims on small acreages, though the railroad at a later date provided a more practical incentive. As this movement progressed, and as the opportunities for achieving control of large and strategic acreages through this movement became apparent, the little partidario was pressed increasingly to find the succulent public pasture he needed to supplement the small land holding he could call his own.

Few individuals took advantage of the government's largesse in New Mexico until after 1880, when the number of claims that were filed jumped significantly. Whereas only 90 claims had been recorded prior to 1881 (and none before 1873), the next 10 years brought an average of more than 200 per year, and by the turn of the century the records show the annual volume of claims to have been running at approximately 400. By 1900, more than 750,000 acres in homesteads had been recorded as final entries in New Mexico.[1]

The change that had taken place by 1904 has been described, in part, by the *American Shepherd's Bulletin.* It marveled at the large tracts that once had been open ranges of government land but which had been absorbed by homestead settlers. "The ranchman," it stated, "can no longer enjoy the boon of letting his flocks wander over vast stretches of grazing country." [2] Two years later, the "Old Observer," traveling correspondent of the *American Shepherd's Bulletin,* found the change most impressive from Puerto de Luna east to Tucumcari.[3] This, in general, had been the munching ground for the sheep belonging to a number of Ilfeld's partidarios. This reporter described a route extending southwest from a point north of Tucumcari Mountain to south of the staked plains then east "as far as one can see" as having "homesteads galore." [4] He facetiously commented that this land was being appropriated by "Oklahoma boomers, irrepressible Texans, and expectant Hoosiers." [5]

Control of the public range. The effect, however, which the Homestead Act had upon the partido system cannot be measured alone by numbers of entries or thousands of acres. The problem of this enclosure movement was not only the engrossing of minor acreages by private interests but, in addition, it was the controlling of vast expanses of public range by those homesteads through monopoly control of water resources. The Public Lands Commission, in 1905, regretted that exceptions to public land policy had been made generally so as to permit "entries being spread out in all sorts of shapes along streams or waterways." [6]

The virtual control of great areas of contiguous lands through strategic claims was made easier by a clause in the original free Homestead Act, known as the Commutation Clause, which permitted the payment of cash of $1.25 per acre ($2.50 within certain railroad grants) after an actual residence on the property of only six months.[7] With a residence requirement of such short duration, it became practicable for one person, restricted as he was to filing on one homestead, to use a nominee, often an employee such as a cowboy or sheepherder, as the legal resident and claimant of a homestead.[8] During that period of residence the building of a fence and the improvement of grass could meet the investment and "cultivation" provisions of the Act.[9] The ownership of many of these holdings proved temporary, and titles found their way into the hands of large cattle and sheep owners. Thus, through a number of small plots of land, each of which effectively controlled water resources, it was possible to hold sway over vast stretches of contiguous public land.[10]

The movement toward private control of the public range was fostered further through the use of government transferable scrip which had been issued as a bonus to the veterans of the Civil War and other wars, and which could be exchanged for public lands without meeting the residence and improvement requirements of the Homestead Act. The "Young Observer" noted in 1902 that much scrip was being purchased by ranchers at $3.50 to $6.00 per acre, which, in turn, was being used to gain ownership of water holes or creek beds commanding control of surrounding range.[11]

Again we are much indebted to the "Young Observer" for the notes he made on the land holdings of many individuals. He wrote of J. R. Aquilar, Postmaster at Wagonmound, who owned and leased 3500 acres "besides his government range." [12] Apparently it was this same reporter who, while in northeastern New Mexico, described a ranch on the Corrumpaw Creek belonging to Edward M. Wight as comprising 3000 acres "so located over this area as to give him grazing privileges over the whole." [13] The Alamocita Ranch, 16 miles north of Clayton, owned by J. L. DeHaven, held 4000 acres of patented land with "government range surrounding it." [14]

Northeast of Santa Rosa, just to the west and north of Cuervo, the "Old Observer" noted four years later that the Llano Sheep Company controlled many sections of grazing land which resulted from its owning a large part of the water in a great area "which practically makes them proprietors of the feed all around." [15] South of this, near Puerto de Luna, the "Young Observer" previously had found Charles Sumner with his 2000 acres of patented land "besides the government range which his ranches" controlled.[16] And, of course, he could not have missed the Salado Livestock Company of Guadalupe County, owned by the governor of the Territory, Miguel A. Otero, and his Territorial secretary, Jefferson W. Raynolds. The land they controlled, which was to the southeast of Pastura, was described by this "Young Observer" as having "water rights for 30 miles along the Salado River" in command of "a fine range of 30 miles square." [17]

The symbol of this control of range was "the fence" and, not unlike its counterpart in the enclosure movements of sixteenth-century England and Spain (though Gras points out the American movement had none of the same serious consequences), it brought resentment and retaliation.[18] Fence-cutting in San Miguel and Mora counties, at least, had become a problem of some import by 1890. The Las Vegas *Democrat* wrote of the threatening notes that many ranchers were receiving—notes that often were followed with depredations. Wilson Waddingham had received a threat to cut fences on his ranch some five miles out of Las Vegas. The La Cueva Ranch, near Mora, also had been warned. A mile of fence was reported to have been destroyed in Mora County and the home and contents of another ranch burned.[19] The *Las Vegas Optic,* a few months later, with a plague-on-both-your-houses approach, editorialized: "Down with the fence-cutters and the land grabbers. Both are alike hurtful to the country." [20] Sympathizing with the little fellow, this Republican newspaper expressed its feeling again. "While fence cutting is wrong . . . fencing up pasturage, water, wood and roadways from the people to whom the privilege of access belongs is a greater crime." [21]

"Another peculiar phase of the present situation," wrote the editor of the *Las Vegas Optic,* "is the fact that some individuals who have no titles have enclosed tens of thousands of acres." [22] It was this latter phase of the fencing movement that brought serious repercussions and gave rise to vigilante groups which took matters into their own hands. Nordhaus referred to them in a letter to Goldenberg: "White Caps are cutting all fences in the neighborhood. . . . Pastures . . . unsafe." [23] This group, like those lawless bands of the same name who terrified the countryside of southern Indiana but a few years before, and earlier in other parts of the country, focused their activities, at first, on some of the large enclosed tracts of grazing land located on the Las Vegas Grant to which the owners did not have clear title.[24]

Marcus Brunswick and the local Republican Party of Las Vegas, of which he was treasurer, tried to make political capital of these depredations by attaching these lawless acts to the People's Party, a reform group of Republicans and Democrats. It was a campaign which he described as "only the good people against the bad." [25] In a money-raising effort he wrote to Wilson Waddingham: "If the People's ticket is successful, I think they will tax everything high and will cut more fences." [26] Earlier he had written to an out-of-Territory resident: "There is nothing new here except fence cutting going on all the time. In my opinion this will stop when the election is over. It is all Politics." [27] It was a blow to Brunswick that the "bad" people won the election, but, to the extent one may surmise that the success of the coalition group was a reflection in part of discontent over the enclosing of land, few would argue that this election was the reason fence-cutting continued to be a problem.[28]

By 1906, however, it was more often the large livestock operator who, like Colonel Brewton in *Sea of Grass*, was being oppressed by the homesteader who nested on "someone else's" public pasture.[29] The firm of Floersheim and Abbott, Solomon Floersheim's sheep partnership in the Springer area, was having just such trouble. Following an interview with the partner, H. C. Abbott, the "Old Observer" noted that this firm had suffered "frightful" losses in its effort to run sheep on open land to forestall settlement, and the situation evidently was becoming more serious as a result of five or six recent claims that had been filed on the Floersheim and Abbott pasture.[30]

This correspondent thought the Floersheim example typical enough to comment that, as a result of such friction on the open range, livestock men "are acquiring vast tracts of land" which seemed to him to push acreage beyond economical operation.[31] Increasingly the public range either was becoming controlled or owned by the large livestock interests.

As for the small rancher, often a partidario, he was being "fenced out" —slowly in the 1890's, but with much speed in the first decade of the twentieth century.

Depletion of pastures. It would be unfortunate and misleading, however, to imply that the baser motives of selfish men were at the root of the fencing problems and thus of the decline of the partido system. Far more important in the picture was the inevitable failure of a policy that had permitted unlimited exploitation of the free government range. In New Mexico and the arid Southwest, where frequently recurring droughts are always a threat to good pasture, nature had not a chance against the prodigal appetites that ate of the common capital. Nor, in general, had the partidarios and small ranchers who, competing for the best forage, quite literally had been eating themselves out of house and home.[32] As a result, the potentially successful rancher was forced to lean upon the only weapon of self preservation he had—the fence.

This was the same weapon that a predecessor of his had turned to (without the barbed wire) on the high, northern plateaus of New Spain some 350 years or more earlier. In an important and recent study it appears that, by the time evidence clearly reveals that the virgin pastures, which had been open to all, could no longer support the multiplication of livestock (1565–1570), the estancia, or fenced ranch, was achieving definite form (1563–1567).[33] In spite of the fact that the establishment of enclosures was a "privilege" (grace), granted by the Viceroy, it is apparent through the restrictions that were placed on the number of grazing head, beginning in the 1550's and 1560's, that enclosures were a necessary part of the survival of this pastoral economy.[34]

In New Mexico, as in New Spain, we find the enclosure movement gaining its greatest impetus as the number of livestock on the range reached its peak and began its decline.[35] By 1890, the animal unit population had reached its peak of more than 2,000,000, from which in the next decade it dropped to a figure only slightly above 1,500,000.[36] Animals on feed, however, rose from almost nil, in 1890, to approximately 100,000 in 1900, and 300,000 in 1910.[37]

In a free and open, eater-take-all approach, sheep and cattle growers ignored the common sense of conservative stocking of the pastures.[38] Assuming conservation might have been practiced here and there, the sheep industry was not provincial in its grazing habits, and public pastures invited distant herders. In periods when drought was not particularly severe in New Mexico but hit with force elsewhere, the movement of sheep from afar increased the stocking. In 1898, for instance, well over 6000 sheep from Colorado were seen grazing on the Santa Fe east mesa and fear was expressed that 12,000 more would soon be there from the drought districts of California.[39]

Whereas Nordhaus was writing in 1895 that plenty of free pasture existed, and a year later that good places could be leased within a radius of 50 miles south and east of Las Vegas, both he and the "Young Observer" commented several years later on the abuse of pasture that had taken place.[40] The latter wrote in 1902 that "either it was unusually dry or the range between Santa Rosa and Las Vegas was badly overstocked. I think, from what I can learn, that the latter was the case." [41]

Overgrazing was noted in 1898 on the government's Pecos Reserve to the northwest of Las Vegas where even the trees were being denuded.[42] A hundred miles or so to the south and east, in the vicinity of Tucumcari, the pastures in 1902 appeared to have been overstocked.[43] A year before, in the central east part of the Territory, in the area of the Salt

Lakes and Seven Lakes, huge acreages of free pasture were stated to have been "clean as a board," causing fear of serious losses because of "the overcrowding of the range and the prevailing drought."[44] All this was prior to the great drought of 1903 and 1904.

As serious deterioration through overstocking continued, the migrations of sheep from winter to summer ranges (reminiscent of the much greater migrations of the Mesta in Spain), over pastures that were being restricted increasingly in area by homesteaders, brought great destruction to grasses on the intermediate and mountain ranges.[45] The tendency of flockmasters was to leave the depleted winter ranges and their feed lots earlier and earlier each spring to take advantage of the fresh shoots that appeared first on the higher pastures.

The end result of this progressive deterioration was obvious to all fair-minded men and even to some prejudiced ones. The Public Lands Commission in its 1905 report admitted that the free range system had been a destructive one and that the question of changing it demanded grave consideration. "Where the carrying capacity [of the range] has increased," the report states, "it has been mostly due to fencing pastures." Even illegal fencing received a back-handed compliment for the improvements it had achieved, and the report added that "some way perhaps should be provided to maintain fences."[46]

In the first years of the century the stockmen who controlled their public pastures were opposed, in general, to the issuance of permits or licenses for the use of government lands and preserves.[47] In 1900, when a number of rules and regulations for forest pasture use were drawn by the General Land Office, prominent men connected with the sheep industry in New Mexico, like Harry F. Lee, secretary of the New Mexico Sheep Sanitary Board, Harry Kelly, Solomon Luna, and W. S. Prager, were reported to have recorded themselves against this move at the 1903 meeting of the National Wool Growers Association.[48] They, like the majority of the industry, soon changed their minds if it is true, as reported, that little was said on leasing of public lands in a meeting of the National Wool Growers Association at Albuquerque in September, 1906. The about-face had been so abrupt in some cases that the "Old Observer," in commenting on the remarks of Solomon Luna and Frank Hubbell to the effect that the Reserve was a good thing, wrote: "Those gentlemen surely are great jokers."[49]

Certainly as Max Nordhaus appraised the changing situation in the light of the deteriorating and shrinking free government pastures on the one hand, and the problems he was having with partidarios on the other, it is little wonder that as early as 1897, with wool and sheep prices promising an end to their long decline, he was pressing Charles Ilfeld to establish a sheep ranching company with A. G. Mills of Puerto de Luna. He wanted to stock this company, in part at least, with sheep taken from "such people as the Maes Bros. & Lucian Trujillo." [50]

Toward Sedentary Sheep Husbandry

In evaluating the change in sheep policy that Max Nordhaus evidently was pressing upon Charles Ilfeld in the latter half of 1897, it is important to recognize that the business environment in which he operated was experiencing a buoyancy that offered a stimulating contrast to the four acute depression years just preceding. All aspects of the firm's business were showing marked upward trends: cash and credit sales, collections in money and kind, as well as prices of sheep and wool. It was a great release to this young man of thirty-two years who, with full responsibility, had fought expediently and successfully to hold the gains of predepression years and who was quick to sense the new opportunities for expansion. The problems with the partidarios, the dwindling quality of the pasture accompanied, as it was, with a faster tempo to the enclosure movement, must have focused his attention on the changing character of the sheep industry in New Mexico. The McKinley tariff and the sharp rise in wool prices touched off that speculative impulse which, though always under control, allowed him to reorient his thinking when the major forces appeared to be pushing in a common direction.

Nordhaus worked off his stronger instincts for speculation on the purchase of large clips of wool, but in planning for the larger and permanent investments in land and fences, windmills and wells, he was slower to move.[51] The drag was not all caution on the part of the young man. Charles Ilfeld had to be persuaded, although not in the sense that this proprietor, now fifty years of age, would be adamant or even stubborn. The older man simply sensed much more acutely than Nordhaus that neither of them was "at home" on a sheep ranch. He had always been reluctant to embark on a venture that he could not control himself when an emergency arose. He was, in the truest sense, a sedentary merchant who kept the bulk of his investment in moving merchandise—compromising as little as possible with the sunk costs of fixed property.

Ilfeld was touchy on any sheep deal that caused a substantial outlay of money, and as Nordhaus presented situations that would open avenues to such commitments, a silence seemed to fall upon any hope of consummation. An opportunity to join with their good friend Prager of Roswell in running a large herd of sheep for speculation did not materialize even though Nordhaus emphasized the chance to ride a new cycle of higher prices and the promise of Prager "to personally look after the sheep in case we bought them together." [52] The time was still not far removed from the prolonged sheep drive of 1895 and 1896, when disastrous losses had threatened almost daily and when but a few months after the closing of that venture Ilfeld had written heatedly to Max Goldenberg stating clearly the company's defensive policy. "I have explicitly impressed on your mind that we dont want to buy cattle or sheep on speculation, we want to collect only." [53]

In August, 1897, Nordhaus was proposing that the company buy out John Gerhardt, whose ranch and equipment in the Santa Rosa area would be attractive for a small operation. Gerhardt had been a slow remitter and the temptation was great. "[It] is a hard problem," Nordhaus wrote to Ilfeld. "I think we better buy him out paying him a good price." [54] The thought of acquiring this property for company use seems not to have blossomed further.

An actual offer was made to A. G. Mills of Puerto de Luna for his ranch properties and livestock in September with the proviso that Mills remain in charge of the outfit at a salary to be agreed upon. Apparently, Mills, who was in need of money at the time and who had requested that an offer be made, wanted a partnership or sharing arrangement—an agreement that Ilfeld seems not to have been willing to make. Ilfeld left the door open, however, as indicated in a later letter from Nordhaus that noted Mills had been informed that "we may go into the sheep bus. together with him next year." [55]

In spite of the fact that no positive steps toward sedentary sheep husbandry were taken in 1897, an indirect approach was followed in the form of leasing lands—a policy which gathered momentum in the years 1898 and 1899. One example of leasing near Santa Rosa occurred in 1897, but in March of the following year Nordhaus was bargaining actively with McDonagh and Associates of Puerto de Luna to rent their land for lambing purposes.[56] Negotiations fell through when McDonagh dropped dead after a siege of pneumonia.[57] In April Nordhaus was advising his agents, Lujan and Pinard, to lease suitable lambing grounds between Liberty and Endee, an area that previously had been noted for its good grass on free government pasture.[58]

Toward the end of 1899, when plans were already under way to start a sheep company at Pintada, and orders were going out to fence some recently acquired land on the Borica Spring, negotiations were being carried on for more permanent leases.[59] Cruz Cedillo, a former partidario in the Lincoln area, offered to lease his ranch and range to the Charles Ilfeld Company for a multiyear period. Nordhaus was enthusiastic because it offered opportunities to lamb 5000 to 10,000 sheep with ample water supplies available through three wells from which the water could be piped short distances to tanks.[60]

A few days later Nordhaus was thinking of leasing the Atanacio Sandoval Ranch, probably in the vicinity of Puerto de Luna, where at the

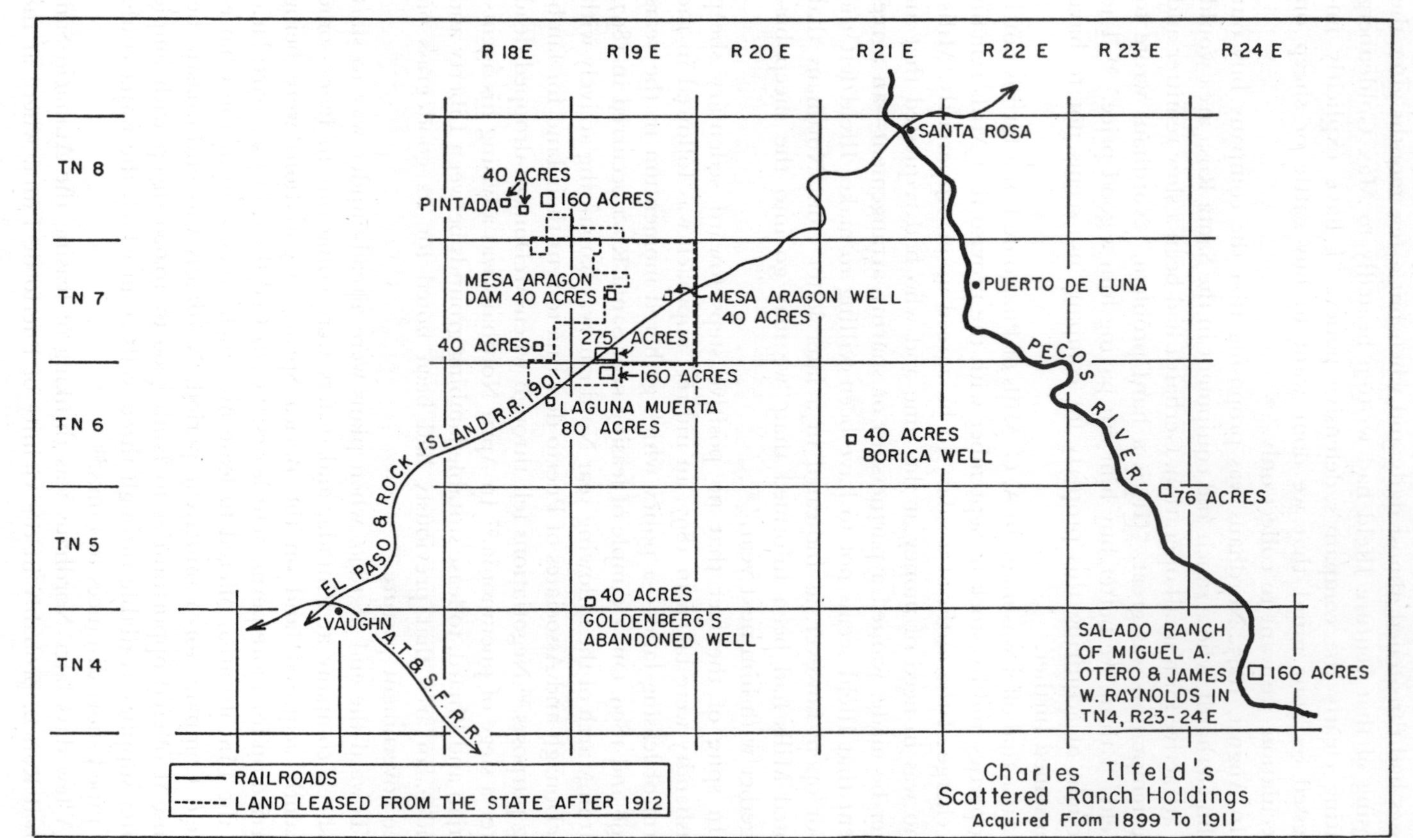

Charles Ilfeld's
Scattered Ranch Holdings
Acquired From 1899 To 1911

well sites he would erect windmills to be left in place when the lease would expire.[61] Neither of these proposals was acted upon. Ilfeld had given in enough when he finally permitted Nordhaus to proceed with plans to acquire land, equipment, and livestock for the launching of a sizable sheep operation some 20 miles up the Pintada, a large draw which drained easterly into the Pecos River a few miles south of Santa Rosa.

Miscellaneous Ranching Properties

The final decision to acquire land for the purpose of establishing a sheep ranch was not made evident until the close of 1899. Prior to that time some ranching land had been taken in payment of accounts receivable though none, with one possible exception, prior to the close of the 1893 to 1897 depression. One pasture, known as the Murillo Claim, which apparently came under ownership in 1896, may have been acquired in this manner.[62] This must have been the property southwest of Vaughn which, in later years, was advertised as the Seven Lakes Ranch. Although it may have commanded government range in addition, the claim amounted to little more than 75 acres.

In the same general area, but somewhat to the south, the Valentin Garcia homestead on 160 acres was accepted in 1898 as payment for his account and was used, perhaps, as part of this Seven Lakes operation until 1902 when it disappears from the records.[63]

Other acquisitions resulting from defaulted accounts were few, and none played any part in the new sheep policy. John Gerhardt's property near Santa Rosa, which in 1897 Nordhaus recommended be bought for a good price, both for the purpose of starting a sheep operation and for removing a bad account from the books, finally was foreclosed upon in December, 1902.[64] The company offered to lease it back to Gerhardt at a nominal figure for three years and then sold it in 1906.[65]

Another piece of property received in payment on account, the José Efren Gonzales Ranch, also in the neighborhood of the Gerhardt land, was a touchy subject to Nordhaus. He had not wanted the land but, having accepted it, was afraid other customers might misunderstand his motives in spite of the many years of demonstratively contrary policy. He wrote sharply to Virginio Casaus: [66]

> I want you to know one thing that I am not here to advance money and merchandise to people hoping that I receive ranches in payment of same. If I can not have the assurance to obtain money of my customers or its equivalent which in time will reduce itself to money, accounts of such customers do not interest me.

Land for Pintada

In November or December, 1899, Max Goldenberg, who had returned to the fold after a year and a half with his brother, Hugo, in Puerto de

Luna, was busy drilling for water at Pintada on the Mesa de Aragon, a high plateau southwest of Santa Rosa where a large area of free government range still existed little marked by homesteaders.[67] Both of the Max's, "Maquecito" Nordhaus and "Big Max" Goldenberg, had each plotted a homestead in the nineteenth range east (see map on page 182). —the former in north township seven, and the latter in north township five.[68] Goldenberg hit water on the Nordhaus stake—"the strongest flow of water," he guessed, "ever struck in this vicinity." He thought he would bring in all the range and water for 50,000 head of sheep inside of two months.[69] He had to abandon a similar effort on his own property, however.[70] Each, of course, was homesteading as a nominee of the Charles Ilfeld Company as both Charles Ilfeld and his son, Herman, who was by that time associated with the firm, would have done had they not already used their privilege in other parts of the territory.[71]

Not being inclined to pay the price of a previously assembled, privately owned ranch, which existed some 30 miles to the southeast in the form of the Salado Cattle Company and which in 1903 was sold to their banker and politico friends, Miguel Otero and Joshua Raynolds, Nordhaus and Ilfeld decided to build Pintada Ranch on government scrip.[72] One exception was to have been the purchase of the William Hoehne homestead and ranch of 160 acres on the Pintada Draw. Their plans were altered somewhat when, having made the purchase for $2500, the title proved doubtful and scrip, later stated to have cost $8.00 per acre, was purchased and placed upon the tract to insure ownership.[73]

This scrip, like a number of similar purchases, had belonged to the Santa Fe Pacific Railroad and had entitled it to lieu lands compensating the railroad for the forest reserves it had been forced to relinquish according to the Forest Reserve Act of 1897.[74] The scrip Nordhaus and Ilfeld purchased originally represented land in the Gila and Salt River areas of the San Francisco Mountains in Arizona.[75]

In explanation of this kind of scrip, Nordhaus wrote Goldenberg: [76]

> As to land scrip you may not be informed that there are various kinds at various prices. The "unrestricted forest reserve scrip" which we have used heretofore is the safest and easiest to apply and therefore, the most costly. Its market value in small pieces is $5.00, in larger tracts $4.00 and $4.50.

Sometimes the application of this scrip turned out to be a dead loss, as when Goldenberg, in another one of his well-drilling ventures, failed to bring up the water. In an effort to control much land with little ownership, scrip was placed upon only 40 acres, but when the water was not forthcoming both Goldenberg and Nordhaus sought an amendment to their scrip hoping to be able to apply it elsewhere. Nordhaus reported straightforwardly in his applicatory letter that he had drilled for water but that he had found none. He wanted to know, however, if the government wanted any other reasons.[77] A week or so later Goldenberg was claiming a surveyor's error had been made in locating the land.[78] Two years later Nordhaus was still trying to influence the General Land Office through a request to Bernard Rodey, territorial representative.[79]

Scrip was bought through Charles F. Easley, Santa Fe broker, and some of it was in the form of Soldier's Warrants issued in return for military service. Nordhaus located an 80-acre tract with a well, for which he expected to obtain a patent within the next few days.[80] A few months later he ordered two 80-acre pieces of scrip through this source but cautioned Easley to guarantee the issue of a patent or to refund the money.[81] One suspects that experience had dictated this precautionary statement.

In 1901 the scrip-buying continued and the effort to control lands through strategic locations became a serious competitive problem.[82] Particularly did Nordhaus find the going rough in vying with his politically strong neighbors, Otero and Raynolds, of the Salado Cattle Company. His efforts to obtain leases on townships set aside for school lands through his lawyer, Charles Spiess, evidently had not been successful, so that it came as a shock when his friends picked the prize plum.[83] In a letter to Goldenberg, he wrote: [84]

> I am going to Santa Fe this afternoon to see Easley & Vance regarding right or wrong of Salado Live Stock Co. taking hold of Normal School Lands without giving other people a show. In the meantime have Rice survey all the important country which we ought to get hold of and control.—Hugo informed me that he has confidential information that Salado Co. will take everything between Moro and Borica so we have to be on our guard, but better do it *on the quiet;* don't make any fuss about it in talking to outsiders as this will do harm only and no good.

The Charles Ilfeld Company had ranches at both Moro, to the south of Pintada, and Borica to the southeast. Nordhaus, from the tone of this letter, had set his eyes on closing the gap between these two and was not happy that Otero and Raynolds might beat him to it. It is surprising, with such evidence of competition, that scrip continued to be in supply. Nordhaus threw some light on this by writing that he would not be able to "get any more for 3 days." [85] Whatever the delay, the price must have remained reasonable because he had just turned down an offer of grazing land at $5.50 per acre as he preferred to acquire it through Easley of Santa Fe if it could be had at the same price.[86]

When William Hoehne, having sold his homestead to Charles Ilfeld, filed on another claim with the Land Office on pasture 25 to 30 miles east of Pintada, an act that was typical of the growing demand for land in this general area, Goldenberg gave vent to his growing appetite for land. Nordhaus, with the restraining hand of Ilfeld on his shoulder, wrote his sheep manager a stern but calming letter: [87]

Filings on the part of other people is something you have no doubt to contend with and if you commence to make other people trouble they will naturally retaliate making us trouble. Now we have to stop some time making further investments or expenses for ranches and as it is not CI's intention or desire to run as many sheep in the future as in the past I think we have enough range; we can not ever-lastingly be building reservoirs and drilling wells and I wish you would manage to get along from now on with investments made up to date.

However, the "scripping" went on and in December, 1903, land was being sought in this manner for acreage near their store at Pastura, the railroad stop for the Pintada Ranch.[88] Scattered plots, embracing four water wells, roughly checkerboarded a much greater area, an area that was gradually filled in with free land over the years.[89]

The holdings remained modest for many years—scarcely exceeding a thousand acres in the Pastura-Pintada area as late as 1919, and in the years 1912 to 1917 most, if not all, of the small and separated ranches about the countryside were sold.[90] A later date brought the fee land at Pintada and its railroad point, Pastura, to more than 27,000 acres, striding the Southern Pacific Railroad—a domain that was augmented by almost 32,000 acres of state leased lands (see map on page 182). Fourteen hundred acres were held under the Taylor Grazing Act, and more than 2500 acres more were under private leases. The maximum area of pasturage within the Pintada Ranch held in fee or lease exceeded 63,000 acres.[91] In the first decade of the century, which was before leased lands became available from the state, such investment was not necessary. Four wells, drilled at strategic points and scattered along the arroyas, improved with reservoirs, commanded ample range.

Sheep Ranching at Pintada

Sheep ranching, in a serious way, was begun toward the end of 1899. To Charles Ilfeld the justification for the project was chiefly as a reservoir for sheep obtained on collections. Upon his return from Europe in the late fall of 1900, having been gone from Las Vegas since January and the country since April, he informed Capt. J. C. Lea of Roswell that he had been "obliged to take in quite a number of sheep on account owing to the slim demand on the outside. . . . I have gone to the expense of buying and making ranches." [92]

In Ilfeld's absence, however, it is apparent that Max Nordhaus was not so defensive in his approach to this acquired part of the business. The closing inventory of sheep at Pintada, in 1899, numbered more than 33,000 head, obtained largely through collections.[93] In February, however, Nordhaus began to make cash outlays for sheep—yearlings, two-year and three-year wethers, as well as numbers of lambs.[94] By the end of the year, with annual figures for "Wool and Stock Collections" exceeding

"Wool and Stock Sales" by more than $15,000 (almost the full amount of which can be accounted for in unsold wool), the number of sheep on hand at Pintada rose to more than 57,000. It seems rather clear that the growing number of sheep had nothing to do with the collection problem as Ilfeld had suggested but rather it had been caused by Nordhaus' speculative purchases.

Sheepherders were being hired in Las Vegas.[95] Their families, remaining behind, bought their needs at the Charles Ilfeld Company on advances made in the form of drafts signed by Max Goldenberg, whose attention to financial controls was somewhat disconcerting.[96] A bookkeeper, H. Reinhardt, was employed later in the year with instructions to set up four basic accounts—Sheep (Purchase and Sale); Ranch Expense (everything sustaining herds); Borica Ranch (Investment and Improvements); and Pintada Trading Company (Merchandise).[97] The "Investment and Improvements" account for Pintada Ranch was kept in Las Vegas.

In addition to the well pump and windmill, supplemented by a gasoline engine, the ranch equipment included five dipping tanks, four wagons, one ambulance (a buckboard), and a cart. As one might expect, there were the usual saddles, harnesses, rifles, camp and pack outfits—24 of them—and a complement of blacksmith tools. Farming implements, which were supplemented in 1901 by three mowers, two rakes, three plows, and one harrow, represented Goldenberg's hope for at least a partial solution to the less-than-adequate range grass.[98] An order for the flag pole, the sine qua non, specified to be light enough to travel economically from the Rociada country north of Las Vegas, was misread, with pardonable optimism, as a hay pole.[99]

The total ranch and camp equipment bore a cost of less than $2000. Sheep lands and improvements had incurred investments of more than $12,000. Both were a small pittance next to the sheep holdings amounting to more than $130,000.[100]

Upon Ilfeld's return from Europe the tune changed a bit. The letter he wrote to Goldenberg in January, 1901, expresses better than any description could otherwise do his ability and incessant desire to sell and turn over investment. It was the first of a series of moves that worked down the sheep inventories.[101]

Dear Max:

I was very much disappointed to see Mr. Garrett return without making a purchase. As customers of his calibre are very scarce. I took him into hand and made him raise his price to 2.45 at which I sold him the herds he wanted as per enclosed contract. . . .

While your calculation of profits may be correct I believe in small profit & turning the money. We have very good use for the cash & have found in the last few years that it is easier to buy sheep than to sell and have always regretted when an opportunity to sell slipped by. We have large accounts on our books again & have to do a whole lot of collecting in sheep next summer and fall . . . now with the comming [*sic*] lambs and the sheep we have to take on account during the year we will have plenty of sheep to take care of. . . .

Yours, etc.

Chas. Ilfeld.

With collections of sheep in 1902 threatening to undo the reductions achieved in 1901, Rodney Schoonmaker, the able bookkeeper, wrote Goldenberg that herd number eight had been sold at prices that seemed to him a sacrifice but, as he expressed it, "in view of short range and scant water supply with possibilities of heavy winter losses I believe it would be folly not to sell at even fair figures." [102] In September, Nordhaus was cautioning not to collect so many sheep as to create an undue risk over the winter.[103] In ordering Goldenberg to make more sales, he wrote again: "C.I. is determined to have our flocks reduced. . . . Not to run or breed more than 5000 good Ewes" and "to give all others out on shares if we can not sell them." [104] Yet at year-end, breeding ewes totaled more than 13,000; wethers, at an all-time high, exceeded 22,000; and total sheep on hand were inventoried at 51,000.

Managerial Problems

The change in policy, though it was slow to be effective, may well have been discouraging to Goldenberg but, if so, this would not have been unwelcome to either Ilfeld or Nordhaus. A combination of factors made it unlikely that they would want to keep their sheep manager much longer. He had not developed into an outstanding sheepman and his carelessness with controls was always a disconcerting element. Ilfeld, in particular, must have been more than a little concerned over the fact that neither he nor Nordhaus could supply the leadership or aptitude in sheep husbandry that, under the circumstances, was necessary.

A ticklish problem, too, was arising in the conflicting business loyalties of Max Goldenberg. He had become a member of the firm of M. B. Goldenberg and Company that had been founded in Liberty in 1900, with his brother Alex and Jacob Wertheim as the other partners.[105] A branch of this firm was opened in Tucumcari early in 1902 just 80 miles east from Pastura down the tracks of the Chicago, Rock Island and Pacific Railroad.[106] At this latter location and at approximately the same time, Ilfeld's branch store was being planned for its opening in December, 1902.[107] It seemed incompatible that Max Goldenberg, whose firm owed a substantial merchandise account to Ilfeld and which also operated a competitive sheep and livestock business, should remain in so important a position of responsibility with Ilfeld.

Goldenberg was surprised in the middle of December to learn that the Pastura store would be under separate managership and that merchandise activities would be taken from the Pintada headquarters. All Pintada supplies were to be obtained through Pastura. With Nordhaus off for a vacation in Germany, Ilfeld preferred to have Schoonmaker reply to Goldenberg's protest with a letter that seemed rather sharp.[108] Relationships appeared to have been more strained in March when M. B. Goldenberg and Company bought some heavy wool for Ilfeld from the Bell Ranch. Max B. promptly was reminded that the instructions were "not to buy any wools for our account . . . looks to us that you can't make trades as per our instructions and we prefer not to buy any wools through you at all rather than to have any misunderstanding." [109]

In September, 1903, or sooner, Goldenberg resigned, pleading poor health, and L. F. Churchill, who until he retired to New York State had been manager of the Alamogordo Sheep Company located some 20 miles north of Fort Sumner, was prevailed upon to return to New Mexico.[110] He could not have come at a more unfortunate time. The great drought of 1903 and 1904 was under way, and although a spirit of caution in the purchase of sheep had prevailed since 1901, influenced to a great extent by the relatively poor condition of the range, the sheep inventory at the end of 1902, approximating 51,000 head, was higher by 7000 than it had been in 1901 and only 6000 less than the peak of 1900.

As the drought year of 1903 wore on, even Nordhaus, fresh from his European vacation, lost a good deal of his enthusiasm for the project he had encouraged.[111] In June, just before the resignation of Goldenberg, he hoped he had found an opportunity to sell the Pintada Ranch although he was suggesting that a corporation be formed in which Ilfeld could retain a part interest.[112] By fall, with sheep collections running high, the situation was rather desperate. The *American Shepherd's Bulletin* reported in December, apparently three months late, that the Charles Ilfeld Company was moving large numbers of sheep from its ranges. "About 65,000 sheep will be moved, the general purpose of which is to lessen the number on the range in Leonard Wood County." [113]

Nordhaus had written Churchill in September, in his effort to persuade him to come to Pastura, that Goldenberg was "disposing of everything a buyer can be found for," but surpluses remained.[114] In November, the company was advertising in the *Daily Drovers Telegram* of Kansas City and the *Drovers Journal,* Union Stock Yards, Illinois, that the range was overstocked and that Ilfeld had 10,000 feeding lambs that "must be sold." [115] In the same month he advised Churchill to offer sheep on shares at 2½ pounds wool rental "if you want to get relieved of the sheep." [116] The year-end inventory listed 28,000 head still on hand.[117]

Churchill had arrived at Pastura in November, 1903, and Charles Ilfeld was there to greet him.[118] A partnership arrangement, known as the Pintada Trading Company, had been agreed to in which Churchill received a one-fifth interest.[119] His tenure as manager, however, lasted less than three years and he, like Goldenberg, resigned for reasons of health.[120] A contributing reason must have been the discouraging outlook for profits. Range conditions, of course, held the numbers of sheep down. The farming-out of excess holdings on partido contract, which showed a steady rise from 1902 through 1905, was an expedient answer that shifted the burden of some 9000 sheep to other hands and to other parched pastures. A. C. Ortega, who in 1903 was a clerk in Hugo Goldenberg's store at Puerto de Luna and who has lived his life in that general area in the livestock and merchandise business, remembers that although the partidarios did well until 1903, they found the going increasingly difficult from that date on.[121]

When the drought of 1903 and 1904 had broken, and even though sheep prices strengthened somewhat, the number of sheep handled by Churchill at Pintada declined by 1906 to slightly more than 22,000, and the numbers of sheep on partido had begun a precipitous drop. The conditions were such as to have made any man sick who had come out of retirement under persuasion. Unlike Goldenberg, however, Churchill left only after Nordhaus had pleaded with him to consider making his leave temporary and after extracting a promise that Churchill would keep at least a part of his interest and would stay on as a member of the advisory board with the freedom to appoint a livestock manager suitable to him.[122] Nordhaus had become as concerned as Ilfeld with their vulnerability to weak management in sheep husbandry activities.

Churchill agreed to the terms proposed and A. P. Grzelachowski, son of Ilfeld's deceased friend, the Padre Palaco, was named manager although some Roswell parties evidently had been considered.[123] The business was incorporated in September, 1907, still as the Pintada Trading Company, and Grzelachowski received $11,000 in stock in return for his Terreros Ranch in the Puerto de Luna area. His tenure, however, was not long, and when he resigned in September, 1908, the Terreros Ranch was leased out, probably to Grzelachowski, at $100 per month.

In his place a Tom Rodgers was appointed at a salary of $100 per month but he, in turn, was dismissed in 1910 to be replaced by an old ranch hand, Pofirio Anaya, who received only $75 per month.[124] Churchill seems to have left by this time, and the corporation was purchased in that year by Max Nordhaus and Charles Ilfeld and his three sons, Louis, Herman, and Arthur, to be operated as a partnership under the trade name The Pastura Trading Company.

This sheep operation, almost from the very start in 1899, had been a discouraging enterprise. From 1903 on, the trend in number of sheep handled had been downward. Twenty-two thousand head were on hand at the close of 1906, less than half the inventory of a few years before, and before 1908 had ended, a temporary bottom of a few hundred head had been reached.[125] Inventory figures are not available for later years, but A. C. Ortega, who in 1908 became bookkeeper and then manager of the Pastura store, remembers that after 1909 the numbers of sheep declined until, in 1913, sheep husbandry ceased entirely and the remaining 7000 head were let out on shares.[126]

Partido contracting turned downward almost as rapidly. By 1913, the number of contracts had fallen from the 1904–1905 peak of 44, to 28, with the same number per contract, although this average had been lower in the interim. Further declines took place in numbers and size of contracts until January 1, 1920, when the partido sheep were sold to the then-formed Ilfeld-Moulton Livestock Company—a second major effort of the Charles Ilfeld Company at sedentary sheep husbandry. These less than 14,000 partido sheep, in 1919, compared with the greater than 75,000 average number at Pintada and with partidarios in the years 1900 through 1902—an annual investment in sheep alone that averaged $167,000. By comparison, this was $13,000 more than had been invested in merchandise inventories in the same years.

The sense of the sedentary merchant, Charles Ilfeld, that this heavy sheep investment was not the wisest risk for the company to take had been borne out. Except as there were minor profits by the partnership prior to 1906, a 15 per cent dividend in January, 1910, is the only evidence of subsequent profitable operation.[127]

The managerial problem had proved a most difficult one. Churchill, apparently, had been the only supervisor who had performed ably, and he faced problems that severely hampered his effectiveness. Louis C. Ilfeld, son of Charles and attorney for the firm, wrote in 1909 before the worst had happened: "Profits in the sheep business depend altogether on the management. The Company I am interested in showed big profits when ably run and ran behind when . . . poor." [128]

Sedentary sheep husbandry had proved foreign to the enterprise of the Charles Ilfeld Company. It required a degree of attention and care that neither Charles Ilfeld nor Max Nordhaus were willing or could afford to give. It required a diversion of capital and time that were needed in the fast-growing mercantile business.

In perspective, too, the purposes for which Ilfeld had made such large commitments of time and money to the sheep division of his business had disappeared or could no longer be served by this approach. The acute collection problem, for which the organization of sheep activities on a large scale served as an heroic protective device, had gone. The need to prevent a collapse of the merchandise market was no longer present.

There was, however, the permanent and ever more pressing problem of a dwindling trade area. The delaying tactics of keeping customers in distant parts committed to Ilfeld through the extension of credit and the placing of partido sheep were no match for the attraction of the new economic centers which continued to arise and to grow along the extending railroads. Other protective devices were needed if the Charles Ilfeld Company was to hold a trade area that Las Vegas could no longer command.

XIII

DEFENSIVE POLICY IN A SHRINKING TRADE AREA

The Beginning Mercantile Capitalist and His Credit Risk

Before we embark on an analysis of defensive mercantile policy, implying as it does an unwillingness or inability to adjust quickly to changing market conditions—a characteristic the American economy likes to think it abhors—it should be recalled that the beginning mercantile capitalist, as an extender of large sums of credit to both distant and isolated markets, was particularly vulnerable to shifts in forces affecting credit risks.[1] He operated in a money barter economy in which, typically, his basic source of income was agricultural. His terms of credit, therefore, were largely geared to a seasonal production cycle in which it was not unusual for settlements on account to occur but once a year. It was imperative, under such conditions, that this mercantile capitalist keep the closest control possible over his customers' financial obligations; in most cases to the point of insisting that these obligations be confined solely to him. He, in turn, would assume the responsibility for supplying, on credit, the reasonable material needs of his customers; for finding solutions to their manifold problems; and for carrying them over long periods of economic hardship. These responsibilities he performed well and they became his trade-mark. In return, however, he often demanded of these customers the exclusive privileges of supplying their needs and of purchasing their produce.

As long as these goods were exchanged in terms of money, but with only a minimal use of money, the control of the petty capitalist by this merchant was nearly complete. As money in trade became more common, however, the petty capitalist, to the extent he had money to spend, became less beholden to his large supplier. As new economic centers arose to challenge the old, his choice of trade centers gave him a competitive leverage.

In this period of transition, when the beginning mercantile capitalist found his control over the petty capitalist weakening and his trade area shrinking, it is only likely he would have been tempted to turn to defensive measures. This was not only because it was human nature for him to attempt to hold on to what he possessed. Equally important was the jeopardy into which he saw many of his credit extensions cast as the produce, that he had anticipated should flow to him, threatened to go elsewhere.

Specifically Nordhaus and Ilfeld

When this transition hit Nordhaus and Ilfeld, it may have been felt more acutely by them than by their counterparts who lived in other times. The transition period which these latter day merchants experienced was relatively short and quite severe—beginning as it did in the 1880's and continuing apace throughout the 1890's. The Las Vegas trade area was being challenged from all directions at the very time that economic conditions for the bulk of Ilfeld's customers became troublesome and then serious. These changes threatened Charles Ilfeld more than might have been anticipated because the very extensions of credit that he had been able to carry through the difficult years of the middle and late 1880's, and in much larger amounts through the depression of the 1890's, were concentrated in support of the sheep industry—an industry comprised of customers who, in large measure, lived on the periphery of his trade area. Sheep and wool collections were his one indispensable source of eastern exchange. Were he in any substantial measure to lose control of that flow, a heavy concentration of his longer term credit extensions would be jeopardized.

Some of these people might have done better, earnings-wise, had they been freely permitted to purchase their goods from the cheapest sources, and to sell their produce at the nearest railroad point. Nordhaus, however, upon whose shoulders the solution to this problem rested, was in no mood to think so objectively. Had he been asked for a rationale of his policies, he probably would have reasoned something like this:

> Our customers (and I speak with particular reference to those located on the edge of our trade area) are heavily in debt to us. Economic conditions are such that we cannot expect these debts to be substantially reduced in the near future. We have gone into debt deeply to extend this credit to our customers. We need a strong cash flow to meet our obligations. Sheep and wool constitute the one hope for this flow. The people who raise sheep and wool need goods to support themselves and their industry. They need credit for this. We shall make certain that they get this from us, for if they obtain it elsewhere, we will lose control over the amount of total credit they will receive. Past experience does not suggest that self-discipline will hold their credit appetites within bounds. We expect to control their total business for as long a period as we can, and certainly that will be at least until they repay their obligations to us.

The Shrinking Trade Area

When the railroad came to Las Vegas in the summer of 1879, Charles Ilfeld's local procurement area, and coincidentally his sales territory, extended over trade routes fanning out from his Plaza store to as far as Roswell and Lincoln in the southeast, to Bernalillo and Albuquerque to the southwest, and through Mora and Cimarron to the north.[2] A few customers as far south as Las Cruces and La Mesilla had dwindling and inactive balances, as they only occasionally had made purchases in Las Vegas.

Eastward a hundred miles or more, Ilfeld acquired some business from the Bell Ranch located on the distant side of an expanding trade area in the Conchas region which extended itself northward to the Tramperos district and southeast to the town of Liberty. This eastern area was the only part of the territory in which trade routes from Las Vegas were extending themselves, and then only temporarily, as natural tributaries to the economy of that town.

The northern sector of the territory was the first to shift allegiance from Las Vegas. Even before the Denver and Fort Worth Railroad had been built across the northeastern corner of New Mexico in the spring of 1888, and through the newly organized town of Clayton, the Atchison, Topeka & Santa Fe Railroad had made it possible for Raton and Springer merchants to capture much of this northern trade. Not too many years after the founding of Clayton, merchants from that town also participated in the competition.[3] Ilfeld, in the face of these economic changes, was able to hold on to only one account of any importance in this northeast sector—the firm of Lujan and Pinard, later Pinard and Romero. This was understandable. Ilfeld leased these men the bulk of their lands, shunted sheep business their way, and, most important, financed them heavily. Even in this case, however, and long after ordinary economics would have dictated, the Charles Ilfeld Company advised Pinard and Romero to trade to better advantage elsewhere.[4]

The Denver and Rio Grande Railway had pushed its tracks southward through western Taos County to Espanola by 1880, and on to Santa Fe in 1885, thus giving Santa Fe merchants easy access to Taos and the Red River country—an area which in the 1870's had been within economic hail of Las Vegas.[5] Nordhaus tried to recapture this territory in the 1890's through the use of a drummer, but he found the competition of A. Staab and the Grunsfeld Brothers (Santa Fe merchants) too keen.[6] He had a little success in selling merchants farther to the north, however, as far north even as some Colorado points near the New Mexico line.

In 1890, the Charles Ilfeld Company had only 27 per cent of its "country" balances (as contrasted with Las Vegas "city" balances) with customers living north of an east-west line drawn through Las Vegas (see Table 15). The "captive" account of Lujan and Pinard equaled one half of the total of these northern balances, and without this account only 14 per cent of the country balances would have been from the northern sector. Three fourths of these represented individuals living in the Mora and Gallinas Valleys within 30 miles of Las Vegas (see Appendix 13).

TABLE 15. DISTRIBUTION OF COUNTRY ACCOUNTS AND COUNTRY ACCOUNT BALANCES, 1880 AND 1890 [a]

Location	Number 1880	Number 1890	Per cent 1880	Per cent 1890	Acct. bals. (dollars) 1880	Acct. bals. (dollars) 1890	Per cent 1880	Per cent 1890
North of an east-west line through Las Vegas								
Pinard Romero	1	1	2	—	—	8,912	—	13
Others	9	51	18	17	936	10,287	20	14
Total North	10	52	20	17	936	19,199	20	27
South of an east-west line through Las Vegas								
East	3	30	6	10	235	3,612	5	5
S. E. to Ft. Sumner	21	131	42	43	1,474	30,268	32	42
Roswell-Lincoln	2	32	4	11	466 [b]	9,093	10	13
Far South	2	6	4	2	306	277	7	[b]
Alb.-Mountainair	2	16	4	5	217	5,528	4	7
Santa Fe–Lamey & Pecos Country	7	30	14	10	456	3,010	10	4
Total South	37	245	74	81	3,154	51,788	68	72
Total country accounts	47	297	94	98	4,090	70,987	88	99
Unknown	3	7	6	2	546	406	12	1
Grand Total	50	304	100	100	4,636	71,393	100	100
Distribution by radius (approximate)								
40 miles	30	102	64	34	1,614	15,255	39	22
40 to 100 miles	13	145	28	49	1,704	46,362	42	65
Over 100 miles	4	50	8	17	772 [b]	9,370	19	13
Total	47	297	100	100	4,090	70,987	100	100

Source: Various ledgers.
[a] See Appendix 13 for detail.
[b] Credit balance included of $490.

To the far southeast Ilfeld suffered a pincers movement. A trail from Roswell and White Oaks and north to Clayton, less hilly than the road to Las Vegas, was an acceptable route in 1888. Over this trail cattle from the Roswell area were driven, and Clayton merchants drew some trade from there and from Lincoln County which otherwise would have gone to Las Vegas.[7]

The other half of the pincers, and much more strong in its pressure, came from Albuquerque and Socorro. Merchants in these centers could make good use of the railroad which, in 1882, had extended a branch

10 miles from the little village of San Antonio, south of Socorro, eastward to Carthage to catch the trade of Lincoln County centers.[8] When Ilfeld Brothers of Albuquerque was destroyed by fire in June, 1898—an event that transferred many of their orders to the Charles Ilfeld Company—the White Oaks area contained some of its customers.[9] Two years before, Nordhaus had used the railroad and freighters of the Browne and Manzanares branch store in Socorro to gain some trade in White Oaks, although the usual shipment continued to be carted in tandem wagons pulled, as one observer described, "by sixteen horses stimulated to their utmost by cursing drivers and welt-raising snake whips." [10]

Ilfeld and Nordhaus managed to hold a good deal of business in the Roswell and Lincoln areas, but it was for the most part in sheep and wool. The accounts receivable from these customers, in 1890, were almost as large in total as those directly north of Las Vegas—being approximately 12 per cent of the country accounts. For all practical purposes, however, these were not trade accounts. They represented ranchers and partidarios whom Ilfeld and Nordhaus found it necessary to support (and incidentally prevent from going into debt to others) until such time as economic conditions would permit full repayment of credit extended. It was McKinley prosperity as well as the railroad, this time the Gulf, Colorado and Santa Fe, which opened from Roswell to Amarillo in March, 1899, that finally made this possible.[11]

The effective trade area for Ilfeld to the south and east could be represented by a 100-mile radius centered at Las Vegas extending from the Manzano region to the southwest, through Fort Sumner, and thence to the Conchas area on the east. This sector, in 1890, held 60 per cent of Ilfeld's country accounts receivable balances, three fourths of which were on or near the road to Fort Sumner through Anton Chico and Puerto de Luna (see Table 15). Throughout the next decade the bulk of Ilfeld's country business came from this sector, although the fringes on the south, from Manzano to Fort Sumner, progressively held less and less importance. The opening of the Rock Island Railroad through the heart of this region at Santa Rosa, and then through Tucumcari south and east of the Conchas area, in 1902, left Las Vegas with little trade area to call its own. The Rock Island thus finished what the Santa Fe had started.

From 1880 to 1902 there had been a constant attrition of square miles that Las Vegas could command though a population increase of close to 25 per cent in the heart of the trade territory tended to obscure the damage that was being done.[12] This population palliative permitted Ilfeld to resist complacently any drastic change in distribution policy—perhaps to indulge in some wishful thinking that no such change would be necessary. Until the Rock Island did add its finishing touches, therefore, we find Charles Ilfeld giving primary consideration to protective mercantile policies aimed at preserving for the Las Vegas emporium as much of its shrinking trade area as credit could hold and for as long a time as possible.

Early Experience with Country Stores

As early as 1870, when Adolph Letcher and Ilfeld established a country store at El Monton de Alamos, some nine miles north of Las Vegas, a policy was being formulated to finance outlying merchants who, in turn, would collect produce from the countryside and trade it to Ilfeld for finished goods.[13] At Tecolote, a few miles to the south, a second store was opened no later than 1873.[14] Upon the establishment of Charles Ilfeld's proprietorship in 1874, this policy of financing country stores became an experiment in the formation of junior partnerships—one at Tecolote, under David Winternitz, and a second at La Junta (now Watrous) managed by Geronimo de Vega.[15] These three outlets (actually they could more accurately be described as inlets) gave Ilfeld some opportunity for control over nearby markets at a time when a few miles of New Mexico roads were effective impairments to communication.

The partnerships at La Junta and Tecolote, however, were dissolved in 1880.[16] The Los Alamos store, which apparently had been vacant since Letcher had left the business, was opened by William Frank, brother-in-law of Letcher, sometime after December, 1877.[17] By 1880, therefore, only Los Alamos remained of the original branches, and its tie to Ilfeld was strictly dependent upon personal relationships.

The pull exerted by the town of Springer on Ilfeld's northern trade area after 1880 gave Ilfeld enough concern that he brought encouragement on his former partner, William Gellermann, who had replaced de Vega at La Junta, to open a store in Springer.[18] This was in the fall of 1882.[19] Gellermann, who had been able to accumulate a sum of $3500 as his share of the partnership dissolution at La Junta, was unsuccessful in Springer.[20] When his financial condition became precarious, Ilfeld moved to protect himself, albeit faster than the law would generally permit one with such inside information.[21] He bought out Gellermann's stock of goods and property for $7000 in March, 1884, and took a mortgage on the store for $1500.[22] This proved embarrassing to Ilfeld, as of course he should have expected, when other creditors hired attorney M. W. Mills of Springer to protect their interests.[23] Ilfeld not only had moved into the mess from a preferred position, but he had done so after having previously described Gellermann in a letter of recommendation as one whom "I have put . . . in Business" and who "will not contract any larger Bills than he is able to pay." [24]

After Gellermann's failure in March, 1884, he remained as manager of

"Charles Ilfeld, Springer" until the first of the year when T. G. Yerby, formerly an employee of John Becker in Belen, was placed in charge for the purpose, it seems, of liquidating the business.[25] In late January the Springer inventory was insured for a period of only 30 days.[26] Two weeks later Ilfeld wrote Yerby to "please try to sell at cost all the goods you can . . . and have circulars printed" for distribution.[27]

The inventory proved not to be readily merchantable, and Yerby complained that he had been unable even to meet expenses. Within a week the safe was sold, and shortly plans were being made to ship the inventory of merchandise to Las Vegas. The wareroom was rented at $15 per month, and the front windows and doors were boarded. The store building was sold to the Springer Mercantile and Banking Company as of June 1, 1888.[28]

Gellermann's failure had been, in reality, the fault of Ilfeld's poor judgment. Ilfeld had put Gellermann in business in an area on which Las Vegas had little competitive hold. He had done this while insisting that Gellermann buy all his merchandise from Las Vegas except "Goods such as Butter and eggs," at cost plus 10 per cent.[29] When Gellermann bought elsewhere, and Ilfeld discovered the breach, a cryptic note would follow against which Gellermann, on one occasion, defensively replied, "Goods have to be bought where they are cheapest." [30] An all-commodity reshipment rate on the railroad from Las Vegas to Springer of 20 cents per 100 pounds, which had been granted Ilfeld as of March 25, 1884, was not, apparently, of sufficient advantage to meet competitive problems.[31]

Gellermann had been caught in the same collection problems that had faced Ilfeld in the early 1880's, but he had been careless and lax in his procedures and finally he proved himself unable to cope with the situation.[32] Ilfeld, on the other hand, with an inadequate system of internal controls and with a penchant for travel without properly preparing for his firm's management in his absence, had chosen the spring of 1883 to embark for Germany, six months after the opening of his Springer store.[33]

What might have happened had Ilfeld abandoned his retailing complex and had established a branch in Springer to be supplied from low cost points, and to be supervised and controlled with effectiveness, we do not know.[34] Ilfeld, however, clearly preferred not to make such a break with his way of doing things even when, with the purchase of Gellermann's assets, he had forced himself into the opportunity.

The Restrictions on Country Stores

The period from 1884 to 1892 brought the collection problem to the forefront because of softness in wool prices and precipitate declines in the price of cattle. The problem was ameliorated somewhat, however, by the strength in markets for sheep.[35] Except that special arrangements were made by Ilfeld to attack this problem through the hiring of Floersheim in 1884, and Goldenberg in 1888, he had no reason to be concerned about the mercantile business as a whole.[36] Throughout this seven-year period sales were strongly on the uptrend and, in 1892, were almost 2¼ times the level of 1886, the first year for which summary sales figures are available. The internal growth of Ilfeld's trade area was obscuring the effects of extensive erosion. It is not surprising, therefore, that we find little special effort in these years to hold trade of country stores except through price and service competition. Several larger store accounts were sold goods on a cost-plus 10 per cent basis, but when, for instance, C. H. "Governor" Moore of Puerto de Luna complained of this arrangement, Schoonmaker, the office manager, wrote a formal letter permitting cancellation of the agreement. "I will endeavor," he wrote, "to sell you all lines of merchandise at the lowest possible prices and would endeavor to merit a continuance of your esteemed patronage." [37]

Before and during the depression years of the 1890's, a few evidences of resentment began to creep into the company letters as a result of discoveries that some merchants, with ample lines of credit from Charles Ilfeld, had been doing some trading with other houses. It is understandable, for instance, that Aniceto Lueras of White Oaks, whose sheep and wool business was coveted by Ilfeld, could purchase his merchandise more advantageously from other sources than Las Vegas and would wish to do so. Nordhaus, however, wrote, "I am entitled to *all your patronage*. . . . You must not believe that I am a banker and that my business is to loan money." [38] He felt obliged to warn Mrs. Chadwick, proprietress of one of the several stores served by Ilfeld in Puerto de Luna, about "trading with other houses." [39] He made his views clear to Preciliano Vigil of Liberty, too, by stating that in return for the credit he was extending customers, "I expect them to buy all their goods that they need from my house." [40] The sauce for the goose came back to the gander, however, when another proprietress, Mrs. Prudencia Hoehne, storekeeper in the little village of Las Colonias north of Santa Rosa, wrote spiritedly, "Why don't you command the feller you got with your sheep to buy hay of me . . . you always pricking me for money, and produce I have to sell . . . you buy of others." [41]

The Charles Ilfeld Company's defensive attitude of using credit extensions as a means of obtaining 100 per cent patronage from recipients was typical of its policy until the railroad, in splitting the trade area asunder, made the failure of such a policy complete. Increasingly, though, the efforts to hold on to distant accounts, and the touchy problems created thereby, brought caution in the commitment of capital to new mercantile ventures that individuals, living beyond or on the fringe of the trade area, were prone to press upon Ilfeld and Nordhaus. An opportunity to start a branch in White Oaks received little consideration.[42] Ilfeld spent more than a year mulling over the chance to buy out a merchant in the Liberty-Endee area in eastern New Mexico, but when Nordhaus returned from Europe in the summer of 1893 the matter was dropped.[43] Max, however, with Ilfeld's consent, was willing to finance his cousin, Henry Nordhaus, in a mercantile venture in Deming, some 60 miles west of Las Cruces in the far southern part of the Territory. The terms as set forth, even for this distance, would have required cousin Henry to buy his goods from Las Vegas at cost plus 10 per cent, and, whether for this or for other reasons, negotiations appear not to have been carried further.[44] A proposition was offered Ilfeld to establish an enterprise in Taos but this was not even considered.[45] However, when C. U. Strong of Mora, a town dependent upon Las Vegas, asked the Charles Ilfeld Company to advance goods for an opening inventory, Nordhaus was more than willing, but again he attached the familiar terms—"it of course being understood that you confine all your trade to our house." [46] Negotiations dragged on for more than a year, but Strong evidently did not wish to be so restricted even though some modifications in the terms were offered.[47]

Use of Negotiable Cash Orders

One advantage Nordhaus had in enforcing his exclusive trade terms on distant stores was the scarcity of money in the hinterland economy. The only effective way these stores had to gain credit with their major distributor was through their delivery to him of produce—principally sheep and wool. Yet, precisely as Ilfeld had faced this problem in the 1870's, these stores eagerly sought out opportunities to acquire negotiable drafts or orders that would be good at face value with their merchant creditor.[48] A golden opportunity, therefore, faced Ilfeld to bring some liquidity into his country store receivables, as well as to solidify the ties of these stores to him, if he could make monetary exchange available to those who traded with him.

As early as the spring of 1887, Ilfeld furnished some of his ranch customers with checkbooks containing both negotiable and non-negotiable forms. The negotiable forms, printed in English, were exchangeable for cash. The non-negotiable, phrased in Spanish, were good only for the purchase of merchandise.[49] This latter type was used more extensively in the depression period of the 1890's. The negotiable checks, however, were most important in the period 1887 to 1893, although they were continued in later years.

The use of negotiable cash orders, payable at the Charles Ilfeld Company, became more common when Nordhaus and Goldenberg were contracting for sheep in the years 1890 to 1892. Nordhaus would furnish key buyers with checkbooks and authorize these individuals to advance money to contractees at so much per head of sheep. If the contractor was also a grower of sheep, he could use these checks to meet his payroll. Although these could be cashed at the Las Vegas store, all contractors were informed ahead of time which country stores had agreed to take these checks. Many of these contractors were merchants in their own right and, it is to be presumed, would deal principally with their own customers, thus being in a position to enlarge the capacity for trade of these individuals.

The storekeeper accepting these checks found himself in a favorable bargaining position. He could, of course, pay out cash when the checks were presented; this service the holder was entitled to receive. He could also sell the holder merchandise which, more than likely, the customer needed at the moment. In such a case it would be profitable for the storekeeper to offer his customer a discount, inasmuch as the check permitted him to reduce his account with Ilfeld including the 12 per cent interest accrual on his overdue balance.[50] Of course, a third alternative was available to the storekeeper in that the customer might wish, or be persuaded, to use the check as a payment on account. At any rate, it was to the storekeeper's advantage, and it is to be assumed he pressed his advantage, to avoid as much as possible a drain on his cash. If, because he could not avoid this drain, he called on Nordhaus for cash, he was charged 1 per cent per month interest on the amount he withdrew, although in later years this was reduced to 10 per cent per annum.[51]

The liquidity Ilfeld and Nordhaus achieved in contracting sheep with Nebraska feeders was thus passed on to Ilfeld's country stores.[52] The effects were to increase greatly the flow of his cash crop—sheep and wool—to produce a greater demand for his merchandise, and to gain a tighter control over his country stores at a time when his trade area was a growing target for other economic centers.

Use of Non-Negotiable Merchandise Orders

Once the depression of 1893 had chilled the sheep-contracting fever, Nordhaus did all he could to discourage the use of negotiable cash orders and to place the emphasis on non-negotiable merchandise orders. Actually from the first evidence we have that Ilfeld was encouraging the use of checks by his agents, instructions always were to keep the cash checks to a minimum and to write merchandise checks whenever possible. When A. G. Mills of Puerto de Luna received his checkbook in the spring of 1887, his instructions were, "Please try to make orders payable ½ in Cash and ½ in Mdse. if you possibly can." [53] In subsequent years the cash proportion was limited before any arrangement was made.[54]

In July, 1893, Nordhaus suffered a large contract revocation by a

Colorado sheep buyer, and it became imperative that he reduce the cash demand against him to as great an extent as possible.[55] He was embarrassed in August when he had to write Lujan and Pinard, "I have not the cash to pay [your orders] and can't procure it at present." Later in the month he begged Grzelachowski, in Puerto de Luna, to arrange with his sheepherders to accept pay in goods.[56]

The advantage of non-negotiable merchandise orders had been obvious for some time, but now it became doubly so. Cash was hard for anyone to come by, and yet should Nordhaus allow his distant customers, all of whom were deeply involved in sheep, to drift away to other markets, his chief source of cash would have been curtailed greatly at a time when his borrowing was reaching greater proportions.[57] The fact, however, that Charles Ilfeld had gained access to lines of credit in New York City, as well as in many other places, permitted Nordhaus to carry large accounts receivable without applying anxious pressure in his collection policy.[58] His offer, therefore, to permit ranch operators (some conducting a general merchandise business on the side) to meet their payrolls with checks exchangeable for goods was more than welcome. With this weapon Nordhaus gained a strong hold on his country stores and insured a greater two-way flow of goods: merchandise to the country, and sheep and wool to the city.

These merchandise drafts, as well as cash orders, when used by employers of labor, could serve the purpose of consolidating a number of small accounts into a few large receivables. The costs of recording and collecting could thus be reduced, and the fewer accounts could be watched and controlled with more effectiveness. This objective was clearly stated by Nordhaus in a letter to Philip Holzman, manager of the Pecos Mercantile Company of Fort Sumner, shortly after the founding of this Charles Ilfeld branch in 1896.[59]

> I am not in favor of your opening the little accounts you opened. If they are for shearers it is better to get orders for the party they shear for. If you continue to open such accounts you will find most will hang to the books and they will soon kill the profit that is made on the good people.

By making the merchandise checks non-negotiable Nordhaus forced those who accepted them to purchase from him, at least indirectly. He was able to make arrangements with designated country stores to accept these checks in exchange for goods and to deposit them with Charles Ilfeld in the same manner that he permitted the deposit of cash orders. In making these arrangements, however, he would inform his stores that a 10 per cent discount would be applied to such deposits before giving credit for them.[60] Nordhaus warned them, as he did Holzman, "Whenever you accept orders drawn on me for Merchandise you must make enough profit on them so you can afford to let me credit them to your acc't with a deduction of 10%. I have to charge them and to wait 12 months for payment without interest." [61]

Some Problems Encountered

Occasionally, a non-negotiable check would be presented to Charles Ilfeld with the phrase "Este Orden No Es Negociable" crossed out, and Nordhaus would discover that it had been endorsed by the original payee to another party who had "cashed" it for merchandise in a store with which Nordhaus had not made arrangements.[62] These he accepted upon first infringements but warned that he would not longer do so. To have permitted this practice to go far would have negated the effectiveness of this tool for encouraging trade through his designated stores.

Most of his trouble came, however, in the use and abuse of the cash orders. He was driven finally in June, 1894, to announce henceforth that he would discount them 10 per cent just as he had been doing on the merchandise drafts whenever country stores sent in these cash orders for credit.[63] It is certain he did not often comply with this directive, and it was more difficult and unfair to apply it the first time to stores that normally did not deal with him. From the lack of evidence of abuse of cash orders after 1894, however, it would appear that this threat was fairly effective in stopping the promiscuous signing of cash orders by sheepmen who had been expected to issue the non-negotiable merchandise type.[64]

One problem that must have been as embarrassing to Nordhaus as it was irksome to his country storekeepers was his refusal to accept checks of customers who were exceeding their credit limitations. Nordhaus was continually writing country storekeepers informing them which customers' checks would be honored and which would not. He safeguarded this problem somewhat by requiring all individuals who were entrusted with his checkbooks to inform him in advance of the amounts of the checks to be written, to whom they were to be given, and the purpose for which they were authorized.[65] Generally he would not permit sheepmen, for instance, to write checks for any purpose other than wages.[66] When he was not forewarned on these items he sometimes refused to honor the checks. An example of this occurred when his agent, Ramundo Salas of Manzano, was "trading and buying and issuing checks" in White Oaks. All of these drafts were honored by Nordhaus except one on which he twice refused payment. This action brought forth a threatening letter from the Business Men's Association of White Oaks, part of which read as follows: [67]

> This action on your part having created a doubt in the minds of our business men, they hesitate to receive checks on you, and in fact, every business house in

town a few days since refused one of Salas' checks. This matter has been presented to our Association for consideration and your reply will decide our course in the matter.

Nordhaus, who previously had explained to Salas that checks would not be honored without prior notification, apparently explained his policy in great detail to the Business Men's Association.[68] The reply to his letter states rather clearly what must have been in the minds of many a country storekeeper: [69]

While we, as business men have no right, nor presume to question your method of dealing with your agents, and which, as explained by you appears to be the only safe course for you to pursue with the majority of Mexican traders, yet you can readily understand how difficult it is for dealers here to know which drafts that are drawn on you by the traders will or will not be honored by you. It is impossible for the dealer to tell where to draw the line.

This was in 1892. Before the depression of 1893 had ended, however, Nordhaus had brought his system of negotiable and non-negotiable drafts into such working order as to cause scarcely a ripple in the otherwise voluminous correspondence.[70] (See reproduction of cancelled checks.)

Another Try at Springer

The Territory, in the spring of 1897, was experiencing a mild boom in sheep prices, particularly of lambs, and Ilfeld's temptation to capture some of the growing market to the north returned. This time, fortunately, there was a young enterpriser on hand who held a strong desire to embark on his own venture to the promising location of Springer. Ludwig W. Ilfeld, son of Charles' older brother William, had come from Germany to work for his "Uncle Charlie" in October, 1891, and, as one might have guessed, was near the age of eighteen.[71] Five and one-half years later, as assistant bookkeeper under Rodney Schoonmaker, he had earned such a reputation for industry and integrity as to make his uncle more than willing to finance the young man's desire.

Ludwig opened his store in May, 1897 (all orders and bills for opening stock going to Charles Ilfeld), and during the next month his sales indicated prospects were good.[72] Solomon Floersheim, then a merchant in Springer, took an interest in the lad and shunted what business he could to him.[73] The bulk of Ludwig's orders was supplied from Las Vegas, but, occasionally, a purchase was made in Raton.[74]

Scarcely a month had passed, however, before Ludwig knew he would not be content to stay in Springer, and his reasons were not financial.[75] This small "one-horse" place was not at all appealing. The marriage Floersheim seemed to be designing for him was creating a certain apprehension. Drunken hold-up men, who forced him to come down from

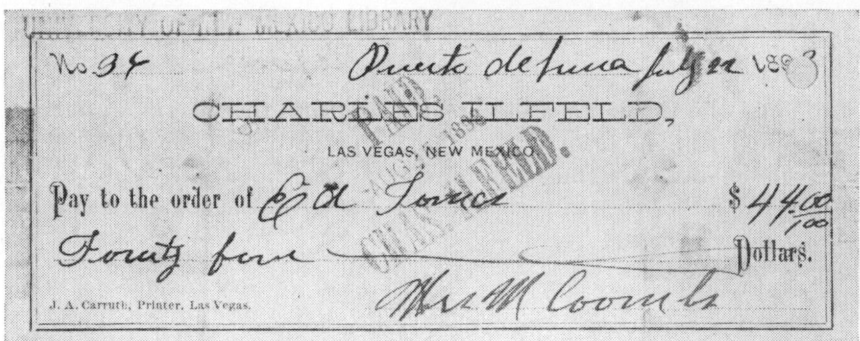

No. 34 Puerto de Luna July 22 1893

CHARLES ILFELD,

LAS VEGAS, NEW MEXICO.

Pay to the order of .... $ 44.00/100

Forty four .... Dollars.

J. A. Carruth, Printer, Las Vegas.

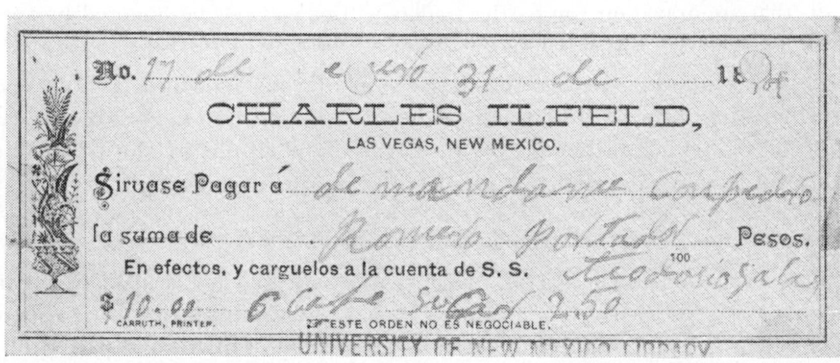

No. 18

CHARLES ILFELD,

LAS VEGAS, NEW MEXICO.

Sirvase Pagar á ....

la suma de .... Pesos.

En efectos, y carguelos a la cuenta de S. S. 100

$ 10.00

CARRUTH, PRINTER. ESTE ORDEN NO ES NEGOCIABLE.

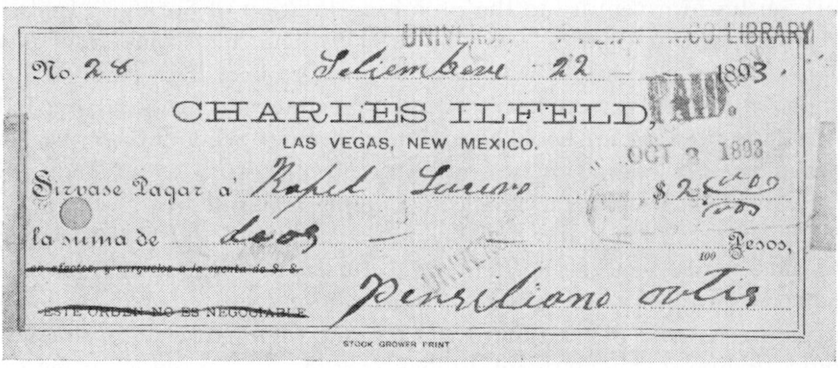

No. 28 Setiembre 22 1893.

CHARLES ILFELD,

LAS VEGAS, NEW MEXICO.

PAID. OCT 2 1893

Sirvase Pagar a' .... $ 2.00/100

la suma de .... Pesos,

~~en efectos, y carguelos a la cuenta de S. S.~~

~~ESTE ORDEN NO ES NEGOCIABLE~~

STOCK GROWER PRINT

Cancelled checks drawn on Charles Ilfeld. *Top:* negotiable cash order. *Middle:* nonnegotiable merchandise order. *Bottom:* nonnegotiable merchandise order with "goods" and "nonnegotiable" clauses crossed out (two endorsements appear on the back).

his over-the-store bed lest they "shoot the lock off the front door," acted like gentlemen when they got in and paid for the goods they wanted, but this was a discouraging experience. Besides, being tied so closely to Uncle Charlie was not really free enterprise.[76]

In the middle of June, Ludwig wrote that "Papa" was ill in Homburg, and, later, that it had been strongly urged upon him that he come home, at least for a visit. Ludwig, however, had made known his intention to resign some time before his father had urged him to come home, although he was not willing to leave before satisfactory arrangements had been made for the Springer investment. Max Nordhaus already had offered Ludwig's inventory at cost to Julius Appel and partner, Max Karlsruher, Red River City merchants. Ludwig would have preferred to sell out the inventory at retail or, being unable to accomplish this in full, to return it to Las Vegas, freight prepaid. He had some misgivings regarding the risk "Uncle Charlie" was taking in selling to these "young men" and, apparently, Ludwig's appraisal caused Nordhaus to attempt a retraction of the offer he had made. Appel, however, either ignored the retraction or left for Springer before the change of plans became known to him. In any event the sale was consummated for a note and chattel mortgage of somewhat less than $2000 on condition that J. Appel and Company would buy exclusively from Charles Ilfeld Company.[77]

In spite of a favorable all-commodity distribution rate of 10 cents per 100 pounds from Las Vegas to Springer, and price terms to Appel of 5 per cent over cost for groceries and 10 per cent over cost for dry goods, it appears that it must have been more advantageous for Appel to make purchases elsewhere.[78] Although Appel's account was very active during the remainder of 1897, the firm found another party willing to refund its mortgage to Ilfeld in January, 1898, and thereafter it proceeded to buy from Ilfeld only in small and infrequent amounts.[79] The account was paid in full in 1900 and closed out completely in 1901.[80]

Puerto de Luna, Liberty, and Tucumcari

The last of the important country stores that Ilfeld and Nordhaus attempted to control through the sheer force of credit, as contrasted with permanent capital, were Hugo L. Goldenberg's general merchandise store (known as M. B. Goldenberg and Company) at Puerto de Luna and the Liberty-Tucumcari enterprises that indirectly grew out of it. Hugo, brother of Max Goldenberg, not only bought all his merchandise from Ilfeld but traded in sheep and wool extensively as his agent. The extent of the obligation which Nordhaus placed upon this firm is shown rather clearly in a letter he wrote to Hugo in 1896: [81]

> I wish you would have Max [Goldenberg] post you on what people owe us and you must use judgment, and some consideration for us in your dealings

with them. You cut us clear off from collecting if you trade their wethers and we think we can expect of you that you look out a little for our interests.

The same problem persisted after Max Goldenberg left the employ of Charles Ilfeld for the first time in May, 1897, and joined Hugo in the Puerto de Luna firm under the style of Goldenberg Brothers.[82] Max Goldenberg evidently had taken his independent employment status to mean he could trade freely in sheep and wool, but Nordhaus disabused him of that idea when he learned Goldenberg had advanced some funds to small ranchers who were heavily in debt to Ilfeld.[83]

Max left his partnership with brother Hugo in April, 1899, and subsequently rejoined the Charles Ilfeld employ.[84] Perhaps the cause was lack of business at Puerto de Luna—at least the growing interest burden of their account to Ilfeld makes it clear that it was difficult to meet the terms of 60 days on groceries and 90 days on all other merchandise that had been permitted them interest free.[85]

Hugo's proprietorship prospered in 1899 with the bulge in sheep trade, but from then on his balance due Ilfeld rose steadily as did the accumulated interest thereon. Whether Hugo's fortunes were affected by a change of policy in which Ilfeld stopped giving cost plus terms to his country stores after 1899 is not determinable.[86]

The coming of the Rock Island Railway, however, in 1901, through the town of Santa Rosa, a dozen miles north of Puerto de Luna, removed the latter location as an important trading point. Hugo Goldenberg, bypassed by the railroad, was doubly encouraged to liquidate because of the great drought of 1903 and 1904. He had been reducing his debt to Ilfeld during 1903, and the account was paid in full in October, 1904.[87]

In the meantime, Max Goldenberg loaned his name, and probably some capital, to his brother Alex and to Jacob Wertheim, who bought the Jarrell General Merchandise Store in Liberty.[88] M. B. Goldenberg and Company began business in that town in February, 1900, agreeing to purchase all its goods from Ilfeld on terms of 60 days for groceries and 90 days for other purchases.[89] When, near the close of 1902, the Rock Island Railway branch to Dawson bypassed Liberty (contrary to early rumor) and took to higher and more level ground a few miles to the east, Alex and Jacob moved their Liberty merchandise to their new store in Tucumcari, which had been operating for a full year.[90] Probably because these gentlemen had accrued a debt to Ilfeld, during the first two years of the Liberty business, of more than $11,000 including interest of $600, the terms for their new stores purchases were strictly "cash." It had become perfectly clear that Tucumcari was no longer in the Las Vegas trade area, and anything that could be done to encourage repayment of this firm's debt was advisable. Real estate interests of the partners in Tucumcari must have paid handsomely, however, because their debit balance with Ilfeld rapidly turned into a credit of more than $9000, causing Ilfeld to pay the interest.[91] The M. B. Goldenberg and Company account was closed in August, 1902.

In the following May, with a branch warehouse well established at Santa Rosa, and the defensive policy in the shrinking trade area now turned to aggressive expansion, Nordhaus could write without emotion: [92]

> When M. B. Goldenberg and Co. started into business we extended them a large credit with the understanding that we were to carry them and that they were to purchase everything from or through us. A new railroad later on cut us off from the section in which they are located and they since purchased goods wherever they pleased.

XIV

RETAIL TRADE AND THE RISE OF JOBBING

The Broader Picture

As the Chicago, Rock Island & Pacific Railway cut its way through the cash cropland of the Las Vegas merchant, it was not, to Max Nordhaus anyway, an unkind cut at all. The defensive mechanisms that were part of the mercantile policy of the Charles Ilfeld Company from the 1880's to the turn of the century, necessary as they were, could not fit closely the aggressive and expansive mood of this young man. Those pressured and formative years following 1886, when at age twenty-one he had had conferred upon him a general agent's power in the fullest breadth of the law, had been fraught with difficulty. When good times returned with protective McKinley prosperity, Nordhaus could see even more clearly that there could be no protection for Las Vegas. When, in the year 1901, he wrote in the first personal pronoun, "I contemplate making an important change in my business the latter part of this year," his letter spoke reams of copy book transcriptions filled with his growing leadership and the change he had wrought toward the ultimate goal of wholesaling.[1] It is perhaps significant that on the same day Max was signing this letter, Charles, home on one of his summer visits to Las Vegas, was signing a number of routine purchase orders—representative of a phase of the business that was close to Ilfeld's heart, particularly when it took him to New York City and its metropolitan attractions.

The "contemplated change" included a warehouse and store on the Rock Island at Santa Rosa, which could be supplied directly from eastern markets, and the establishment of a country store 19 miles down the railroad to the southwest at Pastura. Though this was more an experiment in branch warehousing with retail nubs appended, it was a break from the futile stretching of the limited arms of Las Vegas, and it opened wide the road to wholesaling—a point that was reached in practical fullness but four years later.

Charles Ilfeld had been typical of the sedentary merchant in that he gave up the retailing function slowly. Perhaps because of his love for the store he had built and his "feel" for the merchandise wants of the individual, he had been more reluctant than many would have been to foster a wholesaling business. In spite of the composite evidence that this was so, it would be unfair, in analyzing this change toward jobbing, to attribute to Nordhaus all the forward drive, and to impute to Ilfeld the full drag of an anchor to windward. As early as 1882, Ilfeld had devoted space on the second floor of his store to a department labeled "wholesale dry goods." In June, 1889, he probably acquiesced in a desire expressed by Nordhaus to go more extensively into the wholesale grocery business—a move that shortly afterwards was made.[2] In all cases, however, at this early a date, the term "wholesale" was misleading and seldom amounted to more than the moving of an occasional job lot. The truth seems to be that Ilfeld, though willing enough to permit Nordhaus to develop wholesaling as an arm of the business, did not wish to put his own hand very deeply into it. Nor did he recognize the import of the change that was occurring.

Regardless of personal tastes, however, the real impediment to the development of wholesaling in the Charles Ilfeld Company was the economic structure of the hinterland which the company served. The conditions that dictated an emphasis on retailing in the 1870's were present only in lesser degree in the 1890's, though they were disappearing in a steady undertow. Charles Ilfeld, like many sedentary merchants before him and since, had begun as a retailer when his town was small. He took on the function of wholesaling in limited degree because the country stores around him, literally without money and possessing little capital or access to metropolitan areas, found it necessary to rely on the credit he could furnish them. Also (and Gras has observed it of the sedentary merchant generally), the retail function helped Ilfeld accumulate products for export—products he needed for gaining money exchange in the large financial centers—and customers from the countryside who, also without money, found it equally attractive to exchange their produce at his store for the goods they wanted.[3]

This need for the retailing function finds at least tentative support in the experience of two major wholesale firms in Las Vegas. The predecessors of Gross, Blackwell and Company, as well as Browne and Manzanares, had given up the bulk of their commission business that had constituted so much of their trade as they moved westward with the terminus of the railroad, and, as settled houses, had developed strictly as wholesalers.[4] The larger general merchants, like Ilfeld, had needed these commission houses to take care of the assembling and transferring of their orders from the train to the freighter just as long as the railroad was distant, and the railroad found these houses equally useful as assemblers of the raw materials arriving from the general merchant.[5] When these commission firms settled in Las Vegas, however, and the railroad extended beyond them, they found themselves in direct competition with the very general merchant who had previously supported them, and, to a large extent, this competition was for the produce of the countryside that the merchant credit system had brought so effectively to the general merchant's door.

One can be suspicious that the rather constant financial stringencies experienced by Gross, Blackwell and Company throughout the 1880's, and the reported speculative policies often pursued by this firm in the acquisition of sheep and wool, were in some measure tied to the difficulty the firm must have had in establishing a natural flow of such produce to its doors.[6] The decline in importance of Browne and Manzanares and its ultimate disappearance, though largely attributable to the loss of vigorous management, may well have found much of its cause in the basic handicap this company possessed of not being prepared to trade as a retailer in a money barter economy.[7]

It is important for us, in assessing Ilfeld's retail policy, to keep in mind that the whole character of the area within which he operated would have to change before he could "work himself over to the position of more nearly disposing of his goods to the trade by wholesale." [8] Wholesaling came with the growth of the surrounding economic centers, with the ability of retailers to gain much of the small collections of the country's produce, and with large-scale ranching, particularly sheep ranching. Ilfeld could wholesale to the storekeepers in the expanded economic areas and to the larger landed units, and the time was coming when, through these fewer customers, he could obtain sufficient exportable produce. It was Nordhaus, spending nearly all of his time in Las Vegas, who more clearly felt the undertow of this economic change.

The evidence of this change, and Nordhaus' awareness of it, is surprisingly clear in an analysis of total sales, for which there is a breakdown beginning in 1894 (see Table 16). In that year wholesale revenue was almost 1⅓ times as great as retailing receipts, and this ratio rose rather steadily to nearly 2½ by 1901, the year of the "contemplated change" about which Nordhaus wrote. The rapidity and force with which the wholesaling trend took hold in the 1890's is even more apparent when one compares these figures with the estimate for sales in bulk at discounted prices in the early 1880's—an amount thought to have been less than 10 per cent of total sales.[9]

Even more significant is the fact that in 1890 Charles Ilfeld began construction of his enlarged and refurbished department store that aided in giving a substantial push to retail sales in the years ahead. Yet, three years later, although the records surely could have shown it sooner had they been sufficiently detailed, the wholesale trade was larger and was growing strongly relative to the increase in retail sales which, from 1894 to 1901, grew 50 per cent. In chronicling this trend toward wholesaling, there could be no more logical starting point than Ilfeld's last splurge in retailing when, at the age of forty-three, he was still spending the large por-

TABLE 16. RETAIL AND WHOLESALE SALES, CHARLES ILFELD, 1894–1909 (1000$)

Year	Retail	Wholesale	Ratio	Total sales [a]
1894	87.7	115.8	1.3	203.5
1895	95.5	117.0	1.2	212.5
1896	83.3	119.7	1.4	203.1
1897	93.3	166.6	1.8	259.8
1898	117.6	189.6	1.6	307.1
1899	123.7	229.1	1.9	352.9
1900	129.9	269.2	2.1	399.1
1901	132.7	320.7	2.4	453.4
1902	113.9	310.1	2.7	424.1
1903	119.8	341.8	2.9	461.6
1904	113.1	403.1	3.6	516.3
1905	115.3	554.0	4.8	669.3
1906	33.7	787.1	a	820.8
1907	43.2	852.5	a	895.7
1908	44.6	786.7	a	831.3
1909	65.9	809.3	a	875.2

Source: Annual Summary Book, 1895–1909.

[a] These sales were exclusive of any revenue received from the sale of produce collected on account such as sheep and wool.

tion of each year in Las Vegas, and when Max Nordhaus, at age twenty-five, still may have been exercising a less-than-dominant influence in company policy.

THE ENLARGED DEPARTMENT STORE

The trade slump of the middle 1880's, brought on by the collapse of cattle prices and the weakness in sheep and wool markets, reached its bottom in 1887. The years following, however, had been buoyant indeed. Population growth of about 15 per cent over the decade, with perhaps more than 3000 newcomers to Las Vegas and immediate environs, had offered support to Ilfeld's retail trade.[10] When the sheepman's prosperity returned in 1888, sales promptly reflected the optimism it brought. From a low of $180,000 in 1887, merchandise sales had been rising at the steady rate of $20,000 per year through 1890, making Ilfeld's "Great Emporium," constructed but a scant eight years before, inadequate for the current and envisioned trade.

Negotiations were being carried on with Kirchner and Kirchner, Denver architects, in September, 1890, to more than double the floor space.[11] In October, steel girders were ordered from Chicago, although wooden beams, to be obtained from the Rociada area northwest of Las Vegas, had been substituted in the planning wherever possible in an effort to reduce cost.[12] Local stone, quarried two miles west of the Plaza—red-brown sandstone for the supporting pillars between the large, polished, plate-glass show windows at the first floor, and "creamy-white" stone for the facing of the two upper floors—required the importation of stone masons from Trinidad, Colorado.[13]

Construction was slower than anticipated, and Ilfeld's decision to add a third floor to the new portion, which he had not expected he would need so soon, further slowed things.[14] In June, frantic efforts were being made to complete the roof before the rainy season commenced.[15] By the first of August the third floor was still not ready for occupancy, and the roof had leaked with the first storm and "not in any one or more separate localities." [16] Soon, with the installing of 75 hanging sockets, unmetered electricity was being contracted from the local Gas and Electric Company "to be turned on as soon as darkness requires it." [17] By December, at the latest, the store in its full capacity had been opened to the public, advertising "free car fare to Ilfeld's," and the daily newspaper editorialized with unseasonable effusion: This "Pride of Las Vegas" with its "massive pillars" and "magnificent show windows," "perfectly lighted on every side of its four floors, including basement," fronted "southward upon that beautiful oval of summer verdure, the Plaza." [18]

Retailing to the Ladies

The store of 1891 with 75 feet of frontage was considerably more departmentalized than its predecessor had been, and the greater fragmentation that had taken place was almost entirely to serve the ladies better. When only 32 feet had been available, goods were in such crowded repair that a discerning eye would have summarized no less broadly than the reporter who in 1883 had described the first floor as a "general retail department for dry goods, fancy goods, notions and gents furnishings." [19]

In the new store, the "gents" became "gentlemen," as their furnishings along the west wall of the main room faced two banks of ladies departments, extending more than 100 feet from the front of the store to the rear. In addition to the usual first floor items of linens and laces, silks and satins, gloves, hosiery, and neckwear, newcoming items embraced corsets and underwear, dressmaking, and millinery. The latter group of departments had been brought down from the second floor where they had been associated with dry goods but were now adjacent to the more appealing section of dress fabrics.

Over the years Ilfeld, with the frequent aid of his wife, had encouraged the dressmaking and millinery departments, but he had found it next to impossible to hire fashion-conscious employees in Las Vegas.

He, therefore, often sought recommendations for feminine talent in the larger metropolitan centers. Whenever possible he took it upon himself, when traveling in the East, to interview these young ladies before paying their railroad fares to an area of the country which few, if any of them, had seen before. Evidently he picked them well, because the land of opportunity found many of these adventurous, reliant misses achieving purely personal objectives that led Ilfeld, in his despair at the turnover, to take cognizance of the "marriage bureau" he was running. He even thought some of stipulating in the contract of employment that these employees agree not to *"get married for at least 3 seasons."* [20]

The net profit from the millinery department was large in percentage, about 25 cents on the dollar, but relatively small in sales volume. From 1898 to 1902 it averaged less than $5000 annually.[21] Yet this activity, as well as dressmaking, was additionally profitable by way of the dry goods and trimming that Ilfeld required be purchased from other departments, but even more so because of the feminine trade these departments brought into the store.

An important drawing power, as far as the feminine trade was concerned, was the Butterick Pattern line which Ilfeld had begun to carry as early as 1882 and for which he had secured the exclusive distribution privileges for northern New Mexico.[22] Admittedly, the line was carried "mainly as advertisement," and it proved very valuable over the years in bringing many inquiries for regular goods from customers in areas outside the trading province.[23] Subscriptions to the women's magazine *Delineator,* published by Butterick, were actively solicited, and, in addition, the *Glass of Fashion,* printed by the same firm and containing an advertisement of the Butterick agent—in this case the Charles Ilfeld Company—was mailed directly to subscribers. The *Delineator* in particular became an important enough merchandising tool to cause Nordhaus concern when the patterns it advertised were slow in arriving. The *Delineator* gave the women their ideas but he had found that these ideas had to be capitalized on quickly or the ladies soon made other plans.[24]

The Butterick Publishing Company kept pressure on Ilfeld to stock more patterns and to increase sales of their publications. This they did both by letter and through a traveling representative. In answer to one of these expressions of disappointment in Ilfeld's productivity, Nordhaus felt obliged to explain some of the problems of selling this service in New Mexico. "You do not fully understand the difficulties," he wrote, "of conducting the sale of Butterick patterns in this community. The population altogether, is very sparce and scattered and the large majority have no interest in the changing fashions as their wardrobe from birth to death is composed of a half dozen garments, possibly." [25] The same day he wrote a second letter cancelling an order he had placed for the Spanish edition of *Glass of Fashion* because its cost required it to be retailed at 15 cents instead of the regular 5 cents for the English printing. "Spanish people who buy a fashion book are able to read English," was his comment.[26]

The Native Trade

The native people—"Spanish" when they appeared to offer culture, ability, and motivation; "Mexican" when they gave an indication of irresponsibility and a lack of economic self-discipline—were the backbone of Ilfeld's business. Nordhaus estimated their numbers to constitute more than three fourths of the population and among his customers a majority.[27] Because these native people were so dominant in his trade, and the bulk of them of low economic circumstance, they fashioned, in these early days, much of the inventories that Ilfeld carried. Generally this meant low-cost goods and, frequently, inferior quality.

A letter from Ilfeld to a friend, Levy, who did occasional buying in New York for the firm when Ilfeld was in Las Vegas, is descriptive of the character of buying that kept this trade in mind.[28]

A. Levy
c/o B. Bernard & Son
New York

Dear Alex:

Your Postal just rec'd on the day I returned from New York, am sorry you did not start sooner to meet me there yet. Go to A. Simon Jr. 706 B[road]way, where I bought some Coats at 75¢ and 1.00 & Vests at 50¢ & found them the cheapest in the line. If you don't find there what you are after go to W. P. Ansorge on Bway where I bought some Vests at 50¢ the latter price is *toches auf ian tisch* [bottom on the table]. Go to T. Rothchild 373 Church Str. who sells *Mezies* [bargains] from auction every day & who will treat you right; & has offer Jobs which you can use, mention my name there & he will do his best to sell you, but remember he has more than one price. I wish you buy for me about 25 Coats large size 37/42 dark Colors for about 1.25 to 1.50 & 28 Blue Pen Jackets to cost 1.75 to 2.00 Ansorge has a lot in the Window with red lining & marked out 1.75. . . . In Bargain shoe house you may call on L&C Wise 88 Reade Str. but only for cheap trash. . . . If you need any Dress trimmings go by all means to Wm. Reiss 7 Merser Str. who can save you from 25 to 50%, as he only buys from Auction and Private concerns. Mention my name and ask for Mr. Reiss himself. . . .

El Charles

The "cheap trash" from the bargain shoe house was part of the stuff Ilfeld had purchased a month or so earlier. They were children's shoes and he complained of the billed price of 39 cents a pair. He claimed to have bought them regularly in Boston for 30 cents. "I can use them at 25¢ in the meantime [I] hold them subject to your order." [29]

Ilfeld was proud of his buying prowess and often picked up exceptional bargains. Evidently he was a frequenter of auctions, as indicated in the above and a later letter, or else liked to purchase from merchants who themselves bought at auction. He could not resist the temptations of a low price and, as one of his employees of many years' standing has said: "When Ilfeld was on one of his buying trips we expected to find a lot of junk with the good buys when his shipments came in." [30]

Ilfeld's trade, however, demanded a great deal of bargain buying, and it was reflected as well in the purchase of groceries and staples carried in the basement store. Nordhaus complained when he was unable to buy cheap flour without including some of a higher grade.[31] He was unhappy when, having ordered flour bags from Texas with the imprint "Barata" (cheap), they came stenciled with "Carata" (dear).[32] When an unsatisfactory shipment of prunes came in, someone in the office wrote that they were inferior for anything but the Mexican trade.[33]

However, once a particular brand was recognized for its low price and satisfactory quality, it was difficult for the merchants to sell a competing brand. When a supplier tried to persuade Nordhaus to adopt his brand of coffee the reply was: "My own trade, mostly among the Mexican people could hardly be induced to take anything but Arbuckle." [34] The premiums that were given with the retailing of the product probably had something to do with this loyalty. The same was true of Diamond C soap.[35] When a tobacco company in Richmond, Virginia, tried to introduce competition to "F&F" and "Bull Durham," it was termed "Useless" "no matter how much better or Cheaper." [36]

Price Maintenance and Exclusive Brands

For all the haggling that went on in purchasing—Ilfeld in the market place and Nordhaus by letter—neither of these gentlemen had much love for price-cutting or bargaining at home. In general this meant a desire for a single price system though it often occurred that prices would be differentiated on the basis of customers' credit ratings or with deference to the terms of sale—cash or credit.[37] Distinguishing prices on the basis of credit ratings, however, occurred mostly in the country trade where it sometimes was a source of embarrassment as competing customers learned of others receiving favored treatment and the pressure resulting forced an occasional price change.[38] In over-the-counter retail trade, though, single prices were adhered to except for that infrequent customer who, representing the customs of other days, was permitted to indulge his habit of starting at higher prices and of haggling his way lower.[39]

As early as 1884, Ilfeld was showing his preference for the one-price system through the use of exclusive brands, although it was not for almost a decade that distaste for price-cutting was set forth clearly as a primary motive for seeking these lines. He cancelled an order for patterns and goods in this early year because other firms in Las Vegas were buying the same brands, contrary to this agreement.[40] Charles Ilfeld obtained a two-year exclusive right to the sale of Nipantuck flour; but, when it was learned that others were also selling the brand, it was stated, "I don't object if you sell the other . . . brands . . . if under another name." [41] A threat was made to stop carrying Hills brothers' millinery unless Charles Ilfeld was given an exclusive agency.[42]

Examples of this practice appear with greater frequency in the records, from 1893 on, and in such varied lines as soap and stoves, corsets and men's suits, gloves and waists. The usual cause for bringing to light these agreements, or lack of them, was price-cutting by competitors. Whenever this occurred, Nordhaus promptly reported the fact to the supplier and either the line was dropped or a plea was entered to obtain an exclusive agency as the best way to prevent price-cutting.[43] Nordhaus sent the local newspaper to one supplier as evidence of his competitor Rosenthal's price-cutting practices and threatened to make a change unless exclusive rights to the product could be obtained.[44] On one occasion, at least, when exclusive privileges were not obtainable but the product line was too profitable to abandon, a fair-trading agreement for price maintenance of pharmaceuticals appears to have been agreed to.[45]

One of the developments, occurring by the late 1890's, that added to the need for exclusive dealerships and the desire for price maintenance was the trend toward advertising specific items on a quality basis. Through advertising, placed mostly in the daily papers but also in the Spanish and Catholic weeklies, Nordhaus attempted to reach the full trade area, and especially he tried to pull heavily on the growing population of East Las Vegas from which he claimed to get three fourths of his retail trade.[46] In seeking exclusive control of the Black Cat Hosiery Line, manufactured in Kenosha, Wisconsin, Nordhaus wrote a restrained letter in which he claimed that "the sale of the Black Cat Hosiery in this market is to an extent the result of our having *very liberally* advertised it. As we do not care to advertise for the benefit of competing houses we shall not feel the same interest in the goods as in a brand of which we control the sale for this trade." [47]

Sometimes, when exclusive agencies on valued product lines could not be obtained, Charles Ilfeld persuaded the manufacturer to supply a private brand. In 1885 and 1886 the company was selling shoes, ribbons, and tobacco under its own name.[48] Devoe and Reynolds of Chicago furnished Ilfeld with a private brand of paints, though later an exclusive agency on the regular brands was obtained.[49] In 1899, the company was actively seeking a private brand on a second grade flour.[50]

Beyond the natural desire to obtain or develop valuable brand names, the avoidance of price competition was a major factor in the policy of brand preference.

Jobbing and Bidding

The greater emphasis upon the exclusive retail agency in 1893 and later years was not unrelated to a similar development in the move to obtain jobbers' discounts. The latter developed slowly in the 1880's but was sought and obtained with greater frequency in the middle and late 1890's. Growing economic pressures with increasing force combined to make this relationship of the exclusive retail agency and the volume discount something more than circumstantial.

The onset of the depression in 1893 brought price-cutting to the fore and with it, undoubtedly, a certain amount of distressed selling. Some temptations must have existed among suppliers to seek more intensive distribution as a method of relieving excess inventories. The instinctive reaction of Nordhaus was to protect himself against the threat of demoralized markets, at least in those lines of merchandise where he had expended some effort and cost to promote consumer acceptance on a quality basis. He sought the exclusive agency and its companion, price maintenance—or a more accurate phrase for 1893, orderly price adjustments—as promising tools.

A second set of circumstances, however, blunted the effectiveness of these weapons. The substantial growth in sales to country stores and the increasing competition for their trade from other economic centers made a distribution agency, that was exclusive only for Las Vegas and immediate environs, less effective. Particularly was this so if merchants in Albuquerque and Santa Fe could obtain larger discounts on their purchases. Either because of the shrinking trade area within which Nordhaus was operating, or because of the volume discounts that were being obtained by merchants in other centers, or both, there were brought forth strong efforts to obtain for the Charles Ilfeld Company exclusive agencies for jobbing purposes within San Miguel (Las Vegas) and adjacent counties.

The shrinking trade area most certainly added to the desire, at least, to emphasize genuine wholesaling in those areas that had been lost to retail and where there appeared to be some hope of retaining and developing bulk sales. Two evidences of this occurred in the Roswell–Lincoln–White Oaks area. As a gesture in this direction, Ilfeld referred a retail order received from Roswell to the mercantile house of Jaffa, Prager of that town by shipping the item to that firm with the comment, "I wish to leave all the retail business in your section to you." [51] In 1895, Nordhaus sent some samples of shoes, hosiery, and other apparel to a

White Oaks merchant and explained that he was buying these items "in a very large way" and that his intention was to go "more into the jobbing business and out of ranch trade." [52]

Jobbing discounts were obtained the more readily, of course, in those lines where retail and country store volume had become large. The first instance noted of this development was in coal oil. Prior to 1888, Ilfeld had been buying this product from one of the two local commission houses, but in that year he was able to persuade the Denver office of the Continental Oil Company, because of his volume, to sell him direct.[53] The jobber's price was given him, however, only through the device of a rebate.[54] In 1890, the purchase of a carload of soap became the reason for seeking a distribution subsidy of 10 cents per bar.[55]

Nordhaus' appetite for jobbing over large areas had become quite large by the prosperous year of 1892. The Kansas City Hay Press Company, however, questioned his ability "to handle the entire territory," and Nordhaus was willing to settle for the counties of San Miguel, Mora, Guadalupe, and Chaves, the latter two being new counties and embracing the general territory from Santa Rosa to Roswell.[56]

Charles S. Brown, who went to work for Ilfeld in 1894, remembers that wholesaling had become rather substantial in small wood ranges, Diamond C soap, Arbuckle's coffee, lard, sugar, dried soft bacon, and a cheap line of mixed candies.[57] In that year the firm was also jobbing a line of tobaccos.[58] Hardware items under Charles Danziger rapidly grew into a substantial wholesale department which, with sales of more than $70,000 in 1902, netted a profit of more than $7000, of which Danziger, by agreement, received one third.[59]

Of the three departments in the 1891 store that were advertised as catering to the wholesale as well as the retail trade—dry goods, groceries, and furniture—the last-named, by that year, had been pushed with vigor, and in some respects was worthy of its bulk sales designation.[60] By 1887, a fair-sized retail furniture business had been developed—stimulated, in part, through the devices of installment selling and leasing. The latter became too much of a problem and appears to have been discontinued when a number of leased items turned up frequently in the second-hand stores of the city.[61] Installment selling, however, remained an effective device for many years and was extended to other items than furniture.[62]

The volume of furniture sales generated permitted Ilfeld to buy in carload lots by 1889, and Nordhaus was having some success in outfitting offices, stores, and hotels in Las Vegas and Santa Fe. By 1895, the bidding on volume furnishings, particularly for public buildings, had become an established practice. A distributor's agreement was in force in 1898 with the Wm. R. Schick Company of Chicago, through which purchases from many furniture manufacturers were pooled into carload lots.[63] Evidently, the net cost to Ilfeld was competitively low compared with that of firms in other centers because, among the many buildings that his company furnished through open bids, he was able to obtain the prestige contract, in January, 1900, for the new Territorial capitol building.[64]

In this growing trend toward sales in bulk, either through jobbing or bidding, the country customers were not forgotten. Richard Dunn of Rociada found it easier to meet his account with Ilfeld because, as Ilfeld's agent, he furnished a rather steady flow of lumber for many projects.[65] When Ringling Brothers Circus came to town in October, 1903, Nordhaus obtained the contract for six to ten tons of hay, and Wm. Frank of Los Alamos, whose long tenure as a loyal customer, without so much as a blemish on his record of steady and adequate payments on account, became the supplier.[66]

Drumming

The slowness with which Charles Ilfeld adopted real wholesaling as a positive program is demonstrated most clearly in the late use that was made of the traveling salesman to stimulate trade among the country stores. Floersheim had been employed in the middle 1880's as a drummer of sorts, but his chief function had been that of woolbuyer and collector of accounts. The same had been true even to a greater degree of the employment of Goldenberg.[67] Nordhaus evidently held little appreciation for the value of the drummer's division of labor; probably because the command Charles Ilfeld had over much of the produce of the countryside, through credit extension, brought the country storekeeper more or less regularly to his door. A clue to this attitude is reflected in a remark he made to a Colorado flour miller who had been trying to sell him a carload of his product. Nordhaus had admitted he was in no position to sell flour in that quantity because he had no traveling men on the road. Furthermore, he did not think it worth his while to hire such men (for the sale of flour, anyway) because he did not "know of another article which is more drummed up." [68] He had not entered this type of selling as late as 1895 when, if he felt extra effort should be made, he solicited country store business by mail.[69]

Undoubtedly it was the competition from other economic centers that finally drove Nordhaus to the use of traveling salesmen, although some preliminary experimentation may have had encouragement from his young nephew, Herman C. Ilfeld.[70] Herman, at least, was enthusiastic as the result of one of his early trips in the spring of 1896, for he took time to write his Uncle Noa in Albuquerque about it.[71] Herman continued to make a few selling trips to Mora and nearby territory that spring and summer, always confining his itinerary to points not too distant from the railroad, because he did not seem to have the advantage of a wagon for carting him and a full line of samples.

Nordhaus put little stress on a drummer program as late as 1897, and what little there was of this activity continued to be concentrated in that northern territory where Springer, Raton, and Clayton persisted in taking business away from Las Vegas. Herman made a spring trip to Mora and then, with a helper, to Elizabethtown, but the results were not encouraging. Nordhaus rationalized that business was as good as could be expected for the times.[72] In September, Herman expressed a desire to try his hand in the Taos area, but Nordhaus restrained him, not permitting him to go beyond Guadalupita, a small town about 20 miles north of Mora and 50 miles north of Las Vegas.[73] Herman did take another trip in the fall and went as far north as Springer.[74]

There is evidence that Nordhaus might have been thinking of expanding the program somewhat when he asked Goldenberg in the spring of 1897 to buy a peddlar's license at Puerto de Luna for one Luis Gonzales of Liberty, for a three-month period or "6 months if that is the shortest." [75] This may, of course, simply have been a service he was performing for an independent peddlar who possibly bought some of his goods of Ilfeld. Unquestionably, however, Nordhaus was giving increasing attention to the problem because he seems to have been disturbed by the number of applications for peddlar's licenses in the summer of 1897, presumably made by merchant houses.[76]

The seriousness of drumming competition had been made clear to Nordhaus by September, 1897, when, of all things, he learned that the Ilfeld Brothers, Noa and Louis of Albuquerque, were using drummers to take business right out of his bailiwick. "What do you think about Noa," he wrote Charles, "sending his drummer to Anton Chico where he sold Eduardo & Abercrombie, also was at Mora but don't know whom he sold there. . . . Eduardo told me he bought the goods cheaper than he ever did and how it can pay I. Bro. to send a man with wagon through the country & pay freight up here is a mystery to me, but that is their business." [77]

On the same day he wrote an upbraiding letter to Albuquerque. "Noa, do you think it's right to send your drummer to our customers here in the country?" [78] Noa's capitulation was not only prompt but it went further than Nordhaus evidently expected or wanted. Noa had informed him he would not send a drummer into the Las Vegas area or approach Ilfeld's customers again. Nordhaus stated he would send Noa a list of his customers, thus giving Noa a free hand with other accounts if he wished. And then, with implications that conceivably might have involved more than the extension of drumming, he added, "Perhaps he [Noa] opens a way for us by this method." [79]

Presumably Nordhaus immediately sent the names of those customers that were to be regarded as off the Ilfeld Brothers' premises, but a list of customers and towns sent several months later (February, 1898) indicates that Noa had had some trouble calling off his drummers. "Expect you to give your drummers *strict* instructions not to call on them," he wrote.[80] Perhaps, however, Nordhaus was simply preparing for his spring outings and thought he should post warnings of his exclusive hunting privileges. No claims were made for an extension of his preserves beyond what Nordhaus could rightfully call his trade area, except for the town of Springer.[81] Here, the Charles Ilfeld Company continued a tenuous hold principally through the account of J. Appel & Company which only a month before had shifted its mortgage obligation, and with it its buying loyalty, away from Ilfeld.[82]

Herman Ilfeld, having spent a month or two in New York City studying some of his father's purchasing techniques, was back at his drumming activities in the spring of 1898 and evidently kept his itinerary close to the railroad.[83] It was not until a year later, however, that any reference is made to his complete line of samples of staple dry goods, notions, boots and shoes, and hats that he carried with him in large trunks.[84] This seems to indicate a switch to the traditional sampler wagon of the drummer. The competitive situation apparently had forced this change, for not only had the routes been lengthened—going into the Taos area where Herman had wanted to travel four years before—but an anxiety was present to beat competitors to market. Herman, for instance, was sent post-haste to the town of Penasco in the summer of 1899 because word had come that Staab's men were preparing to leave for that point within a few days.[85]

Drumming became a serious endeavor in 1900, with routes being extended to Colorado points in the San Luis Valley, to Liberty on the east, and to Anton Chico and neighboring settlements to the south.[86] On a trip that started from Las Vegas on March 15, Herman and a helper took a drumming wagon northward, pulled by the horse team of Tom and Jerry, through the villages and towns of La Cueva, Mora, Guadalupita, Cleveland, Penasco, and Trampas. They reached Taos, if they were on schedule, on March 23. It had been planned to spend two days in Mora and two in Penasco with a Sunday stop at Guadalupita. Beyond Taos, stops were scheduled for Arroyo Seco, Arroyo Hondo, Questa, Cerro, and Castillo in New Mexico. The itinerary in Colorado included San Luis, Antonito, and Fort Garland.

The return schedule was more to the west following a route south through Cumbres Pass to Chama with a side trip to Lumberton. Bearing south, Herman was to stop at Tierra Amarilla and then the village of Tres Piedras almost due east of there. From there the route turned south

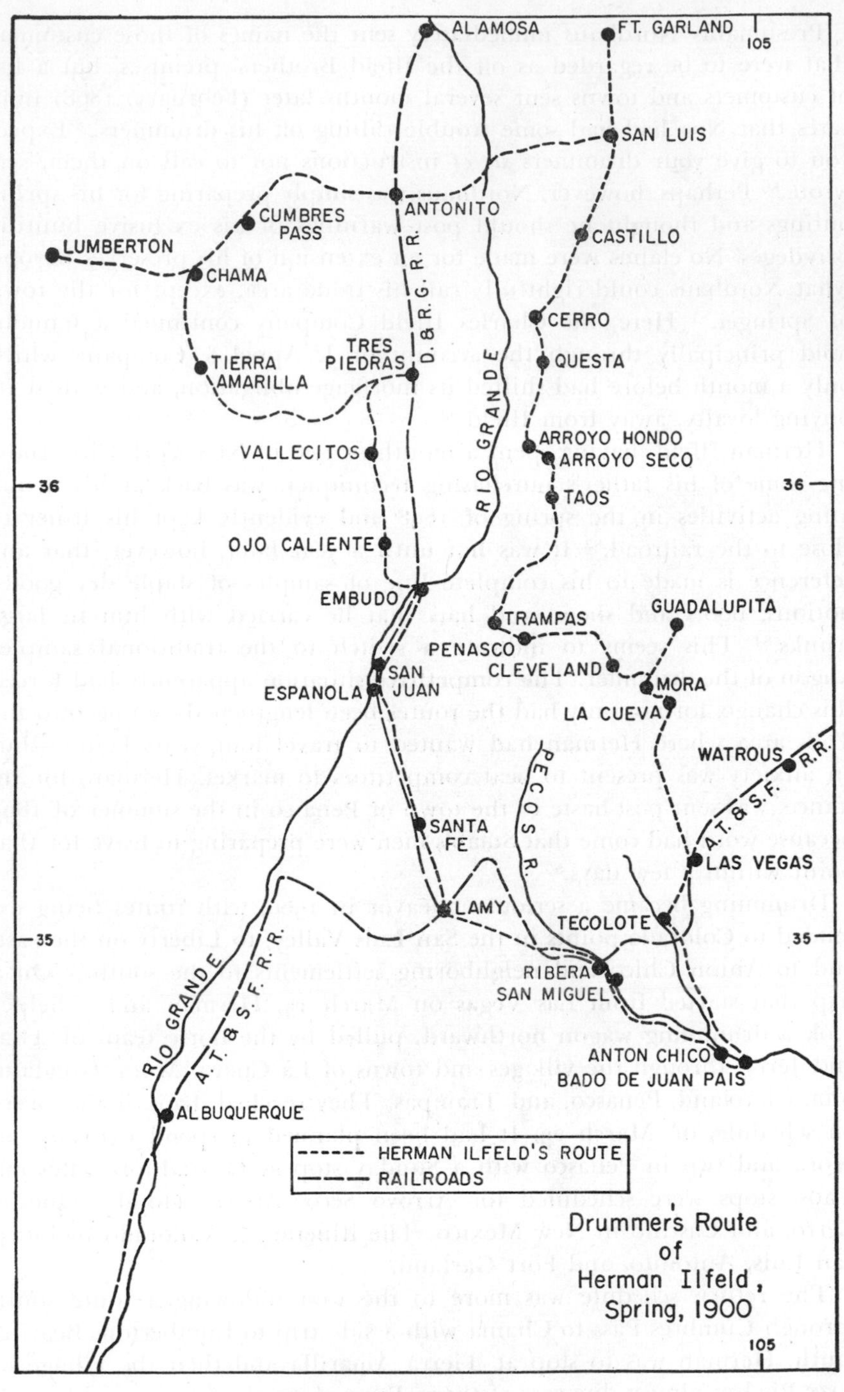

Drummer's Route of Herman Ilfeld, Spring, 1900

through Vallecitos, Ojo Caliente, Embudo, San Juan, Espanola, and Santa Fe. The closing sweep of the route took the wagon south to Lamy and then southeasterly through Ribera, San Miguel, Anton Chico, and Bado de Juan Pais before turning northward through intermediate points on the road to Las Vegas (see map on page 224).[87] The distance covered was well in excess of 500 miles, and the time elapsed could not have been less than eight or nine weeks.

In the fall, with Herman quite ill, a new drummer, Julius Linde, "a short humpbacked fellow," followed a similar route.[88] He was on the road seven to eight weeks before his trip was cut short when his faithful team of Tom and Jerry "played out" at Taos.[89] Upon his return to Las Vegas his route had been planned to cover the Conchas and Liberty country off to the east.[90]

Ten months of business brought in by traveling salesmen in 1902, according to a special financial statement, yielded sales of more than $30,000 upon which net profits were figured to have been over $2600.[91] What portion of these sales would have been made anyway, or what part arose from traveling salesmen handling special lines of hardware, such as steel ranges, or of house furnishings, each sold on the installment plan, cannot be determined. The developing business from the men on the road, however, for the most part with country stores, was of such volume and profitability as to cause Nordhaus to double this effort in the following years. Tom and Jerry, the storied horses, soon had served their time and were replaced by teams of white mules, whose braying as they approached a settlement and a promised stopping place made them heralds of the coming merchandise.[92] Two outfits were used. One team headquartered north of Espanola at Chamita, and the other in the trade territory to the south where routes, greatly extended, fanned out from the new branch warehouse on the railroad at Santa Rosa.[93]

XV

DIRECT INVESTMENT IN COUNTRY STORES

Fort Sumner, Pastura, and Corona

When Nordhaus, in May, 1901, was considering the establishment of a branch warehouse on the new railroad at Santa Rosa as necessary to the extension of wholesaling to the southern part of his trade territory, he also was contemplating the continuance, if not the expansion, of a policy of direct investment in country stores. It had been inevitable that credit extension alone would not prevent defections of allegiance by country storekeepers; but even more important, this device could not have given Nordhaus the needed control over the credits and collections policies of these proprietors or partners. Few of these enterprisers had more than the slightest talent for this all-important business function, and because of the secretiveness with which they preferred to operate—a weakness private enterprise and social pressures have been attempting to overcome for generations—Nordhaus was without influence in transferring any part of the acumen in credit and collection matters that he and Charles Ilfeld possessed to so extraordinary a degree.

Nordhaus made his first move toward direct control of retailing outlets in May, 1896, when he established the Pecos Mercantile Company at Fort Sumner.[1] He chose his friend of more than a decade, Philip Holzman, to manage the enterprise and to participate in the profits.[2] Holzman, apparently, had not been successful as a merchant or enterpriser in his previous experience. When his general store on Main Street in East Las Vegas had burned to the ground in the general conflagration of September, 1880, he had gone to work for a merchant in Trinidad, Colorado.[3] Later, and after a stint near Flagstaff, Arizona, where he had been producing crossties on contract with the Arizona Belt Railroad, he had returned to New Mexico, eventually to become a sheep rancher in the Fort Sumner region.[4] Somewhere along the line he had acquired heavy obligations to the point that, shortly after he had been hired by Nordhaus to manage his new enterprise, Holzman's evidences of debt were given over to an assignee in Las Vegas.[5] Max Nordhaus, in allowing an early fondness for the Holzman family to influence his business judgment, was simply emulating the tendency that had been exhibited by Charles Ilfeld so many times, that of hiring managers and key employees from among friends and relatives.

Holzman's beginning success with the Pecos Mercantile Company did not extend itself into the prosperous years of 1898, 1899, and 1900, and the old problem of credits and collections came to the fore.[6] Only by the most careful supervision of Holzman's credit extensions was Nordhaus able to keep things on an even keel. In spite of the fact that accounts were to be authorized in advance and credit limits established, Nordhaus was unable to prevent the accumulation on the books of many small, slow-paying accounts.[7] In February, 1897, he was using Goldenberg, who was in charge of Ilfeld's sheep ranch and small store at Pintada, to keep an eye on things and to "influence Holzman to drop a number of his customers and be very careful about trusting out so much." [8]

The collection problem became acute in the spring of 1901 when Nordhaus had to impress upon Holzman the absolute need for "an earnest effort to collect *this season* all the accounts you possibly can." By next season, he wrote, "the new R.R. [El Paso and Northeastern Railroad] will probably be ready to cross near your Territory and most people will commence trading along the new road." [9] As time passed and collections were coming in too slowly to suit Nordhaus, he ordered Holzman to settle all accounts in full by October.[10] The following spring, when Nordhaus had decided to use Holzman as manager of the new store at Pastura, a railroad point some 40 miles to the northwest of Fort Sumner, he had to disagree with his friend that these old accounts could be collected easier at the new location.[11] He begged Holzman, as he had on previous occasions, to be frank with the people in pushing collections. "Let the people know that you want to close out," he wrote with some exasperation.[12]

The arrival of the railroad also forced the closing of the Pintada store, although the manager, Goldenberg, was not apprised of the plans to do so until after the Pastura store had opened for trade. With silence thus maintained until after Nordhaus had left for Europe, it seems evident that this was a deliberate tactic to bring an end to Goldenberg's worrisome dual responsibilities as manager of the Pintada Ranch and as part owner of M. B. Goldenberg and Company at Tucumcari.[13] Before another sheep season had ended, Nordhaus' old friend and relative had chosen to resign.[14]

The problem of finding good managers without an arm's length policy of selective hiring was becoming most serious in this period of expansion. The obligation that Nordhaus felt to Holzman as a friend was now deeper because he had been responsible for placing Holzman in the Fort Sumner enterprise that now was dangling helplessly with the advent of the El Paso and Northeastern Railroad. If that store was to be resuscitated it would have to await the fulfillment of a teasing promise of a competitive railroad to build a cut-off eastward across the heart of New Mexico.[15]

Holzman had some misgivings about locating at Pastura but Nordhaus, though he acquiesced in considering other possible places, felt strongly that he had found the proper place for his friend.[16] A contract for construction was let in March, 1902, but Nordhaus was in no hurry to push the work.[17] John S. Calhoun, contractor, was also building the Santa Rosa warehouse project, and that had priority.[18] In addition, the railroad, contrary to the agreement it had with Charles Ilfeld at Santa Rosa, was unwilling to give a lease on its land at Pastura unless Ilfeld would sign an agreement to ship 100 per cent of his merchandise, both in and out, by rail.[19] Yet the store did open on November 12, 1902, with Holzman as its $75-a-month manager.[20]

During the summer after the opening of the Pastura house, Nordhaus made inquiry of H. K. Rountree and Brothers, a merchant firm in the village of Corona located on the railroad almost 60 miles south of Pastura, about the reason why he had not been able to obtain any business from them.[21] Conversations must have continued, because, by December, Nordhaus was planning the purchase of Rountree's "stock of goods and store buildings, lots and real estate." [22] One Thomas DuBois was to "devote all of his time and attention to the management" of this store and "to keep true and perfect accounts" open to the inspection of Charles Ilfeld. DuBois agreed to repay the advances made by Ilfeld at the rate of 10 per cent per year and was given the opportunity to receive all profits "after repayment of all advances and interest and payment of all expenses of carrying on said business." These profits were to be determined at the time DuBois would cease to be the manager, which meant, evidently, when he had actually released himself from an employee status through the purchase of the enterprise.[23]

Toward the end of 1904, Rodney Schoonmaker, who had resigned as Ilfeld's office manager in April, 1903, was asked to accept the managership of the Corona store because DuBois had "not lived up to the terms" of his contract.[24] In the offer Schoonmaker was to take inventory as of January 1, and then to use his judgment whether to retain DuBois after February 1.[25] Schoonmaker accepted the job at $150 a month salary and Nordhaus promptly wrote DuBois terminating their contract. "Under our agreement you have the privilege of purchasing the business of the Corona Mercantile Company. I am ready to sell out all property, assets, and good will of said company for whatever amount may be due me. . . . I would grant you time to February 1st within which to make arrangement." [26] DuBois resigned within a few days.[27]

Schoonmaker, unfortunately, was no manager. He was honest, able as a records keeper, and meticulous to a fault, but he was unsuccessful in matters of business judgment.[28] When Philip Holzman prevailed upon Nordhaus to permit him to take over the Corona store for his boys,

Arthur and Joe, Nordhaus made the arrangement.[29] Presumably father Holzman would keep an eye on things from his Pastura managership.

The situation at Corona went from bad to worse until two acts of God intervened—one helping a little and the other hurting a lot. The Pastura Mercantile Company burned to the ground in 1907, encouraging Philip Holzman to move down the railroad to Corona to keep closer supervision over his boys and, perhaps, to achieve enough success to exercise his option to buy the firm.[30] Some straightening out of matters might have occurred but for the second stroke of fate in the death of Philip sometime in 1910.[31] The solution to the problems at Corona then awaited the arm's length hiring, in November, 1912, of a young, but already successful, enterpriser from the tiny town of Lucy to the northwest. This was Earl L. Moulton, later to become, successively, general manager, president, and chairman of the board of the Charles Ilfeld Company.[32]

The Pastura problem, too, took some time to settle. After the fire, the store was rebuilt almost immediately and a new manager was hired. His dismissal a few months later brought another manager whose tenure approximated two years.[33] In October, 1908, Nordhaus brought in a young bookkeeper, A. C. Ortega, who in 1903 and 1904 had been employed by Hugo Goldenberg at Puerto de Luna, and who had been used at Corona to control the records of the Holzman Mercantile Company. He succeeded to the managership of the Pastura Trading Company in 1910, an event that also settled successfully that managerial problem.[34]

Furthur Retail Store Expansion

The expansion of investment in retail stores continued after the Atchison, Topeka & Santa Fe Railway built its cut-off, in 1908, for an east-west route across central New Mexico, from Belen to Clovis, to connect with its eastern lines at Amarillo, Texas. The Fort Sumner store had been temporarily revived under the managership of A. Brown Harris, a rancher from the Santa Rosa area, who had also served under Holzman, on occasion, as a collector of accounts for the Pecos Mercantile Company.[35]

Brown Harris had not been doing a volume of business satisfactory to Nordhaus, and apparently his record keeping left much to be desired. Schoonmaker, upon his release from Corona, in August, 1905, spent three months at Fort Sumner putting the records in shape and helping out in general in the hope that the store could advantageously profit from the new railroad activity.[36]

As the railroad cut-off neared completion in 1907, Nordhaus laid plans for placing a store 50 miles east of Belen at Willard, where the Bond brothers and John Becker also had mercantile branches.[37] In talking with Carl Dalies, an associate of Becker, while on a trip to

Santa Fe, Nordhaus thought Dalies had implied that, because two large firms in Willard were too many, Becker might be willing to sell his interests there to Ilfeld.[38]

Before approaching Becker on this matter, Nordhaus obtained options on some lots from an agent of Mr. Becker's townsite company. Evidently Becker preferred to wait and test Nordhaus' determination to enter the competition, because Nordhaus had hired a manager "for promotional purposes" and he had opened a store before Becker agreed in May, 1907, to a merger of his interests at Willard with Ilfeld. The Willard Mercantile Company had been incorporated in the spring of 1907 with the issuance of $10,000 in capital stock, two thirds paid in, but upon the purchase of Becker's property, the capitalization was increased to $100,000 with one half paid in. Becker received a 42.5 per cent interest, $33,000 in cash, and a short-term note for the balance of $27,000.[39]

The first dividend of 10 per cent was paid in 1909, followed by disbursements of 1 per cent and 2 per cent in 1910 and 1911, respectively. This less-than-satisfactory performance led to a change in managers, and a reduction in capitalization by one half. The latter was accomplished by the purchase of 250 shares from Becker and by the retirement of a second 250 shares belonging to Ilfeld interests. A surplus account of more than $7000 was written off against certain assets to make balance sheet values more realistic. Becker sold his remaining stock in 1913, and these shares, in large part, became the property of the new manager, Anthony Stanton.[40]

Earnings, as one might expect, became substantial during the war and the years immediately following, 1916 through 1919. In the optimism this engendered, two branches from the Willard corporation were set up in January, 1918—one at Encino, 38 miles down the track to the east, and the other at Mountainair, almost 14 miles up the track to the west. Each received 25 per cent of the working capital of the prosperous Willard enterprise. The Mountainair dowry, however, grew until, in 1926, it absorbed the Willard house and subsequently became the Mountainair Trading Company.[41]

Other investments in retail stores were made in Springer and Roy to the north of Las Vegas, these being a carry-over of the still smouldering desire of the Ilfelds to capture this territory for Las Vegas as a distribution point—this time it being the younger generation of Ilfelds, principally, who held the determination.[42]

The retail store that held on as a profitable enterprise and as a symbol of the sedentary merchant and his mercantile capitalism when all the other retail ventures had disappeared was the Corona Trading and Supply Company. Earl L. Moulton and the contract he signed on November 12, 1912, were both symbols of the more enlightened policies to come.[43] He was among the first of the mercantile managers to have been hired objectively and at arms' length. His contract was the first to permit a manager to purchase goods from the Charles Ilfeld Company only when the price was equal to or lower than other sources. His decision, at first, not to accept the offer of "Mr. Nordhaus" must have whetted the desire of this vice president and general manager for young Moulton's services, because the contract went on to stipulate that grain, flour, and salt would be furnished at cost and all other groceries and provisions at 2.5 per cent over cost at shipping point.[44] This was but one half the mark-up that the Holzmans had been paying on all of the merchandise they had purchased and one fourth the general wholesaling mark-up. Even the interest rate to be charged Moulton for additional funds he might need or for credit he might carry beyond the maturity of his bills was to be but 6 per cent —2 per cent lower than the Holzmans had been charged. On the other hand his rent, at $50 per month, was somewhat higher than that of his predecessor.

Whereas the Holzmans' contract had anticipated the eventual purchase of the store by that family, and thus the retention of any profits that might have been made, this was not the anticipation of the contract with Moulton, although, in case the Charles Ilfeld Company wished to dispose of its investment, Moulton would have had the first opportunity to purchase the assets. Moulton was to receive one fourth of the net profits and a salary of $150 a month, the latter considerably less than the drawings permitted the Holzmans.

The desire Nordhaus held to retain the Corona store as an Ilfeld investment may have been one of the reasons for the more favorable purchase terms accorded Moulton. Another reason of greater weight, however, was the respect Nordhaus held for this thirty-four-year-old enterpriser who had done so well in the much smaller town of Lucy, and the belief that this young man would help him meet the competition of the Gross, Kelly branch at Corona that had captured so much of the trade there.[45]

In March, 1914, the Corona Trading and Supply Company became the Corona Trading Company, a corporation. In its first 14 months of operation, Moulton had produced a profit of $6800 upon a beginning capital of almost $37,000 dollars, accounting for an annual return of approximately 16 per cent.[46] The favorable terms which he had obtained in his contract had helped in these results. Yet, if one considers that 1913 was not, generally, the best of business years and that his predecessors had left him an unenviable "good will" item, this record, in the face of strong competition, must have been impressive.

At the end of the decade when, for personal reasons, Moulton wished to move his family to Albuquerque, there was real need in the Charles Ilfeld Company for this successful enterpriser. Coordination and supervision of the retail stores was calling for the creation of a specialized business function, and Max Nordhaus was anxious that Earl Moulton fill that responsibility. He offered his Corona manager the job at a salary of $5000 per year but added to this the opportunity for Moulton to acquire a one-fifth interest in the projected Ilfeld-Moulton Sheep Company—a corporation capitalized at $200,000. Moulton, somewhat reluctant to return to the sheep industry (he having spent his first five years in New Mexico herding the little beasts while recovering his health), accepted the new positions because he realized the still present need of combining sheep and wool with the country store trade if one were to be successful in retailing at the crossroads in New Mexico.[47]

The story of each of these little country stores—Roy and Springer to the north of Las Vegas, and Willard, Encino, Mountainair, Corona, and Pastura to the southwest—in general setting, at least, would give us the feeling of "this is where we came in." Throughout the decade of the 1920's, and longer at Pastura, Corona, and Mountainair, these country stores traded in money barter, using sheep and wool as the payment in kind; the partidario customers received sheep rented out on partido contract by the Ilfeld-Moulton Sheep Company.[48]

Yet these retail stores were but controlled outlets for the then well-established wholesale business that Max Nordhaus had driven toward so relentlessly since the close of the first decade, certainly, of his association with Charles Ilfeld. By 1920 the Charles Ilfeld Company had been wholesalers, in the true sense of the term, for more than a decade. Only the vestiges of retailing remained, and these were in the hinterland where New Mexico was still very much the New Mexico of the beginning mercantile capitalists.

XVI

WHOLESALING AND BRANCH WAREHOUSES

The Early Extent of Bulk Sales

The emphasis that Nordhaus had placed upon key country stores in the late 1890's, and which grew into an outer structure of company-owned stores, was a manifestation of the growing strength of the wholesaling function. One is inclined to picture it as an old function for the Charles Ilfeld Company—one that grew gradually until it flowered about 1894. Ilfeld's allocation of space in his 1882 store for the wholesaling of dry goods would imply that this function had become of some importance by that time whether emphasized or not. An occasional written expression, particularly in the late 1880's, giving at least lip service to the development of jobbing, indicates this matter was receiving attention. The adoption, though infrequently, of a line of goods carrying a jobber's discount, again in the late 1880's, gives further assurance that the function was being developed at that time. It would be reasonable to assume, however, that had wholesaling in the true sense of the term been a large factor in the business prior to 1894, it would not now be so difficult to find the evidence in the copious records available. It seems likely, too, that the distinguishing of bulk sales in the records would have been detailed sooner than 1894 had this function held major importance relative to retail sales in earlier years.

One clue to the quantity of wholesaling as early as 1886, when total sales began to be recorded on an annual basis, can be gained by estimating the volume of retail revenue relative to the size of cash sales. An interpolation of the percentage trend of cash sales to retail sales for the years 1896 through 1903, extending back to 1886, would indicate a probable relationship of a minimum of 30 per cent in cash to a maximum of 36 per cent (see Table 17). That the lower percentage may not be wholly realistic is indicated in the somewhat higher estimate of retail sales it would produce for 1886 than actually existed in 1894. This, of course, might have been the case because of the extremely depressed economic conditions of the latter year. According to these estimated limits, however, bulk sales in 1886 evidently were 45 per cent or less of total sales and probably less than 40 per cent—perhaps as low as one third.

Yet whatever tenuous conclusion we could reach in this manner, our suspicions would force us to question the accuracy of the application of the term "wholesale" to these other than retail sales acquired by Ilfeld in the 1880's. A far more important clue can be attained from the per-

TABLE 17. Analysis of cash, retail, and wholesale sales (1000$)

Year	Cash sales	Per cent cash to retail	Retail sales	Wholesale sales	Per cent wholesale to total sales	Total sales
1886	$26.9 [a]	30–36 [a]	$89.7–74.7 [a]	$44.6–59.6 [a]	33.2–44.4 [a]	$134.3
1894	35.5	40.5	87.7	115.8	56.9	203.5
1895	37.3	39.1	95.5	117.0	55.1	212.5
1896	39.0	46.8	83.3	119.7	58.9	203.1
1897	48.3	51.8	93.3	166.6	64.1	259.8
1898	64.8	55.1	117.6	189.6	61.1	307.1
1899	68.1	55.1	123.7	229.1	65.0	352.9
1900	74.3	57.2	129.9	269.2	67.5	399.1
1901	77.3	58.3	132.7	320.7	70.7	453.4
1902	64.0	56.2	113.9	310.1	73.1	424.1
1903	68.8	57.4	119.8	341.8	76.2	461.6
1904	69.4	61.4	113.1	403.1	78.1	516.3
1905	82.7	71.7	115.3	554.0	82.8	669.3

Source: Summary Book, 1895–1910.
[a] Estimate.

centage trend of the over-all cost of sales to revenues. True wholesaling, by its very nature, would require a much higher cost-of-goods-sold percentage (a lower mark-up) than the same goods sold at retail. Inasmuch as average mark-ups for merchandise in general, either at retail or wholesale, can be assumed to have changed very little from one year to the next, any substantial change in the relation of cost of goods sold to total sales, including both retail and wholesale data, would be a reflection of the changing proportions of these classifications.

Unfortunately, inventory figures with which to adjust annual purchase data are not available prior to 1894. This handicap can be overcome, for all practical purposes, by calculating percentages of costs of purchases to sales in overlapping bienniums, thus removing reasonably well the influence of changing levels of inventories. Such a method, when compared with the actual cost of sales calculated by Schoonmaker from 1895 to 1902, shows the cumulative error in these eight years to have been slightly more than 0.25 per cent though maximum errors each way of 3 per cent existed. Five of the years, however, show rather minor disparities (see Table 18).

The figures that were obtained in this manner would seem to lend substantial support to the assumption that wholesaling began its marked growth for the first time in the 1894–95 period. The evidence would be stronger, however, were it not for the fact that the single biennium of

TABLE 18. PURCHASES AND SALES ANALYSIS, 1886–1906; COST OF GOODS SOLD AND INVENTORY TURNOVER, 1895–1902 (1000$)

Year	Purchases	Estimated per cent freight of purchases	Estimated freight costs	Total estimated purchase cost	Total sales	Two-year running per cent cost to sales	Actual per cent cost of sales on annual basis [a]	Inventory turnover [b]
1886	$105.8	11.0	$11.6	$117.4	$134.3	—	—	—
1887	97.7	11.0	10.7	108.4	118.6	89.3	—	—
1888	93.2	11.0	10.3	103.5	138.6	82.4	—	—
1889	125.8	11.0	13.8	139.6	159.9	81.4	—	—
1890	126.3	11.0	13.9	140.2	188.2	80.4	—	—
1891	162.4	11.0	17.9	180.3	222.1	78.1	—	—
1892	187.8	11.0	20.7	208.5	267.0	79.5	—	—
1893	124.3	11.0	13.7	138.0	204.2	73.5	—	—
1894	154.5	11.0	17.0	171.5	203.5	75.9	—	—
1895	166.8	10.8 [c]	18.0 [c]	184.8	212.5	85.6	84.6	2.2
1896	147.9	10.0 [c]	14.7 [c]	162.6	203.1	83.6	84.1	1.8
1897	212.4	10.0 [c]	21.2 [c]	233.6	259.8	85.6	82.6	1.9
1898	214.3	11.0 [c]	23.6 [c]	237.9	307.1	83.2	82.7	1.9
1899	277.7	10.3 [c]	28.7 [c]	306.4	352.9	82.5	82.6	1.9
1900	314.6	9.1 [c]	28.7 [c]	343.3	399.1	86.4	89.4	2.2
1901	344.7	8.7 [c]	30.0 [c]	374.7	453.4	84.2	86.5	2.4
1902	359.6	9.6 [c]	34.7 [c]	394.3	424.1	87.6	88.1	2.1
1903	338.4	9.5	32.1	370.5	461.6	86.3	—	—
1904	416.4	9.5	39.6	456.0	516.3	84.5	—	—
1905	570.5	9.5	54.2	624.7	669.3	91.2	—	—
1906	725.7	9.5	68.9	794.6	820.8	95.2	—	—

Source: Summary Book, 1895–1910.
[a] As shown by Schoonmaker's analysis.
[b] Using cost of goods sold divided by average of beginning and ending inventories.
[c] Actual.

1886–87 shows an estimated cost of sales percentage of more than 89 per cent—a figure of 3.5 per cent higher than the 1894–95 biennium. The sudden drop, however, in the 1887–88 biennium, and subsequent declines until 1893–94, would indicate that the earliest biennium had a high cost of sales for other reasons than a possible dominance of wholesaling.

In further explanation, it should be recalled that the 1886–87 period was near the end of a serious decline in wool prices, was at the end of a fall in sheep prices, and was in the middle of a substantial decline in cattle prices.[1] Surely this would have been some deterrent to any relative increase in wholesale to retail sales. Trading with country stores and outfitting of ranches must have been at a lower ebb than retailing activities. The growing population of Las Vegas, supported in degree by the outside income sources of railroad and transients, would have given some strength to local retail trade not possessed by the country business.

Actually, the relatively high cost of sales percentage in 1886–87 must have been caused, not by a high proportion of wholesaling, but by a failure to adjust purchases quickly enough to declining sales. In 1887, for instance, when total sales fell more than $15,000, purchases declined but $9000, giving a percentage cost of purchases to sales in that one year of more than 91 per cent. The much lower estimated cost of sales figures from that time on until 1894–95, based on two-year overlapping periods, evidently resulted from a working off of inventories faster than our method of calculation could detect and from an emphasis on retailing which culminated in Ilfeld's greatly enlarged store which opened in the late months of 1891.[2]

The sharp upturn in these overlapping biennium figures, beginning with 1894–95, from 76 to almost 86 per cent, coincides with the time Schoonmaker began to tabulate wholesale and retail sales separately. In fact, on an annual basis, purchase costs rose as a percentage of sales from 68 per cent in 1893 to more than 84 per cent in 1894. Inasmuch as the depression had been in force a full six months by the beginning of 1894 (locally its beginning can be measured by the break in wool prices in the summer of 1893), very little of the increase in cost of sales can be traced to a failure to adjust purchases to sales. Actually, a surprising increase of more than $30,000 in purchases occurred in 1894—a rise of almost 25 per cent. One can only interpret this as a deliberate stocking of goods undoubtedly for a contemplated wholesale business. The actual cost of sales figures, kept by Schoonmaker from 1895 to 1902, which appear to be consistent with the estimated biennium figures, did not fall below 82 per cent and showed an upward trend, as would be expected, with the rising volume of wholesale business that he recorded (see Table 18).

Charles Ilfeld, Wholesaler

Annual total sales remained approximately the same from 1893 through 1896 at slightly over $200,000, while wholesaling grew moderately. In 1897 a sharp rise in total sales took place, 85 per cent of which occurred in bulk sales. Further substantial increases were attained in the next four years, but wholesaling almost doubled, reaching more than $320,000 or 70 per cent of total volume.[3]

It was at this time, 1901, that Nordhaus was contemplating a change in the character of his business. In March, 1902, he began construction of a building at Santa Rosa on railroad property. Across the street he purchased 75 feet of private land to be used as a corral and stopping place for customers.[4] In August, Juan L. Trujillo of Rociada had been hired to manage the branch, but first Herman Ilfeld and then Max Nordhaus took turns conducting its affairs until Trujillo could make his appearance.[5] Arthur Ilfeld was expected to take charge if the new manager were too slow in arriving.[6] Trujillo finally came in December and began a very successful managership, proving he had been worth the wait.[7]

It is interesting to note that, of more than $46,000 of purchases of merchandise in the first calendar year of operation, only 13 per cent came from Las Vegas, while 15 per cent is recorded as having been bought locally and 72 per cent as having been shipped directly from the East.[8] Nothing could show more clearly, if Nordhaus were to continue to develop his wholesaling trade with country stores, the need to locate warehouses on the railroad closer to these customers—warehouses that could be supplied directly without a first handling of goods in Las Vegas.

In this first year of operation, 1902, the Santa Rosa branch had merchandise sales of almost $37,000 with a cost of sales of more than 86 per cent, indicating a heavy proportion of wholesale trade. Its net profits approximated 4.5 per cent of sales. In addition, the branch collected on account and sold for commissions more than a million pounds of wool at a gross profit barely exceeding 5 per cent. This was almost twice the volume of wool handled at the Las Vegas store that year—another telling experience in the decline of Las Vegas as a distributing center.[9]

By the end of 1904, wholesaling had passed the $400,000 mark and comprised almost 80 per cent of the merchandise business. Under the direction and encouragement of Nordhaus, Charles Danziger had built a substantial wholesale hardware department. Arthur Ilfeld had done the same with groceries, and Albert Stern, manager of the retail store, though not yet twenty-five, was specializing in the dry goods field. The last-named, whose father had been a close friend of Charles Ilfeld, also had created a department for school supplies, which in another year had become the Territorial depository and exclusive distributor for texts adopted by the school system. This 1905 contract became an annual one until 1933 when free schoolbooks henceforth were dispensed by the state throughout the system.[10]

In June, 1905, a series of special sales at retail began. A 10-day clearance sale in the middle of June was followed by "big Bargains" at the end of the month until July 4. On August 10 a "sweeping sale" was announced, followed in that month and the next with "closing out" sales. An announcement, "Going out of the retail business," was made on September 25. On Tuesday, October 17, the store was closed while Lincoln Sale Promoters of Chicago prepared for the final clearance. On Saturday all merchandise was advertised at one-third off. Eight days later it was "$100,000 in merchandise at cost." On November 1 free gifts were being dispensed "$2.50 to $100"—for purchases of listed articles. By November 25 the balance of Ilfeld's retail stock had been transferred to East Las Vegas for a final sale.[11]

Sales volume in 1905 grew at a great pace, and practically the full 30 per cent increase, amounting to more than $150,000, was attributable to wholesaling. By that year this part of the business had exceeded the half-million-dollar mark. With possibilities for further expansion holding much promise through plans for the establishment of company owned retail branches along the Santa Fe cut-off, and a new warehouse in Albuquerque, the incorporation of Charles Ilfeld, proprietor, was being considered.

Incorporation and the Human Factor

Sheer size was a major factor in the move to incorporate. Division of function and delegation of authority and responsibility had been growing so that the flexibility offered by the corporate form must have been inviting. Ilfeld would have been reluctant even to contemplate the addition either of limited or general partners in his major enterprise; and had he done so, the thought of removing and replacing such people as occasion demanded would have discouraged further thought along these lines. Yet, the talents required in an increasing number of managerial positions could not likely be attainable in full without making available opportunities for ownership in the enterprise.

This latter need must have weighed heavily in the decision to change the form of organization. Nordhaus said it did, and there is no reason for believing he was simply making a pleasant sounding statement to his managerial staff. In a letter to his Santa Rosa manager, Trujillo, he wrote: [12]

> I wish to inform you that in very few days the name of the business will be changed to Charles Ilfeld Company which Mr. Ilfeld has organized with the special purpose of giving the trustworthy Employees who have been in our service for some years an interest in the business by offering them shares of the new company. Mr. Ilfeld will allow you to purchase $5,000 (or less if you prefer) of the stock on which you may pay whatever amount you are able to pay and he will carry you for the balance at 5% interest per year. The profit that your $5,000 will earn above the 5% will be your additional remuneration for your services, your salary to remain as it now is with free dwelling. . . .
>
> Yours Very Truly
>
> Max Nordhaus

A number of other employees, including Charles Danziger, his hardware manager, William Springer, the bookkeeper who took Schoonmaker's place, and Albert Stern, his former retail manager but then in charge of dry goods and school supplies, were offered stock on the same terms.[13]

The growth of the company, with its increasing division of function in management, brought with it also a demand for higher skills among the general employees.[14] Higher salaries had been granted all along the line. Whereas in the 1880's, $40 to $45 per month for clerks was a common salary, the usual offer in the 1890's for beginners was rarely under $60 and usually higher. Prompt raises were forthcoming to valuable employees.[15]

Hours of work by 1898 had not shortened much, perhaps not at all. They still covered a span from 7:00 in the morning to 8:00 at night and 9:00 on Saturdays, but Sunday work may have been reduced somewhat and vacations with pay had been instituted by 1896.[16] Ludwig Ilfeld, who was Schoonmaker's assistant in the middle 1890's, remembers working late at night with Schoonmaker, who pored over his books, much like a Bob Cratchit, and who, having a frail physique, often fainted away. Ludwig would throw water on the older man's face, and back to the books "Schooney" would go, never leaving his work until it was finished.[17] By 1900 the store was closing at 6:00, but it was still kept open Saturdays until 9:00.[18] Hours were shortened, of course, after retailing at Las Vegas was abandoned, but the office force still was required to return three nights a week to do billing for Santa Rosa.[19]

It was Schoonmaker, with his Marshall Field experience, who, according to Charles Brown, had much to do with persuading his superiors to permit the innovation of vacations and who also pushed for year-end bonuses. The latter were given in merchandise at the close of a good year and enabled Charles Brown, it is remembered, to obtain his first "set of tails." [20] Prior to Charles Ilfeld's trip to New York in January, 1900, he directed each employee to submit measurements for a new suit or dress.[21]

Picnics, organized by the employees, were held frequently in the summer months at El Porvenir and environs some 17 miles north of Las Vegas in the Gallinas Mountains. Most of the 26 or more employees, on such occasions, would take off in three-seated buggies, hired by the men, to eat the food prepared and furnished by the ladies.[22]

Such outings were but one of the pressures on Nordhaus and Ilfeld to close entirely on Sundays. Yet, it had been against the law since 1887 for all but a handful of businesses to stay open on the Sabbath, but the law had not been enforced and mercantile stores had been among those that had not complied.[23] In 1897 we find Ilfeld pressing Charles Spiess to introduce a bill in the legislature to make a $50 fine (first offense) for opening business on Sunday and, with some thought to an additional public relations twist, to emphasize the benefits these fines would bring, especially to the teaching profession, for which they were to be earmarked.[24]

Schoonmaker had been a constant and gentlemanly goad in such reforms. He had been influential, however, only because, as he pricked from one side, economic forces were pulling from the other. Good labor in Las Vegas had been growing scarcer in relation to the increasing demand brought on by the broader and bigger economic base that mercantile capitalists like Ilfeld and Nordhaus had done so much to create. The need to offer greater rewards than fixed salaries and minor fringe benefits to key employees was being felt as a constant pressure, and profit-sharing seemed clearly necessary if high quality, specialized management was to be retained. Charles Danziger, manager of the hardware department, was one individual who by 1902 had received a share, one third, in the profits he was able to produce.[25] Others undoubtedly had such an arrangement, but the plan was too limited in scope and too difficult to administer to be practical. With the incorporation of the business in January, 1906, an employees' stock plan became a feasible answer to this problem and, as Nordhaus specifically pointed out, this was one of the special purposes of the change in business organization. As the business grew, and as division of function grew with it, the employees' stock plan was greatly expanded so that in 1927, for instance, employees held approximately 27 per cent of the company's Class "A" common stock and 12 per cent of the Class "B." [26]

A second important reason for incorporation needs to be mentioned though it may not have been a consideration at the time. This was the personal desires of Max Nordhaus who, in probability, would sooner or later have need for tangible evidence of ownership as well as a right to transferability of that ownership in an enterprise promising continuity. He was still the general agent of Charles Ilfeld with no agreement, unless perhaps an understanding, of the proportion of ownership, if any, that was his. He was still serving without salary but free to draw what he would from the business, and his board and room continued to be furnished at the Charles Ilfeld residence.[27] As a man of modest tastes with a single loyalty to Charles Ilfeld, no arrangement could have been more satisfactory to him. Max Nordhaus, however, in 1905, was a bachelor, forty years of age, and as fate would have it, he had not long for this single life.

Louis C. Ilfeld, who as Max's attorney was the closest of the Ilfeld boys to Nordhaus, did not believe Max ever questioned or concerned himself with his lack of legal basis for ownership until he took on the responsibilities of a family of his own.[28] In the early fall of 1907, Max Nordhaus married Bertha Staab, the daughter of Abraham Staab, who, in Santa Fe, had created one of the largest wholesaling and general mercantile establishments in New Mexico until his retirement in 1902.[29]

According to Louis C. Ilfeld, Max went to his brother-in-law sometime after his marriage, and probably after the birth of his children, and explained the necessity for some understanding on his share of ownership in the business. Charles is reputed to have asked Max what he thought would be a fair division, and his answer is supposed to have been, "one-fourth for myself and three-fourths for you." The agreement was reached in some such manner and signed on February 18, 1911.[30]

It was an unusual agreement—as unusual, perhaps, as the general agent's agreement of 1886.[31] It was written down in a little black book, and the business organization that was established became known as Charles Ilfeld, Joint Ownership—a copartnership and holding company for the Charles Ilfeld Company and other business investments of the two men.

Expansion of Branch Warehousing

Following the incorporation of the company, plans soon were on foot for expansion of branch warehousing into the growing city of Albuquerque, although it is questionable whether the act of incorporation was more than incidental to the move. The pertinent development had been the decision of the company to specialize in wholesaling. With Albuquerque the point in question, the new character of the business pleasantly removed any obligation Max and Charles had harbored not to compete directly with the Ilfeld brothers in that city.[32] The Charles Ilfeld Company might have established itself there years before it did had it not been for this territorial demarcation along family lines. Gross, Blackwell and Company, with no such deterrent, had moved there in 1893 when the firm of Stover, Crary and Company, located across the street from the Alvarado Hotel, had been purchased.[33] A more satisfactory location on the railroad tracks was obtained in 1902, and a warehouse was constructed.[34]

Charles Ilfeld could not, in concience, have paralleled the move of Gross, Blackwell at the earlier date because his brothers, Louis and Noa, had been well established in Albuquerque for many years. When a disastrous fire wiped out the Ilfeld Brothers' entire merchandise stock in June, 1898, that company transferred its interests entirely to wool and sheep, but a third brother, Bernard, took over the merchandise business that Louis and Noa had given up.[35] Bernard, evidently, did rather well, and when eastern interests were probing Charles Ilfeld for a possible development of a jobbing business in El Paso, Charles suggested the possibility of a merger of his Las Vegas enterprise with B. Ilfeld & Company of Albuquerque as an arm to the larger venture.[36]

When the Charles Ilfeld Company decided that its future lay in wholesaling, there was no longer a family problem. Bernard had been buying much of his merchandise through Charles anyway, and, if warehousing facilities could be located in Albuquerque, so much the better. And so it was. In May, 1906, Nordhaus was seeking a manager for the prospective branch, and in November of that year Louis C. Ilfeld, attorney, was negotiating with the Franz Huning estate for a lease of its property on John Street, east of the Santa Fe tracks, and on the south side of Railroad Avenue.[37] The Charles Ilfeld Company had occupied this space, however, and had carried on business there before agreement on the lease had been accepted.[38]

David Weiller had been hired as manager of the branch.[39] His early operations must have been successful, because the board of directors of the Charles Ilfeld Company, four years later, voted Weiller its thanks for excellent results and sent Weiller and Nordhaus to Chicago to discuss a land lease with the Atchison, Topeka & Santa Fe Railway upon which a larger warehouse could be constructed.[40] A site was selected backing up to the tracks from First Street, north of Central Avenue, and a building was erected there in 1911.[41]

The size of the business is evident from the profits of almost $50,000 earned in the new location the first year, and the fact that the Albuquerque inventory exceeded, for the first time, that of the Las Vegas house.[42] As might be expected from hindsight, the business in Albuquerque continued to be substantially larger than that at Las Vegas from that year on. Max Nordhaus, after making frequent visits to the Albuquerque branch in 1910, moved permanently to that city in 1911, as had Albert Stern the year before.[43]

Further expansion of branch warehousing awaited the prosperous war and postwar years. A lease was signed in October, 1916, for a branch at Magdalena, where the Santa Fe had extended a spur line from Socorro westward many years before.[44] Three years later the Charles Ilfeld Company purchased the assets of Cartwright Brothers in Santa Fe, a mercantile house that had been established there in 1880 and which, in 1902, had become a wholesale business.[45]

The next step in the establishment of branch warehouses seems to have been a long-last admission of prior policy mistakes. The company's repeated failures to gain a foothold in Springer and the northeastern area of the state through credit extensions and monopoly contracts had brought forth new efforts through the establishment of retail stores at Springer and Roy—the latter at the insistence of young Arthur Ilfeld.[46] These stores, too, had been operating failures, so that it must have appeared to Nordhaus that the only practical answer to this long-held dream of a northeastern trade territory would be the placing of a branch warehouse for wholesale distribution at a point where eastern supplies could be obtained at lower cost.[47] This he did by jumping beyond Springer to Raton, a town nestled at the foot of the famous northern pass through which the Santa Fe railroad had won its determined battle with the Denver and Rio Grande into New Mexico.[48] Here he established a small warehouse that was to be used almost strictly for the purchase and distribution of groceries and feed.[49] Las Vegas still was to be relied upon for supplies of dry goods and hardware.[50]

The largest single expansion, however, came in 1924 when, after creating a small branch in Gallup, a city more than a hundred miles west of Albuquerque near the Arizona border, this enterprise was merged with the Gallup Mercantile Company through an outright purchase.[51] This step had not been an easy one to take, for it required a heavy outlay of capital at a time when, as Nordhaus stated, he was having difficulty financing the subsidiaries in the retail business and at the same time the expansion of the wholesale stores.[52]

The Charles Ilfeld, Joint Ownership cash account, which in the three years, 1912 to 1914, had averaged $87,000, had dwindled in the years 1917 and 1918 to an average of about $3600. In 1919, Nordhaus ended the year with only $500 in this account but with investments in United States Liberty bonds of $20,000. These, however, were frozen to the investment account because of the large paper losses sustained as postwar interest rates rose. These were carried from 1918 through 1921 before any portion was sold. The personal interest of Charles Ilfeld, carried at more than a quarter of a million dollars at the end of 1919, was the credit upon which this tight cash position could be supported together with the more than $300,000 in bills receivable which, presumably, were convertible into cash in something called "due time." [53]

In spite of this restricted working capital position, the board of directors was discussing in December, 1919, the advisability of purchasing the Gallup Mercantile Company. Four delegates—Nordhaus, Weiller, Herman Ilfeld, and Albert Stern—were dispatched to Gallup with authority to seek a purchase on the best terms possible.[54] However, Hans Neumann, a German Jew, manager and a major owner of the company along with Gregory Page, evidently was unwilling to entertain a sale on the basis of the offers made.[55]

The result of Nordhaus' failure to acquire the Gallup Mercantile Company was his decision to compete directly with the established firm. After four years of this competition, in which the new outlet had not distinguished itself, Earl Moulton, by that time assistant general manager and director of the corporation, became chief negotiator in arranging for the purchase of the Gallup Mercantile Company, a task he accomplished in February, 1924.[56]

As the end of the prosperous 1920's was nearing, the Charles Ilfeld Company, acting through its wholly owned Gallup subsidiary, purchased the Willis Martin Supply Company of Durango, Colorado, and Farmington, New Mexico.[57] By this move the Ilfeld territory was extended into the northwestern part of the state and over into southern Colorado as

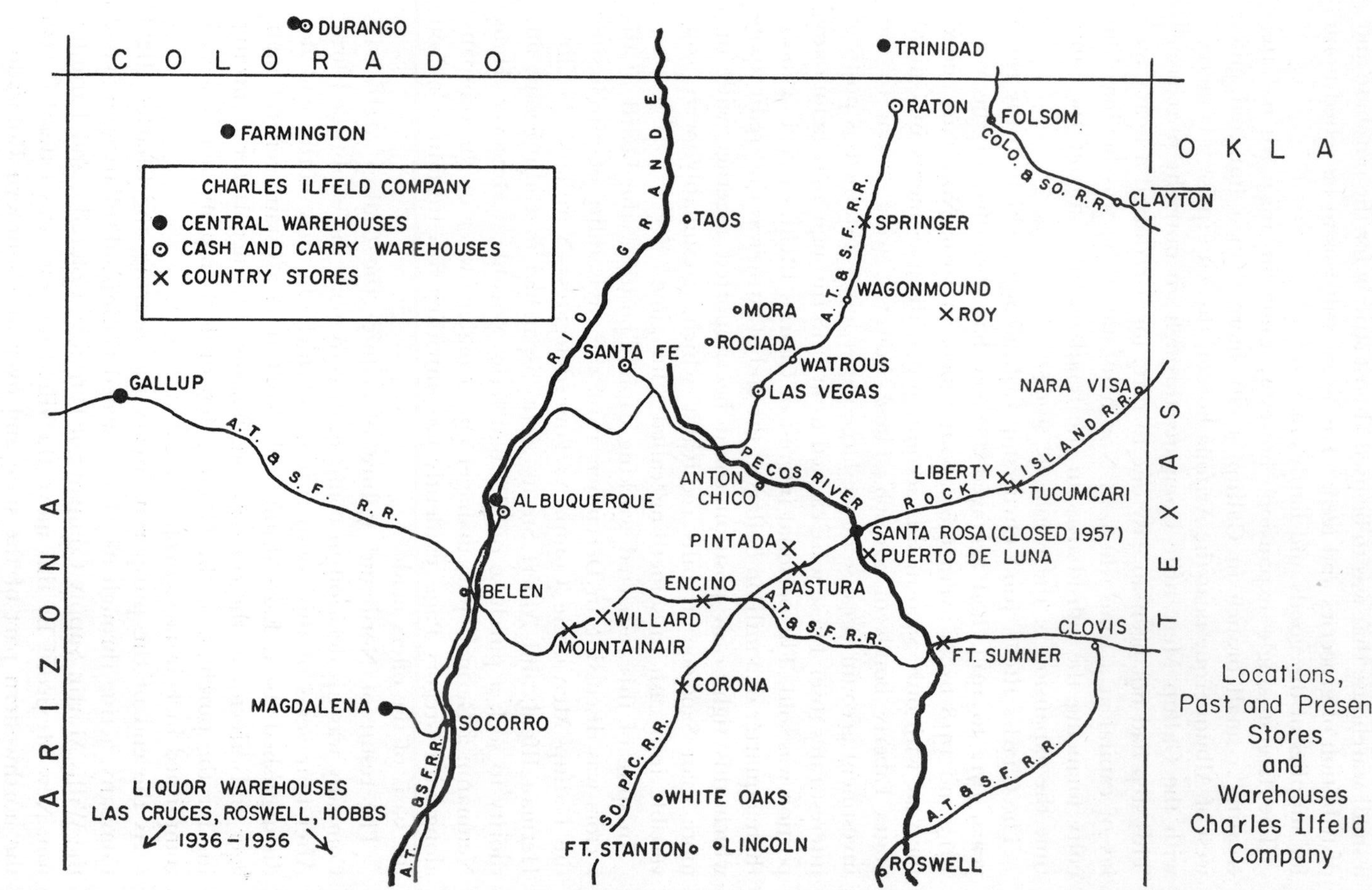

Locations, Past and Present Stores and Warehouses Charles Ilfeld Company

well as to an added portion of its eastern Arizona market that it had already tapped through the Gallup Mercantile Company.

Thus the prewar expansion in branch warehousing, that had begun in Santa Rosa and Albuquerque, had been extended by the end of the 1920's to include the entire northern part of the state through Raton in the eastern sector, Santa Fe in the middle, and Farmington and Durango in the west. Gallup commanded the central far west, and Magdalena was strategically situated to control much of the southwestern, thinly populated area of the state (see map on page 244).

When, in January, 1929, Charles Ilfeld died a few months shy of his eighty-second birthday, he had seen all but the last step in the major geographical growth of his company and, perhaps, he had known of the plans for the Farmington-Durango purchase.[58] With this expansion, driven forward by the inevitable shifting of comparative strengths of economic centers, Las Vegas had been left more to its memories than to its aspirations. Three small branches—Santa Rosa, Magdalena, and Raton—were handling in their group sales of groceries more than the equal of the grocery sales of the Las Vegas house. Albuquerque and Gallup had left the parent far behind. Santa Fe, one of the newer children, was close to the mother house in volume of sales.[59] For a few more years Las Vegas would be allowed to serve as the sentimental center of the business. Even that privilege, however, would soon be allowed to drift away to the centrally located, rapidly growing, city of Albuquerque.[60]

PART FOUR

Decline of Mercantile Capitalism and the Rise of a New Era

XVII

THE OLD ORDER IN A CHANGING ECONOMY

Attacking in Depressions

Had the expansion of the Charles Ilfeld Company into northwestern New Mexico and southern Colorado not occurred at the close of the prosperous 1920's, there is little reason to believe this step would have been thwarted for long by the depression of the 1930's. Charles Ilfeld and Max Nordhaus had never been fearful of economic depression in New Mexico. Protected from the outside by the tariff walls of slow and costly transportation, they were also bolstered from within by a strong and persistent growth in population. As these tariff walls of distance and time cracked in places, the population growth increased in tempo. When a depression plied its strength in this kind of an economy, its cutting edges were dulled. To the extent that economic distress was present, however, the other protective armors of the mercantile capitalist grew thicker. Monetary exchange became scarcer, and indirect lending of capital, principally by the banking specialist, became less effective. Thus, the need for the mercantile capitalist grew in proportion to the economic need of the people. The general merchant, like Ilfeld, unlike the banking specialist who in earlier years, as now, was committed "to pull in his horns" when the near-term profits of his customers were disappearing, met this need by expanding his credit prudently. His faith rested upon a growing population and an ensuing gravity flow of groceries.

The depression of the 1870's was Ilfeld's first experience as an enterpriser in this kind of an economic phenomenon, and so far as the records show he evidently held little disposition to bow to it with short-range strategy. He purchased the interest of his partner, Letcher, in September, 1874, a full year after the failure of Jay Cooke, the investment banker, had precipitated the Panic of 1873 and further economic decline had been manifested.[1] Such an act of independence on the part of Ilfeld suggests the minor concern he held for the depression he was encountering.

There were days, though, when he had entertained his doubts. As economic conditions worsened, his normal exuberance would give way to occasional displays of discouragement. One of these 24-hour affairs came in 1877 when business had reached its lowest ebb. "Vegas is so dull and dead," he wrote his friend Demetrio Perea, "you can be glad to be out of it. If I had only a fair chance to close up my business, I would not think of [*sic*] moment to leave here, but if I would offer my stock 50% below cost I would not find a buyer." [2] His recovery, however, was always rapid, and in this case he was placing orders the next day for a variety of items including bathtubs for babies.[3]

A year later, with commodity prices still dipping downward, occasional despondency had turned to wryness in humor. Richard Dunn and Ilfeld evidently had been commiserating in their economic and social problems but had been preparing to do something about them. These men, with others, had formed a social reading club and, through their mutual friend and publisher, Henry Holt of Chicago, ordered some 17 magazines and newspapers ranging from *Harpers* and the *United States Economist and Dry Goods Reporter* to the *Burlington Hawkeye*. In closing the order, Dunn added: "Excuse this annoyance, Henry, and if you want anything from this Rectum of the world I will cheerfully interest myself in your behalf." The postscript read: "Charley says Me too." [4]

These were words, however, that did not speak as loudly as "Charley's" actions. With the doldrums of 1877 practically upon him, Ilfeld took cognizance of the growing population and brushed aside any personal depression he may have been acquiring from the economic pressures about him. He found the capital and the heart to invest in real estate. He and Tom Catron, prominent Territorial attorney, bought a mortgage on the old Labadie residence on the south side of the Plaza.[5] When Labadie defaulted, the two men bought the house at public auction, and Ilfeld, soon thereafter, purchased Catron's interest.[6]

In April, 1877, when the *Las Vegas Gazette* was complaining "times are hard, money is scarce, everything in the world has depreciated except the wages of sin," Ilfeld began tearing down the old Labadie residence in preparation for a new hotel he planned to build.[7] The fact that a disastrous fire on the Plaza, starting in the Rosenwald wool warehouse, was stopped in its westward path by the Ilfeld demolition was providential.[8] The fact that Ilfeld immediately thereafter began construction on his hotel and was able to lease it in September or October to Charles Jewett under the name of the Jewett House was planning of another kind.[9] This was typical of the expansion that took place in some degree or manner in the business enterprise of Charles Ilfeld or his later corporation through each of the ensuing major or minor economic declines.

Though sales figures are not available for years prior to 1886, we know that the difficulties of the middle 1880's were attacked by an expansion in Ilfeld's sheep activities.[10] The slight recession of 1887–88 was met with further expansion in this field even to the inauguration of the partido system, which placed sheep on rental as one of the means for giving additional support to some of his customers.[11]

The depression of 1893–1897 brought forth a frontal attack with Ilfeld gaining the sources of credit and Nordhaus dispensing it in heroic efforts to hold the hinterland to Las Vegas and to insure the continued growth of the business.[12] Although the merchandise sales dropped sharply in 1893 and remained at that low level through 1896, the greatly expanded wool business brought the total receipts to a figure that certainly exceeded all previous years except, possibly, 1892. By 1897, merchandise sales of $260,000 were but 4 per cent less than the peak of 1892, but wool sales of almost $150,000 exceeded by far anything that had been accomplished before.

The Panic of 1907–1908 left its scar as evidenced by the difficulties in launching the Willard store and in the decline of total sales in spite of the opening of the Albuquerque branch in 1906.[13] Yet the decline in 1908 of 7 per cent was accounted for substantially by a drop in credit sales in the two months of October and November. In spite of this delayed reaction to the Panic of 1907, the year 1908 held to a higher level than 1906.

In the minor recession of 1913–14, earnings evidently slumped the first year as a 5 per cent dividend on the common stock failed to be earned by slightly more than $1000. In the next year, however, earnings returned more than enough to cover a 10 per cent declaration. Substantial dividends declared in the annual meetings of February, 1921, and 1922, offer some evidence that the serious deflation beginning in 1920 did not prove too damaging—although future dividend policies would indicate that Nordhaus and the Ilfeld family tended to be less cautious in years of low earnings or minor losses than many managements would have been.[14]

The ability of the Charles Ilfeld Company to prosper, and even expand, in the rather devastating secondary reaction of 1923–24, is noteworthy. Heavy cattle loans and livestock paper held by New Mexico banks in large proportions to earning assets were generally extinguished when cattle prices failed to rise more than minimally from their 1921 lows. Almost one half of the banks of the state failed from 1920 to 1925—most of them in the secondary economic reaction of 1923–24.[15] From spotty information available, it should be noted that net earnings of the company dropped sharply in 1924 but remained healthy, and the surplus account grew in both 1923 and 1924. Typical of the company's past operations, customers' account receivable balances increased and, logically enough, credit balances carried by a number of customers in the form of deposits rose markedly.[16] This change, probably, in some measure, was related to bank failures. While economic problems remained severe throughout the state, the Charles Ilfeld Company expanded its operations in the western region through its acquisition of the Gallup Mercantile Company.[17]

From 1873 to 1924, depression and recession had been times of opportunity for Charles Ilfeld and his enterprise.

Liquidity and the Great Depression

When the bloom was still on the 1920's, the Charles Ilfeld Company had reached a position of liquidity it probably had never achieved before. A plethora of cash had even caused the board of directors to push the company into the parade of corporations to Wall Street to place time and call loans "for periods not to exceed ninety days" and "for amounts not to exceed three hundred thousand dollars at one time." [18] In 1928 the company had freed itself of bank loans although borrowings of a sort were created through "accommodation deposits"—more than $50,000 that customers preferred to keep with Ilfeld rather than with commercial banks or in high-grade investments. These liabilities bore interest, probably at 6 per cent (it was 4 to 6 per cent a few years later), and were payable on demand. Nordhaus, however, with an adequate amount of cash ($342,000) could meet these or any other presentations that conceivably would be made against him.[19]

This liquidity was carried over into the 1930's. The decline in sales and profits from 1928 had been only moderate by the first year of the decade, and working capital had achieved markedly higher levels. Current assets rose strongly to more than seven times current liabilities (see Table 19). Included in these liabilities were $92,000 in "accommodation deposits"—a figure almost 80 per cent higher than 1928. By 1932 the current ratio had risen to more than nine to one, and the cash position, including United States Treasury bonds, was 1⅓ times the company's short-term liabilities (see Appendix 14). All this occurred even though the dividend policy of the 1920's had been fairly liberal and, in the first three years of the depression, had caused cash payments to exceed net profits by 60 per cent (see Table 19).

Sales and profits rebounded fast in 1933 and 1934, and the company promptly increased its per share dividends in both years, applying the latter appropriation to an additional dividend of 30 per cent in common stock. Thus, from 1930 to 1934, cash payments on capital stock amounted to 111 per cent of net earnings, and although these earnings continued to increase in 1935, and the dividend rate to be cut somewhat, the six-year record shows that 104 per cent of the period profits had been paid to stockholders.

Only a marked change in the character of the business could have caused the astute Max Nordhaus to face about so completely in his recommendations on dividend policy. In the years prior to the United States' entry into World War I, though information and evidence is spotty, it appears that it was more the rule than the exception to keep drawings and dividends below 50 per cent of net profits. Following the war, dividends were stepped up markedly, and it became the exceptional

TABLE 19. SELECTED RATIOS AND PERCENTAGES, 1895–1949

Year	Current assets to current liabilities	Sales to working capital	Sales to receivables	Net worth and long term debt to sales	Net profit to net worth (Per cent)	Drawings, dividends to net profits (Per cent)
1895	5.5	0.9	1.1	2.0	3.1	89.4
1896	6.8	0.7	1.0	2.2	2.5	117.6
1897	8.5	0.7	1.1	2.1	11.5	15.8
1898	7.3	0.8	1.0	2.0	8.6	16.8
1899	7.7	0.9	1.3	1.9	9.9	13.7
1900	3.8	1.0	1.0	1.8	6.3	8.5
1901	5.3	1.0	1.2	1.7	3.4	15.2
1902	4.7	0.9	1.1	1.8	1.3	—
1903	7.6	0.9	1.3	1.8	—	—
1904	9.0	0.8	1.4	1.8	—	—
1923	1.0	—	—	—	8.1	85.1
1924	4.6	—	—	—	4.6	88.8
1925	5.7	—	—	—	10.1	65.8
1928	3.2	2.9	5.7	0.4	14.7	60.5
1929	—	—	—	—	—	88.7 [a]
1930	7.2	2.2	4.0	0.5	7.3	94.5 [a]
1931	6.4	2.8	5.2	0.5	2.2	201.0
1932	9.1	2.4	4.7	0.5	[b]	[c]
1933	6.4	2.3	4.9	0.5	11.5	69.6
1934	5.1	2.8	6.0	0.5	9.0	66.6
1935	6.0	2.8	5.7	0.4	8.1	134.2
1936	3.3	3.0	6.3	0.4	12.1	81.0
1937	2.8	4.1	8.8	0.3	8.6	50.8
1938	3.3	3.6	8.2	0.4	3.6	19.9 [d]
1939	3.3	3.7	8.6	0.3	5.8	102.9
1940	4.3	3.5	8.9	0.3	6.2	88.5
1941	2.6	3.9	10.3	0.3	10.6	51.7
1942	3.7	3.7	17.8	0.3	10.3	59.9
1943	4.0	4.1	16.3	0.3	9.8	71.5
1944	3.6	4.5	21.4	0.2	9.9	58.4
1945	3.7	4.3	19.1	0.3	8.0	70.8
1946	2.5	5.2	16.6	0.2	13.6	46.1
1947	2.8	5.4	18.9	0.2	9.3	53.5
1948	2.9	5.4	15.9	0.2	8.4	63.2
1949	3.7	4.7	31.6	0.3	3.1	149.8

Source: Company records.
[a] Estimate.
[b] Loss of $4300.
[c] Dividends $103,400.
[d] Preferred stock only.

year that retained a majority of earnings for surplus. Throughout the serious depression years, as we have seen, the policy became more liberal.

The about-face may well have been too complete, but if so it is quite understandable. The rate of cash flow through the business had grown measurably. This appears most clearly over the years in the altering relations between sales and receivables and between invested capital and sales (see Table 19). Whereas in the period 1895–1902, annual sales figures approximated the size of year-end net receivables, the late 1920's found sales to be four times as great and to have risen to steadily higher proportions all during the 1930's. In the last calendar year of Max Nordhaus' life, 1935, the ratio stood at well over five to one and, at the time of his death, it was moving above six. In 1895 the average receivable hung on the books for at least a year. In 1936 it was only staying for 60 days. Nothing could be more indicative of the liquidity that had come into mercantile capitalism in New Mexico.

Equally significant in explaining Nordhaus' liberal dividend policy is the changing ratio of capital to sales. In the period 1895 to 1902, $2.00 of capital supported $1.00 of sales. In 1930, 50 cents of capital per dollar of sales was more than adequate, and the trend continued downward to well below 40 cents by the end of the decade (see Table 19).

Probably Max Nordhaus was no less influenced in this policy by the character of his environment. In the mid-1930's there were 470,000 people in the state, of whom approximately 70 per cent were spotted over a hinterland of more than 120,000 square miles.[20] The largest city in the state, Albuquerque, still held but 35,000 inhabitants and its county less than 60,000.[21] To Max Nordhaus and his understudy, Earl Moulton, this environment must have provided very little encouragement to dream of the effects of greatly expanded sales volumes that would require painful adjustments in policies and personnel, and that would strain invested capital to the utmost. In July, 1936, when Max Nordhaus suddenly slumped over his desk, New Mexico was still the land of *mañana* and *poco tiempo*.[22]

The Old Order Continues

The organization that Max Nordhaus had built was deeply engrossed in this slow tempo. Ever since the founding of the company it had been this way. The environment had been infectious. True it was that a Charles Ilfeld could burst to great heights when the emergency demanded it. Acquiring his business and building it strong through the depression of the 1870's, only a few years after he emigrated as a youth from Germany, was an early example. Max Nordhaus, with Charles Ilfeld, had displayed these characteristics of driving and intelligent energy against the deflationary forces of the 1890's. Earl Moulton had risen above great personal odds at an early age, and he would show this determined attack on problems again in company affairs in the 1930's and 1940's.

The Charles Ilfeld Company was fortunate, indeed, to have been guided through three successive generations by such able and potentially forceful men. Yet throughout the period from 1874, when Charles Ilfeld became proprietor, until some years after the death of Max Nordhaus, this good fortune also gave the company a monistic form of administration both in action and ideas.[23] The organization beneath the one or two at the top could be stimulated in emergencies to longer hours and greater energies as part of the game; in general, however, creativity was not its forte. In the 1930's, the long years of service of all the key administrators in Las Vegas and Albuquerque, and the rather static environment in which they had received their training, made certain that, if new patterns of administration were to come, these would occur only after outside pressures had made them obviously necessary.

The training of Earl Moulton, self and imposed, in his rise through executive levels, was tied closely to experience that would make it difficult for him to break away from personal administration and patterns of mercantile capitalism. He had remained as president of the Corona Trading Company and had kept his hand involved in this rural enterprise, though his general responsibilities were much broader. Nostalgia played a great part in this. His country store assignment in 1920, which continued after he became assistant general manager in 1922, entrenched him deeper in the hinterland aspects of the company's business. His personal handling of the purchase of the Gallup Mercantile Company in 1924 was not only an admission by Nordhaus of Earl Moulton's ability in business negotiation; it was evidence of Moulton's rather thorough understanding of people who, as general merchants, dealt principally with customers in the sparsely populated rural areas.

Another side of his training, and one which Earl Moulton frequently recalled, was his early days on the Estancia range when, overcoming the debilitating effects of tuberculosis, he herded sheep for his board.[24] A few years of ranching on his own followed this experience before he chose to enter the mercantile business. His reluctance to return to this early pursuit, however, was not sufficient to prevent him from assuming the supervision of the Ilfeld livestock interests. This experience, too, steeped him more deeply in the country business of the Charles Ilfeld Company. It became indelible with the drought of 1934.

From Mexico on the south to Canada on the north, from the Rio Grande River eastward to points in Kansas, the drought was unrelenting. It covered in some degree or other 75 per cent of the nation and affected 27 states severely.[25] It was, as Moulton thought, much worse because of its extent than either the dry spell of 1903 and 1904 or the subsequent one of 1907 and 1908 that drove him out of the ranching business and into his mercantile proprietorship in the hamlet of Lucy. Furthermore, the ranges in 1934 were stocked heavily so that potential distress was great.[26] The federal government, in an effort to save the situation, instituted palliative measures in which feed was supplied and the least desirable cattle and sheep were purchased and removed from the ranges. This action, however, came late in the year and tended to concentrate more on cattle than sheep.[27] The Ilfeld-Moulton Livestock Company, whose own ranges were conservatively stocked, was threatened with sheep deliveries that would glut its facilities.[28] Yet, if it failed to pasture the herds, thus forcing them to join the distressed marketings from the mountain states, many accounts of the Charles Ilfeld Company would have been placed in jeopardy.

How many times the Charles Ilfeld Company had faced this problem! Was this not further enforcement of Nordhaus' tacit assumption that his company's relationship with its customers would likely be unchanged for some years ahead? Was this not mercantile capitalism placing the fullest responsibility upon the sedentary merchant? In the 1890's, when depression drove sheep and wool to a chaotic market, Nordhaus, with the aid of Goldenberg, had met the problem heroically through the technique of the sheep drive.[29] The same problem, in lesser degree, had been handled through normal marketing procedures on many a later occasion. The situation in 1934, however, spurred on by a combination of drought and depression, called for heroics again. It was a problem finely tailored to challenge the peculiarly practical training of Earl Moulton. He relished the opportunity.

When July, the rainy month, and the first ten days of August passed without moisture, action became imperative. Moulton departed in search of pasture. He traveled through western Arizona and into California and probed the Mexican border at various points. He finally made arrangements for placing 10,000 sheep in Arizona, but the Sheep Sanitary Board of that state closed the borders without warning and practically prohibited sheep importation.[30] A threat, however, from the company to take matters into federal court and the assistance of some good friends in Arizona caused the board to lift the ban.

The problem, though, was only in its infancy. Partidarios and other customers had forced 46,000 more sheep upon the Ilfeld range during the six weeks Moulton had been gone. To complicate matters, the price of feed had soared. Alfalfa in Nebraska, according to Moulton, had jumped from $4.00 per ton in 1933 to $16.00 in 1934. Corn had risen from 15 cents a bushel to $1.00. Wheat in the Texas panhandle was nonexistent. When Moulton thought of the comparatively mild winters New Mexico had been having in the few years past, the probability that a hard one might be due stirred his imagination.

In desperation he hopped off to central Mexico in an airplane. He flew almost 500 miles southeasterly from El Paso to Torreon in the state of Coahuila and "with a good Buick" drove to a recommended ranch in central Durango. Here he was able to make reasonable terms for the care of approximately 12,000 sheep. Delivering them by rail to Ceballos, beyond Chihuahua, and driving them overland through the dense and treacherous *gatuna* brush, however, was a formidable task. The whole process of getting the sheep to the Mexican ranch and of bringing them back to the states the following spring was an episode that consumed eight months. As the herds passed northward, on or near the first of June, through the red tape of the El Paso border officials, their numbers had been lessened by the scabied sheep Moulton had been forced to leave behind—evidently a significant number, though perhaps these were included in one sale of 2000 head south of the border. Three days later, after sorting and dipping, the herds were munching on the Ilfeld range north of Corona where winter snows and spring rain had restored the pasture to weeds and grass.

Upon the death of Max Nordhaus, Moulton's responsibilities grew, though it was not alone because he received the title of general manager. His freedom of movement was to be greater because of his own strong personality and the little competition in this respect he would encounter from other top management. A geographical reason, however, was present also. Max Nordhaus, for personal reasons, had moved to Albuquerque in 1911, and both his leadership and the city's strategic location progressively had diminished the effective influence of the Las Vegas management. The decision of the Ilfeld brothers—Louis, the company attorney and director; Herman, treasurer; and Arthur, vice president—to keep their domicile in Las Vegas, had left the Albuquerque stage rather clear for day-to-day administration of the company. Herman died in mid-1935, leaving but one member of the Ilfeld family active in the daily administration of the enterprise.[31] Upon Nordhaus' death, Arthur became president.

Arthur Ilfeld and Earl Moulton evidently enjoyed a pleasant relationship, though their positions were geographically and functionally separated. Ilfeld was not only happy to remain in Las Vegas; he also was content to confine his main functions to purchases and sales. Moulton assumed direction of "the over-all management of the far-flung organization."[32] There was an obvious thinness in the management structure, however. Communications and internal controls still possessed many of the earmarks of the beginning mercantile capitalist. It may not be surprising, therefore, that the little financial strains that began to show in the company before the death of Max Nordhaus became more obvious in the years immediately following.

Although both the cash and current position of the company appeared sound enough on the surface from 1933 through 1935, their underpinnings were becoming increasingly weakened. The cash position for these three years averaged 75 per cent of current liabilities. The current assets, on the average, remained close to six times the size of the current liabilities. If one were to remove the short-term borrowings from the picture, however, the cash position would have been but 43 per cent of current liabilities, and the absolute quantity of cash assets would have showed a decline in the face of growing sales. Evidently the liberal dividend policy in these years, during which payments on common stock of $650,000 exceeded bank borrowings by almost 50 per cent, had begun to eat seriously into the liquid position of the company. One of the saving graces was the use which management was able to make of customers' funds in the form of "Accommodation Deposits," which accumulatively in these three years approximated the difference between bank borrowings and dividends.

The impact of sharply rising sheep and wool prices as the national economy grew stronger, however, coupled with a steadily rising population in the Territory of the Charles Ilfeld Company, had its pleasant effect upon the sale of merchandise, but it placed an increasing strain upon the company's ability to handle the new volume efficiently.[33] When sales increased 40 per cent from 1935 to 1937, net operating income rose but 26 per cent and net earnings by only 12 per cent. In large measure these unfavorable results were caused by rising operating expenses, a marked slowing down in inventory turnover, and substantial increases in financial charges (see Table 20). These difficulties were made the harder to bear by dividend disbursements comprising 82 per cent of net profits in 1935 in the face of a greater than threefold increase in short-term borrowings. Without these borrowings a cash deficit would have existed of a substantially greater amount than was paid out in dividends.

The sudden but short depression of 1937–38 brought a 20 per cent decline in the price of sheep and 40 per cent in that of wool.[34] The resulting influence on company sales in 1938 was great enough that a full recovery was not obtained until after 1940. This was the first time that recorded sales data show a failure to more than recover predepression sales during the first year of the following prosperous period. The slower inventory turnovers and the higher percentages of costs and expenses that came in 1938 were, perhaps, to be expected. Yet with partial recovery in 1939 and 1940 and with sales at higher volumes than 1936 or before, the rate of net earnings to sales had declined to one half the 1936 percentage.

TABLE 20. Operating percentages of sales and inventory turnover, 1895–1949

Year	Gross profit	Operating expenses	Net operating profit	Net profit	Inventory turnover
1895	18.4	9.0	9.4	6.2	2.19
1896	19.4	10.6	8.8	5.3	1.82
1897	21.8	8.8	13.0	23.4	1.86
1898	20.6	9.4	11.2	16.5	1.88
1899	20.2	9.7	10.5	18.8	1.93
1900	13.1	9.9	3.2	11.5	2.17
1901	16.9	10.0	6.9	5.7	2.42
1902	14.0	10.4	3.6	2.4	2.15
1928	10.2	—	—	5.5	—
1930	9.3	—	—	3.7	—
1931	13.0	10.2	2.8	1.0	4.37
1932	12.3	10.7	1.6	—	4.10
1933	16.3	10.0	6.3	5.8	4.08
1934	14.9	9.4	5.5	4.7	4.22
1935	13.0	9.6	3.4	3.3	4.31
1936	14.0	9.7	4.3	4.3	4.04
1937	13.2	10.2	3.0	2.7	3.92
1938	12.4	10.8	1.6	1.3	3.70
1939	13.3	10.8	2.5	1.9	3.92
1940	13.3	10.9	2.4	2.1	3.84
1941	14.9	10.1	4.8	3.2	3.60
1942	15.5	9.8	5.7	2.9	3.15
1943	14.5	8.9	5.6	2.5	3.74
1944	13.7	8.3	5.4	2.4	4.26
1945	13.4	9.2	4.2	2.0	4.18
1946	13.6	8.7	4.9	3.0	4.62
1947	12.5	9.1	3.4	1.9	4.69
1948	13.1	10.4	2.7	1.7	4.69
1949	12.1	11.0	1.1	0.7	4.80

Source: Summary Books through 1902; annual accounting audits 1928 and later.

In recognition of these discouraging results, the liberal dividend policy became more conservative—the common stock dividend actually having been omitted in 1938—though the rate of pay-out continued to flow at 70 per cent of the net profits for the period 1936 through 1940. The combination of declining profits and fairly liberal dividends led to a fourfold increase in average monthly borrowings during this same period. The average monthly borrowings in 1936 were almost twice the year-end borrowings of 1935, and from 1937 through 1940 this monthly borrowing average had more than doubled again.

Much occurred, however, in the closing years of the 1930's to indicate that the growing troubles of the Charles Ilfeld Company were not alone related to operational weaknesses. An additional and telling factor was the existence of an inbred board of directors, dominated by family ownership that continued the unrealistic policy of liberal dividends, and which kept itself blindly oriented to the old and decaying patterns of mercantile capitalism. Even when a promising step had been taken, as in the acquisition in 1932 of a majority interest in a small retail chain of Albuquerque grocery stores, it seems not to have been grasped by management as a signal for changing direction.[35] The dominating influence of the rural economy, with its slow tempo and its reliance upon the merchant who could furnish a large part of its needs for goods and services (the Charles Ilfeld Company had acquired a mortuary at Mountainair), probably would have appeared much less important to the board of directors in the years following 1935 had this body possessed a quota of urban-oriented members. The strength of the urban economy in New Mexico during the national depression of 1937–38 might have seemed particularly significant to individuals who had not been handicapped by traditional country focus (see Table 21).

The traditions of mercantile capitalism, the secretiveness of a family enterprise, and the training of a selected few for top management had ill-prepared the Charles Ilfeld Company for the turbulent demands of the years ahead.

The War and Postwar Pressures

Less than two weeks before the United States became directly involved in World War II, Arthur Ilfeld died.[36] Moulton became president and general manager of the company in times that were critical enough for everybody.[37] They were particularly so for the Charles Ilfeld Company, though the busyness of a war economy concealed the brunt of the impact. The nuclear age was being conceived, and New Mexico was to be the cradle and the school for its development. Government, with millions and then millions more of capital expenditures, would alter the face and the functioning of the state in ways that private capital would have been content to accomplish more slowly, in different ways, and for other ends. Population was to grow more rapidly than the least conservative could contemplate. Specialized wholesalers, who already had made their appearance and who had been chipping away at the general merchandise business of the large firms of Gross, Kelly and Charles Ilfeld, would make greater inroads as the trade area of Albuquerque became more populous and its per capita income higher. When the change would hit full force,

TABLE 21. New Mexico business indicators, rural and urban

Indicator	1930	1933	1937	1938	1940	1950
			Rural index numbers			
Cash farm income [a]	42.9	22.2	45.5	41.6	49.6	164.1
Cash farm income [b]	—	—	100.0	92.0	110.0	360.0
Livestock income [a]	32.8	16.7	35.9	33.7	41.9	128.0
Livestock income [b]	—	—	100.0	94.0	117.0	356.0
			Urban index numbers			
Business establishments [a]	88.6	82.4	102.0	108.8	114.1	183.8
Business establishments [b]	—	—	100.0	106.8	112.2	180.0
Retail sales [a]	42.0 [c]	19.0	36.9	40.1	48.0	206.5
Bank debits [a d]	33.9	15.9	37.9	37.8	45.4	253.8
			Population (thousands)			
Rural	316.4	—	—	—	356.7	346.9 [e]
Urban	106.6	—	—	—	177.3	344.1 [e]
			Population (percentages)			
Rural	74.8	—	—	—	66.8	50.2 [e]
Urban	25.2	—	—	—	33.2	49.8 [e]
			General index numbers [a]			
Employment	85.8	72.5	86.5	81.4	89.0	130.9
Per capita income	37.8	23.0	41.5	37.8	41.6	130.3
Bank deposits	16.5	10.9	16.7	17.6	21.1	137.0
Bank loans	55.9	24.1	44.2	54.4	57.8	295.8
Electric power production	13.6	28.2	45.7	46.9	56.7	181.6

Source: Business Information Series Nos. 18 and 21, Sept., 1951, and July, 1952. Bureau of Business Research, University of New Mexico, Albuquerque, New Mexico.

[a] 1945 = 100.

[b] 1937 = 100.

[c] Figure is for 1929.

[d] Used as an urban index because of the well-known lesser activity of rural bank accounts.

[e] New definition used. Under old definition, rural would be 53.8 per cent and urban 46.2 per cent. The new definition is more realistic for 1950 as it includes densely populated urban fringe areas which did not exist in significant amount in 1940 and before.

private capital would come to the scene in greater amounts to serve the newer needs in ways that New Mexico had never before demanded. It would be a difficult, strenuous, and painful transition for the much older material and human capital that had been geared to lower speeds and trained for an environment that was rapidly passing.

At the age of sixty-two, Moulton was a vigorous man, and the war called upon him for his utmost energies. It was the local and national community that made inordinate demands upon his time and, in large degree, these obligations shunted his efforts from persistent tackling of long-range company problems. It was true, however, that the problems of maintaining a labor force, of finding adequate sources of merchandise, and of hewing to the myriad of intricate directives of the Office of Price Administration precluded any hope of solving in wartime the deeper and indigenous problems of the Charles Ilfeld Company.

Though many of the long-range problems, particularly in the fields of personnel, administrative organization, and warehouse facilities, could not have been solved during wartime, progress could be made and, in a degree, was made in the area of statistical control. The war did its best to aid Moulton in one crucial aspect by automatically reversing the prewar trend in slowing inventory turnovers. When the impact of price controls and rationing became effective in late 1942 and early 1943, sources of supply were restricted enough, and demands were great enough, to move merchandise at naturally faster rates. This phenomenon caused Moulton to comment at one time on the volume of convenience goods that during this period moved directly from freight car to customer. He wondered, though he spoke without presuming to mean it, if business could not be done more profitably under price controls and rationing than in the so-called "free markets." [38]

From the point of view of speeding up the flow of gross profits on inventory, this was a pleasantly new experience. Whereas the average inventories had been staying in the warehouses approximately four months in 1942, they remained less than three months in the later war years. By estimate, the average grocery inventory was tied to the warehouse for 55 days, a time period, however, that is noteworthy only by the standards of the mercantile capitalist.[39]

Although it is undoubtedly true that the faster movements of goods through the warehouses came at the beginning of the war for very much the reason cited, it was not long before the requirements of the Office of Price Administration and the personal obligation of Moulton as a member of one of its national boards stimulated a system of controls that continued to have a salutary effect into the postwar years.[40] Inventory turnovers in the late 1940's were higher than they had been at any time in the company's history. It is interesting, too, to note that Moulton was soon demanding more frequent and detailed operating reports than had been assembled in the past. In the late 1940's these crossed his desk each week and showed the operating results by both branches and departments. From observation of a few of these, the impression is gained that they were unnecessarily detailed. It is, perhaps, natural that this might have been so. The management was developing a new tool, and it was shaping it with enthusiasm.

When the war ended, Moulton was approaching his sixty-sixth birthday. He was still full of vigor for any problem he thought worth tackling. He had just completed a pioneering book on the economy of New Mexico which incorporated his strong recommendations for a more balanced economy through the development of small manufacturing.[41] He previously had practiced his public advice by establishing a small food-packaging plant at Gallup for chili powder, pinto beans, and other food products.[42] Earlier, upon the urging of a young employee, Frank Mapel of the Gallup Mercantile Company, and with Moulton's persistent backing, this subsidiary company expanded its operations into the Coca Cola bottling business at Gallup and later at Durango, Colorado.[43] During the war the growing sales of Indian jewelry through the Gallup Mercantile Company encouraged the founding of a separate manufacturing corporation—the Gallup Indian Jewelry Company.[44] In 1945, Moulton arranged for the purchase of the Nash automobile agency in Albuquerque as further diversification.[45] Since Max Nordhaus' death, the company thus had continued its expanding ways according to the unwritten policies of the mercantile capitalist: growth without specialization, and diversification without serious consideration of the demands such actions would place upon administrative and capital resources.

Before the first postwar year had ended, if not before, Moulton had isolated three pressing problems that were facing the Charles Ilfeld Company. One was the need for more adequate warehousing; this he could plan to meet squarely. Another, the need for additional working capital, he could approach in a number of ways. A third, the all-important problem of personnel, was too long-range and too fraught with trouble for a man of sixty-seven even to consider pushing as an issue.

In December, 1946, the board of directors heard plans from Moulton for meeting the first of these problems and for attacking the second. The company had been renting a half-dozen warehouses in Albuquerque for the storing of merchandise that had bulged out of the old and obsolete structure on First Street. Not only had the necessity to rent multiple warehouses complicated the problem of inventory control and distribution of merchandise, but the spaces acquired were, for the most part, awkwardly designed for the efficient handling of goods. The main warehouse, the board minutes state, did not "meet a single requirement for efficient operation." It was proposed, therefore, that a large, modern warehouse be constructed soon on land acquired for that purpose.

The related problem of working capital was presented to the board rather fully. The company had become inadequately capitalized, the minutes explain, for reasons that the value of inventories had risen markedly, receivables had grown and would continue their upward trend, and bank debt had reached more than $1,500,000. The immediate solution recommended was to adopt a more conservative dividend policy, a suggestion that was accepted. The underlying hope, however, was that a more efficient handling of merchandise would result when the new warehouse could become a reality.

At about this time, 1946 or 1947, the third problem that Moulton foresaw, that of personnel, was approached secretively and then only from the more narrow point of view of picking the future management from the employees on hand. Moulton refers to this discussion simply as a meeting in his office with Louis Ilfeld and "three of the younger members of the two original families" to outline and to decide upon the future management.[46]

The Albuquerque warehouse plans may well have been slowed, and the working capital situation unduly worsened, by a fire in the Durango warehouse in February, 1948, creating the necessity for immediate construction of a new building at that location.[47] It was not until 1949 that Moulton, with almost an Indian summer of energy, traveled the country to inspect and study the latest advances in warehousing.[48] He had shrewdly purchased ample acreage in a new industrial plot in northwest Albuquerque to meet any foreseeable space needs. When the company's construction plans were nearing readiness, a substantial long-term borrowing from an insurance company was negotiated through a New York investment banker.[49]

Working capital, however, continued to be a plaguy problem as sales rose from the $11,000,000 prewar figure to more than $20,000,000 in 1948. The ratio of sales to working capital, though markedly low by standards of specialist grocery wholesalers, was becoming high for a general wholesaler who still carried substantial balances in slow-paying country receivables. The multiple of annual sales to working capital rose steadily during the decade from 3½ to 5½ times (see Table 19). Not only did this place a financial strain upon the company but, discouragingly enough, the percentage of dollar volume increase was no more than the percentage rise in the price level of the goods handled. Thus, evidently, there was little or no improvement in the physical volume of merchandise sold. Small rises in the cost of goods sold and larger increases in operating expenses, each expressed as percentages of sales, reduced the rate of net profits from 3 per cent of sales in 1946 to less than 1 per cent in 1949. Net profits declined absolutely in each of the years 1947 through 1949 (see Table 20 and Appendix 15).

The Charles Ilfeld Company had been suffering in the midst of what had been New Mexico's most prosperous period. State-wide retail sales in the decade of the 1940's had increased over 300 per cent, while per capita incomes were growing more than 200 per cent and population by approximately one fourth.[50] Yet Ilfeld's dollar volume, only, had doubled with, perhaps, no increase in physical volume. It was not only a serious situation but there seemed to be no coping with it. The specialist wholesalers in liquor, paper, dry goods, and hardware had been established in Albuquerque in sufficient strength to absorb increasingly the jobbing trade in the higher mark-up goods—goods that normally had given the general merchant such a profitable "mix" in his total sales. The Charles Ilfeld Company was finding itself unprepared in personnel and techniques to capitalize on the growing urban trade. In the meantime the country markets, that in 1930 had commanded three fourths of the population and by 1940 only two thirds, engrossed but one half of the inhabitants in 1950.[51]

The general wholesaler, to prosper in this kind of an economy, soon learns he must shrink his functions until he, like his growing competition, also becomes a specialist. He must no longer continue as the supplier of the full spectrum of his customers' needs. As he once had been forced to give up his functions of transportation and banking (Ilfeld had only flirted with the latter), he would now be required to relieve himself of disrelated business activities that were stretching his administrative capacities to paper thinness.

In this changing economic environment, Moulton remained as president of the company until December, 1952, when, still in good health at the age of seventy-three, he retired to the chairmanship of the board of directors.[52] His successor, Frank A. Mapel, had been chosen no later, certainly, than 1947 to attain eventually the top operating position, though, as a director of the corporation and as the manager of the Gallup Mercantile Company for some years before then, his promise had been recognized.[53] His official authority had grown when he became assistant general manager in 1947, and it had increased when his promotion to the position of executive vice president and general manager at Albuquerque was made in 1950.[54] Reminiscent of Moulton's negotiation for the purchase of the Gallup Mercantile Company in 1924 was the choice of Mapel to lead a delegation to Trinidad, Colorado, in the fall of 1951, to investigate an offer to purchase the assets and business of the Azar Mercantile Company, an opportunity that resulted in an expansion of the Ilfeld trade territory to the southeast portion of Colorado in December of that year.[55]

Thus expansion had gone forward even though working capital problems had worsened. In an effort to find more cash from within the company, inventories were reduced at Raton, and the retail outlet at Mountainair, including the mortuary, was sold.[56] Preparations were being made, too, that would take Ilfeld out of the hard liquor business for the second time in the firm's history.[57]

The symbolic sign of the times was the discussions held by the board of directors in the summer and fall of 1952 regarding efforts to sell the company's last retail outlet—Corona.[58] Whether the thought was too heretical to harbor, or the operation in this declining trade center too unpromising to permit a profitable transfer of assets, the store was retained and, with the purchase of minority stockholders' interests, became a wholly owned retail subsidiary of the Charles Ilfeld Company.[59]

XVIII

THAWING THE FAMILY CAPITAL

Awakening to the Problem

There could be no hiding the effects of environmental changes that had occurred in the postwar years. By 1950 the momentum of change had accelerated. The country markets not only were falling behind relative to urban, but 14 of the 22 counties of New Mexico in which Ilfeld had reasonably wide distribution had lost population during the decade.[1] Much of the country trade, too, was coming directly to the cities where the Charles Ilfeld Company was unable, by organization or temperament, to exploit it.

In the country, highways and automobiles had destroyed the isolated feeling of all but a few off-the-road communities. Customers of the small country stores had found it advantageous and pleasurable to drive to the larger centers for the lower prices of convenience goods and the greater variety of luxury items and services. Ranchers, generally operating on large scale, had accustomed themselves to buying their volume needs from a variety of sources including specialized wholesalers and manufacturers' agents. The size of their marketings of livestock and wool had made it more and more certain that cooperative organizations and specialist marketing agents would gain the bulk of their business.

In the city, the larger food markets and systems of chain stores, some of them integrated with the wholesaling function, had cut the share of the market to be obtained by the independent store. Other specialized wholesalers, as has been noted, were taking the higher mark-up trade in ever-greater proportions. When the census of 1950 became public knowledge, and it was clear that the heart of Ilfeld's territory, the metropolitan area of Albuquerque, had jumped in a decade from one eighth to one fourth of a growing state population, outside private capital broke through to destroy the last vestiges of the mercantile capitalist's dominance in the field of distribution. Wholesalers and retailers, specializing in their respective endeavors, beat the Charles Ilfeld Company with almost every punch.

In spite of the acuteness of the situation, the company reacted slowly to the onslaught. Perhaps this was natural for a firm that was still making profits sufficient to permit a small annual dividend. It was even more natural for a firm whose management had lost its youth and whose patterns of thinking had been conditioned by a period of mercantile capitalism in which Charles Ilfeld and his company after him, by 1950, had had 85 years of experience.

The first official evidence that recognition was being given to the seriousness of the problem appears in the board minutes of December, 1950, when the wisdom of seeking a business engineering survey of the company was discussed. The matter, however, appears not to have been pursued. Two years later consideration was being given to devices for holding the retail store trade. A representative of the company, J. C. Boyd, was delegated to attend meetings in Houston and Phoenix where problems of voluntary retail cooperatives were being discussed.[2] Later in the year he was sent to El Paso to study results of the demise of the James A. Dick Company, general wholesalers, whose facilities had been merged with the rapidly growing, integrated retail chain of Safeway Stores.[3] At the same time, another employee, Warren Bresett, reported on his trip to Colorado, where he had studied the cooperative chain, styled Associated Grocers, centered at Pueblo.[4] No actions were taken on these reports, but it is evident that much thought was being given in 1952 to developing markets in urban areas through chain retailing.

The New Regime

When Frank A. Mapel became the fifth president of the corporation, he was the first to possess youth in office.[5] Mapel was forty-five.[6] He was also the first to assume office in an atmosphere of general agreement that serious changes in company policy would be necessary. It is perhaps well to point out, also, that his board of directors (all officers of the company) was dominantly youthful. Five of the eight were under fifty years of age, and this majority grew, in effect, when only seven of the eight directors remained active after 1953.

As though not to take advantage of this favorable situation, Mapel, during his first year in office, chose the sure and convincing pace of small but significant steps that spelled progress without disruption. He revised and improved the employees' medical benefits plan. Dividends were curtailed sharply in the interest of a larger working capital. He began consolidation of hardware inventories from the branches to a central inventory in Albuquerque, permitting only small and basic stocks to be held elsewhere. A perpetual Kardex inventory system was established.[7]

By February, 1954, Mapel was ready to attack on a broad front. The board accepted his recommendation that the management consulting firm of Booz, Allen, and Hamilton be hired to conduct a preliminary survey of the company and, in April, a more thorough study and recommendations were requested. In the meantime Mapel sent Boyd to the Independent Grocers' Alliance meetings in Chicago for study of the opportunities that existed for Ilfeld through this particularly successful voluntary chain group. The board noted that it was "interested" in Boyd's findings.

The need to increase Ilfeld's portion of the urban grocery market, especially in Albuquerque and environs, caused the company to move strongly toward acquiring more trade through retail chains. The majority interest of the Ilfeld and Nordhaus families and associates in Barber's Super Markets, comprising seven local stores,[8] had been treated more as an investment than as a managed enterprise, and this firm had lost much of its potential to the integrated and expanding Safeway chain.[9] It was not until 1955 that the Charles Ilfeld Company even took full advantage of this investment by becoming the sole supplier of Barber's stores of that merchandise which this wholesaler normally carried. It was two years later before a public offering of stock produced the capital to permit the start of an expansion program.[10] By this time, too, a second chain, the Piggly-Wiggly stores of Shop Rite Foods, Inc., had given the bulk of its purchases throughout the Ilfeld territory to this wholesaler, although this chain in January, 1959, withdrew its purchases to attach itself to the Tri-State Grocers Association, a wholesale cooperative supplying its merchandise from El Paso.[11]

By the summer of 1956, Mapel had prepared his organization and its technical operations sufficiently to attempt a full-scale move toward specialization in high minimum volume accounts, and to develop a voluntary chain under an exclusive franchise from the Independent Grocers' Alliance. Twelve stores had signed contracts by the end of the year, and eight had opened for business—five in Albuquerque and three in Santa Fe. This voluntary chain of I.G.A. stores continued to grow under an effective promotional campaign.[12]

This is the façade that in some measure had been foreseen in the years before 1953. It covered and was supported by continuous changes in organization, personnel, warehousing, controls, and retail lines and services.

Emphasis on Administration

The Booz, Allen, and Hamilton study of 1954, and a more detailed report on business organization and personnel by the staff of the Independent Grocers' Alliance in the early months of 1958, gave Frank Mapel the moral strength that comes from the authority of remunerated and expert advice.[13] This was important, but the specifics that these reports set forth, coupled with the careful adaptation that Mapel and his associates made of them, created an atmosphere that promised success in the expensive transition being attempted.

Unlike the problem of many companies of today whose decentralization has caused a need for delegation of authority where little or none existed before, the Charles Ilfeld Company had practiced, long after the necessity passed, an autonomous arrangement as far as the managers of each of its branches were concerned. Charles Ilfeld early had been forced to this arrangement when he created junior partnerships as a method of fixing responsibility where time and distance made direct control impractical. This need for fixing responsibility was only less true when Nordhaus felt it wise to enter into profit-sharing arrangements with his country store managers. Wide freedom for managers was still the practice under Moulton, although the automobile had permitted more frequent trips over greater numbers of miles and the long-distance telephone had grown to common usage. The results of this comparative freedom for branch managers had been that in purchasing, warehousing, and selling there had developed little uniformity of practice from one branch to another.

In the fall of 1954, and as modified later, central merchandising divisions for food, hardware, and appliances were created to operate out of Albuquerque. Divisions of dry goods and beverages were partially organized but eliminated as decisions were reached to abandon these lines.[14] Mapel, however, cautiously felt his way in filling the new jobs that had been defined. Furthermore, he was careful to confine the authority of the new system to Albuquerque until its functioning and its personnel had been proved. Caution in this respect may well have been one of the inherited advantages of mercantile capitalism gained by Mapel from his Gallup experiences. He sensed the need that still existed for much authority at the branch level. And, even when the new organization began to exercise authority over the branches, Mapel placed full responsibility for the carrying out of central procedures upon the local managers.

The food division, in particular, as it was subdivided into a supply and retail division, soon made remarkable progress as the result of controlled procedures. Central purchasing became fairly standard. New lines were added with the employment of managers for frozen foods and meat departments. Facilities for cold storage were improved to permit the handling of cheese products in volume, and the Kraft line was obtained. Local suppliers of frozen foods, ice cream, and meat products—the last-named being carefully supervised by a full-time meat inspector—delivered to guaranteed accounts, centrally invoiced by Ilfeld. This procedure obtained for Ilfeld's customers competitive prices with controlled quality.

By such extension of food lines, the Charles Ilfeld Company approached in sales, on the average, 75 per cent of each customer's potential purchases, and further gains were anticipated through the development of merchandising, advertising, and accounting services for the benefit of these customers.

Warehousing operations had suffered as much as any part of the business because of lack of a central direction. Crowding of merchandise into narrowing aisles had become standard procedure in several warehouses, and grouping of homogeneous merchandise had not been planned well. The use of mechanical equipment in the handling of goods had not been encouraged as a policy, and in some cases little use had been made of these labor saving devices. The warehouses themselves, with the exception of the newer ones at Albuquerque and Durango, were then, as now, two-story operations. Weakness in plant layout, as well as failure to set standard procedures for control of purchases and deliveries, had made undue expense in the flow of goods commonplace.

Among the first actions taken by Mapel in launching his new program was the hiring of a central warehouse manager who would work through branch managers in imposing central procedures upon warehouse foremen. Many immediate improvements, particularly in the grouping of inventories and their placement for easier flow of goods, were made. In Albuquerque, where substantial volume permitted the fullest use of mechanical equipment and division of labor, shifts of employees were established wherein all incoming merchandise was stacked in the mornings and orders for deliveries were filled in the afternoon. Convenience in flow was enhanced by matching the sequence of items on orders with the most efficient routing of the palletized storage battery trucks. Fullest improvements, systemwise, were hampered, however, by a shortage of trained warehouse foremen and by the unsatisfactory design of several warehouses.

An International Business Machines' installation of electronic equipment in the Albuquerque warehouse permitted perpetual control of inventory, and efficient arrangement of stock made possible the physical checking of grocery inventories within a few hours. The problem of out-of-stock items—an old weakness that had been the cause of much customer dissatisfaction—was reduced to reasonable proportions. Grocery inventories, turning more than 13 times a year (much faster than a few years before), manifested this improved control.[15] High minimum buying orders from customers were established at Albuquerque, and, even though the number of accounts was reduced substantially by this decision, total volume soon rose significantly.[16] A major change accompanying this practice required that all orders would be paid for in advance with a blank, signed check. Thus, the Albuquerque operation abolished the cost of customer credit. It deliberately sought high volume with the narrowest mark-ups. It forced its customers to a system of careful budgeting and more efficient methods.

The function of the central warehouse manager was broadened to cover responsibility for delivery and interhouse transportation activities.

To that end one of the early decisions was to hire a central trucking manager. The company had been operating a sizable fleet of trucks for many years—an outgrowth of the inadequate common carrier service of the 1920's and the impossibility of reaching the largest part of the state by railroad. The operation had grown without plan since a customer, about 1925, heavily indebted to the company, was permitted to take on the function as a method of paying off his account. The story has it that he reduced his indebtedness so fast that the company decided to enter the private carrier field. In later years equipment was modernized into a fleet of 95 vehicles, including a number of trailer-type vans for interhouse activities.

Several problems were partially met and solved, including the fuller use of the interhouse private carrier system by a program of branch consolidation and by the establishment of cash and carry warehouses. From 1954 to 1958, central distributing warehouses were closed at Las Vegas, Santa Rosa, Santa Fe, and Raton. At Las Vegas the old problem of transferring goods from rail to conveyance to warehouse, that in the 1890's had created pleasant diversions for employees who played while they pushed horse-drawn tramways, had become too burdensome to endure.[17] Customers even complained that delivery service in Las Vegas was frequently delayed because Ilfeld trucks were being employed at the railroad siding. The general reason, of course, for the closing of these warehouses was the development of the auto-conveyance and the improvement of highways which, having broken the isolation of the smaller New Mexico communities, also caused the decline of intermediate towns as distribution centers.

With the exception of Santa Rosa, a cash and carry warehouse operation was established in each of the above-mentioned centers as well as at Albuquerque and Durango. The advent of minimum orders had effectively squeezed the small buyer from Ilfeld's books. He could continue, however, to purchase in small quantities at low prices if he wished to pick up his own merchandise and, as the larger buyers were required to do, pay cash.

With this closing of branches came a realignment of sales territories in which overlapping of salesmen's efforts were eliminated wherever practical. The general salesman was reinstated after his gradual replacement had taken place over the years by specialist employees who had tried to meet the successful encroachment of representatives of specialist wholesalers. The general salesman became responsible for knowing Ilfeld's full lines and for soliciting orders accordingly. When specialist salesmen had been used, they had received commissions only on the lines of merchandise to which each had been assigned. Serious inconvenience to customers, with accompanying loss of sales, had resulted as these men showed a tendency to accept partial orders—not being enthusiastic to assume a missionary status for their fellow solicitors. Specialist salesmen were still used but were assigned by merchandise managers to promotional projects and to train and to help the general salesman. A few large accounts, however, were serviced by these specialty employees.

Perhaps the most significant improvement in the plan of organization, however, was the creation of the position of comptroller. For the first time, one individual was given the responsibility to formulate policies and procedures in the areas of accounting, budgeting, fiscal analysis, and office management. Not only did this step bring a promise of efficiently controlled operations, but it gave to the president, Frank Mapel, a practical opportunity to implement his long-held desires for methodical progress growing out of written policy, detailed programming, and financial planning.

The last significant change in administrative organization came with the creation of a personnel division. The first step was taken in December, 1957, when the board of directors contracted for studies in job specifications and organization structures to be done by a staff member of the Independent Grocers' Alliance. A training program for retail clerks, as an aid to its three chain customers, was also established at that time. By the spring of 1958, the company was ready to expand its personnel program to the entire organization. A permanent personnel manager and staff were employed whose specific areas of study were outlined to include evaluation of the potential of each employee, the definition of each employee's job, and the establishment of channels of responsibility through which duties were to be performed.

Each of these changes and others entailed a cost that was not immediately reflected in new revenue. No one can doubt, however, that this decision to emphasize administration and to build toward a capable management in depth was the only hope the company had for survival. The fact that these changes were made with comparatively minor strains and friction among personnel, in spite of the necessity to bring in outside talent to fill responsible positions, is a compliment to top management in its careful planning and timing of each step.

It is remarkable, too, that this transition was made with continued profits—profits that rose sharply after the severe adjustments of 1954 and 1955. Common stock dividends, that had been omitted in 1954 and 1955, were resumed in 1956 at higher rates than had been paid since 1952, and they were raised in 1957. Accompanying this outflow was the complete retirement of bank debt and a two-thirds reduction in total debt. The board of directors commented on the "extremely liquid" position of the company. It was, indeed. The thawing of the family capital had produced the most favorable current position since 1936.

The Family Draws Its Capital

The Charles Ilfeld Company had moved a long way from its historical role of mercantile capitalist by the close of the 1950's. Its emphasis on administration through professional management and its tendency toward specialization suggests it may have been close to a full embrace of industrial capitalism.[18] Had it not been for the desire of some members of the absentee family ownership to transfer their capital to more compatible pursuits, perhaps this would have happened. The thought of selling the company had been present in some minds for several years and only the opportunity to press the point of view through a supporting incident had been lacking.

The incident occurred in early 1959, but the groundwork had been laid throughout 1958. A narrowing profit margin during the prior year, brought on by higher operating expenses and severe competition which forced further emphasis on promotional retail services, had caused the board of directors to omit common stock dividends after the spring quarter. In January, 1959, any early resumption of these payments was made unlikely by the announcement that the substantial Piggly-Wiggly retail chain account would be lost to an El Paso cooperative distributor. With this signal the Ilfeld and Nordhaus families actively sought the opportunity to free their capital from this business enterprise whose risks seemed to have an increasingly unfamiliar ring. In this changing atmosphere it was easy for those bred in the traditions of mercantile capitalism to project the declining role of the independent wholesaler as a permanent phenomenon.

The Ilfeld and Nordhaus families were quick to seek potential buyers for their still profitable enterprise. It was to be expected, however, that few parties would step forward to assume the risks the two families were no longer willing to bear. Problems of financing retail store expansion, made worse by tightening money markets; prospects of continued narrowing of gross margins in the wholesale grocery division; the inevitability of lessening usefulness of branch houses serving small urban centers; the necessity for spreading the management organization over two major and dissimilar lines of merchandise (groceries and hardware), over rural and urban marketing, and over a noncognate activity such as the bottling of soft drinks—these factors made it unlikely that a "lock, stock, and barrel" sale could be effected.

Of the offers made, the Kimball Products Company of Fort Worth, a company that already had moved into several centers of New Mexico through an earlier purchase of the assets of Gross, Kelly and Company, Ilfeld's historical competitor, was the only bidder willing to purchase so much as the entire grocery division. To this firm, the wholesale house in Albuquerque was the attractive asset, though the Colorado branches at Durango and Trinidad and the operations in Farmington and Gallup were useful peripheral outlets. The cash and carry warehouses at Albuquerque, Santa Fe, Las Vegas, Raton, and Durango were important for the retention of the small independent grocers' volume. Thrown into the purchase were the Magdalena and Corona establishments—vestiges of other days.

Remnants and Memories of Mercantile Capitalism

Mercantile capitalism had been dying hard in spite of the significant administrative and marketing changes that had been taking place. At the time of the liquidation of the grocery division, the old order of things was still present in varying degrees in many locations of the company's operations. It could be seen in Magdalena and Gallup where the rancher and the small country store continued to buy their varied needs largely from one source and where the extensions of credit permitted were still in some measure carried until the produce of the countryside brought their liquidation. It was present at Farmington where, as in Gallup also, the Indian Trading Posts are a factor. It was present at Corona where Ilfeld's last retail store remains a vestige of Nordhaus' chain of outlets at Fort Sumner, Pastura, Pintada, Corona, Encino, and Willard and Mountainair. Within a few city blocks of Ilfeld's IBM installation in Albuquerque, clerks were still crowded in a small compartment in the main office—some of them posting invoices for handy reference on the blank pages of a Magdalena purchase book.

The new had not yet been able to hide completely the stage of business history to which this study has been devoted and about which Eugene Manlove Rhodes, New Mexico novelist, wrote so appreciatively on at least one occasion: [19]

> I want to modify my permission to put up markers for Billy the Kid, Black Jack and sich like. Because, first of all, I want to put up a marker to Myers of La Luz—"Old Man Myers"—who sold me a suit of clothes on credit— [when credit was an unknown quantity].—The old time merchants: August Roullier of Paraje, Ed Fest of Cuchillo, the Armstrongs of Engle, Brown[e] & Manzanares of Socorro, Winston of Fairview, McClintock of Rincon—Numa Raymond, Theodore Roualt, Phoebus and Morris Freudenthal of Las Cruces, Goldenberg of Tucumcari, Brothers of San Marcial—here's to them!—makers of this country —those named—generous, great souled.—I speak only of those from whom I have bought—on time. Of course I could supply a hundred more at second hand—Gross-Kelly, Jaffa & Prager—Hubbell.

A name is missing from this accolade—that of Charles Ilfeld whose business roots stretch back to 1865 in Taos, less than 20 years after the beginning of mercantile capitalism in New Mexico. His death in 1929 was within 20 years of the rapid disintegration of the dominant phase of this period of New Mexico's business history. His span of years in the Territory and state of his adoption embraced in rough measure the dominion of mercantile capitalism in the economy of New Mexico.

Appendices

APPENDIX 1

Legal Documents of Elsberg and Amberg

The following documents, quoted *in extenso* from the original papers filed in the court house records of the United States District Court in Santa Fe, were a fortunate discovery for one seeking a specific link between the general commercial development of the old Southwest and Charles Ilfeld. To the student of business history, however, their value is not confined to so narrow a setting. Here is a clear outline of the beginning, success, and failure of a prominent mercantile capitalist firm founded in 1855 in Westport, Missouri, but moving to Santa Fe in 1856.

Elsberg and Amberg, with the possible exception of the Beuthners of Taos, was the first enterprise in New Mexico to begin as a full-fledged sedentary merchant firm stripped of all petty capitalist trappings. It was founded for the sole purpose of carrying on two-way trade between Santa Fe and the East with Chihuahua a later objective. No longer was the acquisition of eastern goods for sale in western markets the only planned source of income. The production of the West could be marshaled along with the petty capitalist who produced it, and markets for these goods could be found in the East. Like the German Jewish merchants of the seventeenth and eighteenth centuries who tackled any product or phase of business promising a profit, these nineteenth-century counterparts, Gustave Elsberg and Jacob Amberg, turned their hands to any risk worth taking and helped to bring a new stage of business history to New Mexico.

By 1866, with stores in Chihuahua, Pinos Altos, and Santa Fe; mining properties in New and Old Mexico; a lumber mill to serve the army forts; a partner in New York to take care of all eastern interests, this firm embraced an empire at a time when mercantile capitalism had died in many parts of the world but had only begun in New Mexico.

Bill of Complaint

United States of America
Territory of New Mexico
County of Santa Fe.

In the District Court for the First Judicial District of the Territory aforesaid, in Chancery, July term A.D. 1869, sitting for the trial of causes arising under the Laws of said Territory

To the Honorable Hezekiah S. Johnson, Associate Justice of the Supreme Court for the Territory of New Mexico, and in the absence of the Chief Justice of said Supreme Court, Presiding Judge of the First Judicial District Court sitting in Chancery.

Your orator Gustave Elsberg a citizen of the United States, and a resident of the City County and State of New York, but at present sojourning in the city and County of Santa Fe in said First Judicial District, brings this his bill of complaint against Jacob Amberg also a citizen of the United States, and a resident of the City and County of Santa Fe and Territory of New Mexico, and whom it is prayed may be made a party defendant to this Bill.

And thereupon your orator complains and says, that on or about the seventh day of March in the year One thousand eight hundred and fifty five, your Orator and the said defendant Jacob Amberg, entered into a copartnership, and agreed in writing in manner following:—

This Agreement made and entered into this 7th day of March, 1855, Witnessed that Jacob Amberg of Santa Fe New Mexico, on the one part and Gustave Elsberg of Philadelphia Pa. on the other part have agreed to enter into partnership to conduct the Dry Goods and General Merchandize in the town of Westport Mo. and that both of them agree to the following conditions:—

I. The business to be conducted under the firm of Elsberg and Amberg and to date from 10th of March 1855.

II. J. Amberg of Santa Fe to invest twelve hundred and fifty dollars in cash for the commencement of the business, while G. Elsberg contributes his name and reputation on his part.

III. Both aforesaid parties to have an equal share in the profits of the concern.

IV. The name of the firm to be used by both parties for purchases, sales, obligations or otherwise alike.

V. Should the firm think it advisable, to extend their business to other places besides Westport, in or out of the United States, whether conducted by agents or otherwise the business always to belong to both parties aforesaid in equal shares.

VI. If the parties aforesaid do not agree to extend the partnership any longer the business is to close five years from date.

VII. All speculations, adventures, etc. entered into by either of the partners during the continuance of the business, to be for the good and for account of the same.

VIII. At the expiration of the five years mentioned, or the close of the business the concern to be settled up entirely, stock fixtures and all other appurtenances of any kind found necessary and bought during the continuance and in the prosecution of the business to be sold, all debts paid and all outstanding accounts notes &c collected.

IX. Should both aforesaid parties at the expiration of one year from this deem it best for the interest of their business to have another partner, Albert Elsberg of Sunbury, Northld Co. [Northumberland] Pa. shall be taken in as such, he then from that time onward, to have a third equal share with the other two parties, and to enjoy all the benefits and privileges accorded to the other partners by the within.

In order that all the aforesaid conditions shall be strictly fulfilled and adhered to, in testimony thereof we have both affixed our hands and seals to a copy for each of the partners mentioned.

Read, agreed to and signed this seventh day of March, in the year of our Lord Eighteen Hundred and fifty five at Sunbury Northld Co. Pa.

JACOB AMBERG/s/
GUSTAVE ELSBERG/s/

Witnessed by
ALBERT ELSBERG/s/

Your orator further states that on or about the tenth day of March one thousand eight hundred and fifty five the said copartners commenced their said business at the place in said Articles of Copartnership mentioned, but that subsequently, sometime in the year one thousand eight hundred and fifty six, under and in pursuance of the said Articles of Copartnership, your Orator and the said defendant Jacob Amberg, commenced business in the city and county of Santa Fe in the Territory of New Mexico, and the store and business at Westport in the state of Missouri was discontinued sometime in the year one thousand eight hundred and fifty six. That about the month of October in the year One thousand eight hundred and sixty six the business of the said Copartnership was extended by furnishing a store and commencing the sale of merchandize in the city of Chihuahua, state of Chihuahua, and Republic of Mexico, and that afterwards about the month of April One thousand eight hundred and sixty seven, said Copartners extended their said business further by opening and furnishing a store for the sale of merchandize at Las Vegas in the County of San Miguel in the Territory aforesaid.

Your orator further shows that sometime in the year One thousand eight hundred and sixty five, one Herman Ilfeld a citizen of the United States, and a resident of the County of Santa Fe, and Territory of New Mexico, and whom it is prayed may be made a party defendant to this Bill of Complaint, was admitted as a partner of said firm of Elsberg and Amberg without any change of the name of said firm, with an interest of one fourth of the profits and losses of the said copartnership, business, conditioned that an interest of ten per centum on an amount of capital of One hundred and fifty thousand dollars, part of the capital of your orator and the said defendant Amberg, should be first deducted from any profits accruing; but that the said Ilfeld should not partake in the capital invested in said business of Copartnership. Also that simultaneous to the opening of the mercantile establishment in Las Vegas, County of San Miguel, Territory of New Mexico, one Adolph Letcher and one Carl Ilfeld, both of whom are residents of Las Vegas in said County of San Miguel and Territory aforesaid, and whom it is prayed may also be made parties defendant to this your orators bill of complaint were admitted as partners both of them together to share one half of the profits arising from said mercantile establishment, so opened and carried on in said town of Las Vegas, but that said business was to be conducted under the style, firm and description of A. Letcher & Co.

Your orator further shows, that the said original articles of Copartnership between your orator and the said defendant Amberg were continued by mutual consent from year to year, after the expiration of the said five years, as therein mentioned, and that no further or other articles in writing were entered into between your orator and the said Jacob Amberg.

Your orator further shows, that in process of time from the said commencement of their said business, the same extended, and their capital increased, and so your orator and the said Amberg extended their business operations in various ways and engaged in manifold speculations and enterprizes in addition to their keeping stores for buying and selling merchandize, it became necessary that your orator should reside permanently in the City of New York, for the purpose of making the purchases and liquidating the debts of the said Copartnership, and forward the goods, wares, and merchandize of the said firm to their respective stores and places of destination as aforesaid, and also to transact all other business for the benefit and use of and on account of the said firm, thereupon it was accordingly agreed between said Amberg and your Orator, that your orator should so reside in the said City of New York, and in conformity with said agreement your orator since the year One thousand eight hundred and sixty five, up to the present time, did so reside in said City of New York. It was further agreed and understood that the said Amberg should from time to time, as he might sell the Merchandize belonging to the said Copartnership and collect the money therefor, or realize money from other enterprizes engaged in send remittances thereof to your Orator to enable him to pay the indebtedness of the said firm, and to meet the various liabilities and expenses arising from, and incidental to his operations.

Your Orator further shows that on or about the first day of January One thousand eight hundred and sixty nine, to the best of your Orators knowledge information and belief there were in the possession of said

Copartnership, assets of the following value and description the property of the said Amberg and your orator, to wit:—

At the said city of Santa Fe and in transit to that place, merchandize of the market value amounting to from seventy to eighty thousand dollars.

Moneys due to the firm from responsible persons arising from business transactions in the City of Santa Fe, about the sum of Sixty thousand dollars.

Furniture, fixtures, carriages, wagons, mules &c valued at the sum of about Four thousand dollars.

Money due the firm for corn delivered under a contract with the Government of the United States, about twenty five thousand dollars.

One hundred shares of stock in the Pinos Altos Mining Company, the par value of which is Fifty thousand dollars.

Outstanding debts due the firm, but the collection of which is doubtful, the amount of about One hundred thousand dollars.

At Las Vegas in said Territory, merchandize and collectable debts due the firm of A. Letcher & Co. the amount of about Forty five thousand dollars.

Interest in the Hanover Copper mine situate in the County of Grant, Territory of New Mexico, valued at about One hundred and fourteen thousand dollars, and interest in other mines situate in various localities in said Territory, estimated at about twenty thousand dollars.

Coal stocks of the value of one thousand two hundred and fifty dollars.

Claims against the Government of the United States of various kinds and for various losses sustained by said firm, and for which the Government is responsible, to the amount of about two hundred and fifty three thousand dollars.

At Chihuahua in the Republic of Mexico merchandize valued, (in conformity to facts which have come to the knowledge of your Orator in the latter part of February One Thousand eight hundred and Sixty nine,) at about Thirty thousand dollars, and outstanding collectable debts due the firm, but at the date last aforesaid, not then due, to the amount of about twenty five thousand dollars.

Merchandize in transit to Chihuahua including freight and insurance paid to Port La Baca in the State of Texas, about thirty seven thousand dollars.

Cash, about Four thousand dollars.

Stock in the San Eulalia mine, situate in the Republic of Mexico, standing in the name of one H. Nordwald, worth about five hundred dollars.

Your orator further shows, that the said firm of Elsberg and Amberg is possessed of real estate in the Territory of New Mexico, but that all the deeds, mortgages, documents &c pertaining thereto are under the control of said defendant Amberg, and therefore your Orator cannot now give a description of the same.

And your Orator further represents, that at and about the same time the debts and liabilities of the said firm, principally owing to creditors residing in the City of New York, to the best of your Orator's knowledge, information, and belief amounted to the sum of between two hundred and ten and two hundred and fifteen thousand dollars.

That from and after the twelfth day of March One thousand eight hundred and sixty nine the said defendant Jacob Amberg, wholly ceased to remit any money or funds to your Orator to meet the liabilities of the said firm as he had promised and agreed to do, and it was his duty to do, and that already during the years of One thousand eight hundred and sixty six, One thousand eight hundred and sixty seven and One thousand eight hundred and sixty eight, the remittances sent to your Orator, fell far too short to meet the liabilities when falling due and for necessary expenses, thereby necessitating on the part of your Orator, in order to maintain and uphold the credit of said firm to resort to various expediencies for the temporary raising of money, thereby in the end entailing losses on the firm; and that ever since the month of October, One thousand eight hundred and sixty eight, the said defendant Amberg failed to send remittances in sufficient amounts to meet the liabilities of the said firm, notwithstanding that since that time, (as your Orator has been informed, and has good reason to believe) the sales of Merchandize and collections of money, made by the said Amberg yielded sufficiently to enable him so to do, over and above the necessary expenses for the carrying on of said business. That by reason of such failure, your Orator was greatly embarrassed and was unable to pay the debts and meet the liabilities of said firm, as they became due and payable. That in the month of March One thousand eight hundred and sixty nine, the said defendant Jacob Amberg ceased almost entirely to make any remittances of money whatever, whereupon your Orator left the City of New York, and went to the City of Santa Fe aforesaid: and there had a personal interview with said defendant, about their common interests and business. That said Amberg apologized for and endeavored to explain his said neglect to send said remittances and earnestly promised and agreed to and with your Orator, to faithfully make remittances from thenceforward, as fast as they should be needed: that your Orator relying upon said promises and agreements of said Amberg, thereupon returned to New York City.

Your Orator further states and charges, that said defendant Amberg, since the return of your Orator to New York City, has wholly and totally failed and neglected to make any remittances and has sent no money whatever, by reason of which your Orator, again became greatly embarrassed and involved, being unable to meet the demands of the creditors of the firm, who were pressing for the payment, and some of them commenced suits in the Courts of the city and County of New York.

Your orator further states and charges, that at various times the said defendant Amberg, has stated and given out that it is his intention to convert into money all the merchandize, property, goods, chattels, credits, and effects of the said firm of Elsberg and Amberg, and to appropriate the same to his own use without paying the debts due the creditors of said firm, and without accounting to or dividing with your Orator.

And your Orator further states and charges that he has been informed and believes that the said defendant Amberg in pursuance of the intentions by him expressed as aforesaid, between the twentieth day of April, and the fifteenth day of May, One thousand eight hundred and sixty nine, has made a fraudulent sale of the goods, wares, merchandize, property and effects in and about the store and mercantile establishment at Santa Fe, to one Samuel B. Wheelock, a citizen of the United States, and a resident of the County of Santa Fe and Territory of New Mexico, (whom it is prayed may also be made a party defendant to this his bill of complaint,) and that the said Amberg has transferred the possession of the said store together with the property aforementioned to the said defendant Samuel B. Wheelock, with the fraudulent intention and design to cheat the just creditors of the said firm of Elsberg and Amberg and to defraud your Orator. And your Orator further avers that the said Samuel B. Wheelock, who is a person without much means, if any, combining and confederating with the said defendants Amberg and Herman Ilfeld for the purpose of assisting them to cheat and defraud the creditors of the said firm of Elsberg and Amberg, has taken possession of the said store and the goods, wares, merchandize, &c only for the ultimate benefit of the said defendants Amberg and Herman Ilfeld.

Your orator further states and charges, that he has been informed and believes, that some time in the month of August One thousand eight hundred and sixty eight, the said defendant Amberg fraudulently sold and disposed to Joseph Reynolds and James Edgar Griggs, residents of the County of Dona Ana in said Territory of the interest which the said firm of Elsberg and Amberg possessed in the Pinos Altos Mining Company and other mineral interests, for the sum of twenty thousand dollars; and that the said Amberg took from the said Reynolds and Griggs promissory notes for the said amount, payable two and three years after the date of said prommissory [*sic*] notes. That your Orator was not consulted in regard to the disposal of said mineral and other property, nor did the said defendant Amberg ever advise your Orator of the transfer thereof, nor did he, the said Amberg ever receive or obtain the consent of your Orator for the disposition of said mineral and other property; and your Orator further charges, that he is informed and believes that the interests which the said firm of Elsberg and Amberg own and possess in the mines and property of the Pinos Altos Mining Company, and the other mines so disposed of, exceeds largely in value the amount for which the same were transferred to the said Reynolds and Griggs.

And your orator further avers that the said Pinos Altos Mining Company, at the time of the transfer aforementioned, were indebted to the said firm of Elsberg and Amberg, for goods wares and merchandize purchased and received from them, in the sum of from twenty thousand to twenty two thousand dollars the liquidation of which sum was included in the said sale made by said Amberg to said Reynolds and Griggs, for the said purchase price of twenty thousand dollars, and the said indebtedness was cancelled notwithstanding the said Pinos Altos Mining Company possesses ample property and means to pay the said amount so due the said firm.

And your Orator further avers and charges that sometime in the month of March or April One thousand eight hundred and sixty nine, the said defendant Amberg, has made a fraudulent sale and transfer of the goods, wares, merchandize, property, credits, effects and choses in action, in and about the store and mercantile establishment in the City of Chihuahua, Republic of Mexico, which belongs to the said firm of Elsberg and Amberg, to one Heineman Nordwald, who for the purpose of assisting to defraud the creditors of said firm and your Orator, now pretends to hold the said store &c as his own property, when in truth and in fact the said Nordwald only holds said store &c, for the benefit of the said defendants Amberg and Herman Ilfeld.

Your Orator further avers and charges that he is informed and believes that since the month of March, One thousand eight hundred and sixty nine, the said defendant Amberg has made a fraudulent sale and transfer of all the goods, wares, merchandize, property, credits and effects belonging to the mercantile establishment at Las Vegas, in the County of San Miguel, carried on under the name and description of A. Letcher & Co, that with the exception of but a very small proportion, all the goods, wares and Merchandize which were sold in said establishment were purchased and furnished by the said firm of Elsberg and Amberg, and for the money and credits of said last mentioned firm. That at the time of the formation of said partnership of the firm of Elsberg and Amberg with said A. Letcher & Co, and the furnishing of the goods wares and merchandize by the said Elsberg and Amberg, wherewith to commence the said business at Las Vegas the said Adolph Letcher possessed a capital of but seventeen hundred dollars, or thereabouts, and the said Carl Ilfeld possessed a capital of about five hundred dollars, which said several amounts were credited to them in the books, of the firm of Elsberg and Amberg. That the said defendants Letcher and Carl Ilfeld did not furnish any other capital for the carrying on of the said business at Las Vegas. That during the first year of the carrying on of said business, a profit of eighteen thousand dollars was realized of which one half belonged to the said defendants Letcher and Carl Ilfeld, and the other half to the said firm of Elsberg and Amberg. Your Orator does not know what profits were made in said business during the second year of its existence, but avers that a much larger amount of Merchandize was furnished by Elsberg and Amberg to the firm of A. Letcher & Co. then was furnished during the preceding year. Your Orator avers that according to a statement furnished him by the firm of A. Letcher & Co. in the month of February last, the said firm was indebted to the firm of Elsberg and Amberg in the sum of from fifteen thousand to sixteen thousand dollars, but that in this last mentioned amount the one half of the profits, which up to that time had accrued to the said firm of Elsberg and Amberg was not included, but that said profits are contained in the goods wares and merchandize remaining at that time unsold in the store of the said firm of A. Letcher & Co. That to the best of your Orators knowledge and belief there were in the month of February, One thousand eight hundred and sixty nine, in said store at Las Vegas, and under the control of said A. Letcher & Co, property of the value of not less than thirty five thousand to forty thousand dollars, and there were due to said firm collectable debts to an amount in proportion to the stock of goods on hand and the amount of business transacted by the said firm. That the said defendants Letcher and Carl Ilfeld, combining and confederating with the said defendants Amberg and Herman Ilfeld to cheat and defraud the creditors of the firm of Elsberg and Amberg and your Orator, now claim that they are the sole partners of the firm of A. Letcher & Co. and the sole owners of the property goods effects, credits and assets of the said firm, and that they are in no wise indebted to the said firm of Elsberg and Amberg, but your Orator has been informed and believes, that a secret collusion exists between the said defendants Amberg, Herman Ilfeld Letcher and Carl Ilfeld whereby the proceeds of the said fraudulent transaction is to be divided between them.

Your Orator further states and charges, that since the month of March, One thousand eight hundred and sixty nine, the said defendants Amberg and Herman Ilfeld have fraudulently transferred to one Stephen B. Elkins a citizen of the United States, and a resident of the County of Santa Fe and Territory of New Mexico, (and whom your Orator prays may be made a party defendant to this his bill of complaint) promissory notes, due bills, choses in action and book accounts to amounts, and due and owing by persons to your Orator unknown, and that the said defendant Elkins combining and confederating with the said defendants Amberg and Herman Ilfeld to cheat and defraud the creditors of the said firm of Elsberg and Amberg and your Orator, has been collecting and receiving money on such notes, due bills and book accounts so fraudulently transferred to him the said defendant Elkins. And your Orator further avers and charges that the said defendant Elkins had no interest whatever in the business of the said firm of Elsberg and Amberg nor is the said firm indebted to him in any amount whatever.

Your Orator further states, that in the month of March, one thousand eight hundred and sixty nine, whilst on his way from Santa Fe to New York, he purchased of Samuel McCartney & Co. of Saint Louis, Missouri, for the firm of Elsberg and Amberg, groceries to the amount of about thirty nine hundred dollars, and shipped the same to the house of the said firm of Elsberg and Amberg at Santa Fe, New Mexico. Your Orator is informed and believes that when said groceries were in transit, and near Fort Union, New Mexico, one Philip Elkins the father of the said defendant Elkins, pretending to have a bill of sale of the said groceries from the said firm of Elsberg and Amberg, claimed said groceries as his property, but owing to the fact that the said Samuel McCartney & Co., by their agent had levied an attachment upon said groceries, the said groceries did not come into the possession of the said Philip Elkins. That the said groceries came afterwards in the possession of the said defendant, Wheelock, who as your Orator is informed and believes, caused the mark of Elsberg and Amberg to be defaced and the mark of Samuel B. Wheelock to be placed upon the boxes, barrels, sacks &c, and then had said sacks forwarded to Santa Fe, and placed in the store of Elsberg and Amberg. That the pretended purchase by the said defendant Wheelock was fraudulent and made in connivance with the said defendants Amberg and Herman Ilfeld.

Your Orator further states, that there was stored at Sheridan, State of Kansas, a piano, of the value of about five hundred and fifty dollars exclusive of freight, which said piano was simultaneously with the above mentioned groceries shipped to New Mexico, and was, by the said defendant Amberg fraudulently delivered into the possession of the said defendant Elkins.

Your Orator further avers that he has been informed and believes that since the transfer of the store at Santa Fe to the said defendant Wheelock, the said defendants Amberg and Herman Ilfeld have taken out of said store eight or ten wagon loads of goods wares and Merchandize consisting of the most valuable goods and effects to be found in said store, and shipped the same to Franklin, in the state of Texas, and from thence to Chihuahua, in the Republic of Mexico, for the fraudulent purpose of keeping them for their own use beyond the jurisdiction of this Court. Also that the said defendants Amberg and Herman Ilfeld, for fraudulent purposes have caused to be carried away from said store during the night time, and distributed in several places in the City of Santa Fe, merchandize mostly consisting of silk goods and silk shawls, the property of the said firm of Elsberg and Amberg, with the intent to cheat and defraud your Orator and the creditors of said firm.

And your Orator further avers and charges, that since the month of March, One thousand eight hundred and sixty nine, the said defendants Amberg and Herman Ilfeld have sold and disposed of goods wares and Merchandize belonging to the said firm of Elsberg and Amberg, of great amounts, to various persons at prices far below their market value, and in payment for the same have taken notes and obligations, some of which they have transferred to the said defendant Elkins, which sales and disposition of said goods wares and Merchandize, and transfer of said notes and obligations were made with the intent to cheat and defraud your Orator and the creditors of the said firm. Also for the same purpose and with the same intent, the said defendants Amberg and Herman Ilfeld did sell to one Hyman Rinaldo a resident of the County of Santa Fe, and to others large amounts of merchandize for cash, for prices far below their market value, and that they the last aforesaid defendants, did receive the purchase money for such merchandize.

Your Orator further states, that as soon as he was informed of the fraudulent transactions of the said defendants, Amberg and Herman Ilfeld, he again left the City of New York, and went to Santa Fe, where he arrived on the latter part of May, One Thousand eight hundred and sixty nine. That immediately upon his arrival in said City of Santa Fe, he proceeded to the place of business and the dwelling house adjoining of the said Elsberg and Amberg, but was rudely met by the said defendants Herman Ilfeld and Wheelock, and by one Moses Amberg a brother of the said defendant Amberg, and by one David Loewenstein, the father-in-law of the said last mentioned defendant, and was by them expelled from the premises. That he has in every way possible, through the mediation of mutual friends endeavored to obtain an amicable interview with the said defendant Amberg, but has been unable to effect such an interview: that on several occasions the said defendant Amberg has positively and absolutely refused to meet your Orator for the purpose of amicably consulting together about the affairs of said Copartnership. And your Orator further avers and charges, that on account of the unscrupulous and illegal acts and doings of the said defendants he is entirely excluded from any participation in the transactions of said partnership concern: that he has no control whatever, together with the said

Amberg over the property belonging to the said firm of Elsberg and Amberg; that he has no access to the books kept of the transactions of the business of said firm at Santa Fe Las Vegas and Chihuahua, and that the said defendants Amberg and Herman Ilfeld positively and absolutely refuse to allow your Orator any examination of said books, or any participation in the management of the affairs of the said business. That your Orator has good reasons to believe, and verily does believe, that this strange and inexcusable conduct of the said defendants is prompted by their desire to complete their work of cheat and fraud upon your Orator and the creditors of the said partnership concern.

Your Orator further states that inasmuch as all of the property and the books and papers belonging to the said Copartnership, are now under the exclusive control of the said defendants, he is unable to furnish a more detailed list or description of the goods, wares merchandize and other property belonging to said firm. That the books of the firm of Elsberg and Amberg kept in the City of New York are in your Orators possession, and he is ready and willing and now offers to produce them in Court, whenever he may be required so to do, and your Orator here offers to furnish any other information, concerning the business of said Copartnership, which may be in his knowledge or possession, whenever this Honorable Court shall deem it proper to so direct.

Your Orator further states, that he has not now in his possession or under his control, any money, goods, wares, merchandize, effects or other property of whatever description belonging to the said firm of Elsberg and Amberg.

Your Orator further states that he greatly fears that the said defendants Amberg and Herman Ilfeld will continue to fraudulently dispose of the property belonging to said Copartnership, unless prevented by the remedial process of this Court. That the said defendants Amberg and Herman Ilfeld possess no means whatever except those which they may have concealed for fraudulent purposes and those which are merged in said Copartnership concern, and that unless restrained by the application of the legal powers vested in your Honor, as Chancellor, the acts and doings of said defendants Amberg and Herman Ilfeld will cause irreparable damages to your Orator and the creditors of said firm.

Your Orator further states that he had omitted to pray to have the said Heineman Nordwald made a party defendant to this his bill of complaint for the reason that said Nordwald resides beyond the jurisdiction of this Court, but your Orator now prays that process may issue to cause the said Nordwald to be made a party defendant to this bill, should he come within the jurisdiction of this Honorable Court.

Your Orator further states that all of the said defendants, combining and confederating together with divers other persons at present unknown to your Orator, whose names when discovered your Orator prays he may be at liberty to insert herein, with apt words to charge them as parties defendants hereto, and contriving how to wrong, injure, cheat, and defraud your Orator, and the creditors of the said firm, in the premises, are continually devising means and carrying them into execution, whereby the assets of the said firm of Elsberg and Amberg are to be disposed of in such a manner as to prevent the same to be reached by the process of this Honorable Court. That any delay in the application of remedial process in this cause will be highly detrimental to the interest of your Orator, and to that of the creditors of said firm. That the said defendant Amberg has given out, and your Orator has been informed and believes, that he the said Amberg is now preparing to leave, and will soon leave the city of Santa Fe, and Territory of New Mexico, for the City of Chihuahua in the Republic of Mexico, beyond the jurisdiction of this Court; that if the said defendant Amberg be permitted to thus leave the jurisdiction of this Court, the process cannot be served upon him, and your Orator and the creditors of the said firm of Elsberg and Amberg will be left without any remedy or redress for the wrongs done them by the said Amberg.

All of which actings, doings, and pretences of the said defendants are contrary to equity and good conscience, and tend to the manifest wrong injury and oppression of your Orator in the premises.

In consideration whereof, and inasmuch as your Orator is wholly without remedy in the premises, according to the strict rules of the Common Law, and can only have relief in a Court of Equity, where matters of this nature are properly cognizable and relievable: To the end, therefore, that the said defendants, Jacob Amberg, Herman Ilfeld, Samuel B. Wheelock, Adolph Letcher, Carl Ilfeld, and Stephen B. Elkins, and the rest of the Confederates, when discovered, may, upon their several and respective corporal oaths, full true direct and perfect answer make, to all and singular the matters hereinbefore stated and charged, as fully and particularly, as if the same, were hereinafter repeated, and they thereunto distinctly interrogated, and more especially:

First:—That the said defendants Jacob Amberg and Herman Ilfeld, to the best of their respective knowledge information and belief, do discover disclose and show, what amount of money they have had in their possession, belonging to the said firm of Elsberg and Amberg, since the first day of February, One thousand eight hundred and sixty nine, and the disposition thereof made by them: Also the amount and value of goods, wares, merchandize, chattels, effects or other property of whatsoever description belonging to the said partnership concern was, on the first day of February, one thousand eight hundred and sixty nine, in their possession or under their control, either in Santa Fe, Las

Vegas, New Mexico, or Chihuahua Republic of Mexico, or in any other place, and the disposition they have made of the same, also a statement of the notes, duebills, bills receivable, bills of exchange, or other writing obligatory, and book accounts of moneys due and payable to the said firm of Elsberg and Amberg, and the amounts thereof; by whom due and payable, what amount and from whom collected, since the said first day of February One thousand eight hundred and sixty nine, and the disposition made by them of the same; also what money, goods, wares, merchandize, chattels, effects or other property of whatsoever description either in Santa Fe, Las Vegas New Mexico, and Chihuahua, Republic of Mexico, or in any other place, the property of the said partnership concern, and what notes, due bills, bills receivable, bills of exchange or other writing obligatory, and book accounts of moneys due and payable to the aforesaid firm; the amounts thereof, and by whom due, and owing, are now in their, the said defendants Amberg and Herman Ilfeld's possession or under their control, or in the possession or under the control of either of them, and also what amount of money, goods, wares, merchandize, and other property has either one of the said last mentioned defendants drawn and received on their own private account since the first day of February, One thousand eight hundred and sixty nine, of and from the money, goods, wares, merchandize or other property belonging to the said partnership concern, and what portion or amount of such moneys, goods, wares, merchandize and other property so drawn or received, has been charged to them respectively in the books of accounts of the said firm of Elsberg and Amberg, and what not.

Second:—That the said defendants Adolph Letcher and Carl Ilfeld, to the best of their respective knowledge information and belief, do discover, disclose and show, what amount of money they have had in their possession, belonging to the firm of A. Letcher & Co. since the first day of February, One thousand eight hundred and sixty nine, and the disposition made thereof: also the amount and value of goods, wares, merchandize, chattels, effects and other property of whatsoever description, belonging to the said firm, either in Las Vegas or any other place, was, on the first day of February, One thousand eight hundred and sixty nine in their possession or under their control, and the disposition they have made of the same; also a statement of the notes, due bills, bills receivable, bills of exchange or other writing obligatory and book accounts of moneys due and payable to the said firm of A. Letcher and Co. and the amounts thereof; by whom due and owing; what amount and from whom collected, since the said first day of February One thousand eight hundred and sixty nine, and the disposition made by them of the same; also what money, goods, wares, merchandize chattels, effects or other property of whatever kind or description, either in Las Vegas or any other place, the property of the said firm of A. Letcher & Co, and what notes, due bills, bills receivable, bills of exchange or other writings obligatory and book accounts of moneys due and owing to the said firm, the amounts thereof and by whom due and owing, are now in their, the said defendants, Letcher and Carl Ilfeld's possession or under their control, or in the possession, or under the control of either of them; also what amount of profits were realized in the mercantile establishment of the said firm of A. Letcher & Co. during the continuance of their Copartnership with the firm of Elsberg and Amberg, and if losses were sustained by whom and on what account.

Third:—That the said defendant Samuel B. Wheelock, to the best of his knowledge, information and belief, do discover, disclose, and make known, what amount of goods, wares, merchandize, effects and other property of whatever description he received from the said defendants Amberg and Herman Ilfeld, or from any other person, belonging to the said partnership concern of Elsberg and Amberg at the time of the sale or pretended sale to him of the store at Santa Fe, and what amount of money in cash he paid therefor, and to whom was such money paid, also a statement of the notes or obligations he executed and delivered to either the said defendant Amberg or Herman Ilfeld in payment in full or in part for said goods wares merchandize &c the dates and amounts thereof, when due and to whom payable; if paid to whom were they paid; and if unpaid in whose possession are they at this time. Also what amount of money, goods, wares, merchandize, chattels, effects or other property of whatever description, belonging to the said copartnership of Elsberg and Amberg is now in his, the said defendant Wheelock's possession or under his control: and, if any, what notes, bills, due bills, bills of exchange, or other writing obligatory book accounts of moneys due and owing either to him the said defendant or to any other person, but in which the said defendant Amberg, or the said defendant Herman Ilfeld, or any one of the defendants to this bill of complaint have an interest arising from any transaction of the partnership concern of Elsberg and Amberg, has he, the said defendant Wheelock now in his possession or under his control; and if any what amount of salary or wages he has been paid, or is due him for services rendered in the store of said Elsberg and Amberg in Santa Fe, in any capacity whatever; and also by whom was the money paid for the groceries purchased in March One thousand eight hundred and sixty nine of Samuel McCartney & Co. of Saint Louis, and to whom did the money so paid for said groceries belong; and in case said groceries remain unpaid for, who is responsible for the payment thereof: and also for what reason was the mark of Elsberg and Amberg upon the sacks barrels and boxes of said groceries defaced and that of the said defendant substituted.

Fourth:—That the said defendant Stephen B. Elkins to the best of his knowledge information and belief, do discover, disclose and show what amount of money, (exclusive of Attorney's fees) he has received from either one of his said co-defendants, or from any other person belonging to the said Copartnership of Elsberg and Amberg or arising immediately or remotely from any transaction connected with said copartnership concern and what disposition he has made of the same; also, what notes, bills, due bills, bills of exchange, or other writings obligatory, book accounts for moneys due and payable to said firm of Elsberg and Amberg have been transferred or endorsed and made payable to him, belonging to the said Copartnership of Elsberg and Amberg, by whom were they so transferred or endorsed; what amount of money has been by him collected thereon and of whom, what disposition he has made of the money so collected, and what amount of money he has now in his possession or under his control belonging to the firm of Elsberg and Amberg, and what interest he has in such money; also what goods, wares, merchandize, musical instruments and other property he had received from the said firm of Elsberg and Amberg since the first day of February One thousand eight hundred and sixty nine, on what account and for what consideration and what money has he paid, or what services has he rendered therefore, and for whom were such services rendered.

Your Orator Prays:

First. That the said defendants may set forth an account of all and every sum and sums of money received by them respectively or either of them or by any person or persons by their or either of their order, or for their or either of their use for or in respect of the said Copartnership concern of said Elsberg and Amberg, and when and from whom, and from what in particular, all and every such sums were respectively received and how the same respectively have been applied or disposed of; and also that the said defendants respectively set forth, a full true and particular account of all and singular the goods wares merchandize, chattels, effects, credits, notes, bonds, due bills, bills of exchange, or other writings obligatory, book accounts or any other property of whatever description, and of every part thereof, of the said Copartnership concern, which has been possessed by, or come to the hands of the said defendants or either of them, on and since the first day of February, One thousand eight hundred and sixty nine, or to the hands of any other person or persons, by their or either of their order, or for their or either of their use, with the particular nature, quantities, qualities, and true and utmost value or amounts thereof, and of every part thereof respectively; and how the same and every part thereof, has been applied and disposed of: and whether any, and what part thereof, now remains unapplied and undisposed of; and why; and whether any and what part of the outstanding debts of the said partnership concern remain unliquidated and what amount and why, and that the said defendants Amberg and Herman Ilfeld may also set forth a full true and particular account of the debts and liabilities due and owing by the said partnership concern, in the Territory of New Mexico and on what account and for what consideration were such debts contracted and liabilities created.

Second. That with a view of the final winding up of the affairs of the said copartnership concern, your Orator prays for an account of the partnership dealings and transactions, and that the said defendants Amberg and Herman Ilfeld and your Orator account to each other under the directions of your Honor, of their several acts and doings of and concerning their said copartnership and in like manner account to each other of the assets belonging to said copartnership in their possession, or under their control, or in the possession of or under the control of either of them.

Third. That your Honor forthwith will appoint a suitable person as a receiver to take into his possession all of the goods, wares, merchandize, chattels, credits, effects and other assets of the said partnership concern wherever found within the jurisdiction of this court, who shall hold and dispose of the same as your Honor from time to time may decree and direct; and that the person so appointed as receiver be allowed such fees for his services as your Honor may deem just and proper. That the moneys of said partnership concern which from time to time may come to the hands of the said receiver, after allowing necessary expenses for carrying on said business may be applied to the payment of the liabilities thereof, pro rata, and that upon the final winding up of the affairs of said copartnership and the payment of the just debts of said firm, and the costs of this suit, any surplus should be found to exist, that the same be apportioned and divided among the partners of said concern according to the amount of interests to which they are respectively and each of them seperately [*sic*] is entitled.

Fourth. That your Honor forthwith, will grant unto your Orator the writ of injunction issuing out of and under the seal of this Honorable Court, directed to the said defendants Jacob Amberg, Herman Ilfeld, Adolph Letcher, Carl Ilfeld, Samuel B. Wheelock and Stephen B. Elkins, their Counsellors, Attorneys, Solicitors, and Agents commanding them and each of them, absolutely to refrain and desist from disposing of the property and other assets belonging to the said Copartnership concern, or to collect any money due and owing the same; and commanding them and each of them to deliver to the said receiver, when appointed, all of the property evidences of indebtedness, books, papers, and documents, or other assets of the said copartnership, which now are or may hereafter come to their possession or under their control, or which now are or may hereafter come into the possession and under the control of either of them, and that hereafter said injunc[tion] be made perpetual.

Fifth. That the fraudulent transfer of goods, property, effects, assets, demands, credits &c belonging to said partnership concern, be declared and decreed void, and that the same be ordered to be delivered into the possession, and under the control of the receiver herein prayed for to be appointed.

Sixth. That upon the final hearing of this cause, the premises being found true, and the winding up of all the affairs and transactions of said Copartnership concern, the Copartnership heretofore existing between your Orator and the said defendants Amberg, Herman Ilfeld, Adolph Letcher and Carl Ilfeld be decreed to be thenceforward dissolved.

Seventh. That the said defendant Jacob Amberg may be stayed by the writ of *ne exeat republica,* from departing out of the jurisdiction of this Court.

Eighth. And that your Orator shall have generally such other and further relief as the nature of his case may require, and as your Honor may deem meet and proper.

Therefore, will your Honor grant unto your Orator, the writ of Subpoena, issuing out of and under the seal of this Honorable Court, to be directed to the said defendants, Jacob Amberg, Herman Ilfeld, Adolph Letcher, Carl Ilfeld, Samuel B. Wheelock, and Stephen B. Elkins, commanding them, and each of them, by a certain day, and under a certain penalty therein inserted to appear before your Honor, in the District Court for the County of Santa Fe, and First Judicial District of the Territory of New Mexico, and then and there answer the premises, and abide the orders and decrees of the Court.

And, as in duty bound your Orator will ever pray, &c.

Benedict & Clever/s/
Solicitors for Complainant

Witness to Signature

United States of America
Territory of New Mexico } S.S.
County of Santa Fe:

On this twenty eighth day of July One thousand eight hundred and sixty nine, before me, personally appeared the above named Gustave Elsberg, and made oath that he has read the above bill, subscribed by him, and knows the contents thereof, and that the same is true of his own knowledge, except as to the matters which are therein stated to be on his information or belief, and that as to those matters he believes it to be true.

GUSTAVE ELSBERG/s/

Subscribed and sworn to before me.

HEZEK S. JOHNSON/s/
Associate Justice of the Supreme Court for the Territory of New Mexico.

ORDERS FROM ASSOCIATE JUSTICE OF THE UNITED STATES SUPREME COURT

The President of the United States of America

Having duly considered the foregoing bill of complaint, it is hereby ordered that the Clerk of the United States District Court for our first Judicial District of the Territory of New Mexico do issue subpoena to said defendants therein named, that within five days after service thereof they and each of them, do under the penalty of five hundred dollars, enter an appearance hereto in the office of the Clerk of our said Court, and answer all and singular the matters and things charged against them, and the interrogatories propounded unto them, in said bill of complaint, as therein prayed; and to abide such other and further order and decree, as our said Court may make in the premises.

And furthermore that upon the complainants giving bond in the sum of one thousand dollars with two good and sufficient securities (said bond and security to be approved by said Clerk) he will issue a writ of *ne exeat republica,* with bail in the sum of ten thousand dollars against the defendant Jacob Amberg, as prayed for in this bill.

And furthermore that upon said complainants giving another bond, as aforesaid, in the further sum of ten thousand dollars, the said Clerk will issue writs of injunction as prayed for in said bill.

Given under my hand at Chambers in Santa Fe, New Mexico this 29th day of July A.D. 1869

HEZEK S. JOHNSON/s/
Associate Justice &c

And now in further consideration of the premises of the foregoing bill of complaint, it is ordered that Samuel Ellison of the County of Santa Fe in the Territory of New Mexico, be, and he hereby is, appointed Receiver, to do and perform all and singular the matters and things required to be done and performed by such receiver as prayed for in said bill; and that upon his giving bond, with good and sufficient security, in the sum of twenty thousand dollars, (said bond and security to be approved by the undersigned or by his Honor the Chief Justice of the Supreme Court of our said Territory) and taking and subscribing an oath that he will well truly and impartially do and perform the duties of said Receiver, and as our Court of Chancery may from time to time order and direct in the premises, (said oath to be filed in the office of the Clerk of Our United States District Court, for the First Judicial District of said Territory) the above named Receiver shall have full power and authority to act in the premises.

And upon said receivers filing with the Clerk of our said Court the required bond approved as aforesaid; and the oath hereinbefore mentioned, he will frame and issue such writs as shall be necessary to give said receiver the full power and authority hereinbefore mentioned, and enforcing the same.

Given under my hand at Chambers in Santa Fe this 29th day of July A.D. 1869.

HEZEK S. JOHNSON/s/
Associate Justice &c.

Filed in my office this 29th day of July 1869.

SAML. ELLISON. CLERK./s/

United States of America }
Territory of New Mexico }

I William Breeden Clerk of the United States District Court for the first Judicial District of the Territory of New Mexico, do hereby certify that the above and foregoing is a full and true copy of the original paper on file in my office.

Witness my hand and the seal of said Court, this day of January A.D. 1870.

SEPARATE ANSWER OF ADOLPH LETCHER

Gustave Elsberg
vs
Jacob Amberg
etc. en c.

In Chancery In the District Court for the first Judicial District of New Mexico

The separate answer of Adolph Letcher to the Bill of complaint of Gustave Elsberg filed herein against Jacob Amberg, Hermann Ilfeld,

Adolph Letcher, Carl Ilfeld, Samuel B. Wheelock and Stephen B. Elkins. This defendant now and at all times hereafter reserving all manner of benefit and advantage to himself of exception to the many errors and insufficiencies in said Bill contained, for answer thereto or unto so much or such parts thereof as this defendant is advised is material for him to make answer unto answering says He denies most positively that he and the said Carl Ilfeld were at the time stated in said Bill or at any other time admitted both of them as partners or either of them to share one half of the profits arising from said mercantile Establishment opened or caried [*sic*] on at the town of Las Vegas or elsewhere, and that said Business was to be conducted under the name and discription of Adolph Letcher & Co but here states the fact to be that sometime in the month of May in the year 1867 he became desirous of establishing and opening a store for the sale of Merchandize at Las Vegas New Mexico and in consideration of the fact that he had some money deposited with the firm of Elsberg & Amberg at Santa Fe New Mexico he applied to them for aid and assistance in establishing a store at the place above mentioned which was kindly furnished to the extent and the manner following: that this respondent should purchase from Elsberg and Amberg and they furnish him at cost and carriage a sufficient amount to commence a store with a good assortment, that immediately upon purchasing & receiving goods wares and Merchandize for his business they were to become and were the actual property of the respondent and that said firm of Elsberg & Amberg had no interest whatever in the same. It was agreed further that in consideration of the credit extendit [*sic*] this respondent said firm of Elsberg & Amberg was [to] have a one half interest in the profits araising [*sic*] from the sale of said goods until such time as this respondent could pay for the entire amount of goods so purchased from said firm, at which time the interest of said Elsberg & Amberg in the profits should cease. This respondent further states that he was at perfect liberty to purchase goods of other merchants as he has done, that the firm of Elsberg & Amberg were never in any manner responsible for any debts contracted by this respondent, nor did they have any control whatever over the business or goods of said respondent. This respondent states that the above arrangement was made and entered into between him alone and said firm of Elsberg & Amberg and not with Carl Ilfeld as in said bill stated that after this respondent had commenced business as [*sic*] Las Vegas as aforesaid he without the knowledge of Elsberg & Amberg agreed with said Carl Ilfeld to receive him as a partner in his business. This respondent denies positively that said firm of Elsberg & Amberg at the time stated in said bill had on hand at Las Vegas merchandize and collectable debts due the firm of A. Letcher & Co the amount stated in said bill or any other amount except what might have been due them from the firm of A. Letcher & Co, for goods purchased and the interest in the profits, he denies that said Elsberg & Amberg had any interest in said business except as above stated. This respondent denies that said defendant Amberg has made a fraudulent transfer of all the goods, wares, merchandize, property credits & effects belonging to the mercantile establishment carried on at Las Vegas under the name of A. Letcher & Co as in said Bill stated, but states the fact to be that on the first day of February A.D. 1869 the firm of A. Letcher & Co owed for goods to the firm of Elsberg & Amberg $15150 76/100 and that up to the last of March of the same year said firm of A. Letcher & Co had paid and remitted to said firm of Elsberg and Amberg the sum of 17409 53/100 making a difference of $2258.77 in favor of the firm A. Letcher & Co against which there was a credit of $140 52/100. This respondent states that in consideration of the fact of the payment of said amount, above the amount due by said firm of A. Letcher & Co, and the further fact that said Elsberg & Amberg declared their inability to fill a certain contract with the Government for about seven hundred thousand pounds of corn being in the name of this respondent but without any interest therein and this respondent being obliged to fill the same at a great loss and sacrifice of money it was agreed by said firm to release all claims against the firm of A. Letcher & Co for any proffits [*sic*] that might have accrued in the sale of goods and merchandize up to the time the said firm of A. Letcher & Co paid for the amount of goods purchased and the interest of Elsberg & Amberg in all profits in the future ceased. This respondent admits that most of the goods and merchandize sold by A. Letcher & Co were purchased from the said firm of Elsberg & Amberg, this respondent denies all co-partnership between said firm as in said Bill stated, he denies that he possessed only a capital of about seventeen hundred Dollars when he commenced business at Las Vegas, but states that he possessed a capital of about Eight thousand dollars he admitts [*sic*] there was seventeen hundred Dollars to his credit on books of Elsberg & Amberg and states there should have been about six thousand Dollars additional to his credit as said complainant well knew. This respondent admitts [*sic*] that during the first year he commenced business at Las Vegas the profits of the firm of A. Letcher & Co realized including some debt uncolectable [*sic*] were about Eighteen thousand Dollars. This respondent states during the second year or since January 1868 owing to the general prostration of business in New Mexico and the great scarcity of money he rearly [*sic*] believes he and the said Carl Ilfeld have made little or no profits in their said business.

This respondent admits that of $15000 due by A. Letcher & Co to Elsberg & Amberg in the month of February last, that no part of any profits due said firm were included and states that since this respondent commenced business at the town of Las Vegas as aforesaid until the month of March 1869 at which time he and said Carl Ilfeld fully paid all the firm of A. Letcher & Co owed said firm of Elsberg & Amberg for goods, and was thereby released from paying said Elsberg & Amberg any parts of the profits that might accrue thereafter;—there only accrued to said business during all of said time about twenty thousand dollars clear profits, that Ten thousand Dollars belonged to this respondent and Carl Ilfeld and ten thousand Dollars to the firm of Elsberg & Amberg: that this respondent and Carl Ilfeld has paid in Cash on this amount about two thousand Dollars and counting the loss of money, labor expended and time, in and about the corn contract of said firm of Elsberg & Amberg the [*sic*] have more than fully discharged any and all indebtedness to said firm of Elsberg & Amberg, although they were by said firm in the month of March released in full from all debts they may have owed said firm on any account whatever. This respondent denies that said firm of A. Letcher & Co had at the time stated in said Bill property to the amount of thirty four thousand Dollars at any other time, that said goods and property on hand at that time did not exeed [*sic*] the sum of twenty thousand Dollars that the debts due, collectable and uncollectable did not exeed [*sic*] fifteen thousand Dollars. This respondent denies all combination and confederation with Amberg and Herman Ilfeld for the purpose in said bill stated or for any other purpose. He admits that he and said Carl Ilfeld claim to be the sole partners and owners of the assets of said firm of A. Letcher & Co and that they owe nothing to said firm of Elsberg & Amberg. He denies all combination and collusion secret or otherwise with any of the defendants for any purpose whatever as in said bill stated.

This respondent denies all combination and confederation with any of said defendants or either of them, or with any other persons, for the purposes of cheating and defrauding said complainant or any of the creditors of said firm, or that he has or is doing anything to dispose of the assetts [*sic*] of said firm of Elsberg & Amberg.

This respondent states that he can not now state the exact amount of money he and said Carl Ilfeld have had in their possession since February the 1st, 1869, but whatever amount they may have had, has been paid to Elsberg & Amberg and expended in filling said corn contract.

This respondent further states that since the first day of February 1869 said firm of A. Letcher & Co have purchased from other merchants goods wares and merchandize to a large amount to with about eight thousand Dollars that they have been carrying on their business since said time as merchants and have disposed of no goods exept [*sic*] what they have sold in their ordinary business.

And now having fully answered all and singular the material allegations in said bill contained begs hence to be dismissed with his reasonable costs in this behalf . . . [?]fully sustained.

S. B. Elkins/s/
for Respondent.

Adolph Letcher respondent in the foregoing answer being duly sworn in his oath states that the matters and things set forth and contained in the foregoing answers there stated upon his knowledge and here and there states upon the information of others he believes to be true.

Adolph Letcher/s/

Sworn to and subscribed
before me this the 10th
day of August
A.D. 1869
Wm. Breeden/s/
Clerk

Separate Answer of Charles Ilfeld

Gustave Elsberg
vs
Jacob Amberg
etc c e.

In Chancery in the District
Court for the First Judicial
District of New Mexico

The separate answer of Charles Ilfeld to the Bill of complaint of Gustave Elsberg filed herein against Jacob Amberg, Hermann Ilfeld, Adolph Letcher, Carl Ilfeld, Samuel B. Wheelock and Stephin B. Elkins. This defendant now and at all times hereafter reserving all manner of benefit and advantage to himself of exeption [*sic*] to the many errors and insufficiencies in said Bill contained, for answer thereto or unto so much or such parts thereof as his defendant is advised is material for him to make answer unto answering says:

He desires most positively at the time stated in said bill or at any other time this respondent together with said Adolph Letcher was admitted as a partner with the firm of Elsberg & Amberg at the place stated in said bill or elsewhere, but he states the truth to be that about one month after said Adolph Letcher had established a store at Las Vegas and commenced business, he the said Letcher wrote to this respondent soliciting him to become a partner with him in his business at said place whereupon this respondent consented and became a partner with Adolph Letcher alone to carry on business under the firm name of A. Letcher & Co and in no wise had he anything to do with said Elsberg & Amberg or either of them. This respondent denies that said defendant Amberg ever at any time made a fraudulent sale of the goods wares and merchandize belonging to the mercantile establishment carried on at Las Vegas under the name of A. Letcher & Co as in said Bill stated, he admitts [*sic*] that since he has become a member of the firm of A. Letcher & Co most of the goods and merchandize bought by said firm, have been from the firm of Elsberg and Amberg. This respondent admits that at the time he became a partner of the firm of A. Letcher & Co. he possessed a small capital about the sum mentioned in said bill, which is all the capital he had to put in said firm of A. Letcher & Co. This respondent admits that the profits of said firm of A. Letcher & Co during the first year including some uncolectable [*sic*] debts, were about as stated in said bill. This respondent states that during the second year the profits if any were very small, the exact amount he cannot now state, he denies that a large amount of merchandize was furnished by the firm of Elsberg & Amberg during said year, then the year proceeding. This respondent admits the sum of \$15000⁰⁰ was due the firm of Elsberg & Amberg by the firm of A. Letcher & Co and that the profits of said business was not included in said amount, he states that the full amount of all indebtedness due Elsberg & Amberg by the firm of A. Letcher & Co on any account whatever has long since been discharged and paid.

This respondent denies they were thirty five thousand dollars worth of goods, wares and merchandize on hand belonging to said A. Letcher & Co at the time stated in said Bill, and colectable [*sic*] debts due said firm to an amount in proportion to the stock on hand, but states that said stock did not exeed [*sic*] twenty thousand dollars, he denies all manner of combination or confederacy as in said bill stated with any one or for any of the purposes therein mentioned.

This respondent admits that he and Adolph Letcher claim to be the sole partners and owners of the property, goods and merchandize now under the control of said firm, as they in truth are, he denies any secret collusion exists as in said bill stated, for the purpose as therein set forth.

This respondent states that since the first day of February A.D. 1869 the said firm of A. Letcher & Co have paid said firm of Elsberg & Amberg in full for goods, wares and merchandize, as also in full of all other claims of all kinds. And now having fully answered all and every material allegation in said bill contained this respondent prays hence to be dismissed and his reasonable costs in this behalf . . . [?]fully sustained.

S. B. Elkins/s/
for Respondent

Carl Ilfeld respondent in the foregoing bill being duly sworn upon his oath states that the matters & things set forth and contained in the foregoing answer, those as stated upon his knowledge are true and those stated upon the information of others he believes to be true.

Sworn to and subscribed
before me this the 12th
day of August A.D.
1869

Gustave Elsberg
vs
Jacob Amberg
et al.
Answer of
Carl Ilfeld

Filed in my office
this 12th day of August 1869
Wm. Breeden/s/
Clerk

Separate Answer of Herman Ilfeld

Gustave Elsberg
vs
Jacob Amberg, et als.

In Chancery.
In the District Court
for the first Judicial District
of New Mexico

The separate answer of Herman Ilfeld to the Bill of Complaint of Gustave Elsberg, filed herein against Jacob Amberg, Herman Ilfeld, Adolph Letcher, Carl Ilfeld, Samuel B. Wheelock, and Stephen B. Elkins.

This respondent now and at all times hereafter reserving to himself all manner of benefit and advantage of exception to the many errors and insufficiencies in said bill contained, for answer thereunto, or unto so much or such parts thereof as this respondent is advised is material for him to make answer unto, answering says:

He admits he was admitted a partner of said firm at the time and on the conditions in said bill stated, except that he denies he was to pay an interest of ten per centum on the amount of one hundred and fifty thousand dollars, to be first deducted from any profits accruing, also that he was only to be interested in merchandize, but not in mines or any other speculations.

He denies all confederation and confederacy with said defendant

Wheelock and Amberg for the purposes in said bill stated, and also that said Wheelock holds the store and goods in said bill mentioned for the ultimate benefit of the said Amberg or this respondent, but he states the facts to be that on his return to Santa Fe, from Europe about the middle of April last, and being informed that said Elsberg and Amberg was greatly embarrassed, the said complainant being in the City of New York, and the said Amberg in the Republic of Mexico, and finding his information correct, and with the view of as rapidly as possible, to pay all debts due and owing by said firm, he at once devoted himself to settling the business of the same.

He states he found little or no means on hand, and claims presented for payment almost daily, besides he was compelled to provide ways and means to fill a large contract with the Government, then on hand and unfilled. That at that time there existed and was on hand, goods, wares and merchandise to the amount of about Eighteen thousand dollars, and consisted of an incomplete assortment of goods, as also old remnants and a large amount that was bought when prices were high, during the war; that this respondent finding himself greatly embarrassed for want of funds, was compelled to sell and dispose of such property as belonged to said firm to meet the liabilities, and believing it to be to the interest of said firm to get rid of the old stock on hand, and curtail the expenses incident to a large business with but few goods, he sold all of the goods, wares and merchandize of said firm to said Samuel B. Wheelock for the sum of Thirteen thousand dollars payable in two notes.

This respondent states that said sale was in no wise fraudulent, but was made in good faith for a good and valied [*sic*] consideration, and as this respondent believes from the condition of the depreciated stock of goods vastly to the interest of said firm, and was made to carry on the business, raise means and mantain [*sic*] the credit of said firm, and that said Wheelock has paid for the same, and that said goods could not have brought more under any circumstances, without retailing them out at great expense.

This respondent denies that Adolph Letcher and Carl Ilfeld are or ever were partners in the business of Elsberg and Amberg, but states that sometime in the year 1867, said firm of Elsberg and Amberg agreed to furnish and sell to said Adolph Letcher goods and merchandize to establish a store in Las Vegas; that when said goods were delivered the said Letcher became the sole owner of the same, except that he was in duty bound to pay therefor, in consideration of which fact the firm of Elsberg and Amberg were to receive one half of the profits until such time as said Adolph Letcher could pay for the entire amount of goods so purchased, at which time all interest of said Elsberg and Amberg in the profits would cease.

This respondent states that he has no definite knowledge of any of the business transactions, goods on hand or debts due by said firm of A. Letcher & Co.

This respondent denies all fraudulent transfers to Stephen B. Elkins, of the notes, due bills and book accounts as in said bill stated; he denies all combination and confederacy with said Elkins and Amberg, for the purposes stated in said bill, but states that as he now remembers, he may have transferred one or two notes to said Elkins but with no fraudulent intention.

This respondent admits that said complainant bought groceries from McCartney & Co to the amount stated in said bill, but most positively denies that they were ever attached by said McCartney & Co, but here states the fact to be, that desiring if possible to repair the damage done the firm by the recklessness of said complainant in buying said goods when he knew the firm owed largely, he took immediate steps to have them turned over to the agent of said Samuel McCartney & Co, then in the Territory, which he did; that after said groceries were turned over to said McCartney & Co. he knows a portion of them were sold by said McCartney & Co to Samuel B. Wheelock, but denies that said goods were ever in the possession of said Wheelock previously or that the marks on the boxes and barrels were defaced, and said Wheelock's name substituted. He also denies that said sale to Wheelock by McCartney & Co. was fraudulent or was made in connivance with this respondent and said Amberg.

This respondent denies that the piano stated in said bill was fraudulently delivered to said Elkins, but states that said Elkins received said piano in payment of fees due him for a long time, instead of money, which at that time was a favor to said firm of Elsberg and Amberg, and that he paid the full price for the same, with all costs and charges.

This respondent denies that he and said Amberg at any time before or since the sale to Wheelock, either in the night time or day time ever took out of said store eight or ten wagon loads of goods and shipped them away as in said bill stated; that if any goods were taken from said store it was while this respondent was absent in Europe. He denies the taking away of silk shawls and goods as in said bill stated.

This respondent denies all sales of goods far below their prices, and especially to Hyman Rinaldo, as in said bill stated as also having taken away notes for goods so sold.

This respondent denies positively that said complainant came to the place of business of said firm of Elsberg & Amberg and was rudely met by this respondent on his arrival at Santa Fe as in said bill stated, but states the fact to be that said complainant, on his arrival came to the store of Samuel B. Wheelock where this respondent was, and after knocking at the door and being unable to effect an entrance, proceeded to a window leading into the back yard of said store, and there entered said back yard, and also the back door of said store.

This respondent admits that he did not receive said complainant kindly, for the reason he felt said complainant had not only squandered and fraudulently disposed of the money of the firm, but had endeavored to cheat and defraud this respondent of all he possessed. He denies that said complainant was expelled by him, but states that this respondent informed said complainant that the store belonged to said Samuel B. Wheelock.

This respondent denies most positively that said complainant was by him excluded from seeing the books of said firm.

This respondent denies ever having fraudulently concealed any goods or property belonging to said firm for his own use.

This respondent denies all combination and confederacy with the other defendants, or either of them for the purpose of cheating and defrauding and removing goods as in said bill stated.

This respondent states that Ex "A" herewith filed and made a part of this answer will show the amnts of money merchandize &c drain [*sic*] out of the firm and charged to him on the books of Elsberg & Amberg since February 1st 1869. As the book will show—that if he has had any other transactions that are not declared on said exhibit or in this answer he cannot now remember them.

And now having fully answered all of the material allegations in said bill contained he prays hence to be dismissed with his reasonable costs in this behalf . . . [?]fully sustained.

S. B. ELKINS/s/
for respondent

Herman Ilfeld respondent in the foregoing answer being duly sworn on his oath states that the matters and things set forth or contained therein are true those as stated on his own knowledge and those stated on the information and knowledge of others he believes to be true.

HERMAN ILFELD/s/

Sworn and subscribed before me this the 2 day of August A.D. 1869

WM. BREEDEN, Clerk/s/
for
M. S. Breeden Dept

APPENDIX 2

Letter from Residents of Taos County, New Mexico, to President of the United States

The following letter was copied from the December 5, 1863, issue of the *Santa Fe New Mexican.* It illustrates clearly the difficulties the people of Taos were encountering in their communications with Santa Fe and the depressing effect these difficulties had on prices of grains grown in the Taos area. (See Chapter II.) Céran St. Vrain, storied Santa Fe trader, was the spokesman for these people. The "138 others" were not identified in the newspaper copy of the original letter.

Fernando de Taos,
New Mexico, Sep. 27th '63

To his Excellency, A. Lincoln,

The undersigned, residents of the county of Taos, and loyal citizens of New Mexico, respectfully present the following memorial to the favorable consideration of your Excellency, to wit: Your memorialists believe: (and long experience has shown this belief to be well founded,) that it is greatly to the interest of this Territory of New Mexico,—to the interests of the government of the United States,—and to the especial interest of the Northern portion of our Territory, as imminently involving the former, that by government agency, and sufficient appropriation, an advantageous Public Road, . . . and for more convenient postal intercommunication, should be speedily opened and perfected, between the towns of Taos and Santa Fe. Your memorialists respectfully claim the feasibility of the project, the little time necessary for its practical execution, and in view of the important results manifestly to follow its achievement, the comparatively trivial expenditure required, as primary reasons for their appeal in behalf of the enterprise. The valley of Taos, almost unbounded in extent, unvaryingly fertile, and rich in agricultural products, has long been considered, as it promises ever to remain, the principal granary of this Territory; yet inhospitably shut in by natural barriers, wanting available artificial outlets, and thus, in a great measure, isolated from interior marts of trade, in vain has plenty here reached abundance, and an over-supply cheapened prices far below the demand elsewhere. On this point it will be sufficient to refer your Excellency to the statistics of our last census report, to show our annual grain product, while we beg leave to remark, that corn and wheat which bring at this time $1. and $1.50, a *Fanega,* [about two and a half bushels] in Taos, is from six to eight dollars in Santa Fe; and of course, with easy and less expensive access to places of ready sale, the amount of production would be proportionably increased, with a possible diminution in even low prices. To say nothing, therefore, of immense advantages likely to accrue to local Territorial interests, the direct interest to the government in obtaining supplies from this valley, in all desirable quantities, and at greatly reduced rates, is too obvious to need comment, nor is it matter of less concern, that government troops, in view of any existing or future emergency, would find such a highway as is proposed to be established, the most practicable of all others for their safe and speedy transportation; the route in question embracing, as it would do, not only a central Territorial line, radical for the purposes of military disposition in any desired direction, but also the best settled portions of the country, and affording ample supplies, without the necessity of any particular division of any incoming force, or at most, a resort to ordinary foraging expeditions. As to feasibility, only about twelve or thirteen miles of road would require the principal expenditure of the necessary government appropriation, viz., a section in the most direct line of communication between Taos and Santa Fe, beginning at a point on the east bank of the Rio Grande known as La Cenegilla, and about fifteen miles distant from the town of Taos, being, in fact, a principal outlet of the valley on its western border and terminating at La Hoya, in the adjoining intermediate county of Rio Arriba. Previous surveys, more especially those of Capt. McComb, of the U.S. Army, have shown the grades of this designated section would be easy, the work comparatively light, and that by the circuit made, and the new connections formed, the distance between Taos and Santa Fe would be shortened at least twenty-five miles . . . not more than seventy odd miles, and possibly much less, would have to be traveled, and their freight of whatsoever description, and with an excelerated expedition, at the moment beyond any approximate computation. As to time, from the surveys referred to, it is certain, especially under a competent officer like Capt. McComb, the projected work could be completed, and with no extraordinary application of labor, but with due energetic action, in a period of four months at the outside. As to expense, every reasonable, and every liberal estimate and calculation, has shown that to carry out to successful completion this really important work, an appropriation of $150,000 would be amply sufficient, this sum very probably to be more than made up by the difference in the cost to government of grain already alluded to. Your memorialists presume the citizens of Santa Fe, and indeed, of all other parts of the Territory of New Mexico, are equally interested in the objects of this petition.—Lines of coaches would doubtless soon be established on a direct route between Santa Fe and Denver City, improving our postal exchanges, making the transportation of passengers greatly more convenient and expeditious, and opening up a more familiar intercourse with our sister Territory of Colorado, drawing us into closer and more legitimate proximity to the states of which we are a part. The rich valley of Taos would at once be freed from its present isolated position, and the town of Fernando, deservedly one of the first in the Territory, would likewise receive immediate recognition of its claims to a leading importance. The current of population, naturally flowing into New Mexico from north to south, would be expanded and quickened in its progress, and even the rising attractions of our mineral developments to the adventurous seeker after gold, where travel by direct lines of intercommunications was rendered more convenient and less expensive. These among other suggestions, many of which will doubtless occur to your Excellency's mind, are our reasons for presenting your Excellency this memorial. We most respectfully ask your favorable consideration of the same, and such recommendations as may tend to secure us all necessary congressional intervention in our behalf.

Most Respectfully,
CÉRAN ST. VRAIN,
and 138 others.

APPENDIX 3

A. Letcher and Company Account with Elsberg and Amberg

Gustave Elsberg passed through Las Vegas March 11, 1869. While the stage was waiting on the Plaza he must have told Adolph Letcher and Charles Ilfeld of the financial embarrassment of Elsberg and Amberg, for not only did A. Letcher and Company stop sending money exchange to Elsberg's office in New York, but steps were taken, as soon as Elsberg returned to the East, to obtain releases from all debts to Elsberg and Amberg. Two documents were signed in Santa Fe on March 22, 1869, purporting to accomplish this. (See Chapter III, pp. 22 and 25.) With Herman Ilfeld in Germany, or more probably on the high seas, and Gustave Elsberg in New York, Jacob Amberg must have been the individual who signed these papers. He did not, however, use his own name but merely signed "Elsberg and Amberg."

The first document, a release of Letcher and Company's financial obligations to Elsberg and Amberg, is a recognition of the losses sustained by Letcher and Company in the fulfillment of the Elsberg and Amberg corn contract. The second document refers to a deposit which Letcher made with Elsberg and Amberg in 1865 as partial security against the large credit given him by the Santa Fe firm. (Charles Ilfeld put about $500 on deposit at the same time presumably. See Chapter III, p. 22.) These deposits represented the capital accounts for A. Letcher and Company. Letcher's deposit, at least, was charged off against the amount owed to Elsberg and Amberg by an entry on March 2, 1869.

Release of Letcher and Company's Financial Obligations to Elsberg and Amberg

Santa Fe, N.M.
March 22d, 1869

Received of Mess. A. Letcher and Co. of Las Vegas the sum of Twenty two hundred and nineteen 80/100 dolls being the full amount due by Said A. Letcher and Co. to us in full of all accounts up to date of whatever kind and description and it is understood from and after this date that the said firm of A. Letcher and Co. have paid the full amount due us on account of furnishing them goods and starting them in business, that we have no claim or demand against them whatever of any kind, and in consideration of the full payment of their indebtedness to us we hereby release all claims and demands against them, and especially all claims as profits arising from their business in the future.

ELSBERG AND AMBERG/s/

2219.81
Witness: Morris Brown/s/
L. Plant [?] /s/

DEPOSIT OF LETCHER AND COMPANY WITH ELSBERG AND AMBERG

Santa Fe, N.M.
March 22[d], 1869

Received of A. Letcher the sum of Fifty nine hundred and Seventy 54/100 dollars for and on account of the firm of A. Letcher and Co. of Las Vegas. The above amount being the full amount due by us to said A. Letcher for money loaned us with Interest in the year 1865.

ELSBERG AND AMBERG/s/

5970.54
Witness: Morris Brown/s/
L. Plant [?] /s/

APPENDIX 4

COPY OF DOCUMENT TRANSFERRING OWNERSHIP OF A. LETCHER AND COMPANY TO CHARLES ILFELD

The following is a copy of the original document in Louis C. Ilfeld's office, Las Vegas, New Mexico. It was copied and furnished by courtesy of Louis C. Ilfeld on August 17, 1948.

SALE OF ADOLPH LETCHER'S INTEREST IN A. LETCHER AND COMPANY TO CHARLES ILFELD

This Indenture of two parts, made and concluded this fourteenth day of September A.D. 1874, by and between Adolph Letcher of Las Vegas, merchant, of the first part and Charles Ilfeld of Las Vegas, merchant of the second part, both residents of the County of San Miguel and Territory of New Mexico, witnesseth:

That, whereas, the said parties were lately copartners in the business of selling general Goods and Merchandize, in the Territory of New Mexico, which Partnership was dissolved and determined on the fourteenth day of September A.D. 1874, and whereas many debts, due and owing to the said parties on account of their said co-partnership are still outstanding, and debts due by the said firm are yet unpaid, and whereas it is agreed that the said party of the first part shall assign and release to the said party of the second part all his interest in the stock in trade, goods, and effects, belonging to said firm, and in the debts now owing to said firm, and that the party of the second part shall assume all the debts and liabilities of the said firm and shall discharge and indemnify the said party of the first part, from all liabilities and losses arising from the said partnership:

Now, in pursuance of the said agreement, and in consideration of the sum of Thirty Six Thousand Dollars ($36,000) paid and secured to the said Adolph Letcher party of the first part, and said Adolph Letcher of the first part doth, hereby fully and absolutely sell, assign, release, and make over to the said Charles Ilfeld of the second part all his right, title, interest and share, in and to all the stock in trade, goods merchandise, machinery, tools, books, leasehold premises, effects and household furniture, belonging to the said partnership of whatever kind or nature, and wheresoever situated, also all the right, title and interest in and to all the debts and sums of money, now due, and owing to the said firm whether the said be by bond, Bill, Note, or account or otherwise, and the said Adolph Letcher doth hereby make and appoint the said Charles Ilfeld, his executors, administrators, and assigns to be his attorney and attorneys, to receive all and several the debts and sums of money above mentioned to his and their own use and benefit, and doth hereby authorize the said Charles Ilfeld his executors, administrators and assigns, to demand collect and sue for the said debts and sums of money, and to use his the said Adolph Letcher's name in any way or manner that the collection, recovery and realization of the said debts and demands may render necessary, as well in Courts as out of Courts, but at their own proper costs and charges, and without cost or damage to the said Adolph Letcher.

And the said Adolph Letcher doth hereby further authorize the said Charles Ilfeld to convey and transfer to his own name, and for his own use, and benefit any and all sums of money and effects, real and personal estate, which may be taken or received in the name of the said firm and to hold the same free from all claims by the said Adolph Letcher, his executors administrators or assigns;

And the said Adolph Letcher does hereby agree, and covenant, that whenever it should become necessary to the said Charles Ilfeld, to have his the said Adolph Letcher's signature, to any Deed, Mortgage, or any other class, or description of Instrument of writing, that the said Adolph Letcher hereby agrees to do so at any time hereafter, whenever required, provided the same pertains to aforesaid firm and partnership, and the said Adolph Letcher furthermore authorizes, and empowers, the said Charles Ilfeld to sign his the said Adolph Letcher's name, to any Deed, Mortgage, or other class or description of Instrument of writing pertaining to said firm and partnership, which signature shall be recognized, as his own, and as having been written by his, the said Adolph Letcher's own Hands.

And these presents further witness, that, in pursuance of the said agreement the said Charles Ilfeld, for himself, his executors and administrators, doth hereby covenant, to and with the said Adolph Letcher, his executors and administrators, that the said Charles Ilfeld, and his executors and administrators, shall pay and discharge, and at all times hereafter save harmless, and indemnify, the said Adolph Letcher his executors, administrators and assigns from and against all and every the debts, and liabilities, which at the dissolution and termination of the said partnership, were due and owing by the said firm to any person or persons for any matter or thing touching the said partnership, and of and from all actions, suits, costs, expenses and damages for, or concerning the said debts, and liabilities, unless the said Adolph Letcher shall have contracted any debts or incurred any liabilities, in the name and on account of the said firm, which are unknown to the said Charles

Ilfeld, and do not appear in the books of the said firm, for which, if any such exists, the said Charles Ilfeld does not hereby intend to make himself responsible.

ADOLPH LETCHER/s/

Territory of New Mexico }
County of San Miguel }

Personaly [*sic*] appeared before me the undersigned clerk of the probate court in and for the county of San Miguel territory aforesaid, Adolph Letcher a resident of Las Vegas county and territory aforesaid, who is personaly [*sic*] known to me, to be the same person whose name appear [*sic*] to the aforegoing instrument of writting [*sic*], who acknowledge before me that he signed, sealed and delivered the same freely and voluntarily for the uses and purposes therein mentioned.

Witness my hand and the seal of said Probate Court at Las Vegas, N. M. this 15th day of September A.D. 1874.

ROMAN LOPEZ/s/
Clerk of the Probate Court

(Seal of the Probate
Court)

Pr. Jose S. Rivera/s/
Deputy

APPENDIX 5

Vignette of Alexander Grzelachowski

Because A. Grzelachowski receives far less attention than he deserves in written New Mexico history, the following miscellaneous material is given for whatever value it may have:

Alexander Grzelachowski, a native of Poland, applied for his naturalization papers as a citizen of the United States on October 11, 1855, at Pena Blanca, Santa Ana County, New Mexico, having made his first application in 1850 in Lorain County, Ohio.[a]

He had come to Las Vegas by 1852.

"I wish to make sure about A. Grzelachowski and had to get facts from one of the priests who is my very good friend. Padre Polaco was the name by which Mr. Grzelachowski was known when I came to Las Vegas (1884). He had been Parish Priest in the old church here in 1852 and 1853. I couldn't believe this statement until it was certified by the records, because when I knew him, he was a merchant and rancher at Puerto de Luna, married and father of a son; evidently had apostatized, though that had never been mentioned during the years I've lived here. He was rated a man of intelligence and a good character—a respected citizen. I was well acquainted with his son Adolph." [b]

Grzelachowski served San Miguel del Vado from November, 1851, to March, 1852; San Felipe, September, 1851, and November, 1853, to September, 1856; Cochiti, December, 1853, to November, 1857; Santo Domingo, November, 1853, to November, 1857.[c]

The only reference to Grzelachowski's former profession by Ilfeld was at a time when Ilfeld was having trouble collecting the account of August Klein (Kline) of Roswell and Lincoln. Klein, a prominent rancher, was not willing to pay in cash but preferred to pay in cattle, the price of which was not easy to determine as Ilfeld had not been able to go to Klein's ranch to see the animals. He wrote: "I would like to ask you to deliver 20 cows from 3–6 years old to Padre Polaco in Puerte de Luna for my account." [d]

His trust in Grzelachowski is revealed in a second letter to Klein: [e]

[a] Record Book, 1847–1856, Circuit Court for the County of Santa Ana, New Mexico, University of New Mexico Library, pp. 89–90.

[b] Letter from R. B. Schoonmaker, Las Vegas, New Mexico, Sept. 17, 1947.

[c] Fray Angelico Chavez, *Archives of the Archdiocese of Santa Fe,* Academy of American Franciscan History (Washington, D. C., 1957), p. 259.

[d] Copy Book 3 (in German), Feb. 16, 1878.

[e] Copy Book 4 (in German), Feb. 5, 1878.

In order to come to a decision, I am making you the following proposal: you will take the cattle, if possible mostly in yearlings to the padre in Puerte de Luna and deliver it to him for my account, the price that you and the padre will agree upon I shall be glad to credit to your account. I think this is right as far as you are concerned as well as myself, and if this proposal meets with your approval, let me know at what time you could be at Puerte de Luna, so that I can write the padre about it. If you wish you can take a third man who knows the regular market price.

A. Grzelachowski had the army freighting contract from Ft. Union to other depots in New Mexico, Arizona, and Texas west of latitude 105 degrees for a period ending March 31, 1870.[f]

[f] Report of Secretary of War, 1869–70, 41st Cong., 2d sess., vol. I, pp. 248–249.

APPENDIX 6

NEWS ITEM FROM *Las Vegas Gazette*, JANUARY 24, 1883

The Great Emporium

Charles Ilfeld's New Business House on the Plaza

An Ornament to the Town and a Credit to the Territory

Las Vegas is justly noted among the other towns of the Territory for the substantial character of its business houses, both as regards the buildings and the financial standing of the proprietors.

The Building

Among the new buildings just completed is that of Charles Ilfeld, on the north side of the plaza and adjoining the Plaza hotel. This is without doubt the best business house in the Territory of New Mexico. It is a substantial structure, built of stone, three stories high above the basement and finished off in a manner which gives it an imposing and elegant appearance. It is thirty-two feet wide by one hundred and thirty-two feet long. The basement is the full length of the building and is a most excellent one. The front of the first story above the basement is constructed of brown stone with enormous show windows of French plate glass. The front of the second and third story is constructed of white granite, and is certainly very handsome. The building is covered with a metallic roof, laid by the most skillful workmen. The contractors who were instrumental in erecting this structure were Messrs. Claiburn and Pierce, who did the stone work, Messrs. Taylor & Fowler who did the carpenter work, and Messrs. Finane & Elston who did the painting and glazing. The workmanship throughout is of the best, and reflects credit upon the contractors. The first floor is provided with a large and comodious [*sic*] office, built of imitation walnut, and ground glass amply supplied with large fire proof safes and convenient desks. The office would do credit to a banking establishment. An Osgood elevator affords easy means of carrying goods from the basement to the third floor. The building is provided with water on all the floors, with fireplugs throughout. The cost of construction of this splendid building will reach in the neighborhood of $40,000.

The Stocks of Merchandise

which fills this vast structure is in keeping with the building itself. The basement is devoted to groceries, liquors, hardware and saddlery, all lines of which are unusually complete. The first floor is the general retail department for dry goods, fancy goods, notions and gents furnishing goods. The second floor is practically in two departments, one for wholesale dry goods, and the other for millinery and dressmaking. The latter feature is particularly attractive to lady customers and is presided over by skilled artists in dressmaking and millinery. The third floor is set aside for carpets, oil cloths, matting, etc. On all floors are to be found attentive and courteous clerks, who are especially experienced in the class of goods belonging to their separate departments. The stock of goods carried is immense and would do credit to a Kansas City or Denver establishment.

The Proprietor

of this great emporium is Mr. Charles Ilfeld, who, although yet a young man, commenced business in Las Vegas in 1867, before railroads had yet crossed Kansas. By fair dealing, courteous treatment and a generous disposition he made warm friends and attracted a large patronage. He prospered greatly, made money and has now done a goodly share in aiding to build up the town wherein he made a large portion of his money by the erection of this unsurpassed structure. Naturally a man so well and favorably known and whose personal acquaintance reaches far beyond the territory would control not only a local but a very

General Trade.

This is the case and the house is daily in receipt of orders, not only from the smaller towns in the vicinity, but likewise from the Texas Panhandle, Arizona, and the northern states of Mexico. As Mr. Ilfeld has succeeded so well in establishing a lucrative trade when he occupied the small quarters afforded by the low and dark store rooms which he hitherto inhabited, it is fair to predict that in these new and enlarged quarters his trade will keep pace with the growth and development of the territory.

APPENDIX 7

Explanatory Notes to Maps of the Territory of New Mexico, 1870[a]

The difficulties of preparing a map of the Territory of New Mexico as it existed in 1870 can scarcely be enumerated. It suffices to say that the data had to be gleaned from a series of maps, nearly all of later periods, then verified in census reports, tax lists, statute laws, county histories, general histories, and some monographic studies. It was the original intention that the map show chiefly the Taos and Las Vegas areas since these are of foremost concern in the Ilfeld story. However, when it became apparent that a map of New Mexico in 1870 is either nonexistent or else something of a rarity, it was deemed worthwhile to make a more comprehensive one, though still placing emphasis upon the regions of Taos and Las Vegas. This all-inclusive Territory has been divided into two maps: Northern and Southern New Mexico.

County boundaries. In 1870 in the Territory of New Mexico there were thirteen counties formed out of the seven which had existed during the last years of Mexican and American control, prior to the formation of the Territorial government. As a consequence, several entire boundary lines and some portions of boundaries of the 1870 counties coincided with those of the late Mexican period. The seven counties aforementioned are indicated on a map drawn by James S. Calhoun, who, by order of the U. S. War Department, made a survey of Indian affairs in 1846–47.[b] Since segments of the boundaries indicated by Calhoun were retained as the new counties were created, the 1846–47 survey map was of considerable value in determining several of the 1870 lines.

In addition to the Calhoun map, the following were of considerable use:

Map of New Mexico, 1882, Rand McNally.

Territory of N. M., 1879, Dept. of Interior, Land Office, J. A. Williamson, Commissioner.

Descriptions of county boundaries appear in:

[a] Author's Note: To Miss Katherine Nutt goes the credit for the research as well as for these explanatory notes. She completed her research in August, 1949, while still engaged as my research assistant at the University of New Mexico. Professor Richard G. Huzarski, of the College of Engineering at the University of New Mexico, was the original cartographer. Mr. S. H. Bryant of Marblehead, Massachusetts, prepared the maps for publication.

[b] Map No. 2 of four incorporated in *The Official Correspondence of James S. Calhoun,* published by the government printing office in 1915.

General Laws of N. M., 1880, compiled under the direction of the Honorable L. Bradford Prince, Chief Justice of the Supreme Court of N. M., Albany, N. Y., W. C. Little & Co., Law Publishers, 1880. The quotations from the laws were, however, almost wholly impractical as examples cited later will show.

The 13 counties of the Territory of New Mexico in 1870 were:

Taos	Grant	Socorro
Rio Arriba	Colfax	Lincoln
Santa Ana	Santa Fe	Dona Ana
Bernalillo	Mora	San Miguel
	Valencia	

Of these, nine were established by Act of January 9, 1852; Mora was organized in 1860; Grant in 1868; Lincoln and Colfax in 1869.[c] By this same Act, Taos was bounded as follows: [d]

from the first house of the town of Embudo, on the upper side, where the canon of Picuris terminates, drawing a direct line toward the south over the mountain of Bajillo at the town of Rincones, until it reaches the front of the last house of Las Trampas, on the south side; from thence drawing a direct line toward the east, dividing the mountain, until it reaches the junction of the rivers Mora and Sapello, and from thence to the boundary line of the Territory; from the above-mentioned house of Embudo, drawing a line toward the north over the mountain, and dividing the Rio del Norte in the direction of the Tetilla de la Petaca; from thence taking a westward direction until it terminates with the boundary line of the Territory; and on the north by all the land belonging to the Territory of New Mexico.

Needless to say, few of the points mentioned in this description and none of the landmarks could be located on any of the later maps.

Affecting the Taos County boundaries also was the creation, by the 10th Legislature Assembly, Act of February 1, 1860, of a new county, Mora, which was to be bounded: [e]

on the north and east by the limits of the Territory of New Mexico; on the south by the northern limits of the county of San Miguel; and on the west by the tops of the ridge of mountains which divide the valley of Taos from Mora and Rayado.

In 1868 this was redefined as: [f]

West of the valley of Mora, a line running north commencing at the first hill west of the said valley of Mora and east of the Jicarita, crossing the Vega del Estillero opposite the Canada del Raton, passing through the said canada till it reaches the foot of the Osha hill on the eastern base thereof, thence con-

[c] *Gen'l. Laws of N. M., 1880,* p. 215.
[d] *Ibid.,* pp. 215–216.
[e] *Ibid.,* p. 218.
[f] *Ibid.,* p. 219.

tinuing north along the eastern base of said range, along the eastern side of the head of the Rio Colorado which runs into the Rio Grande, in the county of Taos, and thence in a north east direction to the limits of the Territory.

In 1869 Colfax County was created from the northern portion of Mora, again altering the Taos borders: [g]

All that part of the Territory comprised within the following limits, to wit: To the north and east by the boundaries of the Territory of New Mexico, to the south the boundaries of the grant made to Carlos Beaubien and Guadelupe Miranda, and known as the Rayado grant, and on the west the boundaries of the county of Taos, shall form and constitute a new county to be known as and called Colfax county.

The above statement is misleading, however, for actually Colfax did not include all of the Rayado grant until 1876. The southern tip remained in Mora County, although all of the available maps, 1879, 1882, and 1896, indicate it as part of Colfax.[h] The discrepancy can be verified by the description in the Act of 1876 which described the boundary as follows: [i]

The boundary line between Mora and Colfax counties, is hereby established, to wit: Starting at a point on the eastern boundary of New Mexico and about fifty three miles south of the north east corner of New Mexico, and running west through the center of township twenty-three north from the base line as established by Government Survey, to the western boundary of the counties of Mora and Colfax.

This change extended the area of Colfax by approximately a four to five mile strip, thus retaining within its southern border all of the area of the original Rayado grant.

Of the other ten counties, six defined in 1852 or before 1870 remained unchanged until as late as 1880; hence their lines may be readily established by referring to other maps. These six are Rio Arriba, Santa Fe, Valencia, Socorro, Grant, and San Miguel. Four other counties, however, underwent alterations which would be characteristic of 1870 but not of other maps.

Santa Ana County, the only one of the original counties to be abolished, was dropped in 1876. In 1870, Santa Ana lay between Rio Arriba and Bernalillo, the latter extending westward from the center of the Territory in a strip of four miles or less wide, with Valencia County immediately to the south. The *General Laws* are almost meaningless in their description, for they relied almost completely on local landmarks. The Santa Ana line started west at a point "above the last houses of

[g] *Ibid.*

[h] *Inventory of the County Archives of Colfax County New Mexico,* No. 4, The Historical Records Survey Works Progress Administration, Albuquerque, N. M., Dec., 1937, p. 5.

[i] *Gen'l. Laws of N. M., 1880,* p. 220.

Bernalillo where the lands previously known as those belonging to the Indians of Santa Ana are divided." [j]

The Bernalillo-Valencia line crossed "the Rio del Norte in the direction of the Quelites del Rio Puerco," and continued "in the direction of the canon of Juan Tafoya, terminating with the boundaries of the Territory." [k] Since the Juan Tafoya Canon seems not to have merited recognition on later maps, this boundary remained a hopeless riddle until it was found on the Calhoun map of the original seven counties, though not exactly as they existed in 1870. It is evident from the Calhoun work that following "in the direction of Juan Tafoya Canon" meant a right-angle turn, thus locating the remaining line as due west. When Santa Ana County was abolished, all of its territory was thrown into Bernalillo County.

A small deviation in the Bernalillo line, though evident on later maps, is worthy of note since the change actually occurred in 1870.[l]

All that portion of the county of Bernalillo [a very small area] situated south of a line commencing at a point on the east bank of the Rio Grande where the southern foot of the "loma de Isleta" strikes the Rio Grande and running thence to the "Canon del Inferno," and then following the old line . . . shall be cut off from the county of Bernalillo and included within the county of Valencia.

In 1870, the border line between Socorro and Dona Ana counties was "a direct line to the eastward from the Muerto spring in the Jornada in the direction of La Laguna and continuing" until it terminates with the boundary of Lincoln county, created in 1869. The line went directly west from the spring until it terminated with the boundary of Grant County, created in 1868. The boundary between Lincoln and Dona Ana counties were bordered by the limits of the Territory; on the south, Dona Ana was contiguous with the State of Texas and the Republic of Mexico.

The map of New Mexico in 1870 found herewith was drawn in part from such descriptions as those quoted above. By noting the boundary changes as listed in the *General Laws,* by comparing the post-1870 maps with those of the 1860's to determine what portions of the earlier lines continued to exist, it was possible to extend these segments to find the proper boundary. Some problems, however, were more difficult to solve. The southwest boundary of Bernalillo, that of Valencia County, is perhaps the most striking example. Even after the direction of Juan Tafoya Canon was learned, there was the question of finding exactly where the line proceeded due west. (Probably a matter of less than a mile of variation.) There were, however, a group of border towns which have belonged to first one county then the other; a Valencia County tax list

[j] *Ibid.,* p. 217.
[k] *Ibid.*
[l] *Ibid.,* pp. 219–220.

indicated these particular towns, among them Juan Tafoya and Bluewater, to have been in Valencia in the year 1870. Thus, it was possible to determine where the county line must have been.

Location of towns. If the problem of locating county boundaries was difficult, that of finding the towns existing in 1870 was equally so. Variations in names and spelling because of changing Spanish terms to Anglo ones presented one problem. Ghost towns and those of mushroom growth, typical of the mining and cattle frontiers, further complicated the picture. Thus a town nonexistent in 1865, such as Georgetown in Grant County, became a flourishing community after silver was discovered there in the following year. A town of genuine promise in 1873, by 1893 it had become only a memory. This is only one example among many.

A further problem, and this is especially true of places named by Ilfeld in the records, was that of ranch areas or trading posts which apparently enjoyed the importance of towns, yet were actually only stopping places. "Slocum's" might have been far better known then than such a village as Hot Springs or Hillsboro. Some of these ranches did later become towns, but often under some other name.

One last complication that warrants mention was that caused by the railroad, for it changed many of the old routes of travel and communication. Again, important centers ceased to flourish because the railroad passed them by. Taos may be cited as an example. Other places came to a standstill in their development, as for example Silver City, in the southwest portion of the state. On the other hand, a city such as Albuquerque received a real impetus in growth with the railroad's coming.

Dates of incorporation were of no help in locating the towns of 1870 since most of them were incorporated much later, some of them not until after statehood was achieved in 1912. The 1870 census was of some value, but in some counties it lists only precincts. The towns finally included on the map have been verified from the list in the ninth census (1870) from those mentioned in the Ilfeld records, those included in tax lists, those included as on post roads authorized by Congress previously to 1870, and from those known to have been stopping places on such well-known routes as the Santa Fe Trail and the Butterfield Stage route.

Occasionally Mr. Twitchell's *New Mexico History* has been referred to, and the individual county histories were used if there were actual dates given. Thus, the town of Wagonmound, not included in either the eighth or the ninth census, has been placed on the map. The history of Mora County records that at Wagonmound, in 1857, a mail coach carrying ten male passengers was attacked by Apaches and all of the passengers killed.[m]

[m] *Inventory of the County Archives of Mora County, New Mexico,* No. 17, The New Mexico Historical Works Survey . . . Works Progress Administration, p. 22.

There has been no attempt to indicate the size of the town, only its location. The census list omits many places which were in existence in 1870; it also includes places which cannot now be located.

Routes. Routes indicated on this map are chiefly those of the Santa Fe Trail, the Butterfield Overland Mail, the Chihuahua Trail, deviations of these or connecting trails, and the postroads approved by Congress. Not all were equally important. In general we have assumed that if a trail was once broken, it was probably used again. Many routes were impractical and many were used only according to season. As is evident from the map, the early settlers often had to take a long way around, but they obviously had found the best, if not the shortest routes. One notes with interest that the railroad later utilized many of the routes frequented in 1870 when travel was by mule, oxen, horse, or on foot. Further information concerning these routes may be found in the following:

Lansing Bloom, "The Chihuahua Highway," *The New Mexico Historical Review,* 13:209–216 (July 1937).

Roscoe Platt Conkling, *The Butterfield Overland Mail* (Glendale, Calif.: A. H. Clark, 1947).

Josiah Gregg, *Commerce of the Prairies* (Philadelphia, 1849).

"Postroads Approved by Congress," *U. S. Statutes at Large.*

Rio Grande. The river in 1870 ran a slightly different course south of Fort Craig and Paraje than that shown on later maps, especially those of 1896 and afterwards. Constantly changing with the spring floods, the Rio Grande underwent official changes, as it were, subsequent to the passing of the Land Reclamation Act of 1893 which finally culminated in the construction of Elephant Butte Dam in 1915.

APPENDIX 8

The Arnot Wool Company, Subsidiary of Gross, Kelly and Company [a]

Arnot Wool Company

An important element of the offices of this company is an extensive

Wool Scouring Plant,

which was established eight or ten years ago by the Arnot Wool Co., later acquired by Gross, Kelly & Co., and which is now a coordinate part of the whole enterprise.

This mill scours such quantities of the wool handled by the company as it may desire and in addition does a large order business.

The capacity of the plant enables it to deal with an almost unlimited amount in the wool season.

The vast warehouse of the mill, 200 x 60 feet, alongside the Santa Fe track, is accessible by teams and train, and loading and unloading to and from either can be speedily accomplished, and scales are at hand for weighing the stock as it comes in and goes out.

A million and one-half pounds (or more if necessary) may be easily stored at one time, as was the case in 1904, when the big Ortiz clip, of quite that amount, was received here.

In The Engine Room

are a Nagle boiler and a Hamilton-Corliss engine, 110-horsepower, which runs the whole plant. Adjacent to the engine room is a coal bin with a capacity of six carloads, or about 240 tons.

The Two Sorting Rooms

are in the north wing of the great main building—one on the ground floor and the other in the second story; in the former are tables for 10 men; in the latter for 16.

About 35 men in various capacities are employed in the mill during the wool season.

The wool, having been sorted, goes to the dusters (White's) in

[a] This description was taken from the *American Shepherd's Bulletin,* 11:442–443 (May 1906).

The Scouring Room,

which is 150 feet long and under which—the entire length and width—is a cellar or pit which receives the dust, dirt, and debris.

The dusted wool is conveyed by automatic carriers to the bowls. The two scouring machines (four bowls to the "train") are respectively White's and Sargent's and from the end of the bowls to the feeder are each 145 feet long.

The finest soft water in the country (being nothing else than liquid unpoluted snow) is used in the scouring process, and the soap comes from Warren Soap Company, which is a guarantee of its excellence for the purpose.

A batch of wool is passed through the machines from the self feed to the blower thoroughly cleaned in ten minutes.

By means of the blower, which is an original device of the concern, the clean wool is carried in direct course from the end of the scouring machines to

The Drying Room,

in the second story of the mill, which is 100 feet long.

Here, by means of a Sargent automatic feed, the scoured stock enters the drier, which is 85 feet long and is provided with an endless apron which conveys the aforesaid batch of wool from feed to delivery at the other end in five minutes.

It should be remarked that the steam pipes (there are 4,000 feet of them in the drier) are not directly over the wool, hence all possibility of injury to the stock from leakage or any sort of accident to the pipes is obviated. Moreover, exhaust steam is exclusively used, and the economy of such an arrangement will be apparent when one considers that otherwise 80 pounds to 100 pounds of live steam would be demanded.

Handy to the delivery end of the drier is a packing machine, by means of which close to 100 bags may be stacked in a nine hours' run.

The bags used are new and clean, obtained expressly for the purpose, and hold from 100 to 115 pounds.

Samples of the scoured wool which have come to the packing machine, and which at any time may be seen on this floor, are remarkable for their snowy whiteness and extreme cleanliness.

This concern can scour 25,000 pounds of grease wool in ten hours. All night the mill is at rest.

APPENDIX 9

Description of the Albuquerque Wool Scouring Mill

Albuquerque Wool Scouring Mill[a]
Wool Scouring

It has doubtless occurred to many who have no special interest in wool growing or wool manufacturing that a great waste of means is involved in the transportation of 60 to 70 pounds of dirt and grease in every hundred pounds of wool which finds its way from the range to the seaboard, and probably inquiry has been made as to why, in at least some sections in which large quantities of the staple are produced, cooperation among the growers has not resulted in the establishment of more scouring mills.

Is the failure due simply to the incohesiveness of the growers—their inability "to get together?"—It seems not. The opposition to the establishment of such plants appears to come mainly from the great transportation companies, who easily figure that the business of carrying valueless material is more profitable, inasmuch as by so doing they have a hundred pounds of freight in every instance in which otherwise they would receive pay for but 30 or 40 pounds, and, moreover, the wool in the grease occupies proportionately less space in the cars. So they charge about one and three-fourths times as much per pound for carrying clean wool.

Again, it is said that the worsted manufacturers (some of them at least) prefer to do their own scouring, and decline to buy scoured wool except in cases of emergency—"to piece out"—as they say.

Nevertheless, it appears that during 1905, 4,042,031 pounds of wool were scoured at Albuquerque which subsequently reached the seaboard markets.

Exactly how much of this was included in the 5,000,000 pounds previously mentioned, I do not know, as some of it came from Phoenix, Arizona, but it is certain that all of this was cleaned for the growers and wool buyers, for the

Albuquerque Wool Scouring

mill never owns a pound of wool and does a strictly order business; therefore, the buyers must have found it advantageous to send their stock forward clean, even though they had to pay $3.25 per hundredweight, as against $1.88, which would have been the charge for transportation of the wool in the grease.

[a] This description was taken from the *American Shepherd's Bulletin,* 11:333–334 (April 1906).

This scouring plant is one of the best equipped and ably managed mills of its class in the country, and if in any consideration of Albuquerque as an industrial center I should neglect to give the reader some idea of the scope of the enterprise and its facilities for doing the highly commendable work which it is achieving, my account of the city in which the mill is located would be sadly incomplete.

This thought occurred to me while I was examining the interior of the vast storehouse of the concern, 180 feet by 50 feet, in which there may be over 1,000,000 pounds of wool at one time.

This building stands by the branch track which leads from the Santa Fe road to the door of the storehouse.

From the warehouse an elevator to the sorting room in the second story of the mill building which is just south of the warehouse conveys thither the stock at the rate of 150 bags per hour.

In the sorting room, when the mill is in operation, which is the case from May till December, night and day, one beholds

An Industrial Novelty,

nothing less than an efficient crew of female wool sorters (Mexicans) in charge of a forewoman of the same lineage, whom President Wilkinson, himself an expert sorter, trained to the art.

After the stock is sorted it goes to the wool scouring machine on the ground floor. This apparatus is White's 48-inch parallel rakes, all run by electric power, and by means of it a batch of wool is carried in six minutes from the self-feed to the end of the machine, where, thoroughly cleansed, it is ready for the drier.

The mill is provided with 3,500 feet of steam pipes and has a hot water reservoir or tank which holds 10,000 gallons.

Incidentally, it should be said that this concern uses its own

Pure Potash Soap,

which it manufactures from caustic potash and pure tallow. A soap vat beneath the ground floor of the mill has a capacity of 275 barrels.

Through The Drier,

which is provided with an 80-foot single apron, the aforesaid clean batch of wool is conveyed in five minutes.

APPENDIX 10

DESCRIPTION OF THE RIO GRANDE WOOLEN MILLS COMPANY IN ALBUQUERQUE[a]

Cooperative Woolen Mill

Some of all grades of the wool grown in this section is utilized by the Rio Grande Woolen Mills Co. (Co-Op.), proprietors of a little plant, situated not far from the scouring mill, which comprises two sets of 60-in. cards, 1,588 spindles and 10 looms. It manufactures blankets, dress goods and men's wear fabrics. A portion of the last-named goods is converted into garments in the clothing establishment of the company, which is attached to the mill.

The business—manufacturing and mercantile—is conducted on the cooperative plan.

The president and manager of the company is

Johney H. Bearrup,[b]

an interesting personality, who is "bearing up" a scheme of which I believe he was the deviser, and of the practicality of which he is satisfied. Indeed, he claims that it is already in successful working and yielding results.

The plan, substantially, is this. Any one who is persuaded of the individual benefits which may accrue to the participants in a co-operative industry may become a member of the company by paying $50 into its treasury and receiving a certificate of membership. The company is to make for its members woolen and cotton goods, boots, shoes and harness, for the scheme has latterly been made sufficiently comprehensive to embrace the production of the enumerated articles, other than woolens.

No one is allowed to invest more than $50 unless he is giving his whole time to the company's interests. Goods produced in excess of the needs of the consuming members are sold in the open market.

It is claimed that so far as woolens, boots, shoes and harness are concerned, members can save 50 per cent by using the goods manufactured by the company and participate in a 33⅓ per cent profit.

[a] This description was taken from the *American Shepherd's Bulletin,* 11:334 (April 1906).

[b] Formerly of Ureford, Kansas, a lamb feeder. Incoming Correspondence, Packet 34, Oct. 1896; 36, Dec. 1896; 38, Jan. 1897; 39, March 1897.

APPENDIX 11

Wool data and partido sheep, 1894–1905
(years ending December 31)

	1894	1895	1896	1897	1898	1899	1900	1901	1902	1903	1904	1905
Number of partido sheep	—	—	32,476	33,183	30,901	27,215	24,413	31,174	29,196	32,193	37,651	38,230
Number of partidarios	39	32	32	33	32	30	29	39	43	42	44	44
Partido wool delivered (1000 lbs)	—	—	55	62	54 [a]	57	53	43	43 [a]	31	31	—
Total wool bought (1000 lbs)	1,180	865	987	1,003	614 [a]	1,424 [b]	773	1,109	1,588	1,827	1,552	1,699
Sacks of wool purchased (1000's)	6.0	4.4	4.8	4.9	3.0 [a]	6.8 [b]	3.9	5.4	7.4	7.7	6.4	6.9
Sacks of wool sold (1000's)	6.0	4.3	4.2	5.9	2.7 [a]	7.1 [b]	3.1	7.3	7.4	7.5	6.7	6.9
Year-end partido sheep inventories (dollars)	39,118	41,415	40,910	63,954	72,612	61,234	56,929	62,348	62,771	67,605	82,832	86,018
Net profit on partidos before interest (dollars)	3,926	6,305	3,159	10,463	5,314	8,298	7,839	—	3,307	5,047	13,048	—
Value of total wool bought (1000$)	93.1	87.5	77.0	137.4 [c]	78.5 [a]	180.3 [b]	95.7	122.1	196.8	249.3	224.6	325.7
Value of partido wool delivered (1000$)	—	—	4.5	8.6	8.4	8.2	6.8	4.8	5.5 [a]	4.3	4.7	—
Net return on partido sheep before interest (%)	10.0	15.2	7.7	16.4	7.3	13.6	13.8	—	5.3	7.5	15.8	—
after interest [d] (%)	7.0	12.2	4.7	13.4	4.3	10.6	10.8	—	2.2	4.5	12.8	—
Partido wool delivered to total wool bought (%)	—	—	5.6	6.2	8.8	4.0	6.9	3.9	2.7	1.7	2.0	—

WOOL DATA AND PARTIDO SHEEP, 1894–1905
(YEARS ENDING DECEMBER 31) (*continued*)

	1894	1895	1896	1897	1898	1899	1900	1901	1902	1903	1904	1905
Book value per head of partido sheep (dollars)	—	—	1.26	1.93	2.35	2.25	2.33	2.00	2.15	2.10	2.20	2.25
Average price per lb of wool bought (cents)	7.9	10.1	7.8	13.7 [e]	12.8	12.7	12.4	11.0	12.4	13.6	14.5	—
Average price per lb of partido wool delivered (cents)	—	—	8.2	13.9	15.6 [f]	14.4	12.8	11.2	12.8	13.9	15.2	—
High [g]	—	—	8.8	17.0	14.3	15.0	13.5	13.8	—	—	—	—
Median [g]	—	—	7.8	12.5	13.5	14.5	12.8	11.0	—	—	—	—
Low [g]	—	—	6.0	10.0	11.0	13.5	11.8	9.8	—	—	—	—
Number of sheep per partidario	—	—	1,015	1,006	966	907	842	799	679	767	856	869
Weight per sack of total wool purchased (lbs)	197	197	206	205	205	209	198	205	215	237	243	246
Partido wool delivered per sheep (lbs)	—	—	1.7	1.9	1.7 [h]	2.1	2.2	1.4 [i]	1.5 [i]	1.0 [i]	0.8 [i]	—

Source: Wool and sheep records.
[a] Year incomplete.
[b] Biennium 1898–1899 (incomplete for 1898).
[c] Includes some wool bought in 1896.
[d] After deducting 6% interest on one-half partido inventory.
[e] Exaggerated by overstated total value.
[f] Exaggerated by understated deliveries.
[g] As discovered in the records.
[h] Understated.
[i] A larger proportion of contracts delivered wethers in addition. (One paid cash in 1901–1902.)

APPENDIX 12

Sheep Contract: Charles Ilfeld with Juan Tafoya and Pedro Tafoya

This Agreement, Made and entered into this *18th* day of *October* A.D. One Thousand Nine Hundred and *two* by and between CHARLES ILFELD, of Las Vegas, in the County of San Miguel and Territory of New Mexico, party of the first part, and *Juan Tafoya & Bro* of . . . in the County of *Guadalupe* and Territory aforesaid, of the second part:

Witnesseth, That the said party of the first part has this day given and delivered to the said party of the second part to be cared for by him at his own expense, on shares (partido,) for the period of *Ambos Voluntarios which means for such time as either of the parties may desire giving the other party thirty (30) days' Notice when this Contract shall expire. Give hundred Improved Ewes One hundred ones One hundred twos One hundred threes* from *one hundred* to *five hundred of* years old. And the said party of the second part in consideration of the premises and of the sum of One Dollar to him in hand paid by the said party of the first part, hereby covenants and agrees as follows:

That he will well and faithfully care for and herd all of the said sheep with their increase for the period of this contract from the date of these presents, at his own expense.

That during the period of this contract, he will pay and deliver to the said party of the first part, at his wool house at *Tucumcari,* N. M., during the month of June or July, *two &* (2) pounds of wool for each and every sheep so received on shares, as aforesaid; said wool to be white wool, unwashed, but reasonably clean and free from dirt. . . .

That at the expiration and full performance of this contract, he will deliver over to the said party of the first part, or to his order, at such place in the County of *Guadalupe* as he or his agent may designate; *Five hundred (500) Picked Improved Ewes from One to Five years old One hundred of each age* such delivery to be made positively and unconditionally, during the month of August or September, in the year when this contract of partido shall expire.

That in case of the failure of the said party of the second part to comply fully with all the requirements and conditions of this contract, the said party of the first part shall be entitled to the delivery of the said *five hundred* head of sheep, as aforesaid, to himself or to his order at any time, without giving the said party of the second part any previous notice.

SHEEP CONTRACT.

This Agreement, Made and entered into this 18th day of October A. D. One Thousand Nine Hundred and two by and between CHARLES ILFELD, of Las Vegas, in the County of San Miguel and Territory of New Mexico, party of the first part, and Juan Lafoya & Bro of in the County Guadalupe and Territory aforesaid, of the second part:

Witnesseth, That the said party of the first part has this day given and delivered to the said party of the second part to be cared for by him at his own expense, on shares (partido,) for the period of Ambos Voluntarios Which means for such time as either of the parties may desire giving the other party thirty (30) days' notice when the contract shall expire: Five hundred Improved Ewes One hundred ones One hundred twos One hundred threes from one hundred fours One hundred years old. And the said party of the second part in consideration of the premises and of the sum of One Dollar to him in hand paid by the said party of the first part, hereby covenants and agrees as follows:

That he will well and faithfully care for and herd all of the said sheep with their increase for the period of this contract from the date of these presents, at his own expense.

That during the period of this contract, he will pay and deliver to the said party of the first part, at his wool house at ~~Las Vegas~~ Tucumcari, N. M., during the month of June or July, two ½ (2½) pounds of wool for each and every sheep so received on shares, as aforesaid; said wool to be white wool, unwashed, but reasonably clean and free from dirt.

That at the expiration and full performance of this contract, he will deliver over to the said party of the first part, or to his order, at such place in the County of Guadalupe as he or his agent may designate; Five hundred (500) Picked Improved Ewes from One to five years old One hundred of each age such delivery to be made positively and unconditionally, during the month of August or September, in the year when this contract of partido shall expire.

That in case of the failure of the said party of the second part to comply fully with all the requirements and conditions of this contract, the said party of the first part shall be entitled to the delivery of the said Five hundred head of sheep, as aforesaid, to himself or to his order at any time, without giving the said party of the second part any previous notice.

And it is expressly understood and agreed by and between the parties to this agreement, that the ear-marks of the sheep delivered under this contract are Right

and that the ear marks upon the sheep so delivered are the ear-marks of the said party of the first part, and are to be and remain the ear-marks of the said party of the first part until the full completion of this contract, and that all the increase of the said sheep during the period of this contract, shall bear the said ear-marks, and that all the said sheep and their increase shall during the said period, and until the full completion of this contract, be and remain the property of the said party of the first part, and the title to the same shall vest in the said party of the first part until the full performance of this contract.

And it is further understood and agreed by and between the parties hereto, that in case the said party of the second part should suffer any loss by lightning, Indians or pest, then the said party of the first part herewith agrees to release him from all responsibility for the same, whenever the proof of such loss has been established to the satisfaction of the said party of the first part.

And for the better securing the performance of this contract in all its terms and conditions, and in consideration of the premises herein and the covenants contained, the said part*ies* of the second part does hereby grant, bargain, sell and mortgage unto the said part*y* of the first part, *his* heirs and assigns, the following goods and chattels, to-wit: *Six hundred Ewes belonging to them grazing in Guadalupe County New Mexico and earmarked*

Together with their product and increase. **TO HAVE AND TO HOLD** the said goods and chattels unto the said part*y* of the first part, *his* heirs and assigns forever; **provided, however,** that if the said part*ies* of the second part, *their* heirs, executors and administrators, shall well and truly carry out the foregoing contract in all its terms and conditions, and well and truly pay over to the said part*y* of the first part the sheep and wool as specified herein, for the redemption of the said sheep hereby mortgaged, then these presents to be void, otherwise to be in full force and effect.

In Witness Whereof, The said parties of the first and second part have hereunto set their hands and seals this *twentysix* day of *October* A. D., One Thousand Nine Hundred and *two*

Chas. Ilfeld *By S. H. Beck* [SEAL]

Juan Tafoya y Baca [SEAL]

Know All Men by these Presents, That *we* *Vicente Otero*, *of Plaza Larga, Guadalupe County, New Mexico*

for and in consideration of the sheep given on shares by the said party of the first part to the said party of the second part in the foregoing contract, and in consideration of the covenants therein mentioned, and in further consideration of the sum of One Dollar to us in hand paid, do hereby for ourselves, our heirs, executors, and administrators, covenant and agree to be jointly and severally liable to the said part*y* of the first part, with the said party of the second part, in the faithful and full performance of each and all of the covenants in said contract contained, and to be performed by the said party of the second part, and for the redelivery of the said sheep and repayment of the same, and for any and all loss or losses that the said party of the first part may sustain by reason of the failure of the party of the second part in any respect to perform said contract.

Witness our hands and seals this *28* day of *November* A. D., 190*2*

Vicente Otero [SEAL]

[SEAL]

On 30 days Notice

Ren'd in 1907

SHEEP CONTRACT

CHARLES ILFELD

WITH

Juan Tafoya y Baca

Number of Sheep

Pounds of Wool

Date *Oct 18 1902*

And it is expressly understood and agreed by and between the parties to this agreement, that the ear-marks of the sheep delivered under this contract are [*mark*] *Right* and that the ear-marks upon the sheep so delivered are the ear-marks of the said party of the first part, and are to be and remain the ear-marks of the said party of the first part until the full completion of this contract, and that all the increase of the said sheep during the period of this contract, shall bear the said ear-marks, and that all the said sheep and their increase shall during the said period, and until the full completion of this contract, be and remain the property of the said party of the first part, and the title to the same shall vest in the said party of the first part until the full performance of this contract.

And it is further understood and agreed by and between the parties hereto, that in case the said party of the second part should suffer any loss by lightning, Indians or pest, then the said party of the first part herewith agrees to release him from all responsibility for the same, whenever the proof of such loss has been established to the satisfaction of the said party of the first part.

And for the better securing the performance of this contract in all its terms and conditions, and in consideration of the premises herein and the covenants contained, the said part*ies* of the second part does hereby grant, bargain, sell and mortgage unto the said part *y* of the first part, *his* heirs and assigns, the following goods and chattels, to-wit: *Six hundred Ewes belonging to them grazing in Guadalupe County, New Mexico and Earmarked* [*mark*] Together with their product and increase. TO HAVE AND TO HOLD the said goods and chattels unto the said part *y* of the first part, *his* heirs and assigns forever; provided, however, that if the said part*ies* of the second part, *their* heirs, executors and administrators, shall well and truly carry out the foregoing contract in all its terms and conditions, and well and truly pay over to the said part *y* of the first part the sheep and wool as specified herein, for the redemption of the said sheep hereby mortgaged, then these presents to be void, otherwise to be in full force and effect.

IN WITNESS WHEREOF, The said parties of the first and second part have hereunto set their hands and seals this *twenty-six* days of *October* A.D., One Thousand Nine Hundred and *two*

CHAS. ILFELD
By S. G. BUCK [Seal]
JUAN TAFOLA Y BORS [Seal]

I

KNOW ALL MEN BY THESE PRESENTS, That we, *Vicente Otero, of Plaza Larga, Guadalupe County, New Mexico* for and in consideration of the sheep given on shares by the said party of the first part to the said party of the second part in the foregoing contract, and in consideration of the covenants therein mentioned, and in further consideration of the sum of One Dollar to us in hand paid, do hereby for ourselves, our heirs, executors, and administrators, covenant and agree to be jointly and severally liable to the said part *y* of the first part, with the said party of the second part, in the faithful and full performance of each and all of the covenants in said contract contained, and to be performed by the said party of the second part, and for the redelivery of the said sheep and repayment of the same, and for any and all loss or losses that the said party of the first part may sustain by reason of the failure of the party of the second part in any respect to perform said contract.

WITNESS our hands and seals this *28* day of *November* A.D., 190 *2*

VICENTE OTERO [Seal]

APPENDIX 13

Distribution of Country Accounts and Country Account Balances, 1880 and 1890

Area	Number of accounts 1880	Number of accounts 1890	Account balances (dollars) 1880	Account balances (dollars) 1890
North of an east-west line through Las Vegas				
Northeast				
Ute Creek		7		814
Vaur		1		8,912
Total		8		9,726
North				
Loma Parda		2		7
Hot Springs		3		176
Los Alamos	6	6	423	5,377
Sapello	2	2	401	159
San Ignacio		1		9
Ft. Union		3		33
Mora		3		84
Golodrinas		1		38
Gallinas Springs		1		339
Rociada	1	6	67	1,302
La Junta (Watrous)	1	4	45	972
Wagonmound		2		39
Colmor		1		—
Cimarron		1		3
Springer		1		270
Baca		1		4
Total	10	38	936	8,812
Taos				
Plaza del Llano		4		244
San Lorenzo		1		206
Vallecitos		1		211
Total	—	6	—	661
Total North	10	52	936	19,199

Area	Number of accounts		Account balances (dollars)	
	1880	1890	1880	1890
South of an east-west line through Las Vegas				
East				
Cabra Springs		3		373
Salitre	2	4	77	270
Las Conchas		2		126
La Tremintina		1		3
Bell Ranch	1	6	158	1,746
Fort Bascom		2		643
Trujillo		1		59
Liberty		8		301
Endee		3		91
Total	3	30	235	3,612
Southeast to Puerto de Luna				
Romeroville		1		27
Tecolote	5	10	123	798
La Liendre		2		322
Chaperito	3	9	148	587
Las Colonias		7		493
Carazon		1		3
Bado de Juan Pais	1	2	5	157
Anton Chico	1	7	281	1,445
San Jose		1		1
Las Gallinas		4		223
El Pueblo		1		2
Cedar Springs		1		52
Las Tanas		2		98
Santa Rosa		6		631
Canon del Agua		2		119
Cuervo		1		41
Los Ojitos	2	1	441	3,027
Salado		14		5,811
Puerto de Luna	3	48	333	14,563
La Pintada		1		51
Los Valles	3		56	
Total	18	121	1,387	28,451
Ft. Sumner	3	10	87	1,817

Area	Number of accounts		Account balances (dollars)	
	1880	1890	1880	1890
Roswell-Lincoln				
Roswell	1	6	(490) [a]	705
Rio Bonito		1		53
Red Cloud		2		397
Picacho		1		593
Ft. Stanton		1		1,282
White Oaks	1	9	956	2,504
Lincoln		12		3,559
Total	2	32	466	9,093
Far South				
Alamagordo		1		6
La Luz		1		78
Nogal		1		28
Las Cruces	1	1	185	15
La Mesilla	1		121	
Tularosa		1		105
Carthage		1		45
Total	2	6	306	277
Albuquerque-Manzano				
Bernalillo		1		18
Albuquerque		3		498
Los Lunas		1		3
Manzano	2	2	217	1,486
Punta de Agua		2		167
East View		1		301
Pinos Wells		6		3,055
Total	2	16	217	5,528
Santa Fe–Lamy—North Pecos country				
Los Valles de San Augustin		2		147
San Miguel		2		131
San Pedro		4		246
Rowe		4		232
Lamy		2		705
Ojo de la Baca		2		146
Santa Fe		6		1,329
San Geronimo	7	8	456	74
Total	7	30	456	3,010
Total South	37	245	3,154	51,788
Total known country accounts	47	297	4,090	70,987

Area	Number of accounts 1880	1890	Account balances (dollars) 1880	1890
Unknown country accounts				
El Huero	1		158	
La Monella		1		34
Monte Revuelto	1	2	373	4
Paraje		1		
Pino		3		368
Sangejuela	1		15	
Total	3	7	546	406
Total Country Accounts	50	304	4,636	71,393

Source: Various ledgers.
[a] Parenthesis indicates credit balance.

APPENDIX 14

CURRENT FINANCIAL POSITION OF CHARLES ILFELD COMPANY (1000$) 1895–1949

Year	Cash	U. S. Treasury bonds	Net receivables	Merchandise inventory	Current assets	Accommodation deposits and credit balances	Short-term notes payable	Current liabilities
1895	8.6	—	199.7	89.5	297.8	53.5	—	54.2
1896	29.1	—	206.6	94.4	330.1	47.6	—	48.7
1897	56.9	—	231.7	130.5	419.1	48.0	—	49.5
1898	14.6	—	302.7	133.9	451.2	58.5	—	61.7
1899	44.3	—	266.5	165.1	475.9	62.2	—	62.2
1900	18.6	—	388.0	160.8	567.4	—	—	148.1
1901	26.9	—	367.7	158.7	553.3	—	—	103.9
1902	23.5	—	374.6	186.5	584.6	71.3	52.0	124.5
1903	84.3	—	345.6	181.8	611.7	77.5	—	81.0
1904	122.4	—	373.9	208.1	704.4	68.0	—	78.7
1923	114.2	30.1	535.2	850.8	1530.4	21.9	30.0	139.2
1924	117.7	30.1	539.5	722.1	1411.1	33.2	150.0	307.0
1925	79.7	—	499.5	764.6	1346.2	35.0	61.5	237.7
1928	341.8	—	1075.3	1708.7	3125.9	52.2	164.0 [a]	975.2
1929	—	—	—	—	—	69.0	—	—
1930	245.6	—	1353.9	1200.0	2799.0	91.8	—	389.2
1931	237.3	—	1104.8	1065.9	2408.0	45.8	—	377.5
1932	216.5	101.7	962.0	881.6	2161.8	20.8	95.4	238.0
1933	260.5	73.4	1041.3	1220.0	2595.0	63.7	—	405.1
1934	324.1	75.1	1079.8	1403.2	2882.3	69.9	240.8	560.3
1935	293.8	60.2	1187.2	1313.7	2854.8	65.7	225.0	479.1
1936	350.4	58.7	1291.9	2172.0	3873.0	64.9	438.0 [a]	1172.2
1937	448.6	29.7	1078.7	2046.5	3603.5	14.9	1493.0 [a]	1290.5
1938	355.7	24.4	1014.5	1893.1	3287.6	7.3	819.0 [a]	994.2
1939	336.7	24.5	1030.2	2008.6	3399.9	22.2	835.0 [a]	1022.5
1940	308.8	24.5	1002.1	1998.8	3334.2	14.2	794.0 [a]	784.4
1941	357.4	24.5	1057.6	3126.9	4566.4	16.1	1050.0	1762.8
1942	438.6	68.9	668.9	3276.6	4453.0	—	425.0	1209.8
1943	509.6	99.9	854.6	3098.3	4562.3	—	400.0	1128.8
1944	567.8	256.6	745.1	3360.2	4929.7	—	600.0	1364.8

Year	Cash	U. S. Treasury bonds	Net receivables	Merchandise inventory	Current assets	Accommodation deposits and credit balances	Short-term notes payable	Current liabilities
1945	593.5	485.1	807.6	3022.2	4936.4	—	600.0	1334.0
1946	712.0	222.6	1122.5	3935.0	6006.3	—	1250.0	2450.3
1947	856.8	87.1	1144.2	4128.1	6218.1	—	1100.0	2227.4
1948	741.5	87.1	1352.0	3836.0	6075.1	—	1200.0	2069.9
1949	793.4	87.1	1467.2	3469.8	5870.0	—	890.0	1599.2

Source: Summary Books through 1904, and 1923–1925; accounting audits 1928 and later.

[a] Average monthly borrowings.

APPENDIX 15

Consolidated statements of operating data, Charles Ilfeld Company (1000$) 1886–1949

Year	Net merchandise sales	Gross profits	Net operating profits	Net profits
1886	134.3	—	—	—
1887	118.6	—	—	—
1888	138.6	—	—	—
1889	159.9	—	—	—
1890	188.2	—	—	—
1891	222.1	—	—	—
1892	267.0	—	—	—
1893	204.2	—	—	—
1894	203.5	—	—	—
1895	212.5	39.1	19.9	13.2
1896	203.1	39.4	17.8	10.8
1897	259.8	56.7	33.8	60.7
1898	307.1	63.3	34.4	50.6
1899	352.9	71.4	37.0	66.3
1900	399.1	52.4	12.6	45.8
1901	453.4	72.6	31.1	25.7
1902	424.1	59.5	15.4	10.2
1903	461.6	—	—	—
1904	516.3	—	—	—
1905	669.3	—	—	—
1906	820.8	—	—	—
1907	895.7	—	—	—
1908	831.3	—	—	—
1909	875.2	—	—	—
1928	6,174.0	628.6	—	336.6
1929	—	—	—	327.0 [a]
1930	5,380.0	500.8	—	198.4 [a]
1931	5,691.7	739.1	162.0	56.0
1932	4,555.2	562.4	71.3	(4.3) [b]
1933	5,131.6	838.7	323.2	297.5
1934	6,502.0	967.9	357.7	303.3
1935	6,730.0	878.0	231.8	224.5
1936	8,180.5	1,145.2	353.3	348.7
1937	9,536.6	1,263.5	290.3	253.9

Year	Net merchandise sales	Gross profits	Net operating profits	Net profits
1938	8,310.9	1,026.4	133.3	104.9
1939	8,815.6	1,169.1	223.3	169.7
1940	8,868.9	1,176.9	210.3	185.9
1941	10,845.9	1,617.0	517.1	348.0
1942	11,934.0	1,844.8	675.0	349.8
1943	13,934.0	2,015.3	781.7	350.9
1944	15,930.0	2,181.2	860.7	377.2
1945	15,391.6	2,065.5	641.0	314.1
1946	18,597.5	2,532.7	917.5	559.9
1947	21,628.3	2,703.9	733.0	417.1
1948	21,508.2	2,824.7	589.0	372.7
1949	19,961.0	2,413.3	212.8	130.1

Source: Summary Books and ledgers through 1909; annual accounting audits 1928 and later.

[a] Estimated.

[b] Deficit.

Appendix 16

Ilfeld-Nordhaus Families

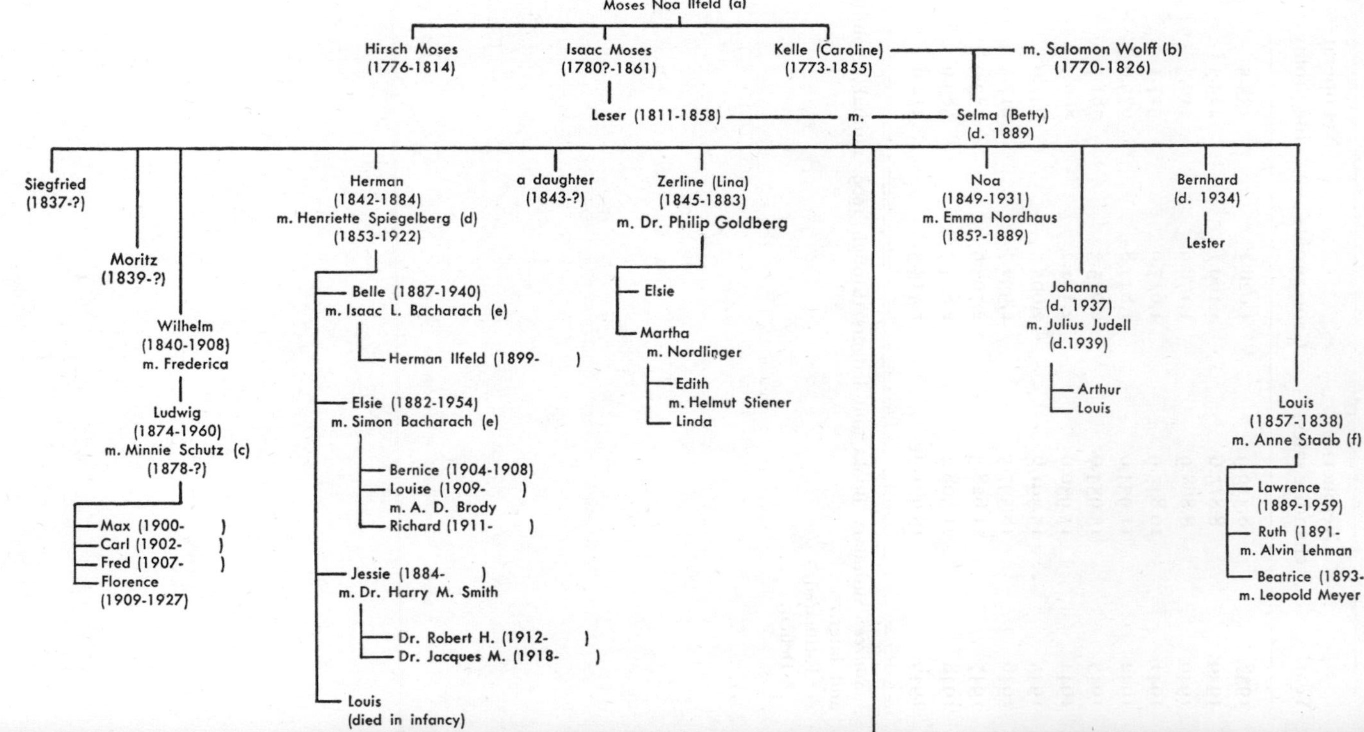

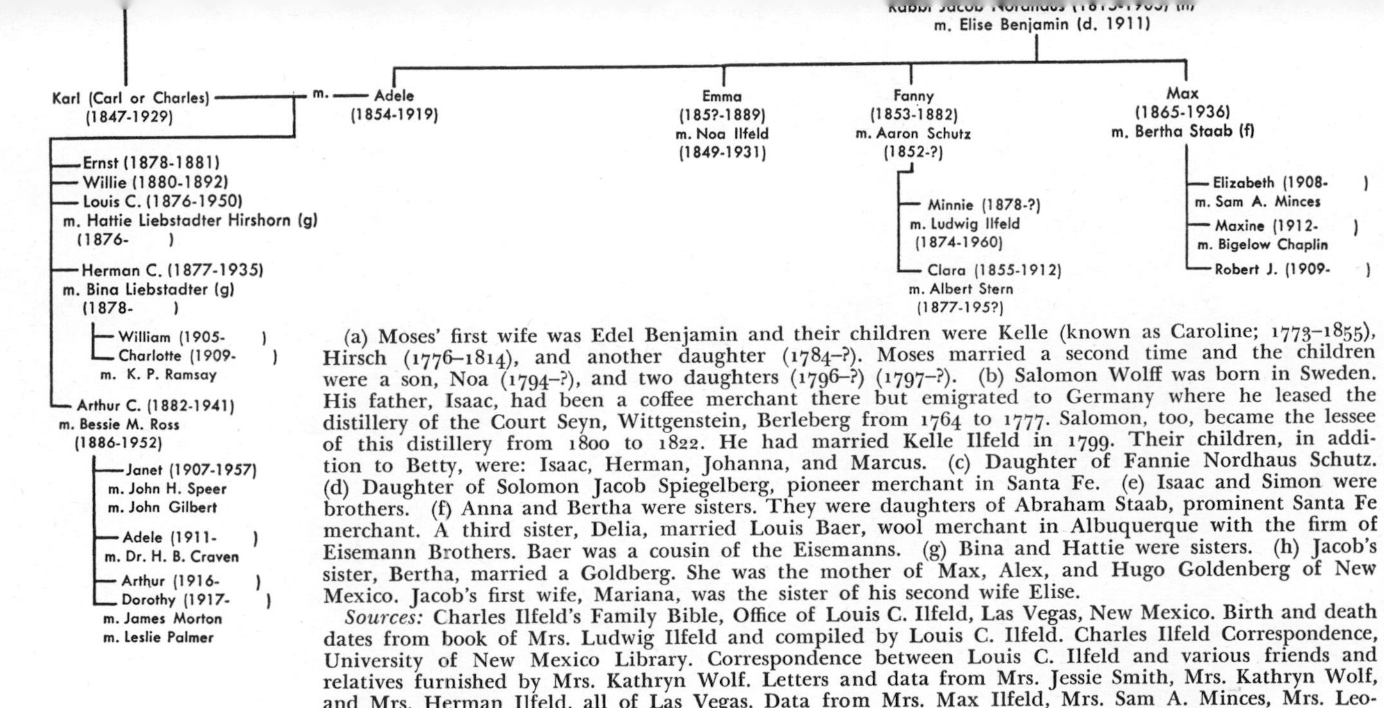

(a) Moses' first wife was Edel Benjamin and their children were Kelle (known as Caroline; 1773–1855), Hirsch (1776–1814), and another daughter (1784–?). Moses married a second time and the children were a son, Noa (1794–?), and two daughters (1796–?) (1797–?). (b) Salomon Wolff was born in Sweden. His father, Isaac, had been a coffee merchant there but emigrated to Germany where he leased the distillery of the Court Seyn, Wittgenstein, Berleberg from 1764 to 1777. Salomon, too, became the lessee of this distillery from 1800 to 1822. He had married Kelle Ilfeld in 1799. Their children, in addition to Betty, were: Isaac, Herman, Johanna, and Marcus. (c) Daughter of Fannie Nordhaus Schutz. (d) Daughter of Solomon Jacob Spiegelberg, pioneer merchant in Santa Fe. (e) Isaac and Simon were brothers. (f) Anna and Bertha were sisters. They were daughters of Abraham Staab, prominent Santa Fe merchant. A third sister, Delia, married Louis Baer, wool merchant in Albuquerque with the firm of Eisemann Brothers. Baer was a cousin of the Eisemanns. (g) Bina and Hattie were sisters. (h) Jacob's sister, Bertha, married a Goldberg. She was the mother of Max, Alex, and Hugo Goldenberg of New Mexico. Jacob's first wife, Mariana, was the sister of his second wife Elise.

Sources: Charles Ilfeld's Family Bible, Office of Louis C. Ilfeld, Las Vegas, New Mexico. Birth and death dates from book of Mrs. Ludwig Ilfeld and compiled by Louis C. Ilfeld. Charles Ilfeld Correspondence, University of New Mexico Library. Correspondence between Louis C. Ilfeld and various friends and relatives furnished by Mrs. Kathryn Wolf. Letters and data from Mrs. Jessie Smith, Mrs. Kathryn Wolf, and Mrs. Herman Ilfeld, all of Las Vegas. Data from Mrs. Max Ilfeld, Mrs. Sam A. Minces, Mrs. Leopold Meyer, and Julius Rosenthal, all of Albuquerque. Various New Mexico Newspapers.

Bibliography

Notes

Index

BIBLIOGRAPHY

Primary Materials

Unpublished Documents

The Charles Ilfeld Collection, University of New Mexico Library, Albuquerque, comprising rather complete business records of the Charles Ilfeld Company, from its founding as A. Letcher Company in 1865, to 1907; the Charles Ilfeld Company business records to date are in possession of the Corporation in Las Vegas and Albuquerque. Included in the collection of business records are:

Albuquerque Wool Scouring Mill Minute Book
Bills Payable Book, 1884–1913
Cash Books, Journals, and Ledgers, reasonably complete, 1867–1907
Copy Books and Letter Books of Louis C. Ilfeld, 1905–1911
Copy Books of Outgoing Correspondence, 1867–1903
A Copy Book as Agent for Studebaker Wagons, 1905–1908
Floersheim Mercantile Company Minute Book
Gross, Blackwell and Company Minute Book
Gross, Kelly and Company Minute Book
Notes Payable Book
Otero and Sellar Letter Book
Packets of Incoming Correspondence, 1883, 1885, 1893–1901
A Special Copy Book for Management's Use, 1890–1907
Summary Book, 1886–1895
Two Wagon Books of Lading and various accounting records of Marcus Brunswick
Wool Record Book

Gustave Elsberg v. *Jacob Amberg et al.,* Bill of Chancery, First Judicial District of Territory of New Mexico, July 29, 1869. Santa Fe County Courthouse, Santa Fe.

Newspapers in Their Depositories

Highlands University Library, Las Vegas: *Las Vegas Daily Optic,* 1880–1884; *Las Vegas Democrat* (microfilm), 1890.

New Mexico Historical Society, Santa Fe: *Rio Abajo Weekly Press,* January 1863–October 1864; *Santa Fe Gazette,* 1864–1866; *Santa Fe New Mexican,* November 1863–October 1867; *Santa Fe Republican,* 1847–1848; *Santa Fe Weekly New Mexican,* October 1871–January 1873; *Santa Fe Weekly Post,* June 1870–June 1872.

Office of Publisher, Las Vegas: *Las Vegas Daily Optic,* 1879–1881.

Private Library of W. A. Keleher, Albuquerque: *Las Vegas Gazette,* October 1872–December 1885; *Lincoln County Leader,* October 1881–May 1890; *White Oaks Eagle,* November 1891–December 1901.

University of New Mexico Library, Albuquerque: *Las Vegas Daily Optic,* 1899–1906.

Interviews and Correspondence

Frank P. Bennett, Boston; Charles S. Brown, Albuquerque; Henry D. Davis, San Antonio; Sydney A. Eisemann, Boston; Ben Floersheim, Springer, N. M.; Carl Floersheim, Springer; Milton Floersheim, Roy, N. M.; Otto Hake,

Albuquerque; Louis C. Ilfeld, Las Vegas; Ludwig Ilfeld, Las Vegas; Dr. Harry E. Kemper, Albuquerque; Floyd Lee, San Mateo, N. M.; Hugh Loudon, Albuquerque; Frank A. Mapel, Albuquerque; Louis A. McRae, Albuquerque; Leopold Meyer, Albuquerque; Earl L. Moulton, Albuquerque; New York Life Insurance Company, New York; A. C. Ortega, Pastura, N. M.; Julius Rosenthal, Albuquerque; Rodney B. Schoonmaker, Las Vegas; William H. Stapp, Las Vegas; Albert Stern, Albuquerque.

Secondary Materials

Adams, Eleanor B., and Fray Angelico Chavez. *The Missions of New Mexico, 1776: A Description by Fray Francisco Atanasio Dominguez with Other Contemporary Documents.* Albuquerque: University of New Mexico Press, 1956.

Alvis, Berry Newton. "History of Union County, New Mexico," *New Mexico Historical Review,* 22 (July 1947).

American Shepherd's Bulletin, 6 (September 1901); 12 (June 1907). United States Department of Agriculture Library, Washington, D. C.

Atherton, Lewis E. "The Pioneer Merchant in Mid-America," *University of Missouri Studies,* XIV (Columbia, Mo., 1939).

Bancroft, Hubert Howe. *The Works of Hubert Howe Bancroft,* XI. *History of Mexico, Vol. III, 1600–1803.* San Francisco, 1883.

Baxter, W. T. *House of Hancock.* Cambridge, Mass.: Harvard University Press, 1945.

Belena, Eusebio Bentura. *Recapilacion Sumaria de Todo Los Autos Acordados de la Real Audiencia y Sala del Crimen de esta Nueva Espana.* 1st ed.; Impresa por don F. de Zuniga y Ontiveros, 1787. Private library of France V. Scholes, Albuquerque.

Bieber, R. P. "Papers of James J. Webb, Santa Fe Merchant, 1844–1861," *Washington University Studies,* XI. Humanistic Series 2 (1924).

Bolton, Herbert E. *Coronado: Knight of Pueblos and Plains.* Albuquerque: University of New Mexico Press, 1949.

Brayer, H. O. *William Blackmore: The Spanish-Mexican Land Grants of New Mexico and Colorado. 1863–1878.* Denver: Bradford-Robinson, 1948.

Brevoort, Elias. *New Mexico: Her Natural Resources and Attractions.* Santa Fe, 1874.

Bureau of Immigration, New Mexico. *Resources of New Mexico.* Santa Fe, 1881, 1882, 1889.

Carlo, A. Milares, y J. I. Mantecon, *Indice y Extractos de los Protocolos del Archivo de Notarias de Mexico, D. F. vol. I, 1524–1528.* El Colegio de Mexico, 1945.

Carroll, H. Bailey, and J. Villasana Haggard. *Three New Mexico Chronicles.* Albuquerque: Quivira Society, 1942.

Charles, Ralph. "Development of the Partido System in the New Mexico Sheep Industry," unpublished master's thesis, University of New Mexico, 1940.

Chevalier, Francois. *La Formacion des Grandes Domaines au Mexiques: Terre et Societe aux XVIe–XVIIe Siecles.* Paris: Institut D'Ethnologue, 1952.

Chittenden, H. M. *The American Fur Trade of the Far West.* 3 vols. New York, 1902.

Coan, Charles F. *History of New Mexico.* 3 vols. New York, 1925.

Dargan, Marion. "New Mexico's Fight for Statehood, 1895–1912," *New Mexico Historical Review,* 14 (January 1939).

Davis, W. W. H. *El Gringo or New Mexico and Her People.* Santa Fe, 1938 (reprint of 1865).

Duffus, R. L. *The Santa Fe Trail.* New York, 1930.

Dusenberry, William H. "Ordinances of the Mesta in New Spain, 1537," *Academy of American Franciscan History,* 4 (January 1948).

El Palacio: Journal of the Museum of New Mexico in Cooperation with the Archeological Society of New Mexico and the School of American Research, Santa Fe, New Mexico.

Ford, Worthington C. *Wool and Manufacturers of Wool.* Washington, D. C., 1894.

Goetz, Otto. "Santa Rosa, New Mexico," *New Mexico Historical Review,* 23 (April 1948).

Grant, Blanche C. *One Hundred Years Ago in Old Taos.* Taos, 1925.

——— *When Old Trails Were New.* New York, 1934.

Gras, N. S. B. *Business and Capitalism.* New York, 1939.

——— *A History of Agriculture in Europe and America.* New York, 1925.

——— *An Introduction to Economic History.* New York, 1922.

——— and Henrietta M. Larson. *Casebook in American Business History.* New York, 1939.

Greever, William S. "Railway Development in the Southwest," *New Mexico Historical Review,* 32 (April 1957).

Gregg, Josiah. *Commerce of the Prairies.* 2 vols. 4th ed.; Philadelphia, 1849.

Haines, Helen. *History of New Mexico.* New York, 1891.

Haley, J. Evetts. *Charles Goodnight: Cowman and Plainsman.* Boston, 1936.

Harrington, V. D. *New York Merchant on Eve of the Revolution.* New York, 1935.

Hendron, J. W. *The Story of Billy the Kid.* Santa Fe: Rydal, 1948.

Hibbard, Benjamin Horace. *A History of the Public Land Policies.* New York, 1924.

History of New Mexico: Its Resources and People. 2 vols. Los Angeles, 1907.

Inventory of County Archives, San Miguel County. New Mexico Historical Records Survey.

Jennings, Sister Marietta. *A Pioneer Merchant of St. Louis, 1810–1820.* New York, 1939.

Jones, F. A. *New Mexico Mines and Minerals.* Santa Fe, 1904.

Jones, John Beauchamp. *The Western Merchant.* Philadelphia, 1849.

Keleher, William A. *Maxwell Land Grant.* Santa Fe: Rydal, 1942.

——— *Turmoil in New Mexico, 1846–1868.* Santa Fe: Rydal, 1952.

——— *Violence in Lincoln County, 1869–1881.* Albuquerque: University of New Mexico Press, 1957.

Klein, Julius. *The Mesta, 1273–1836.* Cambridge, Mass., 1920.

Kupper, Winifred. *The Golden Hoof.* New York, 1905.

Larson, Henrietta M. *Guide to Business History.* Cambridge, Mass.: Harvard University Press, 1948.

——— *Jay Cooke: Private Banker.* Cambridge, Mass., 1936.

Laumbach, Verna. "Las Vegas Before 1850," *New Mexico Historical Review,* 8 (October 1933).

Lee, Floyd. *Bartalome Fernandez: Pioneer Shepherd of the Hills in New Mexico.* New York, San Francisco, Montreal: Newcomen Society of North America, 1954.

Marshall, James. *Santa Fe: The Railroad That Built an Empire.* New York: Random House, 1945.

McCoy, Joseph G. *Cattle Trade of the West and Southwest.* Rev. ed.; Glendale, Calif.: Arthur H. Clark, 1940.

Monthly Bulletin of the National Wool Growers' Association of the United States. 3 (March 1898–November 1898). United States Department of Agriculture Library, Washington, D. C.

Moorhead, Max L. *New Mexico's Royal Road: Trade and Travel on the Chihuahua Trail.* Norman, Okla.: University of Oklahoma Press, 1958.

Moulton, Earl L. *The Odyssey of a Flockmaster: The Story of the 1934 Drought in the Southwestern United States.* Privately printed, Cozad, Nebr.: Noel Cover, 1945. University of New Mexico Library.

——— "From Sheepherder to Director of the Chamber of Commerce of the United States." Unpublished pamphlet, University of New Mexico Library.

——— *Seventy Years of Progress: A Brief History of the Charles Ilfeld Company, 1865–1935.* Privately printed; Albuquerque, 1935. University of New Mexico Library.

National Livestock Bulletin, 12 (July 1907): 13 (May 1908). United States Department of Agriculture Library, Washington, D. C.

National Shepherd's Bulletin, 6 (January 1901–August 1901). United States Department of Agriculture Library, Washington, D. C.

Ogle, Ralph H. "Federal Control of the Western Apaches, 1848–1886," *New Mexico Historical Review,* 15 (July 1940).

Otero, Miguel Antonio. *My Life on the Frontier, 1864–1882.* New York, 1935.

——— *My Nine Years as Governor of the Territory of New Mexico, 1897–1906.* Albuquerque: University of New Mexico Press, 1940.

Parish, William J. "The German Jew and the Commercial Revolution in Territorial New Mexico, 1850–1900," *New Mexico Quarterly,* 29 (Autumn 1959).

Peffer, E. Louis. *The Closing of the Public Domain: Disposal and Reservation Policies, 1900–1950.* Stanford, Calif.; Stanford University Press, 1951.

Porter, H. M. *Pencillings of an Early Western Pioneer.* Denver, 1929.

Quarterly Bulletin of the National Wool Growers' Association of the United States, 1 (July 1896); 3 (January 1898). United States Department of Agriculture Library, Washington, D. C.

Read, Benjamin M. *Illustrated History of New Mexico.* Privately printed; Santa Fe, 1912.

Reeve, Frank D. "The Federal Indian Policy in New Mexico, 1858–1880," *New Mexico Historical Review,* 13 (July 1938).

de Roover, Raymond. *Money, Banking and Credit in Mediaeval Bruges.* Cambridge, Mass.; The Mediaeval Academy of America, 1948.

Ryus, W. H. *The Second William Penn.* Kansas City, Mo., 1913.

Sabin, E. L. *Kit Carson Days.* 2 vols. New York, 1935.

Sauer, Carl. "Colina of New Spain in the Sixteenth Century," *Ibero-Americana,* 29 (1948).

Sellars, Lelia. *Charleston Business on Eve of the American Revolution.* Chapel Hill, 1934.

Shepherd's Bulletin, 3 (December 1898); 5 (December 1910). United States Department of Agriculture Library, Washington, D. C.

Sombart, Werner. *The Jews and Modern Capitalism.* London, 1913.

——— *The Quintessence of Capitalism.* London, 1915.

Statistical Abstract of the United States, 1913.

Stephens, F. F. "Missouri and the Santa Fe Trade," *Missouri Historical Review,* 11 (July 1917).

Taussig, F. W. *The Tariff History of the United States.* 7th ed.; New York, 1923.

Twitchell, R. E. *Leading Facts of New Mexico History.* 5 vols. Cedar Rapids, Iowa, 1911–1917.

——— *Old Santa Fe*. Santa Fe, 1925.

United States Department of Agriculture. *Agricultural Statistics*. Washington, D. C., 1952.

——— *Annual Yearbooks of Agriculture*. Washington, D. C.

——— *Wool Statistics*. Washington, D. C., 1949.

——— Bureau of Animal Husbandry. *6th Annual Report*, 1889; *7th Annual Report*, 1890. Washington, D. C., 1891.

——— ——— *Special Report on the History and Present Conditions of the Sheep Industry of the United States*. H. R. Misc. Doc. 105, 52d Cong., 2d sess. Washington, D. C., 1892.

United States Department of the Interior, *Report of the Secretary*. H. Exec. Doc. 1, pt. 5, 50th Cong., 2d sess. Washington, D. C., 1888.

United States Forest Service. *Material on the Partido System*. Albuquerque, 1937.

——— *The Western Range*. Sen. Doc. 199, 74th Cong., 2d sess. Washington, D. C., 1936.

United States General Land Office. *Annual Report of the Commissioner for the Year 1888*. H. Exec. Doc. 1, 50th Cong., 2d sess. Washington, D. C., 1888.

United States Office of Indian Affairs, Land Research Unit. *Tewa Basin Study*, III. Washington, D. C., 1935–1939.

United States Public Lands Commission. *Report*. Sen. Doc. 189, 58th Cong., 3d Sess. Washington, D. C., 1905.

United States Tariff Board. *Wool and Manufacturers of Wool*. Washington, D. C., 1912.

United States Tariff Commission. *The Wool Growing Industry*. Washington, D. C., 1921.

——— *Wool Prices*. Report 120, Series 2. Washington, D. C., 1937.

Usher, A. P. *The Early History of Deposit Banking in Mediterranean Europe*. Harvard Economic Studies, 75. Cambridge, Mass.: Harvard University Press, 1943.

Van Cleave, Erret. "Credit on the Santa Fe Trail," *Credit and Financial Management*, 41 (October 1939).

Webb, James J. *Adventures in the Santa Fe Trade, 1844–1847*, Ralph P. Bieber, ed. Glendale, Calif., 1931.

Wentworth, Edward Norris. *America's Sheep Trails*. Ames, Iowa: Iowa State College Press, 1948.

Westphall, Victor. "The Public Domain in New Mexico, 1854–1891," *New Mexico Historical Review*, 33 (April 1958).

Wright, Chester W. *Wool Growing and the Tariff: A Study in the Economic History of the United States*. Harvard Economic Studies V. Cambridge, 1910.

NOTES

CHAPTER I

Santa Fe: Development of an Economic Town to 1865

1. Wilfred H. Schoff, *The Periplus of the Erythraean Sea* (New York, 1912), p. 7; Josiah Gregg, *Commerce of the Prairies*, vol. II, chaps. i–viii.

2. C. P. Grant, *The Syrian Desert* (New York, 1938), p. 127; C. F. Coan, *History of New Mexico*, I, 310.

3. N. S. B. Gras, *Business and Capitalism*, p. 41; R. L. Duffus, *The Santa Fe Trail*, p. 136.

4. The bridge across the Missouri at Kansas City, that opened July 4, 1869, removed all future commercial threats from Fort Leavenworth. E. P. Oberholtzer, *A History of the United States Since the Civil War* (New York, 1922), II, 485.

5. See Max L. Moorhead, *New Mexico's Royal Road*, pp. 123–151; Gregg, *Commerce of the Prairies*, II, 161. An interesting side light on the support these profits brought to the "hard" money of Missouri as the silver Mexican peso flowed in is described by F. F. Stephens, "Missouri and the Santa Fe Trade," *Missouri Historical Review*, 11:309–312 (July 1917), and Moorhead, *Royal Road*, pp. 188–189.

6. Charles A. and Mary R. Beard, *Rise of American Civilization* (New York, 1930), sec. i, p. 586.

7. H. M. Chittenden, *The American Fur Trade of the Far West*, II, 520.

8. *Ibid.*

9. Figures are cited showing the extent of this practice. Apparently the fraction of total goods entering Santa Fe from the East and freighted onto Chihuahua was roughly one seventh in the 1820's, reaching two thirds by 1843. This latter fraction represented about $300,000, or roughly one tenth of total Chihuahua trade in that year (Gregg, *Commerce of the Prairies*, II, 160, 162; Moorhead, *Royal Road*, p. 81).

10. Duffus, *Santa Fe Trail*, pp. 175, 199. Henry Connelly was a merchant in Chihuahua from 1828; to 1848 (W. A. Keleher, *Turmoil in New Mexico*, p. 122n38). Later he settled in Peralta, New Mexico, establishing a mercantile business there, and he soon expanded his operations to Albuquerque, Santa Fe, and Las Vegas (Moorhead, *Royal Road*, p. 90n32). Connelly, appointed by Abraham Lincoln, was the Civil War governor of New Mexico.

11. R. E. Twitchell, *Leading Facts of New Mexico History*, II, 137, states that most wagons returned empty in 1866. Duffus, *Santa Fe Trail*, p. 235, mentions that wagons usually returned not more than one-half loaded in the 1850's.

12. Werner Sombart, *The Quintessence of Capitalism*, pp. 155–156.

13. James Josiah Webb, *Adventures in the Santa Fe Trade*, p. 91.

14. Sombart, *Quintessence*, p. 168.

15. The German Jewish immigration began in significant numbers during the depression year of 1836. See Nathan Glazer, *American Judaism* (Chicago, 1957), p. 23. In the decade of the 1820's German immigration was but 6761. The following decade it jumped to 152,454; in the 1840's, to 434,626; in the 1850's, to 951,667. See *Statistical Abstract of the United States*, 1913, 36th number (Washington, D.C., 1914), p. 94.

16. See Barry E. Supple, "A Business Elite: German-Jewish Financiers in Nineteenth-Century New York," *The Business History Review*, 31:149–152 (Summer 1957). See also Glazer, *American Judaism*, p. 44.

17. *American Jewish Archives*, Western Issue, 8:75, 77–79, 98–101 (Oct. 1956); Leon L.

Watters, "The Pioneer Jews of Utah," *Studies in American Jewish History,* 2:4, 5, 16, 37, 42, 50, 52, 58 (American Jewish Historical Society, 1952). L. E. Atherton remarks that the Jewish merchant was not prominent in the early West (*The Pioneer Merchant in Mid-America,* University of Missouri Studies 14 [Columbia, Mo., 1939], p. 19).

18. See W. J. Parish, "The German Jew and the Commercial Revolution in Territorial New Mexico," *New Mexico Quarterly,* 29:307–332 (Autumn 1959).

19. Werner Sombart, *The Jews and Modern Capitalism,* pp. 50–53.

20. Bureau of Immigration, New Mexico, *Resources of New Mexico* (1881), p. 21.

21. R. E. Twitchell, *Old Santa Fe,* pp. 476–477.

22. *Ibid.,* pp. 479–480.

23. Charles Ilfeld, years later, referred to the Elsbergs as relatives. Copy Book 28, May 5, 1894, p. 625. All citations of business records, not otherwise identified, are part of the Charles Ilfeld Collection of business records; University of New Mexico Library.

24. *Gustave Elsberg* vs *Jacob Amberg et al.,* Bill in Chancery, First Judicial District of Territory of New Mexico, July 29, 1869, quoted *in extenso,* Appendix 1.

25. *Ibid.*

26. Twitchell, *Old Santa Fe,* pp. 162–163.

27. Gregg, *Commerce of the Prairies,* II, 160, tabulated the Santa Fe trade from 1822–1843. The average volume of merchandise invested in Santa Fe trade from 1822 to 1829 was $64,000; from 1830 to 1840, $160,000; in 1843 the volume had risen to $450,000. Chittenden, *American Fur Trade,* II, 520, noted a beginning of wholesaling in 1830.

28. Twitchell, *Old Santa Fe,* p. 479. Zoldac and Abraham Staab carried on extensive trade with the Army forts of Utah, Colorado, and Arizona, as well as New Mexico. The *Las Vegas Gazette* (Nov. 16, 1872) records the killing of a buffalo 85 miles north of Las Vegas and adds, "there are plenty in the State Territory."

29. Franz Huning, a German Lutheran, whose mercantile enterprise grew to fair size, deserves credit for initiating the change in the business pattern in Albuquerque. He was the exception to the early domination of mercantile trade by the German Jew. He was born in Bremerhafen and came to the United States in 1848, and Santa Fe in 1849. He established his store in Albuquerque in 1857.

30. *Santa Fe New Mexican,* March 16, 1864.

31. *Santa Fe Gazette,* Sept. 10, Dec. 3, 1864.

32. The Masonic Dedication took place Dec. 27, 1864 (*Santa Fe Gazette,* Dec. 31, 1864). *Santa Fe New Mexican,* Jan. 6, 1865. In 1958 this site was occupied by the First National Bank of Santa Fe.

33. Perhaps the newspaper articles, themselves, were the advertisements.

34. *Santa Fe New Mexican,* Aug. 5, 1864.

35. This incident may have had some connection with the murder of Thomas Mastin by the Apaches in Sept., 1861. Thomas Mastin discovered the first quartz lode, known, later as the Pacific mine, in 1860. The next year his brother Virgil purchased the property. Virgil Mastin was associated with Amberg in the operation of this mine in 1866. From 1861 to 1864 little work was done at the mine because of Indian depredations (F. A. Jones, *New Mexico Mines and Minerals,* p. 48). *Santa Fe New Mexican,* June 16, 1865.

36. *Santa Fe New Mexican,* June 16, 1865.

37. See *Santa Fe New Mexican,* June 30, 1865. Jones, *New Mexico Mines,* p. 51, records this as 1866.

38. The Hanover Copper Mine was near Central City. Discovery of this mine was made by a German from Hanover in the early or middle 1850's. Jones, *New Mexico Mines,* p. 41. Jones also states (p. 51), "It is claimed that J. Amberg, a German metallurgist, did considerable work" on the Cleveland Group of claims on the west side of the mountains at Pinos Altos.

39. *Elsberg* vs *Amberg,* Appendix 1.

40. *Ibid.,* especially reply by Herman Ilfeld.

41. E. L. Moulton, *Seventy Years of Progress: A Brief History of the Charles Ilfeld Company, 1865–1935,* p. 5.

CHAPTER II

Charles Ilfeld Comes to Taos, 1865

1. Charles Ilfeld's passport is signed Carl Ilfeld, and he was so known by his close friends. His birth was verified in a letter from Louis C. Ilfeld, son of Charles Ilfeld, June 16, 1948. William was four years older than Charles (letter from Ludwig Ilfeld, proprietor, Ilfeld and Company, Las Vegas, and son of William Ilfeld, June 29, 1948). Ludwig Ilfeld also wrote that William was largely instrumental in his brothers' coming to the United States. Lester Ilfeld died shortly after the birth, in 1858, of Louis, the last of the brothers to come to the United States (letter from Louis C. Ilfeld, June 16, 1948).

2. Herman became a partner in Elsberg and Amberg in 1865. See Appendix 1.

3. Charles was born in Homburg vor der Hohe, Germany, on April 19, 1847 (interview, Louis C. Ilfeld, Aug. 20, 1947). His passport is in the possession of the Louis C. Ilfeld estate, Las Vegas. It was drawn April 25, 1865, and endorsed April 29 by the United States Consul at Hamburg in the presence of Charles Ilfeld.

4. The structure of his letters, the first available appearing in the 1867 copy book of A. Letcher and Company, is such as to have obviated any likelihood of his learning English that well in two years in his frontier environment. His knowledge of bookkeeping, as revealed in the Taos books, was equal to the standard of the average petty capitalist proprietor of his day.

5. See *Elsberg* vs *Amberg,* Appendix 1.

6. Passenger fare from Missouri to Santa Fe varied with the season of the year. During the Civil War it was $200 and had been $250. Duffus. *Santa Fe Trail,* pp. 237, 240.

7. This was the journey of Alexander Gusdorf from New York to Santa Fe in 1864. Cited by Twitchell, *Leading Facts,* IV, 474.

8. Interview, Louis C. Ilfeld, Aug. 20, 1947.

9. Durango, capital of the State of Durango, Mexico, south of Chihuahua. *Santa Fe New Mexican,* Sept. 29, 1865.

10. *Elsberg* vs *Amberg,* Appendix 1. Blanche Grant tells of Mormons coming to Taos for wheat seed, for Taos still had the title "the granary of the West" (B. C. Grant, *When Old Trails Were New,* p. 172). See also letter from Céran St. Vrain and others to President Lincoln, Sept. 27, 1863; *Santa Fe New Mexican,* Dec. 5, 1863; Appendix 2.

11. Appendix 2.

12. The transportation charges on 10,895 pounds of merchandise from Santa Fe to Taos were $351. Cash Book, 1865–1868.

13. W. A. Keleher, *Maxwell Land Grant,* p. 28. Don Juan Santistevan joined the firm of St. Vrain and Hurst in 1865 (*History of New Mexico,* II, 600). Beuthner Brothers was "one of the largest, if not the largest, mercantile house of the northern portions of New Mexico" (traveling correspondent, *Santa Fe New Mexican,* May 21, 1864).

14. Adolph Letcher was born June 21, 1829. His place of birth is not known. He died in Baltimore, Maryland, Aug. 30, 1903 (letter from the New York Life Insurance Company, Aug. 13, 1947).

15. A cash book and an account ledger are the only extant records of A. Letcher Company. All factual material on this company has been derived from these two books.

16. "One of the brothers is in Europe, another in New York, while Joseph remains in Taos" (*Santa Fe New Mexican,* May 21, 1864).

17. *Ibid.;* E. L. Sabin, *Kit Carson Days,* II, 789.

18. Sabin, *Kit Carson,* p. 961.

19. Scheurich married Terisina Bent, Kit Carson's niece (*ibid.,* p. 799). See also *Santa Fe New Mexican,* June 16, 1865.

20. Sabin, *Kit Carson,* pp. 610, 681.

21. *Ibid.,* p. 786.

22. *Ibid.,* p. 709.

23. *Ibid.,* p. 763.

24. Using the single entry system. Merchandise received on account is debited, and any payment on account becomes a credit.

25. The assumption that this charge is for two people instead of one is based on its size. This would be slightly less than $1.00 a day for each, which approximated the going rate in Las Vegas, in 1860–1870, of $5.00 per week for laboring men. Cited in *Inventory of County Archives*, San Miguel County, Report 24, p. 14.

26. On May 1, 1866, this figure was cut to $50, until the first of the year, when it became $60. A logical explanation would be that Letcher ceased to board. His personal account became inactive for several months.

27. There was no wage account, only a memorandum note at the beginning of Ilfeld's personal account, dated March, 1866, "By Settlement Wages." His charges were not posted to a capital account until Nov., 1867. All of Letcher's withdrawals were subsequently charged against his personal capital.

28. Atherton, *Pioneer Merchant*, pp. 110–111. The experience of A. Letcher and Company in Las Vegas during the last 6½ months of 1867 showed cash sales of slightly less than three fifths of total sales as opposed to two thirds in Taos. No doubt a study of subsequent years would show cash sales of 50 per cent or less, as more charge customers would have been added to the books. This would correspond to the experience of John Beauchamp Jones, Missouri merchant in the 1840's. Jones stated his experience to have been 45 per cent cash sales (*John Beauchamp Jones: The Western Merchant* [Philadelphia, 1849], pp. 49, 70, cited by Atherton, *Pioneer Merchant,* p. 110). Ilfeld's cash sales were 20–23 per cent of total sales in the late 1880's, and 15–20 per cent in the first half of the 1890's. Wilt and Mussina, general merchants of St. Louis, had credit sales in 1811 of 51 per cent of total sales. Sister Marietta Jennings, *Pioneer Merchant of St. Louis, 1810–1820*, pp. 46–47. Leila Sellers (*Charleston Business on Eve of the American Revolution,* p. 91) cites an isolated example of 1786 of 7 per cent cash receipts of total sales.

29. Louis C. Ilfeld wrote to author (Aug. 9, 1948) in reference to this point: "I remember it being said that in C. I.'s experience, over the years, the credit losses did not exceed 1½%." It is possible some of the losses, in Taos, were paid later without a record having been made.

30. Grant, *When Old Trails Were New,* pp. 26–35; "Bishop Tameron's Visitation of New Mexico, 1760," Historical Society of New Mexico Publications in History, vol. XV, Eleanor B. Adams, ed. (Albuquerque, Feb. 1954), pp. 57–58.

31. Chittenden, *American Fur Trade,* I, 363–365.

32. Blanche C. Grant, *One Hundred Years Ago in Old Taos,* p. 12. As an interesting side light, F. T. Cheetham in *New Mexico Historical Review,* 1:378 (Oct. 1926), states: "By the year 1841, the price of furs had so declined that the trappers of Taos were forced to adopt some other means of livelihood."

33. Duffus, *Santa Fe Trail,* pp. 76–77.

34. Appendix 2.

35. *Rio Abajo Weekly Press,* Sept. 20, 1864.

36. Interview, Louis C. Ilfeld, Aug. 20, 1947.

37. Sabin, *Kit Carson,* pp. 300, 800; Grant, *When Old Trails Were New,* pp. 54, 322n, citing Will Records Mora County, I, 185; *History of New Mexico,* I, 185.

38. An effort to bring Taos back to life as a commercial center was made with plans to build the Denver and Rio Grande Railroad south to Taos and Santa Fe in 1871. Taos Junction and Embudo, about 20 to 25 miles away, were as close to Taos as the tracks ever reached. Grant (*When Old Trails Were New,* p. 174) comments: "Taos was fairly pushed off the map" in 1880.

CHAPTER III

Letcher and Ilfeld, Las Vegas (1867–1874)

1. The population of Taos County in 1860 was 14,103; in 1870, 12,079 (*Ninth Census of the United States,* Washington, D. C., 1872).

2. "The larger portion of the merchants of Mora are Germans." *Santa Fe New Mexican,* April 30, 1864.

3. *Ibid.*

4. The population of Upper and Lower Las Vegas in 1870 was 2526.

Trade territory	
San Miguel County	16,058
Mora County	8,056
Lincoln County	1,803
Dona Ana County	5,864
Bernalillo County	
(Albuquerque only)	1,307
	33,088

See *Ninth Census,* Washington, D. C., 1872. The trade territory also served the eastern edge of Socorro, the eastern half of Valencia, and the southern half of Santa Fe Counties. Estimated population: 10,000.

5. The Gallinas River runs through the heart of present-day Las Vegas. Gregg, *Commerce of the Prairies,* I, 109. This "hovel" must have been the future site of Upper Las Vegas just north of the present town of Las Vegas.

6. The first Vegas Grandes Grant was made to Luis Maria Cabeza de Baca, May 29, 1821, by the Spanish Provincial Deputation at Durango. Mexican Independence was not declared until Sept. 28, 1821. The second Vegas Grandes Grant was awarded March 25, 1835, to 29 individuals by Don Francisco Sarracino, governor of New Mexico. Verna Laumbach, "Las Vegas Before 1850," *New Mexico Historical Review,* 8:243–245 (Oct. 1933).

7. W. W. H. Davis, *El Gringo or New Mexico and Her People,* p. 34.

8. Twitchell, *Leading Facts,* pp. 233–234, 238.

9. Interview, Rodney B. Schoonmaker, Aug. 21, 1947. Rodney B. Schoonmaker was born 50 miles south of Chicago on the Kankakee River, May 31, 1856. He was bookkeeper for Charles Ilfeld in the 1880's. He died in Las Vegas on June 13, 1951. In 1887 Romero's business was moved to Wagonmound (Helen Haines, *History of New Mexico,* p. 360).

10. Interviews, Louis C. Ilfeld and Rodney B. Schoonmaker, Aug. 20 and 21, 1947, respectively. Schoonmaker said, "Brunswick had an acute comprehension of past, present, and future."

11. *New Mexico Historical Review,* 18:402 (Oct. 1943).

12. The building still stands. It was the office of Louis C. Ilfeld, Attorney at Law, until his death on March 29, 1950.

13. *History of New Mexico,* I, 583. Kihlberg continued to operate a store in El Monton de Los Alamos until Sept., 1870, when it was leased to Letcher and Ilfeld (Cash Book, 1869–1871, Sept. 2, 1870). He became a partner in a forwarding business in Kit Carson, Colorado, at about this time (Copy Book 1, Sept. 22, 1870, p. 375).

14. Miguel Antonio Otero, *My Life on the Frontier, 1864–1882,* p. 156.

15. Cash Book, 1865–1868; Copy Book 1, Dec. 7 and 27, 1869, pp. 277, 285.

16. Appendix 1.

17. Cash Book, 1865–1868; Appendix 1.

18. Appendix 1.

19. Copy Book 1, p. 91.

20. Based on increase of capital of $1702.14 on $5970.50 from Sept., 1865, through March, 1869. Appendix 3, and Ledger A, p. 24.

21. Ledger A, pp. 24, 37; Appendix 1, Appendix 3.

22. Appendix 1.

23. *Ibid.*

24. See note 38, Chapter I.

25. Appendix 1.

26. *Ibid.*

27. *Ibid.*

28. Reconstructed from letters in Copy Book 1.

29. The "Mr. Amberg" was probably a relative of Jacob Amberg, but there is no assurance this was the case. *Ibid.*, p. 34.

30. *Ibid.*, Jan. 31, 1869, p. 198.

31. *Ibid.*, March 11, 1869, p. 209.

32. *Ibid.*, Sept. 17, 1868; Appendix 1.

33. Copy Book 1, March 11, 1869, p. 209.

34. Appendix 1.

35. *Ibid.*

36. Copy Book 1, pp. 8, 45.

37. *Ibid.*, Dec. 23, 1867, p. 20.

38. Appendix 1.

39. Copy Book 1, Feb. 9 and July 17, 1869, pp. 200, 239.

40. *Ibid.*, Dec. 20, 1869, p. 282.

41. Letter in Letcher's handwriting, *ibid.*, June 16, 1870, p. 308. Letcher returned $80 of expense money, May 6, 1870, Cash Book, 1869–1871.

42. Copy Book 1, May 31, 1869, p. 225; Dec. 10, 1869, p. 278; March 19, 1870, p. 294; Oct. 3, 1870, p. 382.

43. *Ibid.*, Feb. 1 and June 18, 1871, pp. 425, 475; Cash Book, 1869–1871, Oct. 1 and 23, 1871.

44. Phrase used by Charles Ilfeld. Copy Book 1, Dec. 14, 1871, p. 633.

45. *Ibid.*, June 11, 1872, p. 719.

46. Copy Book 2, Feb. 17, 1875, p. 491; Cash Book, 1872–1873, Jan. 5, 1873.

47. Cash Book, 1869–1871, Sept. 2, 1870; Copy Book 2, March 2, 1873, p. 25; Ledger B, p. 170.

48. He bought the property for $2000 (Ledger B, p. 170).

49. *Las Vegas Gazette,* April 19, 1873. "Charles Ilfeld, Esq. of the populous firm of A. Letcher & Co. left Las Vegas today on a six month's trip to Europe. 'O Charles we shall miss you'" (*ibid.*, May 10, 1873).

50. The adjective is sincere. The author has seen an oil painting of Mrs. Charles Ilfeld which confirms in his mind the judgment of an early Las Vegas editor: "She [Mrs. Ilfeld] is the handsomest little lady in New Mexico" (*ibid.*, Oct. 31, 1874). See also letter from Louis C. Ilfeld, June 16, 1948, and Copy Book 4, March 25, 1879, p. 404.

51. Adele Nordhaus was born April 17, 1854. Date taken from a family prayer book which belonged to Charles Ilfeld, Office of Louis C. Ilfeld, Las Vegas.

52. Louis Ilfeld was born Dec. 19, 1857. He reached Santa Fe on his birthday, 1873, after spending three months in New York City. Twitchell, *Leading Facts,* V, 244–245. Since Louis was only 15 when he left Germany and inasmuch as his arrival in New York coincides well with that of Charles, it seems certain Louis accompanied Charles to New York. Noa Ilfeld, older than Louis, was en route to Las Vegas and Santa Fe in Nov. 1871. Copy Book 1, Nov. 29, 1871, p. 628. Bernard Ilfeld, another brother, was in Las Vegas by Sept. 26, 1874. Ledger E, p. 601.

53. Copy Book 2, Nov. 15, 1873, p. 183. Ilfeld's handwriting appears Nov. 19, 1873, p. 186.

54. They were probably married at the home of Charles's sister, Mrs. Philip Goldberg, but the possibility remains that the wedding took place in Baltimore at the residence of Adele Nordhaus' aunt. Letter from Louis C. Ilfeld, July 7, 1948, and interview, Aug. 12, 1949.

55. Copy Book 2, p. 263.

56. "No Life for a Lady" is borrowed from Agnes Morely Cleaveland's autobiography of the same title. This book is a story of Mrs. Cleaveland's experiences as a young lady on a ranch in New Mexico in the 1890's (New York, 1941).

57.

$1544.16	(Cash Book, 1874–1875)
3485.18	(Ledger B, p. 233)
$5029.34	

58. Ledger B, p. 30. Wheelock had given Herman Ilfeld two notes for a total of $13,000, which amounts were paid to Elsberg and Amberg for the purchase of their

Santa Fe store. Appendix 1. After the payment of this cash, July 27, 1871, Wheelock's account became "Ilfeld and Company" under the proprietorship of Herman Ilfeld, Aug. 1, 1871. Ledger B, p. 129.

59. Charles Ilfeld was a member of the New Mexico and Arizona Land Grant and Mining Exchange Agency of Santa Fe which was seeking to market the Cieneguilla Estate in 1873. H. O. Brayer, *William Blackmore: The Spanish-Mexican Land Grants of New Mexico and Colorado, 1863–1878,* p. 199n62. The *Weekly New Mexican* of Santa Fe published some bids on Fort contracts of Charles Ilfeld, May 28, 1872. Marcus Brunswick, who was also bidding, may have been associated with Charles.

60. In 1886, Letcher and Ilfeld formed a ranch and cattle partnership at La Cinta, New Mexico (Copy Book 14, July 15, 1886, p. 230), which was managed by Fritz Eggert (Ledger H, pp. 122–123). Letcher frequently loaned Ilfeld capital in the 1870's and 1880's.

CHAPTER IV

Monetary Exchange, Las Vegas and the East

1. The Navajos were starved out of hiding by Kit Carson's systematic destruction of their crops and cattle and then were driven by forced march to Bosque Redondo (now Fort Sumner), the round-up being completed by the fall of 1866. A treaty was not signed, however, until June, 1868, after an investigation by a commission appointed by President Grant. The Kiowa, Apaches, and Comanches in northeastern New Mexico were defeated in 1864 by Carson, but they gave some trouble until 1866. Twitchell, *Leading Facts,* II, 428–448. The Apaches in the South were not subdued until 1886, when Geronimo, chief of the Chiricahuas, and a portion of his tribe were followed into Mexico by Capt. Lawton and attacked in July. Geronimo surrendered in Sept., and he and his band were entrained for Fort Marion, Florida, to join the more peaceful Chiricahuas who had been shipped there earlier. Ralph H. Ogle, "Federal Control of the Western Apaches, 1848–1886," *New Mexico Historical Review,* 15:327–331 (July 1940).

2. Military force and stations in New Mexico, 1865:

Albuquerque	155	Ft. Sumner	314
Ft. Bascom	325	Ft. Union	807
Ft. Craig	164	Ft. Wingate	135
Ft. Cummings	51	Franklin	217
Ft. Marcy	16	Las Cruces	171
Ft. McRae	49	Los Pinos	46
Ft. Stanton	160	Men en route	443
		Total military personnel	3089

This total is higher by 36 than the actual total of the columns (Coan, *History of New Mexico,* I, 399). Requisition for disbursement by Bvt. Lt. Col. M. I. Ludington, Santa Fe, for the fiscal year 1869–1870, amounted to $384,094.65. *Report of Secretary of War,* I (41st Cong., 2d sess., 1869–1870), 248–249.

3. Compare Atherton, *Pioneer Merchant,* p. 52.

4. The following letter lends further proof of this observation (Copy Book 3, p. 29):

August 4, 1875

Messrs, Chick Browne and Co.
Grenada

Gents: Will you please inform me since when it is customary to charge exchange from Grenada to St. Louis as it was entirely a matter of accommodation to give Mr. Jose Albino Baca the money, besides I would respy. inform you that I am doing a good deal of that business with Messrs. Otero, Sellar & Co., and the first cent of Exchge. has to be paid yet by me.

Respectfully
CHARLES ILFELD

5. *Santa Fe New Mexican,* Feb. 13, 1864; W. H. Ryus, *The Second William Penn,* p. 124.

6. Moore and Adams at Fort Union. *Santa Fe Gazette,* July 7, 1866. Moore, Mitchell and Company at Tecolote, Fort Union, and Fort Bliss. Ryus, *Second William Penn,* p. 124.

7. Ryus, *Second William Penn,* pp. 125, 128.

8. Copy Book 1, Dec. 27, 1867, p. 23.

9. *Ibid.,* Jan. 8, 13, 22, 1868, pp. 27–28, 32.

10. *Ibid.,* Jan. 31, 1868, p. 36.

11. Compare V. D. Harrington, *New York Merchant on the Eve of the Revolution,* p. 115.

12. Copy Book 1, Oct. 2 and 11, 1867; July 11, 1868, pp. 3, 4, 100.

13. *Ibid.,* Jan. 27 and 31, 1869, pp. 193, 196, 198.

14. Keleher, *Maxwell Land Grant;* Brunswick Wagon Bill of Lading Book. *History of New Mexico,* II, 583. Otero and Sellar and Chick, Browne did their heavy freighting to the forts of Kansas and Colorado, but in New Mexico a random contract or two indicates that their commitments were large. One contract was for 300 tons of coal (National Archives, Washington, D.C., photostats in University of New Mexico Library).

15. As noted in Chapter III, several contracts were not recorded; consequently the total must have been larger than this. Cash Books, 1869–1871, 1872–1873, 1874–1875.

16. Cash Book, 1869–1871, April 16, 1871, and Ledger B, p. 100.

17. Ledger B, p. 219; Copy Book 2, Feb. 17, 1875, p. 491. This store building was occupied by protégés of the Spiegelbergs, Nathan Bibo and Sam Dittenhofer, prior to its use by Charles Ilfeld. *Santa Fe Weekly Post,* March 2, 1872.

18. Credit side of Tecolote store account. Ledger B, pp. 206, 219, 220.

19. Their identifiable drafts were on the Vermont National Bank of St. Albans. Cash Book, 1872–1873, i.e., Copy Book 1, Dec. 14, 1868, p. 185.

20. Copy Book 2, March 14, 1873, p. 31; Cash Book, 1872–1873, April 20, July 3, Oct. 1, Nov. 29, 1873. Ilfeld and Letcher had a contract to supply three stations: Nine Mile Hill (Los Alamos); Kearny Gap (known as "Puertacita" or "Little Gate"); and Tecolote. Interview, Rodney B. Schoonmaker, Aug. 21, 1947.

21. Copy Book 2, March 14, 1873, p. 31.

22. *Ibid.*

23. *Ibid.,* March 26, 1873, p. 34.

24. Copy Book 3, July 29, 1875, p. 19. After the railroad came he was bonding T. F. Chapman as postmaster and wished the Postmaster-General to relieve him of this burden. Copy Book 5, Aug. 13, 1880, p. 449; Oct. 23, 1879, p. 71.

25. Copy Book 5, Nov. 5, 1880, p. 558, and Copy Book 6, Jan. 28, 1881, p. 51. H. Sanderson had lost or given up this contract as of Sept. 1, 1880. Copy Book 5, Aug. 19 and Sept. 4, 1880, pp. 458, 477.

26. Copy Book 7, June 24, 1882, p. 216. Alamos was off the beaten track by this time, and Ilfeld claimed some contractors wanted $1000 to $1200 per year (one turned it down because it was a four-year contract), but he had "engaged a Mexican to run the mail for $800" (*ibid.,* July 1, 1882, p. 229).

27. M. W. Mills of Springer had the Springer-Cimarron subcontract from the same firm at $800 per year (Incoming Correspondence, Packet 1, Feb. 1, 1883). Gross, Blackwell and Company operated, as subcontractor, the Las Vegas–Fort Bascom route (*ibid.,* June 19, 1883).

28. Copy Book 28, Feb. 9, 1894, p. 99. Ilfeld sought subcontractors for the Las Vegas–Fort Bascom and Las Vegas–Fort Sumner routes in 1889 (Copy Book 17, Oct. 18, 1889, p. 447).

29. Sena pleaded to be released from this as the cost of horses was so high as to eliminate profits. Besides, George J. Fredericks of East Las Vegas wanted the route on the same terms but wished to use two automobiles which would cut delivery time in half (Louis C. Ilfeld Letter Book, June 29, 1909, p. 105).

30. Keleher, *Maxwell Land Grant,* p. 113. In general, chap. xii, pp. 113–118.

31. Copy Book 1, April 28, June 3, June 25, 1871, pp. 446, 447, 493. Evidence of foreign capital affecting Ilfeld is shown when Ilfeld obtained a Baring Brothers'

draft of £100 sterling for which he received in exchange $535 (Copy Book 3, Jan. 26, 1876, p. 151).

32. Twitchell, *Leading Facts,* II, 483; James Marshall, *Santa Fe: The Railroad That Built an Empire,* p. 398; Copy Book 4, July 7, 1879, p. 555. The first freight train arrived July 5, 1879 (*New Mexico and Southern Pacific Railroad* v. *John Dougher,* Clerk of the Court, San Miguel County, Docket No. 1009, Las Vegas).

33. Coan, *History of New Mexico,* I, 447.

34. *Ibid.,* pp. 446, 447.

35. "All the contractors" is a slight exaggeration but a pardonable one. Brunswick, we know, did most of his business with Ilfeld, and doubtless others shared their allegiance with Jaffa Brothers, the Dolds, Romero, Rosenwald, etc. Otero, *My Life on the Frontier,* I, 162.

36. Copy Book 5, Oct. 18, 1880, p. 543.

37. *Ibid.,* Aug. 14, Nov. 8, Dec. 30, 1880, pp. 453, 560, 657. This was evidently a note similar to that which John Dougher had given the railroad to be paid when the first freight train arrived at the depot in Las Vegas. See note 23 above. To these merchants this meant what is now "Old Las Vegas."

38. *Ibid.,* Sept. 8 and 14, 1880, pp. 484, 490.

39. Copy Book 6, Sept. 27 and Dec. 27, 1881, pp. 440, 594.

40. *Ibid.,* Jan. 31, 1882, p. 648.

41. First National Bank of Santa Fe was chartered Dec. 13, 1870, and was opened for business April 18, 1871. The Second National Bank of Santa Fe was opened for business in Aug., 1872 (Bureau of Immigration, *Resources of New Mexico,* pp. 29, 31).

42. Copy Book 2, Feb. 16, 1873, p. 16. On Nov. 29, 1873, an unidentified exchange rate of 3/4 of 1 per cent was paid (Cash Book, 1872–1873).

43. See notes 5 and 6, Chapter V.

44. Copy Book 4, July 16, 1878, p. 62. See also p. 54.

45. *Ibid.,* Nov. 19, 1878, p. 166. The Stockgrowers' Bank was organized in 1873 by Charles Goodnight and others (J. Evetts Haley, *Charles Goodnight: Cowman and Plainsman,* p. 273).

46. Copy Book 3, May 15, 1877, p. 578.

47. Joseph G. McCoy, *Cattle Trade of the West and Southwest,* chap. xviii, pp. 395–416.

48. Copy Book 2, Nov. 29, 1873; July 2 and Oct. 5, 1874; July 8, 1875, pp. 200, 313, 370, 671. Ilfeld does not appear to have a financial interest in sheep again until his partnership with W. B. Stapp in 1883 (Ledger G, p. 504).

49. Ilfeld sold what cattle he had in 1881 (Copy Book 6, Oct. 15, 1881, p. 461). He bought a small interest in a private brand (Copy Book 7, April 15, 1882, pp. 143–144), and he had a cattle partnership with W. B. Stapp in 1884 (Ledger G, p. 608), as well as with his former partner, Letcher, in 1886 (Ledger H, p. 123).

50. McCoy, *Cattle Trade,* p. 400; Copy Book 3, March 22, 1877, p. 511.

51. Copy Book 3, Feb. 14, 1876, p. 159.

52. *Ibid.,* April 17, 1876, p. 211; June 3, 1876, p. 249.

53. *Ibid.,* June 11, 1877, p. 611.

54. *Ibid.,* p. 511. One day later Ilfeld sought to borrow from Letcher $10,000 at 8 per cent for the same purpose (Copy Book 3 [in German], March 23, 1877, p. 158).

55. Ledger B, pp. 8, 205. Gregg Brothers had an agent headquartering in La Junta, Colorado. Copy Book 4, July 10, 26, 30, Aug. 11, 1879, pp. 567, 597–600, 606–607, 632; Copy Book 5, Oct. 16, Nov. 1, 1879, pp. 65, 80.

56. One shipment of 952 pounds of wool went to Messrs. Pokrantz and Company, Bremen, Germany (Copy Book 2 [in German], Nov. 22, 1873, p. 193).

57. Copy Book 1, June 26, 1869, p. 233.

58. Copy Book 2, Dec. 8, 1874, p. 436.

59. Feb. 28, 1878. *United States Statutes at Large,* 45th Cong., 1877–1879, vol. XX (Washington, D. C.: United States Government Printing Office, 1879), p. 25.

60. *Statistical Abstract of the United States,* 1913, p. 493. The Mexican silver dollar was the successor to the Spanish silver dollar (Lawrence Smith, *Money, Credit, and Public Policy* [Boston, 1959], p. 166).

61. The Act of Feb. 14, 1873, dropped the silver dollar from the list of coins which would be struck at the mint, although a new heavier "trade" silver dollar for export purposes was authorized. The standard silver dollar, of the former weight and fineness, was restored in 1878 through the Bland-Allison Act. This minting of silver bullion at a higher than market value may not have been the only force at work, however. At that time financial conditions in Mexico were still close to the deplorable state they had been in when General Porfirio Diaz first became president in 1776. (*The Encyclopedia Americana,* 18:755 [1950].) It is possible that the favorable balance of trade of the U.S. with Mexico in these years was also true of New Mexico with Mexico and that Mexican silver dollars were more likely to have been used in the satisfaction of U.S. exports than would normally have been the case.

62. Copy Book 4, July 30, 1879, p. 606; Copy Book 5, Oct. 22, 1879, p. 71.

63. Copy Book 5, Nov. 6, 1880, p. 559.

64. William A. Keleher, *Violence in Lincoln County, 1869–1881,* p. 52. J. J. Dolan and Co. became Dolan, Riley & Co. in 1877. *Ibid.*, pp. 56, 267–268.

65. J. W. Hendron, *The Story of Billy the Kid,* p. 8. Fred C. Godfrey, Indian Agent at Fort Stanton, was accused of lending supplies to L. G. Murphy and Co., and later J. J. Dolan and Co., its successors, although without profit to himself. He was replaced in April, 1879 (Frank D. Reeve, "The Federal Indian Policy in New Mexico, 1858–1880, Mescalero Apache," *New Mexico Historical Review,* 13:276–277 [July 1938]).

66. Hendron, *Billy the Kid,* p. 10.

67. Keleher, *Violence,* p. 112, cites a letter of Dolan's published in the *Santa Fe New Mexican,* May 25, 1878: "Mr. Riley and I are in Mr. Chisum's way, because our business conflicts. He wants to control contracts in New Mexico as well as Arizona; in this we have bothered him."

68. The Lincoln County War had, as its immediate and obvious cause, the friction existing between the McSween-Tunstall-Chisum and the Murphy-Dolan-Riley factions as large cattle owners. Each faction bitterly contested for the privilege of supplying government forts—particularly Fort Stanton. Perhaps not provable, but certainly suspiciously present, was the social unrest fostered by the change from petty to mercantile capitalism.

69. Keleher, *Violence,* pp. 82–124, 137–146, 204.

70. It is notable that Billy the Kid (cattle rustler and murderer) had much public support in his Robin Hood-like depredations. When Governor Lew Wallace, author of *Ben Hur,* instigated correspondence with this outlaw, Billy referred the governor to the citizens for a check on his character "for the majority of them are my Friends and have been helping me all they could." *Ibid.*, p. 211. Keleher (p. 215) states that "Governor Wallace was at a loss to understand Bonney's [Billy the Kid's] popularity in the town [Lincoln]." The governor wrote, "A precious specimen named 'The Kid' . . . is an object of tender regard." *Ibid.*, p. 216.

71. Gras, *Business and Capitalism,* pp. 69–70.

CHAPTER V

The Merchant Credit System: Independent of Specialized Banking

1. Compare Atherton, *Pioneer Merchant,* p. 11, and Gras, *Business and Capitalism,* pp. 151, 169.

2. Raymond de Roover, *Money, Banking, and Credit in Mediaeval Bruges,* part I, pp. 9–91; Gras, *Business and Capitalism,* p. 149. The Bank of Deposit of Barcelona, founded as a city bank in 1401, came only after private banking had reached a high stage of development. A. P. Usher, *The Early History of Deposit Banking in Mediterranean Europe,* pp. 237–269.

3. Bank of North America, Philadelphia, 1781; Bank of New York, New York City, 1784; Massachusetts Bank, Boston, 1784.

4. Two banks had existed for a short time. The Bank of St. Louis opened in 1816,

closed in March, 1818, opened again a year later, but failed in July, 1819. The Bank of Missouri failed in Aug., 1821, after a short life (Jennings, *Pioneer Merchant,* p. 172). The Bank of the State of Missouri was established as a state monopoly on May 10, 1837. John Ray Cable, *The State Bank of Missouri,* Columbia Studies in History, Economics, and Public Law 102 (Columbia, Mo., 1923), p. 164.

5. See note 41, Chapter IV. "The first bank to be opened in Las Vegas was established by Jefferson, Joshua, and Frederick A. Raynolds under the name of Raynolds Brothers in 1876. It was located in a building owned by Frank Chapman situated on the west side of the Plaza in Las Vegas. . . . This bank was conducted as a private institution until 1880, when the Raynolds Brothers organized the First National Bank of Las Vegas with a capital stock of fifty thousand dollars" (*History of New Mexico,* I, 414).

6. Jefferson Raynolds and family arrived in Las Vegas to take up permanent residence near the end of Sept., 1876 (*Las Vegas Gazette,* Sept. 30, 1876). The first advertisement of the bank appears in the issue of Oct. 14, 1876. The Raynolds family came to Las Vegas from Pueblo, Colorado (*History of New Mexico,* I, 415). The *Las Vegas Gazette,* June 17, 1876, reported: "Mr. Frank Chapman is now closing up his mercantile business preparatory to opening out a bank. Subscription books have been opened and prospects are now that a large capital will be at once subscribed to establish the institution. Mr. S. G. Collins, cashier of the Exchange Bank of Denver proposes to take a considerable interest. This is an institution which is greatly needed by the business public of Las Vegas and surrounding country." Frank Chapman was accidentally shot at a fandango the night of Sept. 10, 1876 (Copy Book 3, Sept. 11, 1876, p. 336), but was up and about again shortly thereafter. Lack of capital and not the wound was apparently the cause of the bank's failure to get started (*Las Vegas Gazette,* Sept. 23, 1876).

7. It may occur to the reader that it would be too much to expect local items to be listed and described. Inasmuch as Ilfeld listed one such item, however, and was careful to describe all collection items, it seems safe to assume the absence of evidence of Raynolds' checks in Ilfeld's records to be good proof that few people carried accounts. Copy Book 3, p. 945.

8. First deposit was for $200, Oct. 11, 1876. From Oct., 1876, through April, 1877, Ilfeld deposited $11,149.95 and withdrew for exchange purposes $10,678.08 (Cash Book, 1876–1877).

9. His balance on May 31, 1877, was apparently $1372.56, and on Dec. 31, $6366.05. *Ibid.*

10. The first private check of Ilfeld mentioned in his copy books was made payable to Franz Huning in the amount of $2.50 and was dated Dec. 31, 1877 (Copy Book 3, p. 819). The last check of this series, Nov. 28, 1878 (Copy Book 4, p. 190) is numbered 159. Inasmuch as several numbers are given for intermediate checks, we can, by extrapolation, place the date of the first check at a time no earlier than Dec. 1, 1877. On March 26, 1879, Ilfeld wrote check no. 1 of the new series to H. M. Porter of Cimarron in the amount of $52.50 (Copy Book 4, p. 405). Otero and Sellar drew its check, no. 47, against Raynolds Brothers on Oct. 30, 1876 (Otero and Sellar Letter Book, p. 123).

11. Copy Book 3, May 9, 1878, p. 985.

12. The First National Bank of Santa Fe on Oct. 2, 1874, had paid-in capital of $150,000 and deposits of $108,804. On Oct. 1, 1875, the deposit figure was $192,701. The Second National Bank of Santa Fe had a similar experience. *Reports of the Comptroller of the Currency, 1874–1875* (Washington, D.C., 1875 and 1876), p. 759.

13. Analysis of numbered drafts mailed as revealed in Copy Books 3 and 4.

14. Cash Book, 1876–1877.

15. *Ibid.*

16. The Comptroller of the Currency of the United States listed three banks in New Mexico, other than national banks, in existence on Nov. 30, 1876 (*Reports, 1882–1883,* p. 133). These figures may be accurate and yet the other two banks have not been brought to light. The mercantile house of Spiegelberg in Santa Fe is known to have issued its own script (*El Palacio,* vol. XXXI, Dec. 16, 1931, p. 376), though this should

not have qualified it as a bank. The first law regulating territorial banks was passed April 3, 1884 (*1884 Compiled Laws of New Mexico* [Santa Fe, 1885], title III, chap. I, pp. 204–210).

17. Copy Book 4, Dec. 3, 1878, p. 195. This note was discounted Oct. 4, 1879, at 1 per cent per month (Copy Book 5, p. 41).

18. The San Miguel Bank was incorporated Dec. 15, 1879. Twitchell, *Leading Facts,* V, 264. Directors Otero and Gross were associated with Otero and Sellar; L. P. Browne, with Browne, Manzanares. See Otero and Sellar Letter Book, pp. 235–236, for a description of the founding of this bank.

19. Copy Book 5, p. 163.

20. To be discussed in Chapter VII.

21. Copy Book 5, Aug. 14, 1880, pp. 453–454.

22. See Chapter IV.

23. "Credit was obtained without great difficulty from wholesale houses, the usual terms being six months' credit, payable in twelve, with interest ranging from six to ten per cent after the first six months." Quoted by Atherton, *Pioneer Merchant,* p. 11, from John Beauchamp Jones (pen name, Luke Shortfield), *The Western Merchant,* preface.

24. Ledger B, p. 42; Copy Book 2, Nov. 1, 1873, p. 167.

25. Statement of H. B. Claflin Company as drawn up by Charles Ilfeld:

1877			
Sept. 18	To mdse 60 days		$172.84
19	" " "		457.22
20	" " "		560.75
		$1,190.81	
Nov. 5	By Cash	1,190.81	
Sept. 19	To mdse 4 mos.		51.30
22	" " " "		40.45
24	" " " "		35.00
		126.75	
Nov. 26	To mdse 2%	10.50	10.29
26	" " "	33.00	32.34
26	" " "	114.51	108.78
		151.41	
Dec. 17	By cash	151.41	
1878			
Jan. 18	By cash	126.75	
	In payment of 4 mos. Bills Sept. 10/24/77		

Your statement rec'd but does not agree with my books. Above please find my statement & let me know if it is correct.

Copy Book 3, April 1, 1878, p. 939.

26. *Ibid.,* Nov. 8, 1877, p. 749.

27. Copy Book 2, Nov. 13, 1874, p. 407; Copy Book 3, Jan. 14, 1878, p. 841.

28. The First National Bank of Santa Fe paid 4 per cent on a certificate of deposit of Telesfor Jaramillo for $6000 for Feb. 28 to Oct. 1, 1879. Copy Book 5, Nov. 21, 1879, p. 124. The Stockgrowers' National Bank of Pueblo, Colorado, advertised in 1873 that it would pay 6 per cent on money left three months, 7 per cent if left six months, 8 per cent if left twelve months. Haley, *Charles Goodnight,* p. 273.

29. Copy Book 2, March 16, 1875, p. 506; Ledger B, p. 33.

30. Copy Book 3, Dec. 16, 1876, p. 413.

31. Copy Book 2, p. 506.

32. Copy Book 7, June 21, 22, Aug. 2, 31, 1882, pp. 209, 210, 312–313, 376–379. Donnell-

Lawson and Company, private bankers of New York City, were used as a depository for checking funds from Dec. 15, 1877, to July 3, 1878. Copy Books 3 and 4.

33. Atherton, *Pioneer Merchant,* pp. 69–71.

34. Ilfeld dealt with 42 firms in Baltimore and 5 in Philadelphia from 1870 to 1874 (Table 4).

35. R. G. Dun & Co., *Reference Book,* 1869 (*Dun and Bradstreet*); Copy Book 1 (in German), June 16, 1870, p. 308.

36. Ledger B, p. 42. An entry in the Beuthner account prior to this date was made to record the sale by Ilfeld of 50 ounces of gold dust for $962. The gold was shipped in May, 1870, and paid for in June. Solomon Beuthner is listed in *Dun and Bradstreet,* 1869, as "Dry Goods Jobbers" and in 1879 as "Dry Goods Brokers."

37. Interview, Louis C. Ilfeld, Aug. 20, 1947.

38. Ledger B, p. 42. One item of merchandise of $666.06 is followed by "Commission same $16.65."

39. Copy Book 1, Nov. 8, 1867, p. 8; Ledger B, p. 33.

40. Charles Ilfeld used A. L. la Croix of St. Louis as an additional purchasing agent in order to preserve a friendship. Purchases through this source were small and were usually confined to fresh fruit which Ilfeld suggested he buy from that "Italian on Market between 2nd and 3rd." Copy Book 2, June 8, 1875, p. 593.

41. It could hardly have been otherwise. The Census of 1870 lists the number of individuals in trade and transportation: St. Louis 28,219, Kansas City 2806; Census of 1880: St. Louis 36,802, Kansas City 7625. Population of 1870 and 1880 shows St. Louis roughly seven times the size of Kansas City. Chicago was not a factor yet because there was no direct railroad connection until 1888 when the AT&SF Railway finished its Kansas City–Chicago line.

42. Information derived from Copy Books 1, 2, and 3.

43. Ledger B, pp. 38, 114, 164.

44. Atherton, *Pioneer Merchant,* pp. 101–102, states that these commissions in the East during the 1830's had been 0.5 per cent for receiving and forwarding, and 0.5 per cent for insurance, which figure rose to 2.5 per cent for adjusting and collecting insurance losses. A charge of 2.5 per cent was made for buying and holding goods subject to a merchant's call. In the West the charges were generally higher.

45. Example: "In case we have not Freight enough there, forward us 10–15 sacks Coffee, 3 B soda crackers, 5 B soap all to make up weight." Copy Book 1, July 21, 1872, p. 733.

46. Ledger B, p. 229.

47. One other New York City agent, S. Schutz, was used on rare occasions. Copy Book 6, Jan. 31 and Aug. 18, 1881, pp. 54, 361–362. S. Schutz's brother, Aaron, married Mrs. Charles Ilfeld's sister, Fanny. Copy Book 3, July 13, 1877, p. 650.

48. Ledger B, p. 42; Copy Book 3, Dec. 16, 1876, p. 413.

49. "Had a letter of Beuthner a few days ago from Monaco" (Copy Book 3, Feb. 15, 1878, p. 890); *ibid.,* Dec. 15, 1877, p. 798. Donnell-Lawson and Company advertised themselves as dealers in sterling exchange and travelers credits. They received deposits for checking accounts, paying interest thereon, and had special facilities for the transactions of Missouri, Kansas, and Texas business. *The Bankers Almanac and Register,* New York City, 1879.

50. Copy Book 4, July 3, 1878, p. 51a; Copy Book 7, June 21, 22, 1882, pp. 209–210.

51. This Los Alamos should not be confused with the present synthetic town, of nuclear fame, located northwest of Santa Fe.

52. Copy Book 3, Sept. 9, 1876, p. 331; Copy Book 2, Feb. 13, 1875, p. 486.

53. Copy Book 3, Sept. 9, 1876, p. 331; Nov. 10, 1877, p. 751; Nov. 30, 1877, p. 773.

54. *Las Vegas Gazette,* Jan. 29, 1876, and March 1, 1873; Copy Book 5, July 23, 1880, p. 422. Gellerman had been manager of the Isador Stern branch store in Fort Sumner (*Las Vegas Gazette,* May 30, 1874, and July 11, 1874).

55. Law offices of Louis C. Ilfeld, Las Vegas. Photostat in the University of New Mexico Library, Albuquerque.

56. Ilfeld and Dawson was formed to liquidate a cattle receivership (Petty Ledger H, p. 148). Romero, Blanchard, and Ilfeld bought and disposed of the F. B. Wooten sawmill and home in Las Vegas (Ledger G, p. 579). Ilfeld and Brunswick was formed for supply contracts, probably in connection with Ft. Stanton (*ibid.*, p. 560). Other partnerships include: Ilfeld and Stapp, sheep account (*ibid.*, p. 327); Ilfeld and Kronig Ice Co. (*ibid.*, p. 494); Ilfeld and Stapp Cattle Account (*ibid.*, p. 608); Ilfeld and Letcher Ranch Account (Ledger H, p. 123); Ilfeld and Baca, real estate (*Las Vegas Gazette,* Oct. 7, 1882).

57. J. C. Lea was founder of Roswell, New Mexico. J. Evetts Haley, *George W. Littlefield: Texan* (Oklahoma City, 1943), p. 137. Lea County, New Mexico, was named for this merchant and rancher.

58. Copy Book 7, March 8 and April 11, 1882, pp. 40–41, 134.

59. *Ibid.*, Sept. 4 and 19, 1882, pp. 388, 428.

60. Richard Dunn, partner of Grzelachowski, in a store directly west of Charles Ilfeld, sold all his stock to Ilfeld in April or May, 1878, pending "extensive repairs and changes in storehouse," and Dunn assumed charge of Ilfeld's business for a period of six months while Ilfeld was in Europe and the East. Dunn had been employed by Ilfeld earlier, also. Copy Book 3, May 9, 1878, p. 985; *Las Vegas Gazette,* June 29, 1878. Upon Ilfeld's return, Dunn suffered a severe illness, but in Feb., 1879, he and Grzelachowski were in partnership in Puerto de Luna. Copy Book 4, Dec. 31, 1878, and Feb. 1, 1879, pp. 243, 309; Ledger E, p. 132.

61. Copy Book 5, March 23, 1880, p. 277.

62. William Kronig, of La Junta, owned 9 artificial lakes, 7 small breeding ponds, and 400 acres in Mora County. Bureau of Immigration, New Mexico, *Resources of New Mexico* (1889), p. 35. He operated near Ft. Union a woolen mill which was destroyed by fire. Elias Brevoort, *New Mexico: Her Natural Resources and Attractions,* p. 101. S. B. Watrous was a settler in La Junta, now Watrous, long before the American occupation, and he controlled most of the land in that vicinity. *History of New Mexico,* II, 651. Henry Göke had a general store and flour mill in Sapello. He also engaged in the sheep and ranching business. He became president of the Las Vegas Savings Bank and of the First National Bank of Raton, and director of the San Miguel National Bank. Twitchell, *Leading Facts,* IV, 252. Andres Sena was a rancher in El Monton de Los Alamos, where he raised substantial quantities of corn, wheat, and cattle. He acquired most of his backing, however, from his wife, a Baca, which family had a large interest in the Las Vegas Grant. Copy Book 4, Aug. 11, 1879, p. 630; interview, Rodney B. Schoonmaker, Aug. 21, 1947. H. M. Porter was one of the last directors of the Maxwell Land Grant Company. Keleher, *Maxwell Land Grant,* p. 96. Porter was also a rancher, merchant (Porter and Clothier), banker, and builder of telegraph lines (H. M. Porter, *Pencillings of an Early Western Pioneer;* Twitchell, *Leading Facts,* V, 268).

63. Copy Book 3, Nov. 5, 1877, p. 744.

64. Copy Book 2, July 13, 1875, p. 68, and Copy Book 3, Aug. 4, 1876, p. 305.

65. For a succinct discussion of the three stages of capital usage, the usucapital, direct putting-out, and indirect putting-out systems, see Gras, *Business and Capitalism,* pp. 85–86.

66. Charter obtained Sept. 22, 1879 (*Las Vegas Gazette,* Nov. 1, 1879).

67. Qualified Jan. 2, 1880 (*ibid.*, Jan. 28, 1880).

68. See above, note 12.

69. The comparison is not altogether fair inasmuch as the paid-in capital of the First National Bank of Santa Fe was $150,000 while that of the San Miguel National was but $50,000 (*Las Vegas Gazette,* June 24, 1880). However, in less than three years, in a smaller town, in competition with a successful bank, the San Miguel acquired deposits of $167,382 (*ibid.*, July 12, 1882).

70. Otero, *My Life on the Frontier,* I, 235–236.

71. *Las Vegas Gazette,* May 25, 1880.

72. Interview, Charles S. Brown, July 20, 1949.

CHAPTER VI

Significance of Slow and Costly Transportation

1. The more spectacular evidence of this change is seen in the retirement of two large mercantile capitalists from the China trade to the specialized field of private investments. John Jacob Astor withdrew from the Orient trade in 1825, and from all Pacific trade a short time later. John P. Cushing retired in Boston in 1831. N. S. B. Gras and Henrietta M. Larson, *Casebook in American Business History,* pp. 92, 122.

2. Much manufacturing had been established in the 1840's. There was a great surge toward specialization in the next few decades. Walter R. Stevens, *History of St. Louis, The Fourth City, 1764–1909* (St. Louis and Chicago, 1909), pp. 613–650.

3. Copy Book 5, July 23, 1880, p. 422.

4. Copy Book 2, March 14, 1875, p. 504. Sixteen days from Animas represents about 16 to 17 miles per day.

5. Chapter IV, note 1.

6. Copy Book 5, April 26, 1880, p. 312. This, apparently, refers to the activities of Victorio, Apache Chief, which were so severe east of the Pecos at this time that withdrawal of Fort Stanton troops was dismissed as impossible. General Hatch, commanding officer at the fort, disarmed and dismounted the Mescalero Apaches, April 16, 1880 (Reeve, "Indian Policy in New Mexico," pp. 277–278).

7. *Report of the Postmaster General, 1869–1870,* 41st Cong. 2d sess. (Washington, D. C., 1871), pp. 5, 43; *Report of the Postmaster General,* 43d Cong., 2d sess., pp. 68, 69, 1874–1875.

8. Newton, Kansas, Jan. 9, 1873: "The epizootic, or horse disease has immortalized itself in this country." The disease had been in Chicago the year before. William A. Craigie and James R. Holbert, eds., *A Dictionary of American English,* II (Chicago, 1940), 894. The Army's campaign against the Modoc Indians of the Northwest was slowed down because of the disease at this time. *Report of the Secretary of War, 1873–74,* 43d Cong., 1st sess. (Washington, D. C., 1875), pp. 111–112.

9. Copy Book 2, Jan. 21, 1873, p. 2.

10. *Ibid.,* Jan. 30, 1873, p. 10.

11. *Las Vegas Gazette,* Feb. 8, 1873.

12. Copy Book 3, Oct. 9 and Nov. 17, 1877, pp. 707, 758.

13. Probably Ramon A. Baca, member of the New Mexico Legislature, and Speaker of the House, 1876. Benjamin M. Read, *Illustrated History of New Mexico,* p. 729; Copy Book 2, Sept. 4, 1874, p. 650.

14. Copy Book 2, Sept. 20, 1874, p. 361.

15. Benito Baca of Upper Las Vegas, general merchant in 1877, and in 1878 losing candidate for Congress. He died June 21, 1879, at the age of 31. *Las Vegas Gazette,* July 28, 1877, Aug. 31, 1878; Read, *Illustrated History of New Mexico,* p. 732; Copy Book 2, Sept. 27, 1874, p. 365.

16. Copy Book 2, Oct. 11, 1874, p. 378.

17. *Ibid.,* Nov. 28 and Dec. 6, 1874, pp. 419, 432.

18. *Ibid.,* Oct. 5, 1874, p. 370.

19. *Ibid.,* Nov. 28, 1874, p. 419.

20. *Ibid.,* Dec. 6, 1874, p. 430.

21. *Ibid.,* Dec. 12, 1874, p. 440.

22. *Ibid.,* Jan. 6, 1875, p. 453.

23. *Ibid.,* Jan. 6 and 13, 1875, pp. 453, 460.

24. Copy Book 1, Dec. 21, 1869, p. 284.

25. *Ibid.,* Nov. 13, 1871, p. 617.

26. *Ibid.,* Dec. 19 and 28, 1871, pp. 634, 636.

27. *Ibid.,* March 19, 1872, p. 672.

28. Copy Book 4, Jan. 4, 7, 15, 18, 1879, pp. 259, 263, 272, 282.

29. *Ibid.*, Feb. 5, 1879, p. 319.

30. *Ibid.*, Feb. 10, 1879, p. 330.

31. Compare with Otero, *My Life on the Frontier,* I, 192–193. Otero's memory was evidently not accurate on this story. Apparently he has attributed some of the actions of a man named Beckworth to Barela. Charles Ilfeld's letter to Mariano Barela (Copy Book 4, June 6, 1879, p. 503), written shortly after the shooting and hanging, describes the incident:

"On Wednesday afternoon about half after four your brother in passing out of a saloon, drew his pistol and without cause or reason shot one Jesus Morales in the face whereupon Morales' companion, one Benigno Romero remonstrated with your brother who in return shot Benigno Romero twice thro' the body killing him instantly. The police where [*sic*] immediately on the spot and placed Manuel under arrest; who was severely handled by a mob while on the way to jail and it was with great difficulty that the police with the assistance of the sheriff and justice of the peace kept the people from lynching him on the spot.

"When once in jail the sheriff at once put twenty-five men well armed on duty as special guards and dispersed the mob; but about midnight a body of men masked and armed numbering about two hundred went to the jail, forced the door and compelled the deputy sheriff to give up the keys, after the receiving the same they took out Manuel and another person (an Italian) and hung them. . . ."

32. Copy Book 4, July 7, 1879, p. 559.

33. *Ibid.*, June 24, 1879, p. 528.

34. Copy Book 1, June 21, 1870, p. 31.

35. Copy Book 3, Nov. 11, 1875, p. 100.

36. *Ibid.*, April 13, 1877, p. 537.

37. Copy Book 2, Nov. 30, 1873, p. 202.

38. Copy Book 1, April 25, 1872, p. 698.

39. "Boomers" was a term describing itinerant laborers, particularly of the skilled type, who moved to any locality offering job advantages. The wagoners of the 1870's seldom had a permanent home. In a study of Ilfeld's copy books from 1869 to 1879 the names of at least 40 major-domos were noted, and so far as could be ascertained not a single individual's name appeared more than once. It is evident that few of these men tied themselves to a single town.

40. Copy Book 3, Nov. 23, 1875, p. 108.

41. Copy Book 7, March 8, 1882, pp. 40–41.

42. See Chapter II.

43. Copy Book 1, March 5, 1868, p. 45.

44. *Ibid.*, Sept. 7, 1869, p. 255; July 13, 1871, p. 518; June 18, 1871, p. 474.

45. This rule of thumb is quoted frequently by "old-timers," and on the average the facts bear it out. Ilfeld thought such a rate to be minimum when in 1873 the Atchison, Topeka & Santa Fe tried, perhaps at Ilfeld's suggestion, to contract for through rail-wagon rates to New Mexico. Ilfeld replied to the railroad's proposal: "The price you propose, is entirely too low, to justify Freighters, to contract themselves at those terms. The rates for freight paid here are not less than $1.00 one hundred pounds 100 miles." Copy Book 2, April 10, 1873, p. 42. The War Department decided against a policy of permitting through rail-wagon rates by land-grant railroads, as such would violate the "law of Congress prohibiting any payments to such railroads for the transportation of military supplies." *Report of the Secretary of War, 1874–75,* 43d Cong., 2d sess., vol. I, p. 173.

46. Copy Book 3, March 30, 1876, p. 197.

47. Wagon Bill of Lading Books.

48. The substantially higher rate of $3.25 per 100 pounds was justified by the circuitous route required by the government should occasion demand. The route officially went from Las Vegas to Socorro or San Marcial, to Fort Stanton. In none of the trips recorded by Brunswick did his teams follow the longer route. *Reports of the Secretary of War, 1882–83,* 47th Cong., 2d sess., p. 357, and *1883–84,* 48th Cong., 1st sess., p. 538. Brunswick lost the contract to W. H. Chick, formerly of Chick, Browne Company,

commission house, the following year when the bid dropped to $2.00 per 100 pounds. *Report of the Secretary of War, 1883–84*, p. 539.

49.

Pounds carried July 8, 1881, to June 30, 1882	377,960
Pounds carried July 10, 1882, to June 30, 1883	638,210
Total	1,016,170
Contract rate per pound 1881–1882	3.25¢
Average rate per pound paid freighters 1881–1882	1.61¢
Average spread	1.64¢
Contract rate per pound 1882–1883	2.50¢
Average rate per pound paid freighters 1882–1883	1.59¢
Average spread	0.91¢

Gross Profit (2 years) 1,016,170 × 1.18¢ (weighted average) = $11,994.27 = 42.5 per cent. (Brunswick Wagon Bill of Lading Books.)

50. Horses were only used on lighter loads when speed was desired.

51. Copy Book 3, Aug. 4, 1876, pp. 301, 303.

52. *Ibid.*

53. Copy Book 2, June 3, 1875, p. 582.

54. Copy Book 4, March 31, 1879, p. 418; Copy Book 5, April 26, 1880, p. 312. See note 6, above.

55. Copy Book 4, March 21, 24, Aug. 26, 1879, pp. 681, 682, 642; Copy Book 5, Feb. 9, 1880, p. 209; Copy Book 4, April 16, 18, 1879, pp. 443, 452.

56. Copy Book 6, Jan. 10, 1881, p. 2.

57. Marshall, *Sante Fe*, p. 80.

58. *Ibid.*, p. 396.

59. Ilfeld routed goods to Otero and Sellar at Granada, Colorado, July 31, 1873 (Copy Book 2, p. 114). Ilfeld shipped to Otero and Sellar at Kit Carson, Colorado, Aug. 11, 1873 (*ibid.*, p. 118). According to Otero, *My Life on the Frontier*, pp. 69–70, both houses moved to Granada, Aug., 1873.

60. Copy Book 3, July 20, 1875, p. 3.

61. *Ibid.*, Feb. 9, 1876, p. 156.

62. *Ibid.*, March 8, 1876, p. 179.

63. *Ibid.*, p. 407.

64. *Ibid.*, Nov. 21, 1876, p. 402.

65. *Ibid.*, Jan. 13, 1877, p. 431.

66. *Ibid.*, (in German), Sept. 21, 1876, p. 354.

67. *Ibid.*, July 25, 1876, p. 291.

68. Copy Book 4, July 31 and Nov. 18, 1878, pp. 74, 164.

69. Copy Book 3, April 6, 1878, p. 948.

70. Copy Book 4, July 31, 1878, p. 74.

71. Copy Book 5, Feb. 16, 1880, p. 229.

72. Copy Book 3, Dec. 16, 1876, p. 413.

73. Copy Book 5, Nov. 1, 1879, p. 83. It is perhaps noteworthy that Ilfeld stated in 1877 that he had no connection with the A. T. & S. F. R. R. Copy Book 3, Feb. 23, 1877, p. 484.

74. Copy Book 5, Feb. 23, 1880, p. 206.

75. Copy Book 1, Nov. 22, 1870, p. 405, and May 29, 1872, p. 710; Copy Book 3, March 30, 1876, p. 197.

76. Copy Book 5, May 14, 1880, p. 341; Copy Book 7, Feb. 27, 1882, p. 11.

77. Copy Book 12, Feb. 1885, p. 286.

78. Copy Book 13, Dec. 21, 1885, p. 533; Feb. 26, 1886, p. 661.

79. This section declared that it shall be unjust discrimination and unlawful for a common carrier to charge, by any device, a greater or a lesser amount of one person than of another for like contemporaneous services in the transportation of either pas-

sengers or property. Locklin writes that even the Hepburn Act of 1906, which contained a specific provision designed to stop this practice, was not wholly successful. D. Philip Locklin, *Economics of Transportation* (3d ed.; Homewood, Ill., 1947), p. 487.

80. Copy Book 18, July 25, 1890, p. 365. For the usage of "Dennis," see Eric Partridge, *Dictionary of Slang and Unconventional English* (2d ed.; New York, 1938), p. 214; and *The Encyclopedia Americana* (1950), vol. 8, p. 686. It was an insulting or derisive nautical catch phrase of the late 19th century. Name may have been associated with Dennis the hangman of Charles Dickens' *Barnaby Rudge*, 1841, or with John Dennis (1657–1734), the "best abused man in English literature."

81. One such request for his wife, children, and himself was to El Paso by way of Santa Fe, Albuquerque, and Silver City. Copy Book 24, Dec. 8, 1892, p. 433.

82. *Interstate Commerce Commission Reports,* vol. 26, p. 493. (Henceforth cited as 26 ICC.)

83. Special Copy Book, March (?) 1897, p. 48. The "Frisco" was the St. Louis and San Francisco Railway Company (formerly the Atlantic and Pacific). William S. Grewer, "Railway Development in the Southwest," *New Mexico Historical Review,* 32:154 (April 1957).

84. Copy Book 42, May 12, 1897, p. 692.

85. Copy Book 44, Aug. 6, 1897, p. 15.

86. Incoming Correspondence, Packet 38, Feb. 1, 1897.

87. 26 ICC, p. 498. As noted by the Commission, the same conditions existed in Wyoming and Utah. In Utah, practically all the railroads in the state were members of the Utah Pass Committee, which screened all applications for passes. Therefore, the names of all recipients were known to the railroads. In 1913 this Committee agreed to stop the issuance of passes "but within a week . . . some of the Utah lines, yielding to pressure, returned to the practice in effect before the Committee was formed. . . ." *Ibid.,* pp. 503–504.

88. *Ibid.,* p. 496.

CHAPTER VII

Some Early Policy Decisions of Charles Ilfeld

1. For a general discussion of the influence of environment on businessmen, see Robert V. Eagly, "American Capitalism: A Transformation?" *Business History Review,* 33:549–568 (Winter 1959).

2. See Chapter II.

3. Erret Van Cleave, "Credit on the Santa Fe Trail," *Credit and Financial Management,* 41:17 (Oct. 1939), tells the following story:

A salesman from an eastern hardware company called on a native store in Taos but failed to make a sale. Juan, the owner, repeated many times: "Me friend Mr. Ilfeld, me buy of him."

"I have the same axes and the same prices as Mr. Ilfeld. I want the order," pressed the salesman.

"No, me buy Senor Ilfeld."

"What in h—— did Mr. Ilfeld ever do to make you such a friend?"

"A long time ago," replied Juan, "me sold me sheeps, me had four thousand of dollars, me afraid of banks, me afraid me neighbors steals me money, me no sabe what to do, me thinks a long times, me takes the money to Mr. Ilfeld and he keeps it for me, he keeps it long times, maybe ten years and no charge me a cent."

4. Interview, Rodney B. Schoonmaker, Aug. 21, 1947.

5. Copy Book 3, Jan. 17, 1877, p. 434. His Notes Payable Book shows many commitments "endorsed for ——'s benefit."

6. Copy Book 3, Oct. 23, 1875, p. 84.

7. See Chapter II.

8. Chester W. Wright, *Wool Growing and the Tariff,* pp. 214, 209.

9. Washed Ohio fleece wool, per pound, in eastern markets, July 1, medium grade:

1865	73¢	1873	48¢
1866	67¢	1874	53¢
1867	49¢	1875	49¢
1868	45¢	1876	35¢
1869	48¢	1877	44¢
1870	45¢	1878	36¢
1871	60¢	1879	38¢
1872	70¢	1880	48¢

Statistical Abstract of the U. S. (Washington, D. C., 1913), p. 676.

10. Copy Book 2, May 27, 1875, p. 571; Copy Book 3, Sept. 20, 1876, p. 352.

11. Copy Book 6, April 9, 1881, p. 160.

12. Copy Book 2, Nov. 19, 1873, p. 186. Watrous was furnishing Ilfeld with lumber for a railroad contract in 1882. Copy Book 6, Jan. 31, 1882, p. 648. Ilfeld and Kronig Ice Company was formed about this time. Ledger G, p. 494.

13. Copy Book 2, Aug. 17, 1874, p. 343.

14. Copy Book 6, Jan. 20, 1882, p. 631.

15. *Ibid.,* Jan. 19, 1882, p. 630.

16. Otero, *My Life on the Frontier,* I, 235.

17. The first evidence of deposit banking by Ilfeld is recorded in Copy Book 4, Aug. 4, 1879, p. 613: "This is to certify that J. M. Talbot has deposited with me the sum of five hundred and no/100 dollars ($500.00) which will be paid on the presentation of this certificate properly endorsed." No further evidence appears until Copy Book 6, May 18, 1881, p. 225, when Ilfeld mailed Don Pablo Baca a "pass book posted to April 30, 1881." One would assume from the wording of these examples that no interest was paid on the former, but that it was on the latter.

18. Copy Book 5, Dec. 19, 1879, p. 161.

19. Cleland was born in Canada in 1856. He came to the United States at the age of 17, spent 4 years in Detroit, and arrived in New Mexico in 1877. Copy Book 6, June 15, 1881, p. 273. He joined the Charles Ilfeld Company in Sept., 1878, and left in Nov., 1881. Ledger G, p. 160; Ledger E, p. 132.

20. Ledger G, p. 160.

21. *Ibid.,* p. 71. Frank had received $20 per month in 1873 as clerk in a Las Vegas store. Ledger B, pp. 188, 215.

22. *Las Vegas Gazette,* April 28, 1877, Aug. 10, 1879, Nov. 7, 1879; Ledger E, p. 298.

23. Public school teachers of San Miguel County were raised in Oct., 1882, to a salary of $40 per month plus $5 per month rent allowance. Some of the outlying areas paid $30 plus $5 per month rent allowance. *Las Vegas Gazette,* Oct. 25, 1882.

24. Interview, Rodney B. Schoonmaker, Aug. 21, 1947.

25. The 14 other merchants were: T. Romero & Bros.; Richard Dunn; May Hays; Dold & Ellsworth; Charles Emil Wesche; W. A. Clark; J. Rosenwald & Co.; Isadore Stern; Samuel Kohn; Frank Chapman; Charles Blanchard; Geoffrion & Desmarais; Benigno Romero; and F. Knauer. *Las Vegas Gazette,* Sept. 12, 1874.

26. Cash Book, 1876–1877.

27. Gras, *Business and Capitalism,* p. 163.

28. For a development of this point of view, see William J. Parish, "The Spiritual Significance of the Economic Value of Man," *New Mexico Quarterly,* 21:261–273 (Autumn 1951).

29. See "Emphasis on Retailing" in this chapter.

30. Journal, 1882–1884, p. 19; Ledger G, p. 232.

31. Journal, 1882–1884, pp. 319, 473; Ledger H, p. 491.

32. Journal, 1882–1884, p. 245; Ledger H, p. 315.

33. Ledger H, pp. 510, 512.

34. Sol Floersheim, John Prenman, I. Holzman, Rodney Schoonmaker, and Robert Lotz.

35. Journal, 1882–1884, p. 353; Ledger G, p. 270. Delgado was subsequently reduced to $50. Ledger I.

36. W. T. Baxter, *House of Hancock,* pp. 17–21.
37. Ledger B, pp. 194, 233.
38. Copy Book 2, Nov. 1, 1873, p. 167; Ledger B, p. 42.
39. Copy Book 2, Nov. 1, 1873, p. 167.
40. *Ibid.,* Dec. 8, 1873, p. 209; Ledger B, pp. 42, 232.
41. Copy Book 2, June 16, 1874, pp. 300, 301.
42. Copy Book 4, Jan. 4, 1879, p. 256.
43. Ledger B, p. 33.
44. *Ibid.,* p. 64; Journal, 1870–1873, pp. 61, 79, 96, 217, 287, 392, 457, 540.
45. Interview, Rodney B. Schoonmaker, Aug. 21, 1947.
46. Van Cleave expresses the thought this way: "Mr. Ilfeld the salesman, Mr. Nordhaus the executive." Van Cleave, "Credit on the Santa Fe Trail," p. 16.
47. Gras, *Business and Capitalism,* pp. 74–81.
48. Italics inserted by author. *Ibid.,* p. 75.
49. Journal, 1882–1884, pp. 127, 128, 158, 356, 596; Ledger G, p. 372.
50. These terms to Brunswick were granted infrequently and only on small purchases. Journal, 1882–1884, pp. 246, 254, 596, 599, 603. The *Las Vegas Gazette* dates Brunswick's movements in part. He became a partner in a mercantile film with Eugenio Romero, Feb. 5, 1873. On May 29, 1875, he is described as a "former partner." On Sept. 18, 1875, he and Trinidad Romero were supplying sheep to Fort Sill, Oklahoma. On March 25, 1876, he had bought the merchandise stock of Trinidad Romero. Before Dec. 30, 1877, he had become a partner in the mercantile firm of Trinidad Romero and Brothers, which was dissolved on that date. On June 1, 1878, Brunswick leased the Grzelachowski and Dunn store located next to Ilfeld on the Plaza. By April 6, 1880, he was prospecting with F. O. Kihlberg and on May 25, 1880, he is recorded as having a general merchandise store in Lincoln, New Mexico. (Some of his cash books are in the Charles Ilfeld Collection.) By Aug. 28, 1880, he had a gold mine in the Homestake at White Oaks, New Mexico. On Feb. 15, 1881, he sold his inventory of merchandise to Trinidad Romero. On Nov. 11, 1881, Brunswick was advertising for freighters for his Fort Stanton contract (see Chapter VI). On Nov. 26, 1882, he was off with Charles Ilfeld to the coal mines of the Gallinas Mountains. Interspersed with these business dealings, Brunswick made frequent trips to the East.
51. *Las Vegas Gazette,* April 4, 1874; June 22, 1881.
52. *Ibid.,* April 4, 1874 (advertisement). The La Junta property was rented to S. E. Tipton. Copy Book 8, March 12, 14, July 13, 1883, pp. 329, 332, 615; Copy Book 9, Sept. 25, 1883, p. 172.
53. *Las Vegas Gazette,* Sept. 29, 1883.
54. Copy Book 8, Jan. 13, 1883, p. 201.
55. Terms were $15 per month. Journal, 1882–1884, p. 371.
56. Interviews, Rodney B. Schoonmaker and Carl Wertz, Aug. 21 and 23, 1947; and C. S. Brown, June 15, 1949.
57. *N.M. & S.P. R.R.* v. *John Dougher,* Docket No. 1009, 1881, San Miguel County Records; also *Las Vegas Gazette,* March 18, 1881. The railroad claimed the depot was to be not more than one mile from the Plaza in Las Vegas and just south of the Presbyterian Church of Las Vegas.
58. *Las Vegas Gazette,* Jan. 11, 1880, gives Rule 7 of Committee drafting disposition of unoccupied lands of Las Vegas Grandes: "The said Committee shall be and is hereby authorized to donate and concede to the constructors of Railways, such unoccupied lands of the aforementioned Grant as shall be necessary for the tract; provided that the Railroad shall pass through lower town of Las Vegas or in its proximity and that the depot shall be erected in the close vicinity of the town."
59. Copy Book 5, Aug. 14, 1880, p. 453. In a letter of Dec. 30, 1880 (p. 657), what appears to be the same note, perhaps two notes, is given as $750.
60. Copy Book 4, Nov. 20, 1878, p. 175. Albert Alonzo Robinson was chief engineer of the Atchison, Topeka & Santa Fe railway system.
61. Copy Book 5, Aug. 14, 1880, p. 453.
62. *Las Vegas Gazette,* Aug. 2, 1879.

63. *Ibid.*, April 18, 1882.

64. E. L. Moulton, when he was president of the Charles Ilfeld Company, stated that a recent study showed that 50 per cent of the man-hours employed in handling freight at Las Vegas could be saved if a warehouse were on the railroad track. Interview, E. L. Moulton, June 15, 1949.

65. This must have been quite a diversion for the employees. Schoonmaker, Carl Wertz, and Charles Brown, all old employees, each told the story with a good deal of relish.

66. Marshall gives the date as July 4, 1879. *Santa Fe,* p. 398.

67. Coan, *History of New Mexico,* I, 447.

68. *Ibid.*, p. 448; Marshall, *Santa Fe,* p. 420.

69. The extensions were the El Paso and Rock Island Railway to Santa Rosa, and the Chicago, Rock Island and El Paso Railway to Nara Visa near the New Mexico–Texas line. Coan, *History of New Mexico,* I, 448–449.

CHAPTER VIII

Charles Ilfeld and His Management Problem

1. These and all other references in this chapter to Charles Ilfeld as a personality have been synthesized from interviews with a number of people who knew him well.

2. See p. 29.

3. See pp. 55 and 57.

4. Solomon Beuthner was living in Watrous, New Mexico, in 1883 and died there in 1890. Incoming Correspondence, Packet 2, telegram from Solomon Beuthner, June 26, 1883; Copy Book 19, Dec. 16 and 29, 1890, pp. 515, 602.

5. Big and fun loving, Dunn came to Las Vegas from Nova Scotia via Maine and Tonganaxie, Kansas. He played comedy roles in the productions of the Las Vegas Dramatic Society and took part in local quartets. He became president of the Board of County Commissioners and chairman of the Democratic Executive Committee. *Las Vegas Gazette,* Aug. 8, 1874; Jan. 16, 1875; Feb. 12 and Nov. 4, 1876; March 16 and Nov. 16, 1878; Aug. 26, 1879; Sept. 25, 1880; May 3, 1882. Schoonmaker described Dunn as a "Maine Yankee, six feet tall, and well educated." Interview, Aug. 21, 1947.

6. Copy Book 3, April 17, 22, May 18, June 3, 6, July 7, 1876, pp. 211, 214–215, 236, 250, 251, 269; May 9, 1878, p. 985. Copy Book 4, June 22, 25, Oct. 12, Nov. 12, 18, 1878, pp. 39, 43, 147, 160, 163.

7. Copy Book 3, July 25, 1877, p. 659; Aug. 1, Oct. 9, 1877, pp. 671, 704.

8. Copy Book 4. See also page 87.

9. Copy Book 6, March 16, 19, May 29, 1881, pp. 1–6, 131, 243.

10. Copy Book 4, Feb. 1, 1879, p. 309. Dunn had been associated as a partner with Grzelachowski once before while managing the store of Grzelachowski and Dunn on the Las Vegas Plaza. He may have remained as a partner even though the Las Vegas store was closed prior to Dunn's sojourn with Ilfeld in 1879. Copy Book 3, May 6, 1878, p. 980; Copy Book 4, Feb. 14, 1879, p. 343. Letter to J. C. Lea, Roswell, New Mexico, states: "we are only 5 in the house and none of us can leave very well except it must be."

11. Copy Book 6, March 19 and 25, 1881, pp. 131, 145; Copy Book 5, Sept. 25, 1880. John Pendaries, of French extraction, was Dunn's father-in-law. This firm owned lumber mills and a small store. Interview, C. S. Brown, July 11, 1953; also Incoming Correspondence, Packet 1, letterhead, Feb. 12, 1883.

12. Copy Book 7, April 15, May 25, June 23, 1882, pp. 144, 185, 214.

13. See Chapter VII.

14. Colonel Brunswick dropped dead on the Plaza, Oct. 14, 1903, following a hearty meal at the Ilfeld residence. Interview, Louis C. Ilfeld, Aug. 22, 1947. He was buried in the Ilfeld plot, Masonic Cemetery, Las Vegas. His tombstone gives the date of his birth as 1829.

15. After Louis and Noa retired from merchandising (Herman had died), Charles

suggested a possible merger of his firm with Bernard Ilfeld's store in Albuquerque and the establishment of a third outlet in El Paso. Special Copy Book, May 14, 1904, pp. 244–245.

16. Nordhaus was born June 18, 1865. Circular letter sent out by Max Nordhaus on his 65th birthday, which he noted coincided with the 65th anniversary of the founding of the Charles Ilfeld Company. Collection of memorabilia in possession of L. C. Becker, president, First National Bank of Belen. Actually the founding of the firm of A. Letcher Company in Taos took place in Sept., 1865.

17. Letter from Louis C. Ilfeld, June 16, 1948.

18. Copy Book 8, April 21, 1883, p. 429.

19. *Las Vegas Gazette,* June 7, 1883; Copy Book 8, March 20, 1883, p. 348.

20. First day of employment is given as June 6, 1883. Letter from Max Nordhaus to Charles Ilfeld on the date of his 25th anniversary with the company, June 6, 1908. Louis C. Ilfeld files, Las Vegas.

21. See Chapter VII.

22. Ledger E., p. 132; Ledger G, p. 160.

23. Ledger G, p. 469.

24. First letter written July 25, 1884. Copy Book 11, p. 207. Letter from Rodney B. Schoonmaker, Nov. 13, 1947, sets the date at July 20, 1884.

25. Letter from Rodney B. Schoonmaker, March 27, 1950. In another letter, March 31, 1950, Schoonmaker states: "I was office manager, bookkeeper, cashier, and advertising man, preparing the newspaper ads and circulars for house to house distribution. The slogan of my contrivance was 'Ilfeld's—Everything.' "

26. Letter from Rodney B. Schoonmaker, March 27, 1950.

27. Interview, Rodney B. Schoonmaker, Aug. 21, 1947.

28. Solomon Floersheim was born in Hamburg, Germany, Oct. 5, 1856. He came to the United States in 1878 and spent a year in Trinidad, Colorado, before coming to New Mexico in 1879. Typewritten notes of Carl Floersheim, son of Solomon, received Oct. 19, 1953 [Ilfeld Collection]; Ledger G, pp. 276, 279 (balance shows carryover from lost Ledger F); Ledger H, p. 315; Ledger I, p. 166.

29. Interview, Ludwig Ilfeld, Sept. 3, 1952. Ludwig Ilfeld had to deal directly witth Floersheim in Springer, New Mexico, in 1897. A letter from Max Nordhaus to Ludwig, July 12, 1897, speaks in part: "I go a good deal on Mr. F's advice." Copy Book 43, p. 490. Later in the year Nordhaus wrote Charles Ilfeld: "I think it is a good thing for them [Appel Brothers] that F. opened there [Springer] as he draws a good deal of bus. from Wagon Mound and Clayton." Special Copy Book, Oct. 30, 1897, p. 116. Floersheim was often referred to as "Doctor."

30. Interview, Milton Floersheim, son of Solomon, Oct. 19, 1953.

31. Floersheim and Vorenberg of Watrous, New Mexico. First entry in Ledger I, March 10, 1888, p. 166. S. Floersheim, Proprietor, Ocate, New Mexico, Ledger I, Oct. 21, 1889. Floersheim bought the mercantile interest of Henry M. Porter of Springer, New Mexico, in 1897. Special Copy Book, Sept. 8, 1879, p. 87; also typewritten notes by Carl Floersheim, Oct. 19, 1953. The Floersheim Mercantile Company of Springer and later Roy, New Mexico, was founded Dec. 18, 1897. Floersheim Mercantile Company Minute Book, University of New Mexico Library.

32. Letter from Rodney B. Schoonmaker, Nov. 13, 1947.

33. Copy Book 10, beginning March 11, 1884, p. 125.

34. Copy Book 12, March 12, 17, 21, 1885, pp. 330, 342–343, 352.

35. Copy Book 13, July 9, 1885, p. 99.

36. *Inventory of County Archives,* San Miguel County, Book 26, p. 350.

37. Nordhaus-Ilfeld Agreement. Office of Louis C. Ilfeld, Las Vegas.

38. Louis C. Ilfeld once told the author that Max Nordhaus asked for a partnership arrangement in consequence of his marriage in 1907 and in fairness to the future interests of his family. Ilfeld is reputed to have asked Nordhaus what a fair division would be and Nordhaus, it is understood, suggested the one-fourth, three-fourths agreement.

39. Copy Book 45, Nov. 29, 1897, p. 487; Copy Book 48, May 24, 1898, p. 128.

40. Copy Book 16, Dec. 4, 1888, p. 630; Copy Book 25, Feb. 9, 1893, p. 15; Copy Book 40, Nov. 18, 1896, p. 100; Copy Book 77, Feb. 10, 1903, p. 290.

41. Copy Book 25, Feb. 9, 1893, p. 115.

42. Copy Book 40, Dec. 9, 1896, p. 329.

CHAPTER IX

Toward Sheep and Wool Specialization

1. Herbert E. Bolton, *Coronado: Knight of Pueblos and Plains,* p. 1.

2. *Ibid.,* p. 56; Francois Chevalier, *La Formacion des Grandes Domaines au Mexiques: Terre et Societe aux XVIe–XVIIe Siecles,* p. 103. "Soon after the Conquest, Cortés made importations from the Antilles of such domestic animals as did not exist in Mexico" (H. H. Bancroft, *History of Mexico, III, 1600–1803,* p. 615).

3. Chevalier, *La Formacion des Grandes Domaines,* p. 114.

4. *Ibid.,* p. 310. South of Guadalajara, Avalos' eastern boundary cut the western portion of Lake Chapala and its western boundary inside the coastal mountains at about the 104th meridian. Now part of the State of Jalisco. Carl Sauer, *Colima of New Spain in the Sixteenth Century,* Ibero-Americana, 29 (Berkeley and Los Angeles, 1948), p. 8.

5. Chevalier, *La Formacion des Grandes Domaines,* p. 135.

6. Bancroft, *History of Mexico,* III, 616.

7. Edward N. Wentworth, *America's Sheep Trails,* pp. 24–28.

8. *Ibid.,* p. 113.

9. *Ibid.,* pp. 114, 135; also Wright, *Wool Growing and the Tariff,* p. 113.

10. *Special Report on the History and Present Condition of the Sheep Industry in the United States,* H. R. Misc. Doc. 105, 52d Cong., 2d sess., p. 914.

11. *Ibid.,* p. 915.

12. Marshall, *Santa Fe,* p. 400.

13. Thos. D. Keleher began dealing in hides, pelts, and wool with the coming of the railroad to Albuquerque in 1880 and later became a wool commission merchant. Twitchell, *Leading Facts,* III, 13. Eisemann Bros., of Boston, St. Louis, and Albuquerque, appear in the Ilfeld records in 1888. Copy Book 16, Oct. 17, 1888, p. 441. Later specialists were Hamm and Edie and H. M. Hosick & Co., *Albuquerque City Directory,* 1896.

14. Wentworth, *America's Sheep Trails,* p. 312.

15. *Statistical Abstract of the United States* (1913), p. 676. U.S. Dept. of Agriculture, *Agricultural Statistics* (1952), pp. 382–383, 419.

16. Otero and Sellar became involved indirectly in 1880 by extending credit of $10,000 to M. A. Perea of Bernalillo, New Mexico, a large sheep grower. Lesser amounts had been extended to others. Collections became slow and in June or July, 1880, Otero, Sellar, Perea and Co. (a general merchandise firm in Bernalillo) was formed. The purpose, among others, seems to have been to bail out the extended interests of Otero and Sellar. Otero and Sellar Letter Book, 1875–1886, pp. 271, 272, 275, 276. The first merchant of any importance to specialize deliberately in livestock seems to have been the Bond Brothers in Espanola, who began business in 1882. They were not, however, in the classification of the established mercantile capitalists but were actually specialists who took on merchandise as a side line.

17. Warren M. Person, *Forecasting Business Cycles* (New York, 1931), pp. 90, 98, 119.

18. *Ibid.; Statistical Abstract,* 1913, p. 676.

19. *Agricultural Statistics,* p. 419; Wentworth, *America's Sheep Trails,* p. 363.

20. *Agricultural Statistics,* p. 419.

21. See Chapter IV.

22. Gross, Blackwell & Co., successors to Otero and Sellar, struggled through most of this period under the handicap of inadequate capital. Browne and Manzanares lost competitively to the larger firms of Charles Ilfeld; Gross, Blackwell; and E. Rosenwald & Sons. The last-named firm rivaled the other two until it failed in 1923. The old

Santa Fe firms of A. Staab, and Seligman Bros. apparently prospered, but Staab's firm closed upon his retirement in 1902, and Seligman Bros. was losing competitively probably even before the death of Bernard in 1903. The Albuquerque firms of Moore, Bennett; and Stover, McClure were absorbed by L. B. Putney, who failed, and Gross, Blackwell. Ilfeld Bros. turned to sheep and wool, and Grunsfeld Bros. never grew to any great size.

23. Copy Book 10, May 23, 1884, p. 452.

24. Elias Brevoort, author of *New Mexico: Her Natural Resources and Attractions* (Santa Fe, 1874). Copy Book 11, Oct. 4, 1884, p. 414.

25. Copy Book 14, May 5, 1886, p. 68.

26. Copy Book 16, July 25, 1888, p. 182; Oct. 22, 1888, p. 467.

27. Summary Book, 1886–1895. Cash had fallen from $45,523.15 in 1885 to $5488.84 in 1887 and in 1888 had risen to $9341.77 (all January 1 dates). Ledgers H and I.

28. Mr. Floersheim in his later years was wont to tell the story that "Mr. Ilfeld asked me to take a cut in salary to help him finance his family's trip to Germany." Interview, Milton Floersheim, Oct. 19, 1953. The probable truth in the matter was that Floersheim was too able a man to discharge and too independent a man to suit the needs and desires of Ilfeld.

29. Goldenberg's mother, Bertha, was a Nordhaus. Twitchell, *Leading Facts,* III, 490; *History of New Mexico,* II, 884; Copy Book 16, Aug. 3, 1888, p. 211, and Oct. 31, 1888, pp. 516–517. Max Goldenberg had worked for Ilfeld in a similar capacity in 1882 following the resignation, the first time, of Solomon Floersheim. *Las Vegas Gazette,* May 28 and June 8, 1882.

30. Copy Book 15, July 19, 1887, p. 150; Twitchell, *Leading Facts,* III, 490–492.

31. Goldenberg was the successor to Aaron Schutz (Ilfeld's temporary manager in 1877), who had started a general merchandise store in Las Cruces. Incoming Correspondence, Packet 1, Jan. 29, 1883, letterhead, and Feb. 15, 1883; Copy Book 12, May 31, 1885, p. 487; Copy Book 13, March 10, 1886, p. 684.

32. Interview, Sept. 5, 1951.

33. One of the marks of a good sheepman in these days was personal filth. They were men apart. The Range Wars of the 1870's and 1880's between the cattlemen and sheepmen were for the possession of grass, but the disdain with which the cowboy held the sheepherder was accentuated by personal differences. The sheepherder was almost entirely of Spanish-speaking origin and known as "Mexican." The Cowboy was "Anglo." The sheepherder was tagged as "personally filthy," and the cowboy had a reputation, at least, of knowing how to be clean.

34. Copy Book 13, Feb. 15 and March 10, 1886, pp. 643, 684; Copy Book 14, May 4, 1886, pp. 56–57; Copy Book 15, July 19, 1887, p. 150.

35. Copy Book 15, July 22, 1887, p. 161; Aug. 17, 1887, p. 204.

36. Copy Book 16, Aug. 3, 1888, p. 211.

37. *Ibid.,* Sept. 1, 1888, p. 292.

38. Copy Book 17, March 4, 1890, pp. 856–857.

39. Ledger I.

40. Copy Book 16, Sept. 28, 1888, p. 374.

41. Journal, 1893, p. 379.

42. Copy Book 18, May 28, 1890, p. 142; Copy Book 19, Feb. 24, 1891, p. 825.

43. Bills Payable Book, 1884–1913.

44. Copy Book 21, Dec. 7, 1891, p. 312.

45. Summary Book, 1886–1895.

46. Copy Book 17, March 25, 1890, p. 921; Copy Book 18, May 12, 1890, p. 73, and June 18, 1890, p. 216; Copy Book 19, Nov. 24, 1890, p. 376.

47. Copy Book 17, March 26, 1890, p. 917; Copy Book 18, July 7, 1890, p. 282.

48. Copy Book 18, May 7, 1890, p. 43. Scabies is a contagious skin disease of sheep caused by a parasitic mite. It was particularly prevalent among New Mexico flocks in the 1880's. U.S. Bureau of Animal Husbandry, *Special Report on the History of the Sheep Industry,* pp. 925–926; Copy Book 18, May 7, 1890, p. 43.

49. Copy Book 20, July 10, 1891, p. 405; Copy Book 22, May 26, 1892, p. 348.

50. Sheep are now sprayed with chemicals in much the same fashion that automobiles are washed as they pass through an automatic washing plant. The dipping vat has disappeared from the modern sheep ranch. Interview, Floyd Lee, owner and manager of the 250,000-acre Fernandez Company sheep and cattle ranch, San Mateo, New Mexico, Albuquerque, June 29, 1955.

51. Interview, Otto Hake, Frank Bond and Sons, Inc., June 25, 1955. In 1902, Solomon Floersheim had four large boilers in connection with his dipping vat, each holding 650 gallons of dip which kept the solution at temperatures of 105 to 110 degrees Fahrenheit. *American Shepherd's Bulletin,* 7:1702 (Feb. 1902).

52. Copy Book 20, July 13, 1891, p. 41. Floyd Lee suggests that the small vat may have been used only for the rams, which were often hand-dipped and treated with more care than the other sheep.

53. Solomon Floersheim's swimming vat, in which he dipped 2500 to 3000 sheep a day, was 80 feet long. *American Shepherd's Bulletin,* 7:1709 (Feb. 1902). The Chas. Chadwick Company of Albuquerque had a vat 100 feet long, 28 inches wide at the top, 10 inches wide at the bottom, and 5 feet deep. *Ibid.,* 11:354–356 (April 1906). The Roy Land and Livestock Company of Roy, New Mexico, had a vat 70 feet long in which its sheep were dipped three times per year. *Ibid.,* 11:816 (Sept. 1906). John Cole of Picacho, New Mexico, owned a public dipping station which was 40 feet long, 18 inches wide at the top, 6 inches wide at the bottom, and 6 feet deep. *Ibid.,* 12:69 (Jan. 1907). Public dipping stations were common in New Mexico.

54. *Ibid.,* 11:514 (June 1906); 12:69 (Jan. 1907).

55. Copy Book 33, May 24, 1895, p. 119; Copy Book 37, April 24, 1896, p. 410; Incoming Correspondence, Packet 11, July 24, 1893.

56. For one dipping operation Goldenberg ordered 1800 lbs. of sulphur, 900 lbs. of lime, and 3 dozen lye. Incoming Correspondence, Packet 24, March 11, 1895. Lime and sulphur was not the only dip solution used, though it was the most common. Other dips frequently used were nicotine mixtures, often spoken of as black leaf, and creosote preparations. Ilfeld, when he did not use plain lime and sulphur, used trade-name products which he also sold. These were Fernoline, from the Fernoline Sheep Dip Company of Charlestown, South Carolina; Cooper's Dip, from Messrs. Wm. Cooper & Nephews of Galveston, Texas; and a nonpoisonous fluid from Morris Little and Son of Brooklyn, New York, which he once claimed could be used in cold water if mixed with black-leaf preparations. At least one rancher used nicotine and sulphur. Lye was often mixed with nicotine.

57. Incoming Correspondence, Packet 24, March 7, 9, 11, 22, 1895.

58. Copy Book 39, Oct. 6, 1896, p. 378. Nordhaus kept his Vegoso gathering place stacked with firewood. At one time he ordered 18 cords to be delivered immediately "for insurance." Being in May, this could have been insurance either against a cold snap or against a large influx of sheep in need of dipping. Copy Book 34, May 14, 1895, p. 32.

59. Dr. Harry E. Kemper, New Mexico Sheep Sanitary Board, says the lime constricts the fibre at skin point. Leopold Meyer, whose livestock company in Albuquerque was the outgrowth of the Ilfeld Brothers' interests, reports that nicotine washes tend to darken the color of the wool and do not wash out well. Telephone conversations, June 24, 1955.

60. Copy Book 17, March 26, 1890, p. 917; Copy Book 18, July 8, 1890, p. 293.

61. Arroyo Seco was a ranching center nine miles north of Taos. Copy Book 19, Nov. 22, 1890, p. 372.

62. Copy Book 21, Feb. 9, 1892, p. 656.

63. *Ibid.* See also Nov. 19, 1891, p. 178.

64. Copy Book 24, Jan. 11, 1893, p. 620.

65. Copy Book 19, Feb. 9, 1891, p. 778.

66. *Ibid.,* Feb. 8, 1891, p. 775.

67. *Ibid.,* March 2, 1891, p. 845.

68. Copy Book 20, June 29, 1891, pp. 352, 353.

69. Copy Book 20, Aug. 17, 1891, p. 650, and Sept. 15, 1891, p. 669.

70. *Ibid.*, Sept. 13, 1891, p. 734.
71. Twitchell, *Leading Facts*, IV, 474. Louis Baer was a first cousin of Albert Eisemann. Letter from Sidney A. Eisemann, Oct. 28, 1957.
72. Copy Book 21, Oct. 30, 1891, p. 25.
73. Probably only a loss in the sense of not gaining all the revenue expected.
74. Copy Book 21, Nov. 16, 1891, pp. 146–148.
75. Copy Book 19, March 7, 1891, p. 859; Copy Book 20, June 13, 1891, p. 271, and July 29, 1891, p. 514; Copy Book 21, Nov. 16, 1891, pp. 146–148.
76. Copy Book 22, May 11, 1892, p. 193.
77. The "Old Observer," traveling reporter for a national sheep magazine, interviewed Max Goldenberg in 1906 and wrote of these and other drives by "Swift and of Seltenridge and Pebbles." *American Shepherd's Bulletin,* 11:707 (Aug. 1906).
78. At this time Ilfeld was keeping most of his sheep on the Tramperos Creek in northeastern New Mexico where he had acquired several claims next to the Lujan and Pinard property. These claims were obtained from Andres Sena in part payment of heavy debts owed Ilfeld and they were leased in turn to Lujan and Pinard. In later years these lands appear to have been owned by Adolph Letcher and leased to Lujan and Pinard. Copy Book 14, July 31, 1886, pp. 275, 992–994. Copy Book 55, Aug. 26, 1899, p. 232.
79. Copy Book 20, July 29, 1891, p. 514.
80. *Special Report on the History of the Sheep Industry*, p. 924.
81. Copy Book 20, July 6, 1891, p. 382.
82. Winifred Kupper, *The Golden Hoof*, pp. 31–32, 41–43.
83. Copy Book 19, Feb. 14, 1891, p. 801.
84. Copy Book 18, June 27, 1890, p. 250.
85. Copy Book 20, Aug. 1891, p. 551.
86. *Ibid.*, Sept. 26, 1891, p. 851.
87. Copy Book 23, July 18, 1892, p. 130; July 27, 1892, pp. 193 and 209.
88. *Ibid.*, Aug. 1, 1892, pp. 246–247.
89. Two media were referred to in the records: Denver Field and Farm, and Daily Stockman. Copy Book 22, May 5, 1892, p. 158, and May 18, 1892, p. 289. Copy Book 23, July 22, 1892, p. 156; Aug. 5, 1892, p. 280.
90. *Ibid.*, Aug. 30, 1892, p. 447, and Aug. 31, 1892, p. 459.
91. *Ibid.*, Sept. 23, 1892, p. 578.
92. *Ibid.*, Sept. 2, 1892, p. 464.
93. Copy Book 24, Nov. 23, 1892, p. 305.
94. Copy Book 23, Aug. 1, 1892, pp. 246–247.
95. Summary Book, 1886–1895.
96. Copy Book 23, 1892, p. 428.
97. U.S. Dept. of Agriculture, *Agricultural Statistics for 1890's* (1892).
98. The actual receivables figure is not available but the decrease is assumed in view of higher cash collections than credit sales. Record Book, 1886–1895.
99. Copy Book 25, Jan. 26, 1893, pp. 5–7; March 17, 1893, p. 385.
100. *Ibid.*, Feb. 9, 1893, p. 115.
101. *Ibid.*, Feb. 15, 1893, p. 175.
102. *Ibid.*, Feb. 24, 1893, p. 224.
103. *Ibid.*, Feb. 28, 1893, p. 238.
104. *Ibid.*, March 10, 1893, pp. 329 and 330.
105. *Ibid.*, March 11, 1893, p. 342; March 13, 1893, p. 360.
106. *Ibid.*, Feb. 17, 1893, p. 177.
107. Copy Book 26, June 7, 1893, p. 250; July 5, 1893, p. 468.
108. *Ibid.*, July 8, 1893, p. 495; July 13, 1893, p. 516.
109. *Ibid.*, July 7, 1893, p. 482.
110. Copy Book 27, Aug. 19, 1893, p. 63.
111. *Ibid.*, Aug. 23, 1893, p. 86.
112. *Ibid.*, Aug. 26, 1893, p. 108; Aug. 23, 1893, p. 86.
113. *Ibid.*, Aug. 31, 1893, p. 139.

114. *Ibid.*, Aug. 29, 1893, p. 127.
115. *Ibid.*, Aug. 30, 1893, p. 137.
116. *Ibid.*, Aug. 31, 1893, p. 139.
117. *Ibid.*, Aug. 30, 1893, p. 138.
118. *Ibid.*, Aug. 31, 1893, p. 143.
119. *Ibid.*, Sept. 1, 1893, p. 152.
120. Copy Book 25, March 18, 1893, p. 401. The asking price in Folsom was 2½¢ per pound, cash; 2¾¢ per pound, time. Copy Book 27, Aug. 20, 1893, p. 68.
121. *Ibid.*, Sept. 6, 1893, p. 181; Oct. 2, 1893, p. 320.
122. *Ibid.*, Oct. 11, 1893, p. 368.
123. *Ibid.*, Sept. 15, 1893, p. 236.
124. Various weights of sheep were given as follows: 70 to 76 pounds in July for yearlings; 85 to 100 pounds for large wethers. Copy Book 26, July 3, 1893, p. 455. Sixty-five to 75 pounds in late August for yearlings; 85 to 95 for large wethers. Copy Book 27, Sept. 1, 1893, p. 152. In the latter letter, lambs were quoted as 40 to 45 pounds.
125. Copy Book 27, Dec. 16, 1893, p. 768.
126. Ledger K, p. 782.
127. Record Book, 1886–1895.
128. The total amount of borrowings is unknown, but his Bills Payable Journal shows 24 notes of from $2000 to $5000 each. A few of these may represent duplications.
129. Copy Book 28, April 26, 1894, p. 534.
130. Copy Book 31, Nov. 10, 1894, p. 177.
131. Copy Book 33, May 4, 1895, p. 428; May 9, 1895, p. 469; Copy Book 34, July 24, 1895, pp. 532, 547.
132. Copy Book 34, Aug. 7, 1895, p. 638. Copy Book 35, Aug. 28, 1895, p. 56; Aug. 31, 1895, p. 86.
133. *Ibid.*, Aug. 23, 1895, p. 42; Sept. 6, 1895, pp. 106, 109, and 113. According to the traveling reporter of the *American Shepherd's Bulletin,* Goldenberg used one mounted employee for each 1,000 head of sheep. *American Shepherd's Bulletin,* 11:707 (Aug. 1906).
134. Copy Book 35, Sept. 6, 1895, p. 111.
135. *Ibid.*, Sept. 28, 1895, p. 298; Oct. 18, 1895, p. 462.
136. *Ibid.*, Oct. 28, 1895, p. 536.
137. *Ibid.*, Oct. 22, 1895, p. 491.
138. *Ibid.*
139. *Ibid.*, Oct. 28, 1895, p. 524.
140. *Ibid.*, p. 536.
141. Cash Book, 1895–96, pp. 358, 362.
142. Ledger L., p. 87.
143. Journal, 1895–96, pp. 339, 347, 385.
144. Ledger L, p. 101. Copy Book 35, Nov. 25, 1895, p. 782.
145. Ledger L, p. 87. S. M. Newton, purchaser of Ilfeld sheep, ranched in the area of Ogden, Kansas.
146. Copy Book 37, March 9, 1896, p. 14.
147. Copy Book 35, Dec. 14, 1895, p. 966.
148. *Ibid.*, Nov. 28, 1895, p. 799. Copy Book 36, Jan. 6, 1896, p. 205.
149. *Ibid.*, Jan. 13, 1896, p. 249. Apparently Goldenberg's letter to Nordhaus, to which this was an answer, was the one Chas. S. Brown, at that time clerk in the store, remembers reading over Nordhaus' shoulder. Nordhaus turned to Brown and said: "This has been read once. That is enough." Interview, C. S. Brown, July 11, 1953.
150. Copy Book 36, Jan. 1, 1896, p. 157; Jan. 2, 1896, p. 160; and Jan. 7, 1896, p. 206. Incoming Correspondence, Packet 27, Feb. 13, 1896, from A.T. & S.F. R.R.
151. Copy Book 36, Jan. 3, 1896, pp. 172 and 176; Jan. 4, 1896, p. 198. Incoming Correspondence, Packet 27, Jan. 14, 1896, from J. J. Brophy.
152. Copy Book 36, Jan. 27, 1896, p. 380.
153. *Ibid.*, Feb. 12, 1896, p. 513.

154. Cash Book, 1895–96, pp. 450, 458, and 462. Clay Robinson and Co., livestock commission company, sold 2 carloads plus 262 sheep. Incoming Correspondence, Packet 28, March 26 and April 11, 1896.

155. Copy Book 37, March 31, 1896, p. 196.

156. Cash Book, 1895–96; Copy Book 37, May 12, 1896, p. 577.

157. Ledger L, pp. 82–87.

158. Record Book, 1895–1909. Wool purchases, not all representing collections on account, amounted to $87,546. *Ibid.*, sundry exhibits.

CHAPTER X

The Wool Trade

1. Only one contract, and that for 1,000 pounds, appears in the records of this period. Copy Book 1, Oct. 14, 1872, p. 788. Copy Book 2, Feb. 26, 1874, p. 253.

2. Copy Book 2, July 15, 1874, pp. 329–330.

3. See above, Chapter VII.

4. *Statistical Abstract,* p. 676.

5. Copy Book 2, Sept. 6 and 15, 1873, pp. 132, 138.

6. *Statistical Abstract,* p. 676.

7. See above, Chapter VI.

8. Copy Book 3, June 11, 1877, p. 611.

9. See above, Chapter IV.

10. *Statistical Abstract,* p. 676.

11. Copy Book 7, March 8, 1882, p. 40.

12. See above, Chapter IX.

13. Between 1888 and 1903 the following members of the family appear in the records: Virginio, Guadalupe, Leandro, Manuel, Teodoro, Juan, Carlos, Catarino, Perfecto, and Teodorito. Letter from Wm. H. Stapp, Las Vegas, Aug. 14, 1952.

14. Copy Book 77, Feb. 25, 1903, p. 475.

15. Copy Book 16, Sept. 26, 1888, p. 372a.

16. Copy Book 17, Aug. 7, 1889, p. 244.

17. A situation repeated generally by wool merchants. The U. S. Tariff Commission notes: "Consignment years have been 1900, 1903, 1908, 1910 and 1920 . . . all because of weakness in price." *The Wool Growing Industry* (Washington, 1921), pp. 232–233.

18. Copy Book 27, Dec. 18, 1893, p. 771.

19. Copy Book 44, Oct. 7, 1897, p. 615. Gross, Kelly Company made a general practice of consigning its wool from 1896 to 1899. Gross, Kelly Company, *Wool Book, 1896–1899,* Library of the University of New Mexico, Albuquerque.

20. Worthington C. Ford, *Wool and Manufacturers of Wool,* pp. 17, 38–41.

21. *Ibid.*, p. 318.

22. Wright, "Wool Growing and the Tariff," p. 311.

23. Copy Book 27, Nov. 21, 1893, p. 605.

24. Copy Book 48, July 22, 1898, p. 678. Rent was paid to Mrs. L. G. Kihlberg at the rate of $15.00 per month to June 1, 1894; $7.50 to March 1, 1896; $10.00 thereafter.

25. Floyd Lee writes: "It is claimed by our native people, and I think is correct, that Alfalfa was first grown in New Mexico within boundaries of what is now Fernandez Ranch (San Mateo). When the Spanish settlers first came to San Mateo, a village law was enacted requiring that the craw of each wild goose must be saved and the seed therefrom extracted and planted. Thus a strain of alfalfa appeared on the little farms. The people did not know what it was but concluded it to be a form of spinach or greens, and they ate it as such for years." Floyd W. Lee, *Bartalome Fernandez, Pioneer Shepherd of the Hills—in New Mexico.* Copy Book 27, Oct. 26, 1893, p. 459.

26. Copy Book 36, Jan. 8, 1896, p. 224.

27. Copy Book 14, March 19, 1887, p. 869; Copy Book 15, June 11, 1887, p. 87.

28. Copy Book 39, Sept. 9, 1896, p. 140; Copy Book 81, June 20, 1903, p. 32.

29. Copy Book 17, April 7, 1890, p. 951.
30. Copy Book 37, April 10, 1896, p. 254.
31. Copy Book 15, June 11, 1887, p. 87.
32. Copy Book 18, June 19, 1890, p. 224.
33. Copy Book 19, Oct. 15, 1890, p. 168. Ford, *Wool and Manufacturers of Wool*, pp. 62–84. Philadelphia prices on New Mexico wool rose from 18¢ to 22¢ on improved wools, and 16¢ to 20¢ on coarse.
34. Copy Book 28, Feb. 12, 1894, p. 122.
35. Copy Book 34, July 13, 1895, p. 455.
36. Copy Book 18, June 19, 1890, p. 224.
37. Copy Book 24, Dec. 12, 1892, p. 458; Copy Book 32, Dec. 28, 1894, p. 40. This 100,000 lbs. was the largest inventory figure mentioned in any of the records for these years.
38. Copy Book 42, March 6, 1897, p. 62.
39. Four sizes of bags were ordered by Ilfeld in 1891: 58 in., 8 oz. material, 4 bu. capacity; 40 in., 8 oz., 2 bu. capacity; 7 ft., 9½ oz.; and 7½ ft., 9 oz. Copy Book 20, June 9, 1891, p. 246; Aug. 26, 1891, p. 710.
40. Interview, C. S. Brown, March 23, 1954. Average size about 200 lbs. until 1901, thereafter it rose to about 250 lbs. See Appendix 11. Copy Book 19, Nov. 12, 1890, p. 329.
41. Copy Book 29, July 21, 1894, p. 454; Copy Book 30, Aug. 8, 1894, p. 71. Charles Ilfeld thus gained, with sacks at 25¢, weighing approximately 3 lbs., when wool was sold at a price in excess of 8⅓¢ per lb.
42. In 1902 it was newsworthy that the Roswell Wool, Hide and Pelt Company advocated tying of wool by fleeces. *American Shepherd's Bulletin,* 7:3, 169 (Dec. 1902). An editorial in the next issue stated: "New Mexico fleeces which come to this market are not tied. . . . Individual fleeces mat into each other . . . inferior . . . work into the better. [It takes] twice the amount of . . . time in grading New Mexican wools." *American Shepherd's Bulletin,* 8:403 (March 1903).
43. Copy Book 32, Jan. 21, 1895, p. 213. One observation on this practice: "It is more practicable to sort at market centers where midway grades can be thrown into lower or higher grades according to market trend at the time." U. S. Tariff Commission, *The Wool Growing Industry,* p. 229.
44. One Las Vegas wool scourer in complaining about the failure of suppliers to separate wools by quality or grade, is quoted: "The first few layers generally look well." *American Shepherd's Bulletin,* 8:623 (April 1903).
45. Louis A. McRae (interview, July 20, 1955) says that Indian wools almost always were scoured rather than shipped in the dirty state because of the fear of such practices. When Boston wool buyers would ask: "Where did the wool come from?" The seller would sometimes reply: "Where do you want it to come from? Below the shelf or above?" Below the shelf meant below the mesa and south of Cabra Springs and Anton Chico, where it was dustier; as a result, the shrinkage of wool would be greater. Interview, Otto Hake, June 25, 1955.
46. Most of the materials on wool handling have been obtained from miscellaneous notations in the records and from interviews. Those who have contributed a great deal are: Earl L. Moulton, Louis A. McRae, Sr., Leopold Meyer, and Charles S. Brown—all of Albuquerque.
47. Wright, "Wool Growing and the Tariff," p. 226. In writing of the varieties in wools, Wright lists the following qualities: fineness, elasticity, length and strength of fibre, working quality, and shrinkage. Each separate fleece may be sorted into six or eight different grades.
48. Ford, *Wool and Manufacturers of Wool,* pp. 44–48.
49. In 1896 North was selected to be editor of the *Quarterly Bulletin of the National Wool Growers Association.* He had been secretary of the National Wool Manufacturers Association. *Quarterly Bulletin of the National Wool Growers Association,* Washington, D. C., 1:3 (July, 1896). Ford, *Wool and Manufacturers of Wool,* pp. 49–50.
50. Copy Book 16, Nov. 1, 1888, p. 518.

51. Copy Book 18, May 17, 1890, p. 88.

52. Copy Book 22, June 18, 1892, p. 550. The traveling staff correspondent of the *American Shepherd's Bulletin,* writing from New Mexico in 1906, estimated the average shrinkage at 60–70 per cent. *American Shepherd's Bulletin,* 11:331 (April 1906).

53. Incoming Correspondence, Packet 43, March 10, 1897, Keyser Fisler Co.

54. The term "grease" is applied to the raw wool in its oily and dirty state. Actually the weight given for the scoured wool was 62,729 pounds; if correct, this would have meant a shrinkage of 81 per cent. This was, apparently, part of a 1911 inventory.

55. Copy Book 79, April 25, 1903, p. 442. Copy Book 78, March 21, 1903, p. 401. Copy Book 83, Oct. 5, 1903, pp. 518–519.

56. Interview, Hugh Loudon, July 21, 1955. Loudon was born in Scotland on Jan. 3, 1858, and came to Las Vegas, New Mexico, in 1882 as confidential clerk of the Scottish Land Mortgage Company. He remembers George Ludeman as an Australian who came to New Mexico via San Francisco and who had previously a good deal of wool experience.

57. *First Annual Directory of Las Vegas,* (J. A. Carruth, Printer, 1895; Highlands University Library, Las Vegas, New Mexico). In 1896, Ilfeld had 16,592 lbs. of scoured wool on hand from John Robbins. Sundry Exhibits, Record Book, 1896–1909.

58. The two mills in Trinidad were the Primrose and Forbes Scouring Mills. Copy Book 35, Sept. 27, 1895, p. 306; Nov. 13, 1895, p. 665.

59. The stench from the Ludeman plant was the source of newspaper comment. *Las Vegas Optic,* Aug. 23, 1899.

60. Gross, Kelly Company Wool Book. The Forbes Wool Company of Trinidad, Colorado, charged 1¼¢ per pound. This company would absorb incoming freight from Clayton, New Mexico, scour the wool, and deliver the scoured wool to any eastern point for a total charge of $3.65 per 100 pounds of grease wool. This would include also any selling commission. This, Forbes claimed, was 15¢ under the individual charges Ilfeld would have had to pay. Incoming Correspondence, Packet 35, Nov. 19, 1896.

61. Scoured wool freight rate from Las Vegas to Boston in 1906 was quoted as $3.07 per 100 pounds where as wool in the grease was given as $1.87½. *American Shepherd's Bulletin,* 11:432 (May 1906). The comparable rates from Albuquerque to Boston were $3.25 and $1.88. *American Shepherd's Bulletin,* 11:333 (April 1906). Las Vegas, which had been a much larger market for wool than Albuquerque, was given a more favorable rate on scoured wools.

62. *American Shepherd's Bulletin,* 7:1707 (Feb. 1902). Reference is made to "four or five scouring mills in Las Vegas and a new one being erected."

George Arnot, a young Scotsman, had been employed as a clerk by Gross, Blackwell (Kelly) Company but he gained a good knowledge of the wool scouring business from George Ludeman (a fairly old man at that time) for whom he had done some bookkeeping work. Telephone conversation, Charles S. Brown, July 19, 1955. *Las Vegas Optic* (Aug. 23, 1899, Jan. 11, 1900) connects Arnot with the Ludeman mill in 1899 and mentions him as manager in 1900.

63. *American Shepherd's Bulletin,* 11:347 (April 1906). The Wilkinson mill was listed in the *Albuquerque City Directory* for 1897.

64. Minute Book of the Albuquerque Wool Scouring Mill, University of New Mexico Library. J. H. Bearrup, president, and V. P. Edie, formerly a partner in Hamm & Edie, wool dealers, secretary-treasurer; Wilkinson carried the title of vice-president and general manager (*Albuquerque City Directory and Business Guide, 1901*). Bearrup left the firm in 1904 (Albuquerque Wool Scouring Minute Book), to found the Rio Grande Woolen Mills Company of Albuquerque, a cooperative, which manufactured blankets, dress goods, and men's fabrics and clothing (*American Shepherd's Bulletin,* 11:334 [April 1906]). (See Appendix 10.) The company was not in business in 1909 though Bearrup was listed as a resident of Albuquerque. The "Old Observer" of the *American Shepherd's Bulletin* thought a speech by Mr. Bearrup before the National Wool Growers Association on "Cooperation among Sheep Men" was "tinged with socialism" (*American Shepherd's Bulletin,* 12:167 [Feb. 1907]).

65. *American Shepherd's Bulletin,* 7:2666 (Aug. 1902). Mr. Louis A. McRae remembers that Ilfeld Brothers had Wilkinson scour a good deal of their wool.

66. *American Shepherd's Bulletin,* 6:79 (Jan. 1901), 9:1202 (Nov. 1904), 10:934 (Sept. 1905).

67. *Albuquerque City Directories.* Wilkinson left the Albuquerque firm in 1916. W. E. Rogers took over and, in 1922, the last year of operation, he is listed as W. E. Rogers, agent. *Gross, Kelly Financial Statement Book,* Gross, Kelly Collection, University of New Mexico Library.

68. Early wool scourers in Las Vegas were listed in the City Directory as "Wool Scourers and Pullers." The process of pulling was one of soaking the sheepskins in an acid preparation for about 24 hours, then hanging the skins on a stretcher. When dry, a wood pellet scraped across the skin would remove the wool. This was also known as washed wool, which still had to be scoured, but the strands were longer than sheared wool. Telephone conversation (July 25, 1955) with Leopold Meyer, who worked for the Albuquerque Wool Scouring Mill for a period beginning in 1911.

69. These eastern top makers were firms that sorted wools into strands of equal length and quality and tied them in rope-like bunches called "tops."

70. Henry D. Davis, veteran wool buyer of San Antonio, Texas, writes (July 28, 1955): "Nearly all worsted units have always had their own scouring plants in conjunction with their combs. This is not true of woolen mills, nor has it been. So it became a practical procedure years ago to prepare woolen wools [as opposed to worsted wools] for market in New Mexico, with labor which was undoubtedly cheaper than in the east, and in a form which was acceptable to mills for direct shipment."

71. Other discouraging factors that operated against a local scouring industry were the difficulty of getting qualified labor for the scouring process, which is highly technical, of softening the water, and the dipping of sheep before shearing which made quality washing difficult for local plants. The "Old Observer" commented that wool washing in the Territory was often not thorough and that it was complicated by the fact that "some people are swimming their sheep before shearing." *American Shepherd's Bulletin,* 10:827 (Aug., 1905). The Ilfeld records are full of references to the problem of scabies among the sheep. Frequently sheep had to be dipped at times when shearing was still far removed in time. Of course, no sheep owner wanted to do this, because the wool was injured and the fleeces would absorb tremendous quantities of the fluid which was costly. Sometimes the sheep inspectors forced the dipping of sheep before shearing. By appealing to Solomon Luna, president of the New Mexico Sheep Sanitary Board, Max Nordhaus had the ruling of a local inspector that his sheep be quarantined on the eve of shearing, reversed. He received a letter from Harry Lee, secretary of the Board, that this ruling had caused "considerable trouble between the Board and some of its inspectors" and he added that "on account of this favor we ask in return that you will see that your sheep are so dipped that the scab is killed and kept killed and that you keep your sheep clean." Copy Book 54, June 7, 1899, pp. 40–41, and Incoming Correspondence, Packet 68, Aug. 19, 1899.

72. The 1867 duty was 10 and 12 cents per pound.

73. Wright, "Wool Growing and the Tariff," pp. 194–195.

74. *Ibid.,* pp. 197–198.

75. *Ibid.,* pp. 209–210.

76. *Ibid.,* pp. 226, 285. The effective protection may have been no more than 3¢ to 6¢ per pound. According to a statement of one of the presidents of the National Wool-Growers' Association of this period, Australian wool commanded a 5¢ to 7¢ premium because of less shrinkage and the practice of skirting or the removing of the coarser wool of the belly, breech, and legs from the cleaner and lighter wools.

77. Copy Book 16, May 9, 1888, p. 23.

78. *Ibid.,* June 8, 1888, p. 78.

79. Wright, "Wool Growing and the Tariff," pp. 345–346. Eleven to twelve cents per pound on higher class wools; 32% to 50% *ad valorem* on cheaper wools.

80. The raising of sheep has always lost out in the competition for land where metropolitan areas have put a premium on the food and industrial needs of their peoples. The mobility of sheep and the fact that no special forms of transportation are required to transport the by-product, wool, has relegated the industry, typically, to the frontier. It should be noted that even with the historically low sheep and wool prices that

occurred from 1894 to 1897, at which time wool was admitted to the United States free of duty, sheep gained in numbers rapidly in Arizona, Colorado, Idaho, Nevada, and Wyoming where extensive range lands were still available either free or at a nominal cost. Though the rate of growth was faster following the passage of the protective wool tariff of 1897, the absence of protection did not deter the growth of the industry when other conditions were favorable. Wright, "Wool Growing and the Tariff," p. 305.

81. Ford, *Wool and Manufacturers of Wool,* p. 78. Copy Book 19, Nov. 24, 1890, p. 376.

82. Copy Book 24, Nov. 24, 1892, p. 317; Dec. 2, 1892, p. 385.

83. Ford, *Wool and Manufacturers of Wool,* pp. 82–84.

84. Copy Book 28, Feb. 8, 1894, p. 96.

85. *Ibid.,* April 24, 1894, p. 536; May 4, 1894, p. 622.

86. F. W. Taussig, *The Tariff History of the United States,* pp. 289–290.

87. Copy Book 30, Aug. 2, 1894, p. 32.

88. *Ibid.,* Aug. 9, 1894, pp. 78–79.

89. Taussig, *Tariff History,* p. 291.

90. Copy Book 30, Oct. 1, 1894, p. 388.

91. Copy Book 35, Sept. 27, 1895, p. 307.

92. Marion Dargan, "New Mexico's Fight for Statehood, 1895–1910," *New Mexico Historical Review,* 14:20–21 (Jan. 1939).

93. Copy Book 34, Nov. 26, 1895, p. 784.

94. The House tariff bill was introduced as a revenue measure but, before it reached the Senate, the Treasury had raised sufficient funds through the sale of bonds. The Republican Party leadership agreed to make a thorough study of the tariff question and submit a bill later. *The Congressional Record,* Part I, 28:304, 308, 309–326, 331, 29:194; Part II, 28:1267, 1382, 1574, 1690; Part III, 28:2099, 2150; Part IV, 28:3742. Copy Book 36, Dec. 30, 1895, p. 131.

95. Copy Book 38, May 29, 1896, p. 27.

96. *Ibid.,* July 7, 1896, p. 334.

97. Copy Book 39, Sept. 28, 1896, p. 285. Incoming Correspondence, Packet 33, Sept. 24, 1896; Packet 34, Oct. 6 and 20, 1896.

98. Eisemann Brothers was founded by Albert Eisemann who was born in Mossbach, Germany, in 1856. He came to the U. S. in 1872 and to Taos in 1878 where he established a wool business. In 1883, he moved his business to Albuquerque where he was joined by some brothers and by his first cousin, Louis Baer. An office was established in St. Louis in 1888. Letter from Sydney A. Eisemann, son of Albert, Oct. 28, 1957.

99. Copy Book 39, Oct. 20, 1896, p. 486.

100. *Ibid.,* Nov. 5, 1896, p. 665. Strangely enough, T. B. Catron lost his bid for re-election as delegate to Congress from the Territory to a Democrat, H. B. Fergusson. Catron's reputation and influence had been seriously damaged by charges concerning the tampering with witnesses in a law case. An attempt was made to disbar him. His coveted position of National Committeeman from New Mexico was taken from him. The younger members of his party were in open revolt against him. Catron also had been embarrassed by his support of Thomas B. Reed of Maine for the Republican Presidential nomination, which gentleman had been reported to have opposed the admission of any more Territories into the Union—an issue which in New Mexico was probably stronger than that of the tariff. Dargan, "New Mexico's Fight for Statehood," p. 21.

101. Nordhaus was in Europe from Nov., 1896 to May, 1897. Ilfeld was in New York in March and the first part of April, 1897. Schoonmaker signed letters in their absence.

102. Copy Book 39, Nov. 9, 1896, p. 687.

103. Copy Book 41, Jan. 8, 1897, p. 99.

104. Copy Book 42, April 20, 1897, p. 485.

105. Copy Book 43, June 10, 1897, p. 236.

106. *Ibid.,* July 27, 1897, p. 635; passed and made effective July 24, 1897.

107. Taussig, *Tariff History,* p. 427.

108. Ross was referred to by many as a jovial Irishman and a very able wool buyer.

His daughter married Arthur Ilfeld, son of Charles. Special Copy Book, Feb. 24, 1897, p. 34.

109. The A. G. Mills clip was sold for 6⅞¢ per pound—Mills getting 6½¢, Ross receiving ¼¢ commission, and the Charles Ilfeld Company retaining ⅛¢ to cover expenses. Special Copy Book, March 6, 1897, p. 40.

110. *Ibid.*, June 5, 1897, p. 745; Oct. 20, 1897, p. 112.

111. *Ibid.*, Nov. 12, 1897, pp. 130–131.

112. E. Rosenwald and Sons was a large competing firm situated across the Plaza from Ilfeld. Special Copy Book, Nov. 29, 1897, pp. 154–155.

113. Copy Book 44, Sept. 1, 1897, p. 252.

114. Interview, C. S. Brown, March 23, 1954. Pendaries' lots were discovered to be farther east on Valencia Street. Nordhaus refused to buy them but offered to rent them until they could be sold. Copy Book 48, May 31, 1898, p. 183.

115. Copy Book 47, March 16, 1898, p. 122; April 12, 1898, p. 431. Copy Book 48, June 1, 1898, p. 191; July 22, 1898, p. 678.

116. Copy Book 47, April 14, 1898, p. 459; April 25, 1898, p. 575.

117. Copy Book 48, June 2, 1898, p. 238.

118. Wright, "Wool Growing and the Tariff," pp. 349, 342, 336.

119. Person, *Forecasting Business Cycles,* p. 121.

120. Wright, "Wool Growing and the Tariff," pp. 295–296.

121. Taussig, *Tariff History,* p. 336.

122. Wright, "Wool Growing and the Tariff," p. 276.

123. Summary Book, 1886–1895. The figure of 614,397 lbs. given in the records was not for the full year and the drop from 1,003,029 lbs. in 1897, therefore, is exaggerated. However, wool and stock dollar sales, shown as one figure for the 12 months was 51.5 per cent under the previous year in spite of only slightly lower wool prices and substantially higher sheep prices.

124. Copy Book 65, June 5, 1901, p. 467.

125. Copy Book 73, Aug. 12, 1902, p. 116.

126. Copy Book 77, Feb. 2, 1903, pp. 206–207; Feb. 3, 1903, p. 226; Feb. 5, 1903, p. 249; Copy Book 78, March 14, 1903, p. 276; Copy Book 80, May 1, 1903, p. 51; May 19, 1903, p. 303.

127. Copy Book 78, March 21, 1903, p. 401. Wool Record Book, 1903–1907.

128. Copy Book 79, April 25, 1903, p. 442; Copy Book 80, May 1, 1903, p. 51.

129. Wool in the far-western states increased in production from 133,859 lbs. in 1898 to 171,984 lbs. in 1902 but declined somewhat in the period 1903 to 1905. Report of the U. S. Tariff Board, *Wool and Manufacturers of Wool,* p. 64. Figures for New Mexico, alone, do not seem to be available though production of wool in New Mexico in 1903 through 1905 was roughly 13–14 per cent higher than 1899—rising from approximately 15,000,000 to 17,000,000 lbs. *Thirteenth Census of the United States* (1910), *Abstract with Supplement for New Mexico* (1913), p. 352, and U. S. Department of Agriculture, *Yearbooks* (1900–1905).

130. Summary Book, 1895–1910.

131. Pastura was the site of Ilfeld's large ranching project and a branch store. The latter was founded in 1902. Copy Book 79, April 8, 1903, pp. 173–174.

132. *Ibid.*, April 25, 1903, p. 451. Copy Book 85, Dec. 18, 1903, p. 599.

133. Interview, C. S. Brown, March 23, 1954.

134. See Chapter IX.

CHAPTER XI

The Partido System

1. William H. Dusenberry, "Ordinances of the Mesta in New Spain, 1537," *The Americas,* 4:36 (Jan. 1948).

2. *Ibid.* Julius Klein, *The Mesta, 1273–1836,* p. 12.

3. Dusenberry, "Ordinances of the Mesta in New Spain," pp. 347–350.

4. Among a long list of these decrees, the chapter heading summarizing the rules regarding the relationships of the owner of sheep and his sheepherder is as follows: "Que el Pastor no tenga hierro, mas del que le diere su amo, y siendo de un ano el ganado de su partido, lo venda." In view of the fact that these were a series of orders and that this one dealt with problems that owners had with their sheepherders, it has seemed accurate to translate the subjunctive phrase, "lo venda," as "he must sell it." Eusebio Bentura Belena, *Recopilacion Sumaria de Todos Los Autos Acordados de la Real Audiencia y Sala del Crimen de esta Nueva Espana,* chap. 47, p. 45.

France V. Scholes reported to the author that in his researches in the Mexican National Archives he discovered contracts for hog partidos dated as early as 1525. A. Milares Carlo y J. I. Mantecon, *Indice y Extractos de los Protocolos del Archivo de Notarias de Mexico, D. F., vol. I, 1524–1528,* Number 31, Aug. 25, 1525—one-fifth share; Number 167, Oct. 30, 1525—one-half share (?); Number 432, March 14, 1527—one-quarter share; Number 788, Oct. 7, 1527—one-sixth share for hogs and sheep; Number 797, Oct. 11, 1527—one-sixth share.

5. Klein, *The Mesta,* pp. 58–59.

6. The Confraternities of the Blessed Sacrament and of the Rosary each had a capital of 200 ewes contracted to return 32 sheep per year interest. The Devotion of Poor Souls had 300 ewes, stolen or lost, but which apparently continued to yield from some source a return, inadequate for the needs, of 48 sheep per year. Eleanor B. Adams and Fray Angelico Chavez, *The Missions of New Mexico, 1776,* pp. 241–243.

7. *Ibid.,* p. 246.

8. New Mexico Archives Document 600, 1765–66 (University of New Mexico Library, Albuquerque). Cited in free English translation by Ralph Charles, "Development of the Partido System in the New Mexico Sheep Industry" (unpublished Master's thesis, University of New Mexico, 1940).

9. Josiah Gregg, *Commerce of the Prairies,* I, 189.

10. H. B. Carroll and J. V. Haggard, *Three New Mexico Chronicles,* pp. 41–42.

11. Jose Perea was probably a direct descendant of Eugenio Perea of Bernalillo who in 1766 accepted a partido contract from Antonio Baca and Lieutenant-General Ortiz. New Mexico Archives Document 600.

12. Charles, "Development of the Partido System," p. 36.

13. See Appendix 1.

14. Charles, "Development of the Partido System," p. 32. Ferd Meyer, a German-Jewish merchant and sutler to Fort Garland, seems to have used the partido system in the San Luis Valley as early as 1872. H. O. Brayer, *William Blackmore, The Spanish-Mexican Land Grants of New Mexico and Colorado, 1863–1878,* pp. 106, 108, 115.

15. Compiled Laws of New Mexico, 1884, Section 77. Some partido contracts were found by Ralph Charles to have been recorded in the various New Mexico County Archives in the late 1870's though none in any significant numbers until after 1882. Charles, "Development of the Partido System," pp. 31–32.

16. Copy Book 11, June 10, 1884, p. 25. Teodorito Casaus y Benevides had a contract in 1885 but his account, going back to July, 1879, may have been in connection with such an agreement. A cattle partido contract appears in the records in 1884, the first of several through the years. Copy Book 11, June 5, 1884, p. 7.

17. See Chapter IX.

18. Estimated from partido wool received in the amount of more than 35,000 lbs.

19. Taxes on sheep amounted to more than 5¢ per head in San Miguel County and, in the case of partido contracts, Ilfeld paid ½ of this figure. Copy Book 31, Dec. 31, 1894, p. 460.

20. For a summary picture of Ilfeld's partido activities, see Appendix 11.

21. The actual rental collections, however, amounted to but 9/10 of contract terms of 1 8/10 lbs.—an estimated return of 10.8 per cent.

22. Leandro Casaus, Ledger I, p. 71.

23. See Chapter VII.

24. Copy Book 12, Nov. 23, 1884, p. 37.

25. Copy Book 16, Oct. 19, 1888, p. 450.

26. Jose Montano was close to the McSween faction in Lincoln County War days. See, for instance, Keleher, *Violence*, p. 279. In Sept. 1893, when prices were somewhat higher, Nordhaus was unable to sell sheep at Folsom, in northern New Mexico, for $1.50, although Folsom was at least 300 route miles nearer eastern markets with access to two railroads. See Chapter IX.

27. Copy Book 27, Oct. 10 and 20, 1893, pp. 377, 434.

28. *Ibid.*, Nov. 25, 1893, p. 628.

29. Copy Book 55, Sept. 21, 1899, p. 510.

30. Copy Book 17, Oct. 17, 1889, p. 444.

31. Copy Book 14, Sept. 8, 1886, p. 347.

32. Copy Book 27, Jan. 6, 1894, p. 844; Jan. 11, 1894, p. 909; Copy Book 46, Jan. 3, 1898, p. 183. Only one definite exception to this has been noted. The Juan Chavez y Trujillo contract, which began in 1884, stipulated that the partidario pay all the taxes, but in return Ilfeld agreed to absorb all freight costs to Las Vegas. Chavez lived in the White Oaks–Lincoln area. This man rented sheep in turn to other partidarios. Copy Book 20, July 23, 1891, pp. 474–475.

33. Wool Record Book.

34. Copy Book 34, May 24, 1895, pp. 117, 122. Copy Book 46, Jan. 8, 1898, pp. 214–215.

35. In 1905 a notation was made regarding one contract: "37 head allowed for hail." Wool Record Book. In 1892 Nordhaus wrote that the ravages of wolves were more serious that year particularly in the area east of the Red River. Copy Book 21, March 26, 1892, p. 893. This area was dominated by cattle, however.

36. In 1884, Charles Ilfeld had 2000 sheep for sale to shear at 3 lbs. each. Copy Book 12, Nov. 11, 1884, p. 5.

37. Earl L. Moulton (interview, May 15, 1954), who started his career in New Mexico as a sheepherder, believed 6 lbs. to have been a fair minimum estimate in 1903. He remembered that not many sheep sheared as much as 10 lbs. S. N. D. North, wool expert, estimated the average fleece in 1893 in New Mexico to have been 4½ lbs. (Ford, *Wool and Manufacturers of Wool*, p. 50). North's estimate is obtained by dividing the total estimated clip by the approximation of the number of sheep. Neither total is reliable—particularly the number of sheep. Ilfeld's sheep, most of which were in the Puerto de Luna area, probably grew heavier than average fleeces because of the favorable grass stand available. The U. S. Special Report (1892, p. 923) gives the average fleece of improved Mexican sheep as 4 lbs. and of Merino as 6 to 9 lbs. Sixty-one interviews made by representatives of the national sheep and wool publications in the years 1898 to 1906 and tabulated by this writer show fleeces as follows: 2 at 3½ lbs.; 4 at 4 lbs.; 6 at 4½ lbs.; 14 at 5 lbs.; 21 at 6 lbs.; 9 at 8 lbs.; 2 at 9 lbs.; 1 at 10 lbs.; 1 at 12 lbs. The mode, therefore, is 6 lbs. The *Las Vegas Optic*, Jan. 5, 1900, disagreed strenuously with the *American Wool and Cotton Reporter* estimate of an average fleece weight in New Mexico of 3.8 lbs. The *Optic* thought at least 4½ lbs. to be more accurate.

38. Copy Book 52, April 12, 1899, p. 689; Copy Book 53, April 18, 1899, p. 61.

39. U. S. Special Report, p. 923. Almost no evidence appears in the Ilfeld records on lamb crops. One herd of 500 sheep purchased by Ilfeld as a joint venture contained 175 ewes and 100 newborn lambs. Whether the 175 ewes were the mothers of only these lambs is not known, but if this were the case the lambing would have been but 57 per cent. Copy Book 38, July 11, 1896, p. 384. Ben Floersheim, Las Jaritas Ranch (June 16, 1954), remembers a 33 per cent lambing in the early 1900's. Expectations, however, were generally 100 per cent. In 1906, several estimates for the years 1901 through 1905 or 1906 indicate an average for the period of barely more than 60 per cent. Twelve such estimates made by New Mexico ranchers interviewed were as follows: 2 at 50 per cent; 1 at 53 per cent; 4 at 60 per cent; 2 at 62 per cent; 1 at 65 per cent; 1 at 75 per cent; 1 at 85 per cent. *American Shepherd's Bulletin*, scattered issues. It should be explained that the free range was passing rapidly in this period to fenced land and much of the free range was in poor condition from overgrazing. Also, 1903 and 1904 were years of extreme drought. One of these averages included a 45 per cent lambing in 1903 and a zero lambing in 1904.

In the years 1905 and 1906, 44 interviewees of a total of 49 claimed to have had lambing records of 80 per cent or higher; two claimed 100 per cent and two 110 per cent. Two stated 70 per cent and three 75 per cent. *American Shepherd's Bulletin,* 1905, 1906.

40. Typical prices: 1897, $1.25–$1.90; 1898, $1.50–$1.75; 1899, $1.75; 1900, $2.00; 1901, $1.00–$1.25; 1902, $1.15–$1.35; 1903, $1.25.

41. Minimum yield per 100 head of sheep: 200 pounds of wool at 8 cents per pound; 65 lambs at 75 cents each; minimum total income, $64.75. A more typical yield per 100 head of sheep: 350 pounds of wool at 12 cents per pound; 75 lambs at $1.25 each; total income, $135.75.

42. U. S. Special Report, pp. 924–925. One of these estimates was made by F. A. Manzanares, former delegate to Congress from the Territory of New Mexico, and a partner in the merchant firm of Browne and Manzanares. He had become a prominent sheepman in the 1890's. The following figures are for a flock of 2500 sheep:

2 men and provisions, etc.	$ 720
Extra help and provisions during lambing	150
10 per cent losses including meat for hands	650
Total	$1,520

Average cost per head, 60¢ (35¢ without losses).

43. Copy Book 31, Dec. 13, 1894, p. 460; $173.25 for one-half taxes on 6600 head.

44. Copy Book 38, July 11, 1896, pp. 384–385.

45. Costs had risen in the years following 1900. Forty-nine interviewees responded as follows: 4 at less than 50¢ per head; 5 at 50¢–59¢; 10 at 60¢–69¢; 13 at 70¢–79¢; 2 at 80¢–89¢; 3 at 90¢–99¢; 9 at $1.00–$1.25; 3 higher. *American Shepherd's Bulletin,* various issues. Sheep and wool prices had risen substantially, too.

46. The feminine gender, partida, is used when referring to a band of sheep under a partido contract.

47. See U. S. Office of Indian Affairs, Land Research Unit, *Tewa Basin Study,* 3:147; Wentworth, *America's Sheep Trails,* p. 380; Charles F. Lummis, *Land of Poco Tiempo* (New York, 1893), pp. 19–20.

The "Old Observer," traveling correspondent of the *American Shepherd's Bulletin,* expressed the following opinion (11:525 [June 1906]): "I have an idea that a lessor of band of sheep who is at once well posted in regard to such stock and a good business man (especially a good buyer and seller) four times in five, whatever the character of the year, gets a bigger interest on his capital than the lessee receives, net, in compensation for his labor and care, even though he may have been given by the proprietor the best terms known in these parts."

48. The years 1898 and 1900 showed much higher balances because of the inclusion of two accounts—one in each of these years—$10,000 in one case and $5,500 in the other, which were abnormal and, at least in the $10,000 example, not comparable with the others because it involved an expansion in the merchandise and livestock business of Grzelachowski in Puerto de Luna and the account was frozen pending adjudication of his estate following his death in 1898.

49. There were actually 50 contracts, but one contract covered two herds, each with different terms.

50. Nordhaus warned one of his Lincoln County customers: "You ought to take much care in trusting *partidarios* because the majority of them owe an excessive amount to the owners of the sheep." Copy Book 18, June (?), 1890, p. 196.

51. The author asked a Spanish-speaking friend to interview some older partidarios concerning their experiences. The report came back that much of the conversation turned to incidents in which the partidario had taken advantage of the patron.

52. Klein, *The Mesta,* p. 56.

53. Copy Book 22, July 6, 1892, pp. 694–695.

54. Copy Book 23, Sept. 1, 1892, p. 462.

55. Copy Book 24, Jan. 12, 1893, p. 621–622.

56. Compiled Laws of New Mexico, 1884, Sec. 77. A partido contract is actually a mutuum to distinguish it from a bailment. In the case of a bailment, ownership of the

goods remains with the contractor and the same goods are returnable when the purpose of the contract has been fulfilled. A mutuum, however, is, in effect, a bailment of fungible goods—that is, the contract calls for the return of a like number of goods of the same quality and characteristics. In the case of a mutuum, ownership is transferred to the contractee—thus the need for protection against the unauthorized sale of sheep. By being permitted to file such a contract, the contractor places all third parties on notice that he owns a preferred claim.

57. Incoming Correspondence, Packet 40, March 13, 1897.

58. Copy Book 23, Aug. 4, 1892, p. 272.

59. Contracts after 1900 required a mortgage on all real estate, goods, and chattels.

60. Copy Book 17, April 5, 1890, p. 946.

61. Copy Book 46, Jan. 8, 1898, pp. 214–215.

62. *Ibid.*

63. Special Copy Book, Feb. 17, 1902, p. 241. Hugo Goldenberg stayed in ranching near Puerto de Luna. Copy Book 46, Jan. 8, 1898, p. 218.

64. Special Copy Book, Oct. 30, 1897, p. 116; Feb. 12, 1898, p. 165.

65. Copy Book 46, Feb. 12, 1898, p. 492; Feb. 17, 1898, p. 539; Copy Book 54, June 20, 1899, p. 219.

66. W. H. Stapp of Las Vegas writes (Aug. 14, 1950): "The term 'Arab' as I recall, was bantered around considerably. I believe it referred to the Syrian, Turkish and Arab element that migrated to this country with packs on their back and did a lot of trading with ranchers and people in rural communities throughout the County [San Miguel] eventually acquiring ranches and sheep that were given on *partido.* I believe the term 'Arabe' was applied to this element with approbrium. You might say they had somewhat of a Gypsy tendency, but their specialty seems to have been to peddle and trade with the rural population with a view to establishing themselves in the sheep business to which they were particularly adapted."

67. Copy Book 47, May 4, 1898, p. 651.

68. Copy Book 36, Feb. 22, 1896, p. 588.

69. See Debt Funding section above.

70. Copy Book 20, June 22, 1891, p. 310; Copy Book 23, July 22, 1892, p. 158; Copy Book 28, May 7, 1894, p. 643; Copy Book 35, Oct. 25, 1895, p. 505; Copy Book 46, March 2, 1898, p. 659. In the last noted, Nordhaus stated that "Charles has promised already sheep to various customers who we should satisfy first."

71. Thirty-six such requests were noted in the incoming correspondence from 1895 to 1901, though there must have been many more. The majority of requests undoubtedly were made orally to Goldenberg on his travels about the countryside.

72. Copy Book 27, Oct. 4, 1893, p. 326.

73. Examples: Copy Book 20, July 27, 1891, p. 503; Copy Book 23, July 22, 1892, p. 158.

74. See Keleher, *Violence,* pp. 53–54.

75. Emil Fritz was probably a relative of Emil Fritz of Lincoln County fame who died in Germany in 1874. Keleher, *Violence,* p. 33. Copy Book 28, May 7, 1894, p. 643.

76. Copy Book 28, May 7, 1894, p. 643; Copy Book 20, June 22, 1891, p. 310.

77. Copy Book 74, Sept. 27, 1902, p. 103; Copy Book 23, July 28, 1892, pp. 204–205; Copy Book 79, April 24, 1903, p. 422.

78. Incoming Correspondence, Packet 6, Jan. 27, 1893.

79. An amusing example is one from young Selma Letcher, daughter of Adolph Letcher, former partner of Ilfeld, which was answered as follows: "Dear Selma: I am in receipt of your little letter of July 19th and was very glad to hear from you. I notice from the style of your letter, that you are on the way of becoming a speculator & hope all your investments will turn out satisfactory. In regard to the price of sheep would say that they are very high at present, I mean the kind which we can give out to the mexicans on shares & on which they pay the interest in wool. This class of sheep cost at present 1.75 per head & if you wish to buy some you must let me know at once as we have to be on the lookout for a good man to take care of them. I expect to leave for New York in about 2 weeks & if possible will come & see you for a day or two. . . . Yours sincerely, Charles Ilfeld." Copy Book 43, July 29, 1897, p. 674.

Other examples: C. Russell of Lamy; F. E. Fite, Silver City; Ernest Langston, White Oaks; Klasner, R. P. Hopkins, and John Kimball, all of Picacho; C. O. Whitehead, Kansas City but seeking location in New Mexico; Whitmore and Clark, Gallegos Springs; S. B. Harris, Fort Sumner; Alfred and Tom Combs, Puerto de Luna; L. Carpentier, Manzano.

80. Notation scribbled on letter. Incoming Correspondence, Packet 87, July 12, 1901.

81. Copy Book 16, Oct. 3, 1888, pp. 400–401.

82. The Casaus family also placed some of their own sheep on partido. Copy Book 38, Aug. 7, 1896, p. 564. One of their contracts was with an Ilfeld partidario. Copy Book 31, Dec. 8, 1894, p. 382.

83. In June, 1888, Casaus wool was valued at 14¢ per pound. Wool in this year in New Mexico ranged from 11½¢ to 18¢ per pound as indicated in isolated quotations and sales made by Ilfeld. Ford, *Wool and Manufacturers of Wool,* places the range for the year at 14¢ and 22¢; for June, 1888, at 12¢ to 22¢.

84. Copy Book 77, Jan. 27, 1903, pp. 147–148. Brown and Adams of Boston, for whom Ilfeld was buying, wanted the Casaus wool. Ilfeld thought at the time that both a Mr. Hill of Roswell and Harry Kelly of Gross, Blackwell and Co. had made offers.

85. Copy Book 84, Oct. 20, 1903, p. 95. Probably H. N. Jaffa of Jaffa, Prager and Company of Roswell.

86. The partidarios claimed there were no freighters because there was no water on the road. Copy Book 84, Nov. 5, 1903, p. 407.

87. Copy Book 55, Sept. 21, 1899, p. 510.

88. See Charles, "Development of the Partido System," p. 32.

89. See Chapter XII.

90. Copy Book 35, Sept. 25, 1895, p. 270; Copy Book 39, Sept. 28, 1896, p. 290. Copy Book 35, Dec. 12, 1895, p. 940. Ilfeld gave directions to inquire for his sheep at W. H. Long's ranch at Cabra. Copy Book 20, June 13, 1891, p. 271.

91. Copy Book 39, Oct. 5, 1896, p. 375.

92. Copy Book 85, Dec. 7, 1903, p. 374.

93. Copy Book 38, June 27, 1896, p. 269.

94. Copy Book 43, July 26, 1897, p. 623. Copy Book 26, July 6, 1893, p. 475. Location referred to as "Nacimiento del Vegoso." Copy Book 49, Oct. 5, 1898, p. 719. There is some possibility that this ranch was acquired under fortuitous circumstances. It may have belonged to one Benigno Martinez, who was killed by outlaws shortly before Nordhaus began to use the Vegoso ranch. "Benigno Martinez, honest sheep owner . . . pastured . . . about 7 miles east of Las Vegas, at a place known as El Vegoso. . . . On the 25th of May, 1893, both Juan Gallegos, sheep herder, and Benigno Martinez were killed by Cecilio Lucero." Carlos C. de Baca, Vincente Silva, *New Mexico's Vice-King of the Nineties, Based on a Narrative by Manuel C. de Baca* (n.p., n.d.), p. 31 (library of W. H. Stapp, Las Vegas).

95. Copy Book 26, July 6, 1893, p. 475.

96. Copy Book 37, April 24, 1896, p. 410.

97. Copy Book 29, July 14, 1894, p. 398. Copy Book 34, May 24, 1895, p. 122.

98. Copy Book 34, May 24, 1895, p. 122.

99. Copy Book 35, Sept. 25, 1895, p. 270; Wool Record Book.

100. Copy Book 28, April 12, 1894, p. 460; Copy Book 43, July 24, 1897, p. 615.

101. Copy Book 39, Oct. 6, 1896, p. 378. See Chapter IX for discussion of dipping.

102. Copy Book 38, July 2, 1896, p. 305.

103. Special Copy Book, Nov. 9, 1897, p. 127. Copy Book 50, Nov. 15, 1898, p. 483.

104. Copy Book 50, Nov. 15, 1898, p. 483; Nov. (?), 1898, p. 383; Nov. 15, 1898, p. 483.

105. Copy Book 56, Oct. 14, 1899, pp. 154–157. Letter from W. H. Stapp, Aug. 14, 1952. Otto Goetz, "Santa Rosa," *New Mexico Historical Review,* 23:169 (April 1948).

CHAPTER XII

Sedentary Sheep Husbandry

1. *Report of the Public Lands Commission,* Sen. Doc. 189, 58th Cong. 3d sess. (Washington, D. C., 1905), pp. 175–183. See also Victor Westphall, "The Public Domain in New Mexico, 1854–1891," *New Mexico Historical Review,* 33:128–143 (April 1958); for greater detail see Westphall's doctoral dissertation of the same title (University of New Mexico, 1956).

2. *American Shepherd's Bulletin,* 9:696 (June 1904).

3. The "Old Observer" was the pen name used by Andrew Jackson Bennett, oldest of three sons of Levi Bennett, originally from Vermont and later of Cambridge, Massachusetts. Andrew, quitting his position as principal of the Everett (Massachusetts) High School, went to work for his younger brother, Frank P. Bennett, as an editor in 1890 or 1891. Frank had founded at least two magazines by that time—the *American Wool Reporter,* 1887, later to become the *American Wool & Cotton Reporter* and subsequently the current publication *America's Textile Reporter;* and the *United States Investor,* still being published. He also, with the elder Jesse Smith of the Mormon Church, founded the Associated Wool Growers' Company and, in 1896, commenced the publication of a magazine which in January, 1902, became the *American Shepherd's Bulletin.* Andrew J. Bennett was the traveling correspondent and "Old Observer" of this publication. "Andrew, who was a very capable person in many ways, nevertheless, editorially, couldn't write the sort of tariff articles which the [American Wool & Cotton] Reporter required and still does. So my grandfather [Frank P. Bennett] sent his older brother Andrew out into the West to write for the Shepherd's Bulletin." Letter from Frank P. Bennett, Editor of *America's Textile Reporter* and grandson of Frank P. Bennett (grand-nephew of Andrew J. Bennett), Jan. 22, 1958, Boston, Massachusetts.

4. Letter from Frank P. Bennett, Aug., 1906, p. 717. At a later date it was recorded that "extensive homesteading" had occurred in northeastern New Mexico. U. S. Tariff Commission, *The Wool Growing Industry,* p. 152.

5. *American Shepherd's Bulletin,* 11:710 (Aug. 1906).

6. *Report of the Public Lands Commission,* p. 88.

7. Amended to require 8 months, March 3, 1891. The Receiver of the Las Cruces, New Mexico, Land Office thought much fraud could be eliminated if the Commutation Clause were repealed. *Annual Report of the Commissioner of the General Land Office,* 1888, p. 76. (Also see B. H. Hibbard, *A History of the Public Land Policies,* pp. 386–390).

8. Actual cases of this practice in New Mexico are cited in Westphall, "The Public Domain in New Mexico," pp. 30–52; also *Annual Report of the Commissioner of the General Land Office,* p. 48.

9. *Report of the Public Lands Commission,* pp. 89, 107.

10. U. S. Tariff Board, *Wool and Manufacturers of Wool,* p. 601.

11. Efforts to identify this reporter have not been wholly successful. By his own admission he was not the "Old Observer." Several short news items on New Mexico (*American Shepherd's Bulletin,* 10 (April and May, 1905), appearing at times when this correspondent is known to have been in New Mexico, are signed "E. B." and, one, "E. W. B." The latter may have been a typographical error as "E. B." is thought to be the initials of Edward Everett Bennett, youngest of the three Bennett brothers, who could have been the "Young Observer." Letter from Frank P. Bennett, Oct. 27, 1958 (see note 3 above). *American Shepherd's Bulletin,* 7:3167–3168 (Dec. 1902).

12. *American Shepherd's Bulletin,* 7:1708 (Feb. 1902).

13. *Ibid.,* 7:2240 (May 1902).

14. *Ibid.,* 7:2777 (Sept. 1902).

15. Stockholders in the Llano Sheep Company were "Messrs. Robbins, Earickson, and Arnot of the great G[ross] K[elly] & Co. concern though I do not understand that

the great Las Vegas mercantile house as a company has any interest in this sheep enterprise." The "Old Observer," *American Shepherd's Bulletin,* 11:526 (June 1906).

16. *Ibid.,* 7:3020 (Nov. 1902).

17. *Ibid.,* 10:664 (June 1905). According to one source, in writing of the Frank Bond holdings, each land purchase was made so as to control an area approximately 10 times as large. U. S. Office of Indian Affairs, Land Research Unit, *Tewa Basin,* 3:145 (1935–1939).

18. N. S. B. Gras, *A History of Agriculture in Europe and America,* pp. 155–156. Klein, *The Mesta,* pp. 314–315.

19. *Las Vegas Democrat,* June 28, 1890.

20. *Las Vegas Optic,* July 29, 1890.

21. *Ibid.,* Aug. 18, 1890.

22. *Ibid.,* Aug. 4, 1890. In two unnamed counties of New Mexico some 3,000,000 acres of land were thus usurped. *Report of the Secretary of the Interior,* 1:16 (1888).

23. Copy Book 19, Sept. 26, 1890, p. 76.

24. This movement was apparently an extension of the whole post-Civil War craze for vigilante groups. The White Caps had been particularly strong and troublesome in Indiana in the 1880's. Hugh Loudon recalls seeing them sometimes in the streets of Las Vegas with little white caps. Interview, July 21, 1955.

In a letter from W. H. Stapp (Aug. 14, 1952) he writes of this movement in New Mexico as a group who "banded together and under the cover of night to cut the fences." The provocation "was started by some outfits that came into the County and fenced off some large tracts of grazing lands located on the Las Vegas Grant to which they did not have clear title." See note 6, Chapter III.

25. Brunswick Letter Book, Oct. 27, 1890, p. 248.

26. *Ibid.,* Oct. 12, 1890, p. 243.

27. *Ibid.,* Sept. 22, 1890, p. 225.

28. *Ibid.,* Nov. 8, 1890, p. 251. Perhaps a more important aspect of the discontent prevalent in Las Vegas was the corruption-laden leadership of the Romero family that seemed to be giving asylum to Vincente Silva and his gang of outlaws. Again, however, this may have been in part a Robin Hood or Billy the Kid complex that arose from the squeezing out of the native people from their pasture lands on the Las Vegas Grant.

29. Conrad Richter, *Sea of Grass* (New York, 1937), p. 23. The setting of the novel is in the vicinity of Albuquerque in the 1890's.

30. *American Shepherd's Bulletin,* 11:824 (Sept. 1906). Abbott is described as being "between 40 and 50 . . . tall, spare . . . dark complexion, keen but shifty eyes . . . elongated head . . . nervous, billious . . . actions likely to be influenced by his stomach . . . preconceived opinions . . . newspapermen his *bete noir.*" Abbott set his losses in one season at the hands of these homesteaders at 10,000 to 15,000 sheep.

31. *American Shepherd's Bulletin,* 11:825 (Sept. 1906).

32. Goldenberg, in explaining some heavy sheep losses, evidently around the Puerto de Luna area, in 1896, wrote that they were "due to heavy crops of loco weed." Incoming Correspondence, Packet 32, July 8, 1896. Such inroads by this weed is some evidence that the grass had been overgrazed. Nordhaus' appointee, Concepcion Atencio, was accused of doing what so many herders were prone to do. "He displayed poor judgment in grazing such vast herds in a small place of country entirely inadequate and never ventured during the whole winter outside limited scope of country."

33. Chevalier, *La Formacion des Grand Domaines,* pp. 107, 110, 128–130.

34. *Ibid.,* p. 126.

35. By the middle of the 17th century in New Spain the cattle population had reached a level below the 1565–1570 peak. Sheep, however, were growing in numbers on the dry plateaus. Chevalier, *La Formacion des Grand Domaines,* pp. 132 and 135.

36. One animal unit equals any one of the following: 1 head of cattle, 1 horse, 1 mule, 5 sheep, 5 swine, or 5 goats.

37. U.S. Sen. Doc. 99, *The Western Range,* 74th Cong. 2d sess., p. 158.

38. It has been common in New Mexico to permit livestock numbers to reach their

peak in drought periods. *Ibid.*, p. 148. The Forest Service has recommended stocking at 25 per cent below average to preserve semidesert grasses. *Ibid.*, pp. 144–145.

39. *Monthly Bulletin of the National Wool Growers' Association of the United States,* 3:375 (June 1898).

40. Copy Book 35, Nov. 30, 1895, p. 834; Copy Book 39, Oct. 5, 1896, p. 375. In 1898, Nordhaus thought lambing grounds were "pretty good between Liberty and Endee." Copy Book 47, April 2, 1898, p. 316; Copy Book 85, Dec. 7, 1903, p. 374.

41. *American Shepherd's Bulletin,* 7:2369–2370 (June 1902).

42. *Monthly Bulletin of the National Wool Growers' Association* (Aug. 1898), p. 497.

43. *American Shepherd's Bulletin,* 7:2237 (May 1902).

44. *Ibid.*, 6:458 (April 1901). Many strange sheep were driven into the Red Lake area disturbing sheepmen of that section. Seventy-five hundred sheep were thought to be from Pecos. *Ibid.*, 6:1364 (Nov. 1901).

45. U.S. Tariff Commission, *The Wool Growing Industry,* p. 154.

46. *Report of the Public Lands Commission,* pp. 9 and 10.

47. Hibbard, *History of the Public Land Policies,* p. 484.

48. *Ibid. American Shepherd's Bulletin,* 8:257–262 (Feb. 1903).

49. *Ibid.*, 11:1116 (Dec. 1906). *The Shepherd's Bulletin* (Oct. 1900, p. 760), a predecessor, recorded in 1900 that sheepmen were aroused by government projects to lease lands to cattlemen.

50. Special Copy Book, Sept. 30, 1897, p. 100.

51. See Chapter X.

52. Special Copy Book, Aug. 27, 1897, pp. 77–78.

53. Copy Book 38, July 13, 1896, pp. 396–397. For a short period of time in the early spring of 1897, Ilfeld became infected with the speculative fever. Nordhaus was in Germany and Ilfeld in New York and Washington. Ilfeld wrote Schoonmaker to try to make all the sheep contracts he could and informed Goldenberg to buy some yearlings even if he had to pay cash. Incoming Correspondence, Packet 39, March 8 and 22, 1897.

54. Special Copy Book, Aug. 27, 1897, pp. 77–78.

55. *Ibid.*, Sept. 25, 1897, p. 99 and Sept. 30, 1897, p. 100.

56. Copy Book 42, July 6, 1897, p. 450.

57. Copy Book 47, March 26, 1898, p. 237; March 30, 1898, p. 281½.

58. *Ibid.*, April 2, 1898, p. 316.

59. Copy Book 54, June 6, 1899, p. 32. Annual Summary Book 1899–1929. This land was some 20 miles southeast of Pastura known as Borica Draw.

60. Copy Book 56, Nov. 9, 1899, p. 482.

61. *Ibid.*, Nov. 13, 1899, p. 524.

62. Records, Office of Louis C. Ilfeld, Las Vegas.

63. Copy Book 47, March 19, 1898, p. 180; April 19, 1898, p. 502. Annual Summary Book.

64. Special Copy Book, Aug. 27, 1897, pp. 77–78. Copy Book 76, Dec. 23, 1902, p. 222.

65. Copy Book 78, March 23, 1903, p. 410. $30 per annum. Annual Summary Book.

66. Copy Book 80, June 2, 1903, p. 494.

67. Copy Book 56, Nov. 14, 1899, p. 581; Nov. 16, 1899, p. 621.

68. Records, Office of Louis C. Ilfeld, Las Vegas.

69. Incoming Correspondence, Packet 71, Nov. 20, 1899.

70. Records, Office of Louis C. Ilfeld, Las Vegas.

71. Copy Book 57, Dec. 31, 1899, p. 556. Charles Ilfeld was one of many landholders against whom an indictment was brought in land fraud cases prior to 1891. Westphall, "The Public Domain in New Mexico," p. 138.

72. The Salado Cattle Company was originally a partnership, founded Feb. 1, 1883, of Stephen Fuller, Matthew Devine, Campbell Cook, and James P. Gage, Sr.—the first two with a one-third interest each; the latter two a one-sixth interest each. Lands were acquired by Matthew Devine and deeded to above d/b/a Fuller, Devine and Co. at the "Arroya Sellado." Upon the death of the partners, between 1883 and 1891, all interests were sold to James P. Gage, Jr., who incorporated the ranch in Iowa as the

Salado Cattle Company in 1896. Otero and Raynolds bought the ranch, 874 acres, of one Edward G. Austen on Sept. 2, 1903, when it became known as the Salado Livestock Company. This acreage was enlarged through the application of scrip and purchases of homesteads. A part of the ranch was purchased by the Ilfeld Realty Company, July 18, 1928. Records, Office of Louis C. Ilfeld, Las Vegas.

73. Copy Book 58, Jan. 20, 1900, p. 73. The figure of $8.00 was an estimate of Louis C. Ilfeld in a valuation of 1913 property for income tax purposes. Copy Book 58, Jan. 25, 1900, p. 91; Feb. 10, 1900, pp. 285–286.

74. See E. Louise Peffer, *The Closing of the Public Domain Disposal and Reservation Policies, 1900–50*, pp. 43 and 47.

75. Records, Office of Louis C. Ilfeld, Las Vegas.

76. Copy Book 78, March 17, 1903, p. 317.

77. Copy Book 68, Nov. 7, 1901, p. 381.

78. *Ibid.*, Nov. 16, 1901, p. 543.

79. Copy Book 85, Dec. 10, 1903, p. 447.

80. Copy Book 58, Feb. 10, 1900, pp. 285–286.

81. Copy Book 59, May 22, 1900, p. 631.

82. Copy Book 63, Jan. 5, 1901, p. 182.

83. Copy Book 57, Dec. 12, 1899, p. 302.

84. Special Copy Book, March 26, 1901, p. 210. Rice was R. B. Rice of Las Vegas. "Only competent man . . . from here. So busy that we can not get any work done by him . . . Max has been expecting him for over 2 months." Copy Book 67, Oct. 9, 1901, p. 570. No patent on land could be obtained until it had been surveyed. The General Land Office Reports are full of evidence of this demand. Hugo was Hugo Goldenberg, brother of Max.

85. Copy Book 68, Oct. 21, 1901, p. 61.

86. *Ibid.*, Oct. 21, 1901, p. 59.

87. Copy Book 71, March 24, 1902, pp. 679–681.

88. Market for scrip quoted at $4.00 per acre. Copy Book 85, Dec. 21, 1903, p. 649; Dec. 12, 1903, pp. 493–494.

89. Interview, A. C. Ortega, Manager Pastura Trading Post, Aug. 6, 1955.

90. Annual Summary Book.

91. Records, Office of Louis C. Ilfeld, Las Vegas. These lands and leases were sold in 1948.

92. Copy Book 62, Nov. 20, 1900, p. 325. Copy Book 58, Jan. 27, 1900, p. 140. Copy Book 59, April 10, 1900, p. 214. Copy Book 63, Dec. 21, 1900, p. 7.

93. Unless otherwise stated all statistics have been obtained from record books of annual figures.

94. Copy Book 58, Feb. 17, 1900, p. 378.

95. Copy Book 57, Nov. 23, 1899, p. 5.

96. Copy Book 58, Feb. 6, 1900, p. 259.

97. See note 59. Copy Book 61, Oct. 6, 1900, p. 545.

98. "The Company used to own some Pintada bottom land where they used to harvest a good supply of wild hay for use on the ranch. I would estimate that they cut about one hundred tons yearly on the average." Letter from A. C. Ortega, Aug. 22, 1955.

99. Copy Book 61, Oct. 13, 1900, p. 630; Copy Book 62, Oct. 21, 1900, p. 85.

100. A letterhead of the Pintada Trading Company, Max B. Goldenberg, manager, describes the extent of the business. "Dealers in Goods, Boots, Shoes, Hats, Clothing, and General Ranch Supplies. Breeders of and Dealers in Shropshire, Lincoln, and Merino Sheep. [A 1901 inventory listed 52 Rambouillet Bucks] Ranches at Mesa de Aragon, Canoncitos, Seven Lakes, Pintada, Borica, and Carrizo. Earmarks—Paintmarks: Wethers W and Ewes E. Firebrand on Jaw." Members of the New Mexico Stockmen's Protective Association, Office of Louis C. Ilfeld, Las Vegas, New Mexico.

101. Copy Book 63, Jan. 18, 1901, pp. 311–312. The "Mr. Garrett" was Pat Garrett.

102. Copy Book 73, Aug. (?), 1902, p. 326.

103. *Ibid.*, Sept. 3, 1902, p. 440.

104. *Ibid.*, Sept. 4, 1902, p. 501.
105. Copy Book 58, March 8, 1900, p. 543. Ledger L, p. 309.
106. Copy Book 71, Feb. 16, 1902, p. 36.
107. *Ibid.*, March 11, 1902, pp. 467–468. Copy Book 76, Dec. 19, 1902, p. 177.
108. Copy Book 77, Feb. 10, 1903, p. 290. Copy Book 76, Dec. 27, 1902, p. 268.
109. Copy Book 78, March 7, 1903, p. 152.
110. Copy Book 83, Sept. 14, 1903, pp. 116–117. *American Shepherd's Bulletin,* 7:3021 (Nov. 1902). Copy Book 83, Sept. 14, 1903, pp. 124–125.
111. Copy Book 80, April 29, 1903, p. 4.
112. Copy Book 81, June 19, 1903, p. 7–8.
113. *American Shepherd's Bulletin,* 8:1526 (Dec. 1903). Leonard Wood County was the former name for Guadalupe County.
114. Copy Book 83, Sept. 14, 1903, pp. 124–125.
115. Copy Book 85, Nov. 17, 1903, pp. 14 and 15.
116. *Ibid.*, Nov. 27, 1903, p. 196.
117. Annual Summary Book.
118. Copy Book 85, Nov. 17, 1903, p. 14; Nov. 28, 1903, p. 231.
119. Annual Summary Book; Pastura Trading Company Minute Book.
120. Special Copy Book, May 8, 1906, pp. 266–267.
121. Interview, A. C. Ortega, Aug. 6, 1955.
122. Special Copy Book, May 8, 1906, pp. 266–267.
123. General materials on Pastura and Pintada Trading Companies from Pastura Trading Company Minute Book, Office of Louis C. Ilfeld, Las Vegas. Special Copy Book, May 8, 1906, pp. 266–267.
124. One observer who knew both Rodgers and Anaya well rated Rodgers 47 per cent and Anaya 70 per cent of 100 per cent managers.
125. Annual Summary Book, 1899–1929.
126. Letter from A. C. Ortega, Aug. 11, 1955.
127. Sheep profits, which seem to include all dealings in sheep, averaged $2,301 from 1899 to 1902, with a profit of $18,384 in 1901 and a loss of $19,257 in 1902. It is questionable if profitable operation could have taken place in 1903 and 1904, years of drought and contraction. 1905 and 1906 were years of further contraction. Pastura Minute Book I, Office of Louis C. Ilfeld, Las Vegas.
128. Louis C. Ilfeld Letter Book, Oct. 7, 1909, p. 256.

CHAPTER XIII

Defensive Policy in a Shrinking Trade Area

1. See Introduction to Part III.
2. See Chapter V.
3. Berry Newton Alvis, "History of Union County, New Mexico," *New Mexico Historical Review,* 22:247–248, 269 (July 1947).
4. Copy Book 84, Oct. 29, 1903, p. 269.
5. Coan, "History of New Mexico," 1:445.
6. Copy Book 61, Oct. 1, 1900, pp. 477–478.
7. Alvis, "History of Union County," p. 269.
8. Marshall, *Santa Fe,* p. 402.
9. Copy Book 48, June 21, 1898, p. 384; June 22 and 23, 1898, pp. 391–393, 400. Also included accounts in Silver City, New Mexico, and Flagstaff, Winslow, and Showlow, Arizona.
10. Copy Book 37, April 20, 1896, p. 353. Interview, C. S. Brown, July 11, 1953. He further stated: "It was the Bacas of Upper Las Vegas who handled a good deal of this freight from Las Vegas to Roswell. They were vicious with the whip and used loud and foul language. I have seen large welts raised on horses many a time. The horses were trained to turn right or left by the number of jerks of the line. The

wheels were chain locked when going down hill. Care was taken to see that a wheel did not wear out in one place."

11. Marshall, *Santa Fe,* p. 421.

12. Mora, San Miguel, and Guadalupe counties had populations totaling 37,786 in 1900. The figure for 1880 had been 30,389. The gain may have been more than this as Mora and San Miguel gave up some of their territory to Union County in 1891. Guadalupe was formed in 1893 from parts of San Miguel and Lincoln counties. *Twelfth Census of the U.S.* (1900), *Population,* 1:31.

13. See Chapter III.

14. See Chapter V.

15. See Chapter III and Chapter V.

16. Copy Book 5, July 23, 1880, p. 421; Dec. 3, 1880, p. 596.

17. Copy Book 3, Dec. 24, 1877, p. 812.

18. Gellerman had operated a general merchandise store at Fort Bascom, and then at Liberty. *Las Vegas Gazette,* May 18, 1880, and July 7, 1881.

19. Copy Book 8, Oct. 20, 1882, p. 15; Jan. 23, 1883, p. 222.

20. Copy Book 5, July 23, 1880, p. 421.

21. Letter to M. B. Goldenberg: "Was for a week at Springer and bought Gellerman out in order to save myself." Copy Book 10, April 5, 1884, p. 231. Ilfeld's fear indicates this had been another partnership arrangement.

22. Copy Book 10, March 27, 1884, p. 197; Springer Book, March 14, 1884, p. 21.

23. Copy Book 11, Aug. 26, 1884, p. 286. Some claims were settled at 40¢ on the dollar. Most creditors received 40 per cent in cash and the balance in Gellerman's promissory notes.

24. Copy Book 8, Jan. 23, 1883, p. 222.

25. Gellerman was bitter about it all as might be expected, and when he was criticized for what he termed "small matters" he wrote, in part: "Don't you know regardless of my own situation and the worry it [?] me [I] turned over everything to secure you, exposed myself to attachments, and humiliation all for your benefit. Try to remember this and please do not worry about small matters, as you know that I will always look after your interest. You made money by my failing and can not deny it." Springer Book, Aug. 2, 1884, p. 235. This was not true although Ilfeld may have minimized his losses by 1888, to approximately $1,600 (Ledger H, p. 226), plus whatever he may not have collected on Gellerman's personal note of $8481 (Ledger G, p. 272), plus a write-off to Profit and Loss of $433.47 (Ledger I, p. 5). Springer Book, July 2, 1884, p. 165. Incoming Correspondence, Packet 1, June 5, 1883.

26. Copy Book 12, Jan. 24, 1885, p. 218.

27. *Ibid.,* Feb. 5, 1885, p. 249.

28. Incoming Correspondence, Packet 5, Feb. 7, 13, 24, 1885. Copy Book 16, Aug. 9, 1888, p. 230.

29. Copy Book 11, July 31, 1884, p. 225. See footnote 49, Chapter VII.

30. Springer Book, Aug. 2, 1884, p. 235.

31. Copy Book 10, March 29, 1884, p. 212.

32. See Chapter IX. Copy Book 11, June 16, 1884, p. 49.

33. See Chapter VII; Chapter IX; Chapter VIII.

34. See Chapter VII.

35. See Chapter IX.

36. See Chapter VIII; Chapter IX.

37. Copy Book 16, Feb. 4, 1889, p. 761.

38. Copy Book 23, Aug. 24, 1892, p. 422.

39. Copy Book 19, Feb. 19, 1891, p. 814.

40. Copy Book 24, Jan. 10, 1893, p. 617.

41. Incoming Correspondence, Packet 23, Feb. 27, 1895.

42. Copy Book 21, Nov. 11, 1891, p. 110.

43. Copy Book 21, April 4, 1892, p. 930; Copy Book 22, April 20, 1892, p. 45; June 3, 1892, p. 407; Copy Book 26, May 11, 1893, p. 130.

44. Copy Book 36, Feb. 13, 1896, p. 522; Feb. 22, 1896, p. 589

45. Copy Book 42, April 26, 1897, p. 541.

46. Copy Book 49, Oct. 5, 1898, pp. 722–723.

47. Copy Book 58, Feb. 10, 1900, p. 308. At a later date Strong was willing to accept but Nordhaus was no longer interested. Copy Book 81, June 20, 1903, p. 27.

48. See Chapter IV.

49. See photostat, p. 206.

50. A reduction to 10 per cent per annum on overdue merchandise balances occurred for most accounts about 1894.

51. Copy Book 14, April 7, 1887, p. 924. Copy Book 49, Oct. 5, 1898, pp. 722–723.

52. See Chapter IX.

53. Copy Book 14, April 7, 1887, p. 924.

54. Copy Book 17, Aug. 19, 1889, p. 251.

55. See Chapter IX. Copy Book 26, Aug. 3, 1893, p. 658.

56. Copy Book 27, Aug. 22, 1893, p. 77.

57. Bills payable, including interest bearing certificates of deposit, in 1895, amounted to $42,453. The balances in 1893 are not ascertainable. Certificates of deposit numbered 18 in 1893, as contrasted with 8 in 1895.

58. Copy Book 20, Dec. 7, 1891, p. 312. In 1893, Ilfeld had borrowed from 24 different sources. He had 11 notes due to individuals, 2 notes to banks, 10 to merchants, and 1 contingent note with a bank. Four notes carried an 8 per cent interest rate; 6, a 7 per cent rate; 12, a 6 per cent rate; 1, a 5 per cent rate; and 1, an unknown rate. The number of notes in 1891 were 16; 1892, 10; 1894, 16; 1895, 12; 1896, 4. Bills Payable Book. Nordhaus paid off H. L. Waldo's note in 1896 because he had no use for the money. Special Copy Book, Sept. 15, 1896, p. 9.

59. Copy Book 37, May 26, 1896, p. 676.

60. Charles S. Brown remembers that "there was lots of dissatisfaction brought about by the different methods of handling merchandise checks as opposed to cash." Interview, July 11, 1953.

61. Copy Book 38, July 10, 1896, p. 376. In two cases noted, only 5 per cent was deducted but in one of these examples the merchant had not been informed of the practice and Nordhaus took this factor into account. Copy Book 36, Jan. 4, 1896, p. 196; Copy Book 44, Aug. 14, 1897, p. 75.

62. Copy Book 18, May 28, 1890, p. 144. Also see photostat, p. 206.

63. Copy Book 29, June 6, 1894, p. 181.

64. Another minor problem was the presentation of cash orders at the main store after banking hours. Copy Book 43, May 24, 1897, p. 104. Charles S. Brown remembers that the banks normally cleared Ilfeld's cash checks but did not charge them to Ilfeld's account until a collector, sent to the company daily, received permission. Interview, July 11, 1953.

65. Copy Book 24, Dec. 27, 1892, pp. 539–540.

66. Copy Book 23, Sept. 3, 1892, p. 461.

67. Incoming Correspondence, Packet 7, Feb. 14, 1893.

68. Copy Book 24, Dec. 27, 1892, p. 554.

69. Incoming Correspondence, Packet 7, Feb. 23, 1893.

70. The system remained in wide use. The company sought a quotation on 500 to 1,000 counter checkbooks in 1901. Copy Book 65, June 13, 1901, p. 583. E. L. Moulton used the system at Ilfeld's Corona store in 1914 and later. Interview, Aug. 2, 1957.

71. Ledger K, p. 390, Oct. 21, 1891, at $50 per month. Raised to $60 on Nov. 1, 1892.

72. Ledger M, p. 319. Opening inventory was $3,165. Copy Book 43, June 19, 1897, p. 321.

73. Floersheim enlarged his enterprise in Springer by purchasing the established firm of Henry M. Porter on Sept. 6, 1897. He incorporated his firm Dec. 18, 1897, retaining a 50 per cent stock interest. The other 50 per cent was split equally between the officers of Gross, Blackwell & Company of Las Vegas—Jacob Gross, Arthur M. Blackwell, and Henry M. Kelly. Floersheim encountered serious problems through this close tie, and Gross, Blackwell had increased its interest substantially by 1903. During and after World War I, the Floersheim family obtained commanding control. Floersheim

Minute Book. Incoming Correspondence, Packet 43, July 11, 1897. Ludwig to Charles Ilfeld.

74. Copy Book 43, June 19, 1897, p. 321. Nordhaus procured a jobber's rebate on coal oil out of Raton.

75. Ludwig Ilfeld's ledger account with Charles Ilfeld showed a net gain after all charge-offs of $233.14. Ledger M, p. 319.

76. Interview, Ludwig W. Ilfeld, Sept. 3, 1952.

77. Incoming Correspondence from Ludwig W. Ilfeld, Packet 42, June 18, 1897; Packet 43, July 6, 11, 13, 1897. From Appel, Packet 43, July 15, 1897. Copy Book 46, Jan. 11, 1898, p. 233. Appel account, Ledger M, p. 139.

78. The distribution rate of 10¢ per 100 lbs. applied to everything except native produce. Salt, obtained locally, for instance, carried a 17¢ rate. Copy Book 43, July 16, 1897, p. 522. Charles S. Brown says, "The 10¢ per hundred jobbing rate out of Las Vegas extended clear to Silver City. Browne and Manzanares had been instrumental in obtaining this rate. It was cheaper in many instances [wire and nails were cited as examples] to break shipment at Las Vegas and then pay distribution rate than to ship through to Silver City. Ilfeld would prepay the freight charges at the regular local distribution rates and then obtain a refund to make an effective rate of 10¢. These rebates continued until the Interstate Commerce Commission put an end to it." Interview, Albuquerque, July 11, 1953. Usual terms granted were 10 per cent over cost on groceries. Appel was given terms of 40 days net on groceries and 90 days net on dry goods. Interest thereafter accrued at 10 per cent per annum.

79. In a letter to R. G. Dun & Co., Nordhaus wondered how they accomplished this refund. He was suspicious that they borrowed from a relative. Copy Book 46, March 5, 1898, p. 680; Copy Book 49, Aug. 24, 1898, p. 263.

80. Ledger O, p. 741.

81. Copy Book 38, Aug. 8, 1896, p. 567. A chance note that Schoonmaker had written to himself and had lodged in an account ledger indicates a further type of control that was exercised. Goldenberg was authorized, in this instance, to sell to John Gerhardt "not to exceed $60 per month together with purchases here [Charles Ilfeld] and allow us 5 per cent on same when paid or transferred to us." (Note dated Jan. 1, 1897.) Evidently Charles Ilfeld would guarantee some accounts to certain limits and, for this service, would charge 5 per cent.

82. Copy Book 43, May 20, 1897, p. 50. Ledger N, p. 285.

83. Copy Book 43, July 6, 1897, p. 451.

84. Ledger N, p. 292.

85. Ledger L, p. 309; Ledger N, p. 311.

86. Copy Book 51, Dec. (?), 1898, p. 281; Copy Book 57, Dec. 19, 1899, p. 418.

87. Ledger P, p. 921. Letter from A. C. Ortega, who had been clerk in Hugo's store at the time (Aug. 11, 1955). The "Old Observer" interviewed H. L. Goldenberg in Santa Rosa in 1906 and observed his ranches east of Corona in 1907. *American Shepherd's Bulletin,* 11:708–709 (Aug. 1906), 12:263 (March 1907).

88. Alex Goldenberg married a Wertheim. Twitchell, *Leading Facts,* III, 491. *Las Vegas Optic,* March 8, 1900.

89. Ledger O, p. 866.

90. Ledger P, pp. 927 and 931.

91. Wertheim and Alex Goldenberg were two of four individuals who owned the townsite of Tucumcari. *History of New Mexico,* p. 882. Nordhaus congratulated Alex on settling the townsite matter. Copy Book 69, Dec. 5, 1901, pp. 198–199. Ledger P, p. 923.

92. Copy Book 80, April 18, 1903, p. 291. Nordhaus referred to a debt of $20,000 still owed Charles Ilfeld which was probably the capital advance to the Tucumcari firm which Nordhaus had stated "we feel inclined to put . . . into your business." Copy Book 69, Dec. 5, 1901, pp. 198–199.

CHAPTER XIV

Retail Trade and the Rise of Jobbing

1. Copy Book 65, June 5, 1901, p. 467.
2. Copy Book 17, June 28, 1889, p. 70.
3. Gras, *Business and Capitalism,* p. 76. See reference to the advantage achieved by Marshall Field and Company over Wanamaker's in combining the wholesaling and retailing functions. Gras and Larson, *Casebook in American Business History,* p. 495.
4. See Chapter VI. Gross, Blackwell and Company, as well as Browne and Manzanares, specialized in groceries, although the former had a small dry goods business and both developed a jobbing trade in wagons.
5. See Chapter V and Chapter VI.
6. Gross, Blackwell and Company Minute Book. Moulton, while still president of the Charles Ilfeld Company, quoted Max Nordhaus as being pleased that the Charles Ilfeld Company, in acting as a wool broker, had produced as much income, without the headaches, as Gross, Kelly had acquired by speculation. Moulton described Harry Kelly as a "plunger." Interview, Sept. 5, 1951.

Some slight evidence of this general feeling held by older competitors of Gross, Kelly, is found in two letters written by Max Nordhaus. When both Gross, Kelly (and Bond Brothers) were paying more than the market, Nordhaus gladly retreated from the competition on the theory that his customers, by receiving these higher prices, would pay more on their accounts. Copy Book 77, Feb. 12, 1902, p. 321. On another occasion, when Harry Kelly was outbidding Ilfeld's agent in Albuquerque, Nordhaus wrote, "Harry is doing same thing here . . . he paid . . . 13¢ . . . [for wool] I had instructed B[ond] Brothers to pay only 11¾¢ for & we would take it off their hands at 12. As soon as Harry saw it on the streets he phoned B. Bros. that he wanted it." Copy Book 84, Oct. 20, 1903, p. 95.

7. Lawrence P. Browne died in Kansas City on Dec. 5, 1893. F. A. Manzanares died Sept. 16, 1904, in Las Vegas. Twitchell, *Leading Facts,* II, 488–489. Manzanares had turned his interests more to ranching and banking even before Browne's death.
8. Gras, *Business and Capitalism,* p. 75.
9. See Chapter VII.
10. San Miguel County grew from 20,638 in 1880, to 24,204 in 1890. *Twelfth Census of the U.S.* (1900), *Population,* 1:31.
11. Copy Book 19, Sept. 18, 1890, pp. 39–42; Jan. 17, 1891, p. 679. The floor space increased in cubic footage from 104,832 to 255,148.
12. *Ibid.,* Oct. 21, 1890, p. 197; Sept. (22?), 1890, p. 60.
13. *Ibid.,* Oct. 30, 1890, p. 252.
14. *Ibid.,* Dec. 16, 1890, p. 516; March 17, 1891, p. 892; Sept. 18, 1890, p. 42; Copy Book 20, April 27, 1891, p. 46; May 2, 1891, p. 66.
15. Copy Book 20, June 13, 1891, p. 273.
16. *Ibid.,* Aug. 1, 1891, p. 543.
17. *Ibid.,* Aug. 17, 1891, p. 667.
18. *Las Vegas Optic,* Dec. 14, 1891; Dec. 19, 1891.
19. *Ibid.,* Jan. 24, 1883.
20. Copy Book 76, Dec. 16, 1902, p. 136.
21. Summary Book, 1895–1910.
22. Incoming Correspondence, Packet 1, Dec. 1, 1882, Daniels and Fisher, Western Agents for Butterick's Patterns, Denver, Colorado. First record of an order.
23. Copy Book 47, March 16, 1898, pp. 121–122.
24. Copy Book 77, Feb. 19, 1903, p. 411.
25. Copy Book 47, March 16, 1898, pp. 121–122.
26. *Ibid.,* March 16, 1898, p. 123.

27. Copy Book 51, Dec. 16, 1898, p. 170. Copy Book 57, Dec. 23, 1899, p. 471.
28. Copy Book 24, Oct. 24, 1892, pp. 75–76.
29. *Ibid.*, Oct. 24, 1892, p. 98.
30. Interview, C. S. Brown, Aug. 19, 1953.
31. Copy Book 32, Feb. 14, 1895, p. 356.
32. Copy Book 28, May 8, 1894, p. 659.
33. Copy Book 12, May 27, 1885, p. 473.
34. Copy Book 41, Jan. 18, 1897, p. 171.
35. Interview, C. S. Brown, July 11, 1953.
36. Copy Book 20, July 24, 1891, p. 478.
37. Copy Book 40, Nov. 11, 1896, p. 21. Ilfeld and Co. of Albuquerque also followed this practice. Incoming Correspondence, Packet 3, Nov. 16, 1883. Copy Book 12, Dec. 9, 1884, p. 86.
38. Copy Book 27, Oct. 5, 1893, pp. 335–337.
39. Interview, C. S. Brown, Aug. 23, 1957.
40. Copy Book 11, July 5, 1884, p. 127.
41. Copy Book 13, Aug. 15, 1885, p. 185.
42. Copy Book 14, March 9, 1887, p. 821.
43. Copy Book 25, Feb. 14, 1893, p. 153.
44. *Ibid.*
45. Incoming Correspondence, Packet 49, J. C. Ayer & Co., Lowell, Massachusetts, dated Sept. 1, 1897.
46. Copy Book 48, July 7, 1898, p. 536.
47. *Ibid.*
48. Copy Book 12, Jan. 17, 1885, p. 199; Copy Book 14, Sept. 1, 1886, p. 331; Copy Book 13, June 17, 1885, p. 40.
49. Copy Book 49, Aug. 26, 1898, p. 284; Copy Book 65, May 10, 1901, p. 150. Upon learning that Rosenwald "across the street" had the same paint, Nordhaus threatened to drop it "and look for another article."
50. Copy Book 56, Oct. 12, 1899, p. 86.
51. Copy Book 17, July 26, 1889, p. 161.
52. Copy Book 32, Jan. 5, 1895, p. 119.
53. Copy Book 15, Feb. 28, 1888, p. 593.
54. Copy Book 16, Aug. 2, 1888, p. 206.
55. Copy Book 18, May 23, 1890, p. 120.
56. Copy Book 23, Aug. 9, 1892, p. 311.
57. Interview, C. S. Brown, July 11, 1953.
58. Copy Book 31, Oct. 27, 1894, p. 67.
59. Summary Book, 1895–1910.
60. A fourth department, wholesale liquors, was closed out in 1891. The intention to do so was expressed in January, 1890, and was disposed of in April, or thereabouts, 1891. Copy Book 17, Jan. 6, 1890, p. 680; Copy Book 20, April 21, 1891, p. 20. He offered the stock to William Frank but Frank's terms were not as good as someone else's and there was some fear that the stock was too big for Frank to handle.
61. Copy Book 15, Oct. 25, 1887, pp. 364–366.
62. *Las Vegas Optic,* advertisements, March 27 and June 13, 1900.
63. Copy Book 48, June 11, 1898, p. 295; July 28, 1898, p. 710.
64. Copy Book 58, Jan. 24, 1900, pp. 104–106.
65. One valiant effort to help Dunn did not materialize when the well-promoted Las Vegas to Taos railroad did not get beyond the survey. Copy Book 49, Aug. 1, 1898, p. 21; Copy Book 57, Nov. 28, 1899, p. 74. "The Railway Age says that 85 miles of track will be laid from Las Vegas to Taos via Mora. It has already been surveyed." *Las Vegas Optic,* March 23, 1900.
66. Copy Book 83, Sept. 15, 1903, p. 142.
67. See Chapter IX.
68. Copy Book 24, Dec. 15, 1892, pp. 491–492.
69. Copy Book 34, July 30, 1895, p. 577.

70. Herman was the second of five sons born to Adele and Charles Ilfeld. The third and fourth, Ernst and Willi, died at ages three and twelve. The first son was Louis and the fifth, Arthur.

71. Copy Book 37, April 9, 1896, p. 255.

72. Special Copy Book, March 29, 1897, p. 65.

73. *Ibid.*, Sept. 19, 1897, pp. 94–95.

74. Incoming Correspondence, Packet 47, Nov. 4, 1897.

75. Copy Book 42, March 2, 1897, p. 23.

76. Copy Book 43, June 11, 1897, p. 262. The increase in peddlars gave rise to a new law in 1897. Peddlars on foot or with one animal paid a license fee of $250 per year. Those with two or more animals paid $300 per year. The license was only effective in one county. One half the proceeds went to the school fund and one half to the general fund of the county. New Mexico, *Laws of 1897,* chap. 53, March 18, 1897.

77. Special Copy Book, Sept. 4, 1897, p. 83.

78. Copy Book 44, Sept. 4, 1897, p. 283.

79. Special Copy Book, Sept. 7, 1897, p. 86.

80. Copy Book 46, Feb. 7, 1898, p. 438.

81. The towns listed were: Rociada, Ignacio, San Miguel or Ribera, Sapello, Mora, Cleveland, Guadalupita, La Cueva, Ocate, Watrous, Springer, Maxwell City, Anton Chico, Casaus.

82. See Chapter XIII, note 76.

83. Copy Book 46, Jan. 4, 1898, p. 177; Feb. 7, 1898, p. 447. Nordhaus intended to send a man to small towns to sell suits made to order. Copy Book 47, April 9, 1898, p. 396. Copy Book 46, Feb. 10, 1898, p. 480.

84. Copy Book 53, April 17, 1899, p. 15.

85. Incoming Correspondence, Packet 67, June 28, 1899. Letter from Henry Essinger, former whiskey drummer for Ilfeld, 1888–1889. Ledger I, and later ledgers.

86. A letter to a prospective traveling salesman describes the territory as extending to the seven neighboring counties, "having a traveling representative therein at regular intervals." This probably would have meant the counties of Union, Mora, Colfax, Taos, Rio Arriba, Santa Fe, and Bernalillo. Copy Book 60, June 27, 1900, p. 251.

87. Copy Book 58, March 22, 1900, pp. 724–725.

88. Copy Book 61, Sept. 10, 1900, p. 272. Interview, C. S. Brown, Aug. 30, 1957. Copy Book 61, Sept. 12, 1900, pp. 285–290, 292–293.

89. Copy Book 62, Nov. 3, 1900, pp. 131 and 142; Nov. 10, 1900, p. 242.

90. Copy Book 61, Oct. 2, 1900, p. 504.

91. Summary Book, 1895–1910.

92. Interview, C. S. Brown, Aug. 30, 1957.

93. *Ibid.*

CHAPTER XV

Direct Investment in Country Stores

1. Ledger M, p. 387.

2. Copy Book 46, Jan. 31, 1898, p. 399.

3. *Las Vegas Gazette,* Sept. 19, 1880. Incoming Correspondence, Packet 2, May 22, 1883. Ilfeld was evidently taking over some of Holzman's payables resulting from his Las Vegas enterprise. *Ibid.,* June (?), 1883. Letters from Holzman.

4. From C. Barela and Company, General Merchandise, Trinidad, Colorado. Letter Book of the Arizona Mineral Belt Timber Agent. D. M. Rindon, agent, and Philip Holzman, subagent. University of New Mexico Library. Copy Book 35, Oct. 16, 1895, p. 436.

5. Copy Book 40, Dec. 21, 1896, p. 441.

6. Copy Book 52, Feb. 21, 1899, p. 108; Copy Book 57, Dec. 31, 1899, p. 557.

7. Copy Book 37, May 3, 1896, p. 492; May 26, 1896, p. 676.

8. See Chapter XIII. Incoming Correspondence, Packet 38, Feb. 11, 1897; Packet 39, Feb. 27, 1897. Letters from Max Goldenberg.

9. Copy Book 65, May 29, 1901, pp. 386–387.

10. *Ibid.*, June 5, 1901, p. 467.

11. In December he had argued, however, that the new location "can hold a good deal of your present trade." Copy Book 69, Dec. 11, 1901, p. 358.

12. Copy Book 71, March 11, 1902, pp. 467–468.

13. See Chapter XII.

14. See Chapter IX.

15. "It seems now definitely settled that the Portales road will be built; Judge Henry L. Waldo told us that he had advice to this effect." Copy Book 74, Oct. 4, 1902, p. 211. Henry L. Waldo, formerly Chief Justice of the Supreme Court of New Mexico, and later Attorney General of New Mexico, had been Solicitor for New Mexico of the A.T. & S.F. R.R. since 1883. Twitchell, *Old Santa Fe,* p. 399.

16. Copy Book 71, March 11, 1902, pp. 467–468; March 22, 1902, p. 657.

17. *Ibid.*, March 11, 1902, pp. 467–468.

18. *Ibid.*, Feb. 24 and 28, 1902, pp. 139 and 236.

19. Copy Book 73, Aug. 23, 1902, p. 294; Copy Book 74, Sept. 29, 1902, p. 125.

20. Ledger P, p. 1,105. An interruption occurred when the wind blew off the roof. Copy Book 76, Dec. 27, 1902, p. 269. Holzman-Ilfeld Contract, Nov. 11, 1902, Office of Louis C. Ilfeld, Las Vegas.

21. Copy Book 80, June 8, 1903, p. 571.

22. DuBois-Ilfeld Contract, Dec. 17, 1903, Office of Louis C. Ilfeld, Las Vegas.

23. *Ibid.*, also first book entry Jan. 23, 1904, Ledger P, p. 833.

24. Letters from R. B. Schoonmaker, March 27, 31, 1950. Copy Book 80, May 4, 1903, p. 96. Letter in Corona file to Thomas DuBois, Jan. 5, 1905, Office of Louis C. Ilfeld, Las Vegas.

25. Special Copy Book, Dec. (?), 1904, p. 248.

26. See note 24, above.

27. DuBois' resignation, Jan. 10, 1905, Office of Louis C. Ilfeld, Las Vegas. DuBois was paid $450 for release of all claims, Jan. 25, 1905. Lots to the Corona Mercantile Company for $200, Dec. 21, 1903.

28. Schoonmaker wrote of this experience: "The population of the vicinity was a bad mixture of new-comers from West Texas and some transitory railroad employees largely inclined to lawlessness. They led me a merry life for a year resulting in a loss to Ilfeld's." Letter, March 31, 1950.

29. Philip, Joe, and Arthur Holzman contracted with Ilfeld on Oct. 2, 1905, Office of Louis C. Ilfeld, Las Vegas. Special Copy Book, Aug. 11, 1905, pp. 249–255.

30. Louis C. Ilfeld Letter Book, Jan. 28, 1908, p. 27.

31. *Ibid.*, Sept. 30, 1910, p. 105.

32. Moulton was born Sept. 26, 1878, in Leroy, Michigan. He came to New Mexico in 1902 following a short sojourn in California. His trip West had been provoked by poor health which was diagnosed in California as tuberculosis. He regained his health herding sheep near Lucy, New Mexico, where, after almost four years, he purchased a general store in 1907.

33. Holzman was succeeded by James W. Ruane, who in turn was succeeded by Joe Wolf.

34. A. C. Ortega became bookkeeper at Pastura, Oct. 1, 1908, and became manager two years later. He bought the store in 1947. Letter, Aug. 11, 1955.

35. Ledger O, pp. 877–880.

36. Special Copy Book, Aug. 11, 1905, pp. 251–253. Letter from Schoonmaker, March 31, 1950.

37. Willard was incorporated July 25, 1905, by the Willard Town and Improvement Company, John Becker, president. *History of New Mexico,* p. 894.

38. Letter to B. S. Jackson, Willard, New Mexico, from Max Nordhaus, Jan. 30, 1907.

39. Minute Book of the Willard Mercantile Company, Office of Louis C. Ilfeld, Las Vegas.

40. *Ibid.*

41. *Ibid.;* E. L. Moulton, "Seventy Years of Progress," p. 16.

42. Lease of Springer Trading Company to Nathan Weil of Ocate, New Mexico, Oct. 1, 1917, to Oct. 1, 1922, Office of Louis C. Ilfeld, Las Vegas. Upon expiration, Weil had an option to purchase for $6,500. Herman Ilfeld had been president. Charles S. Brown states that the Roy venture was very largely the idea of Arthur Ilfeld and that the branch was a complete failure. Interview, July 11, 1953. Mention is made of the Roy Trading Company and the Springer Trading Company in the Summary Book, 1906–1929, for the years 1917 through 1928. The Public Accountant's Audit for 1928 states that both Springer and Roy stores were in the process of liquidation at that time. Each had a substantial accumulated deficit.

43. Moulton-Ilfeld Contract, Office of Louis C. Ilfeld, Las Vegas.

44. E. L. Moulton in his writing referred to Max Nordhaus as "Mr." His deference and respect for the man who made him general manager of the Charles Ilfeld Company was consistently noticeable. Moulton described his refusal and then acceptance of the Corona position in his unpublished pamphlet, "From Sheepherder to Director of the Chamber of Commerce of the United States," p. 25.

45. *Ibid.*

46. Special analysis for settlement with Moulton upon formation of the Corona Trading Company, Office of Louis C. Ilfeld, Las Vegas. Beginning capital, Nov. 12, 1912, was $36,944.78. Net profits ending Dec. 31, 1913, were $6,801.35. The new corporation was formed March 7, 1914.

47. Moulton, "From Sheepherder to Director," pp. 28–29.

48. Moulton stated that the new sheep company took over 6,400 head from the Pastura Trading Company and 18,000 head from the Charles Ilfeld–Joint Ownership, a general partnership formed by Charles Ilfeld and Max Nordhaus as a holding company for their total joint interests on Feb. 11, 1911. Ilfeld shared three fourths and Nordhaus one fourth in this partnership. Moulton, "From Sheepherder to Director"; Little Black Book, Office of Louis C. Ilfeld, Las Vegas. The Ilfeld-Moulton Sheep Company was dissolved in 1936. In 1935 it had 10,703 breeding sheep, 418 ranch bucks, and 2,061 ewes on partido contract. Records, Office of Louis C. Ilfeld, Las Vegas.

CHAPTER XVI

Wholesaling and Branch Warehouses

1. See Chapter IX.

2. See Chapter XV.

3. See Table 17.

4. Copy Book 71, March 6, 1902, p. 343; Feb. 24, 1902, pp. 139, 140.

5. Copy Book 74, Oct. 25, 1902, p. 577. Copy Book 73, Aug. 7, 1902, p. 43.

6. *Ibid.*, Aug. 12, 1902, p. 116; Copy Book 74, Nov. 1, 1902, p. 678.

7. Copy Book 76, Dec. 8, 1902, p. 5.

8. Summary Book, 1895–1910.

9. *Ibid.*

10. Interview, Albert Stern, July 16, 1953. Actually free textbooks were not made available to all the grades in the public schools until 1941. In 1930 the privilege was made available to the first and second grades, and in 1933 it was extended through the eighth grade. *Laws of New Mexico,* 1941, chap. 76; 1933, chap. 112; 1929, chap. 191. The 1931 Public Accountant's Audit segregated an inventory of school books of $3,516.

11. *Las Vegas Optic,* June 17, 1905, to Nov. 25, 1905, *passim.*

12. Special Copy Book, Jan. 11, 1906, pp. 263–264.

13. *Ibid.*

14. An interesting advertisement in the *Las Vegas Optic,* Jan. 2, 1900, reads as follows: "Business at Ilfeld's has increased such that the present superintendent will be reassigned to one-half of the store's departments and another superintendent will

be hired for the rest. Millinery is in new and larger location. Have new and enlarged office . . . Newly organized shipping department."

15. Inspection of employees accounts in various ledgers.

16. Copy Book 47, March 25, 1898, pp. 218–219. Copy Book 38, Aug. 15, 1896, p. 626. Office employees received two weeks. Clerks received one week. Interview, C. S. Brown, July 11, 1953.

17. Interview, Sept. 15, 1952.

18. *Las Vegas Optic,* Jan. 6, 1900. On Jan. 2, 1900, eight west side (Plaza) firms agreed to close thereafter at 7 o'clock. *Ibid.*

19. Interview, C. S. Brown, July 11, 1953.

20. *Ibid.*

21. *Las Vegas Optic,* Feb. 1, 1900.

22. Interview, C. S. Brown, Sept. 12, 1957. *Las Vegas Optic,* May 28, 1900.

23. *Compiled Laws of New Mexico,* 1897, Sections 1368, 1369, 1372 from New Mexico, *Laws of 1887,* chap. 26.

24. Copy Book 41, Feb. 10, 1897, p. 372. Second offense was to be $75 and the third, $100.

25. Summary Book, 1895–1910.

26. Original capital stock authorized was $500,000, par value $500, 200 shares outstanding. All shareholders agreed to give the company first option on the purchase of the stock of shareholders. The capital stock was doubled in 1916 to 2000 shares of $500 par. Approximately 3/8 of the additional shares were made available to 28 employees outside of the Ilfeld family. Two thirds ($300 per share) was paid for immediately out of surplus and the $200 balance was to be paid in cash by employees. Capital was again changed in 1919 when a $650,000 preferred issue was created; 17,500 Class A common shares, par $100, more than replaced the old 2,000 shares of common; and 30,000 new shares of Class B were authorized. Preferred and Class A held voting privileges and Class B could not be held by anyone not owning some Class A.

27. See Chapter VIII.

28. Interview, Louis C. Ilfeld.

29. The wedding was Sept. 5, 1907. Postcard from Elizabeth Nordhaus Minces, June 23, 1958. Benjamin M. Read, *Illustrated History of New Mexico,* p. 785.

30. Little Black Book, Office of Louis C. Ilfeld, Las Vegas.

31. See Chapter VIII.

32. See Chapter XIV.

33. *History of New Mexico,* p. 530.

34. Gross, Kelly and Company Minute Book.

35. Copy Book 48, June 22, 1898, p. 391; Copy Book 49, Aug. 20, 1898, p. 219; Copy Book 51, Dec. (?), 1898, p. 21.

36. Special Copy Book, May 14, 1904, pp. 244–245.

37. An offer made to J. W. Frankel, Kansas City, Mo., *ibid.,* p. 68. Another letter on the same page is dated May 30, 1906. Louis C. Ilfeld Letter Book, Nov. 13, 1906, p. 262. *Albuquerque City Directory of 1908–09* gives the address as 218–226 East Central Ave. The 1907 *Directory* gives address as East Railroad Ave., and Railroad tracks. These were the same locations.

38. A merchandise inventory for the Albuquerque Branch of $47,530.06 as of Dec. 31, 1906, is listed in the Annual Summary Book, 1906–1929. The lease was accepted Jan. 9, 1907. Charles Ilfeld Company Minute Book.

39. Special Copy Book, Jan. 7, 1907, pp. 269–271.

40. Charles Ilfeld Company Minute Book, Jan. 15, 1910; Jan. 5, 1911.

41. Present site of the company's executive offices.

42. Charles Ilfeld Company Minute Book, Jan. 15, 1910. The earnings of the branch in 1910 had been $19,680.87. At the new location the earnings were $49,892.79. Merchandise inventories were $216,562.50 at Las Vegas and $240,384.66 at Albuquerque. Summary Book, 1906–1929.

43. Moulton, "Seventy Years of Progress," p. 14. As evidenced by the location of regular stockholders' and directors' meetings, Albuquerque did not become the recog-

nized central office until 1947 although intermittent meetings were held in Albuquerque from 1936 on.

44. Charles Ilfeld Company Minute Book, Jan. 22, 1916. Marshall, *Santa Fe,* p. 404.

45. Moulton, "Seventy Years of Progress," pp. 14 and 16. *History of New Mexico,* p. 645.

46. See note 42, Chapter XV.

47. Public Accountant's Audit, Dec. 31, 1928, shows accumulated deficits of $20,140 for Springer and $32,506 for Roy and each was in the process of liquidation.

48. Marshall, *Santa Fe,* pp. 127–143.

49. Charles Ilfeld Company Minute Book, Feb. 12, 1927.

50. Financial Statements of 1927 and Public Accountant's Audits for the following years.

51. Moulton, "Seventy Years of Progress," p. 16. In Feb., 1921, the store was managed by O. H. Gosch. Charles Ilfeld Company Minute Book, Feb. 12, 1921; Feb. 23, 1924.

52. Willard Mercantile Minute Book, Jan. 29, 1920.

53. The Little Black Book, Louis C. Ilfeld Office, Las Vegas; Annual Summary Book, 1906–1929.

54. Charles Ilfeld Company Minute Book, Dec. 9, 1919.

55. Interview, Frank A. Mapel, July 11, 1958. Charles Ilfeld Company Minute Book, Feb. 23, 1924.

56. *Ibid.,* Feb. 11, 1922; Feb. 23, 1924.

57. Public Accountant's Audit, Dec. 31, 1930.

58. Ilfeld died on Jan. 3, 1929. Family Prayer Book, Office of Louis C. Ilfeld, Las Vegas.

59. Financial Statements, 1927; in the case of Gallup the evidence is based on an ending merchandise inventory of $326,000 as against $143,000 for Las Vegas.

60. Albuquerque (old and new) had grown from a population of 15,157 in 1920 to 28,196 in 1930; Las Vegas (old and new) from 8,206 in 1920 to 9,097 in 1930. Bernalillo County (Albuquerque) grew from 29,855 in 1920 to 45,430 in 1930; San Miguel County (Las Vegas) from 22,867 in 1920 to 23,636 in 1930.

CHAPTER XVII

The Old Order in a Changing Economy

1. See Chapter III. Henrietta M. Larson, *Jay Cooke, Private Banker,* p. 410.

2. Copy Book 3, Feb. 18, 1877, p. 474.

3. *Ibid.,* Feb. 19, 1877, p. 477.

4. *Ibid.,* Jan. 25, 1878, pp. 858–859.

5. *Ibid.,* Oct. 4, 1876, p. 369.

6. *Ibid.;* Feb. 5, 1878, p. 876; Cash Book 1876–77, March 27, 1877.

7. *Las Vegas Gazette,* April 21, 1877.

8. *Ibid.,* June 9, 1877.

9. *Ibid.,* Sept. 15, 1877; July 31, 1879; advertisement, Aug. 31, 1879.

10. Chapter IX.

11. *Ibid.;* Chapter XI.

12. Chapter XI; Chapter XIII.

13. Chapter XVI.

14. Corporation Minute Book.

15. Of the 125 commercial banks in New Mexico at the close of 1920, at least 52 had failed by the end of 1925, and 34 of these (21 state and 13 national) closed during 1923 and 1924. Actually, only 60 banks were doing business in 1925 and one of these opened in 1922. *Reports* of New Mexico State Bank Examiner and Comptroller of the Currency. See also Tom L. Popejoy, "Analysis of the Causes of Bank Failures in New Mexico, 1920 to 1925," *University of New Mexico Bulletin, Economic Series,* vol. I, no. 1 (Oct., 1931).

16. Annual Summary Book, 1906–1929.

17. Chapter XVI.
18. Corporation Minute Book, Jan. 23, 1929.
19. Unless otherwise noted all factual data relating to financial operations of the Charles Ilfeld Company have been obtained from the Corporation Minute Book, or Certified Annual Audits of the company.
20. *Business Information Series,* 18 (Sept. 1951), 21 (July 1952), University of New Mexico, Bureau of Business Research, Albuquerque.
21. Figures are above the average for the 1930 and 1940 censuses.
22. Nordhaus died on July 13, 1936.
23. A strange combination of administrative forces existed. The top one or two executives were prone to delegate very little authority although Max Nordhaus seems to have done more of this than Earl Moulton. However, the distance to branch houses from the central offices of Albuquerque and Las Vegas, particularly the western branches, forced a delegation of responsibility to branch managers, independent of controls from the central offices, that was not much less true in the 1930's and 1940's than it had been in prior years. See Chapter XVIII.
24. See Moulton, "From Sheepherder to Director."
25. U. S. Department of Agriculture, *Yearbook,* 1935, pp. 15–16.
26. Sheep on New Mexico ranges averaged some 600,000 more per year from 1930 through 1934 than during the period 1925 through 1929. U. S. Department of Agriculture, *Yearbook,* 1930, p. 864; 1936, p. 232; 1937, p. 271.
27. *Ibid.,* 1935, p. 18.
28. E. L. Moulton, *The Odyssey of a Flockmaster: A Story of the 1934 Drought in the Southwestern United States.* All material relating to the Charles Ilfeld Company experience in the 1934 drought has been taken from this pamphlet.
29. Chapter IX.
30. For an example of the movement of sheep over great distances in days of drought see Chapter XII.
31. Herman Ilfeld died in Las Vegas, July 2, 1935. Family Prayer Book: Died after a short illness. *Albuquerque Tribune,* July 3, 1935.
32. Moulton, "From Sheepherder to Director," p. 32.
33. National sheep and lamb prices per 100 lbs., which had averaged $2.19 in 1932, rose steadily to $4.40 in 1937. Wool prices per lb. had been 8.6¢ in 1932 and had risen to 32¢ in 1937. U. S. Department of Agriculture, *Yearbook,* 1941, pp. 303, 401.
34. *Ibid.;* sheep and lambs dropped to $3.56 per 100 lbs. and wool to 19¢ per lb.
35. This investment was kept secret from the public for fear the independent grocers' trade would be lost. The initial investment of the family was made through R. R. Ryan, trustee, in May, 1932, and in 1933 this certificate for 135 shares and 15 more were transferred to Max Nordhaus, Louis C. Ilfeld, Herman C. Ilfeld, Arthur C. Ilfeld, E. L. Moulton, and W. A. Disque in 25-share lots. Vernon Barber and W. B. Eames were the minority stockholders and the managers of the enterprise.
36. Las Vegas, Nov. 26, 1941. Arthur Ilfeld died after a short illness. *Albuquerque Journal,* Nov. 27, 1941.
37. Corporation Minute Book, Feb. 7, 1942.
38. A casual conversation with the author.
39. Based on actual inventory turnovers of 1936 when for all merchandise the turnover was 4 times but for groceries alone was 6.4.
40. Moulton belonged to the National Retail Council, Consumer Division, Office of Price Administration, Washington, D. C.
41. E. L. Moulton, *New Mexico's Future: An Economic and Employment Appraisal,* Committee for Economic Development Research Study (Albuquerque: University of New Mexico Press, 1945).
42. Del Pueblo Products, Inc., June 1, 1940.
43. Mapel had asked the previous distributor to permit him to sell Coca Cola through the Gallup Mercantile Company. The results were very promising. Mapel, knowing the franchise was for sale, interested Moulton in the opportunity. Moulton called him to Albuquerque (Max Nordhaus was still alive) to explain to the board the

possibilities. "I got a good going over and went back to Gallup with my tail between my legs. Wondered if I had lost my mind. But Moulton stuck with me and soon the money was available." Interview, Frank A. Mapel, July 21, 1958. The Coca Cola bottling business was purchased from O. E. Beck of Albuquerque; franchise dated Aug. 24, 1931. Part of the Durango franchise was purchased from O. E. Beck. Durango Coca Cola Bottling Company was incorporated May 25, 1938.

44. Certificate of Incorporation dated July 17, 1945.

45. The Nash agency was purchased July 1, 1945, and sold to Frank Groesbeeck in Nov., 1948.

46. Moulton, "From Sheepherder to Director," p. 33.

47. The fire was on Feb. 16, 1948. Corporation Minute Book, March 9, 1948.

48. Letters from E. L. Moulton to warehousing managers, Office of Charles Ilfeld Co.

49. The loan was obtained from the Massachusetts Mutual Life Insurance Company through the efforts of Kidder, Peabody and Company.

50. *Business Information Series,* 21 (July 1952).

51. *Ibid.,* 18 (Sept. 1951).

52. Corporation Minute Book, Dec. 18, 1952.

53. Mapel started to work for the Gallup Mercantile Company in 1927. He became its manager in 1938. He became a director of the Charles Ilfeld Company, Feb., 1942.

54. Corporation Minute Book, Feb. 8, 1947; March 15, 1950.

55. *Ibid.,* Oct. 15, 1951; Dec. 3, 1951. *Albuquerque Tribune,* Dec. 1, 1951.

56. Corporation Minute Book, April 14, 1951.

57. *Ibid.* Liquor was eliminated first in 1890. Copy Book 17, Jan. 6, 1890, p. 680.

58. Corporation Minute Book, July 16 and Oct. 15, 1952.

59. Interview, Julius Rosenthal, Auditor and Director of the Charles Ilfeld Corporation, Sept. 4, 1958.

CHAPTER XVIII

Thawing the Family Capital

1. *Business Information Series,* 18 (Sept. 1951).

2. Corporation Minute Book, April 17, 1952.

3. *Ibid.,* Oct. 15, 1952.

4. *Ibid.*

5. It should be pointed out that Max Nordhaus was only 41 when he became vice president and general manager of the corporation at its inception. He had been general agent for Charles Ilfeld since 1886, when he was only 21.

6. Mapel was born at Fort Defiance, Arizona, on Jan. 13, 1908.

7. General information in this section of the chapter, unless otherwise noted, has been taken from the Corporation Minute Book.

8. Offering Circular representing a public offering of common stock, April 1, 1957.

9. See note 35, Chapter XVII.

10. Offering Circular, April 1, 1957.

11. Telephone conversation, Frank A. Mapel, Sept. 6, 1958. Barber's operated 15 stores (Oct. 1958) in New Mexico—all within the Ilfeld territory: 8 were in Albuquerque, 3 in Santa Fe, and 1 each in Farmington, Grants, Los Alamos, and Taos. Shop Rite operated 9 stores in the Ilfeld territory. There was 1 in Farmington, 2 in Santa Fe, and 6 in Albuquerque.

12. In July, 1959, there were 16 IGA stores with 9 in Albuquerque, 2 in Santa Fe, and 1 each in Aztec, Cuba, Farmington, Shiprock, and Cortez (Colorado).

13. The author has been privileged to read these reports and to discuss their findings and interpretations with Frank A. Mapel. Any interpretive statement by the author, however, should be understood to be entirely his own and to have been based upon his own general findings.

14. Beverages, beer and liquor, were being liquidated rapidly in Oct., 1952, and

finally so in Dec. of that year. Corporation Minute Book, Oct. 16, Dec. 18, 1956. Dry goods were closed out after a serious loss of this merchandise had occurred by fire in the top floor of the First Street warehouse on Oct. 4, 1957. "The Cico Analyst" (house organ), Oct., 1957.

15. The last year of Earl Moulton's presidency, 1952, the annual grocery turnovers (figured on cost of sales) were as follows: consolidated operations 7.4; Albuquerque 9.1. In 1957 these figures were: consolidated operations 9.5; Albuquerque 13.4. These latter figures included frozen foods and meats which, as drop-shipments, exaggerated the turnover somewhat. Both sets of figures, however, 1952 and 1957, represent greater improvement than indicated over earlier turnovers when only beginning and ending inventories were available for calculation of average annual inventories. In the past, though not true in present operations, year-end inventories were allowed to fall as low as possible thus tending to exaggerate the annual turnovers.

16. Buying orders were $250 per week. Delivery charges became ½ of 1 per cent in town and higher according to distance.

17. Chapter VII.

18. For a detailed description of this type of business firm in history, see Gras' *Business and Capitalism,* pp. 175–237. For a succinct statement, see Larson's *Guide to Business History,* pp. 112–114.

19. Rhodes was born in 1869. He died in 1934. He is reasonably well known for his writings on late nineteenth- and early twentieth-century ranching life in New Mexico, particularly as he had experienced it, after 1881, in the southern part of the Territory with headquarters at Engle. Letter to E. Johnson, editor of the *Santa Fe New Mexican,* Jan. 15, year unknown. This is a paragraph of a letter written from Alamogordo, New Mexico, a copy of which was furnished the author by W. A. Keleher, Albuquerque, on Aug. 28, 1951.

INDEX